WITTENBERG: An American College

WITTENBERG: An American College

1842 to 1920

WILLIAM A. KINNISON

Library of Congress Control Number:		2008905808
ISBN:	Hardcover	978-1-4363-5309-0
	Softcover	978-1-4363-5308-3

This book was printed in the United States of America.

To order additional copies of this book, contact:
Xlibris Corporation
1-888-795-4274
www.Xlibris.com
Orders@Xlibris.com
42463

Contents

For
Lenore Morris Kinnison
Wittenberg, class of 1959
Violinist, talented musician, and patron of the arts,
Inspiring teacher,
Devoted mother of three and Noni to ten,
Exceptionally fine first lady of Wittenberg,
Enthusiastic hostess
Friend of many students, faculty, and board members
Board spouses, staff and alumni,
Flower gardener extraordinaire,
And
My love, close companion, and friend
Through thick and thin
For over half a century.

Preface and Acknowledgments

The present work and the volume to follow it are the product of many years of experience with Wittenberg University, its constituencies, its board of directors, faculty and students; familiarity with the Springfield community in which the school is located; extensive research in the archives of the school and in the local newspapers from early in the nineteenth century to the beginning of the twenty-first. This has deepened and enriched my understanding of the story of Wittenberg College and its successor, Wittenberg University. In light of all this, it is time for a new history of the institution. I have written earlier works on Wittenberg and on higher education, in general, as well as a history of Springfield. These works—all of which contribute to this one—are referenced in the Bibliography of Sources and References. In this volume, I also incorporate the results of my recent research. I am indebted to previous historians of Wittenberg and to writers on the beginning and growth of higher education in the United States.

Writing the history of a college can be a precarious undertaking. There is a strong expectation that it will trace the evolution of an institution by telling the trials and tribulations of the founders and all the good things that have happened since. Some expect a "marketing" twist, some positive spin. Others prefer a lighter touch in a "coffee table" pictorial view. There is a counter press, however, from the historians always present on a campus for the idea that if you are going to call it a history, you need to adhere to the objective standards of the historians' craft.

That, apparently, is easier said than done. Professional historians today are not as certain, as historians once seemed to be, that objectivity is attainable. Peter Celms, retired professor of History at Wittenberg, recently gave me a book by University of Chicago historian, Peter Novik, in which he records that debate among practitioners of the craft in the 1960s, 1970s and 1980s. Some of them, as Peter pointed out, were my teachers in graduate school at the University of Wisconsin: William Best Hesseltine, Merrill Jensen, Merle Curti, and Howard K. Beale. In his publication *That Noble Dream: "The Objectivity Question" and the American Historical Profession* (Cambridge University Press, New York, 1988), Novik covers the discussion thoroughly.

Can anyone actually tell any story like it really happened? Novik calls Leopold von Ranke's notion of the "value-free investigator interested only in the facts," a myth. Ranke, who is considered to be the father of modern historical scholarship, set goals for the profession that Novik concludes modern historians feel are unattainable. I find one of Ranke's observations sufficient as an overriding principle for this history of Wittenberg. "Every epoch," he said, "is immediate to God and its value in no way depends on what it has produced but in its existence itself, in its own self." Institutional histories may be written to show the evolution of the institution, the way in which its earlier years influenced its later existence. Yet Ranke's suggestion urges us to try to tell the tale of each generation of students and faculty for its own sake, to the best of our ability.

There is another difficulty. Many very fine histories of particular institutions and of the early college movement in general have incorporated some faulty assumptions. Colin B. Burke challenged one of the most serious of these, the generally negative interpretation of the early colleges as falling far short of what they should have been. They were taken totally out of context, he charged, and then judged by inappropriate later-day standards and found wanting. In his work *American Collegiate Populations: A Test of the Traditional View* (New York University Press, 1982), he suggests that insufficient attention has been given to the overwhelming poverty of frontier settlements and the virtual absence of anything resembling adequate primary and secondary schools to prepare students for college. The frontier colleges had to train their own prospective students, if they were to have a college at all. For many years at Wittenberg, and every where else, well over half of the students were in the preparatory academy. The colleges that triumphed over these obstacles, Burke claimed, had achieved a significant objective for the frontier. For many of these schools, the journey from these humble beginnings to widespread service to their communities was a success story and a tale well worth telling.

I would mention two additional studies which have been particularly helpful in this project: Paul P. Kuenning's *The Rise and Fall of American Lutheran Pietism: The Rejection of an Activist Heritage* (Macon, Ga., Mercer University Press, 1985) and Helen Lefkowitz Horowitz's *Campus Life: Underground Cultures from the end of the Eighteenth Century to the Present,* (New York, A. A. Knopf, 1987).

There is a need for a new history of Wittenberg because a lot has happened since the publication of Harold Lentz's *Centennial History of Wittenberg College* in 1945. There have been interim updates from time to time, as indicated in the bibliography, but no general reassessment in light of the research of the past six decades. The Wittenberg story can be instructive, perhaps, in a general reexamination of the development of American higher education, particularly in the West. More recent research has enlarged the body of knowledge available for a new history and suggests the merit of dividing the story into two parts. The first, dealing with the establishment of the college and its early growth, is presented here under the title *Wittenberg: An American College.* It begins with the founders' efforts to Americanize the German Lutheran Church and the six million German immigrants who came to America in the nineteenth century. It ends with the challenges to Wittenberg during the anti-German hysteria of World War I. Simultaneously, it is the story of Wittenberg's adaptation to the emergence of an urban, industrial society and its effort to become a modern institution.

The second volume, *Wittenberg in the Modern World,* will complete the story to the present covering "The Roaring Twenties," the Great Depression, World War II, the great student rebellions of the 1960s, and adjustment to the post-industrial society, globalization, and an information revolution. This division of the material into two parts, as with all such historical divisions, is somewhat arbitrary. But there is a different context for the institution in the years preceding World War I and those which followed the war.

I am indebted to many scholars and to the archivists, librarians, and preservers of documents who make available the resources by means of which the past can, at least in part, be rediscovered. Individual scholars and sources cited in this work are indicated sometimes in the text and in all cases in the bibliography of sources and references.

The first history of Wittenberg was Professor Michael Diehl's 1859 *Biography of the Rev. Ezra Keller, D. D.,* based upon the founder's diary and other papers. It has a long introduction by Samuel Sprecher, Keller's successor. The second was the ambitious undertaking of an enterprising student in the class of 1887, George Gerlaw Clark. His *History of Wittenberg College* dramatizes the important role that students have always played in the life of the school and in making records of their experiences. His energy in interviewing faculty and students, in getting them to sketch their college experiences and to talk about the issues of their day added a great deal to our understanding. He innocently chronicled the rather strenuous transition from the Wittenberg of the founders to that of Samuel A. Ort, a radical redirection of the school to fit new times and conditions

The third effort, in 1895, was also student-inspired and directed. It was the *Semi-Centennial Souvenir,* a yearbook, alumni directory, and history put together by the junior class, the class of 1896, as a celebration of Wittenberg's fiftieth anniversary. That class, with all due modesty, called itself "Wittenberg's First Great Class." The *Souvenir* mined the historical content of the *Wittenberger,* founded in 1874, the school's first official student newspaper. It had collected reminiscences of many of the early students and chronicled events and concerns on campus. A score of underground newspapers called the *Flying Dutchman* appeared between 1863 and 1883. They recorded the peeves as well as the more serious objections of the students to the curriculum and campus life from the Civil War to the exciting days of change under Samuel Ort. It was the voice of the student rebels of several student generations aided and abetted by a Springfield newspaper editor, Clifton M. Nichols. He was a severe critic of all of the "Old Line Colleges" and a strong advocate of educational reform. He was particularly hard on Wittenberg.

A fourth history, never published, is Benjamin Franklin Prince's useful and detailed *Manuscript History of Wittenberg College,* safely tucked away in the university archives. Wittenberg's "Grand Old Man" first wrote it in anticipation of the fiftieth anniversary and revised and updated it for the seventy-fifth anniversary in 1920. He made further revisions and additions up through 1928. It was never published even though the board had approved doing so on several occasions. Apparently, the money to do so was never available, a common fate of institutional histories.

For the Wittenberg centennial in 1945, the college published Harold A. Lentz's history that leaned heavily on Prince's work, bringing it up to date through the first fifteen years of Rees Edgar Tulloss's administration. At the same time Willard D. Allbeck, faculty member at the Hamma School of Theology wrote *Theology at Wittenberg*. This fine scholar wrote many monographs on specific topics in Wittenberg's history. In 1966, he published *A Century of Lutherans in Ohio* that sheds a great deal of light on the beginnings of Lutheranism in Ohio and the founding and growth of Wittenberg. When he retired, he served a number of years as university archivist.

Charles A. Dominick was on the Wittenberg staff for many years. He was director of the important Commission on Mission and Priorities in the 1970s and later served as vice president for Advancement. Our many discussions about Wittenberg and its history over the years were pleasant and instructive times. His doctoral dissertation *Ohio's Ante Bellum Colleges*, University of Michigan, 1987, sheds considerable light on the colleges of the Ohio frontier and the conditions through which they struggled. His research on the life of Ezra Keller and his interaction with students and on the role of the Society for the Promotion of Collegiate and Theological Education in the West and its aid to Wittenberg shed important light on those two very important topics.

The staff of Thomas Memorial Library at Wittenberg and particularly the archive staff deserve the highest praise for continuing, friendly, and unfailing service over many years. Douglas Lehman, director of Thomas Library, and Suzanne A. Smailes, head of Technical Services, with oversight of the archives, deserve special mention. Suzanne A. Smailes worked many hours in support of this project with unfailing good humor. For many past services in this long-running project, I would express special thanks to Regina Entorf, reference librarian. I also acknowledge the late Louis Voigt, librarian and archivist for Hamma School of Theology, whose insights were always enlightening.

The staff at the Fisher Family Library and Archives at the Heritage Center of Clark County, merit high praise. Their unfailing and friendly assistance has been outstanding. Roger Sherrock, executive officer; Virginia L. Weygandt, director of collections; Casey Eichensehr, curator; and Natalie Fritz, archives and library assistant, do a superior job making available their extraordinary collection of papers and artifacts dealing with the area's history. I would also acknowledge the assistance of Karen Drickamer, director of Special Collections and college archivist, Musselman Library, Gettysburg College, Gettysburg, Pa. Gettysburg generously granted permission to quote from the correspondence between Samuel Sprecher and John H. W. Stuckenberg and Frederick Conrad, contained in the Stuckenberg collection: *MS-093: John H. W. Stuckenberg Collection, Special Collections, Gettysburg College, Gettysburg, Pennsylvania.* A readily available guide is Richard A. Hoehn's *Now We See Through a Glass Darkly, But We See: The Papers of J. H. W. and Mary G. Stuckenberg* (Gettysburg College, Gettysburg, Pa., 1987.)

I want to express a special thank you to Wittenberg President Mark Erikson and his wife Lyn who are writing an exciting new chapter of the Wittenberg story. Their enthusiasm for Wittenberg's future is in "the tiger tradition" and holds great promise for things to come. Their interest in and support for this history has been an inspiration. There are others at Wittenberg to be recognized for their generous support. I think especially of Karen Gerboth, director of University Communications and editor of the *Wittenberg Magazine*; Robert Rafferty, director of New Media and Webmaster; Robert Gantt, New Media assistant and gifted photographer; David Long, director of Advancement; and Linda Himes, coordinator of the Wittenberg Fund.

Don Perkins, former director of Public Information, and F. Kenneth Dickerson, former alumni secretary have been supporters of my historical studies. Don has been helpful with advice about this particular project. Former Provosts Sammy Greer and William Wiebenga; Ken and Pat Benne in admissions and alumni affairs; Rev. Ed Brigham and Robert White, past and current directors of church relations; Associate Campus Pastor Larry Houff and the late Pastor to the University Michael D. Wuchter; and current pastors Anders and Rachel Tune have each played their own role in encouraging the completion of this project. I also want to acknowledge the influence of James Klenke who was a real champion for the importance of the student in a school's life and history. In addition, I have had several generations of administrative assistance from Cindy Beacom, Jean Myers, Barbara Korn, and the late Barbara Johnson.

Publishing an institutional history is an adventure all of its own. I am grateful to Jason Paul and Sarah Arizala, representatives of Xlibris for their patient and professional assistance. The Xlibris editorial team was thorough and efficient. Furthermore, by means of modern electronics, Xlibris solves the problem that has prevented so many institutions from publishing histories. Publication on demand means no one has to invest in the initial inventory of books.

Special thanks are due my son, William E. Kinnison, Ph D, Wittenberg Class of 1983, a teacher and professor of English, for his sensitive and critical reading of the entire text and forthright suggestions and corrections. His contributions to the improvement and shaping of the narrative make him my collaborator. I express thanks to Lenore to whom this work is dedicated. She read the work thoughtfully and has lived with the project for more years than anyone should have to.

William A. Kinnison, '54
Springfield, Ohio
April 30, 2008

Chapter One

To Win the West

In 1836, Ezra Keller had just graduated from the Lutheran seminary at Gettysburg, Pennsylvania. At the young age of twenty-four, he set out for the west an itinerant missionary to Indiana, Illinois, and Missouri to report what he found there to the missionary society of the Pennsylvania Ministerium. He left his family and Caroline Routzahn, his fiancée, to undertake the arduous journey. Many in the East were concerned about settlers moving west, worried that they would be lost to the church, cut themselves off from eastern culture and civilization, even organize politically independent of eastern control. Keller traveled over 3,000 miles in six months, mostly on horseback.

He was startled at the number of people he met on the way that he had known in Maryland and Pennsylvania. They had already moved or were moving to the west. He detoured into Kentucky for more than a week to see "a host of aunts,uncles, and cousins" who had done so; so many, he wrote Caroline, that "I have not time to do anything else than converse with them." He then proceeded to Indiana to begin his assignment. Near the end of the journey, he said he was physically undone, totally exhausted, and could go no farther. He advised the missionary society that in the future, they not assign such extensive territories.

Ezra Keller on horseback. Art work by Japanese exchange student, Itsuo Umezaki, class of 1959, Wittenberg University Archives.

Despite his exhaustion, Keller made an insightful report. Confirming Eastern fears, he reported that two-thirds of the people were unchurched. They had abandoned any connection they might once have had. Even those in churches had been so victimized by charlatans posing as ministers that a missionary needed to have the leisure to tarry long enough to become trusted. Otherwise his work was "ephemeral." It was not as easy to bring westerners into the church as it was easterners, he added. "The fervor of enterprise and speculation rages among the western folks to such a degree, that most are unwilling to devote any of their time and much less any of their money, to religious matters." The West, he said, was "a moral wilderness." He wrote Caroline, "I have seen more wickedness . . . than I had seen for six years before . . . I was cast into the worst society and heard and saw much which is disagreeable and which made my heart often bleed . . . But I have always met with some who loved the Lord and respected His commandments."

Among those in a church, he met "anti-mission Baptists" who, he said, detested educated clergy, missionary societies, and itinerant preachers. "Shouting Methodists," he added, shared a similar hostility toward educated ministers; only Presbyterians were understanding and supportive, but they were much less numerous. He was more impressed by the churchgoers he found in Illinois. There were many settlers from New England with a desire for intelligence, good order, good morals, and social improvements which so distinguished the states from which they had come.

Keller's views showed his prejudices and the culture shock that he experienced in the West. The experience awakened in him an understanding that people in the West would have to be approached differently by the formal churches that existed in the East. Open-mindedness and flexibility were required. The territory had settlers from New England, New York, New Jersey, Pennsylvania, and all the mid-Atlantic states as well as generous numbers from the South and lots of European immigrants. As the various cultural and ethnic strains met, there were extreme differences of viewpoint and lifestyle. He began to think about how to reach frontiersmen with the Gospel. The forms and order that appealed to the German Lutherans in the East, he believed, were not going to be as effective in the West.

At St. Louis, Keller sold his horse and booked passage on a steamer down the frozen and ice-laden Mississippi River to Cairo, Illinois. From there he boarded another river boat to travel up the Ohio River—equally treacherous in winter—to Wheeling, Virginia. From Wheeling, he returned home in greater comfort in a stage coach on the Cumberland Road. Back in Maryland, he said that he suffered from a lingering illness and was perplexed as to his duty. Is it the will of God, he asked, that I return to the West and labor there? He had made a "conditional promise," he told his fiancée, to settle at Quincy, Illinois, but his mother and his fiancée, prevailed upon him to remain in Maryland to regain his health.

It was a time of national change and growth for America, a time of national self-confidence. The United States had freed itself from British colonial power at the end of the eighteenth century and, with the rise of Andrew Jackson, had seen the strength and power of free institutions grow in the early days of the nineteenth. It was an America that was increasingly self-assertive and suspicious of those who would preserve European habits and ways. It was expanding rapidly westward overrunning the continent. There were the growing fears that western settlers would throw off all the restraints of civilization. Into this America came hordes of new immigrants to share the bounty, but they would be met with a stiffening anti-foreign nativism. One aspect of this was an indigenous American Protestantism that broke radically with the European tradition of established churches.

From the first colonial settlements in 1607 and 1620 on, many religious viewpoints found their way to America. Often they were groups from outside the established churches. Here, cut off from their European origins and thrown together, they began a distinctive course of development in which each influenced the others, and all responded to the New World's air of freedom and informality. Congregational organization, strong roles for laity in management and evangelism, a sense of freedom of all religious belief, the democratization of church doctrine, and, most uniquely, the establishment of a host of denominational colleges, characterized the innovations.

Alexis de Tocqueville, the French political scientist, described America's democracy for Europeans in a book published in 1835, entitled *Democracy in America*. It appeared in the United States in 1836, the year Keller graduated from the seminary. Tocqueville was amazed at the religious turmoil that he witnessed on his tour of the country. He saw a fervent and Americanized Protestantism unlike anything known in Europe. Even many Catholics, he said, had become ardent proponents of democracy, local ownership of church property, and the freedom of religion from government interference. Religion in America, he said, had few formalities. "Nothing is more repugnant to the human mind in an age of equality," he noted, "than the idea of subjection to forms." The Americans that he met on his tour, he said, were impatient of liturgical forms, saw symbols as artifice that hid truth, and were unmoved by ceremonial observances. Yet, he added, "there is no country in the world where the Christian religion retains greater influence over the souls of men than in America."

The nation's colleges emerged in this same distinctive American culture. Faculty members from Europe's universities were not among the earliest immigrants to the New World. There was no company of scholars or guild of professors to establish a *bona fide* university. The closest thing to it was an occasional body of educated pastors, who from time to time organized schools to train indigenous pastors because too few came from Europe or those that did were unsuited for the American scene. Only a very few early colleges, like William and Mary in Virginia, received a Royal Charter. In the colonies and later in the new republic, local persons hastened to the nearest legislature to obtain some kind of authorization to do what they were doing. The legislatures obliged by authorizing a board of trustees entrusted with operating and perpetuating schools in the public interest. These lay boards were a unique American contribution to academia.

Also by the year 1836, Ralph Waldo Emerson had captured this American spirit and translated it into a philosophy of Transcendentalism and self-reliance. In his first book, *Nature,* published in 1836, Emerson asked why Americans should not have their own distinctive and original relationship to the universe, unfettered by the views and opinions of the less free and less informed thinkers of bygone days. "Why should not we have a poetry and philosophy of insight and not of tradition and a religion by revelation to us? Let us demand," he said, "our own works and laws and worship." In 1837, in a Phi Beta Kappa address at Harvard College entitled "The American Scholar," Emerson made what Oliver Wendell Holmes later called America's intellectual declaration of independence, advising students and faculties to think for themselves, giving up European authority over their minds. Emerson crystallized the national impulse of the day, and it was that religious and intellectual climate to which many in Keller's America responded and so did he.

Ohio had not been part of Keller's assignment, but he had to pass through it to get to Indiana. It was more settled; and in 1818, Lutherans had established a synod which was responsible for the area. There were many recently arrived German Lutherans and many second, third, and fourth generation English-speaking Lutherans being served by the new synod. They were soon at odds with one another. A Lutheran seminary had been established in Canton in the northeastern part of Ohio. It was later moved to Columbus. As Keller headed west he did not travel through Columbus, because the National Road was not completed. He headed southwest to Cincinnati on the Ohio River. Construction of the road stopped just west of Springfield, while the Congress debated whether or not to appropriate funds to continue it.

The English-speaking Lutherans were unhappy with the Columbus Seminary. The German language party had insisted that all instruction be in the German language and that only textbooks written in German be used. They talked of opening Germania College. English-speaking members talked instead of opening an English-speaking college. It was this squabble over language and education that created Keller's second opportunity to go west. According to Benjamin Prince, some of the English synod leaders remembered Keller and invited him to return to Ohio. Those like Keller who advocated the de-Germanization of the church came to be called Americanists, American Lutherans, or "new measure" men. The theological views of the two groups increasingly diverged, and Keller was identified with the so-called New Lutherans.

In 1836, pastors adhering to the English language faction left the synod and organized separately. On October 18, 1842, they voted unanimously to establish a theological and literary institution. "Whereas, we are fully convinced," their action read, "that in this age of light and knowledge, ministers of the Gospel in order to be extremely useful, must be well educated," and since Gettysburg was too far away and they could not encourage the institution in Columbus, "therefore in humble reliance upon God we do ordain and establish the following constitution for the governance of our institution." They then subscribed $1,500 to initiate the project and appointed a board of directors authorized to proceed to found not just a seminary but a college too.

In 1843, the board convened in the town of Wooster in northeastern Ohio. It called Ezra Keller, to come as the first professor of theology. He worried about accepting the call because the new venture was opposed by many Lutherans in Ohio, by those supporting the college and seminary at Gettysburg, and the Ministerium of Pennsylvania which had withdrawn its support for a school in Ohio. But Keller was of a magnetic personality, and his fame as a prophet of the new church had spread rapidly among Americanists. He was seen as a man of dignity, wisdom, austerity, and with an "amazing breadth of intuitive power." Keller, out of intuition alone, decided to accept the call.

Ezra Keller, founder and first president of Wittenberg College, from an engraving by J. Sartain, Philadelphia. Wittenberg University Archives.

Keller's life up to this point seemed to prepare him for a ministry in the West. He was born on a farm near Middletown, Maryland, on May 12, 1812, the third son in a family of five sons and one daughter. He spent his youth laboring on the farm. His grandfather and his mother had a strong religious influence over him, but his father had little interest in religion. A devout farm hand, William Lingenfelter, an evangelical and fundamentalist, had a profound effect on him; and at the age of 17, Ezra decided to become a Lutheran minister. His father objected to the years of preparation and the cost and prohibited him from pursuing his plans.

Keller then left home to live with a Lutheran clergyman, the Rev. Abraham Reck, who strengthened his resolve and helped him to prepare for college. Reck encouraged two of Ezra's friends to join him, David Bittle, who later became the founding president of Roanoke College in Virginia, and Louis Routzahn, whose sister, Caroline, Ezra later married. Reck had been active in establishing the seminary in 1826 and a school which later became Gettysburg College.

He traveled on foot and arrived with only fifty cents in his pocket, a scanty supply of clothing, and a few books. He missed home and family and wrote a long poem about happier days: "I hear the spinning wheel\ and very strange I feel\ I think of home, sweet home\ where once I used to roam." He then recalled, in verse, memories of rolling on the floor, dancing, whirling about, playing games, and other pleasantries of days now gone. In spite of hardships, he did well, finishing his preparatory and collegiate work in five years and entering seminary, where he came under the influence of Professor Samuel Simon Schmucker. A man of great energy and scholarly interest, he had been educated at the Universities of Pennsylvania and Princeton where he encountered the Puritanism of New England and the Scottish Enlightenment.

Keller's father remained estranged. When he was ordained, his father disowned him. Ten years later, he relented, and reconciliation occurred; but Keller had been deeply scarred. It was not so unreasonable for him to have left the farm to become a minister. The younger sons of farmers all over the East were leaving farms in large numbers. Their fathers' holdings were simply not large enough to divide among several sons and many moved west seeking cheap land, while others entered the denominational colleges to pursue new careers.

At the end of his training, Keller made his journey through the west. On that tour he had written to Caroline Routzahn saying it would be a long time before he saw her again. "Yes, we may never see each other again," he added. It was a dangerous journey, yet he earnestly wished to "be able to return and exchange with you once more the sweet kiss of love." He thought of her every day, he said, and asked her to write him at Indianapolis where he hoped to be in a few weeks. He advised her to go to school while he was away to prepare for life as a pastor's wife. As "a token of love," he sent her a book of the collected works of "the pious, amiable, and devoted Hannah More," a popular evangelical writer of the day and great supporter of the Sunday School movement. The letter revealed other traits of the man. Many commented on his "fascinating sweetness of expression" and tenderness of heart. When he returned, Keller began active service in the parish ministry. When he received the call from Ohio, he was pastor of the church in Hagerstown, Maryland, a strong preacher and well-liked by his congregation.

After long and searching prayer, Keller decided to accept the call. "In the West I will labor and toil," he exclaimed, "in the West

I will live, in the West I will die, and from the West I will ascend to Glory!" He seemed relieved to satisfy his earlier desire to go west. He attributed his decision to the influence of his earlier benefactor, Pastor Reck, who had already moved west. "He was one of the wisest and most confidential advisers in all the affairs of the institution, and the church in the West," he wrote in his diary. He prized most of all Reck's "ardent devotion to the church of Christ." Keller's entry in his diary for March 29, 1844, however, was more tentative. "I have at length decided to spend the summer in the West," he wrote, in the service of the contemplated theological institution. "I will not go to housekeeping as I expect the institution will be removed farther west than Wooster . . ." He left his wife and family in Hagerstown.

A joint meeting of the board and the Wooster committee was successful, and the Board voted formally to locate its theological and literary institution there and to apply to the Ohio Legislature for a charter. They continued to call the college the Theological and Literary Institution, but the citizens began to talk about Wooster College and they looked forward to the arrival in town of the Reverend Ezra Keller.

Keller was delayed by an invitation to address the alumni and students of the seminary at Gettysburg. It was his alma mater, and he was serving on its board of directors. He welcomed the opportunity before leaving for Ohio to outline his views on the proper education for a clergyman in the new world. He vigorously defended the importance of a fully educated clergy. He insisted that Moses and the Prophets, Jesus and St. Paul, and all the early church fathers had been thoroughly grounded in the religious literature and traditions of their people and equally well informed about the science and culture of their day. Therefore, he reasoned, today's clergy should have as full an education in the mental culture by means of a thorough and complete college education followed by a most thorough theological training in English.

Such was the mission upon which the church had embarked at Gettysburg, and such was to be his assignment in the West. The zeal with which he delivered his views was criticized by some, but it was the zeal of his mentor, Samuel S. Schmucker, who believed that the church's needs in the New World could not be met without establishing colleges. There were six in Keller's seminary class and all six, reflecting Schmucker's fervor, founded educational institutions. Three colleges survived: Wittenberg in Ohio, Roanoke in Virginia, and Newberry in South Carolina. Schmucker's graduates established at least a dozen schools before the Civil War. One historian tabulated that only half of all antebellum colleges survived.

In the spring the institution opened in Wooster, and a committee was authorized to take bids for a building. When Keller arrived, he found four men waiting to begin theological instruction. The classical department opened with twenty-four students. Mr. F. K. Heisley, from Baltimore served as the first professor. There are few records of the school's operations in Wooster. By July 4 the students organized the Polemic Association and the first debate was on the Whiggish question: should domestic manufactures be encouraged by a high protective tariff?

That fall the English Synod convened in Wooster, and Keller presented his reasons for locating farther west. He wanted to accede to the request of the Synod of the West to locate closer to their congregations in Indiana, Kentucky, and Illinois. On the other hand, the New England Society for Collegiate and Theological Education in the West, from which Keller hoped to receive assistance, urged that the school not be located too far west beyond eastern influences. The number of Lutherans in southern Ohio was increasing rapidly, and the center of Lutheran population shifted in that direction.

The discussion lasted all day, and Keller was in danger of losing his first debate with those who had called him. But he had a view of Lutheran unity that, he hoped, would bridge the differences between English and German factions, and relocation was critical. He wanted to locate the college closer to Columbus and develop a broad and liberal American college like similar schools in New England, where the church could prepare men for the ministry and for all other vocations and callings. He hoped then to prevail upon the Joint Synod to broaden its seminary curriculum so that all could support one college in Springfield and one seminary in Columbus. Such a development, he thought, was reasonable and only a matter of time. As the debate wore on, Father John Stough, an eighty-year-old patriarch of the frontier church, appealed to his brethren to support Keller's proposition. Having seen much of life and having a sense of the growth that was occurring in Ohio, he was willing, he said, to cast his lot with the youthful and enthusiastic Ezra Keller. After Stough's plea, the synod voted to move the school.

Keller's interest in the Western College Society was not mere wishful thinking. The proposed school was of interest to that New England group. They shared concerns about the survival of the Christian church in the west. Theron Baldwin, secretary of the society, noted that Keller's school would be the group's "first open door to the German mind in the West." The Rev. Lyman Beecher, at Lane Seminary in Cincinnati, said the Society's goal was to save the West from Catholicism and from paganism. "If we gain the West, all is safe," he said. "If we lose it, all is lost." Beecher, at Baldwin's suggestion, would visit Keller's school once it was located, to evaluate it and recommend whether or not the Society should extend financial support.

The English Synod sent Keller as an official visitor to the Synod of the West in Fort Wayne, Indiana, to seek support. German-born pastors opposed Keller's English institution, and though the synod passed a resolution of support, nothing came of it. The Synod of the West instead began planning for its own school in Illinois. "I am every day becoming more convinced," Keller wrote in his diary, "of the necessity of raising up an American ministry to spiritualize the millions of Germans who are seeking a home in our happy land." Those educated in Germany, he said, "are not qualified for the work and cannot be persuaded to lay aside foreign prejudices and modes of thought and action."

Keller then boldly took his plan to the meeting of the German Joint Synod of Ohio. His hopes were blasted there too by the synod's continued determination to adhere strictly to German language instruction. Disappointed, Keller then began in earnest to search for a location for his school. He was interested in a place that was central in the state, on main arteries of transportation over which German immigrants moved west. He was interested in locating near Columbus, Springfield, Dayton, Xenia, or Cincinnati.

Visiting the area by horseback and canal boat, he encouraged residents to support a college in their midst. He moved to Springfield in December 1844, with his wife Caroline; their three-year-old son,

Caroline Routzahn, wife of Ezra Keller; photo of a portrait by Robert Gantt.

Martin; an orphan boy, Maurice Kirby, whom they were raising; and their domestic, Mary Stevig, whom they called Polly. They had left three graves in the East of a son and two daughters who had died in infancy. Caroline was soon expecting again and in September, 1845, a daughter Sarah was born. She would be called Sally and be the light of their lives.

Keller spent several weeks promoting the college in the pleasant town of Springfield, the county seat of Clark County and a place of 2,700 people at the terminus of the National Road. It was soon to be a central stop on the railroad from Sandusky, on Lake Erie, to Cincinnati, on the Ohio River. The Erie Canal connected Sandusky to New York City, and the Ohio River flowed into the Mississippi, which flowed all the way to New Orleans. Thus Ohio's first north-south railroad would intersect with the nation's first east-west highway, making Springfield a hub for settlers moving west. It was forty-five miles from the seminary in Columbus. Springfield's newspaper was a vigorous proponent and encouraged the town to respond.

A meeting was called at the Associate Reformed Church on December 2, 1844, to discuss "the propriety of securing the location" of the proposed college. Keller was to be present. "All, without distinction, are invited to attend," the editor advised, emphasizing the broad support which the school's promoters were seeking. The turnout for the meeting was not as large as was hoped, and the group adjourned to meet a week later at the Presbyterian Church. J. H. Gallagher, editor of the *Springfield Republic,* expressed the fear that the beautiful village might become a byword for the want of spirit and enterprise, unless a larger group turned out to hear Mr. Keller. Meanwhile, Keller visited Xenia to see what interest could be raised there.

Springfield attempted to get Baptists to locate Denison University in Springfield in 1832 but was passed over for the smaller, safer village of Granville. In 1841, the Christian Church considered Springfield for Lafayette College but selected the quieter Clark County village of New Carlisle instead. No school opened, however, and the project was abandoned. A few years later, Horace Mann came west for the Congregationalists and located Antioch College a few miles south of Springfield. Some were reluctant to get excited about Keller's college for fear of losing out again.

Keller established his home in Springfield and seemed to have a preference for that location. He continued to cultivate interest in Xenia, however, to keep Springfield's leaders motivated. He sought to ascertain the views and feelings of local residents and the extent to which they would support the venture. He became acquainted with the scattered Lutheran families and visited congregations of Lutherans throughout the area.

Gallagher used his paper to develop greater interest. He advised that the "Lutherans intended to establish a college of the first order calculated to answer all the purposes of college education for that numerous and worthy body of Christians throughout the entire West." He told citizens that it would have moral, intellectual, and economic advantages, and advised farmers that "every foot of real estate within some miles of the village will be more or less enhanced in value." He was hoping to kindle enthusiasm for Keller's proposal, and he warned the citizenry not to be indifferent or lukewarm but to seize the opportunity. "Let the college be founded in Springfield," he advised, "and the effect will be a considerable increase of our population, a proportionate improvement of our market, and a consequent enhancement of the value of real estate in the vicinity." Springfield's expectations for the new school were raised to a high level.

The second meeting enjoyed a large turnout. Charles Anthony, local Whig leader and Ohio Attorney General, presided. Keller discussed the proposed college and the growing German population of the West. William A. Rogers, attorney and area leader in the anti-slavery movement, proposed resolutions to approve the character of the college, asked that it be located in Springfield, and agreed to solicit subscriptions for its support. All passed unanimously. In January of 1845, the *Republic* editor noted that the campaign was having encouraging results, and that the German farmers west of Mad River were subscribing liberally. He called upon others to respond with the same generosity.

Throughout the months in which the college question was on the minds of the local citizens, they were aware of the German immigration issue involved. "A Lutheran college will be of great advantage," said the *Republic* editor, "because of the very rapid increase of that denomination from immigration alone." Charles Anthony, chairman of the subscription campaign, observed that "the members of that denomination, and those connected with them by a common lineage, already own a considerable portion of the soil and substantial wealth of the West." He noted their rapid growth, their perseverance, and diligence. "To everyone acquainted with their history, habits, and character," he observed, "it is very apparent that the rich plains and valleys of the West are destined to feel permanently . . . these traits of German character."

Beyond the benefits of access to a college education, a higher level of learning in the community, access to a library, a stimulus for bookstores, and an ever-ready source of teachers, Anthony saw a special benefit in having this particular institution. "The German could become acquainted with English culture while those of English background would experience the rich heritage of the German." Citizens were aware of the growing nativism and read accounts of riots between American nativists and immigrants. While nativist feelings were not absent in Springfield, they seemed to be milder and more accommodating, if not of the Irish at least of the Germans. An institution devoted to bringing divergent elements together had a strong appeal for many citizens.

Lithograph of Springfield, Ohio, circa 1852, looking south from the north side of Lagonda or Buck Creek. The building in the foreground is the Presbyterian Female Seminary. Clark County Historical Society.

Keller informed leaders of the subscription campaign that the board of directors would meet on St. Valentine's Day, for final consideration of the question of location. When the board met, it had two offers: one from Springfield, the other from Xenia, fifteen miles south. Xenia had the larger population of Lutherans, but the two towns were about the same size. Earlier Xenia had been larger and seemed to be ahead in growth and future prospects. By 1845 Springfield had caught up.

Springfield offered $4,667 and a choice between two locations. The first was an eight-acre plot east of the village, between the National Road and the Lagonda Road, owned by Jeremiah Warder, a Quaker businessman. The second was seventeen acres north of Buck Creek, owned by the Woodshade Cemetery Association. Xenia offered $4,281 and a choice among five small parcels of land. The board toured sites in both towns. Because of the "natural and other advantages of Springfield" and the offered money and property, they voted for Springfield. Railroad and highway connections weighed in their decision along with the abundance of limestone and the town's brick yards and lumber mills.

The Board applied to the state for a charter calling their school Wittenberg College. The name was in use five months before the Board met. While the Board was still using the name Theological and Literary Institution, pastors in the synods were calling it Wittenberg. The *Lutheran Observer* of October 25, 1844, said the school was to be called Wittenberg. Ezra Keller was using the name Wittenberg College in his journal the week before. By tradition, the Rev. J. H. Hoffman is credited with suggesting that the school be named Wittenberg after the sixteenth century German school of Reformation fame where Martin Luther taught. It was to be a new Wittenberg for the new world. It was an act of moderation by Americanists, tying the new institution to historic roots of the church. They did not intend to throw off all old-world Lutheran characteristics, as their opponents claimed, just some of them. Keller still hoped to tie the disparate elements of western Lutheranism together.

The $4,667 contribution was made up of many small donations from local citizens. For every $20 subscribed, the bearer of the receipt for payment was entitled to receive a credit of $10 toward tuition for a student. Thus $2,330 of free tuition was granted in exchange. It was a commitment by Keller that taxed the school's income for several years but had an immediate effect on local enrollment.

On February 28, 1845, citizens of the community and vicinity gathered in the Clark County courthouse to hear Ezra Keller announce the decision. Congressman Samson Mason, a veteran Whig politician, abolitionist, and important community leader suggested a further effort for additional subscriptions. The group approved and the total was eventually raised to $10,000.

There were few Lutherans in Springfield, and they had no church building; but Keller believed that the town had great potential for a college. He selected the location even though the Lutheran church was weak, and he invited those of other faiths to share in building his school. The National Road, he argued, led from Maryland, through Pennsylvania, to Columbus, and then directly to Springfield, the gateway to the West for thousands from Europe and mid-Atlantic America. He had no doubt that the number of Lutherans in the area would increase. Graduates, as pastors, teachers and community leaders would spread out among the newcomers and go west with them in great numbers.

The number of Germans immigrating to the United States before 1820 was unknown. In the decade of the 1820s, less than six thousand were recorded. In the 1830s, however, the number increased to one hundred twenty-five thousand; in the 1840s, it was three hundred eighty-five thousand; but in the 1850s, nearly a million more arrived. By the end of the century over five million had immigrated to the United States. Many of them were Lutheran and many headed west. Their impact on the nation would be immense and they would overwhelm the American Lutherans.

To promote the new college, Keller wrote a series of letters that were published in the *Lutheran Observer* to acquaint the church in the East with conditions in the West and to arouse people to support this new venture. In one letter, he outlined the reasons for promoting education in the West. In another, he explained why a college was needed as a focal point for the church's expansion: the distance from Gettysburg, the lower cost of living in Ohio, the fact that other denominations were establishing colleges there. In other letters, he analyzed the Lutheran population in the West and the conflict between western settlers and German-born clergymen.

In another, he discussed again his missionary trip to the West and the religious needs of the area. In still another, he discussed the English Lutheran seminary and how it would differ from the German school in Columbus. His last letter described the school's location in Springfield. It was, he wrote, "a fertile and attractive part of the state" centrally located with roads to all points. "Here is to be seen bordering on the college grounds the finest scenes in this part of the state. What a delightful retreat for contemplation or scientific research among . . . the rocks, the flowers, the vines of the cliffs, and the convulsion of nature! What a charming home for the muses!"

Lagonda or Buck Creek painted in the mid-nineteenth century by Godfrey Nicholas Frankenstein. Photo by Robert Gantt. Wittenberg University Archives.

Keller found a scattered flock of Lutherans. Since 1841, Pastor John Lehman, from Xenia, had periodically attended to the Lutherans around Clark County. They held services in homes and a variety of other buildings. With Keller's encouragement and the prospect of the new college, they organized more effectively. He started building a church with funds borrowed from the college's small endowment. George Rinkliff, the historian of the church, said that Keller was both architect and superintendent of construction. He believed that he could not build a college without a strong congregation to support it.

As his new measure views became apparent, however, not all Lutherans in the area were happy. For some, his was a rather plain and austere church, his congregation uncomfortable, too puritan and with no emphasis on Christmas and other festival days. Some withdrew to organize St. Johns, but it proved to be too German for some, and they established Zion Lutheran church which took a position between the other two. Thus, within seven years, Keller's flock had become three separate congregations to the dismay of

Springfield's leaders. But Keller had been right in one respect, the influx of Germans and Lutherans was so great that his church grew to 150 members. The others also grew. The divisions indicated the many views which prevailed among Lutherans for most of the nineteenth century and into the twentieth.

The issues were deeper than language. Those advocating English tended toward a less traditional view of theology. They were willing to accommodate more readily to the religious atmosphere in America, which on the frontier was expressed in revivals, a rejection of liturgy, ritual and vestments, an emphasis upon a severe and personal piety, and an insistence upon a lay council to govern the congregation and lay representatives to share responsibility with the Ministerium at Synod. They placed less emphasis on creeds and confessions, which divided Christians, and more on the elements of agreement.

English Lutherans embraced social causes like the abolition movement, temperance, the Sunday school, and the American Tract Society which distributed reform literature. They subscribed to the American protestant notion that though one could not be saved by good works, those who were saved demonstrated their faith in interdenominational benevolent societies that functioned throughout the nation. They were also millenialists, awaiting the second coming of Christ on earth to reign for a thousand years before the final judgment, and they felt an obligation to prepare for his coming by improving society. This led to a social activism foreign to European established churches and to many immigrants who came to America. American Lutherans saw the Christian as a participant in the definition of American citizenship. They advocated participation in political affairs, even the use of the pulpit to help formulate public opinion. Such behaviors elicited negative reactions from the more orthodox. The greatest negative reaction, perhaps, was to American preferences for political activism, Methodist hymns, temperance, and revivals. Their interdenominational involvement led to the sharing of pulpits with Presbyterians, Congregationalists, and Reformed churches.

While other denominations had bypassed Springfield for their college because it was growing and expanding and threatened to become too worldly, Keller thought his college should be in the midst of all this. The Lutheran church, he said, should plant itself in the midst of the growing communities of the West and contend for men whose lives were full and vigorous. He used the words of the Gospel of John to defend his view: "I pray not that thou shouldst take them from the world, but that Thou shouldst keep them from the evil one . . . as Thou didst send me into the world, even so send I them into the world." He argued against locating the college in Columbus, however, because it was a "large, overgrown city, a place of dissipation and expensiveness of living . . . ." He attributed this to the location of the state government there. He hesitated to locate his school there, too close to the German seminary, for fear it would dominate his institution.

"This college is builded for the future," said Keller, "and it must be a place of easy access and centrally located." It did not matter that Springfield was not a center of Lutheranism, or that the church was little known and greatly misunderstood by the other denominations. The days would not all be harmonious, and the town-gown relationship would be both beautiful and stormy, limiting and expanding. Yet in the interplay of the forces of both church and community, Wittenberg's life would unfold unlike that of any other Lutheran school.

Chapter Two

The More Toil, the More Grace

Keller was called to be Wittenberg's chief theological professor; the board called Professor William M. Reynolds of Gettysburg College to be its president. Everyone knew that one man could not do both jobs; that would be expecting too much. Reynolds accepted and said he would arrive on campus in the spring. Later, when the board could not meet his salary expectations, he reconsidered and decided not to come. Benjamin Prince, professor of history, later conjectured that the situation was just not inviting to so prominent a person and would have required him to make too great a sacrifice.

A man of considerable reputation among Lutherans, Reynolds had been Keller's first teacher in college, and the only one he mentioned by name in his diary. He admired him and thought he was a kindred spirit in the effort to Americanize the church and was disappointed when he did not accept. In 1850, Reynolds became the first president of Capital University, the school the German Synod established to rival Wittenberg. He ran into difficulty immediately because the German congregations were suspicious of his moderate English leanings and his effort to accommodate the ambitions of Columbus for a college to meet the town's needs. By 1854 he had resigned.

Jefferson College in Pennsylvania conferred on Keller an honorary degree of Doctor of Divinity. He received the news humbly but was grateful for the boost it gave the morale of Wittenberg's supporters. Their young leader was now to be recognized as Dr. Keller. At the same time, the school also conferred a Doctor of Laws degree on Senator Henry Clay of Kentucky, a leading western statesman. He was author of the "American system" of tariffs and internal improvements, like the national road. As John C. Calhoun spoke for the South and Daniel Webster for the Northeast, Clay was the voice of the West. For Springfielders, it was an impressive development: Ezra Keller and Henry Clay, the preacher and the politician who for them most represented Americanism. Keller was less impressed. He remarked on the mysterious ways of the Lord to take a farm boy from the Middletown valley in Maryland, call him from the plow, send him West and raise him up among the doctors of the church.

On Nov. 3, 1845 classes began at Wittenberg College. The German seminary in Columbus closed temporarily amid continued wrangling over the language issue and remained closed until 1846. Theological classes began earlier in Springfield at Keller's house at the northeast corner of High and Mechanic streets, a block west of where the church was being built. The first step in building the college, he reasoned, was a large and useful church prominently located in the town. Funds for the building were borrowed from Wittenberg's meager endowment and advanced by three members of the congregation and by Pastor Keller, who built the church on their own responsibility.

When the church was under roof, classes began on the ground floor while the sanctuary was being completed. With nine preparatory students and two of Keller's theological students from Wooster, Wittenberg was underway. Classes would be held in the church for five years. There was a large assembly room on the ground floor, and two smaller rooms at the northend where classes were taught. Before the first year ended, enrollment reached seventy-three. An early faculty member reported that his first experience was "in the rough, unfinished basement" of the Lutheran church. The seats were made of log slabs without backs. There was no library except Ezra Keller's library. Two years later the school would boast of 2,800 volumes. Faculty members taught six or seven hours every day. The college paid annual pew rent of one dollar per student per year to augment the church's income.

Unknown artist's conception of the English Lutheran Church on High Street in Springfield, Ohio, where Wittenberg College began, detail from 1852 lithograph. Clark County Historical Society.

The first faculty included "the genial" P. G. Sauerwine of Gettysburg College in languages, and "the faithful" Joseph Welty of Hudson College in mathematics and natural sciences.

The nicknames were those of the students. Keller taught all the theological courses plus mental philosophy in the junior class and moral science in the senior year. There were two tutors, theology student Morris Officer and the orphan in the Keller household, Maurice Kirby, who helped in the preparatory school and the lower classes in the college.

Both Sauerwine and Welty left after a short tenure when Keller ran out of money with which to pay them. One said he would leave because he could not work without steady compensation. The other said he feared that the struggling little school would not make it, and he could not bring himself to make the sacrifices required. Welty later taught at Union College in New York. "Alas, what a want of faith," wrote Keller in his diary, "but youthfulness and inexperience form some excuse!" Keller was but ten years older.

When the session ended with examinations, the two teachers left; and Keller pondered his situation. The new term would start in four weeks, but no teachers had yet been secured. "I will leave this matter," he wrote, "in the hands of the Lord." When the first two teachers left in despair, as some reported, Rev. Frederick W. Conrad, pastor of Keller's former parish in Hagerstown, Maryland, secured two members of his congregation to fill the vacancies. They were Michael Diehl and Hezekiah Reubush Geiger, two Gettysburg seminarians about to graduate. They came willingly to make the sacrifices and to endure the hardships. Together they served a total of fifty-two years and were considered among the school's founders. The connection between the college and the Hagerstown congregation was strong. It sent financial support, library books, and teachers. A number of its members moved to Springfield and joined the church there. Later on, their pastor, Reverend Conrad, came to join the faculty.

The Reverend Diehl came as professor of languages in 1846 and remained until shortly before his death in 1868. Geiger came the same year as professor of mathematics and natural sciences and remained for more than thirty years. He said that the Gettysburg seminary opposed his accepting the call. They saw no need for a competing school and made him a flattering offer to remain in Pennsylvania. With the resoluteness that would mark his whole life, he resisted their blandishments and headed west.

Michael Diehl, professor of Languages, 1860. Wittenberg University Archives.

Hezekiah Reubush Geiger, professor of Mathematics and Natural Science, 1860. Wittenberg University Archives.

Requirements for admission to Wittenberg were outlined in the first college catalog issued in 1847. No one was admitted to the freshman class until he passed examinations in Caesar, Virgil, Bullion's Greek reader, Bullion's Greek and Latin grammars, Latin prosody, ancient and modern geography, English grammar, arithmetic, the history of the United States, and Isaac Watt's very popular *On the Mind*. Watts, an English dissenter, wrote over six hundred hymns including "Joy to the World" and this commentary on John Locke's *Essay on Human Understanding*. It emphasized that the mind was "an empty cabinet" to be furnished by the student. Admission requirements further stipulated that "satisfactory testimonials of good moral character are required, and those who have been connected with other colleges must produce certificates of honorable dismission." The preparatory program was not a high school, but took students where they were in their preparation and sought to get them to the level required for college as fast as feasible. Such programs were common in the early colleges because public schools were slow to develop on the frontier, and there were few private academies.

The original curriculum, as described by Keller in 1846, was ambitious and modern for its time, representing some departure from the classical course then dominant in American colleges. Keller reported that in addition to the normal theological fare, the candidates for the ministry also touched on archaeology and biblical criticism. He described a college course that embraced English and science as well as the usual classic subjects. It included history, art, geography, English, geometry, plane trigonometry, calculus, surveying, navigation, and chemistry. These were mixed with usual courses in Greek, Latin, philosophy, rhetoric, logic, and for seminarians, Hebrew.

The library also had a good beginning. Keller solicited books as well as financial contributions in his travels. The largest gift of books was the Berkenmeyer Collection. William C. Berkenmeyer was a noted eighteenth century pastor in New York and a staunch defender of Lutheran orthodoxy. He preached in German, Dutch, and English and was the overseer of all Lutheran clergy in New York and New Jersey. He collected a library in German, Latin, and Dutch as well as English. At his death, he gave it to his congregation. Responding to one of Keller's appeals, the congregation donated

295 books to Wittenberg. The Rev. Thomas Lape, their pastor, also contributed books from his own library. The Berkenmeyer Collection clearly exposed the seminarians at Wittenberg to the classic literature of Lutheran orthodoxy.

A few years later, after Keller's death, his widow offered to sell her husband's library to the college for a modest sum. A number of persons gave the money to enable the college to buy it and to pay Keller's estate all the money due him for cash advances and back salary. These two collections, Keller's and Berkenmeyer's, formed the basis of the early library. Regular purchases by the literary societies and subsequent gifts steadily enlarged the collection.

Keller gave further evidence of the nature of the curriculum in reporting the growth of the "cabinet of minerals and curiosities," and his request that the board appropriate funds for a "philosophical apparatus," a term used to describe basic scientific equipment of the day. "It will be impossible to give satisfaction in the scientific departments without it," Keller said. He also emphasized the activities of the literary societies which encouraged reasoning, argumentation, writing, and the challenge and debate of ideas. Literary societies were important fixtures in every college in America, and participation was expected of all students.

Just twenty-six days after classes began, thirteen charter members founded the Excelsior Society. The students selected the name from the young American writer Henry Wadsworth Longfellow's poem, "Excelsior." When the newly famous poet learned of their choice, he wrote a letter of appreciation and sent an illustrated copy of his poem which adorned a wall of their hall for decades. The men met every Friday afternoon for reading, declamation, oratory, and debate. They also learned parliamentary procedure, how to keep minutes, and how to give and take oral and written criticism.

Someone conceived the idea of forming a rival society, such as existed at other campuses, and thereby enliven student life through competition. Tradition described the separation as friendly, but that was not the case. "There was," said T. E. Mitchell, "considerable misunderstanding and excitement" which Dr. Keller kindly but firmly adjudicated. Thirteen members, including six of the charter members of the first society, withdrew, taking with them half of the group's resources. On the fourth of July in 1846, they formed the Philosophian Society. To establish its American identity, the group elected the currently popular and sensational, if ill-fated American author, Edgar Allen Poe to honorary membership. He expressed his "grateful acceptance and appreciation" for the honor in a letter to the society dated February 9, 1847.

The two groups, in addition to their internal contests, participated in an annual competition and accepted periodic challenges in debate and in literary contests. They competed for members and in collecting the better library. Their programs attracted enthusiastic audiences of Springfield residents. At first, the societies met in a small room at the north end of the ground floor of the Lutheran church. Later separate rooms were set aside for them in the college building. Their annual celebrations and major competitions were staged in the Town Hall, and many townspeople came to hear them. Usually a brass band was added for effect, and invitations extended to all the young ladies of Springfield. Often the town and campus echoed to the yells, "Excel, Excel, Excel, we do excel, *Altus et altior, Excelsior!*" and "*Philor, Philor, Philor tes Sophias.*"

Not all community influences were positive, and Keller took to heart the need to strengthen his charges for contending with the world. In one chapel talk, he outlined the "sins to which students are liable." He listed first "the love of women" and added "pride and voluptuousness." He was especially troubled, he said, by young men frittering away their college years on courtship, going to parties, and running after and talking about girls. He advised them neither to display themselves in town in fancy dress nor to be pedantic in conversations with local citizens. Their task in college, he summarized, was to form a character and a reputation. Studies, religious piety, and literary exercises ought to receive all of their time and energy.

It was not clear from Keller's notes whether he was admonishing the students for sins they had already committed or whether he was trying to make them not miss it all so much as they adhered to the strict rules governing deportment. One early student, when asked years later about athletics in his day, replied, "We were too busy with study and with prayer to get very good at athletics."

Keller's commitment to the idea of the American college was complete, and he saw it as an essential experience for any man who would serve the church in America. With Presbyterians on his board, an Episcopalian, the Rev. Joseph Stephenson, teaching Latin on his faculty, a Presbyterian among his theological students, and a curriculum that aspired toward breadth and innovation, Keller sought to provide a distinctive Lutheran education for his day that reflected something of America's diversity.

He saw revivals of religion as essential in a well-run school. Though they were becoming less and less prevalent on eastern campuses, in the 1840s any college in western America that did not experience a "refreshing" or an outright awakening of religion at least once every few years was thought to be failing in its mission.

Wittenberg's first revival came in 1847. It followed the death of a student from Springfield, Robert C. McCreight, after a three-day illness. Before his death, he had expressed a desire to feel the full assurance of peace with God. It came to him, he said, just before he died; and the impact of his death and his sense of peace at the end set off a season of revival among the students. He was buried on the future campus, a hundred yards northwest of the site for the college building. Keller conducted the funeral. The campus property had been used originally as a cemetery. The Wittenberg board had set aside three and a half acres in the northwest corner of the original plot for that purpose. Lots were available for five dollars. Burials occurred from time to time until in 1863, Ferncliff Cemetery opened west of the campus and the graves on campus were moved.

Mindful of the pitfalls of extremism and knowing that many Lutherans objected to revivals, Keller defended his views. Openness to life on the frontier, he believed, meant revivals. It was a "new measure" that brought sinners to the church. Once in, more traditional catechetical procedures could allow grace to work. One could be firm in Lutheran doctrine and yet be realistic without being radical. He considered himself educationally, politically, and theologically middle-of-the-road, greeting his world head on, though others disagreed. Still, he often cautioned Americanists about disorder in services and too much emotionalism. A pastor's first responsibility, he observed, was order and dignity, but there was room also for the Holy Spirit.

"Several of the students," he noted, "became afraid of the influence of the Spirit, and to escape its power, left the college." Professor Diehl said Keller was overcome by joy at the school's first revival. "His soul became almost too full for utterance, and the Divine glory seemed to rest upon him in a visible form." He considered revivals "the hope of the church." Keller wrote in his diary, "I regard this first revival as a most precious token of divine favor to our infant Wittenberg." He believed it demonstrated that the school was "doing the will of the Heavenly Father." He believed that the Lutheran church was being revived in America because of revivals.

Keller journeyed over the state soliciting support for the college, acquiring books for the library, and advancing the American Lutheran cause. He was founder of the college, professor of theology, and acted as a "Bishop" of the western territory. "During the year, I traveled three thousand two hundred miles, not including short distances," Keller said in his report to the synod. "I preached one hundred and seventy-two sermons and delivered a number of addresses; organized one congregation, put two churches in process of erection; collected for college $6,000, for churches $1,000; instructed four theological students two hours each day during the summer. For strength to perform this labor," he wrote, "I render my thanks to God. The more toil, the more grace."

The frail little man rode his horse over the rough roads preaching and begging for the school and spreading his Americanist views. "Today I feel exceedingly lonely and dejected," he wrote on a tiring and unproductive trip, "The absence of my family, my bodily indisposition, the obstacles . . . all conspire to weigh down my spirit." After preaching in a small schoolhouse, the frail professor wrote that he thought he heard "the flesh" whispering in his ear. "It would have been better to have remained in your pleasant charge in Maryland." He devoted such uncomfortable and sleepless nights to prayer, asking for meekness, fortitude, and contentment under trials and privations.

On another occasion, he noted, "Some times I feel quite discouraged. The precariousness of such an enterprise, the fear that the expectations of our people will not be realized, the illiberality of many of the wealthy, and the want of unanimity and interest in some of our ministerial brethren tend to discourage me." Yet he took courage, he said, because of the importance of his mission. The care of all the churches, he noted, was one of the burdens of St. Paul and "[t]his burden I, too, have been made to experience."

In his search for support, Keller renewed his appeal to the New England Society. In a visit to Cincinnati, he became acquainted with Lyman Beecher and Calvin Stowe of Lane Seminary. The Society asked those two to evaluate Wittenberg, its curriculum and report on its "soundness of doctrine and thoroughness of education." The two liked Keller and were impressed with his school. They recommended support for Wittenberg. The College joined such schools as Western Reserve and Marietta in Ohio and Wabash in Indiana, as a beneficiary of Presbyterian and Congregational donors in the East. Without this support, it is doubtful the school would have survived. An annual contribution of $600 a year soon increased to $1,000 annually, or ten percent of the school's budget. The President was expected, in return, to find permanent endowment so that it would not continue to need the Society's grant. He was also expected to present the society's mission and need to potential Lutheran donors in the East and invite them to join in support of the society.

Keller preached as often as eight times in a week and three times on the Sabbath. He attributed what he called his "imprudent zeal" to an awareness of the amount of work to be done, and the shortness of the time in which to do it. Such fears had haunted him since his youth. As a college student he had written:

> "The week is past and gone
> No more it shall return
> I'm nearer to the grave
> My soul I wish to save."

Not long after, he wrote:

> "I see the passing, fleeing things of time
> Passing in quiet succession to their end
> I hear a voice, from whence I cannot tell
> 'Here dying man, behold thy fleeting life.'"

"Glad will I be," he wrote in his diary, "when I shall be released from the secular business which necessity now imposes upon me." The time spent in seeing to unplastered walls, faulty stoves, and erection of buildings, he believed, detracted from his ministry. On a happier day, he expressed a different thought. "It requires strong faith to anticipate a large and well-endowed institution from so small a beginning, but

> "Large oaks from little acorns grow,
> Large streams from little fountains flow.
> If God be for us, we shall succeed."

One day, as Keller and the Board walked over the campus property to locate the site for the college building, he pointed to a commanding hill and suggested that it should go there. The trouble was it was not part of the school's seventeen acres. Keller asked Isaac Ward to sell the hilltop to the college. The Board agreed that that was where the building should go and agreed to purchase an additional seven acres to secure the entire hill. Several generous citizens of Springfield contributed funds to make the purchase possible. The campus now contained 24 acres.

Students clearing the site for the first college building. Yearbook art by Itsuo Umezaki, class of 1959. Wittenberg University Archives.

Early in April 1846, students and faculty began to clear the ground on the top of the hill for the east wing of the building. Students were quite handy, if too exuberant, with the ax. An observer from Cincinnati felt the area had been cleared without any regard for good taste or any apparent design for garden or grove. Benjamin Prince confirmed that a large number of trees had to be removed. The area had been covered with magnificent white and red oaks and other trees such as poplar.

Students dug out the basement and prepared the area for the foundation to be built of limestone cut from the cliffs at Buck Creek. The road to campus and the two circular drives up the hill to the left and to the right were cut by the stone-bearing wagons that hauled all the building materials. From bottom to top, the hill had a rising elevation of fifty-six feet in a distance of two hundred yards or so. Footmen could walk it, young men might sprint up, but teams of horses pulling a load of limestone had to take a circular route. In doing so they made a grand circle which later became the historic heart of the campus.

That spring Keller spent a great deal of time on the grounds supervising students in trimming trees, burning brush, removing stumps, taking logs to lumber mills, planting oleanthus trees, and stacking firewood. The students felled trees, peeled bark, and made rails to begin the task of fencing in the college property. "I was reminded of Luther," Keller wrote, "who said he was inspector of a fish pond." After such heavy labor, he and the students looked forward to the restful Sabbath with delight.

In addition to labor, Keller secured funds from his students. Four of them invested up to $100 each for a year to help in the project. It was their money for their next year's expenses. The literary societies raised thirty dollars a piece to help complete their rooms. Some, who thought the college had too much land, suggested that they clear acreage for farming. They could sell the firewood and cultivate crops, onions or turnips, to employ themselves and raise funds for the college.

On September 1, 1846, the board held its first meeting in the partially completed east wing.

East wing of college building under construction, Itsuo Umezaki. Wittenberg University Archives.

They forded the stream, described by Benjamin Prince as a "merry little brook that came from a strong spring" east of the campus. It flowed southwest at the foot of the hill and into Buck Creek. They crossed the brook and trudged up the hill to the east wing. Ten members were present. In a small room, cut off from the world and surrounded by the forest, they considered the design of a college seal and selection of a school motto. The proposed seal showed a hand passing a lighted torch to another. In a circle around the picture, they displayed a Greek motto, *Lampadia Exontes Diadosousin Allelois*. It was a quotation adapted from Plato's *Republic* (Book I).

In Plato's story, Polymarchus, with a group of friends chiming in, is trying to persuade Socrates to stay the night and visit his father. If he stayed, they could see a torch relay race on horseback in honor of a pagan goddess. Socrates exclaimed that was something new to him, a torch race on horseback. How will they do it, he asked? Will riders race with the burning torches and pass them to one another at various intervals? It was that question which held the phrase selected for the motto: "having torches and handing them one to another." At a superficial level, perhaps, it was an appropriate choice for students racing with faculty around the curriculum, a Latin word for a racecourse.

The reason for selecting this as the school's motto, however, is not recorded. It was not a central idea from *The Republic,* but a mere side story in the introduction. The image in *The Republic,* however, is that of Socrates thinking, conversing, and sharing thoughts with others—not an inappropriate picture of the function of a college. Socrates apparently does remain overnight, and in his conversation with Cephalus, Polemarchus's father, engages in a debate about justice and injustice and what the older generation owes the younger generation or what the wealthy owe to society. They are to be the guardians of a free society. Teachers are to be the educators of these guardians of the republic. It was a high purpose for the college teacher to train these leaders.

But if the foundation of education for leadership in western culture was focused on *The Iliad*, the Bible, Plato, and Shakespeare, as was asserted in that era, someone had to select this quotation from that canon. It was Ezra Keller who made that choice. But given Keller's and the school's strong religious orientation, why not a motto from the Bible, like "The Truth will set you free," many might well have asked? Clearly the classical world of Latin and Greek pervaded this little college in the woods if this was to be its motto. The minutes of the board shed no light on the matter. There is no further reference to it until the school planned its first commencement and needed to produce diplomas bearing a seal. In approving the printing, the board approved the seal.

Original seal of Wittenberg College, 1846. Wittenberg University Archives.

But clearly Keller came more and more to the point of view that colleges were responsible for training those who would be the "guardians" of the American Republic.

The motto was, by the mid-1840s however, a familiar quotation concerning the passing on of knowledge from one to another. Harper and Row Publishers in New York City had used it since 1817 to denote the function of a publisher in the society. The phrase had long since moved from a contextual to a symbolic meaning before it was selected by Wittenberg. The school would later translate it into English: "Having Light We Pass It On To Others." The students of 1914, who sought a name for their student newspaper and called it the *Torch*, translated it very well.

At the same 1846 board meeting, having placed themselves so greatly in debt to Professor Keller, the members persuaded him to accept the office of president. Reluctantly he did so. He had declined previously, but "as no one with suitable qualifications could be found who would undertake the labor for the small compensation offered," he noted, "I have with great reluctance accepted it." His private response was, "[m]y sincere prayer is that this act may redound to the glory of God." He still looked forward to the day when the school could afford a full time professor of theology and a president. the *Lutheran Observer* noted that Keller was a decidedly good business man, not a mere bookworm; an excellent choice to head the school.

On Aug. 30, Keller was inaugurated. The board briefly interrupted its session to listen to an address by the Rev. W. H. Harrison of Cincinnati. When Abraham Reck died Harrison had become Keller's closest advisor. Keller said he was "congenial and likeminded." The board watched as Keller and Professors Diehl and Geiger signed a declaration of Christian faith and acceptance of Lutheran doctrine as approved by the General Synod. Then, after prayer, the board returned to its business meeting. The inauguration caused an even less perceptible interruption in Keller's labors. As president, professor, pastor, and western missionary, he continued to exhibit his imprudent zeal.

Keller was highly regarded by the students though one in particular had to overcome an initial disappointment. Looking at the frontispiece of the Catalogue which showed an engraving of a massive building with a pillared porch, a cupola and two grand wings, the student was shocked to find only the east wing standing and it incomplete. He had come five hundred miles and, "I was disappointed in my expectations and, as I thought, deceived." Having given up a chance to attend a flourishing institution in the East, he was startled at the meagerness of this school in the western woods.

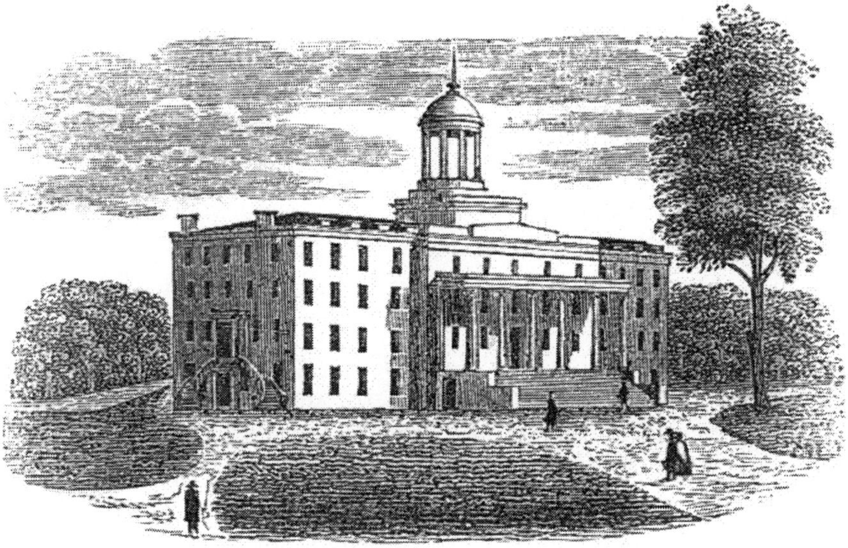

Drawing of proposed first building, from 1848 college catalog. Wittenberg University Archives.

Dr. Keller met newly arrived students at his home or at the church. They were taken by his charm, his grand head, his peculiarly retreating but cordial smile and his soft, sweet voice. Though another who had arrived with him was so disappointed that after a few days he packed up and returned East, the first student was won over immediately. "My mind was made up," he said, "to accept whatever Wittenberg should have in store for me." He regarded Dr. Keller as a foster father and saw himself as a dutiful son. In the spring of 1847, to expedite construction, Keller made himself personally responsible to the various contractors if they would proceed with the work on the east wing and finish it.

The students who remained were captivated by Keller's charismatic personality. His influence, one said, was remarkable. His presence was magnetic, a rare commingling of dignity and austerity with a fascinating sweetness of expression. He was a man of remarkable memory, penetrating insight, and his students never forgot him. Robert C. Woodward, the first Springfield resident to enroll at Wittenberg, and later the town librarian said, "I wish it were possible to transcribe the personality of Dr. Keller." He was a hard task master, but was a living power among the students. Keller was, he added, a man of endurance, fortitude, and superior faith. Peculiarly tactful, very self-controlled, and with high moral standards, Keller was a man, students believed, whose very soul continually shown forth, possessed of "the Christ-life." John F. Mitchell remembered his "firmness and gentleness." If you encountered him only once, he said, you remembered him forever; "so earnest and impressive were his looks and words."

Keller was well received in Springfield. He rapidly became one of the town's leading preachers. He was a man of fine presence, according to Professor Geiger, and an excellent sermonizer. Geiger described his influence in recounting the story of an acquitted murderer. Popular feeling was against the accused, and as he left the court house a free man, a mob of citizens came after him. Keller, recognizing the threatening situation, rolled a store box into the street. Climbing onto the box, he held up his hand to stop the group, and then talked about their intention. His dignity and friendliness, backed by his well-known strength of character, turned the men from their rash act.

In February 1847, Ezra Keller made a progress report to the citizens of Springfield. He needed to do so, he said, because he had asked for their support and they should know how things had gone. The school had been in operation for about fifteen months and enrollment reached eighty-five, nine at the collegiate level and seventy-six at one level of preparation or another—, many from the local area. The library numbered 2,800 volumes. The philosophical and chemical apparatus was nearing completion. The literary societies and German Rhetorical Society were functioning well. He reported that payments on pledges from citizens had reached $5,500, and that nearly all those due had been collected with little difficulty. He thanked all for their support.

But of what benefit had the institution been to the community, he asked? Forty-six of the students were from "abroad"—Virginia, Kentucky, Indiana, Pennsylvania, and more distant parts of Ohio.

Each of these spent $75 per year for a total annual expenditure in Springfield of $3,450. In addition, many visitors, parents, and friends, came yearly to Springfield because of the college. Six families bought or built houses. The dollars spent by students, faculty, staff, and visitors, he noted were in the hands of area farmers, butchers, landlords of taverns and boarding houses, persons who lease houses and rooms to students, tanners, shoemakers, merchants, tailors, seamstresses, physicians, and dentists, draymen, workers in tin and sheet iron, washerwomen, wood sawyers, and so forth. "Every kind of citizen is benefited by such an institution," Keller concluded, "except perhaps the lawyers." He also noted for local donors that tuition grants to students who were children of donors this term amounted to $376.

Another example of the friendly relationship between town and College was the Fourth of July celebration begun on campus in 1848. The community was invited to share in this annual Sabbath school picnic which demonstrated the institution's Americanism and social conscience. The Declaration of Independence was read and addresses delivered by faculty, friends, and students. Refreshments were served and tours of the grounds provided. The editor of the *Springfield Republic* commended the college and observed that the day "was celebrated in a manner becoming the refined intelligence and high-toned morality of the American people . . ."

The literary societies were another popular town-gown relationship. The young men of the societies invited area citizens to attend their anniversary celebrations and contests. They extended special invitations to the young ladies of Springfield to grace the assembly with their presence. The editor observed that the Philosophian Society seemed to have enjoyed the interest and sympathies of the young ladies from its very beginning. At its first anniversary, they presented the men with a beautiful Bible; and this year, he reported, an eighty-one volume set in fancy binding of the choicest of the American Tract Society's reform publications. "This society," noted the editor, "was becoming deeply seated in the affections of the people." Its hall was neatly ornamented with good carpentry and suitable furniture; and it received generous support, not just from the ladies but from other citizens as well.

When the Excelsior Society moved into its top floor room in the east wing of the college building, it installed rich and heavy walnut window casings, marble desks, and bookcases, velvet carpet, and upholstered chairs. The boys figured out a way to remove two posts in the middle of the room without the ceiling collapsing. Similar good reports were given when the Society staged its anniversary program, and when the two met in public competition.

If Wittenberg and Keller influenced the community, they were likewise influenced by it. The school's beginning coincided with growing dissatisfaction in the town with the Mexican War. Keller, already sympathetic with abolition, was deeply influenced by the strong Whig feelings against the war predominant in Springfield. For most of his life, Keller was little concerned about politics. "If men were but as much concerned about making their own calling and election sure as they are about securing the election of their favorite candidates," he observed, "how differently they would live." Keller felt that presidential elections put the community in an uproar, and he was "heartily tired of the noise and confusion" which accompanied the great American quadrennial.

Ezra Keller, by his own admission, failed to vote in any election prior to 1846. He attributed his abstention to a disbelief in the validity of partisan positions as well as to his dislike of political campaigns. Elections seemed to him to be much ado about nothing. He opposed extremes, he said, whether in theology or in politics; and held that a man was probably nearest to truth on any given question when he was abused by both sides.

Keller, like many American Lutherans, abhorred slavery, but he could not accept the extreme tactics of the "abolitionists." Ten years before he moved to Springfield, while still living and preaching in the slave state of Maryland, he described himself as dejected and melancholy because of this one issue. "The foe of my peace is preying upon my soul," he wrote in his diary. "The cause of humanity," his phrase for the plight of the slave, pressed upon his mind. Yet he feared to advocate abolition because of the hatred with which the issue was fraught and the anti-church attitude of many abolitionists. He faced a dilemma of pursuing justice for the slave without becoming an abolitionist.

Once out of the slave state, he came increasingly to view the state of the nation as an appropriate subject for classroom and pulpit. It was a subject that he himself had "too much neglected," he confessed. As he became more aware of "the nation's blessings" and the responsibility which he felt one generation had to transmit those blessings unimpaired to the next, his views about the political role of the Christian changed. "May this land ever more be Emmanuel's land," he told his Springfield congregation. "What a goodly heritage our Heavenly Father has bestowed upon us," he said, and called upon all to show gratitude by working to preserve those blessings. From that day on, Keller played a more active political role. Educators and pastors were indeed guardians of their free society.

As early as 1844, the English Lutheran synod in Ohio had taken a stand against slavery, calling it "an evil, which all Christians should deplore." New School Lutherans in the north, however, were urged to moderate such partisan positions in order not to jeopardize the unity of the General Synod which included many synods and congregations in the south. Americanists, who supported ecumenical cooperation, were also cautioned against agitating the slavery issue because of its affect on other groups. To push for abolition, it was said, undermined the ecumenical movement. How then might a political role for the Christian be accomplished? Keller was not certain, but he gave it extensive thought. In Springfield, in conversation with others, he came closer to a resolution. A program whereby the moderate could oppose slavery was needed. The coming of the Mexican War triggered action for many in this Ohio town and elsewhere.

The power of the slave owners, Keller wrote, undermined the North and destroyed the nation as a bulwark of freedom. Slavery and the Mexican War, which in Keller's opinion was perpetrated against Mexico in the name of slavery, should be opposed by all constitutional means. He, like other evangelical church leaders in the North, after a decade of "dejection and melancholy," was now resolved upon a direction independent of the extremes of slavery or abolition.

The Mexican War, said, Keller, invoking the Church's ancient discipline, was an "unjust war," and every well-informed citizen should endeavor by legal means to change the policy that waged war upon the nation's neighbor to the south. The War and the power of slavery which was behind it, he said, were giant crimes that would "ruin the North by the destruction of our manufactures and the extension of slavery." It was a view that later historians would soften saying that the causes of the war were more varied and less conspiratorial, but it was a view held by many northerners at the time.

Keller and many of his neighbors in Springfield saw the war against Mexico solely as an effort to expand slavery by adding new slave states from Texas and the territory to be acquired from Mexico, thereby strengthening the slave power in the Congress. The year 1846, as historian Bernard De Voto later asserted, became a year of decision for America that would change the course of history.

Very few men from Clark County volunteered for service in the war. The women of the Bible society who visited every home in the county said they gave Bibles to only twenty-one men going off to war. Five Whig congressmen from the area voted against the war. Ohio Senator Thomas Corwin became an outstanding opponent and opposed passage of the military appropriation to supply the army. At the college, Ohio students became involved in heated debate with students from the South and southern enrollments in Ohio colleges began to decline. Every well-wisher of the nation, advised Keller, ought to cast a ballot against the advocates of this war, to defeat slavery and aggression. He ended his life long abstention from politics to vote against the Democratic candidates who supported the unjust war.

In mid-December of 1848, however, the thirty-six-year-old Keller was stricken with typhoid fever. Early in the morning of December 29, he died in the midst of a revival at the church and the college. His death spread a general gloom over the institution, his congregation, and the whole community that had come to love him. The death of Wittenberg's founder raised widespread fears for the future of the school. Unrequested, nearly all the church bells of Springfield were tolled for the "deceased, beloved, lamented Dr. Keller." The editor of the *Springfield Republic* hailed him as a ripe scholar, an exemplary Christian, a patriot, and a philanthropist who gave promise of a brilliant career. As a preacher, few could exceed him, he added. "His language was earnest, impressive and simple in the extreme. A child could understand him; but all felt the power of his words." The fervent advocate of an American Lutheranism and patriotism and president of a frontier college was buried on the unfinished campus.

Official portrait of President Ezra Keller, D D, Wittenberg University Archives. Photo by Robert Gantt.

The students met to draft resolutions about "this melancholy occurrence" but could find no words adequate to express their sorrow and sense of loss. Finally, after long deliberation, they reported, "We make no attempt to express by words our sorrow . . . or to speak the loss we sustain . . . ." They expressed sympathy to the family and agreed to wear "a badge of mourning for sixty days."

By 1848, Keller's "imprudent zeal" had brought fruition to the hopes of the English Lutherans in Ohio, the College Board, friends of the school, and Springfield's residents. Wittenberg was established. One hundred and thirty-nine students were enrolled in the preparatory, collegiate, and theological departments. Fifty-one of them would be candidates for the ministry, and they pursued their studies in English—an American clergy for the Lutheran church in America.

"This is a lovely spot for the location of a literary institution," Keller had said. "It requires some faith to believe that in after years it will be an academic grove to which hundreds will resort to drink at the pure fountains of knowledge and go forth in the world to do good, to bless mankind. And yet I have faith to believe that this will be realized. If my eyes shall not be permitted to behold these blessed results," he concluded, "yet, when they shall be closed in death, others will see them and rejoice and bless the Lord for what He has done in rearing such an instrumentality of Blessing."

Chapter Three

Though the Mountains Shake

Samuel Sprecher succeeded Ezra Keller at Wittenberg and reaffirmed the American emphasis. He was more uncompromising than Keller as conflict among Lutherans grew more intense. He was very close to his brother-in-law, Samuel S. Schmucker, leader of the

Samuel Sprecher, second president of Wittenberg, 1849-1874.
1860 photo. Wittenberg University Archives.

New School Lutherans and president of the General Synod. Sprecher was thirty-nine years of age; and before his quarter-century was concluded, he would be recognized as a provocative and challenging educator and theologian.

Sprecher was a first generation American; and like many, he eagerly embraced his country. He was born December 28, 1810, in Washington County, Maryland. His grandparents had emigrated from Germany before the American Revolution bringing his father and his two brothers with them. The youngest of twelve children, Samuel grew up on the farm, but had abundant time for study. As an expert hunter and trapper, he earned sufficient money from the sale of animal skins to buy what ever books he wanted. He was from the earliest age a delicate, solitary, and studious person. After clerking a short while in a store, he entered Gettysburg College in Pennsylvania.

Like Keller, Sprecher came from a farm in Maryland, had been converted in a country revival, studied under Schmucker, and entered the ministry. He was slight in stature, like Keller, with delicate features and a frail constitution. Each suffered with problems of throat and voice, aggravated by preaching and teaching, yet each was uniquely industrious and zealous. To each, attending to duty was the most hallowed of earthly traits; and each believed that by the grace of God, duty was discernible.

Upon graduation from seminary Sprecher married Catherine, Dr. Schmucker's sister, and developed a close friendship with his former teacher. Catherine bore nine children and was described as practical, heroic, and self-sacrificing; a sturdy companion of Samuel for forty-three years. He began his ministry in Harrisburg, but in 1840 gave up his first charge because of ill health. For two years, he was principal of Emmaus Institute, a preparatory school. Then with renewed vigor he returned to the ministry. A year later he went to Chambersburg, Pennsylvania, where he remained until he came to Wittenberg.

When Keller made his last trip east the summer before he died, he visited Sprecher and asked him to pledge his faithfulness to the doctrines in which they both had stood firm. He noted that others were departing from the spirit which he believed was reviving the church. Having gotten Sprecher's reassurance, Keller considered him a logical candidate to be his partner at Wittenberg. On his deathbed, he wrote Sprecher reminding him of his promise to accept the chair of Theology at Wittenberg

Many thought Sprecher's selection was preordained. They told the story that Keller had called area board members to his bedside to ask them to choose his friend in Chambersburg to carry on the work. The assembled group was probably the Prudential Committee that operated the school between meetings of the board. Later when the board met to elect Sprecher, it was without proper notice. When it met to correct the earlier shortcoming it did not have a quorum. Sprecher was asked in March to accept the presidency; but, aware of Keller's concern that two persons should share the load, he suggested that they look elsewhere. There was no doubt, however, that all concurred in choosing Keller's candidate. Not until long after the call had been issued and Sprecher had accepted did the board get its procedure straightened out.

As the delay continued, the local paper allayed concerns suggesting that the school's charter required that the post be kept vacant for a time. Causes were not very clear locally. As late as mid-April, Sprecher told John J. Snyder, Wittenberg treasurer, that the board should call two persons. Just as Keller wanted Reynolds and then Sprecher to share the load, Sprecher suggested himself as professor of Theology and the Rev. Frederick W. Conrad as president. The work required a two-man team, he felt. The board would certainly do what he asked if the funds were available, said Snyder, but they were not. Once again, one man would have to fill both positions.

Sprecher consulted Conrad by letter and in a personal meeting. He believed that no two men would fit better together at Wittenberg than the two of them. He wanted Conrad's expertise as an administrator and his zeal to put the school on a solid footing, while he would give primary attention to the academic program and the theological department. "Think of the immense good we could do," he said. Between them he saw Wittenberg as shaping the church in the West, determining where new churches should be and training the young men who would make them go. Synods had no full-time staff, and college presidents played a larger role in strengthening their denominations than they would later. Sprecher and Conrad would spread the American Lutheran church among Presbyterians, Methodists, Baptists, and old Lutherans alike. The church would grow in the West by just such measures.

They would build churches to rival the mainstream and give people a sounder theological choice.

In the end, Wittenberg could afford only one of the men, and the two decided that Sprecher should accept the call and, once in Springfield, build toward the day when Conrad could join him. Sprecher arrived in Springfield with his family on June 16, 1849. He assumed his duties from Michael Diehl, professor of languages, who had served as acting president during the six months following Keller's death.

Springfield was pleased, having been assured by Whig party leaders in Chambersburg that they were getting a good man. Hundreds of non-Lutherans joined with his congregation to bid him farewell. "Never have we seen a minister of the Gospel," they reported, "whose hold upon the confidence and admiration of the people extended more widely beyond the pale of his own church." Sprecher's leaving was described as a loss to the community, an occurrence to be regretted, a sundering of deep friendships and great affections; he was held, they said, in the highest regard.

Springfield had high expectations for the college and they were eager for the building to be completed. Samuel Sprecher's choice reassured them. "Although the college is under the protection of the Lutheran denomination," observed the editor of the *Springfield Republic*, "it cannot be called sectarian." Wittenberg's faculty included men of various creeds, and the conduct of the school had gained the patronage of all classes of citizens, he noted. Springfielders expected Wittenberg to be religious in the "exalted sense" not in any narrow or sectarian one. "It has in it," he concluded, "the undeveloped elements of high success, which will one day make it an honor to the town . . . ." Thus in welcoming Sprecher, the editor restated the town's expectations.

A student's view of the transition from Keller to Sprecher was given by William J. Cutter of Jeffersontown, Kentucky, writing to friends in Dayton, Ohio. The previous year, Cutter, a theology student, had taught German in the college. In February, he told his friends that the Lord guarded Wittenberg with special care; and that, while everyone thought everything would end with Keller's death, it had not ended. The school was enjoying prosperity and harmony. In April, he commented, "God has an eye to our beloved Wittenberg, and under His care it will prosper."

In June, Cutter reported on Sprecher's first sermon. "He is an able preacher; but I do not think that he did his best, which is quite wise for it is always better for one to rise than descend." In the evening, an even larger audience came, but Sprecher turned the pulpit over to Professor Diehl who had been serving as interim pastor. Another student, however, thought Sprecher "made a lasting impression upon all who heard him . . . at the close of the service, we all felt sure the right man had been selected."

A third student, John F. Mitchell, was even more impressed.

John F. Mitchell, Valedictorian of Wittenberg's first graduating class in 1851. Photo, Wittenberg University Archives.

"I well remember that first Sabbath, as he appeared where Dr. Keller had such power." He read Psalm 46: "God is our refuge and strength, a very present help in trouble. Therefore will not we fear though the earth be removed and though the mountains shake." As he preached, concerns about the future melted away. "We all at the close of the service," Mitchell concluded, "felt sure that the right man had been selected . . . to take Dr. Keller's place." Sprecher's selection, according to another, "sent a thrill through the whole institution . . . Wittenberg is destined to rise. Believe it. Take courage . . . What everlasting blame would rest upon us if after all the sacrifices [Keller] made, we should permit the institution to suffer . . . and finally run down." All noted the similarity of Sprecher's views to Keller's. The school would move on in an unbroken line.

Sprecher wrote again to Conrad. "If ever our Heavenly Father desired to manifest his sense of the beautiful by the work of His hands, He has done it here!" The town, he noted, was "growing with tremendous rapidity, doubling population . . . in the course of four years," and the students, "[a] more kind, generous, manly company . . . I have seldom seen together." All the place needs, Sprecher told him, was "more money and *yourself*." He added, "Oh! How I would rejoice to have you by my side, planning and working with me in this great and glorious design of God."

Sprecher outlined plans to raise money among the eastern churches, focusing on Hagerstown and Chambersburg. Those churches were already providing enthusiastic support and he urged Conrad to build on that base. He needed money for the college and the churches in the West. Springfield's growth was tremendous, he said, but, if they continued to worship in a basement, "[i]n a small and uncomfortable hole," the Presbyterians and Methodists with their fine, large new churches would gather in the people. A strong college had to begin with a strong Lutheran church in Springfield, he said, and he asked the Wittenberg board to loan the congregation additional funds to complete the church. Sprecher closed a third letter to Conrad saying that Mrs. Keller wanted him to be her husband's biographer and would bring his diary and papers, if he were willing. Sprecher suggested that if Conrad came, it would save her all that trouble.

After completion of the church, Sprecher's major problem was finishing the college building. The east wing was unfinished. A student, in August 1849, said, "Times are somewhat dull around college. Nothing is heard save the mason's hammer and carpenter's saw, and occasionally the eloquence of some remaining student."

On August 14, Sprecher was inaugurated in the Lutheran church in town and, the next day, the cornerstone was laid for the center section of the college building on the campus. The editor of the

Republic took issue with the design of the building which was similar to the main building at Gettysburg. While some in town thought the school was undertaking too large a building and might not be able to complete it, he supported the school on its size but objected to the planned portico. He claimed the press had an obligation to point out errors in public architecture. The portico would "break the front and give it a patchwork appearance. It looks as if it didn't belong there, being stuck on." He suggested revising the plan. The building was completed without the porch because of lack of funds and remained in that state for sixty years. It was the largest structure in the area for years.

A student writing home barely mentioned the event. He noted instead, "the cholera is yet ravaging in town . . . twelve were buried last Sabbath. Some days there are no cases, others a few, then sometimes a large number, many are dead six hours after being attacked. Some of the most prominent citizens have died." Resuming in the morning he wrote, "Thanks be to God, I am still alive and well . . . we cannot tell what moment we may be called to leave the world. There were three deaths last night . . . ."

The following March, the student brought his brother up to date on the building's progress. The workmen had begun again after the winter layoff. The foundation had been laid of limestone rock found in abundance at the southwest corner of the campus, and the same source provided lime for the mortar as they prepared to lay brick. By May he reported, "I have just been on the college building and taking a view." The original plan for a four-story building had been altered. The center five-story section was now three stories above the basement and nearly even with the top of the four-story east wing already in use. Construction had been renewed because the Board had negotiated to borrow $3,000 from Gettysburg to finish. Apparently authorities there were taking a more kindly view toward the western college. Wittenberg treasurer J. J. Snyder completed the loan to be repaid with interest in three years. In the spring of 1850, a tutor in the college and a theology student, Morris Officer, was put in charge of the building's construction; and the project continued uninterrupted until it was finally completed in December of 1851. Upon graduation from the theological course, Officer was named superintendent of the building and principal of the preparatory department.

The first students in the college ready to graduate were two brothers, James and John Mitchell from Clark County. There was, however, no graduation ceremony in 1850. James left for the California gold fields as soon as his classes were finished, responding to Gold Rush fever. John elected to graduate the following year rather than graduate alone. He was named valedictorian of the combined class; and on September 12, 1851, nine men received their diplomas in Springfield's city hall.

Springfield Town Hall, 1848-1878. Site of commencements and literary society exercises for three decades. Clark County Historical Society.

"You are now educated young men," Sprecher told the classes, " . . . may your lives and influence be for good, an honor to your friends, your teachers and your alma mater." That first ceremony was indeed a commencement. It was held at the beginning of the next academic year following completion of senior examinations. Graduates were often unwilling to wait three months for their degrees, yet from 1851 to 1855 the ceremony was in late August or early September. Not until 1856 was it scheduled for June.

In early 1852, Officer supervised moving the preparatory department from church to the campus and with that all of the school's functions had left the church building. When the west wing was ready, the rooms were totally devoid of furnishings. Each student had to purchase furniture in town, make stools and benches, and, as one said, write home to have sent "those things which would occur to a mother to send." The student's day began at four o'clock in the morning when each was required to be up, present and accounted for. Soon the hour for rising was moved to five in the morning. There was a similar muster each evening to see that each student was on hand at the end of the day as well.

One of the most pleasant recollections of students in the early days of the completed building was that of sunsets visible from the upper western windows. On more than one occasion, the scene was so spectacular that students from down the hall gathered at the west end to enjoy the view together. One described the scene: "It was so fine," he said, "rain had fallen and was frozen upon everything it had touched. The forest sparkled in the sunlight like a lake, and the tiny waves of Buck Creek danced in the sun's bright rays. The sun seemingly grew larger and assumed fantastic colors until at last it sank beneath the western horizon, leaving the students in the afterglow of twilight."

A student could walk from the new building to the Lutheran Church at Factory and High Streets. Following the college road south to a spot across from the beautiful waterfall where Mill Run cascaded majestically into Buck Creek, students could cross on stepping stones most of the year to reach the other side just west of the falls. Following a path amid the rocks up the south side they reached Factory Street, which was later renamed Wittenberg Avenue. Proceeding three or four blocks south, they arrived at the church. Later, according to Hezekiah Geiger, the students erected a foot bridge across the creek with their own hands. He was impressed with the students' practical skills. Under Geiger's direction, they also built a small frame building alongside the college brook and piped brook water through a conduit to provide a cold shower bath.

The college building at the top of the hill was a boon to the morale of faculty and students and to the citizens of Springfield, who saw it as a sign that their expectations would now soon be realized.

"Old Wittenberg" completed in 1851. Wittenberg University Archives.

The cost was $28,000 and a lot of contributed time of faculty and students. Geiger, ignoring the school's $8,000 debt for other purposes, including unpaid salaries, made a special point that the building was debt-free. There was little money in Springfield, he said, and almost no surplus capital. Citizens would worry about the school's future if the building were mortgaged. "Springfield was a struggling little place," he added. "I don't like to say that it was exactly a poor town—it was not very good." Friends in Pennsylvania and Maryland contributed generously to augment local contributions, but it would not have been possible without the sacrifice of the faculty.

Sprecher had received a great deal of help from Reverend Conrad. In 1852, he finally persuaded the board to call Conrad as professor of Belles Lettres, Rhetoric, and Homiletics. He would continue to use some of his time to raise funds for the school. He would also relieve Sprecher as pastor of the Lutheran congregation. Sprecher and Conrad then laid plans for the permanent endowment of the college to fulfill the school's commitment to the Western College Society. Prior to 1849 they had received $600 a year from the society. In that year Sprecher attended the group's meeting in Brooklyn, New York, and persuaded them to raise the annual gift to $1,000. In return, he promised to speak to Lutherans of means in the East on the society's behalf. Thus he fulfilled the commitment Ezra Keller had been unable to do before his death.

Benjamin Prince noted that there never was a dedication service for the building because it was occupied as various parts were completed. First, the east wing was occupied as residence hall, dining room, and classrooms. When the main center portion opened these functions were enlarged, adding rooms for the literary societies. Finally with the west wing completed the preparatory school was added. Some rooms remained unfinished for years. Congregations from several states undertook the task of finishing and furnishing rooms until, finally, all were completed.

Funds were short, and Sprecher spent virtually all of the year raising money. It was a serious financial crisis, its full dimensions not widely understood. As Benjamin Prince later described it, "[t]he College had been pushed ahead at a rapid pace, but not fast enough for over zealous and ambitious friends." There were those in the church and in the town who had pushed hard for fast, tangible progress. Leaders in the synods, noting the opening of Capital University in Columbus by the German Synod had urged Sprecher to complete the building at all costs. Leaders in the town were equally assertive. Prince said the two together had pushed Sprecher and the Board to take "greater risks and more uncertain ventures" than the school's resources warranted. Both groups, he said politely, were "somewhat tardy" in providing all the funds their desires for the school required.

As a result of Sprecher's efforts, the meager salaries for the faculty were raised from $700 to $1,000; Conrad was to be paid $600, and Dr. Sprecher's nephew, Isaac, was to tutor for $500 a year. Isaac had come to Wittenberg to study theology, but was put to work so his uncle could travel.

Isaac Sprecher, professor of History and Ancient Languages, 1851-1878. 1860 photograph. Wittenberg University Archives.

Thus salaries totaled $3,300 with $1,000 coming from the Western College Society. To cover the additional $2,300 plus operating costs, the school had to secure gifts or raise tuition and fees.

While Sprecher continued to travel seeking financial support, Conrad wrote articles for newspapers and journals promoting the school and its needs. His work appeared regularly in the *Republic*. His first piece, entitled "Colleges: The Promoters of the Highest Interests of a People," told of the broad educational, moral, financial, and political interests served by western colleges. A second piece argued against the prevalent opinion that students should pay the full costs of their education. A third focused on the benefits that accrued to towns in which such colleges were located, and how continuing local support benefited the community at large. Articles for church publications stressed the advantages to the church in fulfilling its mission by supporting church colleges.

Conrad made direct approaches to the community. At a meeting in 1852, he told local residents that they were not supporting the school as well as other communities with colleges supported theirs. He warned that unless local contributions increased, the institution might have to be moved. It was not the last time that possibility would be raised, but it was not well received. In the first year of this new effort, Lutherans in Pennsylvania gave just $1,000 and citizens of Springfield only $2,500.

By assuring donors that the new gifts would be placed in a permanent endowment so that education could be offered to students at lower cost, the college hoped to see better results. Springfield accepted a goal of $10,000, while $45,000 was to be sought among Lutherans throughout the country. At a town meeting on April 6, 1853, Springfielders pledged $5,125 to be paid over five years with eight percent interest until a pledge was fully paid. The editor of the *Springfield Republic* told readers that a committee would seek to raise the remainder of the $10,000 from those unable to be present. There was sentiment among some, however, that it would be better if the town's $10,000 was applied to physical improvements on the building and the college road.

Plans for the campaign in the churches, however, ran into mounting difficulties. Everything began smoothly enough, but there were concerns expressed by the friends of two other colleges in the General Synod, Gettysburg in Pennsylvania and Hillsboro, later Carthage, in Illinois. So intense was the competition that Sprecher told Conrad that he favored a Lutheran College Society similar to the Western Society that would coordinate fund-raising for all three schools. Before these issues could be resolved, however, a more insurmountable obstacle arose.

Lutherans in America were increasingly involved in the dispute between conservative and liberal views, German and American traditions. Congregations were confused by the competition between the two and the many variations in between. New school Lutherans were pressed for a clearer outline of their position and Sprecher encouraged his brother-in-law, Samuel Schmucker, to make the American position clearer to the mix of people in the West.

In September, 1855, they issued the *Definite Synodical Platform* which outlined their views in plain language.

The advocates of American Lutheranism claimed that their views were fully consistent with the doctrinal position set forth in the constitution of the General Synod. Schmucker, together with Benjamin Kurtz and Sprecher, had agreed on the need for the clearer statement. Paul P. Kuenning, in *The Rise and Fall of American Lutheran Pietism,* attributes the *Platform's* stark and precipitous wording to the fact that Schmucker was ill. It was quite different from his usual careful and deliberate expression of his views. David A. Gustafson in *Lutherans in Crisis,* called the *Definite Platform* an all-out attack on Lutheran sacramental theology and that is how it was perceived by conservatives.

A major part of the *Platform* was "The American Rescension of the Augsburg Confession" which listed alleged errors in the sixteenth-century statement of Lutheran theological positions. Not only were they discarding *The Book of Concord* and other sixteenth century statements of Lutheran doctrine, they proposed to correct "errors" in the Augsburg Confession. The *Platform* revised the confession to exclude errors; asserting, in effect, that the Reformation was unfinished and ongoing and that additional changes may be forthcoming. The *Platform* claimed that it did not omit any "fundamental doctrine of scripture," and was in accord with the General Synod's doctrinal positions.

The authors of the *Definite Platform* were not prepared for the opposition which it aroused. Reaction seemed out of proportion since these were not new ideas and had been expressed before. What had changed was that the part of the church adhering to traditional confessional Lutheranism, because of immigration, was growing larger and stronger. Even a majority of the members of the General Synod refused to accept the *Definite Synodical Platform.* Some expressed strenuous opposition; others ignored it. Only three synods approved it in its entirety: East Ohio, Wittenberg, and Olive Branch in Indiana. The Miami synod approved it in part. All four were synods supporting Wittenberg College and Dr. Sprecher. The Wittenberg Synod adopted it unanimously. As a result, Wittenberg and Sprecher, for a long time afterward, were the focus of orthodox opposition. Fewer students came from other synods, and the school was increasingly isolated theologically.

As Kuenning demonstrates, while the debate focused primarily on theological issues, another major factor in the dispute was the issue of slavery and political activism. Synods in the south distanced themselves from the northern American synods that supported abolition. They had agreed with the northern pietists on many points, but allied themselves with conservatives in the South. Within a few years, they would secede to form the General Synod South. Conservatives in the East would leave the General Synod to form the General Council. Another large body of Germans, the Missouri Synod, refused to recognize the American Lutherans as Lutherans at all. This four-part division of German Lutherans in America would continue until 1917. For Professor Conrad, the controversy meant personal anxiety and despair because, in the end, he disagreed with his friend Sprecher over these issues.

Sprecher asked the Board to change the wording of the declaration of faith signed by the professors, officers, and board members at Wittenberg. In March 1856, he introduced a resolution that "it is of the utmost importance that the declaration of doctrinal views required to be made by the professors of the institution should be as explicit as possible, and the *Definite Synodical Platform* affords such a pledge." Sprecher willingly made Wittenberg College and its theological department the center of the ongoing battle for the American view, but the board postponed action until its June meeting three months later. Not all of Wittenberg's supporting congregations endorsed the *Platform*.

At the June meeting, they crafted a compromise, deleted the term, "the American Recension of the Augsburg Confession," and replaced it with the phrase, "the abstract of the Augsburg Confession." It referred to a shorter form of the Confession, but not a new or altered form. As a consequence of the intensity and complexity of the theological issues, which some of the faculty said they did not understand well enough to pledge themselves one way or the other, the board exempted faculty of the college from taking the oath. It was required of the theological faculty only. It was hoped that all would take the oath, and most, but not all, did. Thus from 1856 on, with brief exceptions in the 1870s, faculty in the college were not required to subscribe to a particular theological position. Active membership in a Christian congregation was sufficient. But if Sprecher consciously looked for faculty who did understand the issues and would sign the oath, and he did, his school in the eyes of some would become increasingly sectarian.

Sprecher was critical of a stagnant scholarship that would not take the Lutheran Church beyond the statements of the sixteenth century. He expressed disapproval of a frame of mind which would "go no further than the instruments of the Reformation," but he also recognized the need for peace and harmony among Wittenberg's supporters. As an old man, in retirement, many years later, he softened his views and became more accepting of the orthodox position; but not while he remained at Wittenberg.

The Lutheran dispute also had far-reaching repercussions for Wittenberg in the Springfield community. The leadership of the town had been attracted to Keller's school and gave it support because of the open and ecumenical views of the founder. They misunderstood this argument among the Lutherans, and they watched the fray with dismay. It seemed that Sprecher and the faculty were preoccupied with these sectarian issues. Many felt that results were slow in coming for the town's investment. They had expected greater growth and expressed disappointment that the Lutheran Church was not doing more. They feared they would be called upon to make up the difference.

With this souring of relationships, the endowment campaign in Springfield floundered like the one in the churches. Funds for the building and the road were provided, but some in town regretted that they had counted on the Lutherans to bring a college to the town. But these were tough years for colleges everywhere. Ohio was now dotted with many weak institutions, twenty-two of them. There were neither enough properly prepared students to support them nor enough financial resources and it appeared that a narrowing sectarianism was capturing every one of them. There were not large numbers of young people for whom parents were seeking a college education. Fewer than 4,000 students attended the twenty-two colleges and over 2,000 of them were preparatory students. Oberlin, with 181 in college courses, was by far the largest.

A new newspaper in Springfield, the nativist *Daily Nonpareil,* editorialized in December 1855 that there were enough colleges in Ohio, and no new ones should be established. To open more colleges before there were enough high schools to prepare students to attend them, the editor argued, was foolhardy. He advised the

Western College Society to add no new colleges to their list, but to concentrate on helping those already open. "There are hundreds already existing," he pointed out, "that are languishing out a miserable existence for want of patronage."

Turning more acidly on Springfield's own local college, the caustic twenty-five-year-old editor Clifton M. Nichols noted that, while the founders of such schools did not mean to become an imposition upon the communities in which they were located, they had in fact become "imposers upon a liberal public." If the church would not come to Wittenberg's support, then Springfield had to; and the beneficiary of that local largesse was hardly living up to what its original sponsors had anticipated. Editor Nichols became a continuing critic of the school and ardent supporter of the community's needs.

But church wrangling, community disappointment and editorial scrutiny were not the only causes of financial difficulty. In 1857, America suffered a severe economic recession; and hard times prevailed for a number of years until the outbreak of Civil War. Enrollment decreased, church support dried up, and community support withered. Those in the community who a decade earlier had hoped for a prosperous college in the town turned their interests elsewhere.

Near the end of 1856, the whole town became energized by Nichol's story that several Presbyterian synods in Ohio planned to pool their efforts to found a major educational institution, one that would rival the school of the Congregationalists at Oberlin. A town meeting was called to explore the idea on November 11, 1856, the eleventh anniversary of Wittenberg's chartering. There it was explained that the Synod of Ohio and the Synod of Cincinnati of the "old school" Presbyterian Church, the conservatives of that denomination, planned to raise $200,000 to start the school in a fiscally sound way. On the 18th, the Synod of Cincinnati planned to meet in Dayton, Ohio, to consider the matter.

Springfield's leaders noted the boon that would accrue to any town that landed that kind of $200,000 investment and they organized as rapidly as possible to respond. The *Daily Nonpareil*, no longer concerned that Ohio had too many colleges, urged all local men of means and all those who loved the cause of Christian education to endorse the idea of the new Presbyterian college and its location in Springfield. While the Whig newspaper, the *Springfield Republic*, had been generally supportive of Wittenberg, the *Daily Nonpareil*, a Whig paper with Nativist leanings was less so. The Nativist movement, which objected to the power of immigrants in America, took a distanced view of Wittenberg in spite of its avowed Americanism, because of its German name, the German names on its rosters and its involvement in anti-slavery politics.

Clifton M. Nichols, Springfield newspaper editor and protagonist for educational reform. Clark County Historical Society.

In 1855, the American Party had been victorious in Springfield's spring municipal elections. Editors Nichols and Hastings, two transplanted New Englanders, had accused the local Catholic priest of political activity. Father Howard denied the charge but was told that denial was not enough. He had to prove his innocence. Nativists took charge of the city school board and picked a new superintendent. After replacing "un-American" teachers, the superintendent required parents of German children, who wanted them to study German twice a week, to request the privilege in writing. Only students of German descent were allowed to study that language.

To such partisans, a Presbyterian school was more American and tied to the British heritage which Nativists cherished.

Community leaders turned out to promote the cause of a Presbyterian university in Springfield. The thought of garnering $200,000 to be spent in Springfield enlisted others as well, and local citizens agreed to raise $35,000 if Presbyterians elsewhere raised the other $165,000. "Is there any one event which could happen to Springfield," Nichols asked, "that would benefit it so much at so little expenditure?" Nichols rationalized that such a step would certainly benefit Wittenberg and the Presbyterian Female Seminary already flourishing in Springfield. With these two and a new Presbyterian university, he mused, Springfield would begin to resemble Oxford and Cambridge in England as a great educational center. President Sprecher and the faculty at Wittenberg were upset by these developments, but their concern went unnoticed for a while in the community.

When the joint convention of Ohio Presbyterian Synods opened in Columbus, it received offers from several Ohio towns including Springfield. After preliminary discussion, the convention dropped all proposals except those of Springfield and West Liberty. After further debate, West Liberty beat out Springfield by eleven votes. Springfield's boosters considered the decision unfortunate and temporary.

In the wake of that decision, friends of Wittenberg in the community announced an effort to raise scholarship funds. All that was needed to enable Wittenberg to fulfill the community's desire for a major college, they said, was increased enrollment. Even the youthful editor of the *Daily Nonpareil* endorsed the campaign. "It is not by any one great event that our city and community are to be built up," he observed humbly, "but by a great number of smaller events . . ." He urged citizens to build up the city little by little, using every opportunity as it came. Wittenberg was certainly one of those opportunities. If we could not have a great Presbyterian university, he averred, let us make the most of the Lutheran college in our midst; it could increase the town's importance too. A year later, the editor of the rival *News and Journal* noted that the school was "out of the woods." He saw Wittenberg as a vigorous school working itself out of "most discouraging circumstances."

But the Presbyterian university idea was not dead. The nation suffered in the economic recession; and if West Liberty's boosters could not raise money for the new school before the downturn, they found the task impossible afterward. Wittenberg and Antioch found the economic times very distressful; and according to the newspapers, the Board at Antioch offered to sell its school in Yellow Springs to the Board of West Liberty University. That Board felt that it could not take such an action because the "solemn covenant" arrived at in Columbus specified a particular location.

The Presbyterians debated again where to locate their school. Springfield renewed its effort. Even the *Springfield Republic* endorsed the new effort. The editor noted that this was not just another college, but a full-scale university with an undergraduate college, a seminary, and medical and law schools. The town could not pass up an opportunity for a "first-class university with an endowment of $250,000." A new committee formed and the town's efforts were again underway.

The new effort strained Wittenberg's community relations to the breaking point. While the Presbyterian group worked to further efforts for the new school, another group of "Friends of Wittenberg College" called a town meeting to consider the predicament Wittenberg was in. They claimed they were friends of both causes, searching for a way to serve both institutions well. They invited the public, the faculty and students of Wittenberg, the Presbyterian university committee, the board of directors of Wittenberg, and the recently appointed committee on valuation to attend the meeting. The committee on valuation was a joint Lutheran-Presbyterian group appointed to determine the value of Wittenberg property in the event the Presbyterians wanted to buy it. Geiger, designated by the Board to negotiate for Wittenberg, had secured a pledge from the Presbyterians that they would buy the Wittenberg property at a fairly established price, if their school were located in Springfield. The committee on valuation was to arrive at that fair price.

While the Wittenberg authorities had no real desire to move, they had decided that Springfield would not adequately support both colleges and that, if the Presbyterians came, Wittenberg would be at a decided disadvantage. The Wittenberg Board, faculty, and student body were dejected; but they felt Professor Geiger had negotiated as good a deal as they could possibly hope for.

The tension in the community was apparent. Local newspapers noted that the citizens were anxious to have the new university but at the same time did not want to be unkind to Wittenberg. They regretted that Dr. Sprecher was convinced that the town could not support both. John F. Mitchell, Wittenberg's first graduate, disagreed publicly with Sprecher and authored several newspaper articles concerning the two college issue. Sprecher, observed the editor of the *Springfield Republic*, "did not support his view of the impracticability of two colleges in our city by either facts or arguments." But he did, according to the editor, "very gravely call in question the sincerity of the professed friendship of the Springfield people for Wittenberg College."

Wittenberg agreed to sell its property for $40,000, the price agreed to by the committee on valuation. Presbyterians discounted it by $10,000, the amount contributed to bring the school to town, and offered $30,000. Geiger insisted that the Committee had already subtracted the $10,000 and called on Presbyterians to keep their word. The meeting adjourned, to resume discussion of a Springfield location separate from the issue of the Wittenberg property. They voted to erect a building in some other part of town, but warned that no work would begin until the full $200,000 had been raised.

Given the hard times and with the coming of the Civil War, the whole matter was dropped. The Reverend Hoge said that if the university project was undertaken later, his synod was under obligation to fulfill its agreement with Springfield. He died in 1864; and when the Presbyterian university idea was revived at the close of the war, Wittenberg was a much stronger institution, and the Springfield location was not seriously considered. Instead the Presbyterians selected Wooster, the town where Wittenberg had first opened its doors in 1843. Calmer voices prevailed among the Presbyterians who questioned the Christian charity of forcing the Lutherans to move.

Some Springfielders, however, were unforgiving. Editor Nichols called Wittenberg's approach "cold hearted." The forty-thousand-dollar price tag, he admitted, accurately covered the value of the school's land and buildings, but the school had put no value on "memories and past associations, special blessings of providence, disappointments and broken pledges, disturbances in the Lutheran church, beautiful location or prayers over the grave of Dr. Keller." The school's attitude, he added, was "contemptible and illiberal indeed!" If the Lutherans did as much for Wittenberg as Springfield had done, he concluded, they would not have to look for a new college to fulfill the town's aspirations. He took special note of a "certain professor of mathematics," Hezekiah Geiger, who failed to calculate the value of a town's goodwill.

As Springfield tried to cope with its failure to attract the Presbyterian school, Wittenberg's friends sought ways to renew the college's image in the town. A first step they thought was to revive the idea of publishing Ezra Keller's biography. Professor Diehl took up the task that F. W. Conrad had left undone. Perhaps the life of Keller would revive happier memories of the earlier decade of hope and harmony for residents of Springfield and the college. The book was printed locally and circulated widely in the hope of restoring earlier good feelings and elevating the spirits of the school's friends.

The college then sought to mobilize its friends in a renewal of its stalled endowment fund campaign. A popular young Springfield attorney and Wittenberg alumnus of 1852, Samuel A. Bowman, accepted the chairmanship. Springfield area farmer and former college treasurer, J. J. Snyder, served as secretary.

Not all of the rancor could be disposed of so easily. Some of it would take time to fade. The idea of moving the college had taken root in the minds of many in the town and in the synods. Benjamin Prince noted that the issue "boded no good for the college." Attachments of long standing had been strained, he said, and only a great deal of time could heal the rupture. Some board members especially resented Editor Nichols' high handedness for years to come; and he was not finished. Nor unfortunately were they.

Years later, Isaac Sprecher would assess the trouble through which his uncle was working. "We were so busy with college work, teaching seven and eight hours per day that we had no time to talk over the youthful part of our lives." His uncle Samuel, he said, continued to be away for long periods pleading for money and "would come home so exhausted and dejected that he would go to bed for several days." After talking with his uncle, at his Aunt Catherine's insistence, to cheer him up, Isaac reported that he went to his own room "so depressed that I was hardly fit for work." Catherine admonished her children, "Don't trouble your father, he has more care than he has the strength to bear."

Chapter Four

Labor Ipse Fuerit Voluptas

In spite of tensions in the college's relations with the Church and the community, students in their daily lives shared a meaningful experience. In the earliest decades, they were exposed to a modified traditional curriculum, participated in the life of the literary societies, and shared in the religious emphasis which permeated it all. Like other American colleges, Wittenberg described its curriculum as being on the Yale plan. Its base was in that conservative defense of the classical curriculum advanced in 1828 by the president of Yale, Jeremiah Day. The announced purpose of an education, he said, was to produce clergymen, gentlemen, and doctors, lawyers, and community leaders.

The most remembered experience for a man preparing for college was the constant translation into and out of Greek, Latin, and English. It was an experience with limited appeal and college enrollments were small. After several years of the ancient languages, the student had more than a passing acquaintance with the Old and New Testaments, Aristotle, Caesar, Cicero, Demosthenes, Herodotus, Homer, Horace, Plato, Plutarch, Tacitus, Thucydides, and Xenophon. All educated men had this common knowledge and rich storehouse of literary references, an elite language that only they fully understood.

This was the curriculum that Yale's president set out to defend. In that year, Andrew Jackson was elected president of the United States. His election represented the elevation, socially and politically, of the less well-educated masses in America. Pressures were mounting from successful farmers, newly successful businessmen and entrepreneurs to make the classical college more responsive to these changes and more comfortable for the upwardly mobile. Colleges for all their classical pretensions were going to be forced to accommodate to a broader spectrum of society. The pressures would grow and expand throughout the century and beyond.

If the curriculum was autocratic and elitist, so be it, said Day. He insisted that "the young merchant must be trained in the counting room, the mechanic in the workshop, the farmer in the field." If they wanted an education, he asked, "[i]s it not desirable," that they should take the regular classic course? They "should be men of superior education, of large and liberal views, of those solid and elegant attainments which will raise them to a higher distinction . . ." Princeton joined Yale in defending the narrower curriculum and sent forth a host of men to preside over schools across the nation. More than any other colleges, these two led American colleges to fall into line and resist the pressures for change. The so-called Yale Plan became the standard and few schools failed to identify with the standard.

Yet in the years between 1828 and the Civil War, faculties everywhere modified the classical course and set off in new directions in spite of the rhetoric. They adopted new ways of proceeding within the older framework and ventured into new historical and philosophical methods. Course titles might remain, but the content and methodologies changed. These were transitional generations between the clergymen teachers of the old line college and the graduate-degreed professors of a modern university. The transition would be hard fought.

The Wittenberg curriculum reflected the Yale Plan, with major modifications. In this college in the southwest corner of frontier Ohio, there were good reasons to adjust the elitist curriculum. Lutherans were not typically members of the elite, and the town in which they were located had needs of its own. Furthermore, if Americanists objected to governing the nineteenth-century church by sixteenth-century documents, they could hardly have endorsed an ancient over a modern curriculum. They identified themselves with the Yale Plan for the same reason they took the German name of Wittenberg for their very American college. They did not intend to abandon the past altogether, only the parts of it that could not be substantiated by current scholarship and experience.

Wittenberg in its catalogs reflected what was called "the new learning." It included natural philosophy or physics and mathematics updated by Isaac Newton and Copernicus. Those influences led to the inclusion of algebra, plane and analytical geometry, plane and spherical trigonometry, differential calculus, acoustics and optics, mechanical philosophy, astronomy, and geology if not all in separate courses, as topics in courses. The emphasis on science proposed for the Wittenberg curriculum was considered by some as excessive. A full and complete science apparatus was a priority expenditure.

The "new learning" also led to natural history, botany, zoology, chemistry, physiology, anatomy, and psychology. Sprecher was a thorough student of Laurens P. Hickok's psychology, and it permeated his teaching. He was the first of several psychologists to preside over Wittenberg, and they stamped the school with a unique perspective. Hickok, president of Union College, was America's ablest nineteenth century dialectician. In the next century he would be forgotten. But in 1848, he published *Rational Psychology*; in 1853, *System of Moral Science*; and in 1854, *Empirical Psychology*, all in use at Wittenberg. The school also included modern languages by teaching German, and it included American history and political science.

In addition to the courses listed in the catalog and regularly offered, the faculty also offered occasional lectures and experimental courses. Student diaries and letters home recorded that, during vacations, when some students remained on campus because they lived too far away to go home, Dr. Sprecher and others would offer occasional lectures on current topics or favorite subjects.

The faculty also put great emphasis on library use to augment textbook memorization and recitation. The experience modified student life and led, in some cases, to real intellectual growth. The literary societies sent students scurrying to the library for independent reading. One student, writing home, implored, "You must not imagine that I am idle . . . I endeavor to improve every moment in reading useful books." He announced proudly that he was in the midst of reading Rollin's eight-volume ancient history, and that the collection of books at Wittenberg was large and growing.

Another student confessed to his diary that he had given up the game of draughts for reading. "The thirst for literary pursuits is becoming strong and the desire to become something in the world, to be an instrument of good to my fellow man is increasing." On another occasion he confided that his studies were becoming a pleasure, and "I would as soon sit down to a lesson as to kick the football or defend the wicket."

While the Yale Plan rejected scientific experimentation and libraries as non-essential, President Sprecher glorified them. Colleges and libraries, he said were within the reach of all; and, therefore, "all may more or less engage in scientific study."

Samuel Sprecher, second president, 1849-1874, engraving from a daguerreotype by J. Sartain, Philadelphia. Wittenberg University Archives.

For Sprecher, scientific study went beyond science itself to embrace all of objective scholarship in which assumptions were subjected to systematic analysis and proof. He believed that the great comforts, conveniences and qualities of civilized life in the 1850s sprung "directly from scientific effort, research and experiment." Science, he said, built the steam engine, the railway, the telegraph and "even helps our wives to cook our food." He was certainly conversant with the Scottish philosophy of common sense. The practical application of knowledge illustrated the value of formal study. Every subject, even theology, could be looked at with scientific discipline.

Sprecher and his fellow Americanists believed that theologians should pursue science in the search of divine as well as general truth. "The man of science must prove all things," he observed. "He must believe the Bible, not because it ought to be true, but because history has shown it to be true." He complained of theologians with limited scientific knowledge who dismissed the wonders of modern geology. As the economic depression of 1857 deepened and the sectional conflict over slavery widened, he conjectured that the nation's problems were exacerbated by the inadequate scientific education of the nation's leaders in business, economics, and politics.

The capstone of any curriculum was a course entitled Moral Philosophy taught by the college president to all seniors. Such a course presented the principles of morality and rectitude that would lead the student in the pursuit of public and private virtue. In it, all of the student's education was to be brought together into a meaningful whole. Wittenberg was no different from other classical colleges, except that Sprecher called his course Moral Science. Eventually moral philosophy moved in the direction of ethics and moral science tended toward the social sciences. As it was taught in most colleges, Moral Philosophy was an attempt to reconcile Lockean empiricism, Newtonian physics, and Christian revelation. The outcome was the knowledge of one almighty, all-wise, and all-good being in whom conflicting ideas and inconsistencies found harmony and reconciliation.

The standard text for the Moral Philosophy course throughout the English-speaking world was eighteenth-century theologian, William C. Paley's *Natural Theology or Evidences of the Existence and Attributes of the Deity Collected from the Appearance of Nature*, published in London in 1802. Fifteen editions appeared in America between 1802 and 1845. Paley's work was a response to the empiricism of

John Locke and it advanced the concept of "intelligent design" by a creator God. Paley, a popular synthesizer of empirical science and reasonable religion, called himself a rational Christian, a man of piety and reason. He was strongly criticized by Calvinists and by Transcendentalists but he dominated college courses in Mental Philosophy until Charles Darwin, in 1859, specifically called his views to account in his *The Origin of Species*.

Even then, Lyman Beecher in Cincinnati, hailed Paley as a major antidote to skepticism and it remained a popular text for many years. Sprecher's use of the term "moral science" reflected his study of Laurens P. Hickok whose text, *System of Moral Science,* was in use at Wittenberg along side Paley's *Natural Theology*. It showed his affinity for that group of transitional scholars, like Theodore Dwight Woolsey of Yale, who also preferred the term "moral science." Noah Porter, another professor at Yale, wrote, "On Moral Science as a Branch of Academical Education," in *the Quarterly Christian Spectator*. He divided college work into three parts: mathematical science, physical science and moral science. For them, the latter included history, political science, psychology, art, literature and metaphysics. It covered a multitude of subjects many of which would later comprise the social sciences.

Sprecher sought to provide principles to guide the conduct of an educated man in society. He applied religion and philosophy to current events; talked of the law of nature, ethics, natural jurisprudence, general economics, politics and the law of nations. He ranged from the idea of morality as a commandment of God to the ignorant to morality as a product of reason for a person possessed of greater opportunities to learn and to know more of the divine plan. Sprecher's baccalaureate addresses, year after year, reflected the tendency of his thought. It was, after all, his last lecture to students about to leave and an opportunity to indicate publicly his most cherished thoughts and highest ideals.

Sprecher told the class of 1855, "Happiness in this life is a reality and the attainment of it a practicable thing. It is not a delusion. It is based upon views and feelings of which we are as clearly conscious as we are of our own existence. It is not a freak of fancy, but will bear the test of rational reflection." He gave the class five principles that guaranteed happiness. And what, he asked, was education for, if it did not lead to happiness? The first principle was that an educated person should prefer that which is necessary to that which is merely convenient or agreeable. Second, the educated man must value the things which qualify him for his profession, his calling in life, above every other attainment. Third, the educated must expect happiness mainly from his mental acquisitions. Fourth, to be happy, he must be active, participating fully in life. And fifth, God made the human's spiritual, not animal, nature the true seat of happiness.

Two years later, Sprecher addressed graduates on the subject of truth. Truth required constant struggle, a great and never-ending effort on the part of anyone who wanted to be educated, he said. One should take neither an ancient declaration nor a modern one for Truth, he admonished them, without subjecting it to the closest scrutiny. The educated person believed no creeds just because his father did. Nor did the educated person accept the modern spirit or current novelty just because it was novel and current or because it enjoyed popular support. Both the ancient and the modern needed to be tested. He advised students not to be of that common class who "picked up and devoured with avidity every new thing, every novel opinion, every bold theory." He reminded them of the legacy of Martin Luther, who, he said, confessed in old age: "If my works would prevent men from investigating great truths for themselves, I would burn them to ashes!" The educated man, Sprecher concluded, had to investigate everything for himself.

Sprecher often told seniors that their education had just begun, that they should never cease studying and investigating. As he phrased it, the life of the mind required constant "silent labor." While it might be distinguished from manual and physical labor, it was labor nonetheless; something should be changed because of it. Energies mightier than any other were unleashed by the active mind, he said. Aristotle and Plato changed their world; Jonathan Edwards, Emmanuel Kant and Martin Luther changed their worlds. The power of the educated mind was the greatest power on earth and every educated man should so live his own life of the mind that something was changed as a result of it.

Not just seniors picked up Sprecher's commitment to mental labor. A freshman, with much less exposure to him, noted each day's lesson showed little progress; but over time, great progress in both literature and science was apparent. "Labor patiently, labor incessantly, and *Labor ipse fuerit voluptas,* he wrote. "Labor itself will lead to pleasure." If Sprecher's Wittenberg had an unofficial motto, that was it: *Labor ipse fuerit voluptas!*

Raising a favorite theme, Sprecher told members of one senior class that they had to be active in an ever-changing and evolving world. In an echo, perhaps of Ralph Waldo Emerson's Phi Beta Kappa address at Harvard in 1834, he told them that the life of the mind was valuable only in a life of constant and untiring action. "The mind of man was not to be idle," he insisted. "It was made for use. And if men will keep busy they will secure happiness." To Sprecher, truth, labor, happiness, action, and the life of the mind were all differing aspects of a single unity. That was the essential thesis in Moral Science as taught by Samuel Sprecher and that was the unity of knowledge to be pursued. Knowledge found coherence in an active mind: *Labor ipse fuerit voluptas*!

Although the school might fall short—because of limited resources, the size and capabilities of the faculty and the limitations and shortcomings of the students—in delivering all that it aspired to or promised in classical and modern education, its commitment was clear. While remaining true to the best of the old curriculum it aspired, as resources would permit, to embrace the best of the new, as well as it could determine what that was, and to respond to the environment in which it found itself. There was ample time in the schedule to attempt such inclusiveness. The day began at 5:00 A.M. The school term was forty weeks long, with two semesters of unequal length, twenty-four weeks for one and sixteen weeks for the other. Summer vacation was short.

Examples of efforts to adapt and expand curriculum to meet the needs of the local environment were a commercial or business course initiated in 1852 and courses for the preparation of public school teachers in compliance with new state legislation. Such deviations from the classical norm were defended in spite of commitment to the Yale Plan. Later, when the business courses were dropped, it was not because they did not belong in the classical college but rather, because students who came to take such courses were not sympathetic to the rest of the classical college experience: the focus on ancient languages, the literary societies, and religious exercises and instruction.

Samuel Sprecher's was by far the dominant mind on the small Wittenberg faculty. A student's education in the early years was predominantly in the hands of but four men; and every student spent many hours with each of them: Samuel Sprecher, Michael

Diehl, Hezekiah R. Geiger and Isaac Sprecher, the president's nephew. They all shared the president's general point of view.

Keller had died after only three years and was replaced by Sprecher. Sauerwine and Welty, the first professors, served less than a year with their positions now filled by Diehl, Geiger and Isaac Sprecher. Conrad remained five years but was less in agreement with Sprecher. This core of four positions was supported by two or three temporary appointments, positions filled by a host of young men who usually were trained at Wittenberg and served only one or two years. Some men of other religious backgrounds in Springfield taught from time to time. These jobs were often given to bright upper classmen, theological students, and recent graduates who had impressed the faculty.

There were also usually a couple of "tutors" who lived in a status between students and faculty. They lived in the dormitory, proctored the dining hall and relieved faculty of many chores, especially day-to-day discipline. They taught in the preparatory program. Morris Officer served in such a position the longest, four years;

Morris Officer, seminarian. Superintendent for construction of the college building. principal of the Preparatory department, Missionary to Liberia. pastor of English Lutheran Church, Springfield. Wittenberg University Archives.

Maurice Kirby, the orphan reared by Keller, served three years; J. F. Reinmund and Isaac Sprecher, before the latter's permanent appointment, for two years.

Thus, with four permanent, two or three changing faculty positions and some tutors, Wittenberg sought to achieve its ambitious curriculum. They all taught several courses for seven or eight hours a day and became drudges, over-worked and underpaid. More than anything else, however, Sprecher's view of life was the basic course, and most students committed themselves to study under him. He was an intelligent man with rare qualities for reflection. When not traveling, he came into contact with the entire student body and lived in a house across the drive from the white-washed college building. He left the routine of daily affairs to Professor Geiger, already heavy-laden, and devoted his time to students. He was remembered for his pleasant, genial smile, a kindly word of greeting, friendly counsel, a sympathetic look, wise advice, and hearty encouragement. It was said that he was loved by nearly all his students and was a builder of character, one who exercised the student's capacities for self-control and self-development.

He was a liberal in theology. A local resident, hearing him preach, said that Sprecher did not put such a strain on reason as other preachers. He did not make literal interpretations of scripture, but talked about the symbolism of biblical texts. Like the faculty at Yale, Sprecher had little difficulty with challenges to the biblical account of creation which were growing more frequent. He was not an advocate of the inerrancy of scripture. The trends in German thought and the revelations of philology, the history of language and man's other cultural achievements, were too real for him for that. Doctrinal views and natural science were to be based on the same truths. An Americanist could make sense of a world of science through a more critical analysis of scripture.

The second major aspect of Sprecher's Wittenberg, beyond the curriculum, continued to be the literary society. The societies served a number of functions. First and foremost, they involved students actively in their own educations. After the reading of dull texts, copious note taking in lectures, labored translations and nervous recitations in classrooms, the preparation for literary exercises immersed the student in a topic of his own choosing.

Student William Settlemyer, class of 1866, recorded in his diary months of independent reading and preparation for an oration on a patriotic theme for one of the Fourth of July celebrations on the campus. His self-doubts, his periods of monumental effort, his writing blocks revealed an intense involvement in learning about himself, his subject and the appropriate rhetorical style to communicate his meaning. It was all energized by his apprehensions as he worried about the judgment of the audience, the faculty, indeed the verdict of the Doctor himself, the opinions of his fellow Philosophians and whether he would uphold the honor of his society.

Dr. Sprecher captured the tension and the value of the experience. "Not a single failure or unpleasant circumstance . . . during the whole evening," he said, describing one program. The students "had made every necessary preparation for the occasion—days, weeks and perhaps months had been spent in doing one thing well, which is the secret of any undertaking." The Doctor's philosophy of education was fully illustrated in such endeavor. "One thing well executed is worth a whole lifetime of weak attempts. The many feeble acts do not make the man, but the one decisive struggle that has in it one's whole mind and heart, determined to reach the mark or fall in the noble effort."

The literary societies also served as social organizations. Every student was pursued to join one or the other of the two groups. Once in, the groups regulated the member's affairs under the supervision of the faculty members in the group and alumni who remained in the community. They selected contest participants for public events after critical evaluation of the member's performances in the group. One's talents, abilities, seriousness of purpose, capacity to perform, popularity, appearance, and general personality were reviewed and judged. The groups provided experience in self-analysis, the evaluation of others, and social and political processes.

For some, this was the group's most important function. Here students developed character, leadership abilities, imagination, and self discipline. Settlemyer made periodic references in his diary to his experiences as a Philosophian. When he joined, he prayed that God would improve his mental faculties and prepare him to preach God's word. Later he complained that he was criticized as the most awkward member of the Society. On another occasion, he gloated that he did better in debate than was expected but complained that

Literary Society Orator. Yearbook artwork by Itsuo Umezaki. Wittenberg University Archives.

he was censured for his sloppy dress. After several years of Society activity, he viewed the awkwardness of the new members and marveled at how much he himself had grown and improved.

Wittenberg's literary societies ventured briefly into journalism. In 1851-1852, the *Excelsior Visitor* appeared carrying the news of the society to members, alumni and friends, but it was short-lived. Later in 1857, John C. Brodfuehrer, published the *Eagle Eye*, a second attempt to put the literary society into print. But in the 1850s the men in the literary societies focused primarily on oral presentations. Editorial interests would become much more important a decade later.

The groups also taught the members parliamentary procedure, how to take minutes, how to write a substantive critique, and to deal with the clashes of personalities and ambitions. They held social functions and evaluated members on the social graces. They developed intense inter-society rivalries, not the least of which was a race to build the larger and better library. They raised money to buy books, wrote to friends at home for contributions and guarded the cache as if it were the arsenal for the next public battle. When the school later proposed that the two collections be merged with the College's to form one library for all, there were years of resistance to the very idea.

The major function of literary societies so far as the town was concerned was the annual public contest when each put forth its best performers. Editors, as educated representatives of the Whig elite, responsible for maintaining its standards, covered the clashes with enthusiasm. These events at which the men put their reputations on the line became major events in the community's intellectual and social life. Young ladies from town and from the nearby Presbyterian Female Seminary were all invited to attend. The romance between the literary gladiators and the ladies blossomed and the men publicly thanked them for assistance in decorating the hall for the occasion and for the gifts they brought to the societies. When an overly critical editor seemed too harsh, one of the ladies wrote to the editor calling him to account and strongly defending the young performers.

Members marched to the town hall parading from the Lutheran church on High Street, north to Main, east to Market, and then south to the hall at the corner of High and Market Streets. They proudly wore their respective badges of satin ribbon: Philo white and Excelsior blue, large rosettes with streamers. As the years went by, the streamers became worn. The students said they were "tadpole-like," round badges with short, tattered tails. The procession was headed by a small brass band and children along the way expressed a preference for one group or the other with cheers they had learned from the young men themselves: "Philo white is always right, Excelsior blue is never true!" or "Excelsior blue is ever true, Philo white is never right!"

Citizens of Springfield and the vicinity crowded the city hall so that it was standing room only. The ladies occupied nearly all the seats with the men standing around the sides and at the back of the room. The faculty added dignity to the occasion by occupying seats on stage with the contestants. After the exercises, free from faculty oversight, Settlemyer wrote of students treating themselves to the pleasure of an oyster supper and the "nice recreation" of smoking.

The annual contest was noticed in the newspapers as early as 1849 and yearly thereafter. The reviews were often cool, occasionally enthusiastic, and often harsh and critical. The exercises "passed off well" said one. This year "considerable improvement was manifest since last year," said another. "The boys exhibited commendable perseverance; and we wish them good speed in their high enterprise," said a third. In reviewing the entries of the Excelsior Society, the editor of the *Republic* observed, "there was more ease in delivery and a perceptible diminution of sophomoric thunder." The editor talked of defects in composition and delivery among the orators but noted that "all will grow better . . . in the crucible of . . . try!" Student John B. Helwig, later the third president of the college, was given low marks as a debater because of a "memory inclined to be treacherous" and a "wanting of clearness of diction." His illustrations, the editor complained, were inappropriate. Isaac K. Funk, later a partner in the publishing firm of Funk and Wagnalls, both Wittenberg graduates, was cited as being "not of sonorous voice" and was blatantly criticized for arguing "the wrong side of the question."

The editors were not always so opinionated and critical. Commenting on the same debate between Helwig and Funk, the rival editor of the *Springfield Weekly News*, observed that Helwig "did well, spoke powerfully, used excellent argument, evinced good sense, research, and a philosophical turn of mind . . . ." Of Funk, he noted, "We expected something good, but were surprised by something magnificent . . . a thorough knowledge of history." He concluded, "So long as Wittenberg bears such fruits as these we shall have a large place for her in our affections."

During the Civil War, an essayist left his work for another to read while he served ninety days in the union army. The critic observed caustically, "If he wields the bayonet half as well as he wields the pen, the traitors are in danger of being occasionally impaled." Students were often criticized for excessive enthusiasm. On one occasion, Michael Hamma, later the benefactor and namesake of the Hamma School of Theology spoke on Hugh Miller, the great exponent of modern geology and a popularizer of science. "Mr. Hamma piled it on," observed the editor, "Hugh Miller became for a time Huge Miller . . . a sort of young deity . . ." He criticized a young Philosophian who spoke on Moses, saying, "He laid it on with a trowel . . . he plastered him. In the mirror . . . the meek old Moses of Mt. Sinai would not know himself."

Students knew their efforts would be judged in the hall and then reviewed critically in the papers. Their reputation, that of their society and of the college itself was at stake. They worked hard to do the best that they could. Their choice of topics to discuss came after long deliberation. To be current and modern and pick a topic they could handle well required sound judgment. One talked about the "Infidelity of the French." Another spoke on the relationship of the Hungarians to European liberty and the threat of Roman Catholicism to the liberties of America, hot topics on the minds of Nativists. George S. Sprecher, the president's son, spoke of the growing role of science in society. John Stuckenberg, described by Sprecher as the best student he ever taught, spoke about the energy unleashed by the mind. They both reflected the teaching of their mentor very well.

The newspapers also noted the purchases of art work by the societies with which to decorate the walls of their meeting rooms: portraits of Presidents Keller and Sprecher by local artist Godfrey Frankenstein, who later achieved a national reputation; a purchase by the Philosophians of a large engraving of that great Whig spokesman for the American System, Henry Clay, delivering his celebrated speech on the Compromise of 1820, surrounded by Senators Webster, Benton and others; copies of Rembrandt Peale's famous portrait of George Washington. The Philosophians acquired a large painting of the twelve year old Jesus in the midst of the doctors and scholars in the Jewish temple. It was a scene recreated years later in stained glass in the Wittenberg window at the Lutheran Church downtown where the college had begun. The art works selected by the societies reflected the patriotic and religious tenor of the institution.

Half a century later, the story of the society's acquisition of the painting of Jesus amid the Rabbis of the Temple surfaced. A group of students sitting under a shade tree "discussing philosophy," as they described it, were approached by a "seedy looking" fellow who said he was in need of money and would leave as collateral his magnificent painting. The group came up with $25 and received the large canvas. It was never redeemed and the students persuaded their fellow Philosophians to take the picture off their hands. It seemed to all to be a quality painting by an artist the teller of the tail recalled as a man named Webber.

The Wittenberg Window at First Lutheran Church, Springfield, Ohio where Wittenberg held classes for five years, 1845-1851. The window was commisioned in 1991 for the church's sesquicentennial. It shows Christ as a child in the Jewish Temple talking with the Rabbis. The University seal as redesigned in 1959 is at the top. Recitation Hall is depicted at the bottom symbolizing the school's decision to remain in Springfield in 1882. Photo by Robert Gantt.

The Nativist editor of the *Nonpareil* made regular visits to the campus and visited society members in their halls. For all his differences with the school and its faculty, he liked the students and the student life style. In 1856, he noted that their halls were comfortably large, handsomely furnished, well supplied with comforts and housed extensive libraries. The Excelsior was in the eastern wing of the college building on the fourth floor, and the Philosophians directly opposite in the west wing. As one approached the halls, he said, it was as if one were approaching the home of some wealthy person. They were beautifully and elegantly furnished. "We had not supposed that there existed in the whole college anything so tastefully arrayed." If there was any doubt about the focus of student interests and energies, the resources invested in these halls removed all doubt. Students, parents, and townsfolk opened their pocketbooks to enhance these facilities.

The speaker's platforms were in the north end of the great rooms, libraries to the right, and the chairs of members in the middle. The rooms resembled small legislative assemblies. Between classes each member could avail himself of his hall. The floors were covered with velvet carpets. The chairs were carved rosewood, high backed with arms and upholstered backs and seats; they were comfortable and "sufficiently nice." The editor called the halls "the lions" of the gentlemanly students, richly furnished and decorated with taste.

In 1858, the editor visited the societies, invited by students Abraham Cummings and John Stuckenberg. He enjoyed the panoramic view of the town and the countryside from the top floor of the building and from the cupola. He reported again on the halls as "fitted up in the most *recherché* style." The word meant furnishings "sought out with care; rare, choice and uncommon." It was used at the time to describe a refined and studied elegance beginning to appear in Ohio homes and institutions as the frontier moved farther west. Editor Nichol's also reported on the drive back over the road between the college and the town, the beautiful scenery, the magnificent water fall of Mill Run and suggested that all should take the drive often just to enjoy the pleasant view.

A major event every year was each society's anniversary banquet at one of the hotels. Typical was the 1858 party of the Excelsior's.

The student, honorary, faculty, and alumni members "partook of a bountiful repast." Leonard Tuttle's Band furnished up-to-date music, and the table was laden with all the luxuries of the season. More oysters were consumed, the members gloated, than had ever been consumed before at a single event in Springfield. The group drank toasts to Dr. Sprecher, whose intellect, they said, probed the very heart and mystery of life, separated reality from pretension and the permanent from the transient. "His words of wisdom will linger with us till the chords of being are unstrung." They toasted Professor Diehl as "True in describing to our minds the brightest gems of ancient lore." And saluted Professor Geiger, "whose mind is as exact and comprehensive as the science he teaches." They then acknowledged Isaac Sprecher, a man most skilled in drilling students effectively in Latin and Greek, as the "founder of our educations." They cited the Springfield Bar Association represented by the estimable Samuel Shellabarger, as "the nursery of the statesmen and the palladium of Freedom." The party adjourned at midnight, but the undergraduates remained, they said, to smoke in private and to return to the college in the early hours of the morning.

The toasts had been more personal at an earlier celebration in 1853. They reflected the close relationship between students and faculty. The Excelsiors saluted Professor Diehl, their instructor in languages: "As he has lately entered the matrimonial state, may he enjoy a long life of uninterrupted happiness; and as we are not prepared to imitate him in this particular instance, may we profit by the Christian meekness, gentleness and humility which to us he daily exhibits." For Professor Geiger, their as yet unmarried professor of mathematics and science, they observed: "Amid the abstractions and abstrusities of mathematical science, may his affections not encounter such an aberration from the orbit of humanity as to prevent him from solving the hymeneal equation, one plus one equal to one." They offered a final toast—to the young ladies of Springfield: "May God bless them and increase their number."

The student's apparent preference for Oyster Bars may have been more than a culinary choice. In 1857, Clifton Nichols, in his *Nonpareil* campaigned against the serving of liquor in oyster bars after hours. "Under the specious guise of oysters and ice cream," he wrote, some were selling "that which tends to ruin in mind and body those whose lives and characters are of inestimable value, not only to friends but to society." Could he have meant the gentlemen of the literary societies, whom he so admired?

If the curriculum and the literary society were two of the major elements in the lives of the early Wittenberg students, a proper participation in religious services remained the crowning piece. There was no escaping an overwhelming Christian focus. Provision was made for non-Lutherans to attend any of the churches in Springfield, but they were expected to attend regularly. If the student or his parents had no preference or if he were Lutheran, he was expected to attend the English Lutheran Church. Daily prayers and church services twice on Sunday were clear expectations. Participation in the "union" Sunday school was a further expectation for those entering the ministry.

The Sunday schools, in the beginning, were an ecumenical and social movement among the poor in which various Protestant churches operated schools for the unchurched to teach them to read by studying the Bible. Gradually, they would become more denominational as church rivalries grew. Wittenberg students by the dozens served in these schools on Sunday mornings. At the movement's peak, students were conducting seventeen such schools around the area, including one for black youths. Sprecher, like Keller before him, preached at the Sunday school picnics on the college grounds.

The most distinctive aspect of the religious climate for students at Wittenberg, however, was the revival. Such events were still prominent among western Protestants although they had become less common on eastern campuses. They were so uncharacteristic of Lutheran schools as to be almost bizarre. Kenyon College, an Episcopalian school, on occasion succumbed to the western atmosphere, but Wittenberg unabashedly called itself a "revival college." The faculty expressed regrets if no such "refreshing" occurred in any year. Dr. Sprecher called such events "special seasons of grace." They occurred on campus and at the English Lutheran Church in town. That church's historian, George Rinkliff, writing at a later time when such enthusiasms were shunned, claimed none had occurred in the church; but contemporary evidence in the newspapers says otherwise. They occurred on campus usually in February or March, after students had been closed in all winter, or they followed a death among faculty or students.

For students, death seemed an almost constant presence. Letters from students carried news of deaths at the college and in the town or reacted to deaths at home that they had just learned about. In 1849 William Cutter reported a bout with bronchial pneumonia. "My light affliction," he wrote, "has enabled me to put additional estimate upon the religion of Christ. As a natural consequence, I thought of death. I viewed it as near, but it had no sting," he said with youthful bravado. Later he wrote of deaths in the town from cholera: seven on Sunday, five on Monday, none on Tuesday, and the students' petition to close the school so they could go home. Alem Hutchins wrote home during the same epidemic. "Thanks be to God I am still alive and well," his family read. But he also noted, "I must say that my religious enjoyment is much purer and more delightful now than it has ever been."

In 1855 another student death plunged the community first into mourning and then into a revival. Edward Harrison, a classmate, presided over a meeting of the students gathered about the death of David Burger, possibly the most lamented student in the annals of college history. For reasons no longer known, he was exceedingly popular. His peers thought they had been deprived "of a most interesting companion . . . a fellow student to whom we were all attached . . . a pious example." One called him "a serious man, yet with the liveliest sense of humor and the very personification of honor and manliness." Yet they acknowledged the sovereignty of God: "Whereas it has pleased our heavenly father to take from among us our beloved brother . . . we must submit to the fiat of heaven." For thirty days, students wore black arm bands in his memory, but they mourned him for much longer than that. He was buried in a grave that he himself had dug for another student. At the last moment, friends decided to take the body home for burial, and the grave remained empty until Burger occupied it. Members of the Excelsior Society placed a monument at the grave and a white picket fence around the mound.

The English Lutheran Church became the center of the revival in which forty persons joined the church. The Springfield newspapers noted, "We understand the students of Wittenberg College are affected and are deeply interested." For whatever reasons, David Burger's influence was overwhelming. Forty years later a classmate, Samuel F. Breckenridge, by then a veteran faculty member and strong leader in the church, felt constrained to devote much of his reminiscence of his college days to a statement about David Burger. He said he wanted to "record a memorial to this gracious man whose head was full of good thoughts, whose mouth was full of good words, and whose heart was full of generous emotion."

The campus again experienced the religious fervor of a revival in 1856 and 1857. One of those converted in 1857 was John Stuckenberg of Cincinnati, who years later became a very influential member of the faculty. In 1858 three students died. Students lamented the deaths of "the genial and devoted" William Gebhart, who had been one of the founders of the short-lived Phi Delta Theta chapter; "the sincere and promising" John R. Harrison; and Martin, the youthful and frank son of the lamented Keller; as well as the "generous and talented David Burger," who three years later, was still so missed by the students that they again included him in their resolutions.

In the spring of 1859, there was yet another revival recorded in Settlemyer's diary. There was a morning meeting for prayer and a conference in the evening, followed by a service. The so-called "protracted meeting" ran for several weeks. Each evening, persons who wanted to be "prayed for" stepped forward. They were encouraged to come the next morning for prayer and instruction. The newspapers noted the great interest among the students and credited the Lutherans on High Street with sparking revivals in other churches in town.

Often when the revivals became extended, classes were suspended. Special preachers, alumni of the school, would return for a visit to recharge their faith as much as the students' and then return to their home churches hoping to carry "the fire" with them. Typically the affairs began with preaching and prayer on one weekend and ended with a communion service at the Lutheran Church on the next. Just such a revival was sparked in 1862 by the death of George S. Sprecher, the president's son and a tutor in the College.

An 1863 revival lasted over two weeks with church meetings and chapel services, according to Settlemyer.

William H. Settlemyer, class of 1866, diarist of student life at Wittenberg during the Civil War. Senior class picture. Wittenberg University Archives.

The excitement continued in student rooms as roommates prevailed upon one another for morning and evening prayer and pressured the unsaved. Such pressure, he observed, led some to seek new roommates who could abide their unsaved state or to escape an overzealous "chum" as roommates were called. As the revival burned itself out, however, some students connived to keep it going to further delay the resumption of classes and the inevitable spring examinations. Settlemyer said he prayed for those sinners and noted the callousness of their sinful state. The revivals always ended just in time for the spring contests and final examinations.

The Lutheran revivals differed from those of other denominations. Once one had had the "experience," sensing his need for God's salvation, he made a public indication that he wanted "to be prayed for" and then to have "conversations" to talk about the restraints that had kept him from receiving God's free gift of saving grace. Soon one was fully engaged in the Lutheran catechism. Thus, out of all the furor, the Lutheran revivalist brought the anxious sinner to Lutheran theology, albeit the American version. The individual could do nothing to save himself; even participating in a revival could not do it. Yet Sprecher firmly believed that God wanted to see some response from man as he acknowledged God's free gift.

One of Sprecher's favorite theologians was Philip Jakob Spener, the founder of German Lutheran pietism. He considered him the second great reformer of the church after Martin Luther and the father of American Lutheran theology. Spener's view that personal experience had to precede any true knowledge of Christianity, and that the doctrines of the Bible had to be "felt" in order to be rightly apprehended were at the root of the Americanist revival. While the beginning of the process looked to the more orthodox suspiciously like frontier Methodism, it was effective, argued the new measure men. Revivalism could be a route from frontier secularism and sectarianism to mainline church orthodoxy, and Sprecher and the Americanists believed that it worked.

Students augmented the official school experience of the classics, the literary society, and religion with some innovations of their own. In 1850, John F. Mitchell noted "a new era" had dawned. It was the appearance of popular music! Professor Leonard Tuttle's Band and his famous quartette, "The Buckeyes," had brought popular music to Springfield. At the same time, Peter A. Schindler, who married Caroline, Ezra Keller's widow, opened his singing school at the English Lutheran Church. Sally, Keller's daughter became the church organist. He conducted singing schools which focused on hymns in virtually all the towns and villages in the county. For a class of hard working choristers, a popular tune by Stephen Foster or a folk song served as a reward. Among the Foster favorites were "Jeannie With the Light Brown Hair," "Come Where My Love Lies Dreaming," "Beautiful Dreamer," or "Nellie Was a Lady." A few popular minstrel tunes might seep in around the edges.

In these singing schools, young men and women found a new activity where they could get together socially. Wittenberg students celebrated these developments and participated eagerly, learning music, studying its principles, and participating at every opportunity. They augmented their literary society programs with music, both vocal and instrumental. For the first commencement in 1851, the class had invited a saxophone band, much to the consternation of the faculty and many in the audience. The instrument had just been invented and students wanted to hear it. "Imagine a time in Springfield when there was no music worthy of the name," observed John Mitchell. "It was almost impossible to find anyone to raise an ordinary tune in church or Sunday school," but no longer. Labor might lead to pleasure, but music did so as well.

Chapter Five

The Sweetest Pleasures of Earth

When twelve-year-old Samuel McCord Crothers appeared on campus with his father, everyone assumed he wanted to enroll in the preparatory school. When he and his father made it clear that he was already prepared for college, even in Greek, and ready to pay all his fees, they were startled. We do not admit twelve-year-old boys for college level work, was their reply. The minimum age for the college was sixteen. Do you have twelve-year-olds on campus, they asked? Yes, for preparatory work. But Samuel has covered all that already, they protested. Can he not attend the college classes and just listen? Until President Sprecher returns and rules on this, they responded, Samuel can stay.

By the time Dr. Sprecher returned, Crothers was doing so well in classes and had become such a young lion in the Excelsior Society in both oratory and debate, that the president allowed him to continue, the youngest freshman in Wittenberg history. Crothers, a Presbyterian, would be a third generation Presbyterian preacher and had come to Wittenberg because Princeton would not admit him because of his age. After completing Wittenberg's course in four years, Princeton relented and with one year's additional work to test him, also granted him a degree. At age 18, he entered the seminary. Later, having become a Unitarian, and something of an embarrassment to a more orthodox Wittenberg, he served for over thirty years as pastor of First Church, Cambridge, and preached regularly to students at Harvard University. He became a famous author and essayist at the turn of the century and was particularly known as an advocate of "the new woman" and supportive of feminist causes and coeducation.

As a student at Wittenberg, Samuel was more poetic about student life than most. His senior year poem, "The Gift of Winter," written in 1872, reflected philosophically on the harsh experiences of young men and boys at college, away from home for the first time. Published in the *Springfield Daily Advertiser*, it was not his earliest work. Poetry, he said, was one of the greatest pleasures of his life. "My mother used to keep a scrapbook for them when I was a boy," he said. "I believe it got quite full."

His poem was much better than what usually passed for poetry in colleges, though all students were expected to make a valiant effort at it. Crothers's poem answered the question, why the New Year at its birth was given to the cold, harsh winter instead of one of the gentler, more pleasant seasons. While Spring would cradle the babe in rosebuds and Summer would have provided lullabies from bright-feathered birds, Autumn would have fed it on ripe fruits under brilliant leaves. But Time, said Crothers, granted the child to Winter because it promised no bed of roses, no soft start in life: but rather would provide the challenge of sturdy north winds and snowstorms. It would teach the child to survive. It was a metaphor for his and others' youthful years at Wittenberg.

There always was more to college than the official, planned educational experiences, and youth was always a time of energy and venturesomeness. It could be a time of challenge, hardship, loneliness; and a time for growing and maturing. The faculty was fully aware of this and sought to keep the student's college life under as much surveillance as possible. The college experience was to be life-shaping, and external distractions were to be kept to a minimum. But students at Wittenberg met life as it was. In their first experience of life on their own, they faced trials and excitements; but, as one expressed it, they also sought "the sweetest pleasures of earth."

When a student boarded the train or stagecoach in Michigan, Kentucky, Pennsylvania, Maryland, or Ohio, he was on his own. Alem Hutchins had to make connections on four rail lines and a lake steamer and stay overnight in a hotel before he finally arrived at school. On the way, he saw a man's foot run over by a train and, in Detroit, listened to entreaties from runners urging him to stay at a public house, a railroad hotel, or a temperance hotel; and he didn't record which he picked.

Once a student arrived in town, he arranged for a wagon to take him and his baggage out to the college. Upon arrival on campus, he was beset by representatives of the two literary societies, each trying to outdo the other in making the new arrival welcome, helping with his luggage, and getting him into a room with a fellow member who would then attempt to persuade him to join his society. Eventually, there was an interview with the President, and arrangements made for examinations and placement in a proper class.

Getting settled in the dormitory was easier for some than others. Those who had been away to school to prepare for college might already know what to expect from the exuberance of a hundred and fifty or so young men housed in one hall, ranging in age from twelve to the mid-twenties. John Stuckenberg, who finished his first year in 1853, told of noise and tumult. "This session," he observed, "we have been troubled by students sent here by their father, the Devil, to disturb the peaceful rest of us all." He told of a chair pushed through a wall, large stones rolled down the building's long halls in the middle of the night, firecrackers set off in a bucket—all activities aimed at the poor tutors who were charged with maintaining order. Others, walking around outside the building, told of flaming paper balls raining down on their heads from a window above. Stringent rules against throwing things out the windows seemed always to be violated.

President Sprecher sought to maintain order by encouraging self-discipline. His approach was reasonably successful; and that was all, perhaps, that he expected. Each student was on his honor to do right from principle; and student John Ruthrauff, who would become Wittenberg's first president in the twentieth century, felt that each was treated with full confidence by the faculty and other students until he proved himself unworthy. He attributed the success of this honor system to the personal character of "the venerable Dr. Sprecher," who inspired students with the desire to prove worthy of esteem. He insisted repeatedly that honor began in self-respect.

Sprecher's sense of fairness and firmness with students impressed them. Because of his fairness, they defended his firmness. One student politely described a part of Sprecher's personality.

"A feature of his character under attack may as well be spoken of here as elsewhere," the senior wrote. Outwardly, Dr. Sprecher appeared to be gentle and quiet. His soft manner encouraged some to think that he might be easily opposed or assailed, the student continued. "To whomsoever it occurred to try to push him from his position," he concluded, "he would have to fight for his own." The longer he fought, "the less likely it was that he should get out of the encounter whole." Clifton Nichols and others could attest to Sprecher's firmness and determination, yet his gentle wisdom enabled him to escape the full consequences of this behavior.

A unique combination of traits characterized the venerable doctor as students saw him: conviction—student George Gerlaw Clark said in 1887 that Sprecher "found rest for the soles of his feet"; determination—Clark believed that he had come to Wittenberg to "endure the trials" and "make it go"; energy—Clark described him as "capable of much enthusiasm and of kindling it in others." Despite the president's influence, however, there was still plenty of opportunity for students in the hall to give vent to boisterousness and to harass an unpopular student or tutor.

More important than a place to sleep and study was the matter of eating meals. Most ate at the college boarding club which began in 1851. Others still boarded with families in town. Some cooked for themselves in their rooms. The college club was an up and down affair, and the steward had to be replaced about every three years. Students complained about the cost, the quality, and the quantity of food. Board at the college cost three dollars per week. A family charged seven cents for breakfast and fifteen cents for lunch or supper, about $2.60 per week. Students cooked in their rooms, on heating stoves, for half that. A student who quit the college club told his parents he was boarding himself on cornbread and molasses. "It goes quite easy . . . . I buy my bread of the bakers in town and get my butter of an old Dutch woman in the country." William Cutter boarded with Caroline Keller until she discharged her boarders because of illness. He then returned to his "former way of living," fixing meals on his heating stove.

The most esteemed early steward of the boarding club was George A. Bender who ran the club in 1857 and 1858. He set such a high standard that no one could ever equal it. He became legendary. When Bender left, the students thanked him for his kindness and good cheer. They told him they would miss him; that he was all they had ever expected in a steward and more. He was interested in them as individuals; and when they were ill, Mrs. Bender brought their meals to their rooms. They hailed the couple as kind and cheerful friends. "Being absent from home," they said, "we found a home" with the Benders. They published their tribute in the Springfield newspapers, and subsequent stewards could never come up to their standard.

One of those successors, the Rev. Jacob Simons, "old Pap Simons" they called him, came and went as steward. He held pastorates in Maryland and Pennsylvania and between calls landed at Wittenberg as steward where he finally settled. Students referred to him as a "broken down preacher." He was called plain, practical, of ardent piety. Religion, it was said, was the central subject of his daily thoughts and the major content of his conversation. He had an overwhelming sense of divine majesty, of the doom hanging over the guilty and of the need to make haste to flee from the wrath to come. Students said he became so much absorbed in religious conversation that he forgot what else he was doing. He never failed to speak a word of reproof, admonition, or encouragement, as he deemed appropriate, to each student as he arrived to eat.

As students changed, Pap seemed increasingly out of touch. Though they treated him with respect, they found his zeal an intrusion on the privacy of their meal times. They described him as a strong man with powerful jaws, large cheek bones, a big nose, quick eyes, shaggy brows, and a mass of hair that had a will of its own. They suspected that he had been a profane man, but now used only one expletive of his own invention: "Byhold You!" When angry he made striking gestures shaking his whole body and with a tossing of his head, shouted, "Byhold You!"

Old Pap had a spirited horse that he rode into town to get supplies. He pastured it on the campus with the college's cows and kept it in the college barn. He took very good care of his horse. Late one night, a group of students, one of whom would later be president of the college, took the horse, muffled its hooves and led him up to the fourth floor of the college where he was found in the morning. When Old Pap learned of it, he was very angry. Someone familiar with the animal helped Pap turn him about and back him down the stairs.

The legendary "Horse in the Copula," yearbook cartoon
by Itsuo Umezaki. Wittenberg University Archives.

Pap mounted the horse in the building and, amid the cheers of students, rode him out the front doors saying that his horse had now been through college and "Byhold You," that was more than the "worthless" perpetrators of this deed would ever accomplish.

There appeared an anonymous poem about "Pap" entitled "Rascal Joe," written by a student that mocked the style of Longfellow's Hiawatha.

Have you heard dear friends, the story,
Which has spread throughout the college
Through the great and pious college?
'Tis about the club of Simons
Where the students get their boarding
Where they feed on good potatoes
Which have never lost their peelings
Which are frozen on the inside
Which are rusting on the outside
Which are huge and rough and ghostly
Which are but a fleeting shadow
Which have stolen the name potato . . .

It went on for another hundred similar dreadful lines. The steward's boarding club lasted until 1867 when it was replaced by a number of "eating clubs" on campus and off.

With all the ups and downs of college life, Wittenberg was a friendly place. Students showed their regard for one another by saying "hello" every time they passed on campus or in town, no matter how frequently. On occasion, a faculty member or student was subject to reproof for "failure to speak." Settlemyer recorded that he was "somewhat amused" when a new student said it seemed "curious" to him that Wittenbergers always recognized one another and spoke a word of greeting. "Upon some reflection," Settlemyer wrote, "it appears to me only another mark of the profound respect we have for each other," for the sacrifices and struggles they were all making to get an education, and he thought that the practicing Christian would always so regard those about him.

Getting mail from home was almost as important as anything else in student lives. The mail arrived with great uncertainty in the Ohio country. One student complained that letters were a month in coming; and, judging from the recriminations and protestations about unanswered letters, many never arrived at all. The Springfield Post Office had one box into which went all student mail, waiting to be picked up and brought to the college. If a newcomer failed to tell the postmaster that he was a student, his mail did not go into the box but rather into the general mail under the initial of his last name. If he did not ask for his mail by name, he did not get it. Conveniently, the local newspaper of widest circulation was paid periodically to run a list of all uncalled for mail. The attentive student, if he read the paper, might learn of his unclaimed mail in that fashion.

Mail was important because many students did not go home for many months. News traveled slowly and they spent many hours wondering about families and maturing as young men on their own. They needed things they did not have and wrote home for cakes, for photographs, for money, for clothing. In return they sent reports on their studies. They had their pictures taken and sent them to show how they had grown. They sent pictures to sisters and female cousins, expecting them to show them to other young ladies at home. They did not want to be forgotten by the girls at home, but neither did they want to be remembered as they were when they left. As soon as they imagined their features showed further maturity, they had a picture taken at Winder's Patent Ambrotype Studio or the Daguerrean Gallery of G. W. Turner, both downtown.

The economics of being a student was frightening to many and indicated that not all students were from affluent families. Alem Hutchins wrote to his parents and his brothers asking for money. "Don't send Michigan bank notes," he told them; "they are highly discounted in Ohio." He and William Cutter sent supplies of religious tracts which they obtained from the College for their friends to sell; they would get a commission on them and be able to make ends meet, if their friends returned the money. If they did not, they would have to pay for the tracts and be worse off than before.

In 1851, the ever-popular David Burger had written his friend and benefactor. "I am entirely out of money . . . . My tuition was $9.93, room rent $3.00. Traveling expenses $5.00; two weeks boarding at $2.00; share of stove $2.25. Matress $2.00; cot 75 cents; books about $5.00." Those were his main expenses, but he also had to buy firewood, a chair, a washbowl, a lamp and oil, and he was now, he said, penniless. "I had no pillow for my bed until brother Yontz gave me one . . . . I have nothing but dry bread for dinner." He closed by saying his need was so great his studies were being affected adversely, but that he was determined to "fight my way through" to the Gospel ministry. He lost that fight when he died on campus.

Sprecher had special words of praise for those who struggled to support themselves. Of Joseph King, who died while getting his education, he said, "While laboring under difficulties incident to such an undertaking, he became the best scholar in his class." His last request was that Dr. Sprecher deliver his funeral sermon.

Settlemyer represented the more affluent among the students and was, perhaps, the most enterprising of all. He was older, twenty-two, when he first enrolled. He served as a financial agent for his father in transactions with J. F. Chorpenning, the college treasurer. They were from the same town in Pennsylvania. Over a period of years, he handled several thousand dollars' worth of business.

To increase income, the college sold lots on the edge of campus. Settlemyer's father sent bank drafts to purchase the mortgages at a standard discount so the college could have cash. The son oversaw the accounts, transfers of title, cancellation of liens, and collection of payments. For his efforts, he was given a portion of the money to meet his college and seminary expenses. His accounts noted all of his educational expenses from preparatory school, through college, and the seminary. On one occasion, he drafted a note promising to repay his father for funds he used in excess of what he was due.

Many students, unable to find work at home or at the college, took summer jobs traveling and selling books, fruit trees, maps, and other products. A few were hired to solicit subscriptions for the college. Some dropped out of school to teach, returning when their funds had been replenished. In their letters they sought jobs for themselves and for their friends and chums, vouching for them with friends at home.

William Cutter expressed quiet desperation when he wrote, "The winter is before me. I need provisions, clothing, house, wood, etc., etc., etc." The synod promised him help, he said, "but where is it?" His books alone cost him twenty-two dollars. The school had little in the way of scholarships. Faculty helped out with jobs around their homes and gardens and with invitations to supper, but were often strapped for funds themselves when salaries were deferred. The lucky student received help from home, but half made much of their own way. Those who thought only the elite sent sons to college were mistaken. Many a second, third, or fourth son of a small farmer was sent on a meager allowance to find a career. Many sacrificed to get an education, inspired by a call to Christian ministry.

It was not just material need that gnawed at them. There was psychological need as well, but they did not have sufficient awareness of the causes of their plight or a modern vocabulary to describe it. "Temptations at times crowd heavily upon me," confessed one. "They assail me from all sides, from within and without." When he overcame one temptation, he lamented, another was ready to attack. He reached the depths of despondency, he said, when he associated "vulgar thought with Deity" itself.

The students were subject to the impact of hormones and the youthful enthusiasm of their peers without any modern understanding of their plight. They had, however, strong social and religious limitations on their behavior. "I am constrained to exclaim," said one, "who is sufficient for these things? It is continual warfare." It was no wonder the college was visited periodically with religious revivals! The pent up frustrations of students coupled with natural youthful exuberance, set the stage for some kind of explosion. Colleges which did not have revivals had fights, serious hazing incidents, and extensive property damage. Some occasionally had all four.

On one particularly gloomy morning, Settlemyer confessed to his diary that he was unwell, having passed a restless night in which his dreams disturbed him. He dreamed of "air loaded with the odor of fragrant flowers," the face of a lady unexpected and pleasant. Then he was at the home of his sister in an unknown part of a strange city. Later he was with his other sister. He remembered this dream as a joyful experience. Most didn't write their dreams down, let alone try to explain them. Upon awakening, he said he spent the day in unpleasant labor and was ill disposed to study. He asked his roommate to have his sister send him a sugar cake. Later when it arrived, he described his fullness of joy and the anticipation of future pleasant associations and formal acquaintance with Julia, "a model of sweetness untainted."

The Presbyterian Female Seminary, located near Wittenberg on the road from the college to town. Detail from 1852 lithograph of Springfield. Clark County Historical Society.

Relationships with women were severely limited, and those that existed were well chaperoned. A student caught entering a saloon or a "house of ill repute" would be summarily dismissed. Some worried about "aberrant affections" and being deflected from the "orbit of humanity." But not all of the students totally repressed all of their feelings. Springfield was rocked by an episode at the Female Seminary, a Presbyterian school for young ladies on the road between Springfield and Wittenberg.

The young men of the college were often on the road past the seminary going into town. The headmaster was concerned that when his ladies were in the yard, Wittenberg students stopped along the way to talk to them over the fence. Some of the girls moved closer to allow the men to reach over and touch them, caressing their hair. On occasion, the men brought gifts of flowers and sweets. In the evening, as the ladies were taking a walk around the area, they were joined by an entourage of Wittenberg men.

Convinced that he had to put a stop to these activities, the headmaster noticed that many of the boys were the brothers of girls enrolled in his seminary. They came to meet their sisters' friends and to introduce theirs. He announced that if one of his pupils had a relative who continued to behave in this shameless manner, he would expel the girl. The behaviors continued, and the headmaster made good his threat and expelled a girl whose brother continued to visit and bring his friends. She was a model student, however, and not involved in any misconduct herself.

When the affair was reported in the newspapers, the town was incensed, not with the students but with the headmaster. Attorney Samuel Shellabarger was president of the Seminary board and adjudicated the matter. In the end, the girl was reinstated, the headmaster resigned, and the men at Wittenberg and the young ladies at the seminary continued their adolescent flirtations. A number, after college, became husband and wife. Apart from Presbyterian and Lutheran concerns for the lack of piety in the behavior of some of these students, there was a more important issue. Parents clearly had a concern that their sons and daughters have the opportunity to meet with at least enough latitude for more permanent relationships to develop.

Members of the faculty provided a more formal and, to their way of thinking, a more appropriate way for the students to meet young ladies. Properly selected off-campus friends were introduced to select sets of college students at "circles" arranged by the faculty. William Settlemyer described one such event held by Professor Diehl. If a student had proved himself to be morally upright, suitably religious and trustworthy over time, the faculty then invited him to a "circle." Settlemyer had been enrolled for two and a half years before he was included in such a party, perhaps because he was so much older than the other students. He told of the deep snowfall that required the college boys to transport the ladies to the party by sleigh. While at the party, he records, "It was my good fortune to become acquainted with some of the ladies of the city . . . the first formal introduction received by me to any ladies of Springfield."

A student met ladies in a few other socially acceptable ways: at the singing school, the Sunday school, and church picnics. At one picnic, Settlemyer said he "fell in" with Eliza, daughter of one of Springfield's leading families. They left the picnic and visited in her home, where he ate strawberries, listened as she played the piano, and admired her drawings. He was impressed, he said, with her "general utility."

Alem Hutchins, who had dropped out of school temporarily to earn money teaching school, and perhaps to escape the school's regimentation, wrote his brother, "There are lots of girls where I teach school, so you must not worry about me."

Students who attended churches in town were invited by families to join them for meals. Picnics were a favorite pastime. A few families living near the school invited a portion of the student body to join them after which there was to be "a feast of reason and a flow of soul." The group ranged over a variety of subjects, but when it turned to politics and growing sectional strife, the ladies excused themselves and left the men to the serious talk. The Wittenberg students may have been disappointed because they were expected to remain for the serious conversation with the men.

Eating was always a way to integrate town and gown. The literary societies included town guests at their banquets. Students often joined friends in town. When snow arrived, young people met at favorite sleighing and skating sites where there were bonfires and refreshments. They ice skated on Buck Creek near the bridge. When the snow got too deep, students complained of being penned up; when the thaw came, they complained that the sleighing was spoiled and their young friends were disappointed. There was a great deal of interest in the outdoors. Picnics gave way to fall walks and rugby football, followed by a season of skating and sledding, which gave way in turn to spring walks, picnics, and competitions in running, jumping, wrestling, and cricket. Cricket clearly captured the enthusiasm of young people both at the college and in town.

In the spring of 1860, Clifton Nichols began to promote the game of cricket—"the greatest and best game in 'Old England' and out of it." He published the rules adopted by the Marlybone and Philadelphia clubs and urged the organization of a club in Springfield. By summer he could announce "a growing interest among our young men in this scientific and interesting game." Three clubs were organized in Springfield and matches became regular public events. The following September, when Wittenberg opened the fall term, the town was in a veritable cricket frenzy. A number of the younger students took up the new game. By November 2, Wittenberg players were ready to challenge the local teams. The students liked the lively physical exercise and the opportunity to compete physically with others. A town and gown skirmish was particularly exhilarating.

In their first match eight Wittenberg students, all sophomores or younger, teamed up with about as many young townsmen to challenge the best players from the two volunteer fire companies. The Wittenberg men lost 78 to 64, but immediately challenged the victors to a rematch. The Wittenberg men on the roster included J. C. Armstrong, George M. Winwood, J. W. Haines, Melanchthon Ort, J. D. Leighty, Asa W. Hatch, Samuel A. Ort, (later Wittenberg's fourth president), and A. P. Mitchell. They were the first Wittenberg students ever to see their names in the newspapers for participation in an athletic contest.

Cricket was a complicated game and students poured over Beadle's *Dime Book of Cricket* to learn the finer points. Nichols was pleased with the interest. He noted growing hazing at eastern colleges, particularly Harvard. Cricket, on the other hand, furnished "the excitement which young men very naturally seek, in their leisure moments, or hours and it is always of a wholesome nature." He assured older residents that profanity and rowdyism were prohibited at the gentlemanly matches. The game's exhilaration, he said, was a natural substitute for drinking alcohol. The game improved the players intellectually and physically and was a "new sensation" for all who came to watch.

The students' interests drew them away from the college grounds to explore the area around the school. They discovered a small Indian mound southeast of the campus near the Indian Spring which was the source of the college brook. Members of the Excelsior Society undertook to excavate the mound. Newspapers reported that others had tried before but without success. The mound was nearly eight feet high and thirty to thirty-five feet in diameter. After digging down a considerable distance, they found a layer of what they described as primitive cement. Upon penetrating this, they found a chamber in which a single skeleton was arrayed. The bones appeared to be in fine condition, but upon exposure to the air began to crumble to dust. With the skeleton were a finely-finished whetstone, a number of very large and highly-polished lance points, and other stones bearing characters which no one, including the faculty, could interpret.

The body had been placed due east and west, following the path of the sun, stretched out on a prepared piece of ground, quite unlike other Indian burials known in the area. The size of the mound for a single burial, the care taken to protect the body, and the relics found by its side led those involved to assume that it was the burial site of a chief whose people predated the Indians more recently in the area. Perhaps it was a burial site of the ancient Hopewell culture, so named because the first remains in Ohio were found at the Hopewell farm. They were the outstanding pre-Columbian people north of Mexico and were renowned as "great earthwork builders." An archaeological assessment of the area years later, reported that at least four different prehistoric Indian cultures were represented by artifacts found at the site: paleo-Indian, Archaic and Adena, as well as Hopewell. The area had been inviting, apparently, to successive Indian cultures over thousands of years.

Once the challenge of the physical exertion and the excitement of the find wore off, the students pondered the age of the burial which did not seem to fit traditional notions of biblical time. They questioned the meaning of their discovery. Dr. Sprecher told them of the values of geology and archaeology for men actively involved in studying the mysteries of the real world. There were mounds throughout central Ohio, and within a few years, additional burials were discovered at Ferncliff cemetery west of the college. Area residents thought they had discovered a pleasant and beautiful prehistoric medicinal garden and burial ground which had served the earliest inhabitants of the area.

The town offered additional opportunities for students to experience the world. In the spring of 1864, Amelia Bloomer lectured in Springfield on women's right to self government. She had gained fame for the individualism expressed in her clothing. She was known for wearing a tunic belted at the waist with a knee length skirt and beneath it, billowing pantaloons that the public called "bloomers." She was billed as an elegant and entertaining speaker, and students willing to spend fifteen cents—the equivalent of a dinner or two breakfasts—joined the "large and attentive audience."

Andrew Black's Opera House, Main Street, Springfield, The Auditorium on the second floor seated one thousand. Site of Wittenberg commencements, 1869-1878. Clark County Historical Society.

Women's issues presented themselves regularly to the men of Wittenberg. Some eagerly identified with the young women of their acquaintance and espoused their cause. The literary societies debated women's suffrage and the editor of the *Springfield Advertiser* warned them that women were a dangerous subject for them to discuss. "Our observation," he added, "is that they had better not meddle with them." At more than one society supper, however, the students revealed their ambivalence on the issue when they included women in the series of toasts in a less lofty vein: "Woman—the edition is large, and everyone should have a copy!" George Rawlins responded and had his fellows in "a roar of laughter." "Woman's rights and the right woman," he exclaimed, or to the young ladies of Springfield, "May God bless them and increase their number."

In 1869, the Philosophian Society sponsored a public lecture by Theodore Tilton, well-known abolitionist, national newspaperman, and lecturer who spoke on women's rights. He argued that women should have the same wages as men; that the law should protect them in their property rights; that they should be equal with men in the control of their children; and that they should be equal with men before the law. To achieve these rights, Tilton advocated woman's suffrage. The editor of the *Springfield Republic* thanked the students for their public spirit in bringing Tilton to town. Tilton, the editor observed in a reference to Amelia Bloomer, was not an "angel in baggy britches," rather he was a man generously "waging battle as a volunteer in behalf of woman."

In Tilton's lecture, he noted man's relationship to women, citing the name of "Jenny" written in very large letters in the snow on the Wittenberg hill. He took the fate of America's "Jennies" as the beginning point of his lecture and offered a copy of a book of poems he had written as a gift to the student who had inscribed Jenny's name in the snow. The next day about twenty students who claimed to have assisted in the snow writing presented themselves to receive the book. Rumor was, however, that they were ribbing one fellow student who was pining for the attention of a local girl named Sarah Jane, nicknamed Jenny. That student received the book.

In 1867, Frederick Douglass, the well-known, former slave and abolitionist from Massachusetts spoke in Springfield at city hall. Proceeds from his lecture went to the Relief Fund of the Grand Army of the Republic. He was one of many outstanding speakers available to the students. Frequently, the famous Horace Mann, president of nearby Antioch College, was invited to speak. A popular and entertaining hometown speaker was Samuel Shellabarger, elected to Congress as a Republican in 1860.

Frederick Douglas, former slave and national abolitionist leader, spoke in Springfield in 1867. Poster in collections of Clark County Historical Society.

Famous performers also stopped at this town on the National Road. Swedish singer Jenny Lind, violinist Ole Bull, and composer-performer Louis Moreau Gottschalk, who sought to capture American Indian music in classical European forms, appeared on the local stage. In 1852, Wittenberg students had the opportunity to hear the Hungarian patriot Louis Kossuth on his tour of America generating support for the revolutionaries in Hungary and arousing nativist, anti-Catholic feelings. They stood in deep snow at the outdoor rally, and sixteen of them became ill. Professor Geiger's younger brother George died. Clearly Wittenberg's location, as compared with smaller college towns, gave its students greater opportunities for culture and entertainment.

The attractions of Springfield brought other students to town. Students at Antioch College, fifteen miles to the south, likewise were attracted to the opportunities in Springfield. Local papers duly noted Antioch vacations and holidays and told residents to prepare for the invasion of "boys . . . calculating on a good time."

One of the first things students became acquainted with was the official town clock in the tower of the Presbyterian Church. It told the correct time and symbolized the social prominence of Presbyterians in the community. To set a watch by Springfield mean time, one was advised to set their time piece at the instant the clock began to strike. The hands were a little erratic, but the chimes began right on the hour. To meet a train, in the days before standard time zones, one had to remember that Springfield time was three minutes and five seconds later than Columbus time by which the trains ran.

Wittenberg was located across the creek and north of town. The road to the college was at first a dirt road which the students and faculty helped lay out along the wagon tracks made during the building construction. Every citizen in the county was required to put in two days per year on road duty, and those affiliated with the college were permitted to put their time in on the college road.

Since the building had been completed in 1851, the area north of Buck Creek had experienced much growth. The first major development east of the Urbana Road had been named Spring Hill by its developers. Leffel's hydraulic mill race, constructed by the Barnetts, emptied back into the creek just below Spring Hill at the foot of what became Limestone Street. A number of mills were developed using the power of the race: a cotton mill, a linseed oil mill, five woolen mills, two flour mills, and two saw mills. It was the beginning of industrial growth for the town. Just above the mills, a number of elegant residences were built: the first by James Leffel, Springfield's first inventor and industrialist; and another by Samuel Shellabarger, across from the Female Seminary whose board of trustees he chaired. Isaac Ward built west of the Seminary. Just northwest of these you could catch a glimpse of the copula of the college building.

The newspapers described Spring Hill as "very much after the fashion of neat New England." It looked down across the creek with its many mills upon the courthouse in what one editor called "Sleepy Hollow." He speculated that soon "all the beautiful knolls about Springfield" would be peopled with "a living, moving population" that carried the city's fortunes forward in spite of the slower-paced lives of the earlier settlers.

The entrepreneurs north of the creek petitioned City Council to extend Market Street across Buck Creek. The improvement could cut a quarter of a mile off the trip from college to town. Isaac Ward provided stone and wood for the new bridge that would span the creek. Wittenberg and Ward built the bridge and gave it to the city in return for a promise that the city would keep it in good repair in perpetuity. Road and bridge improvements were of particular interest to the college because of the constant threat of fire. For a fire in the college building, volunteer fire companies had to come from town, across the creek and out the college road. Anything that made the trip shorter and easier was a top priority. According to Benjamin Prince, fires occurred two or three times every winter. Most were put out by students with water from the well or the brook. In 1856, a large cistern was built behind the building to hold a ready supply of water.

Some fires were too large for students to handle and the fire companies were called. On a cold January morning in 1854, the college building caught fire. A student ran to town for help. Because of the time involved in getting the alarm to town, rounding up the volunteer firemen, and getting the fire engine to the college, only the prompt exertions of the students in the building kept the fire from spreading out of control. The entire open area between the ceiling of the fifth floor and the copula was engulfed in flames. Faculty and students suspected arson, but no clues as to the identity of the culprit or culprits could be found. The faculty expressed thanks to the fire companies; the citizens of Springfield; and the systematic, energetic, and daring action of the students, whose bucket brigades from brook and well to attic saved the building.

Again, in January 1856, the building caught fire. The cause that time was the carelessness of students in setting their stovepipes, a general complaint of firemen about citizens throughout the area. One of the president's complaints about his job was the constant need to check student stoves. Much of the problem was structural. Wood partitions separated the rooms, and the stove pipe openings were too close to the walls. When the pipes became over-heated the wood lath behind the plaster caught fire. The newspaper called for fire wardens to check out the way people set their pipes. It was frightening to think of a separate wood-burning stove in every room in the building. With the variety of student firing skills and a penchant for carelessness among them, it is a wonder the building survived at all.

In March of 1858, Dr. Sprecher was presenting "a beautiful and effective sermon" in the Presbyterian church and about to close with an invitation to the impenitent to be saved. The service was interrupted by the cry of "Fire at Wittenberg College!" The service broke up immediately, and the good doctor with a host of friends headed north. This time the fire had originated in a student's room while he was absent. Once again the prompt and energetic action of the few students who remained in the building subdued the blaze before the fire company arrived.

In still one other way, at least, the Springfield community exerted an influence on the young men of Wittenberg College. Many of the local leaders who had been to college elsewhere had joined one of the new Greek letter societies that were appearing at colleges across America. The local newspapers, as early as 1845, carried stories about such groups and about local alumni who attended anniversary celebrations and conventions of fraternities at Miami University in Oxford, Ohio, and at eastern colleges.

In 1852, eight students were initiated into Phi Delta Theta by friends at Miami University. The eight included an alumnus who remained in Springfield; the school's two tutors, William B. Younce and Maurice Kirby; and five undergraduates. When the chapter was discovered, other students and the faculty objected to a secret and exclusive group within the student body. It cut across class lines, they charged, and leagued some students, staff, and alumni together against the rest of the community.

Dr. Keller had summed up what became the official view about fraternities at the school. "I dislike all secret associations," he had said, "I consider them dangerous to our free institutions both civil and religious. For their pomp and show, I have an utter distaste." He was speaking of the lodges of Freemasons and Odd Fellows, which many American Lutherans had embraced as mainstream American institutions. Had fraternities been brought to his attention, he would have included them in his condemnation.

With the crisis between North and South worsening, students organized a different group which met with great acceptance in town. The local papers heralded a campus military company with the headline, "More Blood." Springfielders were caught up in the growing conflict between North and South over free soil, the extension of slavery, the Fugitive Slave Act, and Bloody Kansas, where pro and anti-slavery settlers were already at war. At the call of Governor Salmon Chase, military companies were organized throughout Ohio. "We are glad to hear that the progressive students of Wittenberg," said Nichols, "have formed their own company." With sectional issues disturbing society meetings, dining hall, and dormitory, regular military drill began on campus.

Chapter Six

The War Unsettled Everything

Wittenberg's position in the sectional crisis was clear. While some congregations split over the issue and a vociferous minority spoke out at synod meetings urging caution, generally those synods related to Wittenberg were opposed to slavery. When Congress established Kansas and Nebraska as territories open to slavery, repealing the Missouri Compromise, two of Wittenberg's synods passed resolutions of disapproval. As early as 1852, the Wittenberg Synod, presided over by Samuel Sprecher, had called slavery "a great national evil and an abomination in the sight of God." The resolution called upon church members to "pray for those who legislate . . . that a plan may be devised for its speedy extinction" and to act in society for slavery's removal. Some were concerned about the character of abolitionists, many of whom were outspoken critics of Christianity but felt that the churches should clearly oppose slavery in spite of that.

After the Dred Scott decision in 1857, in which the Supreme Court declared the Missouri Compromise unconstitutional, Samuel Schmucker at Gettysburg said he would never assist in returning a fugitive to slavery and would assist those trying to flee. In a sermon, "Pray for the Peace of Jerusalem," he said that Lutherans needed to act as well as pray, and urged political action to change laws protecting the despised institution. One synod called slavery "a system of oppression and high handed injustice and entirely contrary to the spirit of the Gospel of Christ." It asked Christians to pray for guidance and to deplore efforts to "extend and perpetuate the stupendous evil."

The firing on Fort Sumter, observed George Halderman, class of 1863, "stirred the old college from dining room to dome." The faculty, students, steward, and janitor poured out for a rally on the college hill. They raised the American flag to the highest point on the building. Every professor made a speech, he said, and each "filled and fired the students' hearts with a love of country." Following each speech, students chanted, "The flag of our country, long may it wave/ O'er the land of the free and the home of the brave!" Sprecher made the last of the many speeches, concluding his remarks with a pledge, "Now we will let that flag hang there until the war is over and the country safe."

The loyalty of Wittenberg alumni was illustrated by twenty-six-year old Rev. John Stuckenberg. He graduated from the college in 1856 and from seminary in 1857. After two years as a pastor, he went to Germany to study at the University of Halle, the place to which the German Wittenberg had been moved in 1815. He returned to a church in Pennsylvania in 1861, where he urged young men to join the army. An outspoken supporter of the North, he enlisted as a chaplain. "War is the business of the present," he said, "and ours is a righteous cause." As a chaplain, he said he learned about human nature and the horror of war and how useless religious creeds were when men faced the carnage of the battlefield. In such dire straits they needed access to God, he said, not to confessions and creeds.

In May of 1861, students reorganized their military company into the Wittenberg Zouaves. It was a popular kind of unit copied from the French Zouaves of the Crimean War, with flamboyant uniforms of baggy trousers, bloused shirt sleeves, bright vests, and curtained caps in bright colors that kept the sun off one's neck. Virtually every northern community had at least one company of Zouaves that lent color and excitement to the martial spirit of a nation that did not expect a long or difficult war.

After the custom of militia, the company elected its officers. It picked a senior student from Altoona, Pennsylvania, James M. Bell, as its captain, initiating for him a distinguished lifetime military career. In June of 1862, seventeen students in the Wittenberg unit joined a newly organized Springfield Company and Bell was elected First Lieutenant. The unit became Company B, Eighty-sixth

Regiment, Ohio Volunteer Infantry. He was sent to Clarksburg, Virginia, for guard duty and training, freeing regular troops to move forward in the effort to separate western Virginia from the rebel state. In September they returned, and students could resume their studies. Lt. Bell reenlisted in a new unit. During the war he achieved the rank of Brigadier General.

Civil War Brigadier General George M. Bell, class of 1862.
Wittenberg University Archives.

Wittenberg's enrollment decreased by twenty-five percent between 1860 and 1863. College level classes declined by one third. The numbers reflected the experience of colleges across the North. In 1860, the school had opened with five theological students, seventy-nine in the college, and seventy-three preparatory students. By

1862, college enrollment declined to fifty-four, preparatory students numbered only fifty-eight, and theological enrollment was six.

On June 5, William Settlemyer noted in his diary that twenty Wittenberg students, seven from his own class, had "filled out" another volunteer unit. Classes were suspended, and all the students joined local citizens for a glorious send off at the railroad station. Throughout the war, Springfield met its quotas for troops with volunteers and did not have to resort to the draft, in part because of the number of Wittenberg students who augmented local enlistments. Sixty-five students left for military service, and many more for shorter tours of three to six months. After 1862, as each new unit left for service or returned, it was saluted with the firing of an old canon from the War of 1812, captured from the Confederates in western Virginia by Springfield's Forty-fourth Ohio Volunteer Infantry. The canon was maintained as an exhibit in Springfield for many years and is now housed in the Heritage Center in downtown Springfield.

The young men who enlisted were prompted by motives of duty and patriotism, said Sprecher. He insisted that the personal and institutional sacrifice had to be made. The school had to show loyalty to the government and he cited reports around the country of Wittenberg's patriotism. "The spirit of patriotism," he said, "which prevails in the institution, leads some of the students to feel that in obedience to their country's call, they ought to enlist in the war. Some of our most pious and promising young men are consequently in the army." The faculty urged students, before taking such a step, to consult with their parents and friends and to "prayerfully consider whether in the order of Providence" it was their duty to enlist at this particular time. Students were urged to do so only from an "overpowering sense of duty," and, if they did so, to "heartily maintain their religious principles and their pious feelings" in the army.

Sprecher received strong community response to his public support of the war. He advised "full confidence in the integrity of Lincoln." He urged their restraint and patience when the war was not going well, when battles were lost and casualties mounted. "We should wait when we are inclined to criticize and denounce the government," he told them. Sprecher was a popular speaker at rallies. He urged citizens to be ready with their purses and persons to respond to their country's call. When they raised a fund to pay bounties to volunteers, Sprecher offered to give twenty-five dollars, which was a week's pay, or a "beef creature" worth fifty dollars. A butcher offered to slaughter it free. Nichols advised, "Eat Sprecher's beef and support the war effort!"

In June, 1864, Sprecher referred to the loss of enrollment caused by the president's call for troops, men for short-term home guard duty to free regular troops for the front. Enrollment was also affected by others going home to assist on the farm or to work in business because of the shortage of labor. Settlemyer left Wittenberg for home in the summer and, once home, joined a thirty-day volunteer company to release regular troops. He told of camp camaraderie and the excitement of life for young men on their own in the army. In October he returned a different person, expecting a little more latitude in his life at Wittenberg. He seemed to himself and others less the boy and more the man. It was a contagious spirit.

Students who remained at school found ways to support the war effort. The literary societies charged admission for their exercises and donated the proceeds to the Ladies Soldiers Aid Society that helped provide assistance to Union soldiers at the front and their families at home. They helped the ladies with funds so they could make hospital garments for the wounded after General Grant's bloody victory at Fort Donelson.

Catherine Sprecher represented Lutheran women on the management committee of the Ladies Soldiers Aid Society. They raised so much money for the Cincinnati Sanitary Fair that they won a flag for their efforts. They united the efforts of women in various denominations who made quilts, sheets, blankets, pillow cases, pillows, bed ticks, towels, shirts, underwear, socks, mittens and slippers for soldiers in the camps. They canned fruits, vegetables and chicken to send to the front. It was the first time that respectable women saw their names in newspapers or managed an organization on so large a scale without male supervision. Ladies work in the churches was never the same.

Melanchthon Ort organized a Sunday school for black children fleeing the south. Many, called "contrabands," were sent north and advertisements in the Springfield newspapers sought homes for them. Agents in Cincinnati sent as many youth to the area as could be accommodated. Isaac Funk went south as a courier taking letters and packages from family and friends to Wittenberg students in the battle of Murfreesboro, Tenn. Students held memorial services for friends who died in the war, noting their "sacrifice on the altar of liberty," saluting those who slept "the slumbers of the brave," and promised that they would be "cherished forever as true patriots."

The loss of students to the army and their coming and going, noted Benjamin F. Prince a senior, was disheartening to the president and faculty. It greatly disrupted their work. Enrollment counts showed 118 in 1862-63, the low point for the war years, 125 in 1863-64, and 155 in 1864-65. The actual number present at any one time was smaller as students left and returned with a greater degree of freedom than ever before. By 1865, discharged veterans came and enrollment reached 195, the highest in history. Former soldiers were present from then until 1874 and helped revolutionize college life.

Faculty noted a steady erosion of student conduct during the war, and it continued afterward. The changes disturbed them. During Settlemyer's second year, as war began, virtually the entire student body was caught up in a religious revival, and the faculty congratulated itself that "there has not been a single case of discipline during the year." Another student who had enrolled at that time observed that "college discipline was really what it claimed to be, that of a good family government. Each student was placed on his honor and expected to do right from principle." But the honor system was to be greatly strained as the war years wore on. Sprecher's disposition was one of gentleness and mildness. He was ill-equipped to deal with the bolder challenges to authority that were to come. One student observed that he could not reprove the student body as a group "without a tear trembling in his eye." He could deal firmly with individual malefactors when their identity was known, but his sense of fairness and justice prevented him from punishing the group or disciplining solely on the basis of suspicion.

In 1863, when the North's cause faltered and Settlemyer, like others, showed greater concern about the war, faculty noted "a relaxation in the attention of students to the exercises and duties of the institution." They had to provide stricter supervision. Prince, one of Settlemyer's classmates, indicated the connection between war and student conduct. Short time enlistments and concern about the successes and failures of the Union cause interfered greatly with their studies. A member of the class of 1865 regretted that he had been inattentive to his studies and preoccupied with daily drills. "The war," he observed, "unsettled everything."

According to Settlemyer, student tensions mounted with the passage of the Conscription Act in 1863. Prior to that, he had kept a rather dispassionate record of the conflict. The Act made unmarried males, ages 18 to 45, and married males, 18 to 30, subject to the draft. With its passage, he noted that it was difficult to keep his mind on his studies and that there was great discussion about the draft among students. In the end most supported the measure because it would equalize the burden between loyalists, who had been carrying the load, and those less supportive of the North. He wrote, "the infernal rebellion: glad that croakers and sympathizers will be compelled to support the cause." Soon after passage, he noted that strong Union supporters paid more attention to students suspected of being Southern sympathizers. Loyalists, he wrote, sent an "under current" to keep backsliders in line. Students began to "take the temperature" of each other's loyalty and one's patriotism had to be apparent. As the war intensified, the Philosophian Society debated the issue which Democrats posed in 1864 as the major Presidential election issue: "that abolitionists brought on this war." An overwhelming majority of students voted for the negative side regardless of the quality of the argument, observed Settlemyer.

When Lincoln issued the Emancipation Proclamation, Sprecher called for a day of prayer and fasting. He urged students to accept the expediency of the act as a part of the war effort and the necessity of emancipation under the Law of God. He also asked students to think of the nation's sin in having participated in slavery. You could not give up sin gradually, he noted, it had to be repented of entirely and at once. On the day of fasting and prayer, Settlemyer added a note of humor. He raised his heart to God in prayer, he wrote, but celebrated the fast "by getting a fast hold on the victuals" at dinner.

In November of 1864, students celebrated Lincoln's reelection with an oyster supper and happy toasts. The first was to President Lincoln: "The personification of loyalty, the champion of liberty, the arch foe of treason, the Fabricius of the present age." Students then toasted the colleges of the nation: "Our colleges, the cradles of American Liberty." They did so with a new sense of their responsibility to assert their own. Wise old Dr. Sprecher responded saying that college boys sometimes construed American liberty to be to do as they pleased, without regard to law or regulations. They practiced the teachings of Thomas Jefferson, he added, whose theory was that a rebellion was necessary every generation or two to promote civil liberty.

The spirit of rebellion among the students was energized by the North's triumph at Appomattox soon after Lincoln's reelection. It could not be dampened even by Lincoln's assassination a few months later, just before Easter. "From the very summit of our highest demonstration of joy over the success of our noble army," a student observed, "we have been plunged into the very depths of sorrow by the malignant assassination of the beloved President of the United States."

One form of student rebelliousness was the student exodus from the boarding hall. It had begun in the middle of the war and grew steadily as the month's passed. Settlemyer left to join Mrs. Steelman's boarding club in town. Others found other accommodations. The faculty was unable to stop the flow. The board of directors was not happy with the situation and called it "a great evil." The mixing of students too freely in the community away from the watchful eyes of steward and tutors, abandoned the student's education to the outside world. This was harmful to the full beneficial mental and moral development of students which the old line college claimed for the undergraduate experience. They asked the faculty to require the students to return to boarding at the College.

It did not work. To make matters worse, as enrollments increased, the school could neither house nor feed all the students. Older ones were permitted officially not only to eat off campus but to live off campus. The steward seemed oblivious to the drop in food prices after the war, according to Prince who was a student at that time. Students then organized independent "eating clubs." Pretheological students and seminarians ate in a club popularly called "The Saints Roost." Another club was called "The Sinners" or "Men of the Pit," because they found quarters in the basement of the building. The split of theological and nontheological students in separate clubs suggests that other factors were involved in the collapse of the steward's club beyond price and quality. It was a matter of self-selected smaller groups within a growing student body.

Theological Boarding Club.

Cartoon, Theological Boarding Club, from the *Cycle, 1895,* yearbook. Wittenberg University Archives.

Settlemyer, though a pretheological student, joined neither campus club. He recorded with great pride an off-campus occurrence in his own little group. A bouquet arrived at Mrs. Steelman's boarding club from an anonymous woman addressed to "the finest looking student there." All agreed, wrote the diarist, that it should go to him. He was unable to conceal his bristling male pride but failed to record who the admirer was.

By 1864, faculty called attention to other kinds of rebelliousness in reporting that, while most students conducted themselves commendably, there were lamentable exceptions: "Some young men who seem to have brought bad habits with them have given us much trouble." Some brought bad habits from the army; some no doubt learned them in town. No one ever listed what the bad habits were because everyone knew. They included smoking and chewing, card playing, alcohol, profane language, and entertaining young ladies in town in suspicious circumstances. Smoking had been practiced for many years. Students celebrated the supreme accomplishment of one of their number who spent more on cigars than he did on food. But there was a new misbehavior involving tobacco which warranted special notice. The new complaint was about chewing tobacco and endless careless spitting. Faculty minutes at western colleges everywhere filled up with complaints about students who ignored or missed the spittoons. Then there were the sins of omission: failure to attend church faithfully every week, failure to attend daily prayer services, and failure to abide by the usually observed standards of Christian piety, humility and gentlemanly conduct.

The faculty lacked the time and the energy to hold students to prewar standards. They mentioned "[t]he necessary absence of the president." He was away raising funds to keep the school ahead of inflation and add to the endowment. The old complaint that one man could not be president and chief theological officer took on new meaning. The president's absence "has perhaps caused us to fail in the reformation of some who could otherwise have been brought to a proper course of student life."

Two years later the faculty reported a growing enrollment, good health, and a high degree of diligence in study by the great majority of students. "But it grieves us to say," they added, "that the state of piety has been comparatively low." Not since the early days of the war had there been a revival. In addition, students seemed less inclined toward earlier standards of pious conduct. In spite of all the efforts by the pastor in town, the president and the faculty, nothing could deflect the students from their preoccupation with the war and new found secular interests. The faculty called special prayer meetings every morning for four months with no marked results.

The reason, they believed, was that the oldest and best students were now living in town; their leadership and example for the younger students was no longer felt. "Doubtless, the influence of war upon morals in general," observed faculty, "and especially upon the character of the returned, unconverted soldiers . . . contributed much to the lamentable state of things." They recommended tougher admissions and graduation requirements and asked that the school admit fewer students who were not religiously committed. The school should no longer accept boys whose parents hoped college could reform them. "We shall have to be more careful even at the risk of having smaller accessions of students," said faculty, "to require certificates of good moral character of all future applicants." The faculty was pleased that it was getting students from non-Lutheran homes and that the academic quality of the institution was being recognized, but lamented that the greater variety led to other problems.

To deal with the situation, faculty rearranged class assignments of seminary professor Joel Schwartz and made him college pastor, the first to hold that title. He preached each Sabbath and looked after his charges through the week, providing counsel and advice. He discovered that he preferred the ministry to teaching and welcomed the change. The board voted to enlarge the chapel to seat the entire student body and organized a campus congregation that all students not living at home were to attend on Sunday. The congregation through its offerings was to pay half of the salary of the Pastor.

Unrest expressed itself in other developments. First was the reappearance of Greek letter fraternities, Phi Kappa Psi in 1866 and Beta Theta Pi in 1867. Jesse O. Davey, a war veteran with an extensive military record, initiated the movement by establishing Phi Kappa Psi and Settlemyer became one of the charter members. It is quite likely that all the charter members came from Mrs. Steelman's boarding club.

Davey spent one hundred twenty days in the army before entering the preparatory course. At the end of his freshman year, he enlisted again and served two more years. He returned in the fall of 1865, a hardened veteran. He had fought at the Battle of Mission Ridge, Georgia, and made a forced march through Tennessee. He had suffered exposure, diarrhea, sunstroke, typhus and smallpox. Some of his comrades were killed in battle and others, like him, were wasted by disease. Upon return to college, he studied classics but prepared to practice medicine. He had a more worldly view of life and planned to enjoy every minute of it that he might have left. He typified a lot of post war students. Davey, whom other students called "the hospitable," was initiated at Ohio Wesleyan University. At Wittenberg he selected seven students to join with him in the new Wittenberg chapter.

Jesse O. Davey, class of 1868, as a sophomore after service in the Civil War. He was instrumental in founding Ohio Beta chapter of Phi Kappa Psi.

George Scholl, Valedictorian, class of 1868, instrumental in establishing Alpha Gamma chapter of Beta Theta Pi in 1867.

George Scholl transferred to Wittenberg from Miami University at Oxford, Ohio, where he had been a member of Beta Theta Pi. He organized a group of Wittenberg students to affiliate with that group. He was a pretheological student from a Lutheran family in Indiana. His parents and other relatives were contributors to Wittenberg's endowment fund. Scholl worked in town with Editor Nichols at the newspaper and elicited and received editorial support for Wittenberg's fledgling Greek societies.

The groups found eager initiates among the students and ardent support among parents, townspeople and alumni. The youthful tutors were enticed to join and provided a semi-official endorsement and a buffer between students and faculty. As earlier, when Phi Delta Theta was suppressed, the board and faculty expressed the hope that students "would not labor to perpetuate" the societies; but this time they did. Secret fraternities became a permanent part of student life on many campuses, arranging for their members to live and eat off campus. Because they were spending their evening hours in town in a lodge room, they provided a meeting place beyond the faculty's view.

Through fraternities students sought to add a lighter touch to what they saw as a dreary existence. Life was not in fact more barren than it had been for earlier students, but it seemed so. These were boys from families in which Puritan standards were obsolete. Many experienced suffering and privation in the war and now sought a life that was richer and more enjoyable. They sought to throw off the restraints of the past. They believed that faculties were hostile to any new form of amusement as a waste of time and a detriment to their studies. But the new students wanted an education for the world in which they would have to live. Even those most serious about their educations deplored the "deadness of the ironbound curriculum," as one expressed it. Many pioneer Greeks, like Benjamin Prince and Samuel Ort, both Phi Psis at Wittenberg, who were destined for academic careers at America's colleges, would later revolutionize their campuses.

The zealousness of Wittenberg's Greek founders was illustrated by George Scholl. In a literary society debate, he had been described as having "a stubborn face, not in any mulish sense, but stubborn as we imagine the face of John Brown was stubborn." People noticed

Scholl's strength of will: "His face is cut into strong shapes and has angles that are arguments." He put his will and his argument to the support of the fledgling fraternity movement and made it go. Supporters noted that it was only at the better schools, in tune with the times, that the Greek letter societies flourished. Schools that successfully suppressed them, they noted, were parochial, unnecessarily narrow-minded, and unresponsive to the winds of change affecting higher education in America.

The conditions which gave birth to fraternities were real, and the Greek letter man was a partisan in a cause. It was a less intellectual movement than the literary society which had dominated campuses before the war. The fraternity brought more of a "this worldly" focus which struck a responsive chord in the rising business and industrial society. Fraternities embraced the secular values of friendship, attractiveness, good grooming, good family connections and the pursuit of success. In doing so they defined a new student life style. The men were better dressed and paid more attention to grooming. They gloated that they took the "best" men in the college and allied them with alumni members of the chapters already in the business community. They focused on manners as a key to success and emphasized getting ahead in this world rather than the next.

At their first anniversary, Wittenberg's Betas celebrated fraternity. Membership, said one, gave students "a solid source of pleasure and mental culture, as well as amusement." The meetings said another, were a relief from the toil of the day. After college, the true Greek would "rise still higher . . . in his encounters with the trials and vicissitudes of the world." Brothers already graduated were spreading the principles of fraternity throughout the land. Another noted, "The young man, far from the parental roof, without the counsel of home, often wrecked a brilliant mind for want of true friends." Fraternity took them in hand, encouraged nobler purposes, "counseled the wayward, assisted the weak, and raised the fallen." The paper called the event "a social and intellectual hour," a "flow of coffee, a discussion of oysters and a ciphering out of cake." Revealing his status as an alumnus of the fraternity, he added, "We shall not soon forget how we sat together in brotherhood and felt the mystic power of invisible cords draw us into unity."

Another manifestation of student discontent was the underground newspaper. As one student described it: "In the month of June, 1863, a new planet, a star of the first magnitude, flashed across the heavens, to the alarm of the faculty. This was none other than the *Flying Dutchman*." It was an underground, anonymously published newspaper in which seniors expressed their pent-up criticisms and perhaps some of those of local residents about the school, its faculty, the academic program, and school rules and policies. It commented on less well-liked members of the student body, especially those who sided with the authorities against their own generation.

The editor of the *Springfield News* noted the student paper's appearance: "the *Flying Dutchman* flew over this city yesterday morning and knocked over several gentlemen by brushing them with his wings and tail." H. R. Geiger, a nemesis to many in town since the dispute over the Presbyterian college, was one of the targets. It was obvious that the students had access to local printers. Throughout the two-decade era of underground papers at Wittenberg, 1863-1883, that relationship was essential. In another reference to the first edition, the editor said, "A package of money and several bouquets have been left with us for the editor of the *Flying Dutchman*."

Students at Wittenberg and elsewhere distributed such papers during the final week of school. At Wittenberg it appeared on Alumni Weekend and was available through final examinations, the annual meeting of the board of directors and Commencement. It was the week when the most people would see the paper and when there was relatively little time left in which to discover the culprits, always seniors about to graduate. The practice spread across the nation in the post Civil War era as students discovered a way to enlist broader support for their pleas for more freedom and to call the attention of board members to their desires for a more up-to-date curriculum. It also enabled editors like Clifton M. Nichols in Springfield, to push for educational reform. Wittenberg students discovered the device ahead of some and stayed with it for a longer period of time.

In 1866 the *Flying Dutchman's Pap* appeared, and, as one student observed, "the ancestor proved worse than its off-spring."

Flying Dutchman's Pap.

Vol. I. "NIX KUM ROUSE." No. 1.

PUBLISHED BY THE SENIOR CLASS WITTENBERG COLLEGE

The Chronicles of Wittenberg.

Flying Dutchman's Pap, one of many underground newspapers at Wittenberg, 1863-1883. Wittenberg University Archives.

The name was used again in 1870 when the *Flying Dutchman's Granddaddy*, appeared; then a couple of year's later the *Flying Dutchman's Grand Mammy*. Some guessed that the paper's name came from a German novel by William Hauff. Richard Wagner told the story in a poem which in 1842 became the basis for his opera of the same name.

By the 1860s, the legend was well known in both Europe and America. A popular form of it involved a stubborn German ship's captain who found himself in a violent storm. The crew begged him to head for a safe harbor, but he stubbornly refused. He defied fate, even daring God to sink his ship and destroy the crew with it. As punishment he was condemned to sail forever, tormenting his crew. For the students, the stubborn captain was Prof. Geiger, albeit assisted by a bevy of junior officers, and the students were his unfortunate crew. In one popular variation, the crew was eventually rescued by a beautiful maiden. The term "Flying Dutchman" was also popular among nativists in derogatory references to German immigrants. It was used in the nativist press during the Civil War alleging that German-American soldiers retreated in the face of enemy fire. It was applied personally to one general of German-American ancestry.

The students used the name in derision of Professors Diehl, Geiger, Isaac Sprecher and Steward Simons. Those who at the school's beginning were hailed by the students as peers were now growing older. They were seen by the newer students as old fashioned and less tolerant of changing student behavior. The paper also took slaps at the college janitor who also kept the key to the library, but never had it with him. Later when the targets of their derision were all gone, the underground papers took different names. Nevertheless, for a time, the generic name for an underground paper was "a Dutchman."

With the second appearance of the paper, the faculty decided it needed to do more than it had done earlier to find the culprits and call them to account. This edition was more scurrilous and represented a growing rebelliousness. Rumor among students was that the faculty offered a $50 reward for the offenders "dead or alive." The sum equaled nearly a full year's expenses for tuition, fees and books. Noting faculty displeasure, more traditional students called an indignation meeting and passed resolutions condemning this act of "misguided persons." What was meant as "a mere sally of wit on the faculty and students" went too far, becoming "slander, vulgarity and profanity." They issued a notice "to show to the public our entire disapprobation of the character of the paper and of the misdirected effort of those who endeavored to create a little sport at the expense of all that is good and pure."

The offenders included a good proportion of the senior class and many senior members of the fraternities. The chief culprit, however, the editor and publisher, was Joshua Shaffer, a non-fraternity man and Settlemyer's roommate. A committee of the Board had examined the seniors earlier and was prepared to make its customary recommendation that "the gentlemen be graduated." This time, however, the motion was tabled pending a discussion of the "editing and publishing of a certain paper known as the *Flying Dutchman's Pap.*" The Board satisfied itself that Shaffer was chiefly responsible and he was summoned to the Board's session at 7:30 a.m., commencement morning. Sprecher and board member Samuel Bowman cross examined him.

Shaffer ventured alone into the room, with the rest of the seniors nervously awaiting the outcome, their degrees hanging in the balance. It was a subdued Joshua Shaffer, who, as the class sacrificial lamb, confessed responsibility. His task was to placate the Board without implicating anyone else and then, if possible, to extricate himself. He succeeded. The Board decided that Shaffer could graduate if he made a written apology which expressed penitence and his promise to avoid slanderous and scandalous publications in the future. When he complied, the motion that "the gentlemen be graduated" was removed from the table and passed. The Board recessed just in time for the exercises to begin, much to the relief of the class.

The class had requested that no honors be given in the class and that orators be selected by the class itself. Shaffer was one of these and he was allowed both to graduate and to speak.

Joshua Shaffer, class of 1866, editor of *Flying Dutchman's Pap*. Class orator, roommate of William H. Settlemyer. Wittenberg University Archives.

His oration was entitled, "The Importance of True Ideals." The reporter covering the event noted the exuberance with which he was greeted. His appearance "at the front, either from his good looks or some other source, was stoutly applauded," he noted. The class saluted its hero, and the reporter feigned ignorance as to why. In his remarks, Shaffer urged the class to pursue what might be before settling for what already was, no matter how practical the tendency of the age.

Conflicts between students who felt liberated by the war and faculties who sought first to maintain and then to restore prewar decorum continued at Wittenberg and elsewhere until major readjustments came in the 1870s. William Settlemyer, Joshua Shaffer, George Rawlins and other members of the class of 1866 left the campus not knowing how it would all come out but having experienced the tension and nearly sacrificing their degrees in the process.

The tenor of the times was illustrated in student reaction to affronts in the world at large. In the spring of 1868, students were agitated by an act of the Ohio legislature which disenfranchised students. In a rally in the college chapel, students said they were "watchful of our interests, jealous of our rights, and desirous to express our disapprobation of this shameful betrayal of trust." Democrats had repealed legislation which allowed soldiers on active duty, in hospitals, and in soldiers' homes as well as students and others away from home to exercise an absentee ballot. Students throughout Ohio called it an affront to intelligence, ability and reason and the college educated class. It was hostile to the very idea of progress. Students at Wittenberg insisted that Wittenberg "link hands with her sister colleges all over the land" to oppose this unfair action.

In June of 1868, the faculty and board of directors were confronted with a more forthright challenge when the entire freshman class petitioned for a change in curriculum. It asked that the study of Latin and Greek be optional after the first year, giving the student the privilege of choosing two courses from among Greek, Latin, German and French or one from the languages and the other from the sciences. The request would mean expanding the curriculum in modern languages and science, allowing electives and an increase in the size of the faculty.

They put forth a brief but well organized case in support of their request. Those preparing for the ministry wanted to put more time on German. They needed German especially because they would be working among the ever growing number of German immigrants. They wanted to be able to read and understand the original German books from Luther's Reformation and its aftermath. "To do this," they said, "we must give less time to Latin and more to German." For those going into law and medicine, the freshmen argued, they needed to drop Greek and replace it with some living language.

All members of the class, the petition continued, were convinced that they gave too much time to the study of dead languages and not enough to the modern, "especially our own great English." They were wasting their time and acquiring bad habits of neglect and carelessness because of their great disinterest in the classics. "We must be measured by our ability to meet the demands of this active scientific age," they argued. Such changes would attract more students. Indeed, it would keep many of those already enrolled who might otherwise depart. "We know that many in our class," they suggested politely, "from their sense of duty and right cannot graduate unless the course is changed." They concluded their request by citing the many institutions that had already made curriculum changes of the type they were requesting and by complimenting the Board for its devotion to the institution and to the best interests of the students. It was a very diplomatically worded petition. In a few paragraphs, they had captured much of the current nationwide criticism of the classical college curriculum.

The Board referred the petition to a committee of three: a young pastor from Dayton, Reverend Luther A. Gotwald, Campus Pastor Joel Schwartz, and President Sprecher. The committee, after due reflection, recommended that the request not be granted. Sprecher did not sign the report. "The chief aim of a collegiate course," the report noted, "is thorough mental discipline, the highest possible cultivation of all the faculties of the mind, and not the mere acquisition of knowledge or the mere preparation of the student for some one sphere of direct or immediate usefulness." This purpose, they said, could best be served "by adhering to the time-honored custom of studying the ancient languages." The second argument against the petitioners was practical and economic. To accede to the request meant hiring additional faculty which, for financial reasons, the school could not do. Added to these arguments were six others about peer institutions, standards and the avoidance of vocationalism.

The committee's final argument shifted the debate from curriculum to methodology. Student dissatisfaction, they said, was with the instruction and not the course itself. They recommended that Latin be taught entirely by Isaac Sprecher and Greek by Michael Diehl. The board agreed to the recommendation that the petitioners' request be turned down but voted against dividing the ancient languages. Professor Diehl, against whom much student criticism was aimed, was affronted by the Committee's report and submitted his resignation. The board accepted reluctantly and voted to award the ailing professor an Honorary Degree. Benjamin Prince described Diehl as "a man of kindly disposition and a friend of everybody." He had been loved and admired by students earlier and saluted for his integrity, high moral character and the genuineness of his Christian life. Prince thought that Diehl, as one of Wittenberg's founders, should have been treated better. Within a year, Diehl died of tuberculosis.

The students met the board's action with mixed feelings. Two freshmen had already left Wittenberg. In the months following the failure of their effort, more left the school. Only thirteen of the original twenty-six members of the class were graduated, showing an attrition rate of fifty percent, much larger than usual. Students had verbalized the growing revolt against the classical curriculum. Many students took only the courses they wanted and left school without a diploma. They objected to Greek and Latin and sought the inclusion of new subjects and methods of study, the replacement of drill and memorization with lecture and laboratory, and oral with written examinations. Would the student study an elitist course focused on ancient civilization or deal with real and contemporary problems? Was one to spend time memorizing the thoughts of others or on original thought and investigation?

The questions the freshmen raised drew attention to the school's dilemma. Faculties had been trained to do things in the old way. A school's reputation with its peers and with much of the society depended upon adherence to the classical program. Certainly there were exponents of reform among them and severe critics all around them but finding a way from the old to the new was not easy and not inexpensive. The freshmen's petition, like the rise of Greek letter societies and the underground newspaper, symbolized the decade of controversy that was emerging. Yet in the years immediately following the war, the Wittenberg Board and faculty were optimistic. Enrollments were up, students enjoyed good health. In 1867 the school experienced a revival, the first in many years, but also the last. "The weekly prayer meeting, though voluntary, is attended by nearly all the students rooming in the college," the faculty reported.

Most gratifying of all, perhaps, the endowment fund effort had reached its goal of $100,000 and faculty were assured, prematurely as it turned out, that they would henceforth be paid in full and on time. The board debated how its new wealth should be invested and created its first standing committee to oversee investments. They changed the existing policy of investing all funds locally, but retained extensive investments in Springfield. Although there were grounds for optimism, unrest continued to disturb the campus and new challenges from the society at-large were on the horizon. One such challenge was a totally new kind of modern, innovative educational institution that would focus on practical education, the Land Grant College.

Chapter Seven

Now for Old Wittenberg

In 1862 the first Republican-controlled Congress in history passed the Land Grant College Act, setting aside land in the Western territories to support the founding of a public university in every state to teach agriculture, mechanics, and military science. The Act created a whole new type of higher educational institution, embodying the industrial spirit of the new age. It took the Ohio Legislature several years to work out the politics of it, but by 1870 it was ready to proceed.

The reaction of the old-line schools in Ohio to this provocation developed gradually. For many years presidents and professors of Ohio's schools had met informally. By 1860 the gatherings had become regular; and in 1866 the group, spurred on by the Land Grant Act, appointed a committee to plan for a more formal organization. Miami University had closed temporarily, but Ohio University provided leadership support for the organization, and Samuel Sprecher was an active participant. On July 2, 1867, at a meeting in Springfield, eight schools organized the Association of Ohio Colleges and elected Sprecher its first president. It adopted standards for colleges that would sustain the requirements of the classical curriculum and exclude schools of agriculture and mechanics as well as institutions of less than college level.

The land grant movement in Ohio would have greater implications for Wittenberg, however, than just its competition with existing institutions. Springfield's boosters led by Clifton Nichols decided to try to locate Ohio's new land grant college in Springfield. In their enthusiasm to capture what was to become the Ohio State University, the town's industrialists created new challenges for Wittenberg.

Springfield was one of the most rapidly expanding centers in the world for the production of farm machinery and the town experienced a real boom after the Civil War. As the War began, it was poised to take advantage of national needs and produced blue jeans cloth for army uniforms, woolen fabric for coats and blankets, linseed oil for an oil-short nation, army wagons by the thousands, and farm machinery to compensate for a shortage of labor on the farms. After the war plows, grain drills, harvesters, binders, mowers and other pieces of needed machinery flowed from Springfield's factories. The town's industrialists made huge profits and put them back into an expansion of their businesses. Their trade was worldwide and they were rare free-traders in a high tariff Republican Party. Where else than in the farm machinery capital of the world, asked Nichols and Springfield's entrepreneurs, should Ohio's land-grant college be located?

The town added two hundred new houses or buildings a year in the post-war decade. A new hotel, a new opera house seating 1,000, and extensive new factories were built. There were six companies in the Champion Reaper interests employing several thousand men. William Whitely operated the second-largest factory building in the world. The city's population doubled and redoubled. One man, who left town for Civil War duty, and did not return until 1872, said he didn't know where he was when he got off the train. "I looked off south and the town was all built up where before the war had been largely swamps. I went north on Limestone Street and could recognize no landmarks . . . . I went on to Main Street before I caught sight of a point by which I could right myself, so great had been the change in a few years."

For two years, Clark County was selected as the site for the Ohio State Fair because of its central location on good arteries of transportation. These events, along with a statewide convention of newspaper editors, also in Springfield, focused Ohio's attention on the prospering city. Springfield's industrialists were confident, self-assured and optimistic. Interest in securing the new land-grant college, however, also arose in Champaign, Montgomery, and

Franklin Counties as well, and campaigns were launched from Urbana, Dayton, Columbus, and Springfield, to persuade local men of means and voters to put up funds to attract the school. Springfield and Columbus emerged as the two main contenders as the Governor pushed for a centralized location.

Springfield industrialists pledged $50,000 to secure the school. Springfield voted 1,462 to 37 in support of a bond issue to provide land and buildings, while county voters opposed the tax by two to one. Because city population so overwhelmed that of the county, the issue passed easily. The vote in Columbus was affirmative, too, 1,259 to 69, in a low turnout. Franklin County voters likewise turned the issue down, but the city vote overwhelmed them. Clearly the proposed agricultural college was more popular in the cities than on the farms.

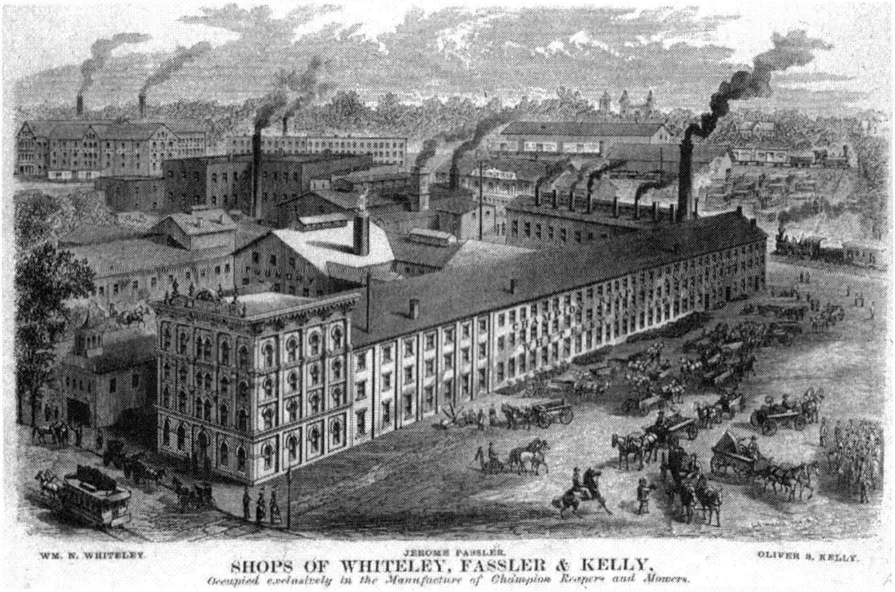

Whiteley, Fassler and Kelly, one of six companies in Springfield producing Champion Farm Machinery after the Civil War. Clark County Historical Society.

On September 20, 1870, the Board of Trustees of the future state university met to consider the various bids and to take final action. Clark County was represented by a large delegation of the leading men in the community. They wired home for authority to add another $50,000 to the city's bid. It took twenty-six ballots to reach a decision and Columbus edged out Springfield by a very narrow margin. Governor Rutherford B. Hayes and farm machinery manufacturers in Akron applied their influence to break the deadlock and secure the school for the state capital. While the businessmen of Akron could not hope to attract the school, they clearly wanted to prevent their Springfield competitors from doing so. Governor Hayes was determined to locate all new state enterprises in the state capital.

The industrial community of Springfield, however, was not to be deterred in its quest for educational facilities geared to the agricultural and mechanical needs of the area. Clifton M. Nichols, editor of the *Springfield Republic* and spokesman for the town's leaders, observed stoically that the town's boosters had done their best. He ran a parallel side story with the caption: "A Good Word for Wittenberg: Ought Not Springfield to Make It a Great University?" He proposed that the town and the college become partners in a new educational venture, with the community adding $50,000 to Wittenberg's endowment for three new professorships in agriculture, mechanics, and political economy. "An agricultural college, at best, is but an experiment," Nichols observed, "but Wittenberg is not an experiment." He would remake it into a rival of the experimental college in Columbus and he advised residents to take better care of what they already possessed. "Let us foster Wittenberg College," he advised, "and make it a better institution than the agricultural college in Franklin County can ever be."

Nichols did not approach Wittenberg leaders directly before he published his proposal. There is no record in the minutes of the Board that they ever received a proposal or discussed it. Instead Nichols called for a general public meeting to explore the Citizens' Endowment Fund idea, requiring Wittenberg to respond in a public forum. He was certain, he told readers, that it would be easier to enlarge the scope, usefulness, and importance of Wittenberg by adding to its endowment and its curriculum than it would be to establish a new institution. It would be a partnership, with the city contributing its resources and Wittenberg contributing its established reputation and public confidence.

Such a merger, he insisted, would provide the kind of modern educational enterprise which the town needed. It was a plan that was working elsewhere in Akron, Cincinnati and Toledo. At this time, each of these three cities established municipal colleges and engulfed already existing small, private educational endowments in the process. Nichols' proposal stirred heated discussion, but before much could happen, word came from Columbus that the Board of the Ohio Agricultural and Mechanical College could not agree upon a site in Franklin County. "Send your offer and try us", said a member of the new college's board, "We are locked and cannot locate here." Springfield renewed its offer, pushing Nichols' Wittenberg plan aside because success now seemed within reach. At this stage, however, Governor Hayes used his influence once more to persuade the Board he had appointed to agree upon a farm north of town.

Flamboyant advertisement for the Warder, Bushnell and Glessner Company, showing President Benjamin Harrison, with his cabinet watching, mowing the south lawn of the White House with a Champion mower made in Springfield, Ohio. Clark County Historical Society.

Nichols picked up his Wittenberg plan where he left it. "Now for Old Wittenberg," he headlined his renewed appeal. The Ohio Agricultural and Mechanical College was now clearly out of the question, he advised; and Springfield should give all possible encouragement to remaking the institution in its midst. He scaled down his proposal, suggesting that thirty to forty thousand dollars and two professorships were sufficient to remake the local institution in the city's image.

It was not just an isolated idea in Nichols' fertile imagination. One of the compromises made in the legislature to get approval for a land grant college was an act allowing cities to organize city colleges. It was the price paid to Cincinnati, Toledo, Akron and other cities in various corners of the state in return for a "centrally located" Ohio State University. The more distant cities, using private endowments already existing, converted them to the support of new municipal colleges. Nichols merely applied the same popular idea to Springfield. If Springfield had won the new university, Columbus would likely have continued its pressure on Capital University to better serve its local educational needs.

An agricultural and mechanical college, however, was an entirely different kind of institution based upon different philosophical and educational assumptions. Clearly, the New England College idea, after which Wittenberg had patterned itself, required that a school serve its region as well as its church constituency. It was a partnership between church and community designed to serve both. That was also the American Lutheran view of the church college's role. Springfield's industrialists saw the land-grant college as the wave of the future and wanted Wittenberg to embrace it.

Wittenberg, however, was grounded in an educational ideal that predated the emergence of industrialized communities and modern agricultural science. It involved a commitment to a modernized classical college curriculum and to the liberal education of leaders for both church and society, not to modern notions of industrial, agricultural, mechanical, professional and military education, all of which were reflected in the land-grant college. It was this challenge that confronted Wittenberg in Nichols' plan for which it was totally unprepared. Many similar residential, undergraduate, liberal arts school's in smaller towns and villages were much less affected by these pressures than Wittenberg. The board of directors stepped forth to defend the institution as best it could in a new, decade-long confrontation with Springfield industrialists.

The Board had been taking a growing role in Wittenberg's institutional affairs since 1855. Originally it was composed of men who wanted a college in the West for an Americanized church. They listened to Keller and Sprecher, the men they had selected to run it with whom they were in substantial agreement. Because of the difficulty of traveling to Board meetings in the early days, they had delegated authority to a local Prudential Committee of seven persons in and around Springfield to operate the school between board meetings. Beginning in 1844, this locally-based Prudential Committee of three area board members and four faculty members had the power to transact all necessary business between meetings, to audit and approve all bills paid, and to meet situations arising from time to time in the operation of the institution. The President was a member but did not preside over it. Virtually all members were pastors. This committee supervised the design, location, and construction of the college building; it approved professorships and picked the men to fill them; it reviewed all financial matters and set salaries. It picked Sprecher to succeed Keller. But it was vulnerable to growing local pressures like those of Nichols.

For nearly two decades college catalogs did not even list the officers of the Board. Beginning in 1864, however, the Reverend Joshua Crouse of Bucyrus, Ohio, was designated as "Board Agent." In 1868, Board officers were indicated. In 1872, the Board appointed a committee of three to review all past records and "to codify the constitution and by-laws of the Board." Evidently, practices had evolved over a quarter of a century without close attention to formal processes of amendment. Many felt it was time to get things in order. One revision was to make the Prudential Committee one of faculty only for internal governance without Board Members in its composition and make all of its actions subject to Board review and approval.

In 1873, Pastor Joshua Crouse, a member of the Board since 1849 and the one real veteran in its midst, was elected to preside over the crucial meetings of 1873 and 1874 in which major changes were made. Crouse could well be considered one of the founders of Wittenberg. Many men served on the Board, like Crouse and

Reck, whose contributions were well above a mere nominal interest.

Born in 1812, Joshua Crouse was a former teacher, carpenter and preacher in frontier Ohio. He began a life of Christian service in a Union Sunday School conducted in his log cabin home, teaching young people to read. He expanded this work into a *bona fide* school for area youth but regularly led his pupils and their parents in prayer meetings. He studied theology on the apprentice system with the patriarch John Stough and others and began preaching as an American pastor in 1842. As an Americanist, he was active in the beginning of the college. He served on the Board and served three times as financial agent. After the important meetings of 1873 and 1874, over which he presided, he became financial secretary and continued his strong interest in Wittenberg affairs. A close associate and resident of Dayton, Ohio, was Alexander Gephardt, who served as treasurer until 1901. Clearly the Board had elected out-of-town, Americanist leadership to preserve the school's original purpose and contend with the growing community pressures and take the pressure off the local Prudential Committee.

The Board's emergence occurred as the college found itself once more in increasing conflict with the town's industrialists. It grew still more in influence as the conflicts became more intense. Campus leaders would find themselves in the middle between Board and community. There were other changes affecting the board which came to bear. Synodical representatives reflected a shrinking majority of men committed to the "New Measures" and doctrinal positions seemed less certain, more open for discussion. The five Synods sent thirty-five Board members from thirty different towns and cities in the five states of Ohio, Indiana, Kentucky, Michigan and western Pennsylvania. Clark County had two members. When the issue of agriculture and mechanics arose, the Clark County representatives were Samuel A. Bowman, a local attorney, and Ross Mitchell, a local entrepreneur, and both members of the Springfield Lutheran Church. Alumni were also speaking up and beginning in 1868, the Alumni Endowment Association had asked for Board representation. It had not yet been granted that privilege but alumni were emerging as another voice demanding to be heard when the future of their college was under discussion. The board, then, reflected a growing divergence of opinion among Lutherans, some of whom were more ardent about the new measures than were others. Alumni among them were sympathetic to the wishes of the Alumni Association. Some were quite in sympathy with the aspirations of the Springfield community. These divisions often led to uncertainty within the board about the school's changing direction.

The Board was strengthened by the development of the Wittenberg Alumni Association in 1869. It was chaired by a young, brash Americanist named John B. Helwig, class of 1861. It established the Alumni Association Endowment Fund with an initial goal of $25,000. When Nichols' Citizens' Endowment proposal arose, the alumni campaign was well underway and meeting with great success. Chairman of the campaign was John C. Brodfuehrer, Class of 1857, and President of Farmer's College near Cincinnati. Wittenberg's 140 living alumni subscribed generously and the fund soon totaled $30,000. "The more we make Wittenberg a first class college," Brodfuehrer said, "the more she will benefit and honor her friends." He sought the names of men who had attended Wittenberg but did not graduate, to increase the size of the alumni group.

The unwillingness of this board to consider the drastic change in its purposes proposed by Nichols put an end to speculation about a citizens' endowment. The decision did not strengthen relationships between the institution and the industrial leaders of the community, and it was the second time Wittenberg had frustrated Clifton Nichols' plans. Community attitudes about the faculty's "old-fashioned notions" spilled over to students and Nichols' partnership with some of the students in publishing underground newspapers continued.

Nichols, now part owner as well as editor of the *Springfield Republic,* was a real nemesis for Wittenberg and the "advisor" behind the series of underground student newspapers of the era. Community animosity was also evident in criticism of the new Land Grant school in Columbus. *Farm and Fireside* magazine, published in Springfield and one of the largest circulating farm papers in America, was highly critical of the Ohio State University for several decades.

FARM AND FIRESIDE.

Entered at the post-office at Springfield, Ohio, as second-class mail matter.

VOL. VII. NO. 24. SPRINGFIELD, OHIO, SEPTEMBER 15, 1884. TERMS: 50 CENTS A YEAR. SINGLE COPY 5 CENTS.

FARM AND FIRESIDE.

ISSUED FIRST AND FIFTEENTH OF EACH MONTH.

MAST, CROWELL & KIRKPATRICK,

PUBLISHERS AND PROPRIETORS.

The Circulation of Farm and Fireside is far greater than any other Agricultural Journal or Political Weekly in the United States, and equal to 400 average weekly papers.

TERMS OF SUBSCRIPTION:

One Year, - (24 Numbers), - 50 Cents.
Six Months, - (12 Numbers), - 30 Cents.

INVARIABLY IN ADVANCE.

The above rates include the payment of postage by us. Subscriptions can commence any time during the year. Send for Premium List and see premiums

The seventeenth annual report of the Ohio State Horticultural Society is a pamphlet of 232 pages, which contains, in addition to the proceedings of the Ohio State Society, brief reports from several of the county societies, and from the Missippi Valley Horticultural and American Pomological societies. Throughout the pamphlet are scattered numerous valuable hints gleaned from the discussions of the practical fruit growers who compose the society, and for the first time these hints are rendered accessible by a copious index. It is placing but a moderate estimate upon the value of this index to say that it doubles the practical value of the report. We have yet one criticism to make upon the index, however, and this applies equally to the Ohio State agricultural reports, and that is that the index is only partly alphabetical. That is, it is only

FARM AND FIRESIDE worthy to enter every rural home in our land, and though we have not yet attained our ideal, and are by no means ready to fold our hands and say "it is good enough," yet we are willing that our work shall be compared with any that is being done in similar channels, for we sincerely believe that no other journal gives so much in real value for the money received as FARM AND FIRESIDE. That we are not alone in this belief is evidenced by the multitudes of commendatory letters we receive from subscribers, and which have never been more numerous, nor expressive of more earnest approval, than during the past few months. With regard to the future, we have only to say that there shall be no abatement of our efforts to merit the good-will which has been so freely shown us in the past.

combing produced by a cross of the Merino upon the Liecester, the medium by the Merino on the downs—now command a higher price in our market than the finest Merino wool, while the sheep which are calculated to produce them are just those best adapted in other respects to the circumstances of farming on high-priced lands, being probably the closest approximation to the ideal of a wool-and-mutton sheep.

It is true, we have not yet succeeded in producing a cross of this kind which will perpetuate itself satisfactorily, the third generation seldom being equal to the second; but the experience of those who have formed the various breeds we now possess, by years of careful and patient selection, shows what may be done, and the problem of producing a breed which shall be as satisfactory a producer of both

Farm and Fireside, published in Springfield, was one of the largest circulation farm papers in the United States in the 1880s. Clark County Historical Society.

The publication helped divert the Second Federal Land Grant appropriated by Congress to a farm station in Wooster, Ohio and away from the Ohio State University.

Meanwhile, on the campus, life among the students seemed normal enough. Student life seemed to proceed oblivious to the school's conflicts at other levels. The interest of the men of Wittenberg turned to less regimented activities in which they could enjoy the company of women. Nichols heartily endorsed their efforts. He clearly advocated coeducation and constantly proposed ways for women and men students to get together. Members of Wittenberg's Philosophian Society with this encouragement initiated an exchange program with students in the Springfield High School and the Presbyterian Female Seminary. First the young men made informal visits to High School and Seminary programs and invited those students to return the visits. Forty young people of both sexes accepted their invitation, with young ladies "largely predominating," according to press reports. The young ladies, said the editor, "by their beauty and grace" so transfixed the college men that their literary performances were flustered and embarrassed. The young ladies from the city, he said, "by their bright eyes and sunny faces" complicated the situation for the men. "We heartily commend this intermingling . . . ," the editor noted. It would, he said, stimulate better education among both men and women and a "warm feeling of friendship" between schools.

The student view of matters as distinct from those of board, faculty and community were expressed in newspapers. In June of 1870, the third edition of the *Flying Dutchman* appeared, this one called the *Flying Dutchman's Grandaddy*. In March students had asked the board of directors for permission to publish an official student newspaper to be called the *Wittenberger*, but permission for such a venture would not come for another three years. Finally, in June 1873, the Board acceded to the request of John C. Kauffman and S. S. Waltz, two graduates enrolled in the theological department. The two had been, more than once, the butt of jokes in the underground papers. They were staunch advocates of their school, but not without criticism. They felt that the best answer to an underground paper was an official one that was at liberty to present a student point of view. An endowed Wittenberg, they said, was soon to take its place among the foremost institutions of the land and all first-class institutions had an official paper. With board approval, the students put together a paper, the *Wittenberger*, which continued into the next century.

The *Wittenberger*, in its first issue heralded "an age of journalism" in a nation which in the Civil War had become flooded with newspapers and magazines. Heretofore, observed Kauffman and Waltz, students had been "shut up within the precincts of the classics." They wanted to "act in a more extended sphere" and the *Wittenberger* would help them expand their horizons. The classic course, they added, did not provide the "intellectual development" or the education "demanded by the age."

Many students publicly disowned the underground papers whenever they appeared. They were usually only a minority voice in campus affairs even though they often captured some of the sentiments of students at large. The June 1870 version they called infamous, obscene, profane, blasphemous, "a libel upon the true sentiments of the students . . . and a gross perversion of their regard for the faculty." Students became seriously divided over the underground papers. From issue to issue, student support ebbed and flowed depending upon how outrageous the editor decided to be and on how much of general student concern he embraced.

An 1867 underground newspaper, called the *Wittenberg Knickerbocker*, described by the students as the Flying Dutchman's cousin, had been fairly innocuous, "begotten in a spirit of generous humor" and "fostered on a diet of wit and fancy." They wanted to expose the "hypocrisies of college life" and focused mainly on students. The paper even apologized to the community of Springfield for the rowdy behavior of a few students and asked that all not be judged by the few who stole lumber, firewood, and chickens; frequented taverns and houses of ill repute; and otherwise prowled around the town's streets at night getting into mischief. It also poked fun at the insincerities of literary society rushing practices and the pretensions of a local fraternity, Pi Eta, whose members, they said, "could not get in the established groups."

The 1870 version of the underground paper, the *Flying Dutchman's Granddaddy*, was much more venomous. It again attacked unpopular professors. The editor was a senior who had prepared, as his graduation oration, a legitimate address on "The Coming Woman" which was critical of the faculty and board for not admitting women students. While his address was a straightforward defense of the emerging American woman and a defense of her rights to an education and fairer treatment, the *Granddaddy* article said otherwise. The senior had craftily written about his coming speech with sexual double entendres and vulgar suggestions. Thus, as he would deliver his serious address at Commencement, many in the class would be convulsed by remembering the suggestive allusions to its parts in the *Flying Dutchman*. The publication, in addition to taking a swipe at every faculty member except Dr. Sprecher, also cast aspersions on the behavior of the daughters of the Steward.

As punishment, before the senior would be permitted to speak at Commencement, he was required to sign a retraction of his statements in the *Granddaddy* and to agree to read his retraction publicly at graduation. The statement was to read: "The object of publishing the paper was sport, and the articles are wholly fictitious. I am satisfied that the paper, contrary to our intentions, degenerated into vulgarity, and I sincerely regret my connection with it."

When the student's time came to address the assembly, Dr. Sprecher rose and occupied the podium. Through a disagreement between the student and the faculty, he announced, the student would not be permitted to present his address. Still, he continued, he was respected and loved as a man; and would be given the opportunity to make a statement. The student stepped forward; but instead of discussing his case or reading the required statement he began his oration: "The Coming Woman, whose dignity has been insulted, whose tenderness crushed, her loveliness blighted by the exorbitant demands of the Board and faculty . . ." The audience, realizing what he was doing, stomped their feet, clapped their hands, hissed, and raised such a noise that he could not be heard. He left the platform and when it came time to confer degrees, his degree was not conferred. In sympathy, another senior refused to accept his diploma.

The fourth edition of the *Flying Dutchman,* the *Flying Dutchman's Grand Mommy,* appeared in June of 1872. It was extremely personal in its references to faculty and continued to harass the members of both faculty and student body most unpopular with the anonymous reporters. In this paper, in which complimentary references to "Cliff" Nichols appeared, the assault on faculty was stronger than ever. The student editors again took pains to exempt Dr. Sprecher from the criticisms: "He is an example of the true scholar. His taste for study would inspire any young man." Students were eager to be in his classes, the article continued, and attended with both profit and pleasure. No one else escaped scathing review. The prejudices expressed reflected Nichols' own views very well: profound respect for Dr. Sprecher, disdain for the rest.

The chief target was, again, "The Heathen Old Geig," Hezekiah Ruebush Geiger. He had been the chief thorn in Nichols' side ever since he came to Springfield. He had outmaneuvered him in the Presbyterian college negotiation and, as Chairman of the Prudential Committee and the "business officer" of the College, had the burden of dealing with the community for fifteen years. He was also "Germanic" in his demeanor, the editor alleged, and his mannerisms were misunderstood and resented. The students, said the editor, considered him affected, stilted, stubborn, and conceited. They said he did not treat them with respect, either in the classroom or on the street; and they laughed at his antiquated views of science. They attributed a new text on *What I Know about Science*, to Geiger, and "not worth a one-cent stamp." Whatever was in it of value, they said, had been plagiarized from other books. It could only be useful to students so young they couldn't recognize plagiarism, bad grammar, and out-of-date science.

Samuel Ort, then a young unmarried faculty member, they accused of philandering, engaging lightly in passing love affairs. His youthful days, they observed, were "rich, rare, and racy." Benjamin Prince was accused of drinking too much beer. "Old Ike," their name for Professor Isaac Sprecher, of currying favor with students in order to get better treatment in the *Dutchman*.

The most Germanic were the "Dutchmen" at whom the writers were aiming: "Old Geig", "Old Ike," and steward Simons, whose alleged German accent received special attention. They were described as ignorant, stupid, churlish, and arrogant. "Old Ike" and "Old Geig" were antiquated fossils with old ideas. They were unwilling to enter the modern industrial age. "May the Lord have mercy on Wittenberg" if it continued to avoid the future. "Goodbye, Prof," they said. "The world is moving, and we are going with it; we do not expect you to keep up."

In February, 1872, Nichols noted with glee an impromptu winter festival of the students. All engaged in "the healthiest and most free-hearted amusement," sledding down the college hill from the dorm, through an arbor, halfway down "science hill," and through the gate at the bottom, and out onto the road to town. On sleds, chairs, boxes, old stoves and clapboards, all were trying the hill. Both sides of the walk were lined with broken boards, stoves, and sleds. The track had been iced to make it faster by the generous application of water on compacted snow. Students tried at breakneck speeds to thread the arbor and the gate. Those who missed nursed bumps and bruises for days. But the more wrecks, the more challengers as winter's doldrums were dissipated.

Nichols' injured pride appeared in other ways. At the Class of 1873 Commencement, Dr. Sprecher remarked that the salutatorian had the choice of giving his address in Latin as was customary or in English. Nichols reported that the student "had the good sense to prefer the latter." Since the student made that choice, Dr. Sprecher also broke with custom and responded in English rather than Latin. Nichols approved. He thought it ludicrous and old fashioned to sit through a Commencement listening to speeches in Latin. Wittenberg's diplomas, however, continued to be written in Latin for almost another eighty years.

When the college catalog began listing students by their full names, first, middle, and last at the request of the students themselves, the editor responded with sarcasm. "This is very nice," he said, "for the Charles Augustines and Alfred Cauliflowers, but the plain Jakes and Jacks can't see it." The school, he implied, had thought itself too good for farmers and mechanics with ordinary names and aimed at those at higher levels that weighted their sons down with big names and inheritances. The charge was not fair. Wittenberg's students for the most part were from families not as wealthy as Nichols himself, and they represented a growing middle class interested in business and the professions. Many sons of farmers still enrolled.

Editor Nichols' coverage of the school was not always negative. He once poked fun at himself in the growing conflict. In an item headlined "Motto of the Republic," he wrote: "Sic (ed) itur ad (Jack) astra! By a gentleman who entered Wittenberg and came out at both ends." Nevertheless, he strongly advocated educational reform, thought faculties too straitlaced, sectarian and narrow minded, felt Wittenberg was unresponsive to local interests and modern trends and ought to be operated in sympathy with local needs. Yet he was pleased with the school's graduates. He insisted that schools should be free from hazing and rioting, and he cited the evil proclivities of students at Harvard, Princeton, Yale, Cornell, and Michigan. Wittenberg, he observed, was a place where the students were "as fond of fun" as anywhere else, "but who see no joke in cruelty or the destruction of valuable property." He advocated a national convention of college presidents to take united action against hazing and other objectionable student practices.

Campus feeling against fraternities grew because they were the advocates of so many of the challenges to the status quo. By the spring of 1874, thirty-seven students signed a petition asking the board of directors to abolish them. A special committee of the Board considered the matter. The petitioners complained that the fraternities claimed to be and did make of themselves a select class creating a spirit of caste that divided every course, department, and association. They perpetuated acts of injustice and propagated hatred and personal strife to an intolerable extent. The committee's final report proposed a resolution: "Whereas, there is reason to believe that secret fraternities in college are of very questionable utility, therefore Resolved that this Board heartily disapprove of the introduction of secret fraternities into the college as detrimental to the highest interests of the institution and hereby express the hope that those who are in these fraternities will not labor to perpetuate them and that new students coming to the institution will only unite with the recognized literary societies of the college."

Board minutes do not describe the debate on the issue; but the resolution, given the circumstances, was a weak one. The absence of a definite proscription, however, made the resolution ineffective. By the time it was passed, fraternities had existed on the campus for nearly a decade. Thirty-nine students and alumni wore the badge of Phi Kappa Psi and thirty-four the pin of Beta Theta Pi. Among their ranks were pastors, professors, benefactors, and sons of some of the prominent families of Springfield. One of their number, Samuel Alfred Ort, a Phi Psi, served as secretary of the Board. Another, Benjamin F. Prince, also a Phi Psi, was later chairman of the Prudential Committee.

Benjamin F. Prince, class of 1865, seen here as a young faculty member. Wittenberg University Archives.

Springfield had taken the groups to their hearts and gave them their sons, helped outfit their halls in downtown Springfield, and attended their public exercises at Black's Opera House. Nichols was a supporter of the groups and gave their activities extensive coverage. Many enjoyed the songs the boys wrote and sang. They also took an interest in their athletic activities. As a result, local supporters misunderstood the opposition of the Board. The groups did after all represent a kind of reform in education that better equipped the young men for the world of business and industry.

Dr. Sprecher's attention had been focused instead on financial problems. The $100,000 endowment could not keep up with inflation and growing college expenses. In June 1872 the treasurer made the financial report indicating expenses exceeding income, and a substantial deficit. Salaries alone exceeded receipts by thirty-three percent. To add to the gloom, Sprecher was considering a call to the theological faculty at Gettysburg College. The Wittenberg Board told Sprecher they could not let him leave at this difficult time and persuaded him to turn down the offer. Nichols agreed that the school could not afford to lose the one man whose mind gave the place meaning and stature. Nichols' criticism of the school, however, was a factor in Sprecher's unhappiness.

It was a difficult decision. Sprecher lamented the decreasing amount of time he had to spend on theology and the impossibility of finding time to write. He felt that the American cause in the Lutheran church was failing and needed to be advanced more aggressively. He wanted to restate Americanist theological principles. The Gettysburg offer was inviting because it would bring together in one faculty a strong proponent of that view, an advocate of the moderately confessionalist view and an ardent confessionalist. Thus it would bring the various dimensions of thought in the General Synod together. S. S. Schmucker had left Gettysburg and Sprecher could restore the American voice there. Nevertheless, his sense of loyalty and the fact that a quarter century of his life had been invested in Wittenberg caused him to decline the offer.

Sprecher and the board worked out an emergency plan to deal with the financial crisis. They proposed to close the seminary for a year, sending their theological students to Gettysburg while that school would consider ultimately moving its seminary farther west. At least one Wittenberg seminarian feared for the future of the

Wittenberg seminary. It was, he said, "virtually extinct" as it was. Four of the students went to Gettysburg and all returned a year later. Three went to Yale and only one came back.

Dr. Sprecher was released from his teaching duties for the year in order to spend virtually all of his time soliciting funds for an additional $100,000 of endowment. It was unlikely that funds of the amount needed could be raised in Springfield. Sprecher and Board members Joshua Crouse and Alexander Gebhart covered thousands of miles visiting churches and individuals within the Wittenberg territory. "All winter long," said Benjamin Prince, "through rain, snow and cold," Sprecher, Crouse and Gephardt pursued their task. Sprecher complained that incessant solicitation of funds wore down his spirits.

By the end of the academic year the three reported $84,940 in pledges, contingent upon reaching the full $100,000 goal. On June 21, in Canton, representatives of the supporting synods met during the convention of the General Synod to review Wittenberg's situation. The Reverend John B. Helwig of Dayton chaired the meeting; Joshua Crouse was secretary. At the conclusion, the supporting synods pledged the remaining $15,000 to reach the goal. At the insistence of attorneys present, they obligated themselves to pay interest on that sum at eight percent until the principal was paid, thus assuming a responsibility for an annual payment to the institution.

It was a great achievement and relatively little had been asked of Springfield. Significant money had been raised in the churches, their efforts crowned by a commitment of the five synods that put the drive over the top. This success, along with the Alumni Endowment Fund, justified and emboldened the Board's resistance to efforts to change the nature and mission of the school. The success reinforced the Americanist party and gave Dr. Sprecher the sense of accomplishment that he needed. Rev. John B. Helwig rose to prominence among Wittenberg supporters because he had been instrumental in securing both alumni and church financial support.

With renewed spirits, the Board voted to reopen the seminary. Sprecher hoped once more for an opportunity at Wittenberg to establish a strong American center. He wanted to enlarge the faculty and extend the seminary course to two years. He also decided to step down from the presidency of the college in order to devote full time to theological education and to writing. Undoubtedly, he thought he had found his successor as president in John Helwig. At the board meeting consideration of a successor began.

It is likely that Sprecher had an understanding with the Board that he could step down as president when he rejected the Gettysburg offer. They called the new funds raised the Samuel Sprecher Endowment in recognition of his quarter of a century of service. From the very beginning of his relationship with Wittenberg, it had been his expectation and his hope that he could one day teach and write theology without other distractions. Now that day had arrived.

At a special meeting, then, the Board took several fateful actions. In view of the endowment fund growth, the board proposed to revise the course of study, to rearrange the professorships, to create new chairs and to elect new members to an expanded faculty. At Sprecher's request, the Board called the Reverend Dr. John H. W. Stuckenberg, Wittenberg class of 1857 and a pastor in Pittsburgh, to the chair of Sacred Philology in the seminary and for a variety of courses in the college. He was Sprecher's choice and his most outstanding student. He had a mind that Sprecher knew would help build the strength of the American seminary. "You were unanimously elected," he wrote him, "and you received every vote on the first ballot."

John H. W. Stuckenberg, class of 1857, professor of Sacred Philology, pioneer in the social gospel movement, who taught and wrote on *Christian Sociology*.

This professorship in Sacred Philology was a bold step forward. Philology at its narrowest was the study of words and linguistics as a basis for criticizing or interpreting a text, in this case, a biblical text. At its broadest, it meant the study of all human works such as language, literature, art, rhetoric, poetry, history, law, mythology, religion, costumes and folklore as aids in reconstructing history and discerning meaning in a text., whether scripture or literature. It was the study of man, and his religion, through all of mans creative endeavor.

In addition, the Board called Dr. Irving Magee to be professor of Belles Lettres and English literature in the college and to be vice president. He had been pastor of the English Lutheran Church in Dayton, a graduate of Gettysburg and a member of the College Board. Formerly an ardent Americanist, like many others, he was now tending toward a more conservative position. Some saw him as a possible successor to Sprecher. To everyone's surprise, he declined the call and accepted a call to a new church in the East.

The board elected alumnus and board member Samuel Alfred Ort as professor of mathematics, taking that assignment from Geiger who would now focus his attention on the natural sciences. Geiger, as one of the school's founders, hoped that he would be selected as President. He had given the college long years of valuable service as teacher, fund raiser and chairman of the Prudential Committee. He felt he was the next logical choice. Others saw Ort as the future president.

Benjamin F. Prince submitted his resignation. Perhaps he was bothered by the harsh words of some over the Greek letter societies or by biting criticism in the *Flying Dutchman*. More likely he was disillusioned by the turmoil and dissension that grew as Sprecher's plans to retire became clearer. He planned to seek a church to pursue the ministry for which he had prepared himself. He had stayed after graduation as a tutor, remained as an instructor and was then hired as principal of the Preparatory Department. Now he felt it was time to move on. By November, however, after a swift succession of events, he was back on the college staff at the invitation of the board. Prince's behavior reflected the uncertainty that gripped the college. In 1872, Prince had begun the construction of a fine, two-story house near the residence of Mrs. Sanderson with whom he boarded and whose daughter he had married in 1869. Yet a few months later, he resigned and prepared to leave town only to change his mind again five months later.

In 1874, Sprecher proposed measures that astounded many and made the 1874 board meeting one of the most important in college history. The increased endowment, he noted, had not allowed as large an increase in faculty as was needed for curricular expansion. Nor would it meet needs for expanded facilities. "The rivalry in education in the state is great," he added, and Wittenberg should not have to compete with inadequate numbers of faculty or less than adequate facilities. He proposed therefore that Wittenberg admit women and African Americans. This, he said, would enable the school to expand its offerings. Public sentiment would support such actions, he said and schools that have taken such steps have larger numbers of students. The Civil Rights Act recently passed in Congress with the active support of his friend Congressman Shellabarger, made mixed-race education the law of the land. He asked the Board to take the necessary actions.

At the meeting in June, Sprecher submitted his resignation as expected and it was reluctantly accepted. The Board also declared the institution open to black students, admitted women, censured Greek letter societies and advised students not to perpetuate them, all in the same session. They replaced Geiger as chairman of the Prudential Committee with the young, thirty year old, handsome, mustached Benjamin Prince who was also named auditor of the college. Prince would hold these posts for over fifty years in the administrations of five Presidents.

In September 1874 a black student, Broadwell Chinn, from Springfield, applied for admission. The faculty, sensitive to mixed sentiments in Springfield as elsewhere, declined to act. When they asked students for their reaction, a majority opposed his admission. The faculty then denied his application on the grounds that they lacked authority to admit him. Clifton Nichols criticized the faculty for their inaction, but local public opinion supported them. At its 1875 meeting, the Board's response was rapid and direct. "The constitution clearly opens the door of the college to all persons of proper qualifications irrespective of color," they declared, and directed the faculty to admit Chinn to the college. Finally, in the fall of 1875, he was enrolled.

Broadwell Chinn, from Springfield, Ohio, was the first African American student at Wittenberg in 1875. Wittenberg University Archives.

In the faculty discussion of the matter, Professor Stuckenberg held that Christian belief should lead to Christian action, and was a leading advocate of the admission of both African Americans and women. Chinn had been banned from the local high school and was given his college preparatory work on the side by the high school principal amid complaints and objections by local citizens. Chinn had been born a slave in Lexington, Kentucky in 1853 and was purchased by his father, William Chinn, who also purchased his own freedom and that of his wife and four other children for $1,900. His owner, after whom Chinn was named, allowed three years for payment. William Chinn was literate and a highly skilled caterer whose owner had made his services available for a fee to others in Lexington. He allowed him to keep some of the money with which he bought his family's freedom. When the contract was completed, the family moved to Springfield where his enterprise continued to serve them well. Broadwell was a talented student and made the most of Springfield's segregated schools.

At the 1874 Board meeting, the admission of women was also approved. It took an amendment to existing documents; the admission of blacks did not. It was hoped this would increase enrollment without further burdening the school's limited facilities since most women students would be from the area and live at home. There was a growing sentiment among more liberal Lutherans in Ohio that women should have access to better educational opportunities. Several women's schools had been undertaken by Lutheran groups: Esther Seminary in Columbus, Hope Seminary in Wooster, and a short lived school in Urbana. All failed, and those interested looked for new opportunities. Several faculty members had daughters whom they felt were capable of handling college work. Professor Stuckenberg had a young wife, Mary Gingrich Stuckenberg, whom he felt should also have the opportunity of getting a college education.

H. R. Geiger's daughters under his tutelage were quite competitive in mathematics and science and proved to his satisfaction that the assumptions of inherent female inadequacy in those fields were not based on fact. He advocated substituting German for Greek in the science course. That would also meet the objections of many of the young men in recent years that there was too much focus on what they called "the dead languages." It also met his daughters' needs; and over the next few years, while most women took selected courses, two of his daughters became not only Wittenberg's first women graduates but also the first women with the Bachelor of Science degree.

The final decision for the historic June 1874 board meeting was to elect a successor to Dr. Sprecher. Geiger was passed over. He knew he was going to be and was so upset that he had taken a leave of absence before the school year ended for a western trip and a trip to the Sandwich Islands with Dr. and Mrs. John W. Bookwalter, a local businessman and entrepreneur. Geiger's unhappiness was so great that he gave up all responsibilities except teaching and became a source of campus discord for years to come. Ort was considered too young and unseasoned to be president and he resigned when the board's choice became known and took a church in Louisville. The freshman class gave him the works of Goethe, the German poet and dramatist, as a parting gift, while the sophomores gave him a gold-headed cane.

The selection committee first brought in the name of Pastor Irving Magee, but the Board rejected the nomination. They turned instead to another Board member, the staunch American pastor from Dayton, the founder and president of the alumni association and its Endowment Fund, and the man who put the Samuel Sprecher Endowment Fund campaign over the top in the church. While many had anticipated that Wittenberg would select a more moderate candidate, Americanists had rallied to select John B. Helwig who would make a tremendous effort to sustain Wittenberg's unique theological position.

Helwig was born near Canal Dover, Ohio, on March 6, 1833, the youngest of five children. His mother died during his infancy and his father remarried and moved to Indiana leaving the infant son with his grandparents. They raised John in an atmosphere their neighbors considered puritanical. He was reared on their farm doing a farm boy's chores and learning the blacksmith's trade. He was good at it, making tools and hardware: nails, hinges, hooks, handles, hammers, pliers, screwdrivers and punches. He obtained only a rudimentary education. Later he was sent to work on his uncle's farm near Bellefontaine, Ohio, where he came under the influence of a Lutheran pastor, Samuel H. Aughe. His pastor interested him in the church and persuaded him to get more education. As his studies advanced, he abandoned blacksmithing to teach school. Reverend Aughe then influenced Helwig to enter Wittenberg College at the age of 22. There with his continuing influence Helwig decided to become a pastor.

As President at Wittenberg, Helwig twice honored Pastor Aughe with an honorary degree: an honorary Ph.D. in 1876, (a practice frowned on once the earned doctorate had become the identification of the new kind of faculty member), and an L.L.D. in 1878. Aughe, he said, changed his life and was the father he never had. George Gerlaw Clark, the student historian, said Helwig was a diligent scholar who "by continued perseverance and patient toil surmounted the difficulties of college one by one."

When Sprecher's term as President ended, Wittenberg owned thirty-three acres of land and was free of debt. The second endowment fund campaign brought cash and pledges to increase the endowment to $200,000. The economic recession of the next few years again made some pledges worthless; but as Sprecher gave Helwig the office, the school's finances seemed to be in good shape. The pulse of change and conflict, however, was reverberating everywhere and Clifton M. Nichols had not been placated.

Helwig would preside over ferment and conflict with strength and resolve, though a softer touch might have been more helpful. Contemporaries would describe his eight-year tenure in simple and direct words: strong, strenuous, thorough, and forcible. They described him as sanguine, ardent, hopeful, and remarkable. The six-foot tall, two-hundred pound, red-haired former blacksmith—the students called him "Old Sorrel Top"—was known as a powerful preacher and a strong administrator. But he was also stubborn, unbending, firm in his beliefs and convictions. There would be a new direction for the college and it came as change overwhelmed him.

Chapter Eight

Not Only a New Thing, But a Good Thing

From out of every window of the college building "was peeping a head with eyes and mouth all standing aghast to witness and drink in the sublimity of the occasion." It was raining, "but what of that? Heads were out the windows nevertheless." A male student described the scene on that drizzly morning of September 4, 1874, when the first women students arrived at Wittenberg. The reporter concluded his article for the *Wittenberger*, saying, "Let the new era be worthy the name important, and then in the great hereafter when Wittenberg shall gather up her jewels, girls in the college will be proven to have been not only a new thing, but a good thing."

Previous to the enrollment of women, the male students had been rather careless about their appearance. Classrooms were filled with "collarless, cuff-less, and coatless boys" and on many occasions they wore only tattered dressing gowns and slippers, frayed and run down at the heels. They came to class, it was said, with their hair uncombed and their "linen not always the cleanest." With the arrival of the women, however, they improved at once and appeared "with all the necessaries of true manliness."

The men expected the women to be gone by lunchtime. After all, they were day students, and none lived on the campus except the president's daughter. When the men ventured out of their rooms "to enjoy some pleasures like the good times of old"—sports,

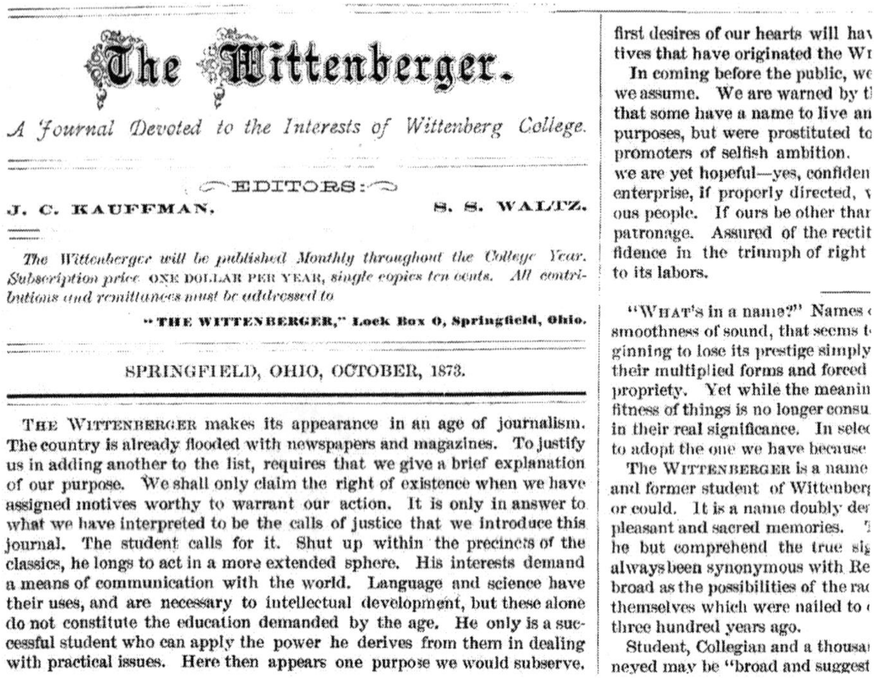

The Wittenberger.

A Journal Devoted to the Interests of Wittenberg College.

EDITORS:

J. C. KAUFFMAN. S. S. WALTZ.

The Wittenberger will be published Monthly throughout the College Year. Subscription price ONE DOLLAR PER YEAR, *single copies ten cents. All contributions and remittances must be addressed to*

"THE WITTENBERGER," Lock Box O, Springfield, Ohio.

SPRINGFIELD, OHIO, OCTOBER, 1873.

THE WITTENBERGER makes its appearance in an age of journalism. The country is already flooded with newspapers and magazines. To justify us in adding another to the list, requires that we give a brief explanation of our purpose. We shall only claim the right of existence when we have assigned motives worthy to warrant our action. It is only in answer to what we have interpreted to be the calls of justice that we introduce this journal. The student calls for it. Shut up within the precincts of the classics, he longs to act in a more extended sphere. His interests demand a means of communication with the world. Language and science have their uses, and are necessary to intellectual development, but these alone do not constitute the education demanded by the age. He only is a successful student who can apply the power he derives from them in dealing with practical issues. Here then appears one purpose we would subserve.

first desires of our hearts will hav
tives that have originated the Wi
In coming before the public, we
we assume. We are warned by t
that some have a name to live an
purposes, but were prostituted to
promoters of selfish ambition.
we are yet hopeful—yes, confiden
enterprise, if properly directed, v
ous people. If ours be other thar
patronage. Assured of the rectit
fidence in the triumph of right
to its labors.

"WHAT'S in a name?" Names
smoothness of sound, that seems t
ginning to lose its prestige simply
their multiplied forms and forced
propriety. Yet while the meanin
fitness of things is no longer consu
in their real significance. In sele
to adopt the one we have because
The WITTENBERGER is a name
and former student of Wittenber
or could. It is a name doubly de
pleasant and sacred memories.
he but comprehend the true sig
always been synonymous with Re
broad as the possibilities of the ra
themselves which were nailed to
three hundred years ago.
Student, Collegian and a thousa
neyed may be "broad and suggest

The *Wittenberger*, first official student newspaper, Wittenberg University Archives.

raucous language, and old clothes—they were startled when one of the "girls" would suddenly come around the corner. "There was a general scatterment. Students shot for their rooms . . . and all noise ceased."

The male students appeared for the most part enthusiastic about the arrival of the women. For years many of the younger men in debate and in oratory had defended or challenged a more liberal view of the feminine role. "The new woman" had been a subject of much conversation, more than a few orations and addresses, and a host of definitions. Alden H. Gilbert, Class of 1865, remembered that during his years in college the men talked about the propriety of admitting women. Some had tried without success to enter the eastern colleges, he said, "but none had dared to try to enter Wittenberg." His fellow students had concluded that "Girls can learn music, drawing, and history, perhaps, and they might study languages with success and possibly comprehend some of the sciences, but they never could become mathematicians." They concluded with a sense of superiority that "if they were admitted they would be distanced by the boys, become discouraged, and soon drop out of their classes."

Now that the fateful step had been taken to admit women to the formerly all-male precincts of the college, male reactions were actually more flustered and adolescent than superior. There was a lot of ribbing and joking at the women's expense and more than a little sophomoric male posturing. In the spring of 1875, two women took Professor Prince's botany class. When he took the class on tour over the campus or to beautiful Ferncliff Cemetery looking for plant specimens, there was confusion and disarray. The men of the class worked a variety of schemes "to get the chance to be the favorite squires of the fair maidens" and paid more attention to the displacement of a rival than to Professor Prince's observations.

To provide the women with a place where they could go, to escape being constantly on display, the faculty set aside a room on the first floor of the college building. The men had their literary society rooms and their bedrooms on the upper floors. The women needed a place, too. The men called it "The Gab Room" because of the sounds which emanated from it as many found reason to loiter in that vicinity to smile at and say hello to each young lady as she arrived or left. In 1880, Wittenberg's first yearbook, the *Aloha,* objected to the name. "Their room . . . ," said the editor, "has been barbarously named the 'gab room' . . . an infamous imposition . . . devoid of justice and wholly inappropriate for a place so comprehensive and important."

The naming of the yearbook was an historical decision. It put the publication in the tradition of the older "Flying Dutchmen" publications. Indeed, this new editorial venture put an end to the long extended metaphor that had existed since 1863. The good ship, *Flying Dutchman,* finally put in at the Cannibal Islands bearing Hezekiah R. Geiger on his famous voyage to Hawaii where he was met with the traditional greeting, "*Aloha.*" The editors stepped off the ship onto the shore holding a sign which read, "An organ of this nature has long been desired by the advocates of student rights and former efforts have bubbled forth in the mysterious and troublesome *Dutchman*". The new yearbook was thus given that exotic title explaining why in its introduction, and attempting to write "finis," as it turned out unsuccessfully, to a seventeen year long story.

Women's activities were not restricted to classes and the "Gab Room." On occasion they spent an evening together on the campus and had dinner. They often enjoyed a program presented by some of their own number in the borrowed rooms of one of the men's literary societies. Relations with the men remained formal, but their growing frequency wore down the stiff and embarrassed interchanges with which the year began.

The faculty had proposed coeducation to the Board in a mild manner. The argument was with members of the Board and with public opinion as much as anything else. The faculty suggested that public opinion was now sufficiently enlightened to permit it. The second reason was that other institutions had admitted women without adverse effects. Third, the college needed more students and the income they would bring. That was the carefully prepared set of arguments the faculty had taken to the Board.

What was left out was the ideological argument put forth by Professor Stuckenberg both for the admission of African Americans and women. More faculty joined him on the issue of women's admission. Stuckenberg felt that Jesus had imparted religious truth directly to women in his ministry and had them transmit it to the men. Even the good news of the resurrection God had allowed women to deliver. Though the world might not be ready for it, God clearly thought women capable of learning and teaching as well. Stuckenberg said it was strange indeed "that where the gospel is professed, woman should ever need emancipation." But many of the truths taught by Jesus that had not yet been realized in the world would need to be realized before the millennium. In God's realm, said Stuckenberg, women were already as free as men.

Wittenberg's leaders were not unaware of changing attitudes about women and their role in society and the Church. Faculty wives had taken an active role in campus life, in the beautification of the grounds and the building, and in the addition of such amenities as the bathhouse. Students called it "Congress", where they gathered, sang, practiced their orations, and carried on heated debates. Women's interests spilled over into area congregations and Bible Societies and Civil War causes. Ever since Ezra Keller's widow had revolutionized the role of women at the Springfield Lutheran Church by ending segregated seating and female silence, Wittenberg wives had made their presence known. During the Civil War, they were prominent in women's war activities, in Sunday schools, and social work. Mrs. Stuckenberg and Mrs. Ehrenfeld organized

Lutheran Church Women, and their husbands led the fight in official church circles for the recognition of the Women's Society in the General Synod. Mrs. Stuckenberg also led in the organization of the Women's Home and Foreign Missionary Society.

Uninspired by any official ideological endorsement of coeducation, the early female students struggled to find a collective identity. At first it was defined by the men. They referred to them as "Wittenberg Girls," then "Ladies of Wittenberg," then "Wittenberg Dames." Early the women copied the men's literary societies, establishing the Hesperian Society. It didn't last. While it did, it was quietly assertive. Its officers insisted, in the *Aloha*, that " . . . a college without girls is only half blessed; it is an orchard without blossoms and a spring without song." There was some concern, however, about women who spoke publicly on current issues. The more forward looking suggested that women be allowed to join the men's literary societies, but the idea was rejected by the faculty. In 1886, with more women enrolled and the issues of propriety settled, the Euterpean Literary Society for women was organized and prospered for decades. A second society, the Olympian, organized in 1891

The ladies of the Olympian Literary Society provided front and back views of their hair styles in the *Semi-Centennial souvenir of Wittenberg College*, 1895. Wittenberg University Archives.

The first women students included Miriam Alice Geiger, who preferred to be called Alice. She was the daughter of Professor Geiger. She began in the select course, but when in 1878 her father received approval for the new curriculum for the Bachelor of Science degree, she switched to that program and in 1879 became the first woman graduate of Wittenberg College. In her graduating class of 1879 no honors were awarded. Students noted that Miss Geiger, John Lenker, and Hamilton Ott were the top three students, but no one wanted to designate that the woman was the valedictorian. There was no precedent for a woman in that role. But no one wanted to pass her over either and designate the top man for that position. Since there was to be no Valedictorian, there would be no Salutatorian. By 1884, however, Alice Mary Mower was honored as the first woman to be Salutatorian. In 1890, Mary Baer was designated Valedictorian, the first to be so honored. In the classes of 1891, 1892, and 1893, as well, the top scholar was a woman, Nellie Schaeffer of Springfield, Rena B. Nelson of Irving, Illinois and Iva Taylor of Galion, Ohio, respectively. The notion that women could not be top scholars was totally discredited.

After earning her degree, Alice Geiger accepted a teaching position in a Lutheran school in Lutherville, Maryland, and later taught in private schools in Nebraska and Ohio. She was then an instructor in mathematics and natural science at Irving College in Mechanicsburg, Pennsylvania. Later she joined the editorial department of the *Farmer's News*, a magazine published in Springfield, Ohio for farmers and advertising the various farm implements manufactured in the city.

Alice Mower, '84, became an instructor in the preparatory school at Wittenberg. Mary Baer became a physician and served as a Medical Missionary in the Lutheran Mission at Gunter, India. Nellie Schaeffer married and raised a family. Rena Nelson became a General Secretary of the YWCA in Gloversville, New York, and Iva Taylor was a school teacher in Galion, Ohio. Effie and Fannie Mitchell were also in the first group of women admitted. Their father, Ross Mitchell, was a prominent Springfield industrialist, active Board member, and generous supporter of the school. There were three Sprecher girls, Ella, Anna, and Mary. Ella was the daughter of the president. Anna and Mary were the daughters of Isaac Sprecher, the president's nephew and professor of ancient languages.

Next on the list was Mary Stuckenberg, who had been married for five years to J.H.W. Stuckenberg, professor of theology. She was one of the earliest married women enrolled in an American undergraduate college. In addition to these seven women in the college, Agnes Zimmerman was admitted as the first woman in the Preparatory Department. Farther down in the Preparatory Department were four other girls: Elizabeth A. Berger, India Crothers, Elizabeth Geiger, and Anna Mitchell. Of these, Elizabeth Geiger later completed the Bachelor of Science course to become the second woman graduate of the college in 1880, a year after her sister's graduation. These twelve young women were from families with Wittenberg connections. All were Lutherans and town residents. Six were daughters of and one the wife of a faculty member. Four were daughters of Board members. Most had brothers who were enrolled or were recent graduates. Several had fathers who were alumni.

M. Alice Geiger, first woman graduate of Wittenberg College, class of 1879. Wittenberg University Archives.

Alice Mower, Salutatorian, class of 1884. First woman faculty member in an academic department. She taught Latin, English and German. Wittenberg University Archives.

Mary Baer, Valedictorian, class of 1890, the first woman to be so designated. After graduation she became a physician and served as a medical missionary in India. Wittenberg University Archives.

One of the objections to a college education for women was "race suicide"; the fear that educated women would remain single and not bear children. In 1878, one student voiced such a concern in the *Flying Dutchman's Great Grandson*. "Several married ladies are attending college," the writer noted. "Wouldn't it be better if they would remain at home and have their husbands teach them to multiply?" Wittenberg's first women students answered that objection. While Alice Geiger remained single and childless, Fannie and Effie Mitchell, Ella Sprecher, Agnes Zimmerman, India Crothers, and Elizabeth Geiger all married soon after their college days. The four unaccounted for may well have married also. In any event, well over half of the women got married and raised children.

At the end of the 1874-75 school year, the faculty assessed the first year of coeducation. "Except for some annoyances of the ladies by the other students, chiefly in sport without any intention of disrespect, the plan of opening the institution to ladies has given very general satisfaction." Nevertheless, two male students were expelled for unacceptable and unspecified immoralities. Three years later the college catalog contained this endorsement: "Thus far, with us, the coeducation of the sexes has been eminently successful and has, in all respects, been fully satisfactory. We invite to our institution all young ladies who prefer a solid to a superficial education."

By 1881 there were eighteen women in attendance, and the class of 1882 was the final graduating class made up entirely of men. In the years subsequent to 1874, more and more women came and they took degree programs in larger numbers. Women from outside the town of Springfield came, and provision was made for them to live with families in town. As the number of women increased, they began to assert their desires more effectively. In 1880, one of them wrote in the *Wittenberger*, "We must have a boarding hall for ladies . . . . we want one or two lady professors."

In 1883 the faculty recommended that a residence hall for women be built south of the campus, across the street from Professor Ehrenfeld's house, later known as the Prince house, and next to the ten room house the Board built for President Helwig. Five years later, in September 1888, the first residence hall for women was opened; its first residents named it Ferncliff Hall. As to the second demand, women faculty members, the school responded in 1886. The first woman on the faculty was Edith H. Gardner, instructor in piano and voice. She was succeeded in 1888 by Miss Anna E. Linn, and she in turn by Mary S. Dunlap who also taught drawing and painting. The first woman faculty member in a regular academic discipline was Alice Mower, '84, a Wittenberg graduate. She came in 1891 to teach Latin and English in the academy. She specialized in German and became an assistant professor in the college.

Ferncliff Hall, first residence hall for women, opened in 1888. The first occupants selected the hall's name. Wittenberg University Archives.

Not everyone was happy about coeducation. One eastern paper referred to the college as "One of those precious products of emancipated and perverted womanhood that demands coeducation." There was some grumbling closer to home. The extent to which Wittenberg's decision to admit women affected the Presbyterian Female Seminary is unclear. A great many Lutheran daughters who might otherwise have attended there were diverted to Wittenberg at the preparatory and collegiate level.

The admission of women became permanent, but the integration of African American students in the student body was much less successful. After Broadwell Chinn's admission, few others came. The president reported that there was no disturbance. "Contrary to what by some was anticipated, few . . . have thus far availed themselves of the advantages of the institution." A student paper reflected greater difficulty, referring to a student in the preparatory department as "an odoriferous African" and suggesting a bath for everyone in the school. In the next issue, the editor apologized and indicated full support of the Board's position. The Board had not violated any rights of white students, he said; but the story indicated that there were problems. African Americans were treated as "outsiders" by much of the campus community. The story indicated "a necessary evil," said the editor, as two races "not adapted to live in the same clime and country" were brought together. Later, the same publication said a black senior was not welcome at Class Day. He was "ungratefully received", the paper reported, and went west "to grow up with the country."

Stories appeared regularly indicating that students harassed the janitors working their way through seminary. "The college Board should pay thirty dollars per month to two or three more colored brethren," observed one anonymous writer, "to sweep the halls of the building once a week and study theology." In spite of student inhospitality, the black seminarians appreciated the opportunity to acquire professional training though none were known to be Lutherans.

Broadwell Chinn remained only for one year. Students spoke of him, however, as a "marvel," and they thought his memory phenomenal. They attributed his leaving to illness. He read law in Springfield and was the second African American to be admitted to the Bar and to the Clark County Bar Association. He died on September 11, 1889, at the age of thirty-six. Gradually, the rise of Jim Crow attitudes in Springfield and among students and faculty, replacing the earlier ideals of civil equality that had prevailed in much of Springfield during the Civil War, temporarily ended the college's experiment in integration. Official policy remained, but practices changed. It would be nearly two decades before the next black students would appear.

The former President began work to revitalize the seminary course. It would be another seventeen years before women would be admitted to that program, and even then, not for ordination, and over some synodical objections. Sprecher also began work on his long thought about book on American Lutheran theology. He finished and published it in 1879. He called it *The Groundwork of a System of Evangelical Lutheran Theology*. Some church writers called it a systematic theology while others called it an extensive introduction to the study of theology. Sprecher did not intend for it to be any more than an introduction or a framework into which further theological study could be fitted. His joy at the completion of his work was cut short by the death of his wife Catherine on November 7 of the same year.

Catherine Schmucker Sprecher. Photograph of portrait by Robert Gantt.

In his five-hundred page treatise, Sprecher dealt with many of the fundamental questions disturbing nineteenth-century theologians. He assessed the relation of creeds and confessions to broader theological concerns; he looked at the psychology of religious experiences; he examined the importance of the personal assurance of salvation; he supported the right of private judgment concerning the scriptures and the centrality of justification by faith in evangelical theology. Fundamentally, however, Sprecher sought to make a direct assault on the growing skepticism of his day by applying scientific methods to theology and calling upon denominations to give up narrower dogmas which he believed obscured the basic truths of Christianity.

Sprecher's *Groundwork* has been called the most articulate expression of the fundamental principles of the Americanist view and a major theological effort. When it appeared in 1879, however, it had little impact on the Lutheran Church at large because more conservative Confessionalists had already won the day. Sprecher's former and current students, however, and others continuing in the American Lutheran tradition were impressed by it.

Stuckenberg called it a work that took the Lutheran Church back to its beginnings and threw light on the philosophical skepticism of the day, a great interest of his. It was pervaded by "a deep and earnest pietistic Lutheran spirit" and proclaimed the truth of Luther and Spener, said Victor S. Conrad. It inspired a new zeal in the clergy and taught laymen the personal assurance of salvation in spite of various creeds and dogmas, said Rev. M. J. Firey in the *Lutheran Observer*. Some ranked Sprecher's work with that of Dorner, whom he translated, and both with that of Luther himself. A Baptist commentator called it "a thoroughly German sort of work," broad in view with masculine vigor and sound faith.

While Sprecher was preparing his book, John H.W. Stuckenberg was also hard at work on one of his own. Before he had joined the Wittenberg faculty, he had published a book entitled *The History of the Augsburg Confession* showing his affinity with his teacher, Dr. Sprecher. It was a scholarly work, based on sources available at the University of Tubingen, Germany, showing careful study of primary as well as secondary German sources. What he had in mind now was a much more ambitious undertaking, a pioneering text on Christian Sociology.

As Stuckenberg reflected on the Civil War and the crusade against slavery that preceded it, the peace movement and the temperance movement, he was taken by the activist role that many evangelical church members had taken in these causes. Later, in his ministry in industrial Pittsburgh, after several years of study at Halle University in Germany, he considered the misery and need in workingmen's communities and posed for industrialists the ethical questions which the new economy raised for him. Halle was not only a center of Lutheran pietism but also a major center of the church's involvement in social welfare activities.

At Wittenberg Stuckenberg had already explored methodically the question of how a Christian society should deal with such issues. In the teachings of Jesus and the example of the New Testament Church, he sought models for the organization of modern society. Both in theory and in regard to specific societal problems, Stuckenberg's *Christian Sociology* anticipated the emerging Social Gospel movement in American Protestantism. His discussion of labor-industry problems, the problems of alcohol in society, and the tendencies in family life proposed a new arena for Church efforts and Christian action.

Those joining the Social Gospel movement were opposed to the ramifications of capitalism as expressed in the "gospel of wealth," and they repudiated that "gospel." It derived from Herbert Spencer's application of Darwin's theory of evolution to sociology, a notion that William Graham Sumner had called "Social Darwinism," the survival of the fittest. Its keystone was, he said, an almost idolatrous conception of private property and the erroneous notion that God prospered those who pleased him and did not prosper those who displeased him. Stuckenberg criticized this "iron law" of property. He argued that unearned wealth should be limited; that all men should work for a living; that it was unfair for one to live off unearned wealth while others lived in poverty. He saw poverty as an inevitable result of the gospel of wealth, and that alone called it into question. He challenged the complacent view in many congregations that the poor were poor because of idleness, debauchery or inherent worthlessness. He saw in American life a more random distribution of wealth and adversity

Advocates of the gospel of wealth saw a limited role for government in dealing with these social issues. Stuckenberg, on the other hand, believed strongly in the positive role of the state in balancing the economic fate of individuals. As an American Lutheran he believed that government was a sphere of God's concerns and Christians were duty-bound to participate as citizens and as politicians. The injustices condoned by the "gospel of wealth," in Stuckenberg's view, were a travesty of God's design for life on earth.

He would replace the rugged individualism of the gospel of wealth with an "interdependent society." He said there were two overriding views of society, and both were wrong. The first was selfish individualism that led to an unbridled capitalism; the other was a dehumanizing socialism that led to tyranny. Christian sociology, as he saw it, staked out a middle ground between the two.

His views were energized by a sense of crisis. The situation of the world, he said, was urgent and rapidly getting worse. This was a particularly troubled age, he added. Injustice was widespread, and something had to be done soon. The primary issues to be dealt with, he felt, were in the areas of world peace, race relations, and labor problems. He called for an international organization to avoid war, advocated the rights of Negroes, supported the right of labor to organize, and promoted arbitration as a way of settling industrial disputes. It was a decidedly progressive platform.

Stuckenberg's desire to apply Christian ethics to day-to-day experiences had come forth in faculty meetings when he advocated the admission of African Americans and women to the college. Had he remained on the faculty, his views on the social gospel would surely have clashed with those held by Springfield's industrialists. His brief presence did not add to the prospect for improved community relations because, during his seven years in their midst, local business and industrial leaders had become quite aware of his views.

To students, however, Stuckenberg was a sympathetic, earnest, large-hearted man. He developed a particular liking for introducing students to new emerging fields of study. He wanted students to be aware of tendencies in European, particularly German thought. Several of his later books were designed to be introductions to such changing fields as philosophy and sociology, and he began to develop their outlines in his teaching at Wittenberg. He was a strong advocate of sociability, and his home was a gathering place for faculty, students, and Springfield residents. He was interested in painting, sculpture, architecture, and music as well, and played an important role in adding an aesthetic dimension to life at Wittenberg. Putting into practice his concern that students have wholesome activities to occupy their time, he organized a concert by the men and women of Wittenberg for the benefit of chapel renovation. The concert raised $235 and helped provide paint for the walls, carpet for the floors, and new furnishings.

Stuckenberg had rather liberal views of proper Christian amusements that commended him to students as well. He pointed to the need for lectures, reading rooms, "ten-pin alleys," and gymnasiums. He saw bowling alleys as "schoolmasters to Christ" and endorsed Christian theater, dancing, billiards, croquet, and all sports as character building and wholesome. It was not enough to condemn vice-ridden entertainments of tavern and brothel, he said. You had to put something wholesome in their place. You had to take young men as they were, and provide diversions, entertainments, recreation, and physical competition. Otherwise they would gravitate to less savory outlets.

The brash young Stuckenberg brought the new and vigorous spirit of European scholarship to Wittenberg. Students in the 1880 yearbook called him an "eminent scholar, able, rich in learning, with broad and liberal views." He was, they said, a teacher deeply in earnest who brought them the results of careful and searching investigation. He was not the first teacher to be thought dangerous because his views were so revolutionary and his personality so attractive to the young.

Stuckenberg's book, *Christian Sociology*, appeared the year after Sprecher's *Groundwork*. With two such works appearing so close together, the richness of evangelical and scholarly thought at Wittenberg should have been apparent to all. But Stuckenberg's work met the same fate as Sprecher's in Lutheran church circles. It was virtually ignored. Charles Howard Hopkins, in *The Rise of the Social Gospel in American Protestantism, 1865-1915*, called Stuckenberg's work a brilliant and pioneering outline, the first and one of the few significant formulations of social theology. He was a decade ahead of other serious scholars in social theology, like Walter Rauschenbusch, said Hopkins; but the Lutheran Church failed to become involved. In their race back to confessionalism, the Lutheran Church forfeited any major role in the social gospel movement until the middle of the twentieth century. It was the ultimate failure of the American movement that it was rejected in its entirety, and most American Lutherans faded away or joined other Protestant denominations. The social gospel movement was just another of those "new measure" aberrations which were viewed with suspicion and open opposition by most Lutheran leaders. Not until the Great Depression of the 1930s would such voices again arise among Lutherans.

Stuckenberg sought to convince the Church of the need for making religion more practical and more sensitive to the physical as well as the spiritual needs of people, especially working people, young people, and the poor. The Church, he insisted, must keep abreast of the times, applying eternal truth to the real problems of people in the modern world. The churches should shuck off worn-out, useless and inappropriate views. Certainly the Church must nurture faith, but it should also teach ethical social behavior.

In these views Stuckenberg again reflected the views of his teacher. Sprecher once observed, "I am fully persuaded the Lord has more truth yet to break forth out of His holy word. For my part, I cannot sufficiently bewail the condition of the reformed churches that are come to a period in religion and will go at present no further than the instruments of the Reformation. The Lutheran Church cannot be drawn to go beyond what Luther saw; whatever part of His will God has revealed to Calvin, they will rather die than embrace it." But both Sprecher and Stuckenberg were speaking to an ever shrinking audience within Lutheranism. Their books represented a final distillation of Americanist concepts as the movement declined. President Helwig would also discover the dwindling away of support for the college as the Americanists drifted away.

Many left to become Presbyterians as Helwig himself would do. Others became Episcopalians. One alumnus, who chose to remain Lutheran, said he came to Wittenberg to be at the center of Americanism. Year's later, as an alumnus, he explained his being at Wittenberg to conservative Iowa parishioners by telling them he went there because of poor health.

The Sprecher and Stuckenberg books, however, represented well the driving spirit that had brought Wittenberg into being, directed its progress for more than thirty years, and gave it a firm foundation and a sense of direction different from any other Lutheran college. As that ideology waned, Wittenberg would experience a crisis far more critical than the financial crises it was used to. With the community of Springfield, for the time being, disinterested, with the Americanist church party waning in strength and influence, the real question for Wittenberg became: to whom does this college belong?

Who cares whether it continues or not? To Helwig was assigned the task of finding a supportive environment for an increasingly isolated American school. He found it among the alumni and within the faculty. In the interim, the growing professionalism of the academic community emerged to pose a new set of goals and purposes for the institution and in that emergence the style and spirit of John Henry Wilburn Stuckenberg became a model.

In 1880 Stuckenberg resigned from the faculty. Several times he had asked for a leave of absence to study again in Germany but his request was denied. It was his intention to return even after he had resigned. He left his library and other personal affects in Sprecher's keeping and stayed in touch with Sprecher and Helwig, but his short sojourn in Germany turned into a fourteen-year stay. There he became pastor of the American Church in Berlin which served a multitude of Americans of various denominations studying or working abroad. He pursued his own studies, making periodic trips back home. His critics noted that his church in Berlin was not a Lutheran congregation and insisted that he was no longer a Lutheran pastor and could not speak as one.

Stuckenberg's impact on Wittenberg College during his time on the faculty had been immense. Shorn of its American theological content, there remained an emphasis on modern German scholarship that would usher in a golden academic age under Helwig's successor. Both Stuckenberg and Samuel Alfred Ort were committed to the new German scholarship and should have been great friends, but their theological views continued to diverge. They had been in college together and their classmates nicknamed Stuckenberg "The Prophetic" and Ort "The Solid." Ort replaced Stuckenberg on the seminary faculty and though he made an effort to encourage his return, it did not happen.

These were disturbing times intellectually and much of the student unrest in the era could be attributed to uncertainty about what their elders had called the "eternal verities," the timeless truths by which society was organized which had been nourished by the classical curriculum. Stuckenberg brought an air of confidence to the confrontation. Scientific theory and growing skepticism which chipped away at Christian doctrine were so much grist for his mill. Darwin's *Origin of Species* was much discussed. Articles by Aldous Huxley and Herbert Spencer appeared with regularity in *Popular*

Science Monthly. Robert Ingersoll, the great doubter, filled the pages of the *North American Review* with challenges to belief. It was as if the underpinnings of all faith were being struck away, and youth left to flounder. But Stuckenberg took on all comers with great gusto.

His style was to take the measure of current trends and translate them so as to attack the very skepticism and unbelief which they seemed to promote. He carefully distinguished the Christian sociology he was developing from the sociology on which Herbert Spencer was busy at work. When Spencer's work was completed, he observed, "It may be found valuable as a study preparatory to Christian social science just as anthropology may be made preparatory to the study of theology." To understand a society in which grace reigns, he told his students, you had to study a society without it.

The trouble with many modern scholars, according to Stuckenberg, was that they treated the mind "like a piece of machinery" which they dismantled, examined and described its constituent parts; but they never reassembled it and studied it as a functioning whole. The task, he said, was to see life whole. Spencer, he elaborated, would treat sociology as a department of physics. "We will find no room in Spencer's sociology," said Stuckenberg, "for the spirit, conscience, free will or for God." Nevertheless, he noted, Spencer's methodology was worth review because, unlike most of his peers, Spencer supplemented the analytic habit of the scientific mind with the synthetic habit of the creative mind. It was a practice worth studying. The role of scientific analysis, he told his students, was to prepare the way for synthesis and it was in synthesis that new directions for action could be found.

For most undergraduate students at Wittenberg, perhaps, Stuckenberg's wrestling with the dimensions of physiological psychology, idealism, and pragmatism were of little interest. Even for most faculty in western colleges, these higher issues affecting the academic world of Europe and some in the eastern American colleges, for which the German university was a model, were of little interest. Philosophy, like most emerging disciplines, was becoming a free-for-all of ideas not immediately relevant to the old style college or to students and faculties therein. There was a challenge to the classical notion that all knowledge could be harmonized and unified. Stuckenberg, however, enjoyed living in the midst of the academic turmoil. The chaos, he was sure, contained the shape of the future, and he wanted to participate in its discovery. His wrestling with the chaos of ideas set a tone for his work at Wittenberg and laid the foundation for strength in the new social sciences at Wittenberg that would be distinctive.

That was the reason Stuckenberg did not return to Wittenberg, that and his growing disagreement with President Ort, Helwig's successor, over the school's direction. Though some students responded to his teaching and his methods, the load in an old-line college was just too heavy to allow thought and research. In the preface to his *Introduction to the Study of Philosophy*, written in Berlin in 1887, he noted that his encounters with graduate students from all parts of the world, of all faiths and none, had been more stimulating to his intellectual career deepening his insights and stretching his understanding. He remained in Germany in the center of the debate and wrote many articles and several books. He authored a *Life of Kant*, an *Introduction to the Study of Sociology*, an *Introduction to the Study of Philosophy*, and *Tendencies in German Thought*.

An equally persuasive reason for not coming back, even though he was invited several times, was that Wittenberg was changing. He became angry at Samuel Alfred Ort, claiming that he insulted the memories of Keller and Sprecher. This was indicative of the great changes that occurred despite President Helwig's strenuous efforts to hold them back. Helwig had been a successful though restless preacher, an efficient administrator, and an effective pastor. He had experience as a teacher and had been active in college affairs for nearly twenty years. He had helped organize and presided over the college's alumni association, and as the Americanists watched their power fade in the synods and their control of the seminary diminished, he shifted their influence to the alumni association and the college. Helwig came to the presidency resolute, but with an impossible task, and under him everything came apart.

If Sprecher and Stuckenberg caught the highest impulses of Americanism in their writings, John B. Helwig captured something less in his. Wittenberg's Americanized founders had been concerned about undue foreign, old-world influences in American society, particularly in education and religion. They favored positive measures to Americanize immigrants while avoiding the jingoism of the Know-Nothing movement. They had founded Wittenberg to Americanize a German church.

In the post-Civil War era, as immigration shifted from Protestant northern Europe to Catholic southern and central Europe, a new wave of nativism and anti-Catholicism arose in the United States. A partial and stunted nativism had survived the Civil War, and it grew gradually until by the 1880s it was again a full-blown movement. Anti-Catholicism flared in several northern states including Ohio in the 1870s. In 1875, the future Republican president, Rutherford B. Hayes, ran for governor of Ohio, suggesting that Democrats were subservient to Catholic designs. Some Republicans, as the party's fortunes seemed to be waning, hoped to turn it into a national campaign issue in the presidential election of 1876.

In that climate, Helwig turned earlier American impulses into a more virulent anti-Catholicism. In 1876, the centennial year of American independence, he published a series of lectures entitled: *The Rise of the Romish Church, Its Results in Europe, and its Designs upon the Institutions of America*. In his preface, he said that he cherished no ill will to any individual member of the Catholic Church, but confessed a steady opposition to the "system of Romanism." He predicted a conflict between the land of civil and religious freedom and the Roman Church. When he first delivered these lectures at the church in Springfield they created a furor in the Catholic community. Springfield Catholics brought a spokesman from the diocesan office in Cincinnati to respond. A Catholic magazine, *The Niagara Index*, took Helwig to task for his assertions. Students on campus noted that Helwig "made Rome howl."

William Lawrence, Republican congressman from Wittenberg's district, wrote a lengthy introduction and a conclusion for Helwig's book. He called him "an able man who has devoted much time, thought, and patient investigation to the subject." He used Helwig's book in the political phase of nativism, hoping to weaken the Democratic Party where Catholics sought refuge. Helwig had given Lawrence an honorary degree in 1875.

With all the changes wrought by the Board in June of 1874, the Board had also created a committee on the relocation of the college. It functioned throughout Helwig's administration. With church and alumni support growing, community leaders suspicious of the school's teachings and its reluctance to change, Wittenberg looked about for a more hospitable and more generous town to which it could move. Twice since Wittenberg began Springfield had sought to bring another college to town. It had most recently sought to change the very nature of the school without regard for its mission and purpose. Perhaps, said Helwig's party, it was time to start over someplace else.

It was not a totally new idea. In 1855 Frederick Conrad had suggested that the school might have to move. In 1865, the Rev. Joshua Crouse, veteran Board member, had told the board of directors that some plan needed to be devised "to bring the citizens of Springfield into practical sympathy" with the college and to disabuse them of "the idle impression which seems to be cherished in the city of Springfield that there is no other place where Wittenberg College can be located than in their midst." We must be generous and just in our attitudes toward the community, he added, but we must also be true to ourselves.

Chapter Nine

A Gem Worth the Setting

Conflict between Wittenberg and the leadership of the Springfield industrial community was attributable to the wide chasm between their views of the role of the college in the community and to the absence of a reconciler in either camp. Springfield businessmen were urged on by the brash Clifton M. Nichols who exacerbated every issue that arose. On the other side, neither Hezekiah R. Geiger nor John Helwig was conciliatory.

Given the economic conditions in the nation and in Springfield from 1873 to 1878, ample opportunity arose for relations between the two parties to worsen. The panic of 1873 cut into the brief prosperity that had followed the recession of 1869 and ushered in five more years of hard times. Economic adversity affected all colleges and universities. The economy was not flourishing; and there was general hardship.

For Wittenberg it meant decreased enrollment, erosion of endowment, slow payment or default on pledges, and tight financial conditions. Salaries were reduced. The small faculty was reduced further and some in Springfield felt the wrong men were let go. Teaching loads were increased. Students wrote in the *Wittenberger* that faculty were overworked, and teaching had become drudgery. Prince described the times as a "melancholy yet heroic part of the story of Wittenberg."

Yet in Springfield, throughout the period, the farm machinery plants continued to operate at capacity. The demand for farm implements was world wide, and business flourished. Businessmen were preoccupied, however, with fears that hardship might soon over take them, with efforts to cope with erratic financial markets, and with desires to make the most of their good fortune while it lasted. They were eager to improve railroad connections. The link between the Sandusky to Springfield and the Dayton to Cincinnati railroads was but a spur and of decreasing importance as other railroads crisscrossed Ohio. They hoped a permanent east-west trunk line could be built through Springfield. In addition, the Champion manufacturing interests wanted a line from Springfield to the coal fields of southern Ohio and West Virginia. They invested heavily in the Springfield, Jackson and Pomeroy Railroad, but lost substantially when the road went bankrupt. To save their investment they bought the road at great additional cost. Nichols described it as a tough time for local businessmen. They were in no mood to talk about other ventures.

The division between these leaders and the relocation party on the Board was a mystery to both. Observers had predicted such an estrangement between the classical colleges and the nation's industrialists. Alexis de Tocqueville had noted that there was no class in America in which taste for intellectual pleasures was transmitted with hereditary fortune and leisure. In America most of the rich were formerly poor; and those who now had leisure had been absorbed in business during their youth. When they might have had a taste for study, they had not the leisure. Now that they had leisure they had not the taste. Charles Francis Adams, New England Brahman and former ambassador to Great Britain, noted that the standards of the classical college no longer prevailed in society and that men, machines and money were in the ascendancy. Those devoted to the former were without influence; those devoted to the latter ignored classical men and passed them by.

Wittenberg's Committee on Removal was chaired by Joshua Crouse, outgoing Chairman of the Board and the acknowledged leader of the Board's reemergence. The committee represented five Lutheran synods supporting the college. Also serving was Helwig and Alexander Gebhart of Dayton, treasurer of the college. There were no Springfielders and no modern industrialists. The action creating the committee was both unanimous and enthusiastic. "We are not astonished at this seemingly radical movement," the

Wittenberger noted. It was not a rash act, but a deliberate one after years of conflict and disappointment. The editor discussed the reasons why such a step, even if justified, should not be taken. He reflected the division among alumni and supporters of the school. He wrote of the sacred memories of every son of Wittenberg and the old campus, "hallowed by the sweet recollection of other days." He talked of a host of friends in Springfield, the graveyard "where sleep some of our fallen brothers," and the tomb of the sainted Ezra Keller. Reflecting the frustrations of the other side, the editor concluded, "The institution cannot live on cherished memories;" it must, in its own interest, outline its needs and ask where such substantial help is to come from.

Students had taken note of the issue in the *Wittenberger*, and expressed their discontents. They reviewed years of unhappiness over the failure to repair the bridge across the creek, to provide a good road or sidewalks. A better bridge at Wittenberg Avenue to connect college and church would be nice, they added. With the arrival of coeds, the editor regretted that they had to "tread all the mud in Clark County with their dainty feet." For thirty years Wittenberg had been a part of Springfield's glory, they wrote. In return citizens had been endearing and showed appreciation in words but seldom in deeds. He calculated that the college in thirty years had added $1.2 million to the economy while the town invested much less in the school. Springfield expended $20,000 while students, over the same years spent $525,000.

In June 1875, the Committee on Removal recommended that the board postpone action for a year, but was asked to develop "some definite plan" yet during the meeting. Proponents of moving felt there should be a standing proposal to present to interested parties. Opponents thought specificity might help expose the whole idea as ill-advised. Willingness to relocate, however, became a standing Board policy. Crouse's committee recommended that the Board ask as a consideration for moving, $100,000, including a site of no less than fifteen acres. The recommendation was tabled. In 1876 it was tabled again, and no action was ever taken on specific terms.

Faced with the board's resolute action, Nichols, for once, seemed conciliatory. "The times having become harder than usual," he noted, "and there being a 'plentiful scarcity' of money," it was no wonder they were not experiencing success in the relocation effort. He advised that they use the hard times to deliberate about the school's real needs and whether Springfield would try to meet them. "Springfield will respond," he promised. "It would, of course, be expected that the institution would improve." Men who could invest in the college, said Nichols, would insist that "it should be in every respect a first-class college." It ought to become a great university with the best teachers in all departments; if they could not be found in the Lutheran church, they should go beyond that source. He talked of a university "under the auspices and care of the Lutherans and yet . . . free from sectarianism."

"Now we beg our friends and neighbors who dwell on the Hill of Science north of the city," he wrote, "to give up all idea of dallying with the Philistines, and to place trust and reliance upon the large-souled, liberal, friendly, and helpful people of Springfield." Nichols was conciliatory and all but guaranteed that Springfield would respond. He promised to help bring such a happy conclusion about.

The failure of the Board to act reflected its lack of consensus. While a number of the members and Helwig favored removal, an equal number plus Ort and Prince favored remaining in Springfield. For this second group, it was a matter of preference and moral obligation. The Board's 1845 acceptance of the offer of Springfield's citizens twice used the phrase "permanent location." It read: "Whereas it now devolves on the Board of Directors to select and permanently fix the location of the institution . . . Therefore, resolved, that Springfield, Clark County, Ohio, be, and is hereby made the permanent location of Wittenberg College . . ." The relocation party, countered that the resolution went on to say, "with the confident expectation, however, from assurances given, that the subscription will be considerably enlarged." That implied continuing support which they said had not been forthcoming. There was a third group, who were unsure of which direction to go, that held the balance of power. One side could not pass nor could the other defeat a motion, and no action could be taken.

A letter to the editor in the *Wittenberger*, gave an alumni point of view. It was similar to that of Editor Nichols and was signed "Eagle Eye." He had written before asking for an accounting of the Alumni Endowment Fund. On another occasion he wrote to advocate a new professor of science.

John C. Brodfuehrer, class of 1857. Alumni Endowment Fund chairman and advocate of educational reform. Wittenberg University Archives.

Eagle Eye had been the name of an Excelsior Society publication in 1856-1857. The secretary of the society and editor was John C. Brodfuehrer, class of 1857. His classmates had called him "The Sarcastic." Wittenberg had only five alumni known to be in New York City and Brodfuehrer was one of them. Brodfuehrer had recently moved to New York but had been present for the crucial Board meeting of 1873. He may have been ambitious to be elected president. Later he accepted the presidency of a small college in South Carolina. By 1895 he became a professor at the German Theological Seminary in Chicago. He, like many alumni, strongly advocated a more modern curriculum.

In his letter Brodfuehrer disagreed with the direction of the college. The school had been a "hesitating, do-little, dilly-dallying" place since 1855, he said, and would continue so until 1881 when what he called the "Egyptian famine" would end. He dated the beginning of the famine with the appearance of the *Definite Synodical Platform* and Sprecher's defense of a failing Americanism. He saw its unexpected extension in the election of Helwig and predicted its end with the demise of the Helwig administration. His prediction was off by a year. During the famine, said "Eagle Eye," a few of the swarms of colleges in America would grow into real collegiate institutions while others would dwindle into preparatory academies and the rest would close. During the interim Wittenberg would have but six professors, some "well favored," others "very ill-favored and lean-fleshed intellectually."

In 1881, Brodfuehrer predicted, Wittenberg would face up to the vital question it had sidestepped in 1873 and 1874, that of meeting the reasonable demands of the age. Only a growing Alumni Endowment Fund and gifts of alumni would save Wittenberg from decline. "Strange as it may seem the soundest counsel and largest gifts," he advised would come from those students who left after two or three years without the classical degree and had become successful businessmen. The course of study and methods of teaching needed to keep Wittenberg from becoming a boy's academy, he said, would have to await a later letter.

The Board, however, was preoccupied with a new proposal to move the seminary west. The General Synod convention in Omaha, Nebraska asked Wittenberg to consider moving its theological school to the Mississippi valley. If it was willing to move the college, perhaps it would move the seminary too. The Board appointed a committee to meet with a similar group from Carthage College in Illinois. The Board ultimately concluded that its endowment could not be divided or a part of it taken somewhere else. Americanists sensed that if they separated the seminary from Wittenberg its unique view within the church was doomed. It was doomed in any location, perhaps, but if there was a chance for survival, that chance existed only at Wittenberg

The situation at Wittenberg had further deteriorated. Enrollment continued to decline in spite of coeducation and the establishment of the Pastor-Parent Scholarship granting sons and daughters of pastors a half tuition scholarship. Income also declined, faculty loads were increased and salaries again reduced. Isaac Sprecher resigned to pursue his career elsewhere. A running debate with the Alumni Association about the use of its funds for his replacement kept the position vacant for some time. The theological faculty wanted to fill its full complement of chairs for its new two-year curriculum while the alumni wanted a professorship of English Literature, modern languages or science.

Professor Isaac Sprecher built and lived in the house now known as the Benjamin Prince House. Photo of a portrait by Robert Gantt.

There was a renewed request by alumni to elect members to the Board, but it was lost in a debate about whether non-Lutherans should be on the Board. The Wittenberg Synod took strong action opposing any non-Lutheran members or any category that might allow for such. The view was interpreted in town and among alumni as narrow and sectarian with a corresponding further decrease in interest and support.

At this point, Helwig's commitment to moving became firmly implanted in his thinking. For him there was no other alternative. He revised the history of the college in the catalog. It had told the story of the founding in Springfield in 1845. In Helwig's revision, the story began with the Oct. 18, 1842 action of the English Synod creating the school. It told of its year in Wooster before moving to Springfield. Adding another sentence later, announcing its move to a third location would be easy. Many college histories could recite just such a wandering beginning.

As the Board reviewed Wittenberg's situation and looked at the other colleges in the state, they concluded that they needed expanded and up-to-date facilities in order to compete more effectively. The resulting plan was for a second building in Springfield or two buildings in a new location. It raised the hurdle for any city wanting to entice the school to relocate. Those who wanted to keep the school in Springfield proposed a campaign for that new building. They took editor Nichol's advice of a plan for a New Wittenberg in Springfield, one that would accommodate an expanded curriculum. They proposed a companion effort to enlarge the endowment to support an enlarged faculty.

The *Wittenberger* complained that "the cause of Wittenberg has been too long treated as a dead letter by the people of Springfield." Yet, it noted that some in Springfield were enthusiastic about the idea for New Wittenberg. The *Republic* ran a series of articles about it, and Nichols wrote what the students called "a neat editorial." A "boom" was developing and the college approached Springfielders for funds for the new building. Success in the effort would settle once and for all the issue of relocation, making it more difficult for other communities to make an attractive offer. The endowment goal would be met by appeals to the churches and alumni outside the town. The Board seemed not to see the naiveté of its position. With its standing Committee on Removal in place, a fund drive in Springfield seemed doomed from the start.

The goal was $100,000, and a well-organized campaign was planned. Local papers were supportive. Industrialist, alumnus and Board member Ross Mitchell committed ten percent of the total. He played a major role in the effort to keep the college in Springfield. At the end of the solicitation, even with that generous gift, the total raised was only $19,000. The Board's reaction was heated and it finally gave the relocation group a majority. They felt the community did not sufficiently appreciate the college and the opportunity it gave to the area or the financial benefits which accrued to the city because of its presence.

The campaign had come in the midst of negotiations with railroad promoters and other towns on a new east-west railroad trunk line. Patience on Wittenberg's part would have been well advised. Local leaders knew that they had to raise an as yet unspecified amount to be invested in the stocks and bonds of the new road. Failure to find allies and investors to get the route built through Springfield would mean the city might lose its last chance to be located on a main line running east and west.

The Board decided to lower its goal to $75,000 and extend the effort until the fall. After August 1, bids would be invited from other communities. For a year, according to Prince, the sentiment for removal was sufficiently strong to prevent any "hearty response on the part of Springfield for the retention of the college." When they saw how hard the Committee for Removal was working, Springfielders waited to see what the outcome would be. They were indifferent, said Prince, "while the billing and cooing were going

Ross Mitchell, Springfield industrialist and philanthropist, partner in Warder, Mitchell and Glessner Co. worked hard to keep Wittenberg in Springfield. Clark County Historical Society.

on" with other cities. A new Committee on the New Wittenberg was composed of members of both points of view. They undertook to raise $75,000 for a building in Springfield and to review proposals for a new campus elsewhere. One way or the other they were to make possible a new Wittenberg. Ross Mitchell, who enlarged his original gift, and Samuel Ort were determined to keep Wittenberg in Springfield. They exerted extraordinary efforts to arouse Springfield and forestall other committee action.

On the basis of the quality of education, Wittenberg was among the state's top institutions. What it did, it did well. Faculty and Board believed that it should be respected as such and be located in a place that recognized and appreciated the fact. The Ohio College Association recognized it as one of the state's top schools. The faculty advised the Board, however, that they needed to sustain that ranking. "The progress which characterizes the age cannot be ignored by institutions of learning . . . . No college can afford for a long period of time to present any appearance of weakness or insufficiency in any of the essential equipments of the good average college of the country." They hoped that the impasse between school and town would be resolved. Helwig noted that Wittenberg had maintained high standards, had earned the respect of "every intelligent community" and of sister institutions. The purpose of the college had been steadily maintained even in the face of financial adversity and other trials. If it were to continue, it needed added facilities in Springfield or somewhere else.

Five months later, the Board convened in special session in the Lutheran Church on High Street. Pledges had not yet reached $25,000 as Springfielders continued to wait. Mr. E. O. Fallis, Toledo architect, presented sketches for two buildings for the Board's consideration. One could be used for the new building in Springfield or both could be used for the new campus. Five other Ohio towns, Bryan, Defiance, Kenton, Lima and Mansfield, had expressed an interest. Bryan offered five acres of land and $20,000, hardly a proposal to excite Board enthusiasm. Most of the others hinted at proposals below Wittenberg's needs and expectations. Only the Mansfield proposal seemed interesting and it was still quite vague.

Mansfield had a large Lutheran population and many were acquainted with Wittenberg. They had been liberal supporters when the school began in Wooster and after it moved to Springfield. In December Sprecher wrote to Stuckenberg in Berlin indicating that it was likely that the college would be moved to Mansfield and that he would be set aside. Students learned of the Mansfield proposal and that it included only one building. Wittenberg was looking "Mansfield-ward," they said. They were aware of the modern plan for students to room and board in private residences; but they were not sure they would like it. Dormitories, they felt, were economical, socially and intellectually more beneficial and enabled them to learn more about human nature.

The Board responded to Mansfield, suggesting that if they would erect two buildings along the lines proposed by E. O. Fallis on a tract of not less than ten acres, Wittenberg would move to Mansfield. They set a deadline of April 1, later extended to May 1. As early as March 19, however, Sprecher told Stuckenberg that he now believed the college would remain in Springfield because Mansfield could not meet Wittenberg's terms. At the same time the campaign in Springfield picked up steam. People of Springfield were gratified by these developments, said Sprecher, and were showing a new interest. Ort and others were now taking subscriptions with greater success.

On May 3, in special session, the Board learned officially that Mansfield had been unable to raise sufficient money to build the two buildings. According to Prince, however, a delegation came to meet with the Board to make a counter offer. They proposed to give notes valued at $50,000 to be paid as the two buildings were erected. That amount of money would not build either one of the buildings as designed.

The special board meeting, however, had been called for a more important reason than consideration of the Mansfield offer, one that indicated the collapse of the relocation movement altogether.

The first item of business was John Helwig's resignation as President remarkably close to the date predicted by Dr. Brodfuehrer. The call for the meeting said that the president had been suffering with severe headaches. "My relief from pain," he wrote, "is not sufficient to enable me to do college work." The pressures of the struggles with Springfield and within the church had finally taken their toll. He asked to be relieved of his duties by the end of June.

Official portrait of John B. Helwig, third president, 1874-1882. Photo by Robert Gantt.

As the effort to move the college faltered and renewed efforts to raise support in Springfield emerged, Helwig found it impossible to rehabilitate himself with the community. As the outspoken advocate of relocation, failure was a psychological blow to this assertive man, from which he could not recover. Two months before his resignation, Sprecher had written Stuckenberg that Helwig would be coming to Europe and would visit him in Berlin. Students said that Helwig's illness was induced by the constant bickering and backbiting of faculty caused by the disgruntled Hezekiah Geiger as the relocation movement exacerbated already existing differences. Ort, who was operating the college in Helwig's absence and pressing the Springfield fund drive, received a telegram from Helwig on March 27 asking that his resignation be presented. Helwig did not plan to be present and if it were accepted, he planned an extended trip abroad. When he returned he would become pastor of Trinity Lutheran Church in Akron.

The Board took matters up in a deliberate if unusual order. First they appointed a committee to pick Helwig's successor. Then they appointed a second committee to consider the resignation. It then adjourned until the committees were ready to report. According to Prince, the mind of the Board was already fixed on the man to be selected. Though the names of several were mentioned, he said, the general trend was to Ort. He was well liked in Springfield, on campus, in the church and among alumni.

Ort received a majority on the first ballot and his election was then made unanimous. Students declared the importance of the action. "As Dr. Keller was the first president of the Old Wittenberg," they wrote in the *Wittenberger*, "Dr. Ort will be the first of the new."

Samuel Alfred Ort, class of 1863, president, 1882-1900. Wittenberg University Archives.

After Ort was elected the Board received the report on Helwig's resignation. His ill health was regretted, attributed to his strenuous efforts on behalf of the college. They recommended that his resignation be accepted. Helwig's career at Wittenberg ended, but not necessarily his influence. Students thought well of the beleaguered president. He had been kind in his relations with them and they respected his frankness and honesty. The stories of his concern for students based on his own difficult childhood were well circulated. Students knew that when Harr Wagner, later editor of the *Aloha*, and his brother, E. R., had arrived without resources, Helwig had allowed them to room and board at his house at no cost for the months it took them to prepare for admission and to become eligible for synodical help.

In 1886 Helwig again became pastor of Springfield's First Lutheran Church. In 1889 he was a candidate for Governor of Ohio on the Prohibition ticket. In 1890, however, he left the Lutheran church to become pastor of Urbana's First Presbyterian Church. He gave as his reason "the constant tendency of the Lutheran church to Catholicism and ritualism." From that time until his death in 1904, he adhered to the Presbyterian Church and lamented the fate of the American Lutheran movement.

The Board then took up the issue of removal to Mansfield. The Mansfield negotiators surprised the Board with a new offer. The new proposal included an offer from U. S. Senator John Sherman, a sharp dealer in real estate in Mansfield as well as in the nation's capital. He offered eighty acres in Mansfield for a sum of $24,000 reduced by a gift to the college of $8,000. This was in addition to the $50,000 in notes offered previously. If this offer had been made six months earlier Helwig's plan to move Wittenberg might well have succeeded. In the present circumstance the Board presented a counter offer closer to its original $100,000. The Mansfield boosters were unable to meet the higher figure. "Thus ended a scheme," said Benjamin Prince, "which should never have had a beginning," the scheme to move Wittenberg out of Springfield.

The Board adjourned to meet again on June 24, at which time the faculty reported that affairs at the college had not improved and enrollment was down farther. The dissension that had existed among Board members and constituents was also prevalent among faculty and students. The Board attributed it to unsatisfactory conditions in the college that existed a year earlier. It involved dissatisfaction of students and the lack of harmony in the faculty. One member suggested the board request the resignation of all the professors to allow them to accept some while not accepting others. Another proposed asking for Geiger's resignation. It was referred to a committee for recommendations.

Getting to the bottom of the turmoil was not an easy matter, and the committee left little information about its proceedings. A letter from the committee to Professor H. R. Geiger called for him to resign. "We were appointed by the Board," they wrote, "with the understanding that, if the causes of the dissatisfaction of the students were carefully inquired into, you would resign." Having conducted the investigation, they said that it was not probable that he could remain "with satisfaction to yourself or benefit to the college." There would be an appropriate financial settlement.

Students were less reticent and told their views in a new underground newspaper, the *Collegian,* in June of 1882. As the students saw it, Geiger had been the power behind the throne in Sprecher's administration. When Sprecher stepped down, he thought he should have been selected rather than Helwig. It was Geiger, then, who exacerbated Helwig's problems on campus and in town. It was Geiger, said the students, whom Ort courted to gain his support when Helwig left. He tried to retain him; but he remained the personification of student and community unhappiness. Of all the "Flying Dutchmen," Geiger had become the chief culprit and target of student unrest.

How sentiments had changed. A few student generations ago Geiger was described as a man of great common sense and knowledge of human nature, a man of science. "My brother considered him the best man on the faculty," said one. "Most of the professors in those days seemed solemn and unapproachable . . . but Geiger had a great sense of humor, and I can see him now with his good-natured smile." But now he was seen as gruff, grumpy, humorless, and out of touch with his discipline and with students.

The lead article in the *Collegian* set a broader context for the campus situation. It was entitled, "Wittenberg and Springfield." The college had been established, it read, when the city was but a country town such as was adjacent to many other colleges. Then Wittenberg was an important part of the town. Since then, Springfield had grown to be a modern industrial city, and Wittenberg had not adjusted to the change in the town and its people. Nor, some alleged, had it kept pace with other colleges. This was at the root

Hezekiah R. Geiger, professor of Natural Science at Wittenberg, 1846-1882. Wittenberg University Archives.

of town-gown conflict. The article did not advocate that Wittenberg add agriculture to its curriculum to match the city's industry, but it did advise that the college broaden its program to meet the needs of a bustling city and postwar students.

"Make Wittenberg a gem worth the setting," observed the *Collegian*, "and Springfield will not be long in furnishing the gold for its base." The writer advised the school to "put men in charge of its business, officers in whose zeal and business ability the people of the city can have confidence . . ." The article charged that faculty were detached from local citizens and their energetic enterprises. It implied that the school discriminated against non-Lutherans on the faculty and excluded them from the Board and thus deprived itself of talent. It should seek the best men, "whether that talent be drawn from Lutheran, Presbyterian or any other source," the writer concluded.

Henry Rodgers and W. H. Wynn, both Presbyterians and Wynn a Wittenberg graduate, were let go in the recent economic crunch rather than those less popular with students and the community. It raised for many the key issue: must a faculty member be an ordained Lutheran clergyman or not? It was not an attack on the church relationship, but an expression of dissatisfaction with the old-fashioned faculty. Would the school hire the new style faculty member with specific academic credentials or the old style, the clergyman devoting his efforts to teaching? The article asked Wittenberg to develop an organization "worthy of the confidence of the citizens of Springfield and the pride of its alumni." If they did, the writer concluded, there would be no lack of students or of financial support from the town.

By calling the paper the *Collegian* rather than another edition of the *Flying Dutchman*, students signaled an important change in their view of themselves and their school. They were part of a new self-conscious national class of students with unique characteristics. There were many indications that Wittenberg was finding a place in the emerging system of higher education as an identifiable type: a residential, undergraduate liberal arts college. Students were thinking of themselves not as students at a uniquely different evangelical Lutheran college, but as collegians on an American campus. Wittenberg's inclusion on the list of Ohio's top colleges was one example. A growing Greek-letter system, with local chapters of national organizations was another. Growing interest in sports and collegiate fads in clothing and behavior were other manifestations.

Geiger departed in the fall. He joined the United States Coast and Geodetic Survey and spent much time in Washington, D. C. and in surveying the Blue Ridge Mountains of Maryland, Virginia and West Virginia. He died in 1899 at the age of 79. For his wife Nancy and their several children at home it was a difficult time. He left for Washington, hopeful and optimistic. "But I must confess," wrote Mrs. Geiger to her husband, recalling his difficulties at Wittenberg, "I have so little confidence in men that I will not feel certain of your position until you are in the field." She worried that it had been so long since a Democrat was in the White House that there would be too much competition for the few jobs available. Geiger was away most of the next four years, and Mrs. Geiger had difficulty managing the household and making ends meet without him. She reflected the general unhappiness of the families of the "Dutchmen." Of Dr. Sprecher she noted, "He looks pretty well but at the same time rather sad, as if he had given up the world and was looking forward to the time of his departure." Professor Diehl's widow sold her house and moved to more modest quarters. She sold household utensils to make ends meet. Eventually she and her son moved to California.

Finally, in 1884, the venerable Dr. Sprecher resigned his teaching position and retired to California. There his health and his morale seemed to improve and in 1887, in partnership with his son-in-law, Frank P. Davidson, and Harr Wagner, class of 1881, he founded a new college with Wittenberg as its model. The San Diego College of Letters, he said, was Wittenberg on the Pacific. It flourished for a while, but was lost in the collapse of San Diego land speculations. Farther up the coast, another Wittenberg alumnus, Samuel H. Weller, class of 1856, founded Occidental College which has had a long and distinguished life as a residential, undergraduate, liberal arts college. With Dr. Sprecher's departure, all of the college's pioneers were gone.

Ort focused his attention on the university movement in America and sought to change Wittenberg by broadening the curriculum, organizing the work into departments and adding graduate-level courses. The changes meant hiring a new kind of faculty. The Rev. S. F. Breckenridge was a carry over. He had joined the faculty in 1874, replacing Ort as professor of Mathematics and logic. He was a representative of the old style faculty, a clergyman with a scholarly bent and a desire to teach. He was better accepted by students than others of that type, however, because he was "fond of athletic sports and games" and was "jovial, enjoyed telling jokes." Students saw him as a person, not just a professor, and noted his medium height, his chunky build, his blue eyes and light complexion, and his willingness to share his life with them. He told students that he had been "sociable and fond of fun," and let it deter him from his studies. In 1860, having experienced a religious conversion, he entered the seminary. He had, however, but a brief career in the ministry, shifting early to teaching. Students distinguished between the older "old style" men and the younger "old style" men; and, in fact, age was as much a factor in student preferences as teaching style and content. In the *Collegian*, one student asked: "How many students will stay if Geiger stayed? Answer: virtually none. How many will stay if 'Brecky' stays? Answer: virtually all." Breckenridge caught some of the fever for the new professionalism and completed a Doctor of Science degree at Gettysburg.

In 1882, as Helwig was leaving and Ort advancing, Charles L. Ehrenfeld was called to teach English Literature and Latin. He was not the new kind of faculty either and resembled the old. A Wittenberg graduate, he was a pastor of the American type, had campaigned for Fremont for president and against slavery. As the Confessionalists triumphed in the church, he shifted his interests from the parish to education. He was one of the last defenders of Wittenberg's American theology and would eventually resign. His father was a graduate of Heidelberg University in Germany, and Ehrenfeld pursued the new Doctor of Philosophy Degree which would become the insignia of the new type of faculty that was emerging. He accepted election to the faculty, he told his students, because "you could not turn down the call of your Alma Mater." In addition, Wittenberg would be a great place for his children to get an education at a cost he could afford and for his wife, it was coming home. He had met her while he was in college

Dr. Ort had his first opportunity to recommend a new style faculty candidate in 1883. His choice, Edgar Fahs Smith, was a brash, young Gettysburg College graduate. He was 29 when he came to Wittenberg with a Doctor of Philosophy degree in Chemistry from Goettingen University in Germany. In 1876 he had been named Assistant in Analytic Chemistry at the University of Pennsylvania. He was a fellow in various scientific associations and academies in the United States and Europe. He was a busy author translating and publishing in America von Richter's *Inorganic Chemistry* in 1883. Subsequent editions appeared in 1885 and 1889. The book was in use widely in the United States. When he arrived at Wittenberg he had twenty-five books and articles to his credit and in five years produced eight more publications.

George Gerlaw Clark, in his *History of Wittenberg College*, described Smith as "[a] man of warm, kindly heart, transparent and open in his nature as the day, unsuspicious and charitable in his judgments of others, true in his loves and friendships as the needle of the pole, governed in all things by a high sense of honor and supreme loyalty to conscience, with loving interest in all and kind regards for all, he merits as he also receives the profound respect and cordial affection of multitudes whose pleasure it is to know him." High praise indeed! And the observation denoted the two attributes students sought in the new faculty: modern competence in their fields and a friendly, open and sociable personality. Call it the genial gentleman scholar, but it clearly reflected the students' ideal. Smith represented that ideal and students were disappointed when he left to return to the faculty at the University of Pennsylvania.

Another student reflected on the kind of professor students wanted in describing the recently resigned Dr. Stuckenberg. "He circulated among us just like a student," he noted. "He made his remarks so simple and direct as to touch the heart of every one of us." A tough task master, he "gave us the consolation that our trials once were his trials" and he urged students to pursue the truth with vigorous dedication.

Ort's second appointment was Herman Mueller as professor of Modern Languages. He was born in St. Petersburg, Russia, and educated at a German Lutheran Gymnasium in that city. His special gifts in languages, both ancient and modern, were cultivated there. He earned graduate degrees at the University of Dorpat in Estonia, and then taught privately among the elite of St. Petersburg, eventually at the court of the Russian Grand Duke, Brother of the Czar. In 1877 he immigrated to the United States and taught languages in New York City and in Pennsylvania before settling in Canton, Ohio.

In 1884 the Alumni Endowment Association indicated a desire to add the Alumni Chair of Modern Languages to the faculty, provided it could select the occupant. After long deliberation and another unsuccessful effort to turn the beneficence to a chair of theology, the Board accepted the terms set forth by the alumni. It was the desire of alumni that the best native speaker of German that could be found should be hired. Mueller was that man. The students described him as "always present, always prepared, always courteous, always exacting, always accurate to the smallest detail." He was helpful to students. His experiences in Russia brought an air of mystery and the exotic to his classes. Two and a half years later, however, Mueller died unexpectedly at the age of thirty-two. Students were shocked. They marched as a class to his funeral and expressed dismay that such a vigorous and talented young man had been taken from them.

To replace Mueller, Ort suggested twenty-five year old Hugo K. Schilling, born in Saalfield, Thuringia, Germany, on March 28, 1861. He had been baptized in a church where Luther had preached. He entered the University of Leipzig as a student of modern philology, studying German, English and the Romance languages under some of the most celebrated scholars of Germany. After two and a half years at the university, he toured England, Ireland and France for several years to experience and study languages in those countries. Upon return to Leipzig, he was the leader of the Anglo Saxon seminar. Finally, in 1885, he was awarded his Doctorate. With his degree, he left for the United States at the invitation of Helwig and Ort. Helwig was certain that Schilling met the desires of the alumni and Ort's requirements for his new faculty.

Clearly Ort was recruiting some of the brightest of the new faculty, but he would have difficulty holding them because of higher salaries, lower teaching loads and better facilities and equipment at eastern institutions. They were leaving Wittenberg to go to the emerging institutions in America. In his effort to build the new faculty at Wittenberg, Ort also sought to persuade John H. W. Stuckenberg to rejoin his friends in Ohio. Indeed, he had sent word via Helwig when he had gone to Europe, indicating that he was wanted and needed at Wittenberg. But Stuckenberg was not ready to return. In 1882 he completed his *Life of Immanuel Kant*, published by Macmillan and Company of London. It was hailed as the most complete biography of Kant in existence at the time. Ort continued to carry Stuckenberg's name on the faculty roster as an occasional lecturer. When he was in the United States to visit or on a lecture tour, he would appear on the campus for lectures and conversation. In 1894 he spent a week at Wittenberg giving a series of lectures on "The Social Problem." Ort wrote him periodically urging his permanent return.

When Stuckenberg visited the campus in 1892 he held seminars on "Tendencies in German Thought" which were well received. One listener recalled that Stuckenberg believed that German thought and action was rapidly nearing a crisis. Much of the old was no longer accepted, but that which would take its place was not yet clear. He spoke of Kant and Hegel. He noted that German scholars no longer accepted the Divine inspiration of the Bible. He told the students of the rise of socialism and the awakening of the consciousness of the German laborer. Students in the German universities, he added, were "entirely without restraint" and that was encouraged for the purpose of strengthening the student's will power. He advised Wittenberg students that their soul aim in college should be the pursuit of truth, disregarding all else, taking the hardest subjects and pursuing them with diligence.

But while Ort and the students alike entertained the hope that Stuckenberg would return, he countered all of Ort's pleas with a negative response. It was not that he was not in sympathy with the school's new aspirations; he agreed with them as far as they went, but they were insufficient. Stuckenberg could not separate American theology from the new scholarship and the new university. He was increasingly critical of Ort and others at Wittenberg who would surrender the theological department to Confessionalists and separate it from the college while focusing their energies on the undergraduate college with an eye to making the school a university.

To Stuckenberg it was precisely the separation of faith and reason that he had argued against in the *Final Science* and which he had tied together as the basis of his *Christian Sociology*. Relating the college to a different theological stance was a move in the wrong direction; but separating theology in a seminary, as a mere discipline, one of many fields of study and not preserving it as the very foundation of all scholarship and the queen of the sciences tore at his notion of learning. He was holding out for a view of university education that was rapidly fading. To him, as to Wittenberg's founders, theology was the integrating force in the entire curriculum. For all his criticism, however, Ort's view was closer to the emerging structure of American higher education; Stuckenberg's, a vain effort to perpetuate a view that would not survive.

Stuckenberg's disappointment with Ort who had replaced him on the theological faculty grew into resentment and anger. He accused Ort of forsaking the principles upon which the school had been founded and maligning the memories of Keller and Sprecher. He severed his relations with the school and at his death, left his papers and memorabilia to Gettysburg College. They included much of Sprecher's correspondence that had been left in his keeping. It was a blow to Ort who felt there was no other practical course for him to take than the one on which he was embarked. Ort felt it was Confessionalists among Lutherans and sectarians everywhere who were withdrawing theology from the emerging structure of scholarship.

Ort was attempting to reconcile differences which had disturbed the school for so many years. In theology he opened his mind to a revival of German scholarship and to the representations of the more conservative theologians. In the community, he opened the school to a reappraisal of its role in a modern industrial society and sought to establish cordial relations. In that too, he fell short of Stuckenberg's expectations. For alumni and students, he showed the way to bring about accommodation and change in curriculum and campus life, gradually and irenically. He was assembling a faculty in the new tradition, increasingly oriented to individual disciplines, each considering itself as important as any other. Ort believed he was ushering in a new golden era for Wittenberg, built upon its past, but not enslaved by it.

Chapter Ten

And the Past Said to the Present, "Go Forward"

The Board moved Wittenberg quickly in a new direction in selecting Samuel Alfred Ort to succeed Helwig. Many of Wittenberg's supporters felt that he was precisely the man needed to lead the school. He had acted with energy and diplomacy to help raise the funds needed to set Wittenberg permanently in Springfield. He was young, friendly, sociable, and well liked. The thirty-nine-year-old seminary professor would take both the college and the seminary into the future with energy and enthusiasm.

His inauguration occurred on a Monday following a stormy weekend in June 1882. There was a sense of crisis facing the college; and large numbers of the school's 300 living alumni came to the ceremony saying, "Now, of all times, Wittenbergers should stand together." Dr. Sprecher prayed for Divine aid to the New Wittenberg, exceeding that which God had extended to the Old. The *Wittenberger* said that Ort was "equal to the emergency" and spoke "in his usual forcible manner" both to Wittenberg alumni and to the community of Springfield.

It had not been a blunder, he said, to have founded Wittenberg in Springfield and, that while her fame had not yet spread widely outside Ohio, as local citizens might like, Wittenberg was yet in her youth and had a great future ahead. Ort referred to the supposed crisis and the critical time at hand, but assured all present that

Wittenberg was committed to moving forward. He believed that educators should clearly understand the world in which they functioned, and he was aware of the rampant materialism of the age and the demand for utilitarian education. Learning must be related to everyday life and to earning a living. But he was also a man of faith who accepted the Bible as the norm of life. Man had a higher calling than survival and ought to hear that calling in his college years. Ort was not a rationalist but believed the mind was just the instrument for the unification of all truth within man's reach—biblical and scientific. The Christian college, he insisted, would educate the student to "lift mankind to the higher plane." There would be "no controversy with science," and no debate with "practical education," but Wittenberg would not lose sight of "the truth that man has within him which craves more than the bread he eats." The nation needed colleges like Wittenberg, he added. "We plead for Wittenberg because she has a right to live" and to "become the institution that she was conceived to be from her beginning."

Ort was born in Lewiston, Pa., November 11, 1843. Before his teens, he spent three years in an academy to prepare himself for college entrance and built a solid foundation in Latin and Greek. In the summer of 1860, not yet seventeen, he entered Wittenberg with his brother Melanchthon, and graduated three years later with high honors. A member of the Philosophian Society, he represented the group as orator. He was active in athletics and was such a powerful kicker in rugby that he could kick the ball over the five-story college building from the depths of the hollow behind it. He achieved a mythic reputation that grew with time and was one of those remembered as having taken Pap Simon's horse to the top of the building. As a tutor, he joined with the students who organized Phi Kappa Psi at Wittenberg over student and faculty objections.

After college, he completed the theological course and was ordained at the age of twenty-two by the Wittenberg Synod. He was dedicated to the ministry by a pious mother who died when he was ten. He studied the catechism diligently and was ready for confirmation well before the normal age. The refusal of his pastor to receive him until he was older angered him; and when he reached the proper age, he refused to be confirmed. He joined the church in Springfield and was confirmed by Pastor Morris Officer.

After completing the theological course, Ort tutored for a year and then served his first pastorate in Findlay, Ohio. He taught at the Hagerstown Academy in Maryland until 1869. For the next five years, he taught English literature and mathematics at Wittenberg. His commanding appearance and friendly manner attracted the attention of the Board and he was elected secretary. From 1873 until his death, he was a delegate to every meeting of the General Synod. In 1873 he became Secretary of the General Synod, reelected twice, serving until 1879. He left Wittenberg in 1874, when Helwig was elected, to become pastor of First Lutheran Church in Louisville, Kentucky. From there he was called to the influential St. James Lutheran Church in New York. He returned to Wittenberg as professor of mental philosophy and sacred philology

Ort demonstrated the improved relationship between Wittenberg and Springfield in the first catalog issued after his election. The 1883-84 catalog dated the school's beginning from March 11, 1845. Gone were Helwig's references to the synod's 1842 action, the classes held in Wooster, and the move to Springfield. Wittenberg began in Springfield, was chartered for that specific, permanent location, and that was that. When other schools were stretching as far back as they could for as early a founding date as they could find, Ort gave up three years to demonstrate the commitment to Springfield.

The peace that Ort sought with Wittenberg's constituencies was illustrated in the ceremonies surrounding the construction and dedication of New Wittenberg. Students dubbed the building "Recitation Hall," a name which stuck because it was where they recited daily. They named the older building "Boy's Dorm" because it was where they lived. That neither structure was going to bear a man's name was a given. The school's theological stance would not allow it. In good pietistic tradition, no man should be so conceited, so boastful of his achievements that he would allow a building to be named after him. Immodest it was, but modesty was not the issue. Right out of the Book of Romans, the part of the Bible from which the basic principle of Luther's Reformation came—salvation through grace alone—came the admonition against boasting. No man was to be justified by his works, therefore why boast of what he had done. Without grace, no achievement was possible. It was a view that the gilded age would soon get over. But for the moment, that was it: Boy's Dorm and Recitation Hall; not a Mitchell Building to honor the largest donor, Ross Mitchell; not even a Sprecher Hall to honor the man who had firmly established the college. Neither would have agreed to it.

On January 30, 1883, the Board authorized construction. Gifts had reached $50,000 with more to come. With that promise, the Board approved the architect's plans at an estimated cost of $60,000. Prince was named chairman of the building committee. It would have recitation rooms, faculty offices, a library, laboratories for chemistry and physics, commodious new meeting rooms for the literary societies, and a chapel.

On a clear, bright afternoon in February, Prof. Prince, the contractors, and interested students and faculty marched southwest from the old building to a beautiful knoll. They stood silent for a few moments, according to George Gerlaw Clark, meditating on the event about to take place. Here, finally in the school's fourth decade, a second building was underway. Bearings were taken, and the place for the first stake marked. A seminarian Reuben Wagner, Wittenberg class of 1882, offered a $5 gold piece for the privilege of driving the first stake.

Fish and Crist of Springfield submitted the low bid to excavate the basement and do the stonework of the foundation. When they finished, the bricklayers began. By late May, the cornerstone could be put in place. Because of spring rains, the ceremony was postponed until May 24. Actually, according to Dr. Prince, the cornerstone was laid twice. Members of the junior class stole into the building the night before and conducted their own ceremony to confound the senior class who were to share in the official ceremony the next day. The official event symbolized a new beginning for the college, the town, the church, and the alumni. "The weather could not have been more delightful," observed the *Globe Republic*. "The sky was perfectly clear, not a cloud to be seen in it. The sun was pleasantly warm, and there was a refreshing breeze from the west."

The same pleasant and optimistic report could be given about the crowd gathered for the day, more than a thousand people. Churchmen in town for a meeting of the General Synod recessed to show support for the college. Alumni mingled with townspeople in a spirit of camaraderie; all cognizant of the small band of faculty and the host of students gathered in an air of friendship and common purpose. The event began in the grove in front of Old Wittenberg on a gentler part of the hill with spring flowers and greening grass underfoot and new green leaves overhead. Ort opened the ceremonies by reading the Psalm 113, "Praise ye the Lord. Praise, O ye servants of the Lord, praise the name of the Lord," he began. And ended by reading, "He maketh the barren woman to keep house, and to be a joyful mother of children. Praise ye the Lord." It was a day to praise God that Wittenberg's friends had come to her aid. For others who had waited for this day for so long, it was as if a barren woman had given birth. That such should come forth from the generosity of formerly estranged friends seemed miraculous.

The Rev. W. H. Webb, pastor of Springfield's Second Presbyterian Church offered the day's prayer. He thanked God that this was a land of liberty, knowledge, and Christian education, and for the past history of Wittenberg because from its halls and groves so many had gone forth to bless God and mankind. He asked God's blessings upon the Board, faculty, and students, and asked that they be a continuing power for good.

Ort introduced G. C. Rawlins, a local attorney, to speak on behalf of the citizens of Springfield. He commented on the cornerstone itself, dug like the building's foundation stones from the limestone shelf on which both college and town were built. The cornerstone represented the promise of the future, "hung round with memories coeval with the city." The stone told of the common past of town and college. The limestone had also enriched the soil of the area making a sweet alkaline, limestone-laced soil that was the basis of all the area's prosperity.

Wittenberg existed in this grove where the speaker and his listeners stood. But it also existed in the town's mercantile establishments, the area's farms, and in the streets and byways. It existed in all those places where its graduates had gone as teachers, missionaries, preachers, or in Federal army blue to die to save the union. Wittenberg needed to see itself larger than it had been prone to do, with a sense of place that was Springfield and a mission that embraced the world. Rawlins concluded with the town's pioneers. "We speak of George Rogers Clark, of Charles Anthony, of William A. Rogers, and of Samson Mason . . . we say Macpelah and Ferncliff are ours; that this fertile valley yonder bright city with its people happy, prosperous, and free are ours; and by the same token, we cherish this college as part of our heritage."

Dr. Michael W. Hamma, of Baltimore, MD, Lutheran pastor, and one of the bright young lights among the schools' alumni was next. He praised Keller and Sprecher, Keller for his foresight in picking the school's location, Sprecher for the sense of academic purpose which he had conferred upon the place. A graduate owed more to Dr. Sprecher than to any other person beside his mother, Hamma asserted. Under his influence, the school became a place of serious pursuits, respected by other institutions, acknowledged as one of the West's better schools. "During these forty years," he added, "graduates have gone out equipped for the battle of life to every state, destined to positions of profit and power and good." The children of Wittenberg had emerged to take their places in the world, and the future would be even more fruitful than the past.

The next speaker was George Scholl, class of 1868, now a Lutheran pastor also from Baltimore. As an undergraduate, he had been one of those who were instrumental in establishing the Greek letter system at Wittenberg, in spite of Board and faculty opposition. He was one of editor Nichols's allies in the battle for modernity and had assisted with the underground newspapers of his day. It was part of the remarkable nature of the occasion that he—a former student rebel—was present on the same platform with the officers of the Board and the faculty. With the frankness of youth, he spoke bluntly of his gratitude that Wittenberg was to stay in Springfield. There were only two spots on earth that he felt compelled to revisit, he said. The first was his childhood home, "where cluster the memories of a mother's Christian teaching." The other was the Wittenberg grove, "my Alma Mater" and its setting in Springfield, Ohio. He was glad, he said, that this union of town and gown, where he and all the other "old boys" had received both their formal and their more practical educations was not to be broken.

Next among the speakers was Dr. F. W. Conrad, of Philadelphia, formerly of Dayton and Springfield; the man who Sprecher had so earnestly sought for Wittenberg and with whom he had a falling out over *The Recension of the Augsburg Confession* back in the 1850s. They had patched up their differences and became friends once again, in a friendship that would last to the end of their lives. Conrad began by reminiscing and comparing the old with the new Springfield. "Memory takes me back thirty-eight years," he said. "Then Springfield had only seven thousand people, now it has thirty thousand. Then its wealth was computed by tens of thousands, now by tens of millions." Then it could subscribe only a few thousand dollars for the beginning of the college, now it could offer more than $60,000 for one building. Then the Lutherans were a small body in "the rear guard of the religious host," now they occupied a leading position.

Conrad stressed the significance of the ceremony of the cornerstone laying. The scriptures, he said, put special emphasis on beginnings. He stressed the importance of the occasion for Wittenberg's future. He saluted the venerable Dr. Sprecher, and the crowd was moved. Even more they must have responded to his perceptive observation that on this day, when Wittenberg's history had been so thoroughly reviewed, the past had finally said to the present, "Go forward!" It was time for Wittenberg to move into a new era. He ended with the prayer *Esto Perpetua*—may Wittenberg live forever!

Ort expressed thanks to the people of Springfield. This day, he said, was only possible because of the generosity of the people of this fine city. Then he asked the group to move to the southeast corner of the building. When they had found a comfortable position, students and workmen perched on the unfinished walls; the stone was moved into view. Conrad opened the ceremony with prayer. Then Ort read the list of articles as they were placed into the copper box that would be placed in the stone. The contents illustrated the reconciliation that was taking place just as much as the speeches of the day.

First into the box were the constitutions of the Excelsior and Philosophian Societies and a list of their members. Next was a list of the faculty and members of the building committee. Then, copies of the *Beta theta Pi*, the Phi Kappa Psi *Shield*, and the *Alpha Tau Omega*, Greek letter society magazines were added. A copy of the 1845 charter and the constitution of the college were next. Demonstrating the influential role which the press played in Wittenberg life, a group of church and area journals was added: the *Lutheran Observer*, the *Springfield Republic*, the *Weekly Republic*, the *Wittenberger* and the *Transcript*, student papers, the weekly and daily Springfield *Globe*, *Springfield Journal*, the daily and weekly Springfield *Gazette*, the 1882-83 college catalog, and the *Missionary Journal*. Lists of the names of all students currently enrolled in the preparatory, college, and seminary classes were added. The collection was completed with the addition of a copy of the *King James Bible*, the *Lutheran Book of Worship*, with the common service, and sketches of the lives of Keller and Sprecher.

Dr. Sprecher had been chosen to put the box into place and to set the stone. It was a dramatic moment. Because of his health, he had asked for a leave of absence; within a year, he would retire and move to California.

Samuel Sprecher near retirement after a lifetime of service to Wittenberg. Wittenberg University Archives.

Taking the box in his hands, he rose, his white hair tossed by the breeze, his twelve-inch beard obscuring his notes. One observer said the old doctor looked like an Albrecht Durer painting of one of the patriarchs. His voice trembling with age and emotion, Sprecher said, "About an ordinary generation ago, we laid the cornerstone of the old Wittenberg in what was then almost a wilderness." Now the new Wittenberg, like the old was to be dedicated to the cause of religion and science. Since the days of Melanchthon, he noted, it has been the custom of the Church to keep faith and reason together. That would later be called the Protestant Principle, the juxtaposition of Faith and Reason.

For a moment, all of the "old boys" in the audience felt transported back to a Friday afternoon lecture in Moral Science, a lecture such as the good Doctor often delivered at the end of a week of exemplary recitations. He was quietly reviewing the educational philosophy that had always motivated him: the combination of faith and learning, religion refocused by modern science, a commitment to the new mode of thought wherever it might lead men of faith. It was a Sprecher the crowd could respond to because many had responded in their youth, even those who had now adopted a more conservative theological stance; in his words, they sensed the essence of their college.

"We therefore lay the cornerstone of the new Wittenberg," Sprecher said, "in the name of the Father, Son, and Holy Ghost, the God of Christians, and in the interest of true religion and true science." He then offered words of prayer. The box was moved into position and the stone put in place. He tapped each corner with his hammer. Ort gave the benediction. It had been a day of deep meaning and great joy.

Later, at the other end of the building, the northeast corner, another smaller stone was put into place by the class of 1883. It bore the belligerent Latin inscription *Aut Vincere aut Mori*. Perhaps it reflected the spirit of those who would have Wittenberg remain in Springfield or the intensity of the battle between the two factions, or perhaps it was a reference to the increasingly vigorous student athletic competition or the ever present bravado of students. The English translation was, "either vanquish or die."

The brickwork was continued throughout the summer and finished by the end of December and the building under roof. Windows were put in to secure the building from winter weather. Work had been slowing down to await the arrival of funds for its completion. In the winter of 1884, work ceased altogether and the building stood incomplete, a mockery of the new day heralded at the cornerstone laying. Finally in the spring, funds arrived for the completion of the building. Springfielders had provided $60,000, but final costs were $67,300. The building itself, according to Benjamin Prince's figures, exceeded $62,800. The remainder was the costs of furnishings and equipment. The overrun for furnishings and equipment caused the problem and the delay.

At commencement in 1886, the new building was dedicated and ready for use.

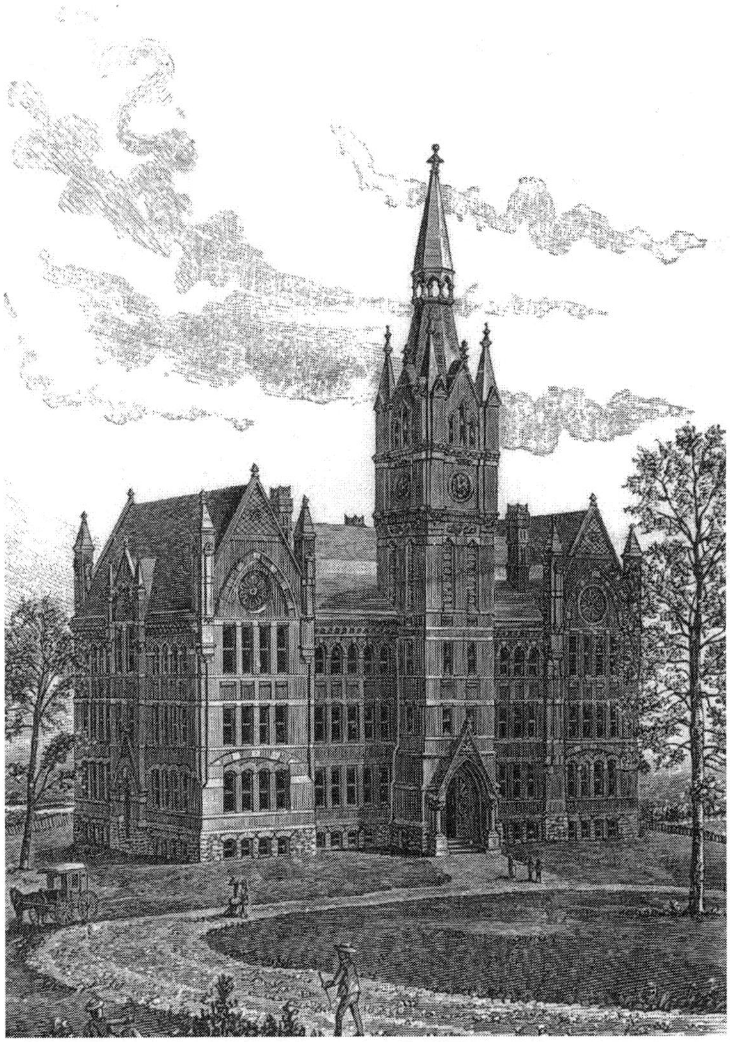

Contemporary sketch of Recitation Hall, circa 1886. Wittenberg University Archives.

There was general rejoicing, according to Prince, that the building for which all had waited so long was now complete. Once again a celebration was held in the college grove, in the center of the campus, the same grove in which commencements were now held. It was the very heart of the campus. President Ort was the master of ceremonies and made brief remarks welcoming the crowd of visitors. The college, he said, had passed its fortieth year and was now prepared to do even greater work. He then introduced former president John B. Helwig for the main address. He had not been present at the cornerstone laying. His life story had not been placed in the copper box with those of Keller and Sprecher. Now he was ready to join in the public display in which diverse parties showed support for the college.

Helwig's address was entitled "The Needs of Wittenberg." In it, recognizing that he had lost the battle to move the school, he laid out the needs that had to be met to create a first-class modern institution in Springfield. What he didn't quite say was that he did not believe Springfield had in the past or would in the future provide its fair share toward meeting those needs. He began by quoting from a Springfield newspaper article that had appeared in 1880 in which the editor, his personal nemesis, had insisted that Wittenberg needed to be enlarged and improved, to be made broader and stronger and better. Only money could do it, Helwig asserted. Prince approved of the "forcible" way Helwig had put the issue. Some thought that, as usual, he had been far too blunt in his statements.

While Prince remembered how Helwig put it to Springfielders one last time, George Gerlaw Clark, that invaluable student chronicler, remembered something else. Helwig, he said, talked about the ideal New Wittenberg that the new building symbolized. This new Wittenberg, according to Helwig, had certain characteristics: a concentration of study in new emerging fields of social science and a more thorough study in individual disciplines because the new age would demand it. Students would have to discipline their minds more rigorously than before. The new education, he said, had to be the education of "the whole man." This building, he said, was dedicated to the new Wittenberg, to the whole person, to the new learning, to head and heart, to temperance, and to hard work. It would be a nurturing place seeking to bring out the best in every student.

Helwig was probably the first person at Wittenberg to use the phrase, "educating the whole person." It represented a shift in curriculum based on the self-development of the student in class and out. Noah Porter and Theodore Dwight Woolsey, at Yale, in 1846, talked of the role of education in developing a student's true freedom and wholeness. They repudiated the Yale report of 1828 and its defense of the old line classic college course. Their objectives were inspired by the same German idealism and philology that Stuckenberg brought later to Wittenberg. The variety of new disciplines that comprised the curriculum would find their unity in the concept of the "whole person."

After Helwig spoke, an offering was taken. Then Oscar T. Martin, an alumnus and an attorney, spoke on behalf of area citizens. He spoke eloquently of the industrial and educational growth of the city and the state. He took special note of what Wittenberg had accomplished in just a few short years. "As I stand at the foundation of the new Wittenberg," he said with rising emotion, "I look to the future with heart-throbbing pleasure and most earnestly yet reverently wish her Godspeed."

In spite of Helwig's continuing doubts about the local community, many townsmen felt a sincere concern about the school's future. For those who loved the college and the town, whatever their other perspectives, this was an emotional day. When they said they wished the best for Wittenberg, this may have meant different things to different people, but they were all well-meaning and sincere.

Benjamin Prince then gave a month by month and dollar for dollar accounting of the building process. While he might have wished that he would someday be president of the college, he served an invaluable function as he increasingly took charge of the business affairs previously handled by Professor Geiger. He presented the keys to the new building to the Rev. A. J. Imhoff, president of the Board. Pastor Imhoff thanked the citizens of Springfield once more for their enterprise and their generosity. Prince later confided that it was a great day for the college, and that the new building was an inspiration to students and faculty to do even better work as they did it under more favorable conditions.

Moving into the building was no easy matter. The three libraries had to be moved—the college's, the Philosophian's, and the Excelsior's—and they had to be merged in one single library room. It was located in the first-floor oval-shaped space under the second-floor chapel. This was a great step forward, achieved after much wrangling and negotiation. It gave all students, including the ladies, access to all the collections. Regular hours were now set for the library to be open, and a library fee of $1.50 per year was charged to provide for the purchase of books and magazines.

Furniture for all the classrooms and faculty offices had to be acquired and moved in. President Ort occupied Room 1 on the first floor, southeast corner. The heating system had yet to be installed, but each of the main rooms had its own fireplace. All of the windows had to be fitted for shades. The ladies "Gab Room" had to be moved from what was now the Boy's Dorm. Their new room was much larger and located next to Dr. Ort's office. The women needed a large new carpet and better furniture, and they set out with all the persuasive powers they possessed to raise money from friends in town and on campus. They also considered a new name for their new room. "Grotto of Graces," was one suggestion. Some liked the ring of it; but "Gab Room" was too deeply rooted in the popular vocabulary, and it persisted.

Moving the literary societies presented a different problem. As the new building was completed, the burning question was which one, Excelsior or Philosophian, would occupy the south end of the third floor, above the cornerstone and with its great view of the city of Springfield, and which the north end. President Ort and Prof. Breckenridge received the conflicting views of the two societies on the lawn in front of the Dorm. "Every window on that side of the building," said student Charles Heckert, "presented an interested spectator." Heckert, who would later become president of Wittenberg, said he argued his cause, but in vain, that the older society should have the preferred location. Ort and Breckenridge opted for flipping a coin. Heckert said he was cut short in his attempt to assert the immorality of casting lots when Breckenridge asked him for a coin. Philo lost the toss, and the Excelsiors won the preferred southern location.

The two societies had new spaces to outfit and decorate. They did them up in the finest style of the era. The YMCA acquired the old Excelsior hall in the dorm and was assisted by First Lutheran Church in outfitting it for their use. The old Philo space was converted into additional dormitory rooms to house more students.

Springfield's Lutheran Church was now being called First Lutheran because in January 1884, fifty members departed to establish Second Lutheran on Clifton Street. The English Lutherans began numbering their congregations like the Congregationalists in New England. The official history of First Lutheran suggests that it was an amicable separation. Keller's widow, now Mrs. Peter A. Schindler, her new family, and daughter Sally Keller, now Mrs. Ross Mitchell, provided the nucleus. It was as if when the Dutchmen left the faculty, the remaining original families left First Lutheran Church. Both congregations remained Americanist and declined to use the Common Service.

The department that benefited most from the opening of the new building was Science. After years of laboring under severe handicaps, the presence of running city water and artificial gas meant that real experiments could be undertaken. The one thing that differentiated the new from the old science was the laboratory and the experimental method of study. Both chemistry and physics blossomed in the new environment.

Only one thing was missing in the new building. The clock tower had no clock, and there was little hope in getting one because of cost. The four open circles were boarded up with small round windows in the center and would remain so for a hundred years. The opening of Recitation Hall, however, set the tone for the Ort administration as one of growth and progress.

Ort would be the first president to be called a "building president." In 1887 he asked the Board for a ladies' hall, and they approved borrowing money to do it. The project was delayed while the Prudential Committee debated sites. Finally they agreed upon a site north of the house they had built for President Helwig outside the main entrance and across from the Prince House. In 1889 Dr. Michael M. Hamma, Ort's good friend, provided money to erect a separate building for the seminary. Also in 1889, students petitioned for a gymnasium. Ort supported their request, but the Board said that he would have to raise the money to do it; they would not borrow for that purpose. Then in 1892, Wittenberg added the Zimmerman Library. Alumni gifts built three of these structures.

The Hamma proposal called for a special meeting of the Board where it was received enthusiastically. There were strings attached. Almira Crothers Hamma, whose family's money was to be the source of the gift, had insisted that the building be named for her husband. More orthodox Lutherans, like Mrs. Hamma, had less of the pietism of the Americanists and were willing to name buildings for persons other than themselves. Pastor Hamma had something else in mind. He wanted the Wittenberg Seminary to pay particular attention to older men who later in their lives felt a call to the gospel ministry, who, because of their age, had unique issues to be taken into account. He was concerned about a shortage of ministers and was certain that there were many men in their thirties or older who had changed their view of life and purpose. It became a unique program among Lutheran seminaries when the Board accepted the gift and its two conditions. It would not be Hamma's last gift to his Alma Mater.

In 1889 Ort proposed renovating the Boy's Dorm, the first of many renovations in the building's long history. Needed repairs and improvements were estimated at $3,000: new flooring, new windows, painting inside and out, lots of minor repairs in every room, and, miracle of miracles, inside toilets and showers. It was at this time that the building's white-washed exterior was traded for red brick paint to better seal the porous brick. For thirty-eight years, it had been a large white building at the top of the hill. The red, all said, looked better, since between whitewashings, the building had often looked gray and dirty. Over summer all of the work was completed at a cost of $3,250. In 1899 Ort proposed a further upgrading. Modern students, he said, insisted on more amenities. He suggested a steam-heating system, but it would be up to his successor to get that job done. He also left to the future the pillars and the massive front portico not yet built. The merely decorative feature, like the clock in "Reci's" tower or the portico on the dorm, always seemed to give way to that which was more necessary.

The Zimmerman family sought to meet another of the school's pressing needs, a library building. They wanted a memorial to their deceased brother, Rev. Joseph Clark Zimmerman, Secretary of the Board for Church Extension of the General Synod. John L. Zimmerman, class of 1879, was the leading figure in the enterprise, and he thought it could be named for his brother without any compromise of principle. It was not that he was naming it after himself. It was a salute to pastors who wore themselves out in service to others.

Sketch of the original Zimmerman Library built in 1892. Wittenberg University Archives.

Construction began in late summer of 1891 following local architect R. C. Gotwald's plan, and was completed the next year. It was a beautiful stone gem in the Richardson Romanesque style so popular in Springfield. The architect sited it at the top of a rise over the hollow northwest of the dormitory. When it was finished, students moved all of the books from "Reci" to the new library building. As they were carried in, they were reclassified and assigned to stacks by a new subject index. Wittenberg gained, at least briefly, the distinction of being "the only college in Ohio that had a building devoted exclusively to library purposes," said the *Wittenberger*, for March 6, 1894.

In reporting the dedication, Springfield journalists fell into the new florid mode for describing college settings. There was a way of writing about colleges emerging, and local editors adopted it. "'Neath the spreading branches and leafy boughs of Old Wittenberg's classic campus," they wrote, "the dedicatory exercises of the Zimmerman Library were held . . . The patter of raindrops, the chirping of a bird, or the picking strokes of a woodpecker tended to disturb the exercises." Use of the passive voice and a focus on the rural and natural, even bucolic country scene in phrases that gave campuses an aura of being a natural, preserve outside the hustle and bustle of the harsh urban industrial society became the norm. The illusion of quiet, of being detached, of being lost in the groves of academe was a popular myth to be cultivated.

A few months later, fifty students petitioned the Board for an athletic field. They were eager to enter intercollegiate athletic competition and needed a place to practice and to entertain visiting teams. They had been using the city YMCA fields on the shores of Buck Creek, but they were giving way to new housing developments by builders of the houses east of Limestone Street on Sherman and Stanton Avenues and further north.

The Board approved the request and looked at the Hawley property north of the campus as a probable site. They authorized the purchase of an adjoining parcel of land to widen the field sufficiently to accommodate football and field sports. The project received immediate attention because John L. Zimmerman stepped forward to provide the necessary funds. The result was Zimmerman Field, so named by the students in their exuberance to honor their friend and champion. In addition, to complete the breadth of their generosity, the Zimmermans provided the funds to plaster and paint the new chapel in Recitation Hall. Nothing symbolized the new emerging Wittenberg more than the generosity of this Springfield and alumni family in providing almost simultaneously the new chapel, the library, and the athletic fields for the college.

While the school developed new buildings and playing fields, it was natural that the Board turned its attention to campus planning. Finding a site for each new project meant laying out a campus. In the beginning, the school had located buildings in the woods, clearing land around them to enable them to function. Now there was growing interest in developing a real campus. This was the

A youthful John L. Zimmerman, class of 1879, Springfield attorney and long time treasurer, Wittenberg University Archives.

era of the development of great parks like Central Park in New York City, Rock Creek Park in the nation's capital, even Snyder Park in Springfield, Ohio, that stretched from the center of town to the western city limits, meandering along Buck Creek. With Snyder Park, Ferncliff cemetery, and an 18-hole golf course on Springfield's west side, there was an immense green space adjoining the Wittenberg property of which it was a part. Landscape architects like Frederick Law Olmsted were at the peak of their popularity. The development of campuses as parks, even arboretums, was a growing trend. At Wittenberg the Board and faculty had been selecting sites for buildings and houses without very much attention to the grounds along the connecting paths. The area possessed such a natural beauty that their oversight was not too noticeable.

In 1890 a special committee was appointed to recommend action. It proposed a landscape gardener to develop plans by which the entire grounds of the college might be developed into a campus. This ambitious idea, however, would not come to fruition until the 1920s. Not having funds for it in 1890, the Board proposed to keep up the drives and the roadways, take out dead timber, and plant 150 young trees. This minimal action pleased Professor Prince. He had become nervous as the Board talked of having a landscape gardener to beautify the campus. The Wittenberg grounds, he knew in his soul, were already among the most beautiful in the nation: the hills, the cliffs, the brook, the streams, and the monarchs of the forest, giant hickory, elm, linden, sugar trees, black oak, and white oak. Nothing could improve such natural scenes. Even the Indians and the mound builders appreciated the area's natural beauty, its plentiful fruits, berries, nuts, and herbs, and its constant flowing springs.

Prince knew civilization was catching up with the area. Soil was being packed down by heavier traffic, and the water table was dropping. Hard winter freezes, tornadoes, severe thunder storms, and droughts combined over the years with human factors to bring down the giant, aging monarchs. Tree replanting was essential. A new period was at hand for the college grounds, said Prince; but the natural configuration should never be destroyed. No self-respecting landscape gardener would think of altering nature's basic design of the area, he assured himself, but he was fearful of the risk. All Wittenberg needed to do, he was certain, was to help nature here and there with a gentle touch.

Students participated in the planting of the trees. Beginning in 1872, each senior class planted class trees somewhere on the campus. Virtually every class planted at least one tree and some planted more. Students and faculty have also planted trees in memory of a deceased friend or staff member.

There was another natural facility on the campus that had to be dispensed with. In this case, Prince recognized the need for change, but he regretted it. He put into words the sense of loss that many felt. It was the college well, now to be replaced by indoor running water. It had stood at the back of the dorm for nearly forty years, furnishing cool and refreshing water for every student generation. Springfield's many natural springs gushed forth water at a constant fifty-seven degrees Fahrenheit, winter or summer. It was the reason Springfield was given her name; springs everywhere. The town's one unlimited natural resource: a pure, unending supply of cool water.

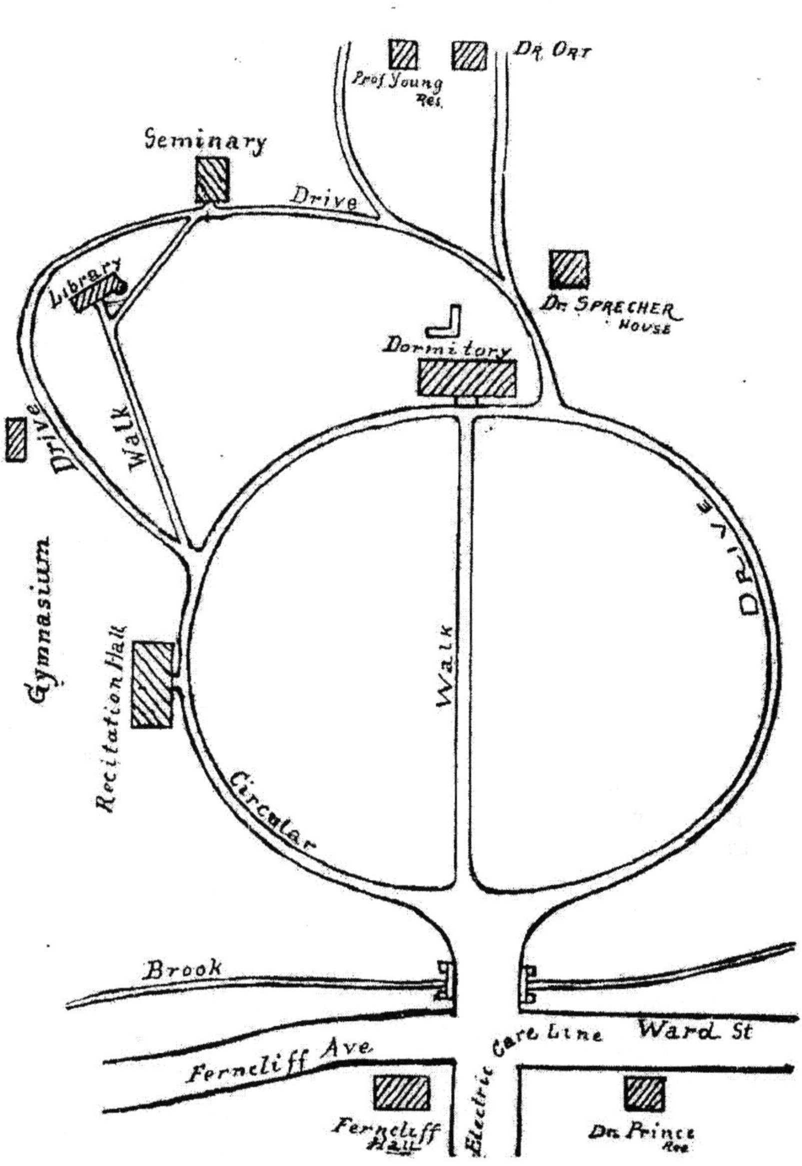

PLAT OF CAMPUS SHOWING LOCATION OF BUILDINGS.

Map of the campus in 1895. The Springfield Electric Street Rail Line stopped at the campus entrance. Wittenberg University Archives.

There was no fabled "moss covered bucket by the well," noted Prince; but there was an iron handle, which, with but a slight stroke, brought up "the cooling drink for the thirsty lad." There was an iron cup fastened by a chain to the pump stock. The cup was cold to the lips in winter; you had to watch to see that your lips did not stick to the rim in freezing weather. Yet in summer, as the cup hung in the hot sun, it reached a temperature high enough to nearly fry your lips, if you forgot to run the cool water over the edge for a few seconds before drinking.

Those who used the well day after day could never forget it, said Prince. Subsequent generations would have no conception of how many memories clustered about the old pump that quickly lifted the sparkling water from the depths of the hillside every morning, noon, and night for every student. It was a place of meeting, a place of conniving and plotting, of confessing and confiding, or just conversing, trading a story, or settling a dispute. The well was a figure of speech in orations and debates and in private conversations; it was as if an entire lifetime transpired "at the well." At least one campus playwright included a scene "at the pump." But the sad day for the old well, said Prince, came all too soon. A little outbreak of typhoid fever in the area brought all wells under suspicion. City water with its summer variations in temperature took the place of the ever cool water of the college well.

By 1900, after a series of disastrous fires in the city, Springfield's fire department sought permission to run a water main onto the campus to the top of the hill, placing a fire hydrant next to the dorm. The college gladly consented and gave the city a right of way and free access to make repairs. In spite of this, a couple of years later the seminary building—a hundred yards from the hydrant—burned to the ground. They then extended the main the rest of the way through the campus to the housing area developing to the north with an additional hydrant between the seminary and the athletic fields. There was also an effort to extend lines for artificial or natural gas.

The area around the campus experienced great urban development from 1874 to 1900. That in large part accounted for the dropping water table and other environmental changes. The Urbana road, known in town as Limestone Street, had been a rural road north of Buck Creek; but by 1874, there was extensive subdivision and development east and west of it. By 1875 the intersection of McCreight Avenue and

Limestone Street, a mile northeast of the campus, represented the northernmost thrust of city development. That same year, Market Street (renamed Fountain Avenue for the beautiful wrought iron fountain on the esplanade), was extended north as was Center Street (called Woodlawn Avenue), which bordered the eastern edge of the campus.

Several streets crossed Buck Creek carrying the town north: Spring, Limestone, Center, Factory, Wittenberg, and Plum. All but one had a bridge. It was a rich town that built four bridges, all within a few blocks of one another, to provide easy access from south to north. Taxpayers on the south side resented the cost of making Springfield a town on two sides of the creek and saw it as a boon mostly to real estate developers.

Around Wittenberg all of the side streets connecting the new north-south streets were laid out: College Avenue, Cecil Street (now Bill Edwards Drive), and Ward Street. Park Place was cut through and divided into building lots by S. A. Bowman. Much of the subdividing was done by George H. Frey, J. Ward Frey, and other heirs of Isaac Ward who for years had held the lands bordering the campus. It was they, perhaps, who gained the most from Wittenberg's decision to remain in Springfield. By 1900, all of the streets from Limestone to Plum and from the cliffs at Buck Creek to McCreight had been laid out and houses had been built in great numbers.

In 1887 a group of members from First Lutheran Church had formed the Fourth Lutheran Church Corporation to purchase lots on north Fountain Ave., a block from the campus. The congregation is now known as Good Shepherd Lutheran Church. The growth in the campus area included the homes of many faculty and staff members, and meant that a new church would be needed. Organizational meetings were held in Prince's house, and Sunday services were held in the college chapel in Recitation Hall. The congregation was established on May 23, 1897. Most staff and faculty joined and students began attending. The congregation was Fourth Lutheran because a third congregation had grown out of First and organized in Springfield's south end.

In 1895 the Phi Kappa Psi fraternity ventured into the college neighborhood, the first group to abandon quarters downtown for the campus. They rented the old Isaac Ward house southwest of campus as Wittenberg's first fraternity house. Many residences on the side streets were modest bungalows and double houses. Springfield developed more double houses than any other city in America, as Harry S. Kissell, Wittenberg alumnus and real estate developer, sold people on the idea of living in one-half of the structure, while allowing income from the other half to cover the mortgage.

On the main thoroughfares, citizens built magnificent Victorian homes, some in Queen Anne style with large turrets and round porches, others in Italianate style or Greek Revival or Colonial. The heavily wooded area with gently rolling hills made a variety of styles readily compatible. Alleyways cut through the square blocks at right angles so that service and trade calls could be made discretely to the back doors in good Victorian style.

The changes wrought on campus and in the surrounding countryside from Ort's inauguration in 1882 to the turn of the century seemed phenomenal indeed. Modern Wittenberg had clearly emerged. The college in the forest some distance from town was now located in the midst of one of Springfield's finest residential neighborhoods. But Ort's development of the modern Wittenberg looked easier than it was and, after 1895, the President's tasks became more difficult. The economy took a turn for the worse, his top faculty was often enticed away, seminary issues again heated up, and personal tragedy visited Ort's family circle.

Chapter Eleven

Educating the Whole Person

Ort's plans for the new Wittenberg were not concerned primarily with new buildings and neighborhood development as important as these were. Simultaneously he focused on bold advances in the undergraduate curriculum and a major redirection of theological education. In 1883, in the first catalog issued after he became President, significant change was apparent. The classical course leading to the bachelor of arts degree was joined by a scientific course with the bachelor of science degree. A literature course leading to the bachelor of literature degree was later combined in the B. A. program.

Wittenberg introduced limited elective studies for juniors and seniors, the first Lutheran college to do so formally. Faculty action followed years of student agitation and petitions for an elective system. A strongly worded petition from students urged an even wider availability of electives. By 1890 there were electives for all four classes, and the faculty designed a required basic course of literature, languages, mathematics, and science required of all students with a variety of electives to complete the degree of choice.

Entrance requirements were increased after Ort's election. All entering students were examined in the areas of Latin, Greek, Mathematics, English, History, and Geography; and the examinations were more extensive. Allowances were made for differences in preparation for science and literature. Candidates for admission to the classical course were examined in Latin and Greek; those entering the science program were tested in Latin and German; and those pursuing the literature course could elect to be examined in any two languages selected from Greek, Latin, German, or French. The school calendar was changed from two unequal semesters to three unequal terms.

Ort and the faculty were aware of the rapid changes underway in higher education and worked hard to bring the Board along. Wittenberg should stay abreast of the general progress of the times, said Ort. He called for an ever larger faculty, better facilities and equipment, a larger endowment, higher standards of performance, and scholarships to attract the better students. All progressive colleges were doing all these things, he told the board, and "Wittenberg must fall into line and keep step to the music of the onward march of today." He would lead them into the mainstream if only they would go.

In 1885 the faculty moved all classes forward one year and dropped the freshman level of work to the realm of entrance requirements. Freshmen began in what had been the sophomore course. A new more advanced senior year was added. By 1887 oral examinations were replaced with written comprehensive tests. Gradually written tests became the standard, causing a major shift in student life. Forensic prowess gave way to English composition as the chief tool for giving evidence of learning. The literary societies waned further in importance to students.

Finally after five years of fast paced curricular change, the school required for admission evidence of a four-year college preparatory course taken in an academy or at a first-rate public high school. All the changes made between 1883 and 1888 at first discouraged enrollment. In his first year as President, Ort greeted thirty-five new freshmen. The following year only seventeen were admitted. The demands of the times justified higher requirements to Ort's way of thinking. He sought not the plaudits of "the generation now in the midst of the toil and battle of life," but that of the generations to come.

If the student presented evidence of proper preparation, passed the entrance examinations, and had good recommendations, he was admitted as a "probationer." At the end of three weeks, if conduct and studiousness met with faculty approval, he became a fully matriculated member of the campus community by signing the student pledge to obey the rules of the institution. "Colleges are founded for the purpose of educating those who come to study," said Ort, "they are not places of amusement or houses of correction." Each was to prove his good character and willingness to study.

Rephrasing Samuel Sprecher's honor system under which he himself had studied, Ort pointed out that every student was received as a lady or gentleman, "trusted to conduct himself in truthfulness and uprightness, in kindness and respect, in diligence and sobriety, in obedience to law and maintenance of order, and regard for Christian institutions." These were high expectations indeed. To Ort student honor meant that the student lived up to the code of what was honorable. If he did not, the matter was no longer in student hands. The privileges of the college community, he observed, outlining conditions for dismissal, could not be retained by those who violated the college code.

At matriculation students had long been expected to sign the following pledge: "I sincerely promise, while I remain connected with this institution, to obey all its rules and regulations and treat my instructors, fellow students, and others with respect." An editor for the *Wittenberg Weekly Wasp*, student newspaper, noted that by 1893, the school had gotten lax in enforcing the signing of the pledge and was endeavoring to find all those who had escaped. "It is an experience every student ought to have," observed one faculty member. The editor remembered marching down the center aisle of the chapel to sign the card in front of the whole student body and "under the dread eye of the doctor himself, feeling the full weight of obligation we labored under."

Students pushed for reform and leniency. They objected to the grading system as "a meaningless form to which students must submit and which encouraged cheating, cramming, and the use of ponies."

The "pony," originally, was an English translation of a Greek or Latin text that saved a student the hard work of making his own translation. They later appeared for a great variety of college subjects. Students rehearsed the "inconsistencies and absurdities" of a grading system which, they said, was too subjective. In its place they advocated the German system in which a student studied until ready to take final examinations for his degree. Not succeeding, they petitioned to eliminate honors at commencement based, they said, on slight variations in grade averages earned by dubious means and asked to march in alphabetical order rather than by class rank. Only the latter request was granted.

Yearbook cartoon by Harry Trotwood Blount, class of 1896, *"95 Cycle."* Wittenberg University Archives.

"Wittenberg College is always ready to recognize whatever in the new education is valuable," said Ort, mulling over the ferment in higher education. Still, he continued, Wittenberg adhered firmly to the original intent of the college course: "the highest unique development of the several powers of the human mind." True to its German heritage, it must also enlarge the area of man's knowledge in science, philosophy, and religion. Through it all, the Christian scholar was to learn to live effectively in society and in cooperation with his fellow man.

In defining the new Wittenberg, Ort embraced new trends in education and the new experimental sciences. He sought to define Wittenberg as an undergraduate college in the emerging system of colleges and universities. But he was also receptive to many of the changes that students would make in their lifestyles. He took seriously Stuckenberg's admonition that colleges take young men as they are and allow an array of activities to absorb their energies. He was unwilling to accept, however, the total liberty of the student as practiced in the German university where all were allowed to rise or fall, sink or swim, by their own personal, adolescent choices. Ort reflected Helwig's phraseology about developing the whole person by a well-rounded educational experience.

He amended the part of the catalog which dealt with "religious exercises." After disciplined behavior, this was the next step in his program for achieving what he called the disciplined soul. "There cannot be any deep culture or any truly healthful mental progress," he observed, "separate from a genuine spirit of religion and worship." He was aware of the number of non-Lutheran students and was responsive to complaints that students had been required to attend Lutheran services regardless of their preference. He was also aware that Lutherans no longer agreed on what the religious requirements should be. He abandoned the campus congregation, and parents of each student were asked once again to designate the church in town which their son or daughter was to attend. Only if they failed to do so was the student required to attend services at the college church, still conducted very much in the American pattern.

Daily chapel services, however, were another matter. Many students objected to these required services. In an approved student paper called the *College Stylus*, the editor in February 1883, noted that Harvard and Cornell had given up compulsory chapel as part of the official educational program. "The tendency among the leading institutions," the editor observed, "seems to be toward making the student more of a free agent and less of a machine." He advocated similar progressivism for Wittenberg. A year earlier, the editor had been more insistent. The compulsory chapel rule, he said, was virtually dead, killed by student resistance and noncompliance. It was more difficult to enforce than it was worth, he added, and "our faculty would do well to strike it from the list." Students came to acquire knowledge and did not expect forced worship. The matter should be left to the student's free will. "Sooner or later," he concluded, "it will come to that."

Ort was willing to make chapel a voluntary matter, and the faculty supported him. He was willing to go even further in liberalizing matters of religion, suggesting that Sunday Bible study no longer be required but be made available as a voluntary activity. The more professional approach to theological studies emerging in the seminary made that faculty eager to abandon teaching the Bible classes which had been part of their responsibility to students in the college.

This new direction was criticized by both laymen and clergy outside the institution and by both Americanists and confessionalists. Ort spoke bluntly in response. You did not establish Christian education by holding chapel services and requiring Bible study on Sunday afternoon. Nor was it merely a matter of campus environment and faculty commitment. All of these might be a part of the whole, but "that education is only Christian," he observed, "which apprehends the truths of science and philosophy . . . in the light of the Christian view of all reality." He believed that students could not comprehend the universe of truth apart from Christianity and teachers could neither comprehend nor teach apart from Christianity. Christian education in the final analysis, then, depended upon the faith of teachers and students, not upon requirements. It was an advanced position; and it implied that once the faith of faculty and students disappeared, the church-relatedness of the college went with it.

True Christian education, Ort believed, was not narrow-minded and restrictive. There was no place in it for what he described as dogmatic or oracular instruction. It involved no limitations upon curriculum or upon course content. It was a matter of viewpoint and attitude. The task of the Christian scholar was still to reconcile faith and science. It was not a matter of avoiding issues or protecting students from areas of conflict; it was a matter of meeting situations directly with the earnest conviction that the teacher in a Christian college would reach the heart as well as the mind. Ort's views were reminiscent of those of his mentor, the venerable Dr. Sprecher; but they were redefined to fit the needs of the latter part of the nineteenth century. He did not talk of disciplining the faculties of the mind, a theory of education under attack. He talked of disciplining the faculties of the soul. Difficult subjects studied with diligence for an extended period of time in the face of specific tests graded on a high standard set by a competent and Christian faculty in an atmosphere of freedom and responsibility provided the discipline of the soul about which he spoke.

It was parents and the general society who set the overall dimensions of the religious community. In the school, a variety of provisions attentive to religious differences would fit in with that proper nurturing climate. Something of a model for him was the original University of Wittenberg in Germany. It was founded without the permission of any ecclesiastical authority, though it was approved five years later by Papal endorsement. It was the first university founded by a German prince. It was established in 1502 by an edict of Frederick III, called the Wise, one of the Electors of the Holy Roman Emperor The seal bore his likeness and read: "Wittenberg began teaching under my auspices." This independent character of the institution played an important role in the school's future and in the life of the young scholar Martin Luther. From its beginning traditional scholasticism and the new Italian humanism lived side by side. Should not the school's namesake in America maintain a similar openness and independence?

The Young Men's Christian Association emerged in 1883 to sustain an ecumenical and experiential element in campus religious life. If the college was to be somewhat neutral in order, not to embrace the new orthodoxy of the seminary and not to disregard the plurality of views in the student body, the YMCA at least became a way to unofficially maintain some American practices. It grew out of the United States Christian Commission which had brought aid and refreshment to Union Army troops during the Civil War. Prince was the instigator in Springfield. He had become active in the city YMCA movement and started the program in the First Lutheran Church where it continued for several years before establishing its separate town identity.

Prince believed that through a Y on the campus he could preserve certain American principles while supporting the new emerging Wittenberg under Dr. Ort. When Bible study became voluntary, he encouraged students in the Y to continue the practice. He encouraged them to send representatives to the state YMCA convention, and they returned to organize the Wittenberg chapter. Later they sent representatives to Dwight L. Moody's Bible School at Mount Herman, Mass., at Moody's invitation, to better prepare them to lead Bible study sessions.

The campus YMCA had begun with thirty members in 1884, expanded to sixty in 1885, and to ninety in 1886, a substantial proportion of the male enrollment. With help from First Lutheran Church, the group flourished as a rival between the fading literary societies and the rising Greek letter movement. These three explored the dimensions of student life in and around the new curriculum. While Wittenberg gave up revivals, the campus Y took up the cause with enthusiasm and held annual preaching missions. They organized a Young Women's Christian Association to cooperate with them in religious activities. It would be the campus Ys then that would embrace the emerging enthusiasm for college athletics to carve out its unique role in campus life.

Cartoon saluting the YM and YWCA, by A. K. Mumma, class of 1893, the *Cycle, 1893*. It depicts the Ys as the lighthouse guiding ship-wrecked students to safety from the stormy sea of college life. Wittenberg University Archives.

By June of 1892, the new education had taken hold and the institution flourished. In his report to the Board, Dr. Ort reported the largest enrollment in the school's history. A total of 363 men and women, including 117 of college rank and 25 seminarians, were in attendance. The changes required a larger faculty, more specifically prepared. It opened the way for specialization in the sciences, history, political science, and modern languages. It made the elective system necessary. It also reduced the emphasis on more traditional studies and required accommodation to the emerging system of public high schools. By 1890 entrance examinations were dropped for anyone who graduated from an approved high school.

The expansion in the sciences illustrated the changes underway. Science as a field of study had expanded greatly since the 1859 publication of Charles Darwin's *Origin of Species*. He had raised the crucial issue of whether each species was a particular creation of God or had they not evolved over time in response to the challenges of survival. The Lutheran Church's attitudes toward the new sciences were expressed in their publications. One writer in the *Lutheran Standard* observed, "Science has become haughty and arrogant. Reason usurps the place of faith . . . The attacks made upon the church and her doctrines by the Darwins, Huxleys, Spencers, and Tyndalls of our day are the oppositions of science falsely so called . . . It is not facts which they oppose to the scriptures but false theories illegitimately deduced from facts." In 1873 another in the same magazine asserted, man is not "a highly developed beast, related to the gorilla and the orangutan." Still a third, writing in 1876, noted, "He, then who reads nature aright reads what the finger of God has written there; but God did not write one thing in nature and its opposite in the Bible. Correct scientific investigation will therefore inevitably result in coincidence with God's word." Yet an article entitled "Darwinian Theology" asserted in 1878 that the Genesis account is literal history and is opposed to Darwinian evolution.

Other writers in other journals took a different stance. An editorial by W. H. Singly, a man known to Wittenberg and Secretary of the Board that selected Ort as President, said, "The modern discussion of the relation of science to religion is producing most gratifying results. The evidence of the truthfulness of the Bible is becoming stronger just in proportion to the clearness obtained in a science." But this was in the *Lutheran Evangelist*, Dr. Stuckenberg's paper. Of the Rev. J. A. Hall, a lecturer on geology, the editor said, "Like every true conservative scientist, he maintained the perfect harmony of revelation with thoroughly established scientific truth." Thus while some writers expressed animosity toward science, there were other Lutheran voices advocating the reconciliation of religious and scientific truth, and Wittenberg responded to the latter.

The school's movement to modern geology caught some students by surprise. In an editorial in the *Wittenberger*, one student objected. He believed, said the writer, in "a certain development," but would utterly deny the evolution of species. He questioned the wisdom of "substituting Le Comte's in place of Dana's manual of geology." Le Comte, he said, was an avowed evolutionist, an "uncircumcised Philistine." While some were proud to trace their ancestors to the monkey, he preferred to accept the Bible and recognize Adam and Eve.

Ort had long ago reconciled such conflicts in his own mind and worked to strengthen the study of real science. In 1874 he published an article in *Quarterly Review*, entitled: "The Controversy between the Theist and the Scientist." In it he observed: "What folly would it be for the naked eye to say to the telescope, 'there are no worlds beyond the limits of my vision . . . ' Would it be sensible for the ear to tell the nose, 'there are no odors,' or for the nose to say to the ear, 'there is no sound'" beyond what they could hear or smell. The senses and what they could know, augmented by new scientific apparatus, discovered truths the mind had to accept. Judgment had to be reserved over seeming conflicts with scripture that those discoveries suggested. On the other hand, Ort assured his readers, science as well could not "declare the whole field of knowledge is circumscribed by its limits," and deny that there was truth beyond what the senses and the scientific method could assess.

Dr. Prince observed that Ort committed himself fully to the strengthening of the sciences at Wittenberg. College presidents throughout America, he observed, were working hard to keep their institutions abreast of the rapid expansion in biology, chemistry, physics, and geology. It was a new age of science, and the college that could not keep up would languish. Ort committed himself so fully to meeting these needs that he alienated persons in support of other programs.

In June 1885, Ort asked the Board to take the money they were setting aside for a ladies dormitory and use it to buy science equipment for Edgar Fahs Smith, his new professor of chemistry. It delayed housing for women another two years. The donors consented. One of them, Alexander Gebhart, an Americanist Lutheran from Dayton, Ohio, provided additional funds so that Smith could have a graduate assistant to help in the department of natural sciences. With the prospect of a gift from his friend Rev. Hamma for a seminary building, Ort asked that funds earmarked for a theological building also be directed to the sciences. The Board approved an additional effort to raise $6,000 for the science department. The three actions represented a major commitment to the expansion of science at Wittenberg.

These efforts were made to fulfill Ort's commitment to Smith that the college was serious about expanding its program and reputation in the sciences. But more than that, it reflected Ort's views that the new sciences should be at the heart of the curriculum of any self-respecting college that sought to educate students to live and work in the modern era. Science was the cutting edge, and without it, a school languished in the past.

In 1887 Smith began the publication of "Contributions from the Chemical Laboratories of Wittenberg College," and his reputation as an outstanding chemist grew throughout the country. As a result, he was enticed away by the University of Pennsylvania. Ort experienced this kind of loss frequently as many of his prized new faculty members were hired away. It caused him to increase his efforts to make Wittenberg more attractive to talented teachers.

Continuing its commitment to science, the Board approved two positions to replace Smith. The first, offered to Alvin F. Linn, class of 1884, was a professorship of chemistry, zoology, and botany. Linn had done advanced work under Smith and attended Johns Hopkins where he earned the doctor of philosophy degree in chemistry. Samuel Keller, class of 1888, taught mathematics in the academy. The Prudential Committee asked him to fill the second position. He was not only a brilliant mathematician but was also well versed in other fields. He served on the Wittenberg faculty for fifteen years, leaving in 1905 to establish the Mathematics Department at the new Carnegie Institute of Technology in Pittsburgh. He left because his broad assignment in the physical sciences at Wittenberg had deflected him from his growing specialization in mathematics.

Another area of curricular expansion at Wittenberg was the social sciences. As Benjamin Prince observed, Wittenberg began to take a broader look at society in the 1870s with Dr. Stuckenberg's presence on the faculty. The study of the constitutional development of the United States, the history of western civilization, sociology, economics, international law, political science, and psychology all became to one degree or another new areas for exploration and new courses in the curriculum. It was a logical outgrowth of American theology as applied to society in Stuckenberg's *Christian Sociology*. As the social gospel movement grew in America, it called for greater attention to current issues and to the status of life in an emerging urban and industrial society.

From time to time in the 80s and 90s, John H. W. Stuckenberg returned as a visiting lecturer. George P. Krapp, class of 1893, recorded in his diary Stuckenberg's description of the university enterprise: " . . . our aim should be solely the truth . . . suffering, denying ourselves, working, if necessary dying for it . . . Our purpose is not merely to get knowledge but to get knowledge and apply it in the solution of the great problems of the day." It was at the heart of the social scientists' objective.

Samuel Sprecher had been very much interested in the study of psychology and the effort to better understand human behavior. When that philosopher talked about the mind, he was talking psychology. Now Ort himself was referred to more as a psychologist than as a philosopher or theologian. It was inevitable that the Wittenberg curriculum would have an emphasis in that area. Ort's psychology was neither the new experimental psychology that was emerging in the German universities nor that of William James or G. Stanley Hall at Harvard or John Dewey at the University of Chicago. It was still the Scottish mental philosophy or mental science.

By this time, with the rise of the new learning, the old courses in Moral Philosophy and Moral Science were disappearing from college curricula. The very effort to reconcile science and religion collapsed as the sciences expanded so rapidly that they could not be assimilated. The educational environment was no longer as receptive to notions about the unity of knowledge as it had been. Nevertheless, Ort retained the mental philosophy course with its focus on the evidences of Christianity and the natural theology of William C. Paley. He still offered Moral Science as a course in which rational psychology, the history of philosophy, and logic were emphasized. The course titles were there but, in what became a standard academic practice, the content was changing, focusing on man's reaction to diverging fields of knowledge. If there were any longer, any unity or coherence of knowledge, it had to be in the mind of the student.

There was a third major new direction in curriculum and that was the area of art, music, and general cultural enrichment. Ort said the addition of these courses was a result of the admission of women, but they were available and recommended for all. He indicated faculty interest in expanding the music program as early as 1887. His reference to "keeping step to the music of the onward march of today" in his report to the Board that year was more than figurative. He spoke of cultivating the heart as well as the head, responding to the trend in collegiate education toward a broader cultural dimension.

Robert H. Hiller, Salutatorian, class of 1889, wrote the words and music of the Wittenberg Alma Mater. Wittenberg University Archives.

Robert H. Hiller, class of 1889, was the man called to fill these chairs of culture. He came technically as a professor of Greek; but his far ranging interests in art, architecture, and music made him the chief advocate of liberal culture. In him, personally, the idea of the culture as a coherent family of studies was embodied. He was a Wittenberg graduate and had done advanced study at Hartwick Seminary and Columbia University. In 1891 he wrote the music which would be used later for Wittenberg's Alma Mater, set to the words he would write in 1913. While in graduate school, he wrote the tune for use by his fraternity brothers in a campus show. The beat of the tune was said to be that of New York City's elevated railroad as the wheels clattered across rail sections. Hiller heard it riding from Columbia to a church on Fifth Avenue where he sang in the choir and played the organ. The "clickety clack" of the elevated became the beat of that campus musical, and later, slowed down a little, as the Alma Mater, punctuated campus convocations and other events.

Dr. Hiller also brought fine arts to Wittenberg as a result of his New York experiences. While the literary societies had invested in some works of art, the campus had been generally rather plain. Stuckenberg had brought some focus on art to his courses and to student activities. Wittenberg, however, had its first art exhibit on May 28, 1895; and it was the first adornment of the plain grey walls of Recitation Hall. The following year, a public reception initiated the school's effort to link campus art to the art interests of the elite of Springfield. Hiller was named head of the Art Department in that year at the age of thirty-one. He coordinated the work of five faculty members.

One of the five was D. Orrin Steinberger who left at the turn of the century to become the "hermit of Mad River," living in a tree house called "Camp-a-loft." He was a graduate of the Wittenberg academy and taught art at the National Academy of Art League Schools in New York before coming back to Springfield. He was a successful illustrator for the *Youth's Companion* and *Farm and Fireside* magazines, the latter published in Springfield. Students noted with pride that he had designed a new cover for the *Wittenberger*.

He was known at the time, as America moved toward the Spanish-American War, for his water color entitled "The Accolade," depicting the United States as Miss Liberty embracing Cuba suffering through its revolution against Spain. While at Wittenberg, he drew a political cartoon, "Bleeding Cuba," which was very popular in the months preceding the war. He offered students drawing with pen and ink, technique in watercolor, blackboard art for teachers, and commercial photography. He also taught art as a medium of communication for grand ideas and political issues as in the political cartoon. His family said he was escaping the reality of losing a sweetheart when he left abruptly to live in solitude in the woods, in a tree house high above the ground.

In 1887, with Hiller's enthusiastic support, Wittenberg announced the establishment of a Conservatory of Music. The Lutheran Church had embarked upon a program to encourage better music for worship services and the demand for better-trained church musicians was growing. From the beginning there seemed to be some confusion about the kind of music program various parties desired. A conservatory implied training for professional musicians. After two years, the program was renamed a School of Music offering professional courses for performers, teachers, and church musicians, as well as music for general liberal arts students. Professor H. O. Farnum was director. By 1891 the school had fifty students, and the campus was enriched by recitals in organ and piano. The director organized a glee club that toured neighboring towns and churches to advertise the college, promote good church relations, and demonstrate better choral music.

In 1892 Philander N. Cook of Boston became director. During his two year tenure, Irene Spangler taught piano and Robert Braine, director of the Springfield YMCA orchestra and the Grand Opera House orchestra, taught violin. The school's objective was to teach "proper and solid foundations" in pianoforte technique and in voice culture, "based on the Italian school of singing." Cook lectured on music history. Students presented recitals and performances every three weeks. A public concert was given in the college chapel at the end of each term.

Leroy Lambert replaced Cook in 1894 and the school again became a conservatory and remained so for over a decade. It was then designated a department of the college. Lambert was a graduate of the Boston Training School of Music and former associate director of the Commonwealth Conservatory of Boston. He brought to Wittenberg and to Springfield a sense of the century old musical culture of Boston. Other members of the seven person department included Robert H. Hiller who taught vocal culture and sight reading. William W. Arnold, an advanced student of the director, taught piano. Sylvester Hulburt taught organ. Charles E. Dunnebacke, catering to a popular student interest, taught guitar and mandolin. Alex P. Bunker taught violin, theory, history, and ensemble playing. Georgia Shaw, a local organist, was accompanist in the vocal classes. Springfield responded enthusiastically to the Department of Music.

Men's Glee Club, 1900-1901. Wittenberg University Archives.

The Wittenberg Glee Club separated from the instrumentalists, and the two organizations assumed separate identities. On January 26, 1894, the sixteen voice choir made its formal debut at an oratorical contest in Springfield's Grand Opera House. Charles L. Bauer was director. The group's first out of town concert was in Urbana, fifteen miles north of Springfield. The following fall, the group made the first of what became annual tours and visited churches in Mansfield, Akron, and Ashland in Ohio and Columbus, Indiana and Louisville, Kentucky. It was Ort who saw value in sending the choir during vacations "among the churches to bring the name and spirit of the new Wittenberg into the homes of the people of the church."

Ort's plans for theological education were equally ambitious. After forty years as a department of the college, Ort envisioned a separate seminary independent of the college. He proposed reorganization, and a separate building to house the school. It would offer a curriculum in line with that at other General Synod Seminaries. He would be accused of forsaking the Americanists and of repudiating

Ezra Keller and Samuel Sprecher, but it was only partially true. While he would have his new seminary embrace the unaltered Augsburg Confession, *The Book of Concord* and the Common Service, coming visibly closer to the orthodoxy of the General Council and many in the General Synod, still he retained many distinguishing aspects of the New Measure men. Lutherans in Wittenberg's territory were long identified with a continued emphasis on piety, a strong role for laity, ecumenism, and a firm resistance to centralized authority at Synod and national church levels.

His first appointment to the seminary faculty replacing the venerable Dr. Sprecher telegraphed his revisionist position. It was James William Richard, a forty-two-year-old graduate of the Gettysburg Seminary widely known as a strong proponent of Confessionalism in the General Synod. He asked that his oath of office should pledge him to the current doctrinal position of the General Synod. He had written, however, in support of "the essential unity of Protestant Christianity," a view not foreign to Americanists. His arrival at Wittenberg, as noted by Lutheran church historian Donald L. Huber, in his *Educating Lutheran Pastors in Ohio*, "marked the end of 'American Lutheran' theological instruction in the United States." After 1885, no Lutheran seminary taught the Americanist doctrine. That Sprecher should be replaced by Richards rankled many.

Richard's stay at Wittenberg, however, was brief. In 1887 he joined with Ort in recommending the addition of a third professorship and a separate endowment fund for the seminary. The third chair had long been sought and was now granted. The separate endowment fund idea met with resistance, since the Board had already decided that the Wittenberg endowment could not be divided. By 1887, however, Ort was referring to the school as Wittenberg Theological Seminary. Richards left in 1888 before the third position was filled to accept a post at Gettysburg Seminary. There may have been pressures to return the Wittenberg Seminary to its earlier Americanist theological position, but Ort was only briefly deterred from his course. He recommended two new faculty: Luther A. Gotwald for Practical Theology and Samuel F. Breckenridge for Exegetical Theology. He would teach Systematic Theology.

Ort's theological utterances were much drier and more obscure than his comments on the new education, but he clearly had shifted his view from his earlier days as an Americanist. Prince implied that rumblings about what was being taught in the seminary had bubbled up from the Americanist churches on the college territory beginning in the mid-1880s and reached a peak in 1892. The Board had tried to reassure the discontented that seminary teaching was fully in accord with the current doctrinal position of the General Synod. When Americanists sought to challenge the new direction at Wittenberg, however, they attacked one of his faculty appointments, not Ort himself.

On April 4, 1893, a special meeting of the Board reviewed a charge of heresy brought against Luther A. Gotwald. He was accused of having departed from the doctrinal basis on which Wittenberg had been founded and that the General Synod had approved. The protagonists were Alexander Gebhart, who had originally nominated Gotwald, his former pastor, for the faculty position; Earnest E. Baker, class of 1884 and current pastor in Dayton, and Joseph R. Gebhart, Alexander's cousin. All three were members of the Board. Baker was editor of the *Lutheran Evangelist*, a paper opposed to Confessionalsim at Wittenberg. The Gebharts were partners in the company publishing the paper. The three attacked Gotwald through their paper; but when the Wittenberg Board and the Miami Synod defended him, decided to raise the issue with the Board.

Involved with them in the charges were Prof. Ehrenfeld, who had resigned from the faculty under pressure in 1892, and the venerable Hezekiah R. Geiger, still disgruntled with recent trends at the college. Gotwald was convinced that Stuckenberg was also involved behind the scene. The charges in Gotwald's estimation were vague and general, and he asked that they be made more specific. He was accused of teaching in the spirit of the General Council rather than the spirit of the General Synod to which the churches supporting Wittenberg belonged. But the two were moving closer together and within fifteen years would reunite, and Gotwald felt the accusers should delineate more clearly where he supposedly transgressed and was heretical.

If Gotwald were guilty, some believed that Ort was as well. On Reformation Day in 1891, Ort had said in a sermon in Springfield that to know the Augsburg Confession was to know what the Lutheran Church teaches and believes, and that its confessional doctrines found their source entirely in the scriptures. But the plaintiffs supported Ort's views about the college and did not want to weaken support for it by attacking him. To single out Gotwald focused the issue where they wanted to effect change.

The Board agreed that the charges should be made more specific but the plaintiffs refused to do so. A Board committee then made them more specific and the complainants had nothing further too do with the trial. With clarified charges before them, the Board proceeded to acquit Gotwald of any wrong doing. When the verdict came to a vote, the three who brought the charges abstained, thus allowing a unanimous decision in favor of Gotwald. It was a strange sequence of events that led many to wonder what the affair was really about. It challenged a change of direction that had been initiated eight years earlier. Those who brought the charge failed to prosecute it with any sustained effort. Gotwald described it as the last gasp of the recensionists, those who had sought to amend the Augsburg Confession, but he never understood what their objective was in raising the issue at this late date.

Stuckenberg took the acquittal as a final sign, a public demonstration, that Wittenberg had abandoned the views of Keller and Sprecher. Former faculty member Ehrenfeld called the trial a farce. Ehrenfeld's biographer, who favored the more conservative direction, called the trial, from all perspectives, "sad and amusing and useless . . ." It was, he said, "a solemn comic farce from beginning to end." It appeared to be an elaborately staged event to show once and for all that the seminary at Wittenberg was in line with all the other General Synod seminaries and ahead of some in recognizing a growing unity with the General Council. The end result was the strengthening of historic Lutheranism at Wittenberg, but it was a painful and distressing event that affected many supporters. There were financial repercussions that cost the college some financial support. In spite of it all, suspicions about the school's Lutheranism still lingered for decades in the minds of many in other synods.

For all his achievements, Ort's presidency was not without its challenges. He had struggled throughout to find the resources to make his new Wittenberg a reality. After the Gotwald trial and in the face of the panic of 1893 and the ensuing depression, he wore himself out trying to make ends meet. The depression brought decreased enrollment, decreased operating income, and decreased endowment income. By the end of the century, Ort's energy failed him. Worn out and discouraged at the age of fifty-seven, Dr. Ort would resign.

Samuel Alfred Ort, Valedictorian, class of 1863, fourth president, 1882-1900. Photo of official portrait by Robert Gantt.

The depression that followed the panic spread deeply throughout the nation affecting nearly everyone. Labor unrest and strikes ensued. Not since the Chicago Haymarket riots of 1887 had the nation seen such widespread unrest. Coxey's army of the unemployed set out to march on Washington. Similar groups from all over the nation began to march. In some places, they commandeered trains and robbery and looting were said to follow the trail of the "commonwealers" as they were called in the press. In 1894, frontrunners of this movement arrived in Springfield; and by the end of the month, Aubrey's army from Indianapolis was expected to arrive 200 strong. When it appeared just before commencement, it numbered only fifty or so and passed through town, camping overnight in the park just below campus along the foot of the cliffs, without incident.

That June, Ort spoke to the graduating class about the "industrial situation." He told them that while bad men were giving in to violence, "good men are standing still, fearing to move." And both were responsible for the unrest because there had to be a new order of things; and those who refused to leave the past and proceed were as responsible as those who had become impatient. "It is no wonder that society is disturbed," he added. "What can you expect when man treats his fellowman as if he were no more than the ox that browses in his pasture?" The root cause was not wages; it was a moral question of how we treat our fellow human beings. Ort suggested that both capitalism and socialism were wrong. It was management mistreating labor and labor mistreating management and both acting out of the sinful nature of man. Reflective of the pessimism current in German thought, Ort saw no solution to growing problems except in changing men's hearts. The German philosophers, however, saw nothing in man's history to suggest that a change of heart was possible. Ort, outwardly, seemed more optimistic. Missing, however, was any ringing endorsement of the idea of orderly progress that heretofore had characterized his thinking. Progress would continue only with the concerted effort of men with a great many disparate points of view to find common ground.

Ort's reports to the Board, said Prince, were always hopeful throughout his tenure of eighteen years. While disappointment in gifts not forthcoming sometimes chilled his ardor, he had always been able to rise above the cloud. His spirit of hopefulness and optimism gave energy to the faculty, but the repeated effort to recharge his own enthusiasm in the face of insufficient resources slowly wore him out. Prince remembered one of Ort's statements to the Board which summed up his educational program: "It is wise always to aim at large results. The standard should be high. There should not be any disposition to build this institution on small ideas and out-of-date notions. The steady purpose on the part of all should be to make Wittenberg College a grand institution of higher Christian education. With this steadily in view, let us plan and work."

After 1893 the Board never again lived up to Ort's expectations. Large grants received after that date were for the seminary and its new conservative theological direction. An endowment fund goal for the college was approved by the synods but not raised. Ort had already seen the high-water mark of college advancement, and a period of diminished support ensued. Had the financial resources equal to his plans been available, said Prince, Wittenberg would have leaped to the forefront of American higher education.

Income was insufficient to provide the kind of resources which the new Wittenberg needed to sustain the expanded programs. The crisis triggered a reassessment by the board. Having turned down a proposal to reduce its size, they created a standing committee "for the better control of the finances, both permanent and current." Its duties were "to examine into and report to the Board the financial affairs of the college and recommend appropriations separately for the several departments of expenditures: salaries, labor, repairs, new buildings, incidental expenditures, etc." The report indicated the unsophisticated nature of the school's accounting system by later standards denoting that they had not yet divided accounts into separate funds for operations, physical plant, and endowment. President Ort and Dr. Prince helped in the design of new fiscal policies. The expanded campus and curriculum were costly, and the effort of faculty to keep up with the new education taxed the Board's capacity to find the resources. The board's work had to be more specialized and a clearer role for administration was needed.

In another action, the Board plumbed the complex issue of financial support from the synods. They discovered that members elected by synods saw themselves as responsible not to Wittenberg but to the synods from which they came. They saw themselves as overseers of college activities; and, while they had historically presented the cause of the college to the churches, they had not accepted a personal responsibility to fund the institution. They saw themselves as their name indicated as a board of directors, not trustees. The new Wittenberg, driven by the growth and expansion of faculty specialization, was taking them beyond their traditional commitment. The editor of the *Wittenberger* asked, "Why cannot the Lutheran Church support at least one university in this country? Why not at Springfield, Ohio?" He suggested that the Church had too narrow a view of its educational responsibility.

To alter the member's perception of his responsibilities, the oath administered to new members was revised. Upon election to the Board, and as often afterward as he was reelected, the director subscribed to a declaration: "Sincerely approving of the object of

Wittenberg College, I solemnly promise faithfully to endeavor to carry out the provisions of its charter and constitution, and thus promote the great design of the institution."

The only group that seemed ready to accept a clear responsibility for financial support was the Alumni Association but it was not yet officially represented on the Board. As a result, even its efforts were faltering. Ort again asked that the Alumni Endowment Association be given seats on the Board. After due deliberation and objections by several synods, the request was withdrawn. The *Wittenberger* observed, "Persons are seldom loyal where there is not complete representation." The Alumni Association continued to control its fund to maximize its influence. After another decade, the Board would relent; but not until 1895 were alumni representatives authorized, and they had to be Lutheran. The first two were the Rev. M. W. Hamma of Washington, D.C., and the Reverend E. W. Simon of Springfield's First Lutheran Church.

Chapter Twelve

A Vast Chorus of Dissent

The three most prominent aspects of student life on eastern college campuses in the 1890s were the popularity of business as a career, the Greek letter societies, and intercollegiate athletics. There was a focus on getting a "practical education" and getting ahead. The deeper social, economic, and political issues affecting the nation were indeed well beyond most students' interests.

The approaching turning of the new twentieth century had attracted everyone's attention. Lloyd C. Douglas, who entered the Wittenberg Academy in 1894, would be in the college class of 1900. Upperclassmen, he said, stopped him as he crossed the campus to inquire what class he belonged to just to hear him say "nineteen hundred." When he added that he planned to spend three years in seminary, they exclaimed, "nineteen oh three," and laughed exuberantly.

Wittenberg students were drawn to that eastern mainstream and Douglas said he was the only pretheological student in Phi Gamma Delta fraternity. All the other members looked to business, law, and medicine as life careers promising material success. The number of fraternities had doubled, and even the women were looking at the possibility of a "fraternity" for women. The school caught athletic fever, and intercollegiate sports took on great importance. Ort, with his concern for the whole man, looked with favor on all these developments; but, with the theological battles in the church and the search for funds for the college, the new spirit of student life on campus would not be enough to sustain his energy.

Lloyd C. Douglas, class of 1900.
Wittenberg University Archives.

The literary societies seemed to dwindle even more and this was the source of much criticism from alumni. In his reports to the Board, Ort mentioned the students' devotion to the literary work of the societies. He gave them a major and official part in college life encouraging their participation in the State Oratorical Association, founded in 1886 to promote state wide intercollegiate competition. The groups developed yells and cheers and a rooting section in the audience to support and encourage their contestants. The practice developed simultaneously at athletic contests as well.

Ort allowed the literary societies, rather than the Greek groups, to produce the official student newspaper, the *Wittenberger*. At many Ohio colleges, fraternities took control of the journalistic revolution among students, either through the student newspaper or that new invention, the college yearbook, or both. At Wittenberg both were entrusted, at least at first, to the literary societies. In 1884, the Greeks surrendered the *Wittenberger* to non-Greeks but established the *Stylus*, a college yearbook under their own control. When the *Stylus* mounted a campaign to bar preparatory students from membership in Greek societies, it was with Ort's blessing. When it took up agitation for ending compulsory chapel, that too, surprisingly, had met with Ort's support.

These developments did not preclude one last appearance of the underground newspaper, the *Flying Dutchman*. It appeared in Ort's first year on January 28, 1883, as the *Student Review* or the *Flying Dutchman*. The motto on its mast head was: "The Press Has Always Been a Reform Agent." It called the *Wittenberger* an official student publication; the *Wittenberg Quarterly* an official faculty publication; and the *Dutchman* the only publication "in which the plain, unvarnished truth is told." It noted that Ort was the homeliest man on the Board and charged that his membership in Phi Kappa Psi alienated a large number of students. In fact, the editor claimed, so many faculty were Phi Psis as to create an unhealthy alliance. This final issue of the *Dutchman* renewed the racist attacks of other recent editions. The comments reflected the continuing change from the egalitarian ideals of the Civil War to the rise of "Jim Crow" policies of racial discrimination in American society and in the Springfield community.

Official College reaction was swift and harsh. The editor of this "anonymous and slanderous paper" was suspended, and faculty asked the Board for the authority to annul any degree conferred at a commencement if it was learned afterward that the recipient had been engaged in the publication of such a paper. They asked that the Prudential Committee be authorized to pay $300 for evidence that would convict any person having a part in editing, publishing, or circulating a paper "reflecting in a scurrilous manner on the college, its faculty, or its Board of Directors." The profane nature of the final edition caused those in town and on campus who had condoned earlier editions to abandon it.

The *Dutchman* prospered more under Helwig because it focused general opposition to Helwig and the old order. Helwig had come to the college at the earnest solicitation of his friends to save Americanism in the Lutheran Church, said Prince, and not because of his own love of college teaching. Ort, on the other hand, was very popular with students. Tales of his student years were widely circulated: his athletic prowess, the story of the horse in the cupola.

The yearbook dredged up his old literary society fines: not wearing shoes to meetings, wearing muddy boots, chewing tobacco, using improper language. When he was a young professor, students noted his smoking, borrowing of cigarettes, drinking root beer—and the real thing. When such a president was vilified, students came to his defense.

Clearly students had changed. The class of 1882 described itself as follows: "None of them have any religion, but all prefer the Lutheran church except one, thereby showing the nonsectarian character of the institution. One begins theology next year. The quicker he is sent amongst the cannibals, the better for Christianity. He prays six days in the week, but the seventh he gets mad and swears like a Texas Ranger." Only one member of the class was said never to smoke, chew, play cards, drink, or disobey any of the rules; and he hid under his bed when faculty came to the dorm to put an end to "a college racket." Bicycling, with its various attendant mischiefs, and following the horse races, said the observer, brought further discredit to the group. The topics of student discourse had certainly changed; and traditional discipline was being put to new tests.

The class of 1892 picked as its unofficial motto: "Get Plenty While You're a'Gittin," and as its yell, "I am, I am, I am a Hun; everyone else is a son-of-a-gun." The presence of an official student newspaper put an end to the outrageousness of the underground papers, but the rhetoric of the approved papers was astounding enough to those not normally privy to everyday campus life.

Alumni, too, spoke openly of a different side of campus life. When the "old boys" get together, said one, "we dwell not so much upon the regular work of the college course as upon treasons, stratagems, and wars" between and within the classes. Alumni seldom recalled to one another "the grade we received in calculus, the interest we took in a critical study of Macbeth, or the grind in roots, affixes and suffixes." Rather, the spokesman continued, "we bring to mind the war on Sophs, the bombardment and fall of a sophomore door." Another cited "united bolts" against established authority, contested elections in the literary societies, secret fraternity incidents, and sports. Alumni gloried in the emerging collegiate lifestyle and came vaguely to support a "modern" Wittenberg without much sympathy for the more radical reforms in the land grant college movement.

Window over the doorway to the Excelsior literary society hall in Recitation Hall. Photo by Robert Gantt.

Even with all the effort to extend the life of the old literary societies, their work dwindled. Gone was the kind of enthusiasm for them that just a few years earlier had prompted Harr and Reuben Wagner, to set out for Boston to meet their honorary fellow member, Henry Wadsworth Longfellow. They reported that the elderly Mr. Longfellow received them cordially and spent about a half hour with them. He asked them about the Excelsior Society and about Wittenberg. He also wanted to know how many colleges there were in Ohio. When they told him thirty-three, Longfellow exclaimed, "That is too many!" and he urged educational reform. The state's policy did not change. There was to be a college, it seemed, in every city and town; some would have two or three. The state was to rank first in the nation in the number of colleges per square mile. Enrollment and financial resources would be spread thin. Competition would be intense and a particular school could excel only by attracting unusually strong support from its community, church, or alumni.

In 1895, the undergraduate historian for the Excelsior Society lamented that the societies were weakened by the desire of the men to be outside playing sports. When sports did not cancel a meeting, he added, fraternity rivalries arose to disrupt the proceedings.

They became the arena in which the Greek societies contended for preference, blocking candidates—for office, editor, orator, or whatever—if they belonged to a rival fraternity. "We can hear yet," he said "the vast chorus of indignant dissent swell upon the air with a vehemence that would have washed the president from his chair."

The historian for the Philosophians took a different view. "The past is dead," he wrote. To recite the enthusiasm of bygone days and point to illustrious alumni, he added, missed the point. "We doubt if there were those other attractions of college life, today regarded as necessary, to draw the time and attention from society work." He meant fraternities, sports, and the campus YMCA, among others, which competed for student time and interest. The literary society was not going down, he concluded; it was adapting to the changing times. He confessed that memberships in the societies were rather small.

Entrance to Philosophian Hall, now room 311 in Recitation Hall. Photo by Robert Gantt.

The Greek societies, however, were growing steadily. In November of 1883, Alpha Psi chapter of Alpha Tau Omega was founded, encouraged by N. Wiley Thomas, professor of Natural

Sciences. The following year, Sigma of Phi Gamma Delta was established. From 1884 to the turn of the century, there were several attempts to establish a fifth fraternity without success. Women students talked of forming a group, but that would not occur until 1902. The life of men on the campus, however, was dominated by the four fraternities.

Yet Lloyd C. Douglas told his father that he was the only Phi Gam who was taking Greek. His father asked what the Greek letters Phi Gamma Delta stood for; since there were no such groups at Wittenberg when he had attended. Douglas replied that he could not tell him because it was a secret. "You undoubtedly had a secret society," his father replied. When a student who knew no Greek whispered Greek into the ear of another student who knew no Greek, it surely was a secret that would never get out.

The earliest fraternity school in Ohio was the state university, Miami, with two chapters in the decade of the '30s and six groups by the 1860s. The most prolific fraternity school was Ohio Wesleyan with nine chapters by 1890; and it was from Ohio Wesleyan and Miami that the Greek "virus" reached Wittenberg and other Ohio colleges. Ohio State had eleven chapters by 1900. Kenyon and Wooster reached a total of seven chapters each by 1890, but Wooster abolished all such groups at the behest of a major benefactor. Students at Wesleyan were most strident in their advocacy of fraternities. "The best educational centers are where the societies flourish most successfully," they said, "Old Yale is teeming with them. Young Cornell has grown with their strength. The finest universities of the West . . . are full of them." Schools without fraternities, they insisted, were insignificant or religiously fanatical.

As the nineteenth century entered its final decade, however, the campus YMCA movement effectively challenged the Greeks for campus domination at Wittenberg and at other schools where religion remained a major interest. With its original focus on religion and a new found interest in athletics, it muscled its way between the literary societies and the fraternities to carve out a special niche. It capitalized on Wittenberg's unique religious environment. Soon Y members were talking of building their own building as YMCAs had done on other campuses.

The college YMCA movement began at Princeton in 1877 and appeared at Wittenberg seven years later. It spread rapidly to 231 colleges and had 15,000 members. Coaches, also trained at Princeton, fanned out across the country to preach about God and to teach physical fitness. The central figure at Wittenberg in the emergence of the Ys, as in so many other areas, was Benjamin Prince, president of the Springfield YMCA board and an active proponent of the Y in the city and on campus. It had functioned for several years in the First Lutheran Church.

Members compared the Y to the literary society, calling it a group of "higher aim, more extended usefulness, and with a more emphatic imperative." It had much to do with the decline of the literary societies, perhaps more than the fraternities. Its appeal was that it was "work for young men by young men," and, like fraternities, not faculty dominated. It was ecumenical, with pietistic emphases mixed with an appeal to youthful strength and vitality. Its three major programs were Bible study, missionary causes, and athletics.

A very popular event was the weekly joint meeting of the college Y with the women of the college YWCA on Sunday afternoons on the fourth floor of the men's dormitory. Bringing the women into the men's dorm on a regular basis was revolutionary indeed. Willard Hackenberg, class of 1901, was assigned to secure speakers for those Sunday afternoon meetings. In addition to Lutheran pastors, there were a number of other ministers the students liked to hear. Two of the most frequently requested were Rev. John A. Story of High Street Methodist Church and Rev. R. H. Hume of United Presbyterian Church on South Limestone Street. The most popular, he said, was "our own beloved President Ort, but he was away so much on weekends that he was the hardest speaker to get." Students watched his house to see when he was home.

The Y also held daily prayer services and assumed responsibility for the daily chapel with hymn singing, scripture reading, and a marvelous prayer by Dr. Ort. "Even though the services were not compulsory," said Hackenberg, "the chapel was always packed. Who of us can ever forget those wonderful prayers offered by Dr. Ort for us students, for whom he felt such personal responsibility." The students petitioned the Board for academic electives in Old and New Testament Bible, as regular courses for college credit, taught by a qualified faculty member. The Board was happy to comply.

Another group within the Y was the Student Volunteer Movement. These were students planning to serve in the world as missionaries. It had branches on campuses across the nation. A large group from Wittenberg attended an SVM rally in Cleveland. "What a wonderful convention that was," Hackenberg noted. "I can shut my eyes and see that great streamer stretched across the front of the hall: "The Evangelization of the World in This Generation." Many subsequently served in Africa and Asia.

What most caught the college man's attention perhaps was the Ys focus on Jesus, the man. He was, said the group's leaders, "a perfect man in body as well as in mind and spirit." It was a more human, masculine view of Christianity than previous views, and it had special appeal to the male adolescent entering college. It was a particularly appealing rationale for the education of the whole person, body, mind, and soul. Y leaders warned students not to be "parodies of the crowning work of creation" by neglecting either physical, mental, or moral development. A strong physical constitution was only part of being a real man or woman, but it ought not to be neglected.

In his report to the Board in June 1889, Ort, responded to growing student interest in athletics, asking for a gymnasium, a plain simple building devoted to physical fitness.

Old Gym, built in 1890, north of Recitation Hall where Koch Hall now Stands. Wittenberg University Archives.

The Board approved and voted to raise the $1,400 needed. Walter Pierce, class of 1890, marked the beginning of Wittenberg's athletic emphasis with the building of that little gymnasium, northwest of Recitation Hall where Koch Hall now stands. Writing five years after the event, he said, "The athletic fever, from which Wittenberg had never suffered to any alarming extent, began to infect the boys." Soon, he added, it became chronic; and Wittenberg which had "absolutely no place in the athletic world prior to 1890, by 1895 had become one of the leaders in the state."

The football team was a contender for a number of years, Hackenberg recalled. It went to Ohio State University and came home with a victory. "We need to understand," he added, "OSU was just getting started, and her student enrollment was about the same as Wittenberg's." All institutions interested in intercollegiate sports were equal and in the same competitive field. The college took official notice of athletics in 1890 with a catalog reference to the Athletic Association and the gymnasium. It announced that physical culture was a "prominent feature of the students' education." Within another year, gym classes were compulsory, without credit, for freshmen and sophomores.

Prince noted that the Wittenberg faculty had always recognized the need for exercise and good health and an even greater need to satisfy the play impulse of youth. He described early athletic activities as crude and unsystematic. First, he said, there were "various intramural contests, sometimes a game in which one class played against another or the members of one literary society against the members of the other." In the 1850s, games were "like stolen fruits," observed one student. "We had no gymnasium, no athletic field . . . no teams or clubs, but boys will have their fun." Sledding, ice skating, cricket, and rugby predominated. Croquet had a large following and grew more popular with coeducation. Samuel F. Breckenridge, class of 1860, observed that student games included "football, in which the ball was actually kicked," meaning rugby, "town ball," which was a game midway between cricket and baseball, quoits, running, and leaping. Quoits was a sophisticated game but some of the farm boys substituted horseshoes for the rings of rope.

Alden H. Gillett, who graduated five years later, said the north part of the campus was the football and cricket grounds. He talked about "gymnasium football" which was rugby regulated into a safer game. "It was not debauched," he said, "by hitting and brutality like rugby, and the ball, not the players, was kicked, and the play never terminated in a prize fight." In 1868 faculty tried to substitute cricket. "Our gymnasium," Gillett observed, "consisted of a horizontal bar suspended between two trees, and it was well supplied with pure fresh air and nothing else." Open fields, fresh air, and a shower in the cold waterfalls of Ferncliff Cemetery was the gym of those early days.

Prince also noted the quickening interest in sports in the Gay Nineties. Athletics, he said, increased greatly among students, faculty, rival institutions, the citizens of Springfield, and other college towns all at the same time. The spirit was infectious. In 1889, students adopted official team colors—cardinal and cream—and an official college cry or yell "without which no college is fully equipped," they insisted. The catalog noted that "in connection with gymnasium work, there is also much interest taken in baseball, football, and track athletics."

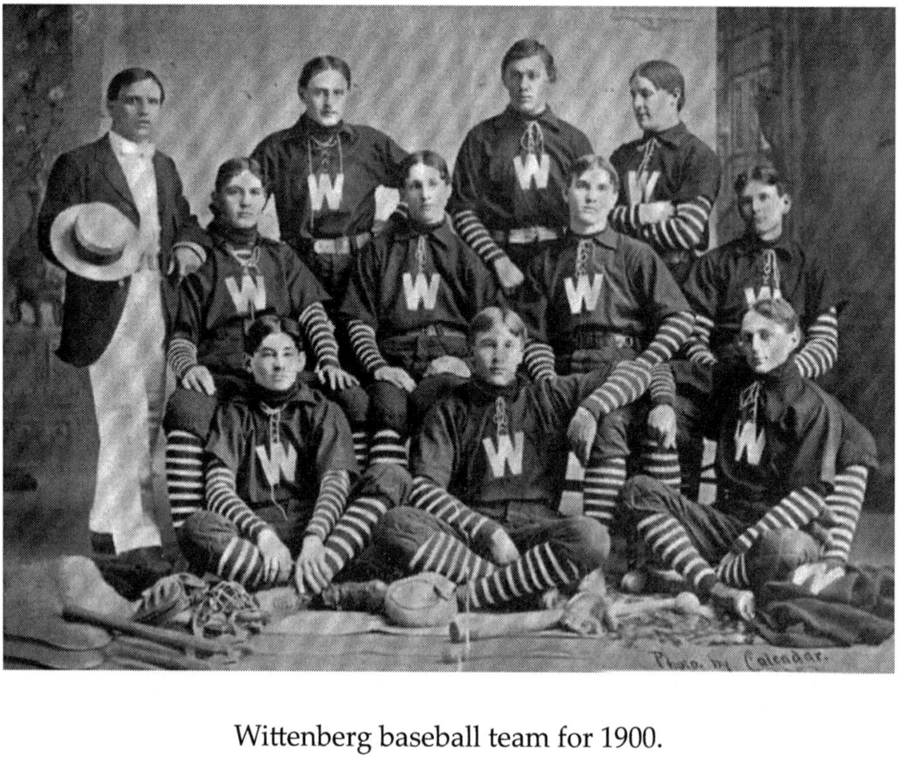

Wittenberg baseball team for 1900.
Wittenberg University Archives.

In 1892 the college established a ladies' gymnasium in the spacious and convenient third-floor attic of Ferncliff Hall. The yearbook editor described it as a "roomy, well-lighted, and well-ventilated gymnasium sufficiently furnished for the present needs." The school hired the director of athletics at the Springfield YMCA to provide physical education for twenty coeds who signed up. The first recorded women's athletic contest was a baseball game in the spring of 1893. Ferncliff Hall lost 24 to 4 apparently to coeds not living in Ferncliff Hall.

The Wittenberg Athletic Association was formed in 1890 but faltered because of a lack of financial support. After that, physical education was more formally organized. A special athletic fee of $1.50 was charged of all students to support the institution's commitment to health and physical development. The campus YMCA collected twenty-five cents annually from members to finance the student athletic association.

At an 1892 meeting in Akron, Ohio, Wittenberg students helped organize the Athletic League of Ohio Colleges which consisted of Ohio and Miami universities, Otterbein, Marietta, and Wittenberg colleges. Some others were represented but not permitted by their schools to sign the agreement. Its first action was to arrange schedules for the coming season. It scheduled baseball games and planned a statewide field day for track and field events. It was held in Springfield and hosted by Wittenberg at the city YMCA field on the north shore of Buck Creek northeast of town. The Athletic League of Ohio predated the Ohio Conference by a decade. Wittenberg joined the OAC in 1909. It was a conference that included virtually every college in Ohio.

Students at many Ohio colleges organized football competition and bicycle clubs. Wittenberg offered intramural competition in baseball and tennis. Students also formed a Hare and Hound Club to organize fall and spring hunting. On the occasion of a successful hunt, the various boarding clubs featured feasts of fresh game, a practice that continued for well over a half century. Earlier students had engaged in hunting and fishing as casual pastime activity since the school began.

Mounting sports enthusiasm culminated in a student petition to the Board of Directors asking for an athletic field large enough to enable students to engage in intercollegiate sports. They wanted designated facilities both for practice and for hosting visiting teams. The students lost one makeshift baseball field when construction began on Recitation Hall. They lost their replacement field when Ferncliff Hall was built. Still another site was taken over by the gymnasium. Every time the students found a clear flat space, it seemed, the Board put a building on it. Their request was referred to a committee that responded favorably; and, in short order, lands north of the campus that had been given by Mr. Hawley were made available and prepared for use. Around the periphery of the field, a cinder track was constructed; and the students invited other schools to come to Wittenberg to compete in baseball, football, and track.

While the field was being prepared, the school used the city YMCA field. Through the goodwill of Dr. John Rodgers, the Y had secured the tract of land between Stanton Ave. and Cassilly St. from Buck Creek inland a few hundred yards. Areas for swimming and boating were designated. It was a popular area for students and townsfolk alike for picnics and recreation. Students said it ushered in "years of struggle . . . high above the rushing waters of Buck Creek," where college students contended with city boys for the use of the grounds on any given afternoon. The controversy was never settled until the grounds disappeared in urban development. The field consisted of ball diamonds, tennis courts, a running track, a football field with bleachers seating 250, and a small field house. Wittenberg rented the field for official games from 1890 to 1894, and the facility was described as "the second best athletic park in the state." In 1894 the city Y lost its lease to real estate developers, and Wittenberg shifted its play to its new field on campus.

Wittenberg initiated regular schedules in football, baseball, and track in 1892, just a few years behind many other Ohio colleges. Ralph Miller, student, player, manager, coach, and trainer, arranged for the first intercollegiate football game against Ohio University. It was a widely heralded event that never took place; O.U. did not show up. After that disappointment, Miller contacted Antioch College; and the first game was played on Oct. 8. Antioch won 6 to 4. In two other games that season, Wittenberg tied Marietta 0 to 0, and lost to Otterbein by a score of 50 to 0. One of the highlights of the season for students was that President Ort attended all the games.

Wittenberg's first football team, 1892.
Wittenberg University Archives.

By 1893 a Mr. Barnett came from Princeton to be the team's coach. He was a great quarterback. With Barnett coaching, Wittenberg won its first football victory 16 to 4; but it did not count since it was a practice game with the Springfield YMCA. The team beat Heidelberg twice, 64 to 0 in the first encounter, and finished the season with two wins and three losses. There were two controversial encounters with Ohio State and DePauw. In the first, OSU was accused of "every illegal trick in the book" while winning 36 to 10. The DePauw game, Wittenberg's first out-of-state opponent, was called by the press "the dirtiest game ever played on the YMCA field."

The next year, Wittenberg posted its best early record, winning seven and losing only one game. It was an achievement that would not be equaled again until 1918. The season began with a victory over Ohio State 6 to 0. Wittenberg won eighteen complete football uniforms as a prize. The team participated in a State Fair tournament with Ohio State, Akron, Denison, and Miami. The prize went to the team with the highest accumulative score. The long rivalry with Ohio Wesleyan also started in the 1894 season with Wittenberg winning 24 to 0. The first win over Otterbein, 30 to 4, ended with a brief riot when an Otterbein player came off the bench to tackle a Wittenberg man running for a final touchdown. In the season, Wittenberg outscored opponents 116 to 28. Wittenberg had arrived.

The absence of eligibility rules and the informal nature of sports at the time were illustrated by one of the legends that grew out of the Ohio State Fair football tournament. The story was told by John L. Zimmerman, class of 1879, a strong booster of Wittenberg athletics that the students stopped by the Big Four Railroad yards on the way out of town to pick up two burly young yardmen to beef up their line. Willard Hackenberg of the class of 1901 claimed that players were hired freely at Wittenberg and elsewhere in his student days. He entered Wittenberg preparatory school in 1895 and graduated from the seminary in 1904. During his nine years on campus, he said, "Some of the best men would stay after graduation just to be on the football team." O. O. Lipe, he added, after graduation, was hired to be director of the band but played right halfback on the team.

In a return match with OSU, Wittenberg won by a score of 18 to 6. A second interstate game in 1896 saw Wittenberg lose 28 to 0 to the University of Michigan at Ann Arbor. In 1897, the Lutheran team lost to two out-of-state foes: Earlham in Indiana, 8 to 6, and Michigan, 32 to 0; but their ambition and enthusiasm seemed undaunted. The team did not always lose. In eight seasons before the turn of the century, the "Fighting Lutherans" had four winning seasons and four losing seasons, winning 27 games and losing 27 for a respectable percentage.

The fights, injuries, use of nonstudent players, and similar abuses aroused faculties at Wittenberg and other Ohio colleges to the need for rules governing this vigorous and relatively unsupervised student activity. Some sought greater control with faculty athletic boards of control within institutions and intercollegiate athletic associations for collective action. The movement attracted enough attention to be reported in *Harper's Weekly*, on October 21, 1896: "Last winter the Ohio Intercollegiate Association, composed of Denison, Miami, Cincinnati, Ohio State, Kenyon, Marietta, Oberlin, Otterbein, and Wittenberg, drew up eligibility rules." The rules reported were four in number: (1) each player must attend at least eight hours of recitations per week; (2) no student holding a degree was eligible; (3) no student could receive any form of compensation for engaging in athletics, and (4) managers, at least ten days before a game, must exchange lists of eligible players certified by the presidents of the colleges.

President Theodore Roosevelt took the lead for reform nationally, calling college and university sports leaders to meetings to deal with violence and injuries on the gridiron. The very existence of collegiate athletics was threatened by the number of serious, even fatal injuries to players. Out of this effort came the organization of the National Collegiate Athletic Association, the NCAA, in 1905. The group sought to control the rules, to establish better standards for the conduct of sports, and to serve as a clearing house for the exchange of ideas about improving student participation in athletics. College and university athletic competition was here to stay.

Faculties were not without interest in sports. In the 1890s, the Wittenberg faculty had its own baseball team; and it challenged each of the four classes to a game. Prof. Prince played left field and managed the faculty team. Charles G. Heckert, professor of English and later president of the College, was the faculty's ace pitcher. E. O. Weaver, professor of science, played second base. President Ort was the umpire of choice by both faculty and students. The faculty beat all four classes in 1895. Pitching star for the students was Charles W. Maggart, who it was said, twirled the ball with such remarkable skill that no other student team ever defeated him. By 1895 Charles Maggart and Charles Heckert were campus legends. The "two invincible Charleys" they were called. "One," said the yearbook editor, "was a grandstand player and could only play when ladies came to witness the game; the other was more remarkable in practice than in a match game." The report neglected to say which Charley was which.

Other sports prospered. The four fraternities organized tennis clubs, and there was regular intramural competition. Occasional challenge tennis matches with off-campus opponents were scheduled. The most popular sports activity, however, was bicycling and the Bicycle Club claimed the largest membership of any group on campus except the Ys.

Bicycle clubs were very popular with students and townsfolk alike. Many excursions began and ended at Recitation Hall. Wittenberg University Archives.

So great was the craze that the student yearbooks of the era were named the *Cycle*. The bicycle was a great liberator of students. It gave the individual student, pairs, or groups the capability of going further and further away from the campus whenever they wished. One's range of freedom was only limited by one's physical stamina.

By 1902 the athletic field had been enlarged and regraded. The area was designed to support all outdoor sports with a track, baseball diamond, and football field with a 250-seat stadium. The first touchdown on the new field was made by an African-American student named Oliver "Ollie" Gregory. He went on to become one of the early greats on the Wittenberg gridiron. He graduated in 1906.

Through the turn of the century, athletics were closely allied with the religious emphasis of the extra curriculum. The chief proponent of sports remained the YMCA. "You will find college life a strenuous one," said the officers to the entering freshmen; and they urged new students to get started right by pursuing a complete development: physical, mental, and spiritual. "The noblest strength is the gentlest," they advised, and "a sound mind, a sound spirit, but these in a strong body," that was the Wittenberg ideal. "Every man who is physically able," they told freshmen, "should esteem it a privilege and an honor to try for a place on the team." If they could not make the team, they were to cheer from the sidelines and encourage the team by every possible means.

Both player and spectator were to put the crowning touches on the campus ideal by behaving as ladies and gentlemen. Anyone could lose control in the heat of battle, the student handbook advised, but the educated always remembered that they were to be gentlemen on and off the field of combat. Thus, good character, a cultivated intellect, a sound and well-developed body as the temple of God, loyalty to one's team, and a good school spirit together with the attributes of gentlemanly behavior were the hallmarks of the Wittenberg man or woman as advanced by the student culture.

Coaching was on a part-time basis. The combined coach and athletic director was usually a student who had training in physical education, often a seminarian who had been active in sports as an undergraduate. The first individual listed in the catalog as teaching physical culture was Benjamin Greff Printz, who came as instructor in 1891. He remained until 1898. A different person handled the coaching chores each year until 1899 when "Coach Wood of Princeton" arrived for the last one-year term. In 1900 and 1901, Charles M. Rogers of Dartmouth coached all sports. Clearly colleges that pioneered in physical education and varsity sports in the East were continuing to carry the cause westward.

In the eastern schools, alumni dominated sports while faculty generally washed their hands of the responsibility. In Ohio, faculties viewed matters differently and took a firm hand in sports affairs. Sometimes tension developed between faculty and students and with area boosters. From 1845 to 1898, the Wittenberg faculty had functioned without any committees except for the Prudential Committee. In 1898, however, a faculty committee on matriculation and class standing was created to keep track of student progress though an increasingly complex curriculum and to keep an eye on player eligibility for sports. In 1904, they created a committee on athletics.

As Wittenberg students moved into the national mainstream by embracing Greek letter societies and intercollegiate athletics, the school's friends talked about how the school had changed in five decades. There was a great sense of accomplishment as the fiftieth anniversary approached. Professor of English, Charles Heckert, summarized the faculty's view. "This period has been the richest in our history. New buildings have been erected, the curriculum has been advanced steadily, the teaching force has been increased, the music and art departments have been added, the number of students has been doubled, and the endowment fund has been augmented by many thousands of dollars."

The Board called upon Dr. Prince to write a fiftieth anniversary history of the college to be published by the Lutheran Board for Publication. He complied beginning what became known as the "Prince Manuscript History of Wittenberg College," but it was never published. The Prudential Committee requested that 350 cloth-bound copies be published; but for reasons unknown, it was never done. It was probably not printed for financial reasons. Furthermore, Prince's literary style was not all that exciting; and his narrative in places sounded like the minutes of the Prudential Committee. The manuscript remained unpublished, but became a valuable resource for future historians as he periodically revised it and extended it. It was the story as told by a man who, at that time, had spent more years at Wittenberg than anyone else.

Students produced their own publication, the *Semi Centennial Souvenir*, a yearbook of ambitious proportions. It included historical essays by alumni from the 1840s through the 1890s, articles reprinted from various issues of the *Wittenberger*, a complete alumni directory with brief biographies of all alumni, and photographs of many. There were longer biographies of outstanding alumni and of all the presidents and members of the faculty. Not since George Gerlaw Clark's 1887 History of Wittenberg College had there been such a collection of information about the college. It was ambitious indeed, well conceived, well executed, and very well received. Perhaps after its appearance, publishing Prince's history seemed less urgent.

In the afterglow of the semicentennial celebration, the class of 1896 called itself "Wittenberg's First Great Class." It was the largest to date, comprised of twenty-nine men and seventeen women. It achieved signal honors in athletics, fielding the first football team wearing regular uniforms. It was the first to wear caps and gowns, or to plant ivy next to a college building. Planting an oak tree and ivy became long-lived traditions accompanied by orations by members of the senior classes. The class revived the tradition of the class gift. The classes of 1876 and 1877 were the first to make class gifts but subsequent classes discontinued the practice. Wittenberg was a real American college, the class of 1896 insisted, and they reveled in it.

The practice of wearing caps and gowns did not meet with universal approval. One student was prohibited by his father from participating in a ceremony of such pomp and showmanship. By and large, however, Wittenberg students enjoyed being among America's college elite. For most, college meant good times, pleasant friendships, and enjoyment of the lifelong prestige that came to the selected four percent of American youth who were fortunate enough to attend college.

One student, at least, seemed not to fit in with the new Wittenberg spirit; and he was misled by the national spirit of material success. Sherwood Anderson whom H. L. Mencken would later call "America's most distinctive novelist," left Wittenberg in 1900. He, like many of his generation, was attracted to a career in business hoping for great material success. But his business career was a false start that he would painfully struggle to correct. As a student, he was too thin for athletics. His brother said he was all skin and bones. He was twenty-three, older than the average Greek letter man, but at the end of his preparatory year, he was eligible for pledging. He later recalled that the Betas, who "rushed" him, were too boyishly eager as they smoked their pipes, and he turned them down. He had enrolled in the academy, after the Spanish-American War, to complete his preparatory work and get ready for college. His classmates saw him as attractive but retiring, eager and intelligent, yet too energetic. He carried fourteen courses in one year and did well. He irritated classmates by keeping classes after the bell, asking questions.

Anderson later recalled his uneasiness about the quiet calm of the classroom and the dispassionate discussions of great social issues while the world outside groaned in conflict and growing disorder. In his literary society, Anderson spoke about England and the Boers in the Transvaal, the Dreyfus Case, and the Mormons. His interests were in how people organized themselves and in social justice or the lack of it. In a later novel, *Marching Men*, which appeared in 1917, he reflected on his time at Wittenberg. He implied that his teachers had not given him the answers he had been looking for, though he admitted he and they might not have clearly understood that at the time. While he might have continued in college, he did not. At the academy graduation, he spoke on "Zionism." The advertising manager for *Woman's Home Companion*, a magazine published in Springfield, was so impressed that he offered him a job in the Chicago office. Anderson accepted the offer, getting a fast if false start in a business career rather than finishing his education.

The new Wittenberg emerged because Samuel Alfred Ort had willed it into being. It was the realization of the aspirations of his classmates in the Civil War college which first emerged in the Greek societies and the underground newspapers. It was the Wittenberg many alumni and local Springfield citizens had agitated for, which they said the times demanded. But Ort had been able to bring divergent aspirations together and gave them form. He nurtured the new science in the face of church opposition, sought to straddle theological disputes, but in the end moved boldly in new directions. In subsequent years, he was less happy. It was a trying time, economically; and gifts were slower in coming. A friend said that the problems were so severe that in his more depressed moments, Ort believed Wittenberg was done for.

Yet Wittenberg advertised itself as the largest college in the Lutheran Church with 363 students and 21 faculty members, "as thorough as any college of New England at half the expense." It had six buildings, a library of 30,000 volumes, modern laboratories for physics and chemistry, a gymnasium, and eight courses of study: theology, classics, science, literature, a ladies course, music, art, and a preparatory academy.

The resources available to sustain Wittenberg seemed harder to come by. In 1888, Ort had asked the Board to create the post of Financial Secretary to oversee fund raising. It did so; but five years later, the post was left vacant. A new view of administration was emerging in the Board that redefined the president's role. In the past, the president had been a faculty member teaching in college and seminary, presiding over faculty, handling student discipline, and doing what fund raising he could. Now the fund raising role and other off-campus duties loomed larger as presidential responsibilities. With a more professional faculty and a dispersal of daily functions among various ones of them, the Board felt the

President could play a more strategic role for the college. It planned a Semicentennial Endowment Fund campaign and saw it as the President's major responsibility. Only increased resources would make possible the twentieth-century school they all envisioned

In 1899, with the death of his son, Ort's own health failed. In an address to the senior class, he made but a brief reference to his loss saying, "It is with unspeakable sadness that I rise to address you on this occasion." The Board approved a short vacation for him. At their meeting the following June, Ort gave an overview of the eighteen years of his administration. The Board seemed not to notice the valedictory tone of his address. They referred his report to a special committee with the recommendation that he be relieved of his teaching duties in order to concentrate on fund raising. He was thinking in just the opposite direction, giving up fund raising, to focus more on teaching. The committee returned to the Board with his resignation.

There were other factors in Ort's leaving, showing other differences between the president and the Board. When Ort led the faculty decision to abolish graduate work because of insufficient resources and facilities, it was not a popular decision with some on the Board. Increasingly, they harbored the growing hope among Lutherans for a great Lutheran university with graduate work, a law school, and a medical school as well as the undergraduate school, a music conservatory, and the seminary. Ort was convinced that there would hardly be resources enough to sustain a first-rate undergraduate liberal arts institution and a thorough theological seminary. He cited the faltering support of synods and the slow progress in the endowment campaign.

In May of 1895, in the school's fiftieth anniversary year, the Board had appointed a committee, chaired by John L. Zimmerman, to consider officially the feasibility of changing the college into a university. Ort considered such a move ill-advised, and most of the faculty agreed with him. Three years later, in 1898, the Board passed a resolution calling for the opening of law and medical schools in the fall term. Ort resisted doing so without further planning and new financial resources. The Board believed that they had waited long enough for such an expansion.

Interest in expanding the institutions scope was also strong in the community and in the synods. Church interest related to unhappiness over the state universities, particularly Ohio State University. Many were shocked at their rapid progress and the secular nature of their programs. The effort of state universities "to monopolize the education of the young people of the state" and to offer a "Godless environment," they said, alarmed them. The Board asked the president to prepare a leaflet setting forth "the perils of attending secular and state institutions" for circulation among Lutherans. He refused. A year later, he was asked, "Has this been done?" He replied, "It has not."

In 1900, Ort resigned as president and assumed full-time duties in the seminary. He did so partly because of this disagreement with the Board; partly because he did not want to give up teaching; partly, perhaps even mostly because of his grief over his son's death. In his public announcement, he said that he thought the new century and its new expectations should begin with a new president. He was not the man to take a "Greater Wittenberg" into the new century. "The twentieth century is almost here. The twentieth century! Everything must be new. The old is no longer serviceable nor agreeable," he said sardonically. Speaking to the graduating class in 1899, he stated succinctly the philosophy of education that had guided him as Wittenberg's president. He addressed the class with a heavy heart because of the death of his son just before he was to graduate in this class. He described the education they had received. "And now to have all these, a beautiful body, an improved mind, a tender conscience, a warm heart, and a Christian soul, what a solid basis for a true and honorable life." This was Wittenberg's mission: to prepare youth not just for a job, but for a true and honorable life.

Ort's comments about the importance of physical fitness fit well with the emerging athletic emphasis of the school. But his meaning was deeper than that. The soul, the human character had no other instrument through which to express itself in this world than the body. He told the class of 1900 that man was the union of body and spirit, the union of nature and grace. "The natural cannot be divorced from the spiritual and still permit the creature to become what it ought to be." He thought again of his deceased son all of whose great promise had vanished in his death. "If in the evening time of your days," he said, "you can still chant your morning song, it will be because unimpaired vigor of body, strength of heart, firmness of muscle, steadiness of nerve, healthy assimilating forces of your physical organism are part of the capital with which you start to do the business of human life." The student should be a healthy animal that "boasts of something more," he said; and he urged them to have a sympathetic soul and a loving heart, to help the needy, the careworn, the weary, the unfortunate, and the outcast. Then they would be men—and women—prepared for the dawning century and all its problems and challenges.

Chapter Thirteen

A Great Lutheran University

The Board of Directors moved quietly and deliberately in selecting a successor to Samuel Alfred Ort. Their choice, a man now nearly forgotten, was one of the most outspoken advocates of Lutheran higher education at the turn of the century. His presence on campus was to be so brief, however, that his name was misremembered at the school's Diamond Jubilee in 1920 as James instead of John.

The fifth president was John Mosheim Ruthrauff. Benjamin Prince always referred to him as J. Mosheim, but he preferred to be called Mosheim when in college. He was an accomplished horseman, a man hardened by farm work in his youth, a skilled mechanic, and a Civil War veteran. He rose to the top of the list after months of careful deliberation by the committee. They passed over a board member who was a graduate of Gettysburg and later became president there, to pick a Wittenberg Beta to replace the retiring Phi Psi, Samuel Ort. He was a veteran of the postwar student reform movement at Wittenberg and a product of the fraternity rivalries of the day.

J. Mosheim Ruthrauff died nineteen months after his selection, too soon to make any major contribution to the institution. Prince called his death "an event of sorrow in the college circle." It was an interruption of the school's momentum; it allowed uncertainty to return. He was a man of great promise who laid out a sure course forward. He had been received with great expectations.

John Mosheim Ruthrauf, fifth president of Wittenberg, 1900-1902. Wittenberg University Archives.

Yet his brief tenure was an important transition for the college primarily because it was such an extended interruption. It led to an incongruous sequence of events. Ruthrauff came as a vigorous exponent of Wittenberg as a university but would be replaced by a man who was equally vigorous in advocating Wittenberg as an undergraduate liberal arts college. They were good friends and they were fraternity brothers. This would not be the last time that the institution would vacillate between the concepts of a Big and a Little Wittenberg. Ruthrauff came as the spokesman for the Board's authority to determine the mission of the college, but he would be succeeded by a faculty member who spoke for the institutional role of the emerging academic profession.

Ruthrauff was born January 13, 1846, the third son of Henry and Lydia Ruthrauff. His great grandfather had worked with Samuel Schmucker in the founding of the Lutheran Seminary at Gettysburg, and he served on its first Board of Directors. Mosheim spent his early years on the farm where he developed skills as a mechanic. His prosperous father had in addition to the farm a well-equipped work shop, a flour mill, a saw mill, and a small coal mine. He had also invented a successful mowing machine and encouraged his son's mechanical skills. He seemed far more at home in the world of mechanics than that of theology, and the son seemed to be stranded between the two.

Mosheim developed skills in athletics and as a horseman. He had the skills for being a jockey, though he was a bit too large. He was known as a man with an exceptional physique. Ort called him "a manly man." He stood five feet ten and a half inches and weighed 185 pounds. After a preparatory education, he enrolled for two years in Mount Union College but left in 1864 for the Civil War. After the war, he went to Oil City, Pennsylvania, to seek his fortune in the boom resulting from the discovery of oil. Mosheim's mother thought her son had interests in the ministry that he had not asserted, and she persuaded his father to let him return to college. He enrolled at Wittenberg under the influence of his pastor. There he was fond of debating, active in athletics, and an eager member of the new chapter of Beta Theta Pi.

While a student at the college and seminary, he indicated a preference for his middle name and asked to be called Mosheim instead of John. He inscribed his notebook "Dr. Sprecher's Lectures and Mosheim's History," identifying himself with the famous Lutheran scholar, Johann Lorenz von Mosheim, an eighteenth century theologian much admired by Samuel S. Schmucker and his grandfather. In his notes, taken in Sprecher's class, he wrote about "the impotence of theology." Presumably he had meant to write "the importance of theology," and the slip may provide insight into his lifetime concern about the physical weakness of pastors and their need to be physically stronger.

When he finished seminary, Sprecher sent him to Louisville, Kentucky, to organize a mission congregation of the Americanist persuasion. He was there until 1874 when he was succeeded by Samuel A. Ort. Having gotten the new congregation started, Ruthrauff turned it over to the more experienced man to bring it to fruition. As Ort had succeeded Ruthrauff in Louisville, Ruthrauff would succeed Ort at Wittenberg.

In the next several years, Ruthrauff served in several other parishes, and in May of 1879 married Sarah Ellen Morrison of Constantine, Michigan. He described her as "a charming, cultured, Christian woman, a devoted wife, a Spartan mother, and a great help and inspiration." The couple had three children Will, Nellie, and John Mosheim, Jr., who, when they arrived in Springfield, were nineteen, sixteen, and fourteen years of age.

Both Ruthrauff and his wife had contracted malaria while serving a church in southern Ohio. They moved to a church in Dixon, Ill., and there sought to rebuild their health. He became a fearless and active worker for temperance for all and physical fitness among pastors. He organized summer camping and fitness programs among the hills and along the bluffs of the beautiful Rock River Valley. With fitness activities as the central focus, he added Bible study and musical and literary entertainments to the program, replicating the great New York Chautauqua movement. He served as president of the Rock River Assembly, as well as president of the Illinois synod and a member of the Board of Directors of the German Theological Seminary in Chicago.

In the spring of 1895, Carthage College faced a difficult situation in which its indebtedness almost equaled its assets. As they discussed closing the school, Ruthrauff expressed his belief that the college was essential if the Lutheran Church were to continue to grow in Illinois. The Board then asked him to accept the presidency and to save the school, if he could. In five years, he left Carthage with its confidence restored, with an endowment, free of debt, and with funds for campus improvements. The friends of Carthage attributed his success to perseverance, unusual organizing ability, and a personality that inspired confidence. It was just these qualities that recommended him to the Wittenberg search committee.

He persuaded the General Synod, in spite of growing opposition, to advocate increased support for all its colleges. In the Synod, authority was still decentralized; and it could only recommend increased support; it could not require it. Ruthrauff encouraged the central body to recommend it as strongly as it possibly could. As the new century began, however, the organization and structure of the church was becoming more apparent and more specialized. There was, in addition, growing criticism of the cost of church colleges. Some advocated that the church abandon the increasingly secular work of the modern college. Up until this time, the colleges had been central institutions of church identity and the major engines of western church growth. Now central church offices and officers increasingly took on greater authority, taking over many of the functions that college presidents had fulfilled unofficially for fifty years. Some spoke in glowing terms of what could be done in other fields, like theological education and foreign missions, with the funds consumed by the colleges.

Some are only colleges in name said several critics. We have too many schools, more than we can properly endow and equip, said others. They marshaled statistics to prove their point. In doing so, they demonstrated the abject poverty of most of Lutheran higher education. The Episcopalians, with only five colleges, had 90,000 members per school as a basis for support. The Baptists had one college for every 80,000 members and the Methodists, one for every 55,000. The Lutheran Church, divided as it was into so many small and separate synods, each with its own college, was burdened with one college for every 30,000 members. The weight of this burden was evident in endowments. The colleges of the Congregational and of the Episcopal Churches had an average endowment of a third of a million dollars. The nation's 111 private, nonsectarian schools averaged $600,000. The Baptists endowed their colleges fifteen times better than Lutherans endowed theirs. The Lutheran colleges of the nation were at the bottom of the list with an average of less than $20,000. Under the circumstances, Wittenberg's $250,000 was a marvel to behold.

The average American college in 1899, according to Professor F. V. N. Painter of Roanoke College, had 25 professors, 142 students, a scientific apparatus valued at $33,000, buildings and grounds worth $244,000, and an endowment fund of $228,000. His figures were based on a study of 485 institutions. Not one Lutheran institution measured up to these averages in all areas, though Wittenberg came closest.

There was another side to the story according to Ruthrauff; and at a meeting of the General Synod, he insisted on telling it. Grudgingly, he was allotted fifteen minutes; but when his time expired, the audience insisted that he be given more time. He appealed for continued church support of Christian education. To him it was not a question of the availability of resources; it was a question of the judicious use of the resources available. While it might be difficult for Lutherans to support all of their schools, he observed, they could not well get along without each of them. He might have suggested reducing the number by closing the weakest and shifting support to the stronger ones, but instead he encouraged greater support for all.

Defenders of the Church's role in higher education, he observed, could summarize the case for support in four salient points. First, the Lutheran Church was born in a university and should retain the intellectual stimulation of that relationship. Second, in the United States, the Church was placed in an atmosphere of intellectual freedom where its progress depended on its access to university resources and audiences. Third, in America without strong institutions of learning, the Church could not make a deep impression on the life of the nation. Fourth, the Lutheran Church, with a well-defined theology and a noble educational ideal, was well qualified to superintend educational enterprises. It brought a positive view of faith and reason to the world of education.

A more positive outgrowth of these discussions was a hope for a great Lutheran university in America to rank with the strongest and most venerable institutions of the world. It would rival the growing secular state university. Such an institution would never materialize, however, because of Lutheran disunity in the university-building years. With this background and cherishing these hopes, however, Ruthrauff returned to his alma mater to serve as its fifth president, the man the Board believed could lead Wittenberg in the new century. At his inauguration, on June 12, 1901, he spoke on the subject, "The Christian College," but his message was about the Lutheran University. He outlined a new relationship between church and college. He set new goals for Wittenberg in the new century. It should educate a professional ministry with an intellectual culture second to that of no other class of professional men. The church must see to it that her servants were neither physical nor intellectual weaklings by providing a demanding preparation.

Schools like Wittenberg, he told his listeners, were also important and necessary to provide trained Christian leaders in all of the professions and vocations of life. The church was obliged to support Christian colleges in sufficient numbers and with sufficient endowment and equipment to do first class work in all the areas of a modern university curriculum. Our children will not long be content to study in inferior schools, he told them. The sons and daughters of Lutherans should be able to secure, under Lutheran auspices, the general, special, technical, scientific, and professional training needed in any legitimate sphere of life. It was a clear call for the denominational college of broad scope that many on the Board and in the churches were asking for.

"The Christian College," said Ruthrauff, "should be under denominational control and stand for some definite statement of religious truth." Yet, in its courses and programs, it should not teach denominational tenets. He tried to put into words a very complex definition of the church relationship that he saw developing. It was one in which a definite theological position was acknowledged; but where the responsibility for a broad educational program would be fulfilled, recognizing the greater role and secular function of a college serving its community and open to all.

He likened the modern Christian college to a constitutional government. It would have an elected board answerable to synods which operated under their own constitution and offered a particular theological point of view. The religious stance would be defined by the church while the college's board would preserve the school's resources and its objectives in harmony with the controlling church. The educational program, however, would not be controlled by the church. It would be under the aegis of the College Board. "The Christian College," said Ruthrauff, "must compete with the purely secular school . . . in the scope and quality of its work . . . If the Church had been neglectful of this great cause," he concluded, "she must be aroused from her lethargy."

In brief, according to Ruthrauff, the synods would determine the theological stance of the Church, not the Wittenberg Board or faculty as they had been used to doing in the past under Presidents Keller, Sprecher, and Helwig. The Wittenberg Board and faculty, however, would determine the educational program of the college independent of direct synod action. Later, in accord with developments in the universities of the nation, the Board would delegate greater and greater control of the academic program and student life to the faculty, under the authority of the president. Both synod and College Board would be governed by written constitutions spelling out the respective rights of each group. It was a bold statement of institutional autonomy and academic freedom in the church college in a day when some Lutherans thought that decisions to hire or release faculty and those regarding curriculum should be voted on in the synods.

In Dr. Ruthrauff's view, because of the greater resources already accumulated at Wittenberg, it logically should be that great university for its branch of the Lutheran Church, competing with the purely secular university in the quality as well as the scope of its work. Many on the Board were pleased with Ruthrauff's views and the phrase, "a greater Wittenberg," became a permanent part of the school's vocabulary.

Ruthrauff assumed that the resources for such a school could be found. He told his listeners on that inaugural day in 1901 of the many new buildings needed: a YMCA building with a modern gymnasium, an art and a music building. "And in time," he concluded, "medical, law, and other departments should come. Indeed, I hardly know which should come first." Clearly he saw a university with a liberal arts college, school of music, theological school, law school, medical school, and graduate study. Included in the undergraduate college would be specific vocational and professional fields. The Board saw in Ruthrauff's plan "a full comprehension of the needs of higher education," and they pledged to carry out his vision.

The new president would be the first in the school's history without teaching responsibilities either in the college or the seminary. Technically, he was still president of the faculty, but the Board expected him to spend most of his time administering the schools, seeking friends, financial support, and students. He studied Wittenberg's needs, its weaknesses, and its strengths. He analyzed its unique opportunities. "His coming was without blare of trumpets," said Professor Heckert, the friend, faculty member, and fellow Beta that Ruthrauff selected to help him in his analysis. "Indeed, that was characteristic; he cared nothing for the purely spectacular." Heckert, who in effect became the president's assistant, said further, "In everything that touched our complex institutional life, he was both intelligently interested and active. He had a masterly way of compelling one to believe him, and that was probably the secret of his success in securing aid."

Ruthrauff delegated responsibility for the seminary to Dr. Ort, and the theological faculty was organized separately with Ort as dean. But at commencement, when the new president elected to award the degrees, the students in the seminary objected, insisting that they be awarded by their dean. The college faculty developed a greater sense of its own collective responsibility for day-to-day activity. With Charles G. Heckert's assignment as the president's chief faculty colleague, he must have had some special role of leadership within the faculty, if not an official one.

Students in the college made repeated references in the student newspaper to President Ruthrauff's absence from the campus visiting synods and congregations in the interest of the college and the seminary. He spent a major share of his time getting acquainted with the Wittenberg territory, creating goodwill for Wittenberg, presenting the school's needs to potential benefactors and recruiting students.

Before moving his family to Springfield, Ruthrauff had visited the campus staying with Dr. Ort. He then spent the month of October off campus visiting and preaching. Not until mid-November did his family arrive. They all stayed with Benjamin Prince and took meals at the women's dining hall across the street until their house, Helwig's former residence south of Ferncliff Hall, was ready. In December, January, and February, he continued to travel. In one week, he said, he rode fully 150 miles by sleigh, as well as greater distances by train and carriage. On one cold February day alone, he traveled eighteen miles by sleigh to preach in three churches.

In his ledger, he wrote suggestions for the approaching commencement week, "Meet the senior classes in both the theological and collegiate departments early enough to arrange the programs with them. Have Dr. Ort march with the class and the faculty sit on the platform with the class. Have not less than one thousand invitations printed and sent to members of The Literary Club and all prominent citizens, to all the graduates of the city high school, and to all high school pupils in the surrounding towns."

Anticipating the opening of the next school year, Ruthrauff wrote, "Give lecture to students in chapel about the importance of the literary society work, urging all to enter." He also noted that "athletics must not interfere with the work of the literary societies," and that "boys who play match games must make passing grades and secure consent of parents or guardians." To this he added, "See that all match games are guaranteed before played. Must contract no more debt." A match game was an intercollegiate contest. In disciplinary actions for his first year, he ruled that three baseball players were ineligible for away games because they had damaged the dormitory.

In his first year, Ruthrauff found most student misbehavior to be the kicking in of doors in the dorm and in the gymnasium. One student, however, was disciplined for "shooting through the door" in the dorm. He wrote no comment about the level of destructive aggression that such behavior indicated. In exerting greater control, Ruthrauff tried unsuccessfully to put an end to the long-time practice in which students "owned" their rooms for the duration of their stay in college. He decreed that students should remove their furniture when they graduated, and the college thereafter would furnish the room. When students left for the summer, the college would rent the rooms to summer students. Students resisted these changes as an invasion of their rights. Lack of funds forestalled the plan, but not before several doors had been destroyed.

It was a whirlwind start for the vigorous Dr. Ruthrauff; and students, faculty, community, and synods knew that a new man was at the helm. Before another year passed, however, the president was dead. He did not live to see the spectacular changes in American culture and in higher education that he predicted for the twentieth century and their affect on Wittenberg. Along with his talents, his experience, and his enthusiasm, he brought with him a physical constitution weakened by malaria and labor and a developing kidney problem that went undiagnosed. On a trip in the Northern Indiana Synod, he collapsed across the threshold of the place where he was staying. He was confined to his bed for weeks. His wife pleaded with him to take a vacation, but he replied, "When I have raised the necessary money for Wittenberg, I will."

The basis of his pleading was thorough knowledge of Wittenberg's needs. He had made a thorough study of the school's needs, its weaknesses, and its challenging opportunities. "I was more than once surprised," said Professor Heckert, "by his deep grasp of our situation." Alexander Gebhart was persuaded to retire after thirty-three years as treasurer; and John L. Zimmerman, also a Beta, was elected to replace him. It brought the president, the treasurer, and the chair of the Prudential Committee into closer proximity and harmony, and gave Ruthrauff a full access to financial information and greater control of fiscal decisions.

Fire damage to Hamma Hall, the seminary building, Decenber 28, 1900. Wittenberg University Archives.

Shortly after he arrived on campus, the new seminary building burned. While campus fires were not uncommon, most had been minor affairs. This one was devastating. Willard Hackenberg, remembered three fires during his eight years on campus. One was deliberately set by two students from Indiana in the student coal bins lined up behind the Boy's Dorm. "What a fire that was," said Hackenberg. "Think of the many tons of coal that were burned, my winter's supply with the rest," he noted. The two students were caught and expelled. Another fire badly damaged the gymnasium. This too was considered arson, but the culprit was never discovered. The third fire was at Hamma Hall early in the evening of December 28, 1900. The fire was discovered too late for the water from the new hydrant to make much difference. By nine o'clock, it was a complete loss. Students lost all of their property except what they had taken home with them for the Christmas holiday. It was an even greater loss for Dr. Ort; his notes for a book were also consumed in the fire.

The president sought immediately to have the building rebuilt. The Rev. Michael W. Hamma who had provided the funds for the original building announced that he would replace it at no cost to Wittenberg, making up the difference between the insurance proceeds and the cost for a new building. The fire also brought another issue to the fore. Ort's earlier recommendation for a central heating plant moved to the top of Ruthrauff's agenda. It would connect Hamma Hall, the old dorm, Recitation Hall, and the library, and eliminate separate fireplaces, stoves, and furnaces in all four buildings. Ruthrauff pursued the project with energy and solicited gifts of $6,000 in Springfield to help pay for it. Hamma contributed the cost of including the seminary in the project.

When the system was installed, students complained of the loss of control of the temperatures in their rooms in a poem about the chief custodian, Scott Swearingen:

He's known to every student,
For he's been here quite a while.
By nature he is cheerful, and
He always wears a smile.
Ker-choo! Ker-choo! Ker-choo-oo!
Excuse me if I sneeze!
He keeps us warm in summer,
But in winter he lets us freeze!

With equal energy, Ruthrauff served as editor of the *Wittenberg Quarterly*, a journal designed to acquaint the school's friends with its strengths and needs. It augmented the student paper with one more directly responsive to institutional needs for communication with the constituencies of church, alumni, and the Springfield community.

Dr. Ruthrauff also put Wittenberg's annuity concept that had begun with the Hawley gift in 1872 into a more formalized program. In the past, the Board had entered into such agreements without actuarial tables or any formal procedure for estimating appropriate levels of annuity payments. The school issued a brochure encouraging wider use of the charitable gift annuity by means of which friends could make a gift to the school while retaining a lifetime retirement income. The school would guarantee the payments. It raised the level of responsibility of the Board and its finance committee to properly manage and guarantee such funds, a task which it has performed in exemplary fashion for well over a century.

Ruthrauff's activities and interests on campus were the more remarkable in light of his total schedule of duties. A great enthusiast for student athletics, he found time to enjoy Wittenberg's first intercollegiate basketball team and to express his pride in an undefeated season. The growing athletic program, he felt, was good for students and promised a stronger and healthier generation of pastors. He hoped that every candidate for the ministry would participate in vigorous physical activities.

It was a busy year and a half for the new president. A few months after the seminary fire, the rebuilt structure was ready for occupancy. In the spring of 1902, a dedicatory program gave the campus a festive and a confident atmosphere. From April 30 to May 4, 1902, a series of lectures was presented by prominent Lutheran educators and leaders in the church, culminating with the seminary commencement address by Dr. Hamma. The program was designed to show the growing unity among the German Lutherans in the General Synod, the General Synod South, and the General Council with representatives from the colleges and seminaries of all three groups.

The Rev. J. H. Culler, D D, representing the General Synod, presented an address on "The Substantial Unity of the Various Branches of the Lutheran Church in this Country." Dr. H. E. Jacobs, representing the General Council, delivered the closing address on "A Word for the Day." He was gratified by the fact that two great bodies of the Lutheran Church were uniting in fellowship and friendship. "There may be two wings of the Church," he said, "if there be but one heart that beats between them." President Ruthrauff gave the dedicatory address describing "Specific Training for the Lutheran Ministry." The ceremony was an elaborate affair designed to tell a large audience that Wittenberg had not only rejoined the mainstream of American Lutheran thought but hoped, in fact, to assume a leadership role in building Lutheran unity.

The previous month, Dr. Ruthrauff had become ill and was confined to bed in Canton, Ohio. He had just returned from a trip to the east soliciting support. He was tired, he said, but refused to admit that he was ill. The hopeful news of promised support from eastern friends encouraged him, and he attributed his pain to fatigue. He continued to require the attention of his doctor, and his family and friends were concerned.

The elaborate program rededicating Hamma Hall was an additional strain on the president. In May the annual commencement exercises for the seminary further tired him, but he was pleased at the thought of new men entering the active ministry. Some thought a number of the graduates were disrespectful in their pique that he rather than Ort conferred their degrees. He seemed not to notice. On the following Tuesday morning, he promised his wife that he would see his doctor after chapel. Sarah had noticed his feeble and sometimes-dazed appearance during the recent events on campus. She suspected that he had difficulty reading and seeing as the week wore on.

After a short chapel service, the brevity of which attracted student attention as much as did the president's gaunt appearance, Dr. Ruthrauff went downtown to see the doctor. On the way, he stopped at the law offices of John L. Zimmerman to talk about his recent trip east and the promise that it gave for additional financial support for their new university. When he rose to leave, he fell into Zimmerman's arms. Later that afternoon, at the age of fifty-six, J. Mosheim Ruthrauff died of a kidney ailment.

A student of sociology and economics as well as theology, Ruthrauff had believed that he could see the trends of his times. The next generation, he said, would see the union of the different German-American Lutheran bodies in one church. It would see the development of ever larger social organizations, both religious and secular, and Wittenberg would share in that growth. The trend of social and industrial evolution was toward greater centralization and more complex organizations. The ultimate end would be an international economic and political organization coordinating the maturing cultures of the nations of the world. To him this was the direction man must go to solve the problems of the twentieth century. He told his older son, "The great problems of your generation are going to be in the field of economics and sociology. Whatever vocation you choose, make a careful study of these subjects."

The Wittenberg Seal as redesigned by John M. Ruthrauff in 1902. Wittenberg University Archives.

What had seemed too many a minor issue was Dr. Ruthrauff's strong desire to revise the college seal. He had the arms and hands redrawn to show a firm, more masculine grasp of the torch and added "Founded in 1845" and "Springfield, Ohio." In spite of his insistence, the old form continued in use. The seal on the commencement program and the diplomas for his daughter Nellie's class in 1903 was the old one. Sixty years after his death, when his daughter Nellie gave the college a portrait of the fifth president for its gallery of presidents, she insisted that his revised seal be a prominent part of the painting. In 1926 President Tulloss, formally established Ruthrauff's corrected seal, with a few more embellishments, as the official one. As early as 1915, students began to use an English translation rather than the Greek: "Having Light We Pass It On To Others."

Official presidential portrait of J. Mosheim Ruthrauff, fifth president, 1900-1902. Photo by Robert Gantt.

John Ruthrauff was a student of his times and a vigorous thinker. His early death denied Wittenberg and its constituencies any full understanding of his depth and promise. He was quiet, unassuming, manly, and persevering. He was also keenly aware of the need to contemplate the shape of things to come and to build a Wittenberg that fit into the new day. He hoped to make his Alma Mater the leading Lutheran university in America, but that would fall to other hands. Like Ezra Keller over a half century before, he would bequeath his hopes and dreams to others for fulfillment.

While students were shocked by the president's death, they were not as shocked as might have been expected. He had been in office not quite nineteen months. For a large part of that time, students were away on vacation. For the remainder, Ruthrauff was away raising funds. Dr. Ort was in charge of the seminary, and

Prof. Heckert seemed to be in charge of the college. When he died, Benjamin Prince as chairman of the Prudential Committee continued to attend to the day to day operation of the school. Ort was named dean of the college and acting president as the presidential search got underway.

The sadness of the 1903 commencement was most real for the students in the grief of the president's family and particularly his daughter Nellie, who was vice president of the class. As Ruthrauff's death was noted and a new president inaugurated, it was a sad occasion for the class even as it was a joyous one as well. For the seniors, the day was enlivened by the fact that, after years of effort, the practice concerning student addresses had finally been resolved. For nearly two decades, students had petitioned to be excused from the ordeal of preparing and delivering orations for the occasion. Once or twice, the Board had relented as an experiment but always returned to the old practice. Now, finally, the old custom was abandoned.

The students did not escape entirely. Six or eight members of a class, depending on its size, would deliver orations while the others would write a paper on an assigned topic for faculty review. A number of years later, the practice was further modified to have one student orator selected by the faculty to represent the class and one distinguished person from off campus, also chosen by the faculty, to deliver the commencement address.

The June 1903 commencement week included an alumni banquet and marked the beginning of a practice that continued for a century. On the occasion, the members of the graduating class were formally received into the Alumni Association. Benjamin Prince noted that such an event had been attempted as early as 1868, but there were not enough alumni able to return to sustain the event. The purpose of the revived event, he said, was to cultivate good fellowship among "old Wittenbergers." Around the event grew class reunions and a greater loyalty to the college.

In succeeding months, Mrs. Ruthrauff had a difficult time. One of Nellie's classmates recalled Mrs. Ruthrauff's problems. "She did everything to keep her family together and educate them," she said. "She gave physical culture lessons, did fine embroidery, and kept roomers." There was at that time no provision for faculty retirement and no provision for the families of men who died young.

Mrs. Ruthrauff kept ten male students in her house, served them breakfast, and had them join her family in worship every morning. "That money kept my family in food," she confided to a friend.

Her older son moved to Tucson, Ariz., and after a while sent for his mother and younger siblings. After great struggle, the last of the children finished college; and she was overcome with emotion "because Dr. Ruthrauff was not there to see it." Some felt the college never really appreciated Mrs. Ruthrauff's situation nor expressed any proper concern for the family's loss or its sacrifices for Wittenberg. But the Board had provided significant assistance for the times. They voted to allow her free rent in the college house and her husband's salary for four months. They also voted to grant free tuition for her children. Such well-meant assistance, however, was both temporary and inadequate. It may have been better than the standard for the day, but it called attention to a serious and growing problem. No one on the faculty or staff had any greater security.

Chapter Fourteen

Weltanschauung: A World View

After nearly a year's deliberation, the Board chose a new president. The selection committee proposed a forty-year-old, fun-loving, sociable, almost light-hearted, professor of English. He had worked so closely with his predecessor that many wondered why it took the Board so long. The nominee accepted the nomination with one condition: on the day faculty salaries were again discounted, his resignation would be in their hands.

He had studied for the ministry, but never served as a pastor. While he preached occasionally, more after becoming president than before, he had been a teacher all of his professional life. When interviewed about religious views, he gave an unusual response: "I really don't care much what you think of my views, possibly just as little as you are concerned about my opinion of your viewpoint." Modern religion, he continued, had more love in it and less envy and hatred. "Christians are not so opinionated today." His part of the church, he said, expected to see Catholics and Methodists in heaven as well as Lutherans. "Sure," he concluded, "they all have their creeds and believe many things," but he did not worry much about creedal differences.

The English professor went further. The college, he said, should provide a climate of respect and support for all beliefs. "The modern idea of religion is so reasonable, so kindly, so all inclusive, so persuasive that I challenge any man to come in touch with it without being made better." He advised students to try various churches and find one they liked. In this more tolerant climate, Wittenberg's first Jewish students enrolled; and a Newman Club for Catholics was established.

Charles Girven Heckert was born on March 22, 1863, to Benjamin and Sarah Jane Durst Heckert. His father was a successful merchant. He enrolled in 1880 at the age of seventeen. After two years, he left to teach. Returning in 1884, he completed the Classical Course and was graduated, valedictorian of his class. He was active in the Excelsior Society and the State Oratorical Association, was the manager of the football team, and a legendary baseball pitcher. Like Ruthrauff, he was an energetic member of Beta Theta Pi fraternity. His brothers described him as the shortest member of the class, the brother "nearest to mother earth." He entered seminary and tutored in the preparatory department. On July 24, 1889, he married Ada Royer and accepted appointment as instructor of Greek and history in the academy. He was soon promoted to principal and pursued graduate work in Mental Philosophy. In 1893 he became professor of English and Logic in the college.

In 1899 he received an honorary doctor of divinity degree from J. Mosheim Ruthrauff, president of Carthage College in recognition of his service at Wittenberg. The two had become acquainted through Beta activities. During Ruthrauff's short tenure, he became close to Heckert and College Treasurer John L. Zimmerman. It would be this team of "Betas," plus several more on the faculty and the Board, that led Wittenberg for the next several years. After decades of Phi Psi rule, the Betas gloried in their triumph.

Ruthrauff and Zimmerman had endorsed the idea of Wittenberg as a university, while Heckert was an advocate of Wittenberg as a liberal arts college. Debate over that issue may have caused the delay in the committee's selection, and an important compromise was arrived at that influenced the school's future course greatly. With Heckert's election, there was little further talk of law and medical schools or graduate-level programs. There was, however, an expanded view of what should be included in an undergraduate curriculum. It should go beyond traditional liberal arts to include certain kinds of vocational training at the undergraduate level. Parish pastors wanted the options for their youth to be expanded so that they would not have to attend a state university.

Heckert was aware of the emerging structure of American higher education with undergraduate colleges, universities, graduate and professional schools. With limited resources, he was content that Wittenberg be one of the state's quality undergraduate colleges, but with a program that was broader than most. He resisted the efforts of some "to call this college a university . . . We are not a university and make no pretension to do work other than that which comes within the proper sphere of a well-equipped college."

Charles Girven Heckert, sixth president, 1902-1920,
Photo by Robert Gantt.

Heckert began his service as president with a record of active service in civic and church affairs. He had served as secretary and as president of the Miami Synod, and for three years, managing editor of the *Lutheran World*. He and his wife had been active in the organization of Fourth Lutheran Church, now Good Shepherd near the campus. He was also known as a man of good business sense. Capitalizing on his youthful experience in his father's business, he was a founder of The James Carson Company of wholesale grocers in Springfield. He served as a member of the Board of Directors of the American Trust and Savings Bank of Springfield, where

Wittenberg maintained its accounts; and he was a board member of the Ohio State Life Insurance Company in Columbus.

His inaugural address, "The Rationale for the Denominational College," revealed the depth of his commitment to Christian higher education and his sense of anticipation about the shape of the new century. He noted that much had changed with the close of the nineteenth century and urged his audience not to be alarmed when they discovered that the judgments and policies of their fathers had been "peremptorily banished to the limbo of things that were good enough for their day" but not this. The relationships of people and the social, political, and economic developments of the nation called for new judgments and new policies. Things were going to be different, he conjectured, in as yet unperceived ways. "The demand of this age is for things modern," he said, and in the world of education, the church college had to be as progressive as the state university.

What a person meant when he used the term "modern" in 1904 was not easy to say. Alain Locke, the first African American Rhoades Scholar in 1907, in his *Lectures on the Theory and Practice of Race,* a decade later, defined "modern" as a society that no longer merely repeated and extended its past, but changed in unforeseeable directions. The modern person, he said, could not see his role in life in advance, but found it as he coped with the new, evolving course of events. When Heckert talked about the modern in 1904, he referred primarily to new behaviors, actions, and solutions that replaced those of "our father's times." But he would need a decade to determine exactly what that meant.

For one thing, the modern included a more open and public enjoyment of leisure. His photo album was full of casual snapshots of the Heckerts at parties, at home, in parks, at the horse races, in the countryside, and on beaches. The difference was at least in part the result of the appearance of cheaper cameras and his enthusiastic use of them. For students modern meant the more public demonstration of joy, romance, and playfulness. Heckert and the faculty accepted that. They replaced a Victorian dichotomy of a public and a private life with a modern notion of being yourself at all times.

More formally, the modern had to do with the new music of Stravinsky and Schoenberg, the art of the cubists, the poetry of T. S. Eliot, the antiheroic novels of James Joyce, and Virginia Woolf's definition of a new cultural climate. The pursuit of the modern by creative artists such as these began with the new century, but would not be apparent until after World War I. In science there was Einstein, in political economics Karl Marx, and in psychology Sigmund Freud. All of these new voices appeared soon after the beginning of the twentieth century; and as a group, as T. S. Eliot said of James Joyce, they "destroyed the whole of the nineteenth century." For perceptive persons close to the world of the intellect in colleges and universities, these were the harbingers of a modern era whose dimensions were as yet unclear. Heckert shared in the anticipation of this unknown, emerging new world and sought to define its meaning for Wittenberg. Modernism was not just cubism in art and modern poetry and literature. It was also new ways to structure enterprise: business, politics, education, even society itself.

Wittenberg needed to see itself in the context of modern higher education, Heckert said; it needed to take into account the revolutionary changes that continued to alter learning. He left little doubt that Wittenberg must be part of the greater whole as it unfolded. The address revealed the essential elements of his philosophy. He had what philosophers called *"weltanschauung,"* said Professor V. G. A. Tressler, a world view. Tressler taught Greek in the college and theology in the seminary. For Heckert, Tressler continued, "it was a great thing to live, to be part of this beautiful, wonderful, awe-inspiring world; he leaped with joy at the motion of it." His world view was enlivened by the divine and the human spirit, and he fought unflinchingly to be a part of it.

And tackle the world for Wittenberg, Heckert would; but first, he needed to get some things reordered on campus. In the *Cycle*, the yearbook for 1902, the students said that Heckert's motto was "Order is Heavens' first law;" and as president, he sought to reorder the way the school's work was done. But first, he had electric lights installed in all the buildings. When he was a youth in Sunbury, Pa., Thomas Edison built there the first three-wire, central station, electric light plant in the world. Twenty years, he thought, was long enough for Wittenberg to wait for this modern marvel. He also had the dirt pathways between buildings replaced with cement walks. Students were excited by such advances. In appreciation, the sophomore class refurnished his office in Recitation Hall. The student who made the presentation was Rees Tulloss,

Rees Edgar Tulloss, class of 1906, shown here as captain of the football team in 1904. He would succeed Dr. Heckert as president in 1920.

who would succeed Heckert as president of the College. The most recent class gifts had refurbished classrooms or offices. Beginning with Heckert, classes extended the cement walkways or contributed to Professor E. O. Weaver's magnificent new design for the campus entrance.

Heckert had inherited a system which required faculty members, during summer vacation, to travel over Wittenberg's territory interviewing and recruiting students, counseling with vacationing students and their parents, and soliciting financial support. The practice was disliked by the new faculty, and Heckert looked for a better way to do this work. He asked the Board to create the post of field representative and hired the Rev. C. S. Ernsberger to fill it. He was to visit among the churches and area high schools to acquaint students, parents, and teachers with Wittenberg. This made admissions more efficient and relieved faculty of a major interference with their study and research.

Heckert's modern college also called for the better organization of the faculty. He named Charles G. Shatzer, a Beta from the class of 1900, as dean so that he could spend more time off campus. In his first report, Shatzer defined the college as the larger unit of which the departments were the parts. He asserted what became the defining principal of faculty organization at Wittenberg: "The success of the college depends upon the individuality of the departments in matters pertaining to the content of courses and methods of instruction." As curriculum expanded, departmentalization grew. Each department referred to itself as a school. Neither Shatzer nor Heckert discouraged the presumption.

Faculty came together, said Shatzer, for matters of overall efficiency and those requiring unity of procedure and common standards. Their role in governance was still focused in the Prudential Committee. Shatzer spoke as if faculty were just discovering a collective role and were uncertain about it. When the faculty was smaller, most served on the Prudential Committee and sat in on meetings of the Board. As the faculty grew larger, those practices were less satisfactory; but what would take their place was as yet unclear. "Much has been begun," said Shatzer, "that may be developed as time passes."

The next year was more difficult than the first, said the dean. In a lament that would be heard repeatedly from faculty called to administrative posts, he complained that his duties as dean kept him from meeting the needs of his department and his students. He initiated weekly meetings of faculty, which they resisted. The professors recognized their responsibility to attend, but showed a great desire to delegate matters to committees. He asked for a stenographer and bookkeeper to relieve faculty and himself of clerical duties and record keeping not related directly to classroom teaching. The dean also began reporting on faculty members' professional activities, papers delivered at professional meetings, and their publications of articles and books.

Charles G. Shatzer, class of 1900, first Springfield professor of Geology in 1904. He was named Dean of the College in 1912 and served for thirty-five years. Wittenberg University Archives.

As faculty became more organized, Heckert looked toward a clearer administrative structure as well. He saw a need for better alumni relations and added that responsibility to the field secretary's duties. The emerging "administration" consisted then of Heckert as president; Prince as vice president and chairman of the Prudential Committee; Dr. D. H. Bauslin, a Beta from the class of 1876, as dean of The Divinity School; Charles G. Shatzer, dean of the College; and C. S. Ernsberger, as field representative.

In 1906, Rev. Michael Hamma made his most significant gift of $175,000 for theological education. He received an annuity income until his death. All income, with that exception, was to go to the seminary. The gift was made in Almira Hamma's memory. In her will, if her husband had died first, the funds were to go to Wittenberg on condition that the seminary pledge to teach in accordance with the "unaltered Augsburg Confession and Luther's Smaller

Catechism, without modification, amendment, or evasion," and that the school be named Hamma Divinity School. He made the gift with the understanding that his wife's wishes would be honored.

In 1910, Heckert made his boldest proposal for reform: reducing the size of the Board. "Every detail entering into the life and conduct of the college," he said, "has been subjected to the keenest examination." It was time for the Board to examine itself. It was too large, he said; the whole tendency in modern business was toward boards of a few strong and active men. He did not propose to change the balance of power among synods, Springfield, and the alumni, he said, but the proposal did alter the balance slightly. He proposed merely to reduce the Board from forty-two to twenty-four members: two clergy and two lay directors from each of the five synods, two directors from Clark County and two from the alumni. Twenty-four was still too many, he said, but it was a step in the right direction. A year later, he withdrew the proposal. While it had support from leading businessmen, some clergy opposed it. He felt they misunderstood the plan; but, since it could not get unanimous approval, he would withdraw the idea. "It is bound to come," he said, "the proposition is undoubtedly right." The Board continued to grow as the church grew; and, unfortunately, action to reduce its size would not come for many years.

Heckert also made small changes in the character and nature of commencement. The seminary graduation was separated from that of the college and held in the chapel a week earlier. The college ceremony had been moved to the campus in 1878 and continued in the grove below the men's dorm. Heckert continued the policy dispensing with speeches by all graduates. He revived the procession from Recitation Hall up the hill to the dormitory then down the east drive and west to the campus circle where a platform had been erected. The procession stopped at the dorm to honor the founders: Keller, Sprecher, Geiger, Diehl, and Isaac Sprecher, a worthy tribute to those who had expended their lives for the college in its early years. "The Flying Dutchmen" were redeemed.

Heckert presided over a changing curriculum as vestiges of the old classical course decreased, and a more modern list of courses appeared. When he made the annual report of the faculty, he did so by department: the History and Political Science Department with Benjamin Prince; Chemistry with A. F. Linn; Greek with Robert H. Hiller; Mathematics with W. E. Anderson; Latin with Jens A. Ness;

German with K. F. R. Hochdoerfer; Geology and Biology with Dean Charles G. Shatzer; French with Madame Hochdoerfer; English with J. P. Schneider assisted by Miss Rose Caddwgan; Physics with E. O. Weaver; and Psychology, Philosophy, and Education with T. Bruce Birch. He used newly designated ranks of instructor, assistant professor, and professor.

The president of the class of 1913 noted Heckert's progress toward modernity. "More has been accomplished in the past ten years than in the preceding forty," observed Lloyd Wallich. He noted Wittenberg's commitment to hiring university-trained men. Noting feelings in the churches against the practice, Heckert defended the policy at the General Synod's 1909 and 1913 conventions. The editor of the *Springfield Morning Sun* wrote, "Dr. Heckert's dream is to put this hall of learning on a plane where it will be recognized as among the most important educational institutions in the whole country." He captured Heckert's aspirations very well. But it could only be achieved, Heckert believed, by attracting and retaining the best of the new faculty available.

The first faculty member to be hired by Heckert was a professor of Greek, Victor G. A. Tressler. He was a *summa cum laude* graduate of Gettysburg College. After earning a master's degree, he spent two years in law school before entering McCormick Theological Seminary, a Presbyterian school in Chicago. Afterward he went to Europe to study in Berlin, Paris, and Leipzig, receiving his Ph D *magna cum laude,* from Leipzig in 1902. He was one of the first Americans to ride the Trans-Siberian Railroad. He had a quick mind, knew several languages, and wrote poetry for fun.

He was willing to begin as a teacher of Greek in both college and seminary, but hoped eventually to teach theology. Hamma and Heckert promised him the first opening available at the seminary and then worried about how soon they might be able to fulfill their commitment. They made the promise because Tressler was a bright young star in the Lutheran sky. In less than a year, he was offered a college presidency. Hamma wrote Heckert, "On your urging," I assured him of a place teaching Biblical Criticism. "You and I are under obligation to put on our thinking caps to see what can be done to meet the expectations that we inspired." When Tressler was promoted, Robert H. Hiller, fresh from Columbia University, replaced him in the chair of Greek.

Heckert's second appointment was his own replacement. He surrendered his position in English to J. Philip Schneider who had grown up in the German neighborhood on New York's lower east side. A Phi Psi, he had graduated from Wittenberg in "the great class of 1896," received a masters from Columbia in 1898, and his Ph D from Johns Hopkins University in 1904, where he was inducted into Phi Beta Kappa. In recommending him, his graduate advisor wrote that he had "more than the average share of enthusiasm" and he "believes in sound work above everything else." He predicted that Schneider would be a "professor of exceptional power." At Wittenberg he taught Shakespeare and Dante, was involved in student activities, and an active sports fan. He had great impact on students.

Heckert's third appointment, also in 1904, was Jens Anderson Ness, professor of Latin. He was a scholar with interest in Indo-Germanic philology; and he read Sanskrit, Avestan, Greek, classical and Medieval Latin, Lithuanian, German, and the Romance languages. He taught at St. Olaf College, the Universities of South Dakota, Minnesota, Chicago, and Johns Hopkins where he earned his Ph D.

Heckert's fourth faculty decision was to promote Charles G. Shatzer to acting professor of Geology and Biology while he solicited business and industrial leaders to endow the Springfield chair for those subjects. In 1905 Shatzer was appointed to the endowed chair and in 1912 was named dean. These new faculty members joined Alice Mower in languages and Samuel Ort and the seminary faculty. The growing list included emeritus faculty member Samuel Sprecher, but his name would soon be removed from the roll in 1906 and Ort's five years later.

Heckert talked about the old giving way to the new and nothing symbolized that as clearly as the passing of these two giants. Ort eulogized Sprecher "as the man, the preacher, the theologian, the teacher, and the president." He was a rare man, he said, and a powerful preacher. His sermons were "logic on fire!" For all his emphasis on saving grace, said Ort, Sprecher could not reject a role for human will. God, he said, expected man's response. He was a distinguished teacher, fresh, vigorous, forceful, and innovative, imparting something of himself, his personality, his mind to his students. As president of the fledgling school, said Ort, Sprecher made Wittenberg permanent. "Wittenberg was a little college and, comparatively speaking, had scarcely any friends; nevertheless, he loved this college with all his soul and gave it the best of his strength, the best of his life. He lived himself into its very existence; and so it is that the two are forever inseparable."

Five years later Ort, too, died. Tributes poured in from New York to California and from foreign mission fields. Alumni observed that early students called him "Doc;" later students called him "Old Doc;" no other faculty member was to be called by that shortened form. Older alumni, Ort's classmates, and his earliest students had called him "Sammy," with great familiarity. In his mathematics classes, he was considered blunt. In bachelor days, he lived in the dorm; and students learned of his kindhearted disposition. "I can still see that Grand Old Man of God," said an alumnus, "drawing himself up to his full tiptoe stature . . . as he shouted, 'My young friends, no man has a right to do wrong.'"

He was a "fun-mixed-with-religion" man, said another, lessening the austerity of it all. Many noted that his mind was "supported by a strong, vigorous, and healthful body. His moral and spiritual nature took active and permanent possession of his vigorous body and mental powers." Others noted his personal interest in each student. A close friend said, "I wish his latter days had been happier than they were." Another said, "A man never looked so gigantic and masterful in a soft, felt hat." Elizabeth Stanley McCauley, class of 1900, a missionary in India, remembered one of his chapel prayers: "Lord, help us to serve well the day and generation in which we live.'"

Clearly Heckert sought to serve as well in his day and generation as Sprecher and Ort had served in theirs. In the old-time college, the president more than anyone else had personified the institution. As the modern era emerged, that focus on one strong personality in the life of the school was waning. Sprecher's Wittenberg and Ort's were identified with them to such a great extent that Helwig's failure to achieve that identification for want of skill and Ruthrauff's for want of time, stood out starkly in public perception and in Heckert's.

Heckert had traveled to California in 1905 to meet Sprecher and learn more about the part of the institution which he embodied. He already knew that which dwelt in Samuel Ort. Sprecher and Ort spent more time on campus than Heckert would be able to do.

They taught at every class level, in several subjects in both college and seminary. After many years of teaching, Heckert's contacts in the classroom would now be zero. Students would increasingly personify the institution in the lives of the various faculty members who most influenced their lives.

Heckert lost little time in setting to work to increase support for the faculty and their programs. One of the outcomes of Ruthrauff's inspired pleading was The Million Dollar Education Fund. At the Synod's convention in Baltimore in 1903, a campaign was approved for a million dollars for colleges and seminaries. The colleges included were Carthage, Gettysburg, Midland, Susquehanna, and Wittenberg. Their presidents and vice presidents were appointed a committee "to devise and execute plans." The General Synod strongly recommended support and asked the committee to secure the cooperation of the district synods. This meant that Heckert had to persuade each of Wittenberg's five supporting synods to join in the effort.

Wittenberg sought other avenues to new sources of revenue. The president began a long and productive relationship with a leading alumnus, a fellow Beta Theta Pi, Federal Judge Peter S. Grosscup. President Benjamin Harrison appointed Grosscup a United States Federal District Judge in 1872. President William McKinley named him to the Circuit Court of Appeals in Chicago in 1884. He achieved national prominence through a number of cases that came before him. In the Chicago World's Fair Sunday Closing Case, he upheld laws requiring that certain services be withheld on Sundays. He issued the injunctions that broke the Great Railway Strike in 1894. Over Illinois Governor John Altgeld's objections, he endorsed a call for President Grover Cleveland to send Federal troops to suppress the riots. While Clarence Darrow defended Eugene V. Debs and strike leaders, Grosscup sent them to jail for violating his injunctions.

At Wittenberg, Judge Grosscup had been an active member of the fraternity movement as a Beta and a member of the Excelsior Society. He was a champion debater. His love of his alma mater was strong; and in his desire to help increase the school's resources, he was willing to use his prominence and influence in the school's behalf. His reputation for positions in support of business and industry won him friends among the leaders of American enterprise. He tried to get Heckert together with Henry Clay Frick, a steel magnate in

Pittsburgh and ally of Andrew Carnegie. Frick wrote Heckert that he would be out of town most of the summer and added, "If it is the desire of the judge and yourself to see me in connection with the contribution to your college, I think it would be a waste of your time." Grosscup advised Heckert not to take him seriously. When times improve, he said, Frick would consider Wittenberg for a gift.

Grosscup scheduled a meeting with Nicholas Murray Butler, president of Columbia University and member of Rockefeller's General Education Board. "Before going to Mr. Rockefeller personally," he said, "we shall see Mr. Butler," since he would refer us to him anyway. Later, he reported seeing Harry Pratt Judson, president of the University of Chicago, also a member of the General Education Board. The Board, said the judge, would send someone to evaluate the school. "If they do," he added, "I have asked that they let me know so that I can be present." The approach to Mr. Rockefeller took many years and did not bear fruit until the year after Heckert retired, but he kept up the effort. In 1915 Grosscup wrote, "I have written Mr. Rockefeller an insistent letter." Wittenberg submitted a formal proposal to the General Education Board. It was deferred first by the Board, pending an evaluation of the school, and then by World War I.

While the Frick and Rockefeller approaches worked their way out, Grosscup approached the McCormick family, rich and famous because of the McCormick reaper, a major competitor of the reaper made by the Springfield Champion Agricultural Works. Later the two, along with three other companies merged in the International Harvester Company. Throughout Heckert's administration, he and Judge Grosscup engaged in these kinds of complex financial cultivations. While the judge's conduct was acceptable, apparently, in the Gilded Age, today, such actions, no matter how well intentioned, would fall outside of the code of ethics for appropriate behavior for a Federal judge.

An early success for Heckert was his approach to Andrew Carnegie. He began his cultivation of Carnegie for a gift for a new science building. Finally, on July 10, 1905, he received a terse letter from Mr. Carnegie's private secretary saying, "Mr. Carnegie desires me to say that he will be glad to pay for the erection of a science building, at a cost of $30,000, provided the amount of $30,000 new endowment is raised toward the upkeep and carrying on of the

Science Department in this building." Heckert had asked for $40,000 and continued to negotiate for the rest of the money while seeing if he could raise the matching funds.

Carnegie Science Hall, 1909.
Wittenberg University Archives.

On September 5, he wrote alumni asking them to raise $5,000 of the $30,000 goal. On November 1, he wrote to Lutheran congregations in Wittenberg's territory. He personally solicited individuals he thought could make gifts of $1,000 or more. It appeared that the response would be good, and he approached The Commercial Club of Springfield asking if they would commit $10,000. If so he would accept Carnegie's challenge. They agreed.

The program for the building was completed by Professor E. O. Weaver, a Beta from the class of 1889 and professor of Physics. It was clear that the cost would be closer to the original request of $40,000. Heckert wrote Carnegie accepting the challenge for the $30,000, but adding that he still needed the additional $10,000. After some delay and the exchange of insistent letters, Carnegie approved an additional $5,000. Heckert responded with gratitude and accepted the increase, but said that he still needed $5,459.65 to complete the building needed. He told Carnegie that he had tried to raise the additional money elsewhere. "I can get money to endow or equip it, but men decline to give funds to help pay for a building that is generally thought to be erected by Mr. Carnegie. This surely must be evident to you." The exchange of letters suggests that the frugal Scotsman and the stubborn German thoroughly enjoyed their tug of war.

Heckert told Carnegie that science enrollments at Wittenberg were already increasing in anticipation of the Carnegie Science Hall with its up-to-date equipment. "We get the German and Scandinavian young men," he added, "and they actively make good citizens when Americanized." In late December 1907, after several more letters, Carnegie's secretary asked if Heckert was prepared to match a further gift from Mr. Carnegie, if it were forthcoming. Heckert said "yes" to this Christmas present. The final gift of $5,549, dropping the sixty-five cents, brought the grand total to $40,549. Wittenberg friends added an equal amount to endowment plus the funds for furnishings and equipment.

The beginning of the new entrance to the campus. Class gifts over two decades would complete the project. Wittenberg University Archives.

It was the gentle and kind E. O. Weaver, teacher at Wittenberg for half a century, who defined the needs of the sciences and supervised construction. Springfield architect Robert C. Gotwald designed the building taking Weaver's program into account. Weaver designed stairs and walks from Carnegie Hall to "Reci's" south doors. While he was at it, he proposed a new campus entrance. He persuaded the class of 1909 to build the stairs and lobbied later classes for the various sections of the new entrance.

Heckert's cultivation of industrialists and foundations reflected the competition among colleges in the major expansion under way in higher education. Enrollments were growing and institutions needed to improve facilities and add equipment and endowment. Changes were instigated by new associations like the Carnegie Foundation and the General Education Board and by businessmen serving on college boards. In some universities, a struggle began between faculties and boards, between intellectuals and corporate chiefs. Modern faculties, particularly at the large universities, adopted the autonomy of European faculties. They saw that American invention, the state-chartered board, as an obstacle in defining modern higher education. These tensions were not yet apparent at Wittenberg. Earlier conflicts with Springfield industrialists had subsided, and no one currently on the faculty irritated businessmen as Dr. Stuckenberg had done. Faculty, who had been in need for so long, welcomed the new resources. For Wittenberg the clash over corporate support came not from faculty, but from the church.

In the midst of the campaign for the science hall, another issue involving Carnegie's benevolence arose which caused concern in the Lutheran churches. The story broke in the *Springfield Sun* on June 7, 1906, but had been simmering for some time. "Tempest in a Teapot Stirred up in Lutheran Circles," read the headline. The story asked, "Had Wittenberg forsaken her faith for Carnegie's gold?"

At the same time that Heckert sought the science building gift, he wanted Wittenberg to be included in the Carnegie Foundation's plan for faculty pensions. There was no greater problem facing faculty, he felt, than the prospect of retirement, declining health or early death with no provision other than private savings. Given the low salary scales, savings were hard to accumulate. It meant that many stayed at their jobs beyond the point of effectiveness. Heckert was convinced that Wittenberg's faculty should be in the retirement plan which Carnegie proposed. But the Foundation required that participating institutions be nondenominational. "When Mr. Carnegie established a fund for the pensioning of aged professors," said Heckert, "it was his intention to exclude the denominational school entirely. No school under the control of any church was to be allowed to partake of his benefaction." Perhaps Heckert believed he could change Carnegie's mind on this as he had on the gift for the building. He went with a group of church-college leaders to see Carnegie to persuade him and was overly optimistic about that possibility. As the costs of carrying out the plan rose, Carnegie restricted it even further and then replaced it with a different plan altogether.

In the changed plan, said Heckert, the only condition was that the college which applied to participate must not teach denominational doctrines in its collegiate department. He asked the Board to approve a resolution stating: "In the collegiate and academic departments of Wittenberg College, the following is and has been the policy of Wittenberg College, that no denominational test is imposed in the choice of trustees, officers, or teachers, or in the admission of students, nor are denominational tenets or doctrines taught to the students." This resolution, said Heckert, would enable Wittenberg to be on the approved list of schools.

The Board approved the statement but many believed it went beyond the actual state of affairs at least in the matter of qualifications for board membership. The action led to considerable discussion, argument, and misunderstanding. Many insisted it was a major change in policy, that Wittenberg had forsaken its Lutheran origins, that Heckert had indeed sold out for Carnegie's gifts. The Board felt that while the school was supported primarily by Lutherans, its service was by no means to be restricted to that denomination. Perhaps it had dropped the theological oath for board members, but clearly all synod elected members were required to be Lutheran. Heckert was arguing that it was not necessary that alumni board members or those from Clark County be Lutheran, and that the executive trustees were selected without reference to religious affiliation. But the synods had not all subscribed to that liberalization.

Keller's Wittenberg had never been narrowly denominational. The first faculty included an Episcopalian; the first Board included Presbyterians. The Americanists had been interdenominational, and

Congregationalists, Methodists, Episcopalians, and Presbyterians, as well as Lutherans and nonchurch members were enrolled. Now there were Catholics and Jews would be enrolled within the decade. As theological education had become more denominational, the college and the seminary had become separate. Since 1855, faculty had been exempt from taking a theological oath. There were growing pressures from Lutheran circles to maintain the narrower focus that had emerged after 1855, but the Board spoke boldly to sustain the statement they had passed.

The Wittenberg Synod formally asked the Board to rescind its 1906 statement. The Board debated the request at length and then reported, "After thorough reconsideration, it is the opinion of the Board that it would be unwise to rescind the action taken on this question a year ago." All but four of the Board's members had been elected by the five synods relating to Wittenberg; and though their action was not unanimous, it showed strong board support for Heckert's more liberal interpretation.

Wittenberg, however, was not going to be eligible after all. Heckert had not been able to change Carnegie's mind this time. When the regulations appeared defining what the ban meant, none of the nation's church-related colleges could qualify. The stipulation was "only colleges, universities, and technical schools of requisite academic grade, not owned or controlled by a religious organization, whose acts of incorporation or charters specifically provide that no denominational test shall be applied in the choice of trustees, officers, or teachers, nor in the admission of students, shall be eligible." Heckert joined a new delegation of presidents of church colleges to call upon the foundation. It included Brown, Denison, Gettysburg, Haverford, Heidelberg, Lake Forest, Monmouth, Ohio Wesleyan, Richmond, Parsons, Wooster, and Wittenberg.

The group met with representatives of Carnegie on Mar. 4, 1909, but there was no change in the decision. Faculties of church-related colleges were not eligible. Some schools continued to negotiate, even altered their constitutions in hopes of qualifying; but Wittenberg dropped the matter. Later, in 1918, the Foundation put forth a new plan which developed into the Teachers Insurance and Annuity Association (TIAA). Wittenberg later joined this program, enabling faculty to contribute a percentage of salary which the institution matched, to a retirement fund to be independently managed.

In the midst of the furor over the retirement plan, Heckert obtained a major gift from a local industrialist. While visiting Carnegie in 1906, Heckert said the thought occurred to him to visit John W. Bookwalter, a Springfield resident then located in Lakeport, N. J. In 1908, Dr. and Mrs. Heckert left for Europe to again visit Bookwalter who was traveling there. The *Springfield Sun* called it "Dr. Heckert's mysterious trip abroad." He made the trip, he said later, because given the state of Bookwalter's health, he might never again return to Springfield. They visited with the Bookwalters in Nice, France, for several days, having stopped in the Canary Islands, Gibraltar, Algiers, and Italy on the way. Following their visit, they stopped in Rome and then returned home with Bookwalter's gift of $30,000 for the John W. Bookwalter, chair of Philosophy and Psychology.

The man called to fill the new chair was T. Bruce Birch.

T. Bruce Birch, first Bookwalter professor of Philosophy, 1908-1937. Wittenberg University Archives.

He did his undergraduate work at Gettysburg College and graduate studies at the University of Pennsylvania, earning the Ph D. He continued a traditional philosophy program at Wittenberg but introduced modern psychology. Drs. Sprecher and Ort had had a continuing interest in the field of psychology and an ongoing curiosity about human behavior. Birch carried these interests further in a study of the experimental works of the new generation of psychologists. He was also instrumental in designing a new course in pedagogy and educational psychology replacing the old normal school program. In 1922 he turned this area of work over to a newly created Department of Education. The changes kept pace with new state teacher certification requirements.

Birch's primary area of research was the study of William of Ockham (c1300-1349), a fourteenth century English scholastic who undermined the basic assumptions of Scholasticism and was acclaimed as the standard bearer for free thought in medieval universities. He produced a torrent of books challenging the authority of the popes. If the Americanists who founded Wittenberg argued that the Reformation of the church did not end with Luther, but was ongoing, Birch reminded Heckert's Wittenberg that it had begun long before Luther in the universities of the Renaissance. Ockhamists called his philosophy *via moderna,* the modern way; and they were influential in educating both John Hus and Luther, reformers of the church. Ockham insisted that faith might hold to beliefs for which science and philosophy could find no evidence, but that philosophy and science could depend only upon reason and experience in arriving at secular explanations of cause and effect. The universities of Ockham's day were pursuing the modern nearly seven hundred years earlier.

Birch wrote his dissertation on Ockham and spent a lifetime deciphering and translating Ockham's Latin abbreviations which had obscured so many of his writings. After studying photographs of manuscript pages from Europe with a magnifying glass, he built Ockham's shorthand into a Latin text which he then translated into English. In 1930, he published *De Sacramento Altaris,* one of the most scholarly works produced by a Wittenberg faculty member, one widely acclaimed in the United States and in Europe.

To honor the man who endowed Birch's chair, the Wittenberg class of 1910 redecorated and refurnished the philosophy classroom in Recitation Hall. It was to be a model classroom recognizing Bookwalter's gift. "We have," said the class president, "taken upon ourselves to embellish slightly that splendid and princely gift."

Birch then held forth in the Bookwalter room all of his professional life. Students remembered him as a tall, English sort with a face that never changed expression. He accepted faculty membership in one of the local fraternities, *Sadhe Aleph*, a Hebrew letter society, primarily for pretheological students that sought to reform the fraternity movement. He liked to walk and carried little pieces of wood for whittling. He watched football practice, whittling all the while and pondering some mysterious abbreviation in Ockham's text.

Heckert's efforts to bring Wittenberg into the modern world were not yet finished. In June of 1914, at the urging of Phi Beta Kappa members on the faculty, he wrote to Professor Edwin A. Grosvenor, president of Amherst College and of the United Chapters of Phi Beta Kappa, inquiring about a chapter for Wittenberg. He received no response. Finally in Dec. 1916, Grosvenor wrote that he had just found Heckert's letter "in a book which I had not opened for months." Apparently he had placed it there, perhaps as a book mark. He apologized and indicated that he would forward it to the secretary of Phi Beta Kappa. In 1917, as Europe's war finally engulfed the United States, Heckert's ambitions for a chapter of the premiere honor society had to be deferred. War restrictions prohibited groups from holding conventions. There would no opportunity to apply until 1920.

There was yet another item on Heckert's agenda: accreditation. American higher education had been variously termed a hodgepodge, a chaos, a dispersed confusion that was no system at all. There was growing urgency among leaders in higher education to replace the confusion with system and order. Heckert wanted Wittenberg to be a part of the solution to that problem. More students were coming from an increasing number of secondary schools to enroll in a rapidly proliferating number of postsecondary institutions. There was no commonly accepted standard of performance, or of academic sufficiency. There were no common criteria for admission or for graduation. There was no definition of a college or of the program properly belonging to such an institution. And, apparently, there was no authority in government or education empowered to establish standards or agree on definitions.

By 1885, colleges and secondary schools had begun to associate regionally to protect themselves and the public from pretentious, shoddy, or fraudulent institutions that called themselves colleges but were not in the eyes of their peers. Sprecher had been a leader in the forming of the Ohio College Association in 1867, an attempt to set standards for colleges in his day. It continued to serve that function as the North Central Association of College and Secondary Schools organized in 1895. The regional association movement, with Carnegie's encouragement, however, gained momentum and spread rapidly. It allowed for regional variations within a national system. "We are on the eve of a period of reconstruction," said Woodrow Wilson, speaking in 1907 as president of Princeton. He hailed the dawn of a new day. "We are going to set up standards," said the future president of the United States. "We are going to put things together into something like a connected and thought-out scheme of endeavor."

The Carnegie Foundation for the Advancement of Teaching was a strong ally of the accreditation movement. In providing its retirement program for college professors, it had faced a major problem in deciding which of the many institutions interested could properly be classified as colleges. At first it accepted the definition of a college used by the New York Board of Regents. Later it became an active force in promoting the regional accrediting agencies to establish more exact criteria on a regional basis.

By 1913 the North Central Association published a list of accredited schools for an area that included Ohio. Any institution seeking membership had to be examined and approved. Heckert was willing to participate because it was clear to him that foundations and philanthropists would use these approved lists to determine who was eligible for financial support. Surrendering the minimum of autonomy entailed, in Heckert's view, was not too great a price. He convinced the Board of the wisdom of the move.

By 1916 Wittenberg was examined and approved by the North Central Association, one of the earliest Lutheran institutions to be so listed. A number of schools, older or younger, resisted accreditation for several decades. They were suspicious of the "critical scrutiny of outsiders" and convinced that it was an attack upon their autonomy. But college and university accreditation, the struggle over standards, spread rapidly. Wittenberg entered that mainstream early and with enthusiasm.

Another association appeared with little fanfare in 1915. It was the American Association of University Professors, the AAUP. It would advance the standards, ideals, and welfare of the academic profession. More specifically, it sought the development and protection of academic freedom and tenure for teachers. The concept of academic freedom was that a properly credentialed faculty member was free to teach the subjects in which he was proficient and to express the conclusions arrived at in his research without censorship and without restriction by institutional, governmental, or church authorities. It was a concept from the ancient universities as far back as William of Ockham and before. Tenure in the modern university meant that after a suitable probationary period, a faculty member, if not previously terminated for cause, would receive tenure after which date he could not be terminated except for very specific offenses or financial exigency. The AAUP originally did not include faculty at church-related colleges. Not until later did Wittenberg and similar schools have faculty who were members. The organization had influence, however, as church colleges considered modern personnel policies.

After a decade of constant effort, Heckert asked the Board for a leave of absence to recuperate his energies and to contemplate the further demands of modernization for Wittenberg. In the spring and summer of 1911, he and Ada, her sister and her mother, toured Europe for nearly five months while Benjamin Prince served as acting president. That long suffering servant was pleased to be so recognized by Heckert and the Board. The Heckert party visited Italy, Switzerland, Germany, Holland, Belgium, France, Luxemburg, and England. This trip, his earlier trip to Europe, and his trip to California made Heckert the most widely traveled president thus far in Wittenberg history. That in itself marked him as a very modern college president.

The family spent over a month in Germany. Ada noted in her diary that while they were all very fond of "dear old Germany," their favorite city was Dresden. Yet her longest inscription was about Wittenberg. They visited the Luther House, the old university buildings, the Castle Church, the Melanchthon House, and all the other sites of interest to Lutherans and Protestants. It was a delightful trip for anyone caught up in the great German revival in America as the Heckerts had been. She bought ivy plants so that the ivy covered halls of her Wittenberg would have a link to the Wittenberg of Reformation fame. Her husband purchased a gavel, with a hammer from an oak tree in Wittenberg where Luther taught, and a handle from an oak tree at the Wartburg where he translated the Bible into German. It would add to meetings of the Board and the faculty.

At the end of the trip, they arrived in England in time for the coronation of George V. It was "the trip of our lives," Ada exclaimed. It was a perfect Edwardian summer, she said, but the large number of soldiers in Germany and England, and the many military band concerts and parades prevalent in both countries, did not escape her notice. She made no extensive commentary about these ominous signs. Nevertheless their joyous experience had been marred by an ever-present militarism. Within three years, Europe would be at war, though it would not involve the United States for seven years. It was an intrusion on Heckert's reverie and his contemplation of Wittenberg's future, but he did not seem overly concerned about its implications. He was in the midst of the struggle toward Wittenberg's form and organization for the modern era and looked eagerly toward home. Their departure was delayed by the glut of travelers in England for the coronation at which all of the crowned heads of Europe were in attendance, representing a past that was as surely as unexpectedly to vanish in the modern era.

Chapter Fifteen

Three Cheers for the Varsity Life

Rah, Rah, Rah,
Rah, Rah, Rah,
Rah, Rah, Wittenberg
Bang, Boom, Bah-h-h

Meanwhile, in 1904, students were well ahead of their elders in grasping for the shape of the new modern world. They were much less burdened with experience in the old nineteenth century and found themselves in the midst of the newness of the twentieth.

The increasing numbers of students at Wittenberg were preoccupied with a growing array of activities and social events that made some faculty wonder what their purpose was for being in college. In 1898, even a student asked, "What are we here for?" and lamented that "many students seem to over estimate the side issues of college life." There was emerging in the early decades of the new century, a national collegiate culture of gaiety and, what the older generation called increased promiscuity. The future dimensions of the "Roaring Twenties" were already apparent. It was a focus on the "modern," and Wittenberg students reveled in it. They adopted the eastern students' shortened form of the words "university life" and pursued what they called "the varsity life."

G. Stanley Hall, professor of Pedagogy and Psychology at Harvard said that students at the turn of the century lived in a "play world" displaying "psychic infantilism" or "babyism." He cited baby talk in student plays and nonsensical slang, cheers, and songs. A student at Ohio State noted, however, that "Student life is not as might be supposed by the outside looker-on." There were two sides to it: a routine of reading, recitation, and investigation, and a strong reaction against all that in sports, joviality, and general good times. Out of the latter grew a focus on fraternities, activities, and sports. Students comprised two groups, those more or less focused on academics. "Scholarship," said R. S. Bourne in *Atlantic Monthly* in 1911, "fails to provide a satisfactory field for honor and reputation" for everyone. Fraternities and athletics expanded the options. There was a social and a physical as well as a mental aristocracy. If one could not or preferred not to make his mark in the classroom, he could do so elsewhere.

In summary, he said, the turn-of-the-century student was predominantly of middle-class origin, reflected a parental hope for material success in the new world of business or in the professions and possessed a strong interest in youthful good times and self-indulgence. He was practical, romantic, and high spirited, only passively involved in politics and religion with little intensity or conviction. Nevertheless, said John E. Bradley of the National Council on Education, the average young man or woman was better off in college than out because faculties at least exerted a beneficial influence. The council's report was entitled, pejoratively, "The Higher Life of the College."

Bradley reported that some believed faculties should avoid interfering with the independent initiative and self-direction of students, exercised outside of the classroom in activities. There they learned habits of self-guidance and self reliance, making their own decisions and living with the consequences, characteristics of great value in a modern industrial society. Indeed, said another, attacking those who deplored student extravagance, "a boy in college ought to spend $1,000 a year if he can have it." Many wanted today's students to suffer just because they had suffered.

Colleges were changing. Standards were higher; courses were extended and more difficult. Freedom of choice had grown with the elective system. Planning one's course of study was more complicated and put more responsibility on students. New methods of instruction were in use. Conduct was freer and fraternities, athletics, and musical organizations changed campus life. College life was, on balance, a better life; but there were misgivings. President Lowell of Harvard, said "athletics has beaten scholarship," in public and student opinion. Woodrow Wilson, at Princeton noted, "The sideshows have swallowed up the circus, and we in the main tent do not know what is going on."

At Wittenberg, "varsity life" was not something to be opposed so much as something to be monitored. Heckert reported the faculty's view: "The modern college community," he said, "is a small world in itself. There are the common social events, athletic interests, religious organizations, literary associations, and the daily grind of the classroom." Sensing that even with all this some students were still on the outside, he suggested that teachers needed to interest students in a wider range of activities as well as in their studies. It was in keeping with a goal of developing the whole person. It was a new kind of college experience in an ever growing and changing society.

The following year, Heckert further explained the "varsity world" to a board that did not fully understand the new undergraduate. "Probably there has never been a time," he said, "when there has been so much college spirit and student activity of the right kind." He reported briefly on disciplinary problems but focused always on the positive side of student life. "There have been the usual college pranks and many innocent attempts of diversion," he told them. "All persons familiar with college life can understand and enjoy these manifestations of college spirit." Later, he said, "I would not have the Board think that our student body is of the goody-goody type. On the contrary, it is made up of a vigorous, fun-loving, and entirely human set of young men and women." He indicated general faculty approval. "One of the puzzling problems of the modern college," he said, "is the control or regulation of the many features that lie just outside . . . the classroom, the laboratory, or the literary society hall."

Heckert's outline of classroom, laboratory, literary society, revealed a change in the perception of things troubling to some. If curriculum, religious exercises, and the literary societies comprised the core in Sprecher's Wittenberg, classrooms, laboratories, and literary societies did so in the modern school, said Heckert. His use of the word "classroom" in place of "curriculum" reflected greater specialization and less integration in the academic program. Use of the word "laboratory" instead of "religious exercises" focused the issue of science versus religion. The focus on the literary societies was an overstatement because everyone knew of their dwindling importance.

Religion was now included with student activities outside the core structure. It was not yet less important; there was not yet less emphasis on it. There was not yet much change to be seen by the casual observer, but religious life was no longer at the center of the curriculum. Heckert lamented the "unrest and spiritual indifferences" of the world around him; but both faculty and Board had been obliged to recede from a central, active role in determining the theological stance of the church. The seminary faculty was now separate. The college faculty, though all were still practicing Christians, was mostly untrained in theology and increasingly focused on specialized fields of study. Religion was no longer central to every course and was instead a part of the extracurriculum. This was all reinforced, in Heckert's view, by growing diversity in the religious backgrounds of students. It was a natural evolution of the changes at the denominational college.

YMCA members rallied in the fall to rake leaves on the campus. Wittenberg University Archives.

Religious exercises were as much in evidence as before, but the YMCA and YWCA were the focal point. There was an effort to establish a Luther League on campus to rival the Ys. Supporters argued that since Wittenberg was a Lutheran college, the program of the church for young people ought to replace the Ys. Supporters of the Ys argued that their programs were developed by college students and were more inclusive. They were open to all students regardless of denomination. By 1910 the Luther League, unable to sustain itself, merged with the more poplar student organization.

The Ys continued to promote Bible study and missionary activities, even in the various fraternity houses. While some faculty felt qualified to assist in these activities and some seminarians were also involved, faculty as a group placed increasing emphasis on bringing visiting pastors to campus with their fresh faces and voices, and their better qualifications to speak on religious matters and to counsel students.

Faculty inaugurated an annual address on the call to the ministry and invited leading pastors in Springfield and in the synods to present it. They organized a special week of preaching, inviting a guest minister to spend the week on campus. It was the beginning of an event that would endure for more than forty years: "Religious Emphasis Week." One such guest included these topics designed to pique student interest: "What Are You Going to Make of Your Life?" "Did God Make A Mistake?" "The Delusion of the Life of Least Resistance!" Others spoke on the Prophet Jonah, The Right Attitude about Community Problems, The Augsburg Confession, The Miracles of Healing, and the Mosaic Code.

"The chapel service," said the faculty "is one of the universally perplexing problems." Any service held every day, was certain to become more or less formal or routine. It was difficult to maintain freshness and to keep students involved spiritually and not just bodily. Pastors who were critical did not have to face their parishioners daily, complained the faculty, and they were not all young people. When class rivalries bristled, it was in chapel that they conveyed their challenges, indicating a certain disregard for the purposes of the service. "The frequent clashes of the classes in chapel," reported the *Wittenberger*, "when the gauntlet, 'We run this place,' is thrown down," showed how great Wittenberg's varsity spirit was. Wittenberg had been slow getting into college spirit and hazing, the editor observed; but now that it was under way its growth was to be encouraged and commended. Pranksters from the lower classes removed the four pews in the chapel reserved for seniors and hid them in one of the literary society halls. The student newspaper said they were removed because seniors were not using them.

The *Torch* deplored the student "who goes to chapel for other than a religious purpose." Since services were voluntary, students should not be there if they were not in a worshipful mood, it implied. There were all kinds of misconduct: conversation, laughter, tossing of books and other things, and mild forms of scuffling. Later the same publication reported on faculty attendance. While it was possible to find some students who had attended only a half-a-dozen times during the year, some faculty had not attended at all. Only two, the dean and Prof. Hiller, had perfect attendance records; and they had charge of the services. The score for the faculty over the period measured was forty-three appearances out of ninety-five opportunities for a forty-five percent rate of attendance. The editor of the yearbook listed among the Seven Wonders of the World "a professor who goes to chapel."

As the churches on Wittenberg's territory moved further into Lutheran liturgy and tradition, many pressed the school to adopt a program of Lenten observance for the forty days before Easter. Wittenberg complied, first with a series of special services in which pastors from the Springfield area participated. Later, "in further compliance with the desires of our church in the observance of Lent," the college asked students to end all social activities for the forty days. This was a difficult matter, Heckert reported, because "the student body represented many denominations, very few of which make any special feature of the Lenten season." The degree of cooperation obtained, he said, spoke highly for the "spirit of religious respect" in the student body. It was especially gratifying, he emphasized, when students "are so completely at liberty to do what they choose." In fact, many arranged alternative social activities off campus.

The dean noted that "the religious attitude of the average student is better than is generally attributed to him." He was not as active in church nor as easily influenced to become so. "He has a free, easy, and happy bearing," causing adults to misinterpret his behavior. The modern student was as serious as the young had ever been, he said; they just appeared to be less so. A regent of the University of Miami attributed such behavior to the college man's embarrassment at matters of emotion or faith. They hid such feelings, denied them, or laughed them off. An example was the "Prophecy of the Class of 1904" which saw all of the class in hell, "the men shoveling and the ladies fanning."

In the 1913-14 school year, Wittenberg replaced elective courses in religion with required courses in English Bible for juniors and Christian Apologetics for seniors. They created a Department of Religion staffed not by seminary faculty, but by regular appointees to the college staff. Heckert advised the Board, "There is a magnificent opening in this" for the endowment of a chair. The president taught the course for juniors; and board member, Rev. Samuel E. Greenawalt, taught the seniors. The faculty said that its intent in requiring these two courses was to make the students "better scholars and better citizens:" The first because it made their education more complete; the second, because it would strengthen their concept of Christian behavior in personal honesty, morality, and conduct. The position was made permanent when Dr. Greenawalt and his wife contributed funds to create the Ross Mitchell Professorship of Bible and Comparative Religion. The second course, for seniors, was changed from Apologetics to Comparative Religions in response to student requests.

That there was concern about the religious emphasis on the modern campus was clear from the amount of time given to the topic in Heckert's and Shatzer's reports to the Board. "The religious life of the student body is a constant concern of the faculty," Shatzer assured them. "Efforts are made to encourage proper living and thoughtful consideration of the serious problems which students are likely to encounter." But he also told them that the problems of sustaining a religious focus were not just local. "The roots of it, lie in the general state of unrest" in society. Two decades earlier, Ort had said that the church relatedness of a college depended upon the religiousness of the students and the faculty and of the homes from which they came. Shatzer's response was essentially the same. The supporting synods sensed that the nature of their school was changing as it entered a more public and a more competitive phase of development. They wanted Heckert to reassure them that all was going to be well.

What Heckert and Shatzer said was true as far as it went, but it was not the whole story. The driving force behind change in student life, including religious activity, at Wittenberg and other church-related colleges was the rapid increase in undergraduate enrollments and the expansion of educational services which the denominational colleges were expected to provide. Wittenberg, in response to Synod insistence, had broadened the scope of the program so that nearly every student could find what he was looking for and would not have to attend a "Godless state university."

As Wittenberg changed from the old classical curriculum to a modern one focused on liberal arts, sciences, social sciences, humanities, selected professional fields, music, and fine arts, many things had to change. A larger faculty was necessary. More facilities and increased equipment were required. More than anything else, however, a larger student body was needed to provide enough students in each specialized area to make programs viable. The need for a larger, more specialized enrollment led to greater competition among Ohio's many institutions. All institutions that sought to develop modern programs needed to expand their student bodies beyond their church constituency. If they did not grow, they could not provide the breadth of program expected; and they would become less attractive even to members of their own denomination.

As Heckert contemplated the changes his school was undergoing, he said he needed a thousand students to accomplish what was envisioned; and he spoke of a "consuming desire" to reach that goal. When he took charge, the school had but 235 persons enrolled, and only 210 of these in the college. Five years later, when he hired a field secretary for admissions, undergraduate enrollment was still only 212; but special programs like art, music, teacher training, and summer school had grown more rapidly. The faculty added a Saturday College providing further opportunity for nontraditional students, particularly area teachers needing to meet newly enacted state teacher certification requirements.

By 1910, enrollment was 279, but the total number of students served was 703. Enrollment increased in every year of Heckert's administration until the World War began. The number served in the 1910-11 school year was 760; in 1911-12 it was 821; in 1912-13 it leveled off at 826; in 1913-14 it rose to 922; in 1914-15 the school served 972; and by 1915-16 the total number of students in all divisions was 1,119. Heckert said the goal was to serve 1,000 students in order to provide the modern curriculum wanted; and by 1915 the goal was achieved, and Wittenberg would never be the same.

Heckert gave credit for the increase to C. S. Ernsberger, the field secretary, and to active, loyal alumni. The college was printing and distributing large quantities of literature about the school. In addition, the field representative had been diligent in visiting high schools, churches, and homes in Ohio, Indiana, Michigan, Kentucky, and Pennsylvania. "The competition was never so keen as now," Heckert noted, "and the state of Ohio has more educational institutions than any other state in the union." Only with the support of alumni, he added, could Wittenberg meet its enrollment goals.

As Heckert reported on enrollment, he stressed the competition with other colleges and the loss of students who should have enrolled at Wittenberg. He called on alumni, pastors, and friends to direct worthy young people to the college. "Our efforts to secure students," he said, "are not by any means limited to the young people of our own particular branch of the church." Wittenberg had "all shades of church belief" in its student body, and "this is as it should be." Alumni and friends should not hesitate to recommend Wittenberg to any young person seeking a higher education. By 1914, according to the *Wittenberger*, only fifty-two percent of the entering class was Lutheran, in a state in which only five percent of the population was Lutheran.

An alumnus, writing to the *Wittenberger*, noted that the college was growing beyond the church and no longer "a mere parochial or synodical department of the Church." Rightly so, he added, if Wittenberg were to attain the full measure of a college, it needed to be independent. "The Church is concerned with inculcating but a limited part of truth, while the college is or should be interested in the whole field of knowledge." There were those who would argue with his concept, but his point was clear. Wittenberg's appeal was no longer only that of a church institution to its church constituency, rather its appeal was its standing as an educational institution for a public constituency. He called for a stronger alumni association to support that role.

Heckert noted that special attention was being given to alumni and that they were being sent all college publications. Dean Shatzer was collecting items of information about alumni for a special edition of the *Wittenberger*. Both men were quietly urging an expanded voice for alumni on the Board of Directors. In the same issue, the editor took the pulse of the school's nearly 1,100 living graduates. Just over fifteen percent voted for the alumni board member in the last election. That was far too low a percentage. A survey of alumni secretaries at fifty-three other colleges and universities showed greater levels of alumni participation at twenty-eight of the schools than at Wittenberg. Twenty-seven of them charged annual dues of from $1-$5.

C. S. Ernsberger reported the concentration of nearly half of all Wittenberg alumni in just twelve cities: Springfield, Mansfield, Galion, New Philadelphia in Ohio, and Fort Wayne, Ind., Louisville, Ky., and Three Rivers, Mich. He raised the question of including nongraduates in the Wittenberg Alumni Association in order to increase its size. Dr. Brodfuehrer, two decades earlier, had predicted that Wittenberg would find the support it needed among this group of nongraduates who left because they could not get the courses they wanted. Of the fifty-three alumni associations surveyed, only twenty-two required a degree for membership. The other thirty-one allowed nongraduates to be members. The report also noted that colleges with active alumni groups had a paid alumni secretary. For Ernsberger there was a clear connection between active alumni and increased enrollment.

There were other steps to be taken to attract students. In 1911 Mrs. Lovina Openlander gave funds for an addition to Ferncliff Hall.

New Ferncliff Hall, dedicated June 1914.
Wittenberg University Archives.

The old frame building was moved to the rear of the lot and turned to face north and a new brick building was erected. New Fernncliff was dedicated in June 1914. Soon it too was filled.

Heckert told the Board that to be competitive, the men's hall needed repair as well. A student described it as "a huge old building that had seen its best days." He told his parents that it looked like one of the abandoned old cotton factories in central New York. A member of the class of 1904 called it the "last relic of the Keller age." Heckert asked the Myers brothers, Lutherans, and industrialists in Ashland, Ohio, to underwrite a thorough renovation. F. E. Myers and P. A. Myers agreed to do so. Their gift also enabled Wittenberg to add the impressive pillars and portico to the front of the building sixty years after it was first built. On November 18, 1916, the sparkling red building with its massive white porch and cupola was rededicated and named, Myers Hall.

The keen competition among the denominational colleges for enrollments led to other developments affecting rates of tuition, entrance requirements, and expanding programs for financial aid. Larger numbers alone were not enough; one had to attract students for specific programs. Wittenberg's tuition had been $60 for decades; but in 1911, Heckert asked the Board to increase it to $75, an increase of twenty-five percent. Later, he noted that enrollment was not adversely affected. The college could increase the size of the faculty, expand the courses offered, and increase laboratory facilities. Even then, said Benjamin Prince, the student was only paying half the cost of his education. With costs rising and competition from state universities as well as other denominational colleges growing, Heckert advised the Board that Wittenberg now needed to offer scholarships. The Board approved a free scholarship to every first honors graduate of any high school. The plan worked well in attracting the highest grade of students. Other schools, said Heckert in 1910, were offering more in scholarships than was Wittenberg.

Mr. E. J. Young and Mr. J. L. Clark established the first of a number of organizations in Wittenberg's history that bore the name The Wittenberg Guild. The first guild was a group of Lutheran businessmen, who contributed annually to a fund to pay college and seminary tuition for young men planning to enter the ministry. The plan continued for nearly three decades and assisted a great many young men. Alexander Moore of Defiance set up a trust fund, the income of which was to provide loans to students at an interest rate of three percent. It was the school's first student loan program. Financial aid enabled the school to better recruit students for specific programs.

Wittenberg found itself lagging behind in relaxing entrance requirements. In 1910 Heckert noted that Wittenberg still required four years of Latin and two years of a modern language, well in excess of other Ohio colleges. Faculty amended the requirement, reducing it to four years, with at least two years in Latin. Other colleges counted high school electives in the sixteen courses required while Wittenberg still specified what the courses were for admission. Such changes, represented a modernization of requirements, but the competitiveness in the state could also lead to a lowering of standards. It clearly led to a segmentation of the field into more and less demanding schools. Heckert sought competitive requirements without lowering standards.

Liberalization of entrance requirements, enhanced enrollment in the college, but decreased it in the academy. It served students from areas where the high schools were not up to par. As the public high school system expanded and improved, there were fewer college-bound students with deficient records in need of repair. Public high schools, particularly in the larger towns and cities, were improving steadily. With the construction of Springfield's new central high school, academy enrollment dropped by one-third.

Demographic factors were substantially altering the size and composition of the Wittenberg student body. The religious diversity of the students and their geographic origins were also changing rapidly. There were fewer younger preparatory students and more in the traditional college ages of seventeen to twenty-one. The new homogeneity enabled students to mold the student body together by promoting all-campus social events and activities. They sought for a unity and coherence by stressing the dimensions of the "varsity life." The purpose of these events, said Dean Shatzer, was to unify the student body, eliminate sectional animosities, and enable students to appreciate "one another's true worth." Regardless of such efforts, there were always some who felt like outsiders.

Dean Shatzer's philosophy of education, which focused on what he referred to as "a man's true worth," was reflected in his jovial and sympathetic treatment of students. Such a view was expressed in remarks he made to the YMCA about "college ethics." He was convinced by experience, he said, "that men are inherently better than they are usually considered to be." He looked on the bright side of matters and gave students the benefit of the doubt, and he encouraged them to do likewise. Whether you were an optimist or a pessimist, he said, was up to you; but if you were critical and ungenerous and derogatory in your treatment of others, you became egotistical, jealous, suspicious, and unhappy. To do the opposite made life easier, happier, and more constructive.

The dean treated students as young men and women with rights, feelings, and opinions. It worked well for him and the school. While on occasion, some students took advantage of him, by and large, they responded well. He took up once again the issue of the ownership of student rooms which had been raised before and never resolved. "The sensible methods of the dean," observed the men in the dorm, secured their agreement to "surrender" their rooms over the summer so that they could be used for summer school students. He allowed the residents, now mostly members of "The Dorm League," to vote on the issue, and it passed unanimously. He treated us like men and not like children, they reported. He gave us the reasons for the school's request, and therefore we could weigh the matter like reasonable persons and respond. The rooms would be available for summer school, but the regular occupants retained ownership of the furniture. In addition the dean allowed the men their own meeting room in the hall and granted them the right to enter teams in intramural sports to compete with the classes and the Greek groups.

For three decades, students at Wittenberg had taken note of various schemes for student government developing on eastern college campuses. The Amherst experiment with a student congress in 1886 was reviewed in detail in the Wittenberg student newspapers. Wittenberg's student journalists, however, doubted that colleges in the west would give up "their privileges of government." Later, when the Lutheran college at Gettysburg adopted a form of student government, the *Wittenberger* endorsed the idea, but to no avail. At Wittenberg the faculty remained firmly in charge of the governance of students. Some saw in Shatzer's collaborative approach; some hope for change.

By June of 1915, faculty had in place a complete set of regulations governing eligibility for participation in the varsity life. The *Torch* noted that faculty had the erroneous idea that student activities constituted a privilege which they could extend or withdraw. To the contrary, the writer argued, activities were the essential core of the varsity life and every student had a right to participate. He suggested that perhaps students earning top grades should be limited so that more students could be involved. Under the faculty system, academic leaders monopolized positions of leadership to the detriment of other students. The real appeal of Greek life and athletics, was that in them leadership was apportioned by students on a different scale. Students volunteered to be involved, and selected their leaders on the basis of personal appeal and style.

A similar student view of the matter came from Ohio Wesleyan. There the faculty adopted a point system. Each activity was assigned a point value: president of the student body 15, president of a class 10, editor of a college paper 14, cast of a play 6, a lead part 10, and so forth. A student was limited to a total of twenty-five points at any one time. The idea was to spread honors around and prevent students from getting overloaded to the detriment of their academic performance. A writer for the *Torch* objected to the plan as misunderstanding the facts of student life. There were not great numbers of students eagerly pursuing the hard jobs, he said. Student leaders were, in fact, "the goats" of the rest of the students, men who had shown reliability, trustworthiness, and ability to get things done. These "pluggers," were imposed upon and needed to be saved, he said, but the jobs they were doing would go undone in any plan to spread opportunities around.

The most conspicuous activity of varsity life, the one least under faculty control, was athletics. Wittenberg's YMCA leaders told entering students, "The spirit which pervades athletics determines in large measure the spirit in general college life." That was the barometer; a school without athletic spirit lacked spirit generally and was not a part of the real varsity scene. "While mental development is the chief end of a college course," conceded the YMCA *Handbook*, "the man who neglects the physical side of his being cannot claim to be a man entirely." The handbook made "friendly suggestions" for new students, and the list included: "Learn the Wittenberg songs and cheers; attend athletic and oratorical meetings; join the athletic association; if you play football, come out, you will help make a winning team; make yourself heard at athletic games."

Athletics arose so fast and spread so rapidly that it grew outside of normal channels of authority. All of a sudden, playtime games became a major vehicle of student culture. Its desire to be free of faculty control was only modified by its need for outlays of college resources of land, buildings, money, and equipment. The two had to find a way to coexist. Heckert inherited a program that functioned largely outside of any rules and was governed by a zeal that made the contests spiritual events. Indeed, both athletics and religious activity were under the auspices of the Y. The spirit of one affected the other.

One of the great stories of Wittenberg athletic tradition was that of the handsome and energetic Curtis Laughbaum, later a Lutheran pastor, who through college and seminary played football for Wittenberg in eight seasons under three presidents. He played in 1897, 98, 99, 1900, 01, 02, 03, and then again in a postgraduate year in 1905. He had his collarbone broken in the nineteenth century, his nose in the twentieth.

Curtis Laughbaum, class of 1900. Handsome and rugged football player through eight seasons while in college and seminary. Wittenberg University Archives.

Another star player early in Heckert's tenure was Bob Bescher who came to Wittenberg in 1905, having played for Notre Dame.

He was described as a lusty athlete, a great give-and-take fellow, rugged and full of fun. In two seasons, he carried the ball 1,700 yards in twelve games, scored fifteen touchdowns, and did all the punting. At six feet, 190 pounds, he was the fastest man on the field. His real love, however, was baseball; and he played for Wittenberg and for semiprofessional teams in the area. Heckert suspended two men for playing professional baseball on Sunday, which was illegal at the time; and one of them may have been Bescher. He later played outfield for the Cincinnati Reds. His speed at stealing bases led Grantland Rice, the sports writer, to call him "the ghost of the bases" and gained him a place in the record books.

Another great story of the era concerned six-foot, two-hundred-pound pretheological student, Ross Stover. He did not so much "go out" for football as get "recruited." The coach saw a potential tackle or fullback, and persuaded this outstanding vocalist in the choir to play ball. Coach designed a new "pass" play for Stover and another big player involving their diminutive quarterback, "Tid" Schaeffer. When the team was near the goal line but facing a formidable defense, the two big men grabbed Schaeffer's belt, stepped forward and tossed him over the line into the end zone.

These stories grew out of situations that arose when athletics was a student run enterprise with few if any rules and driven by a great desire to win. There was only casual, indirect, or unofficial faculty involvement. To make matters worse, the teams were relatively unsuccessful; and there was general dissatisfaction all around. The basketball team had very low morale. By 1904 the school was playing a full schedule of games, but the sport was not popular. Bruce Young, who played from 1906 to 1909, recalled unheated courts with low beams, no showers, and few spectators. "What few games we could play at home," he said, "were played in a roller skating rink at the southwest corner of Mulberry and Limestone Streets. A ball thrown too high was lost in the rafters."

There were instructors in physical culture for all students. The first woman, June Izora Gannett, came to teach physical education for ladies. The first person to be listed as a coach was Leo DeTray, and it was hoped that a coach would bring the teams under greater control. DeTray joined the staff in 1908 after serving as assistant to coach Alonzo Stagg at the University of Chicago. In 1909 Wittenberg joined the Ohio Athletic Conference. De Tray left in 1910 after two unsuccessful seasons as coach of all Wittenberg teams. In the fall of 1910, J. B. Longwell came as coach; and Joseph H. Keyser was listed as athletic director, the first in the school's history.

Joseph H. Keyser as a student and football player in 1898. Wittenberg University Archives.

Rev. Joseph H. "Big Joe" Keyser, class of 1900, first director of athletics, 1910-1916. He helped design the structure that preceded Wittenberg's "Golden Age" of sports. Wittenberg University Archives.

Keyser had graduated from Wittenberg in 1900 and had served for ten years in YMCA programs in Ohio and Illinois. He would bring even more of the Christian values of the YMCA to the Wittenberg athletic effort, but the teams were still unsuccessful. In addition to Keyser and coach Longwell, Laverne G. Ogden taught physical culture for men, and Marguerite Hursey taught physical education for women. It was a large staff and indicated that Heckert wanted to build a successful program. He was disappointed in the results. "In athletics," he reported, "we have had probably as much success as we are entitled to." He cited inadequate facilities and a limited number of students from which to select teams. In athletics, as in everything else, a larger enrollment was necessary. Heckert told the Board the school needed improved athletic fields and a new gymnasium to attract the students that could make those programs successful.

Faculty gained some order in athletics by becoming directly involved. A. F. Linn, of the Chemistry Department, became treasurer of the Athletic Association and sought to end fiscal mismanagement and deficits. Dry, dour T. B. Birch of the Philosophy Department became sports manager, remaining quietly above the excitement. He whittled as he kept an eye on scheduling and arrangements for the contests. Team property was given over to the care of the efficient Oliver Roller, custodian at the seminary.

It had been a difficult period, only one winning football season since 1908. In other sports like basketball, baseball, track, and tennis, enthusiasm continued but results were sporadic. Eventually, however, Heckert found the man he was looking for to bring order and success to varsity sports, but only after considerable conflict and dissension. It all came to a head in the spring and fall of 1914.

The *Wittenberger* opened the discussion advocating athletic scholarships. Wittenberg was the laughing stock of the Ohio Conference, said the editor, because it had not done so. "It has become almost a necessity to offer some inducement to high school athletes of known ability to enter any college." The larger schools were so persistent in offering athletic grants that small schools had to do the same. Wittenberg players met those at other schools who said "[t]hey were not playing for nothing." The *Wittenberger* specifically cited Denison, as a school at which the coach was authorized "to make offers to men who will help his school in athletics," and implied that Ohio University and Ohio State were doing so as well. Rumors were rife about Oberlin, the reigning athletic powerhouse of the day among Ohio colleges.

Another complaint was that in the Ohio Conference, freshmen were ineligible to play; and Wittenberg did not have enough upper classmen to play without them. Furthermore, since the coaching staff was small, there was no one to work separately with the freshmen. When they became sophomores, they were not ready to join the varsity.

The root of Wittenberg's athletic problems, said the editor of the *Wittenberger*, was coaching. In an editorial headlined "The Athletic Problem," he told of coaching turnover and inadequacy. The most successful coach had been replaced because the students did not like him. Now that Keyser was on board, there was continuity; but he needed an assistant to get the job done.

Keyser recommended that Wittenberg leave the Ohio Conference over the issue of freshman eligibility, but the faculty unanimously rejected that proposition. The *Wittenberger* endorsed the faculty action, noting that the "faculty has decided we are to remain in an organization whose sole object is the uplift of college athletics and the elimination of professionalism." The faculty endorsed the conference as the proper place for Wittenberg among the best schools in Ohio. They also endorsed "manly and sportsmanlike conduct" in games, the requirement of good classroom work for all participants, limits on the number of contests in all sports, the promotion of minor sports like tennis, and the encouragement of campus intramurals for classes and groups. The *Torch*, on the other hand, took a less supportive view of the faculty's broad pronouncement on athletics. "If the student body here at Wittenberg doesn't wake up," said the editor, "they will wake up one of these fine days and find that the faculty is running athletics." He predicted that the awakening would come the following fall.

The *Wittenberger* took a less belligerent stance and tried to help the faculty sort out a number of issues about varsity sports. In an editorial entitled "Morals and Athletics," the editor gently approached what was for students a delicate issue. A point of view was developing, he noted, that concluded that good athletic performance and high moral values were antagonistic. More specifically, it was seen as a matter of presuming high moral values, and retaining Coach Keyser on the one hand, or a better coach and lower moral standards on the other. This was, said the editor, a wrong phrasing of the question. The real issue was "Can we find a coach of athletics who has all the moral qualities of the present director and, in addition, a superior power of teaching his branch." There, the issue was out in the open. Coach Keyser was a fine man, a likeable man, a religious man, a man well versed in the philosophy and ideals of the YMCA, and who upheld the highest standards in the athletic conference; but he could not coach.

A week later, advocates of better sports received a very forthright answer from Athletic Director Keyser himself. Writing in both the *Wittenberger* and in the *Torch*, he entitled his piece, "Food for Thought along Athletic Lines." Frankly, he said, "What students, athletic board, and the public want are a winning football team, a winning baseball team, and a winner in basketball." Unlike the faculty, they had no apparent concern for the minor sports or intramurals. To give them what they want, he continued, the school needed a new coach, a larger coaching staff, better equipment, new facilities, and a larger enrollment. One of the state's sports writers, he said, was saying, "Alonzo Stagg himself could not produce a winning team at Wittenberg." The view outlined by Keyser compared with that passed earlier by the faculty, posed what were to become the classical conflicting positions on sports of boosters and faculties at good liberal arts colleges everywhere.

By April, Keyser had developed a full scale proposal for athletic reform along what he called "up-to-date lines." He called for a Department of Athletics or of physical education headed by a director of athletics. He asked faculty to recognize that no system of education was complete without proper attention to the physical needs of all the students. He indicated the need for a proper gymnasium and for a set of courses for credit in physical education. He suggested that faculty recognize that they were too busy in their own disciplines to give direction to the physical development of students. That was a specialized field requiring persons professionally trained to take responsibility. He recommended that a director of athletics be the head coach of all sports, but that an assistant coach be hired for each individual sport. He suggested that a faculty member continue as treasurer of athletics. He concluded by recommending that the Board of Athletic Control be abolished and that an executive committee be appointed. That committee would consist of the student manager of each sport, the president and secretary of the Student Athletic Association, the faculty treasurer, and the athletic director.

Both the *Torch* and the *Wittenberger* carried Keyser's proposals and all seemed for the most part to agree with his assessment. It was his major contribution to sports at Wittenberg. While it was not adopted in its entirety and faculty concerns for the depth and breadth of athletic opportunities continued, it laid the groundwork for decades of progress in physical education and sports. With the acceptance of many of his suggestions, Keyser resigned at the end of the 1915-16 school year, clearing the way for Heckert to look for a new director and head coach.

Ernest Godfrey, a young Lutheran and recent graduate of the Ohio State University, began what came to be known as Wittenberg's first Golden Age of Sports. He came as athletic director and head coach in the fall of 1916.

Ernest Godfrey, athletic director and coach, 1916-1917 and 1919-1929. Called by Knute Rockne, of Notre Dame, the best line coach in America. Students called him "The King" of college football. Wittenberg University Archives.

Students celebrated his coming. In the 1917 yearbook, they gloated: "Talk football to an Ohio athlete, and he begins to talk about Godfrey; talk college, and he talks Wittenberg." The students called him the "King," of intercollegiate sports. He gave them visions of an excellent football field, a massive stadium, a new gymnasium, tennis courts, complete equipment, and an indomitable varsity spirit. He told them of enormous crowds coming to Wittenberg to see athletic competition as they were beginning to do at the Ohio State University and at the University of Michigan. He set everyone's sights on a first-class program at Wittenberg to compete with the best teams in the nation. He told them that the Wittenberg varsity would be on the athletic map for years to come.

In Godfrey's first year, results were not much better than before; but student and team morale was. The football team won 2, lost 5, and tied 2; but students lauded Godfrey's conduct on the field and his masterly methods. "Great is the praise and esteem for Coach Godfrey," they said. The "King" was the busiest coach in the state. "He has interviewed many men in this and neighboring states with the idea of getting them into the camp of the cardinal and cream." The World War would postpone Godfrey's revolution in sports at Wittenberg as it postponed many other plans the school had for the future. He left in 1917 for military service and did not return to coach until 1919.

Godfrey coached at Wittenberg until 1929 when he left to be line coach at Ohio State. In ten consecutive seasons at Wittenberg, his football teams won sixty-one games, lost nineteen, and tied six, a winning percentage of .744. His football teams were undefeated in 1919 and 1920, and only once did he fail to win the league title. Later a member of the College Football Hall of Fame, Godfrey coached such outstanding players as Wilson "Wib" Etter, who led the nation in scoring in 1920 with 170 points. Knute Rockne, famous coach at Notre Dame, called Ernie Godfrey the best line coach in America.

Godfrey also produced fine basketball teams and started a winning tradition in that sport as well. He took over a team that had posted a record of one win and eleven losses in 1918, and guided it to five straight winning seasons, including one of eleven wins and one loss in 1922. His career record in basketball was 100 wins and 72 losses. In 1921 Wittenberg lost to Ohio State by 1 point, 27 to 26 and defeated Princeton the following week, 33 to 10. Wittenberg lost the title in the Ohio Athletic Conference to Ohio University. The "Fighting Lutherans" had twelve victories in fifteen games.

Wilson "Wib" Etter, shown here as right-halfback in 1918-1919. In 1920 he was the nation's leading scorer in college football. Wittenberg University Archives.

John Heberling of the class of 1922 represented the Godfrey product in sports and exemplified the ideal of the varsity life in the eyes of students. After graduation he was freshman coach and assistant to Godfrey. Heberling, according to students, "exemplified the finest spirit of the athlete; in that he has played fairly and squarely and with beautiful modesty; in that he has played hardest when defeat seemed imminent; in that he has taken punishment when it came and never winced nor cried aloud; and because in every way with his mates, with his fellow students, and with the faculty, he has always been the gentleman: clean, courageous, honest." The description carried spiritual, almost worshipful overtones and posed the image of the athlete as the ideal in the varsity life.

Chapter Sixteen

A Perilous Resemblance

The apparent disorder that existed in varsity sports was reflective of the high-spirited, even rambunctious physical involvement of youth at play. Their hazing and their mock battles were symptomatic of the age. The historian of the class of 1904 recorded details of the 1900 battle of his class with the class of '03. Such an altercation of classes was called, "the rush." Freshman and sophomore classes regularly battled it out for "supremacy" in this traditional fall ritual. Most freshmen entered college well-informed about the fate that awaited them at the hands of the upperclassmen. This freshman class gathered at the back of the chapel on the opening day of school, determined not to wait to be hazed by the sophomores, but to strike first. They constructed an effigy of the class of '03 and proposed to defend it from that class and hang and burn it. "Like all class fights," said the historian, "although supposed to be kept secret, the word was passed along."

Two days later, narrowly escaping capture by the sophomores, the freshmen gathered at "The Arcade" downtown. The Arcade was a recently built enclosed street of shops with a fish pond and small fountain in the center. It was adjacent to the new Arcade Hotel and across from the new city hall on the other side of the Esplanade. Between the two buildings on the esplanade was a fountain that rivaled the one in Cincinnati. When William Whitely moved his farm implements factory out of the center of the town, his huge building was converted into this showy new shopping area which in a later time would be called a mall. It was the very center of Springfield's vigorous, prosperous, industry-based, social, and economic life.

Fountain Square in downtown Springfield, circa 1898. The Arcade and hotel are on the left. The City Building, now the Heritage Center of the Clark County Historical Society is on the right. Water color, Clark County Historical Society.

By 3 a.m., a party of thirty to thirty-five freshmen had gathered, and the class started to march to the campus. It was an all-male affair, because the women were under much closer supervision and were not allowed out at night. The men regathered below the cliffs near the Fountain Avenue bridge that connected downtown Springfield to the campus area. "At a little after four," continued the class chronicler, "we left our fortifications behind the cliffs and began our east flanking movement to the campus."

The class circled all the way to the east side of the campus and entered it by Dr. Ort's old house, which had been Sprecher's house, at the top of Myer's Hollow. "No enemy was in sight," the account continued. Marching down past the library, the group then hanged their effigy of the sophomore class on an elm tree in the hollow between the library and the men's dormitory. "As morning dawned," continued the historian, the warriors of nineteen three made their appearance at the west of the dorm, giving their battle cry of "Rick ro rick, rai ro ree; Wittenberg, Wittenberg, nineteen three." The freshmen responded, "Chi-bim, che-boom; chi-bim, boom, bore; Razzle dazzle zizzle zazzle, ra ra roar; Wittenberg, Wittenberg, nineteen four."

The sophomores, bent upon freeing the effigy of their class, rushed the freshmen who were arrayed around the tree to defend it. The sophomores planned to rescue the effigy and it cut down, but after fifteen minutes of rough and tumble, the battle was over; the freshmen had triumphed and the sophomores were tied up with rope. The fight occurred so early that none of the women were out in time to participate. A group of freshmen coeds, not to be left out entirely, captured and tied up a sophomore girl on her way to class. The freshmen took photographs of the humiliated sophomores as a record of their victory. "The class then attended chapel in a body," gloated the freshmen historian. After chapel the group moved to the steps of the old dormitory for more pictures, this time of the victors. The dummy of 1903 was then burned amid cheers and gloating.

In 1904 in downtown Springfield near where four years before the freshmen had gathered for the class rush, a real mob lynched an African American man and proceeded to a black neighborhood known as the "Levee" which they set on fire. In the newspaper coverage of the terrible event, a reporter wrote: "It looked more like a crowd of college boys out for a lark than anything else." It was perhaps just an insensitive trivializing remark that did not take the terrible incident with the seriousness it should have had. The paper even captioned a part of the report: "Yell Like Students," comparing the rallying cries of the mob to students circling the campus in a "rush." The reporter continued, "There was a perilous resemblance between the mob and college students."

The Springfield riot conformed perfectly, said historians, to the pattern of racial violence occurring at the time in other parts of the nation. In an altercation, an African American allegedly shot a policeman. A mob gathered, broke into the jail, seized the prisoner, and proceeded with the lynching of the accused. The mob then spent its energies wreaking destruction in a black neighborhood conveniently defined as a "center of vice."

The news coverage gave rise to rumors that Wittenberg students had been involved. Heckert issued a denial, although he suspected there may have been some students in the crowd watching. "While the college students occasionally have rushes on the college grounds," he noted, "they have never been known to engage in any lawlessness in the city." He assured the community that, after personal investigation, he was certain that students "were in no way responsible for the work of the mob this week."

As for the acts of murder and violence, Heckert called them a crime and a stain upon the name of Springfield. "This was an instance," he told students in chapel, "where men's lower feelings of anger and revenge suspended their sense of justice and respect for law." He urged the students in their conversations with others to condemn the lynching in the strongest possible terms. In referring to higher and lower instincts, he was reverting to a Victorian vocabulary that seemed strange to modern ears.

Two years later, in 1906, Springfield, unfortunately, suffered another racial disturbance. This time authorities got the prisoner safely away to jail in nearby Dayton. The frustrated mob turned its attention instead to an area called "the Jungles." When the fire department arrived, the mob cut the hoses. When the State Militia arrived, the crowd was dispersed. One student was among those arrested. Heckert gathered the male students in the chapel and again denounced mob spirit and lawlessness. He asked them to condemn the action of the rioters and to pledge themselves not to countenance or participate in such lawless acts. They were not to be present at, act in, or speak in favor of such behavior. Students passed resolutions and expressed sympathy for the victims.

The riots of those two years and the campus rushes were not without some similarities: the language of war and battle, the real and feigned hatred, the hanging of effigies, and a lynching, the yells, the mass maneuvers of numbers of people as if with a single mind, ringleaders, followers, bystanders, the sense of mob camaraderie, the inability of authorities to maintain order, the loss of individuality in the group, the rush of adrenaline. But the events revealed serious problems in the community, not just in Springfield, but in America, that would not be easily resolved. It was a major problem in modern culture.

These tensions in the nation were also apparent on campus. Not every student was welcome to enjoy the varsity life. The two or three African American students were excluded from the residence halls and from student life. The school had been one of the early colleges to admit such students following the Civil War, but it regressed as a spirit of Jim Crow rose in the north. After school, African American students were relegated to black neighborhoods in segregated Springfield. In small towns nearby, they had to be out of town by sundown. They found life difficult. Ollie Gregory, the football hero who scored the first touchdown on Zimmerman Field in 1904, was ostracized from the rest of campus life. His father was the jailer who had faced the angry mob and whose own life had been threatened. Upon graduation, Gregory had difficulty securing employment. Even educated African Americans found little opportunity for appropriate placement.

Students in general were oblivious to the plight of these students while other white students also outside the varsity life felt no solidarity with them. These conditions would remain unacknowledged on campus well into the middle of the new century and would not yet be fully resolved when the century ended. It was what Gunnar Myrdal, in 1944, would label "the American Dilemma" in his book of the same name. It posed as great a challenge to modernism as any other problem in the culture.

By 1910 the fall "rush" of freshmen and sophomores had given way to a tug-of-war across Buck Creek. The term "rush" was applied instead to the surge of upper class members of the Greek letter and literary societies trying to persuade white and Christian freshmen to join their organizations. In the tug-of-war, freshmen lined up on one side of the creek and sophomores on the other, on opposite ends of a rope. Each tried to pull the other into the creek. Regardless of who won, the affair ended in a rough house through the night in the dorms and, for the men, around the campus.

In 1914 the editor of the *Torch* described the tug-of-war as a splendid custom and an improvement over the hazing of earlier years. "Men in any group," he said, "demand that newcomers show

The losing class in the waters of Buck Creek in the annual Freshman-Sophomore tug-of-war. The tradition began in 1910 and continued for nearly four decades. Wittenberg University Archives.

their fitness to become members, and college is no exception." Before the advent of the tug-of-war, the freshman was caught unawares and required to undergo a random series of tests to prove his fitness. On the modern campus, said the editor, freshmen were challenged to develop the cooperation needed to participate successfully, in a predetermined activity. In a tug-of-war, the freshmen showed their fitness to be Wittenbergers, he concluded; and both the freshmen and the sophomore classes were forged into permanent functioning organizations. The same argument was used by fraternities to justify their systematic as opposed to haphazard hazing practices.

Campus and fraternity hazing were discouraged, but found lots of support in student publications and among alumni. The *Wittenberger* reported that freshmen were required to wear unusual clothing and to submit to certain rules prescribed by the upperclassmen. An article about "unknown persons" maliciously vilifying "smut-faced worms" appeared in the *Torch* for October 8, 1914, heralding another fall-hazing season. The warning, the notice said, "smelled of obituaries and foretold mangled limbs." The vocabulary of violence and demeaning prejudice reflected the national collegiate culture. Between the rush of the organizations to befriend freshmen and the hazing by the student body at large which harassed and belittled them, the new students wearing their red beanies with a big white "W," might have been more than a little bewildered.

To the contrary, most arrived knowing what the freshman gauntlet would be like and eager to participate in the near free-for-all. Some gave back full measure everything they received. At pep rallies, for instance, freshmen were expected to provide the horsepower to pull the college's large wagon through town with seniors as the cargo. In 1914 students gave little attention to the outbreak of war in Europe, but focused on their own little world. As the noisy procession of the pep band, with seniors aboard the freshman-powered wagon and cheering middle-class men and fraternity men marching through downtown Springfield, the freshmen plotted revenge. All of the elements of varsity life came together in this October spectacle. The freshmen, lumbering up the Fountain Avenue hill to the Esplanade, turned the wagon at full speed into the wall of the Arcade Hotel, letting go and jumping aside just as the wagon with its load of seniors crashed. Seniors flew unceremoniously into the air and onto the ground. According to one chronicler, seniors "nursed black and blue remembrances of the occasion" for some time.

There were quieter manifestations of student unruliness. By 1913, Stunt Day had become popular. On that day, students as individuals and as groups dressed and behaved outrageously; some, oblivious to the racial tensions around them, appeared in minstrel blackface. The various classes adopted special distinguishing items of attire: straw hats, scarves, spats, fur coats, canes, anything to make them stand out as a group. Classroom work came to a standstill. Amid it all, a freshman without his red beanie had his nose painted green. Probably the most distinctive of student group identifications were those of the "Knights of the Jeweled Letter," the members of the Greek letter societies. Alpha Tau Omega "preps" or pledges were required to attend classes carrying something conspicuous. Their parade was headed by one member playing the mandolin. Others carried dinner pails, suitcases, newspapers, huge dictionaries, and pillows to class to mixed reactions among their professors.

Stunt Day, 1913. Wittenberg University Archives.

In 1910, the campus was shocked by a student's death, allegedly in a fraternity hazing incident. Newspapers spread the story over the state. President Heckert regretted the death but denied reports that it was caused by fraternity hazing. "Sensational stories in the public print concerning college escapades," he charged, "are usually to be taken with a grain of salt." The president said the reports were "absolutely baseless."

The growing number of such stories throughout the state, however, led to turmoil on campuses and calls for action by the legislature. At Ohio State University, a new anti-Greek newspaper attacked the *Lantern*, controlled by fraternity members. The new rival advocated abolishment of fraternities. They caused the student body to disintegrate, claimed the editor, as fraternity "collusion" blocked non-Greeks from positions of trust and honor. The *Wittenberger* took an anti-Greek position while the *Torch* came to their defense. "The fraternity question," said the editor of the older publication, "seems to be reaching the acute state." Fraternities, he complained, sought to dominate politics, athletics, and every enterprise on campus. He charged fraternities with responsibility for the lack of success in athletics and the eminent demise of the literary societies.

As the storm grew statewide, a bill was introduced in the legislature to abolish fraternities at state universities. They brought it all on themselves by their conduct, charged the *Wittenberger* editor. Whenever an organization placed itself above the institution of which it was only a part, he added, trouble and sorrow would come into that organization's life. He recommended a thorough housecleaning. "The fraternity is here to stay," he admitted. It was a major part of the whole varsity scene. "Men must organize into mutual groups according to a social law," the editor added. But, he concluded, the system was not beyond correction. By the spring, the furor around the state had diminished and the Anti-Fraternity Bill was quietly tabled. Extensive hearings had allowed the concerned to air their views, but the politicians declined to act.

A bigger story on the Wittenberg campus was the decision of the trustees at the College of Wooster to eliminate fraternities by forbidding further initiations. The outrageous part of the story, from the Wittenberg Greeks' point of view was that they did it for money. The *Wittenberger* alleged that Wooster had received a quarter-of-a-million-dollar gift conditioned upon the antifraternity action.

Just how the faculty was attempting to deal with the fraternities at Wittenberg and get them under control during this period was outlined in Heckert's annual report to the Board in 1910. "One of the problems confronting every conference of professors and presidents," he said, "is the relation of the fraternity house to the college authorities." The faculty at Wittenberg, he added, had undertaken a year-long study and was now "quietly but persistently" dealing with the matter. A member of the faculty was assigned to visit each house monthly and report to the full faculty on the conditions they found.

The faculty set a limit on the number of social functions each group could have. They outlawed membership for students enrolled in the academy or area high schools. They prohibited initiation before the first of November. The groups agreed to review regularly the class standing of their members and to adopt house rules on member conduct and house study hours. In every case, the pretext for regulation was the faculty's overriding concern for the academic performance of students not any inherent right to regulate student organizations. They began publishing grade averages by group affiliation, honoring the top groups, and circumscribing the activities of those ranking too low.

The Greeks remained the institutionalized rowdies of varsity life. In one student publication, the *Rap*, the Greek groups were classified for general campus consumption. "To be an ATO," said the classifier, "one must be an ass, an athlete, or an encyclopedia." To be a Beta, "one must be adept in the use of the double cross, a bore, a wit, or a backslider." To be a Phi Gam, "one must hail from a town of 360 inhabitants or less, be proficient in the use of the plow, and give some attention to the coeds, but more to the clergy." To be a Phi Psi, the writer further advised, "One must be lazy, handsome, indifferent, grumpy, and conceited." To be a nonfraternity man, he concluded, "One must be either too proud, too particular, too poor, too pious, or too unprepossessing," to be a Greek. Turning to the sororities, he wrote, "To be an Alpha Xi, one must be pretty and almost a prude." A Tau Delt, however, was "a society belle" with a family tree of lemons. A nonsorority girl living in Ferncliff "must be able to live on tough beef and prunes."

The women were energetic at organizing sororities, first called fraternities for women, and their groups caused the faculty less concern. April 17, 1902, the Tau Delta Theta local was founded. In the winter of 1903, Sigma Pi local was established; and on May 11, 1904, it became Zeta chapter of Alpha Xi Delta, the first national sorority on campus. In the 1911-12 academic year, women were permitted to withdraw from Ferncliff Hall to live in the school's first sorority house, Alpha Xi Delta. On March 4, 1913, Gamma Beta Gamma local was founded, and in the fall became Chi Chapter of Alpha Delta Pi. In 1915 another group of Wittenberg women received a charter as a chapter of Aloquin, a national sorority without a Greek letter name. In 1917, however, the group gave up its national affiliation to become the local Theta Gamma Rho.

The existence of sororities focused attention on one of the most rapidly changing aspects of varsity life, the social calendar. A campus party in 1874 was such an unprecedented event that it was front page news and was acknowledged as the first party ever held on campus. Interestingly, it occurred in the year women were first enrolled. By the time of the Heckert administration, nearly three decades later, social events were so plentiful as to require regulation, scheduling, and limitation. There were four fraternities, four sororities, Myers Hall, Ferncliff Hall, the two Ys, and a score of other associations and clubs and each, to one degree or another, pursued a social dimension in its work. Heckert defended the social scene. "The modern college community," he said, "is a small world in itself." The only way to tie together all the divergent groups of a larger and increasingly diverse student body, he said, was by a common social life.

Another topic of wide discussion was the double standard in morals. "Women were not made inherently better than men," observed one chapel speaker. Their lives were cleaner, he concluded, because they were held "in leash" by public sentiment. The vices of men resulted from the double standard, he continued; and the human race would be lifted from moral degeneracy if the one higher standard were applied to both.

Much of society feared, however, that both women and men were adhering increasingly to the lower standard of behavior and calling it "sophisticated." One of the distinguishing characteristics of the emerging national collegiate culture was the more public display of suggestive conduct by the "in" group and an inclination to talk and write about it openly. In the midwest, perhaps, there was more the appearance of promiscuity than the substance but the more open behavior made adults nervous. Both the city newspaper and the *Torch* told of boys and girls meeting at night on other college campuses, but then noted that student behavior was about the same in all institutions.

In an editorial, poking fun at the growing interest in women's athletics, one male student noted, "Muscles formerly soft as velvet will now respond to loving caresses like bands of unyielding steel. Soft biceps that were originally ordained for gentle response will now swing around with a resounding smack. Alas! And before long the poor masculine who endeavors to call on his lady love may be subject to rough treatment." He was likely, he concluded, to slink home as if returning from a "prep" initiation.

There was flirting in class; students rushed to class to sit side by side, holding hands if they could get away with it. Some couples were so close that when quizzed by the professor, they answered for one another.

The College Brook in 1917. This area, located west of the lighted main campus entrance, was a favorite alternate route to and from the women's dormitory. "Kissing Bridge" was constructed by students in this secluded area. In 1927 it would become the location for commencement exercises, and be renamed Commencement Hollow. Wittenberg University Archives.

Students constructed "Kissing Bridge" across the college brook in the hollow to the left of the lighted entrance, an alternative, more secluded route to and from the women's dorm. A student wrote a poem about the proctors at the women's hall. Its fourth verse:

So beware of midnight parties
　　And of revels late at night,
For if the proctors get you
　　They'll give it to you right!
So when you get a "campus,"
　　There's no use to cry or pout,
For those proctors they got you
　　Cause you didn't watch out!

To get a "campus" meant that a girl caught violating curfew would be restricted to the campus, not allowed to leave for a specified period. Dancing parties were one of the "in things" and, though not permitted on campus, they occurred at special places in town designed to attract the dancing crowd, like Neff's Grounds and the Park Pavilion. As more and more student social life involved going off campus, being "campused" was a serious interference, indeed. The class of 1904 recalled a late night illicit dance held in the college gym with an African American jazz band. The music was loud enough unfortunately to arouse Professor Prince and President Heckert who shut it down.

As revolutionary for student social life in the Heckert years as the bicycle had been in Samuel Ort's day, was the advent of the new motion picture theater. In 1908 Philip Chakeres opened his first of many movie theaters in downtown Springfield, The Princess. It was advertised as "Springfield's theater beautiful, cozy, and comfortable, the theater of courteous treatment." The Chakeres family opened a second theater, The Majestic, in time for Christmas in 1912. They called it "Springfield's first Christmas gift" because it opened on Christmas Day. By 1916, the town boasted of eight movie houses showing up to sixteen different motion pictures on any given day of the week. Students frequented them regularly alone, by couples, and in groups.

Not every one accepted the new "modern" social life emerging on the campus. In 1914, Heckert explained the stance of the Lutheran Church on a variety of issues. His observations explained some of the rising conflict between the church and the campus. Lutherans, he said, came from America's great middle class; they were progressive and conservative, progressive in adapting to the urban, industrial, and scientific age, but conservative in politics, religious beliefs, and morals. Its four distinguishing characteristics, he said, were (1) "Save the children," by emphasis on Sunday schools and the catechism, (2) an emphasis on an educated clergy, (3) interest in foreign missions, and (4) an insistence on good order in worship. Lutherans were liturgical, he said, but not "high" church; they followed the traditional calendar, believed in infant baptism with later confirmation, and accepted the Bible as the sole and infallible rule of faith and practice. Most, he said, had hardly been touched by the higher criticism or by the rationalistic tendencies of the modern age. These points of view and the tendencies in campus social and religious life were destined to be in conflict on and off the campus.

In 1915 the Wittenberg Synod took action instructing its members of the Board to protest vigorously Sunday picture shows, dancing on campus, and certain advertisements in student publications that promoted "dandying." By that latter term, they meant stylish dress, slicked back hair, the mustache, fancy shoes, and similar modern styles. A year later, a group of recent graduates petitioned the Board for a hearing. They wanted to make recommendations about the spiritual life of the students. All nine of the petitioners were theological students and became active pastors in Wittenberg's supporting synods and devoted a lifetime to raising the moral and spiritual issues of campus life.

When granted the right to speak, they had two resolutions to offer for board consideration. First, they asked that the college appoint a campus pastor to direct the spiritual life and activities of students and to "conserve to the Gospel ministry," a larger percentage of the young men who came with that calling in mind. The temptations of a varsity lifestyle, they claimed, led too many astray and into other careers. Second, they asked that campus organizations be under faculty supervision and that all be prohibited from activities which tended toward spiritual indifference. Which activities did so?

Cartoon by Harry Trotwood Blount, class of 1896, *Cycle 95* yearbook. Wittenberg University Archives.

Cartoon by unidentified student, *Cycle, 1902* yearbook. Wittenberg University Archives.

"Dancing, card playing, and the like," they said. The Board referred the recommendations to a special committee.

At the June 1917 meeting, the special committee brought "Resolutions Concerning Moral and Spiritual Interests of Students." The first expressed disapproval of dancing and card playing, and called upon faculty to restrict such practices. The second expanded the role of the professor of Bible, Samuel E. Greenawalt, naming him campus pastor. The third asked faculty to make Sunday church attendance a requirement. The fourth recommended that attendance at chapel for faculty and students be required. The fifth asked that reports "on these four items" be made to the Board annually.

The following year, Heckert reported that faculty had limited students to one dance per group per semester and one off-campus formal dance in the spring. That action allowed at least two dozen dances to occur annually. So far as requiring students to attend Sunday services, the president reported that the school had supplied the names of all students to the appropriate denominations in town asking the pastors to call on them. It was action, but far short of the compulsion which some desired. Chapel services, he continued, were well attended; and every effort was made to maintain "churchly ideals." But he urged the Board to remember that it was also a gathering of the community with conversations and announcements about all that was going on in student lives. As a general convocation of the student body, chapel served a multitude of purposes; and worship was only one of them.

The report fell short of what the Board expected. Limiting dances was not the level of regulation anticipated. The president failed to mention card playing at all; and it seemed he sidestepped the matter of required worship as well. As pressure continued, Heckert bluntly reported that if compulsory chapel was what was wanted, the Board, through its secretary, should notify members of the faculty that attendance was required. He suggested further that board members rotate among themselves the matter of conducting the services. Clearly he and the faculty, who lived with the students daily, were becoming irritated with board members who sought to govern campus life from afar. The conflict between church and campus on these matters would be postponed by the World War, but the institution would have to come to grips with them sooner or later.

There were other aspects of the emerging varsity life about which students were enthusiastic that elicited little or no church or board opposition, and engendered great support from a public eager to be part of the "varsity spirit." The first was the revival of the college Glee Club. The glee club began under President Ort, but interest had waned. In 1911 it was revived under the direction of student Ross Stover and Professor Hiller. It began public concerts in Springfield and toured throughout Ohio and Indiana. It was used for student recruitment and fund raising. It was hailed as one of the best men's singing groups in the state, one which had a "delightful spirit of comradeship" and was recognized for the gentlemanly conduct of its members wherever it went. It added a brass quartette and a comic orchestra to lighten its repertoire. One special program that became increasingly popular was called "Warblings of War."

The second activity was the class play. The junior and senior classes regularly presented a spring play. When the new Springfield High School auditorium became available, the plays moved from the college chapel to High Street, southwest of the Lutheran church. The plays became community events. In 1916 Professor Hiller staged the newly translated Greek drama, "The Alcestis of Euripides," on an outdoor stage built in front of Recitation Hall. The play was presented in the Greek fashion with a chorus. The editor of the yearbook called it "really a remarkable production." The Senior Class Play was "The Runaways," and it pleased a large audience with the antics of an "old maid hired girl" in pursuit of a man. In 1917 the junior class said that it sought to avoid the lighter, modern farces as "too unsubstantial to be worth the effort," and yet avoided older plays which were "too difficult" for them to perform. They chose Percy Mackaye's "Mater," which they presented in the high school auditorium.

Two later class plays were comedies which featured plots based on English family life. The seniors presented "Green Stockings," which made fun of English courting and marriage traditions, while the juniors performed "All-of-a-Sudden Peggy," featuring an unlikely marriage quadrangle of Peggy and her mother with Lord Anthony and his younger brother. Both focused on heroines of decidedly modern and "fresh" behavior and dissected established marriage customs.

Another popular activity was *Der Deutscher Verein*. The German Club required a high standard of language achievement for membership and attracted local residents as well as advanced students and faculty who enjoyed the celebration of the German language and culture. Wittenberg graduates, those of other colleges who had studied German, native Germans who lived in Springfield, and many of the town's descendants of earlier German immigrants joined one another monthly to use the language in formal and informal discourse. They read plays in German, sang German songs, played German music, read and discussed German poetry and literature, and discussed the developing crisis in Europe. The outbreak of war in Europe in June of 1914 between Germany, England, and France cast a shadow over the group and everything German in America.

Students and faculty, particularly those in *Der Deutscher Verein* along with their friends in the city, were hard pressed to handle growing antagonisms. Those of German and British decent were increasingly at odds with one another. A senior, Hugh Stewart

Fullerton of the class of 1915, attempted to summarize the situation in an essay entitled "Neutrality" in the *Wittenberger*. "We are very much in the position of the 'old woman in the shoe,'" he wrote. Unruly German-Americans and unruly Anglo-Americans were "set to turning out explosive pamphlets" that undermined President Woodrow Wilson's policy of neutrality. The result, he was certain, would be a nation split into bellicose factions. All of this was unfortunate, he said, because "none of the propaganda from either side can be believed;" and America's own best interests would not likely be served by either party. As to whether England or Germany had "the just cause," he said, it was too soon to tell. In any event, he concluded, the war in Europe was becoming a "people's war, affecting everyone far beyond what it did when it began." Upon graduation, Fullerton pursued graduate work and a career in the diplomatic corps.

Fullerton's analysis was prophetic. Little did he know how serious the clash would be for his college with its German name and its rediscovered heritage. The intensity of the conflict and the effort to get the United States into the war on one side or the other was a catastrophe for Wittenberg. It consumed the energies of students, faculty, and the Board, and set all other issues and concerns aside. President Heckert's effort to adapt Wittenberg to the modern era, it seemed, was stalled.

As the United States was drawn closer to involvement in Europe's war, Lutherans in America were planning for the celebration of the Four Hundredth Anniversary of Luther's Reformation in Germany. The two events, the Lutheran Quadra-centennial and America's entrance into the war, had significant impact on the new Wittenberg in Ohio and shaped its future for years to come. When Heckert reflected on the events of 1917, 1918, and 1919, he observed: "Our position as a college was threatened;" and he talked about the "solemn duty resting on me to maintain our beloved school and at the same time to show the country that people with German blood would be intensely loyal."

Spurred by the immigration of six million Germans in the nineteenth century and the unification of Germany in the 1870s, there had been a tremendous growth in German culture in America. One of every six immigrants in the century had been German. Americanized Lutheranism at Wittenberg and elsewhere had been overwhelmed by German Lutheran orthodoxy. Wittenberg shared in that rediscovery of the German. Indeed all of American higher education adopted reforms based on the German university model. The music of Bach, Beethoven, and Wagner, among others, had become increasingly popular, but would soon be dropped from concert programs. Gymnasiums and physical education programs bore a definite Germanic stamp. Kindergartens had appeared as an integral part of a progressive elementary school program. German societies blossomed: benevolent groups for welfare, societies to foster German music, and social clubs like Wittenberg's *Der Deutscher Verein*. The German newspaper was a familiar part of larger cities. German treats such as the beer garden, the Sunday concert, and the Christmas tree had become common. But the climate for them changed rapidly.

That some were pro-German before the United States entered the war was to be expected. The nation was officially neutral; and various ethnic groups naturally included many who were inclined to support the nation from which they or their parents had immigrated: England, France, Germany, Austria, Ireland, or Italy. Nearly one out of every four Americans had German blood in their veins. Because of their number, their German names, the extensive German-language press, and the sheer number of their lodges and clubs, they seemed a more formidable challenge than the others.

Plans for the celebration of the 400th anniversary of the Reformation involved eastern American Lutheran churches of German origins: the General Synod to which Wittenberg related, the General Council, and the United Synod South. Their plans were ambitious. There were to be joint Lutheran worship services, many of them in the German language. They planned lectures, publications, a special church-wide offering, all designed to heighten awareness of the Lutheran Reformation in Germany.

As these events were planned, the sequence of events leading the United States into war was also unfolding. In May 1915, German submarines sank the unarmed British passenger liner *Lusitania* with more than a hundred U.S. citizens among the nearly 1,200 who perished. President Woodrow Wilson protested the outrage with no effect. Germany's policy of unrestricted submarine warfare against neutral ships, and the killing of civilians on unarmed vessels aroused American public opinion and moved the nation to opposition to Germany. Early the following year, after the sinking of another unarmed ship, the French steamer *Sussex*, Wilson issued an ultimatum saying that the United States would enter the war if Germany continued the policy. In May Wilson thought he had Germany's agreement to cease such attacks on neutral or unarmed vessels. To move the nation toward preparedness in the event of war, however, Congress passed the National Defense Act to increase the size of the army.

Faculty, said Heckert, was anxious to do what was right in the matter of military service. They suggested that there was no need for men to rush at once into service; but if a student wanted to enroll in a reserve officer's training corps, they would receive letters of approval and credit for their work. A large number of men were also approved to leave campus early to do farm work because of the need to increase food production for aid to the hungry in Europe where farm production had been seriously disrupted by war.

On January 31, 1917, Germany announced the resumption of unrestricted submarine warfare. The United States broke off diplomatic relations. Tensions mounted and anti-German sentiment grew. British intelligence revealed the so-called Zimmerman Note in which Germany instructed its ambassador to Mexico to incite that nation to conflict with the United States to keep the nation preoccupied at home. They offered to support Mexico in reclaiming lands lost in the Mexican War. The revelation further shifted public opinion toward the British and French. After the sinking of more American ships, the president asked for a Declaration of War.

While Wittenberg and her students sought to redefine what college in the twentieth century would be like, America and the world found themselves in the midst of a struggle to determine what form a new world order would take. For the next few years, thousands of Germans in America would be arrested and detained on suspicion of spying or disloyalty. More than a few would be mobbed and some were lynched.

Chapter Seventeen

Teddy Rah!

As anti-German war hysteria rose in America and affected Wittenberg, the irony of it was that the school had begun as an institution committed to Americanizing the German church and the German immigrants who poured into America in the nineteenth century. By the time of World War I, Wittenberg had participated sufficiently in the celebration of German culture that it came under suspicion. Every one of the school's presidents, most of its faculty, and a majority of students and alumni had German names like Keller, Sprecher, Helwig, Ort, Ruthrauff, Heckert, Hochdoerfer, Zimmerman, and Brodfuehrer.

The prejudice was not just informal and unorganized. Surveys of opinion among college officers, newspaper editors, and government officials indicated widespread fear of German influences in America among these educated groups as well. There was a War Council to mobilize the state of Ohio and ensure adequate labor for the war effort. Ohio Governor James M. Cox appointed a Publicity Committee to marshal patriotic sentiments and put the state on a maximum war footing. It put pressure on German-Americans to demonstrate their loyalty. This committee influenced news about the war through daily bulletins to the state's newspapers.

To "educate" Ohioans more effectively, the State created a Patriotic Education Committee, chaired by William Oxley Thompson, president of the Ohio State University. The bureau enlisted speakers from the state's academic community, but it quickly attracted a wide variety of persons with an interest in patriotism. Some of the speeches deteriorated into jingoism and brought protests from some educational institutions, but not many. Some resigned from the committee because of the coarse and uninformed propaganda it sometimes disseminated.

Even the fledgling Association of American University Professors, the defender of academic freedom for university teachers, faltered in the anti-German hysteria. In a special report on "Academic Freedom in Wartime," it asserted its own unqualified loyalty and deplored "sinister forces" supporting the German side. They argued that in wartime, freedom of speech and academic freedom had to be temporarily suspended. Rather than a reasoned voice that urged avoidance of blanket accusations and jingoistic assaults on the innocent to get at the guilty, the AAUP lent credence to a national assault on every college or university with German antecedents

The Declaration of War came on April 6, 1917, eight months before the Lutheran Quadra-centennial was to occur. As the anti-German sentiment swept the country, the Lutheran celebration and the mood of the country collided. From the months leading up to war to the Armistice in late 1918, Germans and Lutherans suffered. Some Lutheran pastors were accused of allegiance to the Kaiser. Some were tarred and feathered by irate neighbors. Schools and churches which conducted services in German were attacked. The hysteria grew and intensified. In many places, Springfield High School and the Wittenberg Academy included, the German language was dropped in midsemester. At the College of Wooster, students broke into the German classroom and defaced the picture of the Kaiser hanging there. At Wittenberg, the German professor, Dr. Hochdoerfer became ill and took a leave of absence. The class of 1917, to show their support of him, elected both Dr. and Mrs. Hochdoerfer to honorary membership in their class. Sauerkraut and schmearcase, two standard German grocery items in Springfield, were renamed "liberty cabbage" and "cottage cheese." German-Americans who had been outspoken in their support of Germany in the months leading up to war now found themselves in an awkward position. Patriotic citizens, once the United States became involved, saw such expressions as evidence of possible treasonous behavior.

The war of words in America grew intense as the war became more costly in lives. There was a demand for more aggressive efforts at Americanization and the rooting out of German treason. Ohio's Governor appointed an Americanization Committee, a group that would undertake to reeducate all of Ohio's foreign-born population. It was chaired by Professor Raymond Motley of Western Reserve University. Rooted in the assumption that all of the foreign born might maintain loyalties to the European nation from which they had come, the committee sought to organize special education programs for them. It influenced what was taught in local schools and advocated the elimination of German language instruction. It circulated lists of pro-German books to libraries and asked that they be removed from circulation. The committee also circulated a list of approved books that could be kept in circulation.

To protect Wittenberg in the anti-German climate, Dr. Heckert recommended active support of the allied cause so that the school's loyalty could readily be seen. Wittenberg, he said, was not German in any narrow sense of that word. Rather, it represented the best of the German heritage in America's melting pot culture. Even this mild defense of German culture brought criticism and found few defenders in the broader educational world. German-related institutions were immediately relegated to a second-class level in American higher education from which they had difficulty extricating themselves. It was hard for Heckert to understand how people could just assume that persons of German ancestry would be disloyal.

"Wittenberg is loyal to the core," said Dean Shatzer. "Her loyalty is in works and not words." Heckert's list of good works to show loyalty was extensive; work for the war effort in Liberty Bond drives and the YMCA Fund and Red Cross activities both on campus and off; work to collect clothing and supplies for soldiers. He counseled pastors to be active in such work and to drop services in German. He conducted religious services in nearby training camps. He promoted war savings stamps and said every faculty and staff member had bought war bonds.

When Congress passed the Selective Service Act, all of higher education reacted, but Wittenberg had reacted faster. Pre-induction military training was organized on campus to get students ready for actual service within five days of the declaration of war.

Three days later, all Wittenberg men marched in Springfield's "Preparedness Parade."

The War Department advised students, at least for the present, to remain in school. Coach Godfrey, Captain Estel Steward of Co. B, Third Regiment of the Ohio National Guard, local resident Charles B. Zimmerman, and Charles Meyer of the Ohio National Guard conducted campus drills. Later in the year, the Federal government indicated that it would establish regular army training courses at approximately six hundred colleges and universities. Heckert told the Board that the faculty had approved applying for a unit; and in December, Wittenberg was approved for a Student Army Training Corps detachment.

Student Army Training Corps (SATC) cartoon by John Wilbur "Wib" Dorst, class of 1922 in the *Wittenberger*, 1918-1919. Wittenberg University Archives.

Heckert felt that more needed to be done to keep Wittenberg from suffering permanent damage in the anti-German furor. What was needed, he was convinced, was widespread press coverage of Wittenberg's loyalty; and he undertook to get it. He secured Governor James M. Cox as Commencement speaker for the June 1918 ceremony. Cox was launching a bid for reelection based upon his record as a strong war governor who had hunted down disloyalty and turned Ohio into a strong force for national victory. Increased production on Ohio's farms and factories, a strong response to the call for troops, and a thorough plan of Americanization were the planks in his platform. His record was so strong that he was being talked of as a leading contender for the Democratic presidential nomination to succeed Woodrow Wilson. Indeed Cox and vice presidential running mate Franklin Delano Roosevelt would be the unsuccessful Democratic slate in the 1920 presidential race. Surely, thought Heckert, if Governor Cox agreed to speak at Wittenberg, it would be testimony enough to the loyalty of the school and could not be misunderstood. He appreciated Cox's willingness to come when not coming might have been better politics.

There was another, even stronger boost for the college's morale and reputation. Dr. Heckert and Harry S. Kissell, a Springfield banker, realtor, and member of the Wittenberg Board of Directors were involved with the Clark County War Chest drive. Springfield, because of its identification with Wittenberg, was also accused of pro-German sympathies, and both were eager to demonstrate their loyalty. The suspicions lingered. As late as 1933, Ford Maddox Ford, in his novel *The Rash Act*, depicted Springfield in 1917 as a pro-German town. Heckert and Kissell asked former President Theodore Roosevelt, known for his vigorous Americanism, to speak at a war fund-raising rally in Springfield. Receiving a reply that was reasonably encouraging, the two men left for Sagamore Hill for an interview.

Roosevelt explained to the two men that he did not see everybody who wired for an engagement. "I agreed to see you because I noticed you both have German names," he said. "He brushed aside our arguments as to why he should come to Springfield to help in the War Chest drive with apparent indifference," said Heckert. "If I come," Roosevelt finally said, "I want to come because Wittenberg College is located there." He asked if Wittenberg was a Lutheran institution and, when told that it was, explained that he had been looking for an opportunity to address people of German extraction in the United States from an appropriate location. Wittenberg, he said, with its German name reminiscent of the birth of Lutheranism, gave him the perfect setting.

Harry Kissell said afterward that he rather resented the former president's remarks since his family had been in the United States since the American Revolution. But, he concluded, if Roosevelt could be gotten by this route, he would not disabuse him. The two tried to persuade Roosevelt to come earlier in the week than Saturday; but the former president explained that he already had a western trip planned so, if he came at all, it would have to be a Saturday in May. After discussing the possibilities, Roosevelt kept the two for almost an hour talking about "the great questions of the day with a freedom which rather astonished me," observed Heckert. As they left, Roosevelt said, "Meet me at the Harvard Club tomorrow afternoon, and I will give you my final answer."

The next day they met a very assertive Roosevelt who told them that he would come on May 25, arriving at 9 a.m. and leaving that night for Chicago. He had three conditions which would set the stage for his speech which had to be met. First, he said, Dr. Heckert was to preside. Second, a German Catholic Priest had to give the invocation and a German Lutheran pastor the benediction. Third, no one was to be on the platform unless he had a German name or German blood in his veins. Heckert said that he demurred at chairing the event because he did not want the people of Springfield to think that he personally was trying to get into the limelight. "Unless you preside," said Roosevelt, "I don't come."

Colonel Roosevelt had agreed to address college students at 10:30 in the morning, followed by lunch with a small group. He would address a city-wide war chest rally that afternoon at Springfield's new Memorial Hall on Main Street, followed by a short speech on the Esplanade between the Arcade and City Hall. Following that, he and Dr. Heckert would drive out to the Wilbur Wright Air Field, near Dayton, to view the Army Air Corps squadrons. On that trip, Roosevelt's secretary pulled Heckert aside and pleaded with him to make sure that the Colonel did not go up in an airship.

Roosevelt expected to talk with a rather small student group. The campus visit was to have been "a sort of private function." When the former President arrived, the editor of the *Wittenberg Torch* observed that "it looked as though every person who had ever been graduated by Wittenberg was on hand." Friends of the students had clamored for admission "until the faculty was almost beside itself," the student paper concluded. The Springfield paper felt that the most extraordinary aspect of the visit, besides Roosevelt himself, was the presence in the Lutheran college chapel of Monsignor Vattman, a Roman Catholic priest from Cincinnati and a military chaplain. The monsignor was pleased with the loud standing ovation with which the students, not unaware of the historic importance of his presence, greeted him. Surely he was the first Roman Catholic priest ever to grace the Wittenberg chapel, and a monsignor at that!

It was midmorning as Theodore Roosevelt entered and was introduced to each member of the college faculty and others seated on the platform. Amid the formalities, the students boomed forth a single ringing "Teddy, Rah!" Roosevelt turned from his duties to wave to the students and to give them the famous Roosevelt grin. Students and their friends were packed into every seat and standing along the walls, in the aisles, in the doorways, in the hall, and up the stairs to the third floor on either side of the chapel.

Former President Theodore Roosevelt leaving Recitation Hall flanked by Charles G. Heckert, left, and Harry S. Kissell, right, Springfield businessman and Wittenberg Board member. Wittenberg University Archives.

Roosevelt told the students that he was eager to come to the campus. He explained why he came several times in a relatively short address because, he said, many will wonder. "The reason I am glad to come here," he said, first, "is shown in your service flag there and your honor roll there." He pointed to the symbols of alumni war service near the pulpit from which he spoke. "For three quarters of a century," he continued, "Wittenberg College has held an honorable position among educational institutions of the country. It has taught high ideals."

The raspy-voiced American was not uncritical of the German tendency to exclusiveness; and, expressing the views that he had come to Ohio to expound, he recommended that German be a foreign language, taught as a foreign language, and not used in Lutheran services. His own church, the Dutch Reformed, he pointed out, had faced a similar problem. The ex-president, recognizing that not all of the anti-German clamor was misguided, insisted that loyal citizens of German descent oppose the German-American Alliance, a subversive national organization, as an "alliance of treason" bringing harm to the nation. Their activities, he said, caused unwarranted injury to loyal Americans of German ancestry. It was they, he implied, who were responsible when loyal German-Americans were badly treated.

The real reason he had been eager to come to Wittenberg, however, said the former president finally, was that this embattled college afforded him a peculiar opportunity to inculcate the doctrines of true Americanism from the pulpit of a loyal German-American institution. He added, in an aside to the students, that he used up a great deal of his time declining invitations to visit colleges and could now be in trouble with the students at Rutgers, his own church's college. "I decline to recognize any discrimination . . . because of the creed any man professes or because of diverse nationalities," he told them. It was infamy, he continued, for a man to discriminate against another because his ancestors were born in Germany, and added, "No greater crime has ever been committed."

When he left the campus, Roosevelt continued to use Wittenberg as an example for his claim that most German-Americans were loyal. In an article entitled "No Half Measures" in the *Metropolitan Magazine* in August, he addressed a larger audience. "The other day," he wrote, "I spoke in Springfield, Ohio . . . . I was introduced by the President of Wittenberg College, a Lutheran college founded by Germans but now straight-out American . . ." It was as American as Harvard, Yale or Princeton, he continued, with two hundred of her sons in the Army or Navy. It illustrated clearly why it was unfair and unwise, he said, to condemn everything that sounded German.

"At last our answer has gone back," said the editor of the school paper; Theodore Roosevelt struck at the "ignorant and insidious remarks" about the school. Never, he said, had Wittenberg rendered such service to America as now in this "great war for civilization and humanity." And, when Dr. Heckert had asked him to come, related the editor, Roosevelt said, "I jumped at the chance."

With Roosevelt on the campus in May and Ohio's governor, James M. Cox, there in June, Heckert felt that he had gotten widely publicized testimonies to Wittenberg's loyalty. A few of Wittenberg's friends felt that Heckert and the school might be going too far to demonstrate loyalty to a doubting nation. Others agreed that any effort to win public approval in the current climate was necessary and justifiable. A college was no longer an isolated community removed from the broader life of the nation. It existed in the real world and needed to be responsive to opinion in the community at large.

The school's experience with the anti-German sentiment of World War I sensitized Wittenberg to the new field of public relations; more so, perhaps, than most colleges. Some criticized the school's penchant for public self-explanation and, as they saw it, self-promotion. But Heckert's patriotism should be seen in a broader context. The American Protective League and other super-patriotic groups scrutinized institutions for pro-German and anti-war sentiments. Schools of the Anglicans, Presbyterians, Baptists, and Methodists were seemingly given the benefit of the doubt. The new nativists, however, were quick to identify sympathizers with the Germans and with the Bolsheviks in Russia. Heckert believed Wittenberg had to be seen as neither the one nor the other.

Even if many American colleges before the war had failed to capture widespread support from business, government, and the general public, the war was changing all that. The nation's war experience in general and the establishment of the Student Army Training Corps (SATC) in particular, led to the development of a new national consensus on the value of higher education. There was recognition of the greater need for "skilled intelligence" and specially trained experts. As recognition of that need grew, colleges and universities were given the opportunity to show a new usefulness. Heckert wanted Wittenberg's new usefulness to be as unfettered as possible.

The SATC was conceived as a program for examining, training, and classifying nearly all of the men in America's colleges and universities, mobilizing them into a corps of leaders for the various branches of service and for commissioned officer and noncommissioned officer schools. It was a gigantic mobilization of college men in their colleges, and an effort to appraise how best to use their skills in the nation's service. It was an effort to avoid the errors European nations had made in stripping their universities of students and sending them all into battle. The large number of them who had been killed in grinding trench warfare had repercussions for all of Europe after the war was over. A generation of Europe's future leaders was decimated in four years of carnage.

The SATC was also a response to the appeals of educators. The better organized system of higher education that had emerged in the new century pressed Congress and the President for assistance in the face of war demands. Society needed not only soldiers and sailors but also engineers, architects, physicians, surgeons, chaplains, nurses, accountants, and thousands of other skilled men and women. The new kind of warfare in which the nation was engaged, and the postwar era, would require some to complete their degrees before service. If higher education was a partner with business, industry, and government, it needed to be strengthened and preserved.

In September of 1918, Wittenberg's detachment of the SATC was established under the direction of Captain Abraham J. Somes. To be included among the colleges that received detachments, a school had to guarantee a place in the SATC unit to any male high school graduate who requested one. In return, qualified institutions were to receive $900 per student-soldier to cover tuition, room, and board. More than 140,000 male students were sworn into the U.S. Army in ceremonies in 525 colleges and universities across the United States. Men in colleges not participating in the SATC program transferred to colleges that were or went directly into service.

At Wittenberg the men who were to be sworn in marched to the front of Myers Hall where a new flag pole had been erected.

Wittenberg men assembling in front of Myers Hall for induction into the Student Army Training Corps (SATC), November, 1918. Wittenberg University Archives.

After induction, students marched to the football field for first assembly as soldiers and division into four platoons. Wittenberg University Archives.

Officials of the school and the army were arrayed on the steps. After addresses by Springfield's Civil and Spanish American War General J. Warren Keifer, Dr. Heckert and others, they were sworn in. A crowd of friends and area citizens witnessed the ceremony. At the national level, President Wilson and Secretary of War Newton D. Baker spearheaded the effort to keep young men in college to complete their courses while being trained for service. As Baker expressed it, the nation needed "to keep the lamp of learning burning among the young." Finishing a degree was patriotic because the army and the nation needed educated men.

Two hundred and fifty men formed the Wittenberg SATC unit. The fraternity houses were depleted as the students moved into the newly renovated Myers Hall. All of the colleges and the student's furnishings and belongings were removed, and only army cots and trunks and other officially issued equipment and clothing were allowed in the dormitory. As Benjamin Prince noted, if there was any lingering argument about student ownership of rooms, it vanished with arrival of the army.

The men gave the great majority of their waking hours to drill and other military duties. They were given the rudiments of military tactics, both practical and theoretical. They were trained in the principles of interior guard, the offensive use of the bayonet, the nomenclature and use of the rifle, the use of small arms, the fundamentals of military law and courtesy, and the role of the individual soldier, the squad and the company. As the unit developed a high level of morale, they talked excitedly of "the battle of Wittenberg" as they tried to combine all of that plus endless drill on the athletic field with their regular school work.

The football team, with the encouragement of the SATC officers and under the coaching of "Buckeye" Hobt, organized and went undefeated for the first time in college history. The student-soldiers were ecstatic that the SATC had attracted many good athletes to expand the school's usual force. The military physical fitness program increased the strength, agility, and discipline of the team. On the other hand, the literary societies dwindled to their lowest level of activity anyone could remember. Heckert complained that the war interfered with the religious spirit on the campus, and he feared that the military students expected only entertainment from the religious organizations.

The impact on the college was far-reaching. "The extra amount of work caused by the SATC," said Heckert, "was carried by all members of the teaching staff with great cheerfulness." Many new courses were introduced, professors were shifted to cover programs affected when four young assistant teachers were drafted, and the hours of duty for remaining faculty members were extended.

Heckert complained that academic standards had been seriously interfered with. Dean Shatzer was more specific. "The college year has been one of confusion and extreme difficulty," he said. First, the faculty had to completely reorganize itself and the curriculum to incorporate the military program. Next, it had to deal with a violent flu epidemic which terminated classroom activities for three weeks. Then, finally, with the armistice on November 11, 1918, the faculty again had to reorganize the curriculum to accommodate demobilization. The SATC had lasted only a few months. Indeed it had been an exhausting year that had wrenched every tradition of good academic practice. The faculty gave credit for courses that had never before been part of a liberal arts curriculum and gave grades for interrupted and incomplete work that, under any other circumstances, would never be acceptable. And they did so in the name of patriotism and in support of the national war effort.

The flu epidemic hit Wittenberg during the second week of October, shortly after the SATC program began. More than 150 students suffered, but unlike many institutions Wittenberg could boast that not a single student died. There was one casualty, a volunteer nurse, a member of First Lutheran Church who had worked diligently to ease the suffering of the students. The Red Cross, the Springfield War Camp Community Service, wives of faculty members, and neighbors near the campus provided hours of service.

The SATC was barely underway when the armistice was signed, bringing the war to a close. At first the government indicated that the units on college campuses would be continued to the end of the academic year. Instead, the Wittenberg unit was disbanded on December 20. Faculty and students tried to return to "things educational and religious." The unit had been given high ratings, and Wittenberg was offered a unit of the new Reserve Officer Training Corps (ROTC). Faculty studied the matter. President Heckert noted that "there would seem to be good reason for such a corps here, but the students who were in the SATC are practically a unit against it." What they were willing to undertake in wartime, apparently, they were unwilling to continue when the war ended. In the final chapel service for the school year, Heckert announced that Wittenberg would have regular, compulsory military training the following year and that Secretary of War Baker had indicated that an officer would be stationed on campus to direct the program. Taking note of student and faculty opposition, however, Heckert submitted the matter to the Board which voted against ROTC at Wittenberg. Many men who had enrolled because of the military subsidy were unable to remain without it.

Students dedicated the 1918-19 year book, the *Wittenberger*, to the SATC, the 248 alumni who had served in the armed forces, to nine who died in service, and to the volunteer nurse who died on campus. But it did not linger long on the somber theme of death and sacrifice. Instead, it reported the experience of the living and its liberalizing effect on student life. It noted the temporary end of the *Torch* and its replacement by the *Wittenberg Reveille*, the only SATC paper at an Ohio college. It was published for and by the students in training.

The postwar *Wittenberger* featured a great many cartoons by a prolific freshman, John Wilbur "Wib" Dorst, class of 1922. One of his cartoons was entitled "Taps: Then and Now." For "then" he drew a silhouette of a soldier blowing a bugle, for "now" he showed two beer kegs with taps inserted. In another effort, "Favorite Indoor Sport," he drew a couple "necking" on the sorority house couch.

Cartoon by John Wilbur "Wib" Dorst, class of 1922, the *Wittenberger* yearbook, 1918-1919. Wittenberg University Archives.

Advertisements in student publications demonstrated the changing times. Ads for such places as the Fairbanks Billiard Parlour, Meeks Sporting Goods Store, and Remington Typewriters indicated some of the new dimensions of student life. There was a picture of a four-door, top down roadster in an ad for the Westcott Motor Car Company, an automobile built in Springfield. Wurlitzer Corporation advertised pianos, Victrolas and music instruments with the slogan "Add pep and vigor to the music."

A new style of music was one of the more apparent changes in campus life. As the Wurlitzer ad suggested it was a peppier, more vigorous music the students called jazz. Another example of the effect of the SATC on student life was the SATC Jazz Band. When the military company gave its first ball, music was needed. Several musicians who emerged from the ranks were described as "a real surprise," and, it was said, they had been "going ever since." It was an odd combination of two saxophones, a clarinet, a violin, tenor banjo, banjo guitar, and piano. The group's motto was "We keep 'em happy," and it presaged the Roaring Twenties. As the SATC unit prepared to disband, the group played for a farewell ball. After being mustered out of the army, it renamed itself "The All Ohio Six Novelty Jazz Orchestra." It was soon joined by eight coeds who added a little jazz to the girls' glee club that had been organized to fill in when the men's glee club disappeared with the war. The new group called itself "The Wittenberg Jazzettes."

SATC Jazz Band, 1918. Wittenberg University Archives.

The Wittenberg Jazettes, 1918.
Wittenberg University Archives.

There was informal music as well. A yearbook writer, discussing the women's residence hall, noted that "Chief among the nocturnal events" there was the "melodious harmony of bass voices blending with the wail of the ukulele and the strumming of the guitar." Ferncliff, he noted, was where the men students "give proof" to the Darwinian theory of the survival of the fittest as they tried to catch the girls' attention without arousing "the rigid police system" of the hall's matrons. The hall, in the jargon of war, was known as "No man's land," open to young men only at rare intervals. Music helped the young men make the most of those occasions, suggested the student writer.

Amid the frivolity of the postwar campus, there was a quiet and more dignified event focused on restoring prewar campus spirit. For the first time in history, wrote the yearbook editors, Wittenberg College held a May Festival. Such events appeared at eastern women's colleges before the turn of the century. Earlham College in Indiana was among the first in the West. On May 23, 1919, Miss Esther Homrighaus of the junior class was crowned Queen of the May. The day began early that morning with the crowning of the queen. Then from her throne, she reviewed the day's festivities: "aesthetic dancing," a wand drill, and a dance around the May pole. It was an aspect of that modern world that emerged with the new century. Modernism promoted sport, exercise, and dance; and for the women, it meant outdoor synchronized dance. Wittenberg's coeds danced around the hollow behind Myers Hall—students called it the "gulley"—in self-designed costumes, leaping and dancing until they would rename the hollow itself.

It was a magnificent exhibition of song and dance directed by Miss Ella Wilcox, director of the campus YWCA. Undoubtedly, some objected to a May Day celebration as reflective of the world socialist movement's May Day demonstrations. But the event was rooted first in the German customs of Cincinnati and Springfield and elsewhere of spring musical festivals which revived following the World War. The event in the hollow was renamed the Alma Mater Pageant, and the queen was named The Alma Mater, the highest distinction that could be conferred on a junior woman at Wittenberg. She would preside over the pageant as her first responsibility and then reign throughout her senior year, crowning her successor in May. Engrafted onto the ancient medieval celebration of spring and life and youth and the German celebration of music and dance was Wittenberg's celebration of its highest ideals of faith, learning, and service to others. The women selected were chosen for academic achievement, personality, character, service, leadership, and appearance.

The Alma Mater Celebration began in 1919 as a May Day Festival. Wittenberg University Archives.

It put a finishing touch on the Varsity Life of the postwar campus and in just a few years, the hollow behind Myers Hall was renamed Alma Mater Hollow.

The war affected Wittenberg in other important ways. The Lutheran churches supporting Wittenberg became a part of a larger and more centralized synod. As the celebration of the Reformation approached, a joint committee of the German Lutheran churches proposed their merger into one new church. John L. Zimmerman, a lay member of the committee, a member of Springfield's First Lutheran Church, and treasurer of the Wittenberg Board, was one of the chief advocates of merger on the joint committee. Many of the clergy were less enthusiastic, but Zimmerman led lay delegates in a strong effort of persuasion. The Rev. Henry Eyster Jacobs, president of the General Council's Lutheran Theological Seminary in Philadelphia, entered the debate on Zimmerman's side; and the merger idea prevailed. "If it had not been for John L. Zimmerman," said George Neff of York, Pa., to George Rinkliff, historian of Springfield's First Lutheran Church, "it is very doubtful whether we would have the United Lutheran Church today."

On November 11, 1918, the day of the Armistice in Europe, the three general Lutheran bodies each held their final meetings in New York. On Nov. 14, the first convention of the new United Lutheran Church in America was called to order. It was a historic event and had special meaning for the heirs of the Americanists in Ohio. The General Council had split off from the General Synod in 1868 because of a ruling against them by Samuel Sprecher who was presiding at the convention. The General Synod South had withdrawn during the Civil War. After a half century, these rifts had been healed. In Ohio it led to a consolidation of several separate synods into a new Synod of Ohio which would speak with a single powerful voice in postwar Wittenberg affairs, far outweighing that of the other supporting synods and other constituencies.

There were other factors that pushed Lutherans toward further unity. The U. S. government would not deal with a multiplicity of spokesmen for the various divisions of the Lutheran Church in arranging for wartime chaplains nor would it, in the postwar period, in the matter of European relief. There were still twenty-one separate Lutheran bodies with congregations conducting services in eighteen different languages. Federal authorities wanted to deal with one Lutheran chaplain-sending authority. For that purpose and others, groups representing two-thirds of all Lutherans in the United States organized the National Lutheran Commission for Soldiers and Sailors Welfare.

The Commission evolved into The National Lutheran Council which continued after the war. It first represented Lutherans in Washington in other cooperative efforts like the prevention of a ban of the German language in worship. It continued thereafter to represent the churches' interests in public affairs and promoted cooperation in dividing up mission fields to avoid duplication as Lutherans expanded in communities with defense industries. It also focused on the needs of Lutherans in post war Europe and overseas relief activities. As representatives of the Council met other world Lutheran leaders, they helped organize the first Lutheran World Convention in 1919. It set up the first world-wide gathering at Eisenach, Germany, in August of 1923; and representatives attended from twenty-two countries.

These beginnings—the United Lutheran Church in America, the National Lutheran Council, and the Lutheran World Convention—clearly suggested a new, more complex and intricate structure for American Lutheranism in national and world affairs than had previously existed. The Lutheran colleges and seminaries, from a variety of Lutheran synods, had already organized in 1910, a decade ahead of the churches. They met periodically to deal with church and secular issues confronting them. Prewar meetings of the Lutheran Educational Conference in North America had been held first at Wittenberg in 1912 and at Maywood, Illinois, in 1916. The meetings resumed in 1918 and continued annually thereafter.

But the war had a greater effect on churches, the colleges, and the nation. Society had been shaken to its very foundations by the horrors of total war. The merciless toll on the battle fields and the deaths of unarmed civilians shattered public confidence in the institutions of Western civilization. A more cynical postwar generation questioned the very claims of Christianity. How could God allow such atrocities to occur; how could any nation that called itself Christian commit such acts? These were questions which struck at the very core of Western thought and opened the way for spokesmen for a "modern" world to command greater attention. The theories of Freud gained greater popularity as the world faced the mental breakdown of men at the front and found traditional treatment barbarous or ineffective. The theories of Marx were gaining greater popularity as the Bolshevik revolution in Russia elevated them to greater prominence through implementation, and many in their disillusionment looked at the new secular faith.

H. G. Wells startled the postwar world with his new work *The Outline of History,* which began not with traditional Christian creation stories or with the five thousand years of recorded history but rather with the ages of geological development and evolution. He suggested a harder, colder, more scientific, less personal basis for life and its evolution. His work became popular and controversial.

Benjamin F. Prince, Wittenberg's "Grand Old Man." In 1916, Prince celebrated the fiftieth anniversary of his graduation from Wittenberg and fifty years of service to the college. Wittenberg University Archives.

A recent Wittenberg graduate wrote Benjamin Prince to ask if he should read it. "I have a copy of Wells's late book lying on my table," Prince responded. He liked what he had read of it and was sure it would benefit the alumnus to read it as well. Wells was a good historian, he continued; and his facts were generally correct. "Before he gets to man," he observed, "he reviews the great geological ages and states the evidences of life, animal and vegetable, as exhibited in the rocks. Of course, man, in his estimation, is a development from an earlier animal."

Prince also told the former student that he had read Darwin and other modernists as well, and they could not shake his own faith and should not shake his. "As to the geological ages mentioned in every work by our geologists, I do not think we can challenge them," he confessed. "There is a mystery here we do not understand," between the biblical story of creation and the science of geology. All in all, Prince observed, Wells's work exhibited a novelty of expression and offered views that were truly refreshing and should be read by educated persons.

As the war ended in Europe, Heckert's efforts to save Wittenberg from the anti-German furor continued as if he were unable to stop what he had set in motion. He had Senator, and later president, Warren G. Harding lined up to deliver the commencement address in 1919 and was in correspondence with Secretary of War Newton D. Baker and World Relief director, and later president, Herbert Hoover for future appearances. He was appointed by Ohio Governor Cox as an honorary delegate to the Great Lakes Conference for a League of Nations to be held in Chicago. Gradually, however, Heckert began to relax his strenuous efforts and turned his attention to the celebration of Wittenberg's seventy-fifth anniversary on March 11, 1920.

Six years before the Diamond Jubilee was to occur, before World War engulfed America, Heckert had suggested that the 1920 commencement take special note of the day, and that an extra special effort be made to have all of Wittenberg's friends celebrate the school's seventy-fifth anniversary. As he revived these plans, Heckert's health failed. A weakened heart, overtaxed by his strenuous war efforts, caught up with him. He took a long spring vacation in the south to rest, but returned to campus knowing that he would not get well. He set about as methodically as he had done everything else to plan for an orderly transition.

At the June 1920 meeting of the Board, Heckert tendered his resignation; and the Rev. Dr. Rees Edgar Tulloss, his choice as his successor, a member of the Board and a Pastor in Mansfield, Ohio, was elected. It was a well-planned, orderly transition. On May 21, preceding the board meeting, President Heckert met the students in an assembly to present the "Literary W's" to the outstanding debaters, orators, and writers for the year. It was an award like the Varsity W letter given to outstanding athletes. In presenting the coveted wooden shields with the large carved "W" on their face, Heckert reminisced with the students telling them how life was at college when he had enrolled over forty years before. He closed his remarks with an appeal to fraternity men to be more supportive of the old literary societies whose activities had loomed so large in his days. It was a final appeal to revive an old order that was dying.

Heckert constructed a financial statement of the assets of the institution, in part as a report to the Ohio Department of Public Instruction, a new government requirement, and in part for his own pleasure. He valued the grounds at $100,000; the buildings at $270,000; furniture, $7,500; apparatus, $8,000; the library, $16,000; the museum, $1,000; investments, $698,000; total assets, $1,100,500. It was a solid million-dollar institution he would turn over to Dr. Tulloss, and he was well satisfied with the job he had done.

When the weekend for the Diamond Jubilee celebration arrived, Heckert was too ill to participate in very many of the activities. He made an appearance at the great banquet in Springfield's new Memorial Hall. Fifteen hundred were seated for dinner; and an overflow crowd of five hundred watched the proceedings from the balconies. The hall was richly decorated in the college colors of red and white, and Wittenberg pennants and American flags were tastefully arranged in abundance. An orchestra played delightful music; and student cheerleaders, Paul Laughner and John Kuhns, led the audience in "yells" that reverberated throughout the great hall and in the singing of "America." The men's and the women's glee clubs entertained the proud and happy crowd.

When Heckert arrived, he was greeted with a long, standing ovation and cheers. If there were a hero of the "battle of Wittenberg," he was it. He asked the audience to pay tribute to the memories of all the former presidents and professors of the college who had "passed to the great beyond." He listened to long and sincere tributes, the general theme of which was that he had been a moving power and a great force in the college which he had served so faithfully, and in the community. Heckert then presented Dr. Tulloss. He told the audience that Tulloss was his choice. "He was my best student in college."

"The king is dead, long live the king," said the departing president as he talked about the transition. This was not a cheerful way to begin his remarks, he noted, but he was closing his own life's service with a full measure of satisfaction. His eighteen years as president, he said, had a rather doleful start, with the death of President Ruthrauff, and had ended with the difficult days of the war. Then he added, "I suddenly awoke to the surprising fact that my active career was about ended." Was he shocked, he asked. "No, not exactly," he replied, "only mildly startled."

A few months after the event, President Tulloss issued a jubilee edition of the *Wittenberg Bulletin* recounting the events of the celebration and presenting several historic addresses.

Rees Edgar Tulloss, class of 1906, seventh president of Wittenberg, 1920-1949, at the time of his election to the office. Wittenberg University Archives.

The first was by the Rev. S. E. Greenawalt, professor of Bible, who had recounted the years of Ezra Keller and Samuel Sprecher. Second, the Rev. Harlan K. Fenner of Louisville had reviewed the years of Helwig, and Ort. Dr. Tulloss had then reviewed the years of Ruthrauff and Heckert. The publication ended with a brief look at the future by the Rev. Charles S. Bauslin of the seminary faculty who projected a Wittenberg "moving on to higher and even better things."

Left out of the publication was the special Diamond Jubilee address of Dr. Charles Franklin Thwing, president of Western Reserve University and one of the nation's leaders in higher education, who Dr. Heckert had personally invited. They had agreed that the subject of Dr. Thwing's address would be: "What Have the American People a Right to Expect from the American College in the Next Seventy-Five Years?" Heckert saw it as a long look into Wittenberg's future. It was a broader theme and a broader definition of the school's constituency, and it reflected Dr. Heckert's world view that had guided him throughout his presidency. For Heckert, it was the question that needed to be asked. Wittenberg was part of America and it ought to ask what that meant for its future.

Thwing outlined five expectations that the public might have for any college or university regardless of its ownership or sponsorship. First, he said, people had a right to expect that the American college would educate students to have a disciplined mind responsive to the needs of society, and that it would undergird national liberty, equality, and unity. Second, said Thwing, America had a right to expect rational and sympathetic interpretations of the doctrine of the value of work. Labor, he said, should be lifted as one of the great purposes of life. It was an old theme, a reprise on an earlier Wittenberg era, *Labor Ipse Fuerit Voluptas*; labor is its own reward.

Third, said Thwing, the American people have a right to expect that the college will develop in its students a sense of social responsibility, since the educated were responsible for social leadership. They were the guardians of American democracy. Fourth, said the Western Reserve president, the people have a right to expect a commitment to truth, the truth of nature and of men, the truth of history and philosophy, the truth of economics and of literature. America, he said, was imperiled by a narrowing vision and a growing sentimentalism. There was too much living for the day only. The antidote, he said, was the college committed to the pursuit of truth. *Veritas*, the recently adopted new motto of Harvard University, he said, should be written over every college gateway in the nation. "Without fear and without prejudice," he observed, "the scholar is to seek to know. The college is a force to discover and to declare truth."

Finally, Thwing observed, "The American people have a right to expect . . . the spiritual interpretation of America's future." He was not talking about sectarian or denominational religious views, he said; he talked of the spiritual essence of America, that which made America more human and more divine. Heckert liked Thwing's address; it posed a broad challenge for the great college he had always envisioned. He died before he could see it develop. He never knew that Tulloss dropped the speech from the Diamond Jubilee report. Ten years earlier a reporter for the *Springfield Morning Sun* had noted Heckert's dream to put Wittenberg among the most important institutions in America. His successor, at his inaugural, said it was destined to become the leading college of the Lutheran Church in America. It was likewise an ambitious goal, but one with a slightly narrower, some said, more realistic emphasis.

On Thursday, Dec. 7, 1920, six months after the great seventy-fifth anniversary celebration and a month after the inauguration of Rees Edgar Tulloss, Dr. Heckert died. The students saluted him on a memorial plaque in Hiller Chapel in Recitation Hall as "Scholar, teacher, preacher, loyal citizen, and friend." He left his estate in an annuity with the college for his wife's support after which it was to endow a chair in English.

During the next twenty-nine years, Tulloss would guide Wittenberg through the "Roaring Twenties," into the Great Depression of the thirties, and through World War II—three decades of challenge and change. On that chilly day of Dec. 7, 1920, however, he presided over an institution of great strength. The momentous events that occurred from the Civil War through the World War had made Wittenberg a different place from what it was in the beginning. It now resembled undergraduate, residential liberal arts colleges all across America that reflected the emerging global, secular, urban, industrial society.

"This is a lovely spot for the location of a literary institution," Ezra Keller had said three-quarters of a century earlier. "It requires some faith to believe that in after years it will be an academic grove to which hundreds will resort to drink at the pure fountains of knowledge and go forth in the world to do good, to bless mankind. And yet I have faith to believe that this will be realized."

Wittenberg, after Charles Heckert's stewardship and that of his predecessors, had become that pleasant academic grove and held the promise of greater things to come.

Bibliography of Sources and References

Ahlstrom, Sidney. *A Religious History of the American People*. New Haven, Conn. Yale University Press, 1972.

Allbeck, Willard D. "Women at Wittenberg" unpublished monograph. Wittenberg University Archives.

_________. "Books from Ezra Keller's Library." *The Wittenberg Bulletin*. vol. 42, no. 3. December, 1945, p. 29.

_________. *Theology at Wittenberg, 1845-1945*. Springfield, Ohio. Wittenberg Press, 1945.

_________. *A Century of Lutherans in Ohio*. Yellow Springs, Ohio. the Antioch Press, 1966.

Allmendinger, jr. David F., *Paupers and Scholars: The Transformation of Student Life in Nineteenth Century New England*. New York. St. Martin's Press, 1975.

Anderson, Sherwood. *Marching Men*. New York. John Lane Co., 1917.

Austin, W. G. *History of the Manufactories of Springfield, Ohio*. Springfield., Ohio, 1938.

Barnes, Harry E. "The Social and Political Theories of J. H. W. Stuckenberg." *Lutheran Quarterly*. October, 1921.

Bauslin, David H. "The Genesis of the 'New Measure' Movement in the Lutheran Church in this Country." *Lutheran Quarterly*. vol. 40, July, 1910, pp. 368-91.

Bell, P. G. *A Portraiture of the Life of Samuel* Sprecher. Philadelphia, Pa. Lutheran Publication Society. 1907.

Billington, Ray Allen. *The Protestant Crusade, 1800-1860: A Study in the Origins of American Nativism*. Rinehart, New York. 1938, 1952.

Bledstein, Burton J. *The Culture of Professionalism: The Middle Class and the Development of Higher Education in America*. New York. Norton and Co., 1976.

Board of Directors of Wittenberg College. Minutes, 1842-2007. Wittenberg University Archives, Springfield, Ohio.

Bosse, Richard O. *Origins of Lutheran Higher Education in Ohio*. Ph.D. dissertation. The Ohio State University, 1969.

Bracher, Peter. *At the Center: A Sesquicentennial History of First Lutheran Church, Dayton, Ohio, 1839-1989*. Dayton, Ohio. First Lutheran Church, 1989.

Breidenbaugh, E. S., ed. *The Pennsylvania College Book, 1832-1882*. Philadelphia, Pa. Lutheran Publication Society. 1882.

Broome, Edwin Cornelius. *A Historical and Critical Discussion of College Admissions Requirements*. Columbia University Contributions to Philosophy, Psychology and Education, vol. XI, nos. 3, 4. New York, 1903. reprinted, College Entrance Examination Board. Princeton, N. J., 1963.

Brubaker, John S. and Rudy, Willis. *Higher Education in Transition: A Popular History of American Colleges, 1636-1956*. New York, Harper and Bros., 1958.

Bryan, Rev. W. S. Plumer, D. D. *The Church, Her Colleges and the Carnegie Foundation*. Princeton, N.J. Princeton University Press, 1911.

Burke, Colin B. *American Collegiate Populations: A Test of the Traditional View*. New York. New York University Press, 1982.

Cebula, James E. *James M. Cox: Journalist and Politician in Modern American History*. New York. Garland Publishing, Inc., 1985.

Chessman, G. Wallace. *Denison: The Story of an Ohio College*. Granville, Ohio. Denison University, 1957.

Clark, George Gerlaw, '87. *History of Wittenberg College, Springfield, Ohio, with Portraits and Sketches of the lives of her most Prominent Men*. Springfield, Ohio. J. A. Work Printer, 1887.

The College Stylus. student newspaper, 1882-1884.

The Collegian. student newspaper, June, 1882.

Collins, David R. *Archaeology of Clark County*. Springfield, Ohio. Clark County Historical Society, 1959.

Conrad, Frederick W. papers, in Stuckenberg collection, Gettysburg College archives.

________. *A Plan for Wittenberg College*. Springfield, Ohio. G. D. Emerson and Co., 1851.

Cramer, Clarence H. *Case Western Reserve: A History of the University, 1826-1976*, Boston, Mass. Little, Brown and Company, 1976.

Curti, Merle E., and Nash, Roderick. *Philanthropy in the Shaping of American Higher Education*. New Brunswick, N.J. Rutgers University Press, 1965.

Cutter, William I., student letters, Archives, Wittenberg University.

DeVoto, Bernard. *The Year of Decision: 1846*. Cambridge, Mass. Houghton Mifflin Company, 1942.

Diehl, Michael. *Biography of Rev. Ezra Keller, D. D., Founder and First President of Wittenberg College, with an introduction by Rev. Samuel Sprecher*. Springfield, Ohio. Ruralist Publishing Co., 1859.

Dominick, Charles A., *Ohio's Antebellum Colleges*. Ph. D. dissertation, University of Michigan. Ann Arbor, Michigan, 1987.

Douglas, Lloyd C. *Time to Remember*. Boston, Mass. Houghton Mifflin Co., 1951.

________. *Forgive Us Our Trespasses*. Boston, Mass. Houghton Mifflin Co., 1932.

Dunkelberger, Harold A. "Gettysburg College and the Lutheran Connection: An Open-ended Story of a Proud Relationship," Historic Series No. 3. *The Gettysburg Bulletin*, vol. 66, Dec. 1975, no. 5.

Eckelberry, Roscoe Huhn. *History of the Municipal University in the United States*. U. S. Dept. of Education., Bulletin No. 2. Washington, D. C. U. S. Government Printing Office, 1932.

Eisenberg, William Edward. *The First Hundred Years: Roanoke College. 1842-1942*. Salem, Va. Trustees of Roanoke College, 1942.

Emerson, Ralph Waldo. *The Collected Works of Ralph Waldo Emerson*, Centenary Edition, 12 vols. Boston and New York. Houghton Mifflin Co. 1903.

Ernsberger, Rev. C. S. *A History of the Wittenberg Synod of the General Synod of the Evangelical Lutheran Church*. Columbus, Ohio, 1917.

Evjen, John O. *The Life of J. H. W. Stuckenberg: Theologian, philosopher, Sociologist*. Minneapolis, Minn. Lutheran Free Church Publishing Co., 1938.

________, "The Berkenmeyer Library, A Two Hundred Year Old Church Library Found at Wittenberg College," *The Lutheran Quarterly*, April, 1925, pp 132-147.

________, "The Berkenmeyer Library: A Two Hundred Year Old Church Library Found at Wittenberg College," *The Wittenberg Bulletin*, vol. 22, no. 17, Springfield, Ohio, 1925.

Ferm, Vergilius. *The Crisis in American Lutheran Theology: A Study of the Issue Between American Lutheranism and Old Lutheranism.* New York. The Century Co., 1927.

Findlay, James. "The SPCTEW and Western Colleges: Religion and Higher Education in Mid-nineteenth Century America," *History of Education Quarterly*, spring, 1977, pp. 31-62.

Fischer, Robert H., ed. "Franklin Clark Fry: A Palette for a Portrait," supplementary number, *The Lutheran Quarterly*, vol. XXIV. 1972. Wittenberg University. Springfield, Ohio, 1972.

Fisher, Ilo D. *The Coming of Age of a College Library: Wittenberg College Library, 1945-1965*. Springfield, Ohio. Wittenberg University, 1978.

Fletcher, Robert S. *A History of Oberlin College From Its Foundation Through the Civil War*, 2 vols. Oberlin, Ohio, 1943.

The Flying Dutchman, underground student newspapers, 1863-1883, with variations in title, archives, Wittenberg University.

Ford, Ford Maddox. *The Rash Act*. New York. Ray Long and Richard R. Smith, Inc., 1933.

Geiger, Hezekiah Reubush, papers, Wittenberg University Archives.

________. "Another Talk on Life in Early Springfield," *Yester year in Clark County*, vol. 3, pp. 2-3. Clark County Historical Society. Springfield, Oh., 1949.

Gerber, David A. *Black Ohio and the Color Line, 1860-1915*. Urbana, Ill. University of Illinois Press, 1976.

Gotwald, Frederick Gebhart. *Early American Theological Education, 1745-1845*. York, Pa., 1916.

Gotwald, Luther A. *Trial of L. A. Gotwald, D. D. Professor of Practical Theology in Wittenberg Theological Seminary*. Springfield, Ohio, 1893.

Gotwald, Luther A., Jr. *The Gotwald Trial Revisited*. Davidsville, Pa., Luther A. Gotwald Jr., 1992.

Granstaff, Viola. *Harr Wagner, California Educational Publicist*. dissertation, University of California. Los Angeles, Calif., 1965.

Gustafson, David A. *Lutherans in Crisis: The Question of Identity in the American Republic*. Minneapolis, Minn. Augsburg-Fortress Press, 1993.

Hackenberg, Willard M. "The Wittenberg of My Day: 1895-1904," unpublished typescript. Wittenberg University Archives. Springfield, Ohio.

Hall, G. Stanley. "Student Customs," *American Antiquarian Society Proceedings, 1900-1901*. Worcester, Mass. American Antiquarian Society, 1901, pp 85-91.

Harding, Thomas S. *College Literary Societies: Their Contribution to Higher Education in the United States, 1818-1876*. New York, 1971.

Harper, William Rainey. "Trend of University and College Education in the United States." *North American Review*, CLXXIV (1902), pp. 457-65.

_________. "Higher Education in the West," *North American Review*, CLXXIX (1904) pp. 584-590

Hatch, Nathan O. *The Democratization of American Christianity*. New Haven, Conn. Yale University Press, 1989.

Hayes, Rutherford B. Correspondence, Manuscript collection. The Ohio State University Library, Columbus, Ohio.

Hayes, Rutherford B., Alexis Cope and William Henry Scott Correspondence. Rutherford B. Hayes Library. Fremont, Ohio.

Heckert, Charles Girven, papers. Wittenberg University Archives.

Hefelbower, Samuel G. *The History of Gettysburg College, 1832-1932*. Gettysburg, Pa. Gettysburg College, 1932.

Helwig, John B. papers. Wittenberg University Archives.

_________. *Lectures: The Rise of the Romish Church, Its Results in Europe and its Designs Upon the Institutions of America*. Dayton, Ohio, United Brethren Publishing House, 1876.

Higham, John. *Strangers in the Land: Patterns of American Nativism, 1860-1925*. New Brunswick, N.J. Rutgers University Press, 1955, 1963.

Hiller, Robert H. *Along the Way and Other Poems*. New York. Fleming H. Revell Co., 1940.

Himmelfarb, Gertrude. *The Roads to Modernity: The British, French and American Enlightenments*. New York. Alfred A. Knopf, 2004.

Hoehn, Richard A. "J. H. W. Stuckenberg: American Lutheranism's First Social Ethicist." *Dialog*, 22 (winter, 1983) 15-20.

_________. *Now We See Through a Glass Darkly—But We See: The Papers of J.H.W. and Mary G. Stuckenberg*. Musselman Library. Gettysburg, Pa., Gettysburg College, 1987.

Hofstadter, Richard and Metzger, Walter. *The Development of Academic Freedom in the United States*. New York. Columbia University Press, 1955.

Holifield, E. Brooks. *Theology in America: Christian Thought from the Age of the Puritans to the Civil War*. New Haven, Conn., Yale University Press, 2003.

Hoover, Mary Ruthrauff. *History of the Ruthrauffs: 1560-1925*. Kansas City, Mo., 1925.

Hopkins, Charles Howard. *The Rise of the Social Gospel in America, 1865-1915*. New Haven, Conn. Yale University Press, 1940.

Horn, Francis H., editor. *Go Forth, Be Strong: advice and Reflections from Commencement Speakers.* Carbondale, Ill. Southern Illinois University Press, 1978.

Horowitz, Helen Lefkowitz. *Campus Life: Underground Cultures from the End of the Eighteenth Century to the Present*. New York. Alfred A. Knopf, 1987.

Huber, Donald L. *Educating Lutheran Pastors in Ohio, 1830-1980: A History of Trinity Lutheran Seminary and its Predecessors*. Studies in American Religion, vol. 33. The Edwin Mellen Press. Queenstown, Ontario, Canada, 1989.

_________. "Ezra Keller's Missionary Journey to the West, 1836-37." *Trinity Seminary Review*, vol. 12, no. 1, spring, 1990, pp 14-25

_________. "Producers of Big Things: Funk and Wagnalls," *Timeline,* the Ohio Historical Society, vol. 16, no. 5, Sept-Oct, 1999, pp 36-49.

_________. "The Hermit of Mad River," *Timeline,* the Ohio Historical Society, vol. 16, no. 5, Sept-Oct., 2000, pp 50-54.

Hutchins, A. J. student letters, Wittenberg University Archives.

Johannesen, Eric. *Ohio College Architecture Before 1871*. Columbus, Ohio. Ohio Historical Society. Historic Ohio Building Series, 1969.

Johnson, Paul. *Modern Times: The World From the Twenties to the Nineties*. New York. Harper Collins Publisher, 1983.

Keller, Thomas A. "A Brief Sketch of the Negro in Springfield," unpublished monograph.

Keller, Ezra. Papers. Wittenberg University Archives.

_________. "To the Missionary Society of the Theological Seminary at Gettysburg, Pennsylvania." *The Lutheran Observer*, Jan. 6, 20, Mar. 17, 24, Apr. 21, 28, 1837

________. "The Importance of a Thorough Theological Education to Eminent Usefulness in the Ministry," *An Address Delivered Before the Alumni and Students of the Theological Seminary of the Lutheran Church at Gettysburg, Pa., April 16, 1844*. Baltimore, 1844.

________. "The Church in the West." *The Lutheran Observer*, vol. 12, nos. 18-32, Jan. 3 to Apr. 4, 1845.

Kinnison, William A. "The More Toil, The More Grace: Wittenberg's First President, Ezra Keller." *The Wittenberg Alumnus*, Feb., 1963.

________. "Wittenberg's Second President: Dr. Samuel Sprecher." *The Wittenberg Alumnus*, Apr., 1963.

________. "A New Departure: Dr. John B. Helwig, Wittenberg's Third President." *The Wittenberg Alumnus*, Oct., 1963.

________. "A New Wittenberg Spirit Emerges: Dr. Samuel Alfred Ort, Wittenberg's Fourth President." *The Wittenberg Alumnus*, Jan., 1964.

________. "A Student of His Times: Dr. John Mosheim Ruthrauff, Wittenberg's Fifth President." *The Wittenberg Alumnus*, May, 1964.

________. "Weltanschauung, A World View: Dr. Charles Girven Heckert, sixth President of Wittenberg." unpublished monograph. 1964.

________. "Outrage and Bewilderment: An Account of the Early Days of Greek Letter Societies and their One Hundred Year History at Wittenberg." *The Wittenberg Alumnus*, vol. 18, no. 6, Nov,-Dec., 1966.

________. *The Impact of the Morrill Act on Higher Education in Ohio*. Ph. D.dissertation. The Ohio State University, Columbus, Ohio, 1967.

________. "And Other Meritorious Distinctions." *The Wittenberg Alumnus*, vol. 20, May/June, 1968, no. 33, pp 4-8.

________. "The Wittenberg Board and How it Grew (and Grew)." *The Wittenberg Alumnus*, vol. 21, Jan/Feb 1969, no. 1, pp 16-20.

________. *Building Sullivant's Pyramid: an Administrative History of the Ohio State University, 1870-1907*, published in observance of the 1970 centennial. Columbus, Ohio. The Ohio State University Press, 1970.

________. *Wittenberg in Clark County, 1845-1970*. Springfield, Ohio. Clark County Historical Society, 1970.

________. "Notes On Six Wittenberg Authors: Lloyd C. Douglas, John H. W. Stuckenberg, Isaac Funk and Adam Wagnalls, Samuel

McCord Crothers, and Sherwood Anderson." *Ohioana Quarterly*, vol. 15, no. 4, Winter, 1972.

________. *Wittenberg: A Concise History*, published for the United States Bicentennial. Springfield, Ohio. Wittenberg University, 1976.

________. *An American Seminary: A History of the Hamma School of Theology, 1845-1978*. Columbus, Ohio. The Ohio Synod of the Lutheran Church in America, 1980.

________. "German Lutherans in the Ohio Valley." *Queen City Heritage*, Journal of the Cincinnati Historical Society, vol. 42, Fall, 1984, no. 3, pp 3-11.

________. *Springfield and Clark County: An Illustrated History*. Northridge, Calif. Windsor Publications Inc., 1985.

________. "The Past as Prologue in Lutheran Higher Education." *Papers and Proceedings, 1985, Lutheran Educational Conference of North America*. Washington, D. C., 1985, pp 7-29.

________. "Wittenberg; Prototype of the Mature Church-Related College." *Tradition and Change: Toward A Mature Relationship Between Church and College*. A Symposium Celebrating Wittenberg's Sesquicentennial, ed, by Richard P. Veler, chairman, Springfield, Ohio, 1993.

Knight, George W., and Commons, John R. *The History of Higher Education in Ohio*, U.S. Bureau of Education Circular of Information no. 5. Washington, D.C. U.S. Government Printing Office, 1891.

Kuenning, Paul P. *The Rise and Fall of American Lutheran Pietism: The Rejection of an Activist Heritage*. Macon, Ga. Mercer University Press, 1988.

Lasser, Carol A. *Educating Men and Women Together: Coeducation in a Changing World*. Chicago and Urbana, Ill. University of Illinois Press, 1985.

Laue, Theodore H. *Leopold von Ranke: The Formative Years*. Princeton, N. J. Princeton University Press, 1950.

Lentz, Harold H. *History of the Social Gospel in the General Synod of the Lutheran Church in America, 1867-1918*. Ph. D. dissertation. Yale University, 1943.

________. *A History of Wittenberg College, 1845-1945*. Springfield, Ohio. Wittenberg Press, 1946.

________. *The Miracle of Carthage College: History of Carthage College, 1847-1947*, Lima, Ohio. The C. S. S. Publishing Co., 1957.

Levine, David O. *The American College and the Culture of Aspiration, 1915-1940*, Ithaca, N.Y. Cornell University Press, 1986.

Locke, Alain LeRoy. *Race Contacts and Interracial Relations: Lectures on the Theory and Practice of Race*. Ed., Jeffrey C. Stewart. Wash. D. C. Howard University Press, 1992.

The Lutheran Observer, 1831-1865. Lutheran Theological Seminary Archives, Gettysburg, Pa.

Manning, Libby Davis. "Almira Crothers Hamma: A New Paradigm for Women's Leadership in Nineteenth Century." *Trinity Seminary Review*, Vol. 20 (fall-winter, 1980) No. 2, pp. 111-118.

Markley, Mary E. *The Lutheran Church and its Students*. Muhlenberg Press. Philadelphia, 1948.

Marsden, George M. "The Secularization of Higher Education." *Tradition and Change: Toward A Mature Relationship Between Church and College*. Wittenberg Sesquicentennial Symposium. ed., Richard P. Veler, chairman. Springfield, Ohio, 1993.

_________. *The Soul of the American University: From Protestant Establishment to Established Non-belief*. New York. Oxford University Press, 1994.

McMillen, Theodore C. *The Springfield Y.M.C.A., 1854-1954*. Springfield, Ohio. Springfield Tribune Co., 1954

Menand, Louis. *The Metaphysical Club: A Story of Ideas in America*. New York. Farrar, Straus and Giroux, 2001.

Montgomery, John Warwick. "The Colonial Parish Library of Wilhelm Christoph Berkenmeyer." *Papers of the Bibliographic Society of America*. Vol. LIII, Second Quarter, 1959, pp. 114-149.

Morris, Robert W. "The Shouvlin Center Site, Wittenberg University, Springfield, Ohio." *Ohio Archaeologist*. Vol. 39, no. 3, Summer, 1989, pp 9-16.

Myrdal, Gunnar. *An American Dilemma: The Negro Problem and American Democracy* New York, 1944.

Nelson, E. Clifford. *Lutheranism in North America, 1914-1970*. Augsburg Publishing House. Minneapolis, Minn., 1972.

_________. ed. *The Lutherans in North America*. Philadelphia. Fortress Press, 1975.

Newman, John Henry. *The Idea of the University Defined and Illustrated*. London. Oxford Clarendon Press, 1976.

Notestein, Lucy I. *Wooster of the Middlewest*. two vols. Kent, Ohio. Kent State University Press, 1969.

Novik, Peter. *That Noble Dream: The Objectivity Question and the American historical Profession*. New York. Cambridge University Press, 1988.

Ohio College Association. *College Entrance Requirements*. Wooster, Ohio, 1913.

Ort, Samuel Alfred. Papers. Wittenberg University Archives.

________. "The Controversy between the Theist and the Scientist," *Quarterly Review of the Evangelical Lutheran Church*, vol. 4, 1874.

________. "Our Educational Institutions." *The First General Conference of Lutherans in America, held in Philadelphia, Dec. 27-29, 1898, Proceedings, Essays, and Debates*. Lutheran Publishing Society and General Council Publication Board. Philadelphia, 1899.

________. *Selected Sermons and Addresses*. ed., Leander S. Keyser. Seattle, Wash. H. C Stafford Publisher, 1914.

The Ohio State University. Archives. Columbus, Ohio,

Owens, David B. *These Hundred Years: The Centennial History of Capital University*. Columbus, Ohio. Capital University, 1950.

Painter, F. V. N. *Luther on Education*. St. Louis, Mo. Concordia Publishing House, 1889.

Parsonage, Robert Rue ed. *Church Related Higher Education: Perceptions and Perspectives*. Judson Press. Valley Forge, Pa., 1978.

Pelikan, Jaroslav. *Obedient Rebels: Catholic Substance and Protestant Principle in Luther's Reformation*. New York. Harper and Row, 1964.

________. *The Idea of the University: A Reexamination*. New Haven, Conn. Yale University Press, 1992.

Pershing, Benjamin H. "Fourth Lutheran Church History." *Fiftieth Anniversary, 1897-1947*. Springfield, Oh., 1947.

Persons, Stow. *The Decline of American Gentility*. New York. Columbia University Press, 1973.

Pfnister, Allan O. "A Century of the Church Related College." in *A Century of Higher Education*. ed. by W. W. Brickman and Stanley Lehrer. New York, N. Y. Society for the Advancement of Education, 1962, pp 80-93.

Phillips, Mary E. *Edgar Allen Poe, The Man*. Philadelphia, 1926.

Prince, Benjamin F. "History of the First Lutheran Church, Springfield, Ohio." In *History and Services in the Observance of the Fiftieth Anniversary of the First Lutheran Church, Springfield,*

Ohio, Feb. 20-25, 1895. The New Era Co., Printers. Springfield, Oh., 1895.

_________. "Theological Education in Wittenberg College." Unpublished monograph. 1916, Archives, Wittenberg University.

_________. *Theological Education in Wittenberg College*. paper read at the dedication of Hamma Divinity School, Nov. 10-11, 1915, reprinted from *The Lutheran Quarterly*. Jan., 1916.

_________. ed. *The Centennial Celebration of Springfield, Ohio, 1901*. Springfield, Ohio. Springfield Publishing Co., 1901.

_________. *A Standard History of Springfield and Clark County*. 2 vols. New York and Chicago. The American Historical Society, 1922.

_________. "History of Wittenberg College," unpublished manuscript. 1928. Wittenberg University Archives.

Pritchett, Henry S. "The Place of the College in American Education." *Annual Report*. New York. Carnegie Foundation for the Advancement of Teaching, 1907.

_________. "The Relations of Christian Denominations to Colleges." *Educational Review*, vol. XXXVI, Oct., 1908, pp. 217-241.

Quillen, Frank U. *The Color Line in Ohio: A History of Race Prejudice in a Typical Northern State*. Ann Arbor, Mich. University of Michigan Historical Studies, 1913.

Ranke, Leopold von. *The Theory and Practice of History*. Ed. Georg Iggers and Konrad von Moltke. Indianapolis, 1973.

Renick, Marion Lewis. *A Long Bright Shadow*. A play in two acts about the Life of Ezra Keller and the Founding of Wittenberg University. Performed for the 125th Anniversary of the Founding. March, 1970.

Rinkliff, George L. *The First Evangelical Lutheran Church of Springfield, A Centennial History*. Philadelphia, Pa. Muhlenburg Press, 1941.

Robards, Calvin E. *150 Years: From Buckets to Diesels*. Springfield, Ohio. Miller Printing Co., 1978

Rockel, William M. *Twentieth Century History of Springfield and Clark County, Ohio*. Chicago, Ill. Biographical Publishing Co., 1908.

Roseboom, Eugene H. and Weisenburger, Francis P. *A History of Ohio*. ed. by James H. Rodabaugh. Columbus, Ohio. The Ohio State Archaeological and Historical Society, 1956.

Ross, Earle D. *Democracy's College: The Land-Grant Movement in the Formative Stage*. Ames, Iowa. Iowa State College Press, 1942.

Roosevelt, Theodore. "No Half Measures." *Metropolitan Magazine*, Aug., 1918.

Rudolph, Frederick. *Curriculum: A History of the American Undergraduate Course of Study Since 1636*. San Francisco, Calif. Jossey-Bass Co., 1977.

_________. "Neglect of Students as a Historical Tradition." *The College and the Student*, ed. by Lawrence E. Dennis and Joseph F. Kauffman. Washington, D.C. American Council on Education, 1966.

_________. *The American College and University*. New York. Knopf and Co., 1962.

_________. *Hopkins and the Log*, New Haven, Conn. Yale University Press, 1956.

Ruthrauff, John Mosheim. Papers. Wittenberg University archives.

Sanderson, John P. class of 1869. "Memoirs." Wittenberg University Archives.

Savage, Howard J. *Fruit of an Impulse: Forty Five Years of the Carnegie Foundation, 1905-1950*. The Carnegie Foundation. New York, 1953.

Schmucker, Samuel S. *Fraternal Appeal to the American Churches, With a Plan for Catholic Union on Apostolic Principles*. 1838. reprint by Frederick Wentz. Philadelphia, Pa. Fortress Press, 1965.

_________. *The Christian Pulpit, The Rightful Guardian of Morals, in Political No Less Than In Private Life: A Discourse Delivered at Gettysburg, Nov 26, The Day Appointed by the Governor for Public Humiliation, Thanksgiving, and Prayer*. Gettysburg, Pa., 1846.

_________. *The American Lutheran Church Historically, Doctrinally, and Practically Delineated, In Several Occasional Discourses*. second ed. Springfield, Ohio. D. Harbaugh, 1851.

_________. *Definite Synodical Platform, Doctrinal and Disciplinarian for Evangelical Lutheran Synods: Constructed In Accordance with the Principles of the General Synod*. Philadelphia, Pa. Miller and Burlock Publishers, 1855.

_________. *Elements of a Popular Theology, with Occasional references to the Doctrines of the Reformation Avowed Before the Diet of Augsburg in 1530*. 1st ed., Andover, Gould and Newmann, 1834. 9th ed., to which is added an appendix *The Formula for Government and Discipline of the American Lutheran Church*. Philadelphia, Pa.

Schwiebert, Ernest G. *Luther and His Times: The Reformation from a New Perspective*. St. Louis, Mo. Concordia Publishing House, 1950.

Sears, Jesse B. *Philanthropy in the History of American Higher Education*. U. S. Bureau of Education. Bulletin No. 26. Washington, D. C. U. S. Government Printing Office, 1922.

Seilhammer, Frank H. "The New Measure Movement among Lutherans" *Lutheran Quarterly*. Vol. 12, May, 1960, pp. 121-143.

Selden, William K. *Accreditation: A Struggle over Standards in Higher Education*, New York, Harper and Row, 1960.

Settlemyer, William H., class of 1867. *Reminiscences of Wittenberg College, 1860-1867*. student diary. Wittenberg University Archives.

Sheldon, Henry Davidson. *The History and Pedagogy of American Student Societies*. New York. Appleton Co., 1901.

Shephardson, Francis W. *Denison University, 1831-1931: A Centennial History*. Granville, Ohio. Denison University, 1931.

Sloan, Douglas. *The Scottish Enlightenment and the American College Ideal*. New York. Columbia University, Teachers College Press, 1971.

Smythe, George Franklin. *Kenyon College, Its First Century*. New Haven, Conn. Yale University Press, 1924.

Society for the Promotion of Collegiate and Theological Education in the West. Papers. Congregational Library. Boston, Mass., 1843-1869.

Solberg, Richard W. *Lutheran Higher Education in North America*. Minneapolis, Minn. Augsburg Publishing House, 1985.

Solomon, Barbara Miller. *In The Company of Educated Women: A History of Women and Higher Education in America*. New Haven, Conn. Yale University Press, 1985.

Song Book Committee. *Wittenberg Song Book*. Springfield, Ohio, 1926.

Sprecher, Samuel. Papers. Wittenberg University Archives.

_________. *An Address Delivered to the Candidates for the Baccalaureate of Wittenberg College at the Anniversary Commencement, August 18, 1851, published by the class*. Springfield, Ohio. G. D. Emerson and Co., 1851.

_________. *The Groundwork of a System of Evangelical Lutheran Theology*. Philadelphia, Pa. Lutheran Publication Society, 1879.

The Springfield Nonpareil.

The Springfield Republic.

Stauffer, John N. "The Christian College, Its Future Prospect," *Wittenberg Bulletin*. LXII, July, 1965, No. 5.

_________. Papers. Wittenberg University Archives.

Stevenson, Louise L. *Scholarly Means to Evangelical Ends: The New Haven Scholars and the Transformation of Higher Learning In America, 1830-1890*. Baltimore, Md. Johns Hopkins University Press, 1986.

Stuckenberg, John H. W. papers. Gettysburg College Archives.

_________. *Christian Sociology*. New York. I. K. Funk and Co., 1880.

_________. *The Final Science, or Spiritual Materialism, Being A Strict Application of the Most Approved Modern Scientific Principles to the Solution of the Deepest Problems of the Age*. New York. Funk and Wagnals Publishing Co., 1885.

_________. "What Can The Church Do For The Laboring Classes." *Lutheran Evangelist*, Aug. 23, 1878.

_________. *Life of Emanuel Kant*. London. Macmillan and Co., 1882.

_________. *The Social Problem*. York, Pa. Social Problem Publishing Co., 1897.

_________. *Introduction to the Study of Philosophy*. New York. A. C. Armstrong and Son, 1907.

_________. "Greetings from the Fatherland." *Lutheran Evangelist*, July, 1892.

_________. *Orthodox Lutheranism in Germany and the Confessional Position of the General Synod of the Evangelical Lutheran Church in the United States. Testimony of Leaders. An End of Controversy*. Dayton, Ohio. Groneweg Printing Co., 1892.

_________. *Tendencies in German Thought*. Hartford, Conn. Student Publishing Co., 1896.

Swaim, James E. *A History of Muhlenberg College, 1848-1967*. New York. Appleton Century Crofts, 1967.

Taylor, Mary Jane. *A Walking Tour of Wittenberg Architecture*. Wittenberg University Archives, Thomas Library. Springfield, Oh., 1988.

Tewksbury, Donald G. *The Founding of American Colleges and Universities before the Civil War: with Particular Reference to the Religious Influences Bearing Upon the College Movement*. New York. Archon Books, 1965.

Thornburg, Opal. *Earlham: The Story of the College, 1847-1962*. Richmond, Ind. The Earlham College Press, 1963.

Thwing, Charles Franklin. *What Have the American People a Right to Expect from the American College in the Next Seventy Five Years?* address at the 75th Anniversary of the Founding of Wittenberg

College, Mar. 11, 1920, Heckert Papers, Wittenberg University Archives.

_________. *The American and The German University: One Hundred Years of History*. New York. The Macmillan Co., 1928.

Traver, Amos J., Class of 1910. "Wittenberg, A. D. 1907-1910," unpublished reminiscences, June 27, 1972, Wittenberg University Archives.

Tobias, Marilyn. *Old Dartmouth on Trial: The Transformation of the Academic Community in Nineteenth Century America*. New York. New York University Press, 1982.

Tocqueville, Alexis de. *Democracy in America*. 2 vols., {1835}, with an introduction by Daniel C. Gilman. The Henry Reeve translation, revised by Francis Bowen 2 vols., New York. Century, 1898. Philip Bradly. New York. Knopf and Co., 1945.

Todd, Edwin Smith, class of 1870. *A Sociological Study of Clark County*. Doctoral Dissertation, Columbia University. Springfield, Ohio. Springfield Publishing Co., 1904.

Townsend, Kim. *Sherwood Anderson*, Boston, Ma. Houghton Mifflin Co., 1987.

Tulloss, Rees Edgar. Papers. Wittenberg University Archives.

Turner, James. *Without God, Without Creed: The Origins of Unbelief in America*. Baltimore, Md. Johns Hopkins University Press, 1985.

Veblen, Thorstein. *The Higher Learning in America*. New York. B. W. Huebsch, 1918.

Veler, Herbert W., class of 1929. A Life of Ezra Keller, D. D. STM thesis, Chicago Lutheran Theological Seminary, 1951.

Veysey, Lawrence R. *The Emergence of the American University*. Chicago, Ill. University of Chicago Press, 1965.

Wagner, Edwin R. "Half an hour with the Sage of Cambridge," *Pacific Coast Magazine*. Nov. 18, 1881.

Waite, Frederick Clayton. *Western Reserve University: The Hudson Era*. Cleveland, Ohio, 1943.

Weisenberger, Francis P. *Ordeal of Faith: The Crisis of Church-going America, 1865-1900*. New York. Philosophical Library, 1959.

_________. *Triumph of Faith: Contributions of the Church to American Life, 1865-1900*, Richmond, Va. William Bird Press, 1962.

Wentz, Abdel R. *History of Gettysburg Theological Seminary*. Philadelphia, Pa. United Lutheran Publication House, 1926.

________. *Pioneer in Christian Unity: Samuel Simon Schmucker.* Philadelphia, Pa., Fortress Press, 1967.
The Witt From Wittenberg, campus humor magazine, vol. 1, no. 1, Nov., 1922.
Wittenberg College, *Aloha.* Springfield, Ohio. Daily Times Printing Office, 1880.
Wittenberg College. *The Cycle.* vol. I, June, 1892; vol. II. June, 1893; vol. III, June, 1894.
Wittenberg College. *The Cardinal.* Springfield, Ohio, 1913.
Wittenberg College. *Annual Report of the Faculty.* Springfield, Ohio, 1910-1921.
Wittenberg College. *Catalog of Wittenberg College,* 1845-1959.
Wittenberg College, 1902-1903, Student Handbook, Presented by the YMCA and YWCA. Springfield, Ohio, 1902.
Wittenberg College Students' Handbook, 1912-1913, Young Men's Christian Association. Springfield, Ohio, 1912.
Wittenberg College, Class of 1896. *The Semi-Centennial Souvenir of Wittenberg College.* Winters Art Lithographic Co. Springfield, Oh., 1895.
Wittenberg College. *The Thesis.* Springfield, Ohio, 1915.
The Wittenberg Reveille. Student Army Training Corps newspaper. 1918.
The Wittenberg Torch. 1914-1917, 1919-20.
Wittenberg University. *Catalog of Wittenberg University,* 1960-1996.
Wittenberg University. *Constitution and Bylaws.* 1845, 1854, 1880, 1894, 1906.
Wittenberg University, Sesquicentennial Symposium Committee. *Tradition and Change: Toward A Mature Relationship Between Church and College.* Feb. 17-18, 1993. Richard P. Veler, Chairman and editor. Springfield, Ohio, 1993.
Wittenberg University Luther Symposium. (1983). *Luther and Learning,* ed. Marilyn Harran. Cranbury, N. J. Associated University Press, Inc., 1985.
Wittenberg Weekly Wasp. student newspaper. Vols. 1, 2. 1893-1894.
The Wittenberger. Vols. 1-40. 1874-1920.
Wittke, Carl. *German-Americans and World War I.* Columbus, Ohio, 1936.
________. *The German Language Press in America.* Lexington, Ky. University of Kentucky Press, 1957.

_________. *We Who Built America: The Saga of the Immigrant*. Cleveland, Ohio. The Press of Western Reserve University, 1964.

The Wooster Democrat. 1842-1844.

Wynn, W. H., class of 1851. "Reminiscences of Wittenberg. A Quarter of a Century ago," *The Wittenberger*, vol. 1, no. 4, Jan., 1874, p 25.

_________. "Dr. Samuel Sprecher, Philosopher, College President, and Man of God: An Appreciation," *Lutheran Quarterly*, vol. 36, April, 1906, pp 281-293.

Index

B

C

D

G

H

I

J

K

L

M

V

W

X

Y

Z

FILMMAKERS SERIES
edited by
ANTHONY SLIDE

1. *James Whale,* by James Curtis. 1982
2. *Cinema Stylists,* by John Belton. 1983
3. *Harry Langdon,* by William Schelly. 1982
4. *William A. Wellman,* by Frank Thompson. 1983
5. *Stanley Donen,* by Joseph Casper. 1983
6. *Brian De Palma,* by Michael Bliss. 1983
7. *J. Stuart Blackton,* by Marian Blackton Trimble. 1985
8. *Martin Scorsese and Michael Cimino,* by Michael Bliss. 1985
9. *Franklin J. Schaffner,* by Erwin Kim. 1985
10. *D. W. Griffith and the Biograph Company,* by Cooper C. Graham et al. 1985
11. *Some Day We'll Laugh: An Autobiography,* by Esther Ralston. 1985
12. *The Memoirs of Alice Guy Blaché,* 2nd ed., translated by Roberta and Simone Blaché. 1996
13. *Leni Riefenstahl and Olympia,* by Cooper C. Graham. 1986
14. *Robert Florey,* by Brian Taves. 1987
15. *Henry King's America,* by Walter Coppedge. 1986
16. *Aldous Huxley and Film,* by Virginia M. Clark. 1987
17. *Five American Cinematographers,* by Scott Eyman. 1987
18. *Cinematographers on the Art and Craft of Cinematography,* by Anna Kate Sterling. 1987
19. *Stars of the Silents,* by Edward Wagenknecht. 1987
20. *Twentieth Century-Fox,* by Aubrey Solomon. 1988
21. *Highlights and Shadows: The Memoirs of a Hollywood Cameraman,* by Charles G. Clarke. 1989
22. *I Went That-a-Way: The Memoirs of a Western Film Director,* by Harry L. Fraser; edited by Wheeler Winston Dixon and Audrey Brown Fraser. 1990
23. *Order in the Universe: The Films of John Carpenter,* by Robert C. Cumbow. 1990 *(out of print; see No. 70)*
24. *The Films of Freddie Francis,* by Wheeler Winston Dixon. 1991
25. *Hollywood Be Thy Name,* by William Bakewell. 1991
26. *The Charm of Evil: The Life and Films of Terence Fisher,* by Wheeler Winston Dixon. 1991
27. *Lionheart in Hollywood: The Autobiography of Henry Wilcoxon,* with Katherine Orrison. 1991

28. *William Desmond Taylor: A Dossier,* by Bruce Long. 1991
29. *The Films of Leni Riefenstahl,* 2nd ed., by David B. Hinton. 1991
30. *Hollywood Holyland: The Filming and Scoring of "The Greatest Story Ever Told,"* by Ken Darby. 1992
31. *The Films of Reginald LeBorg: Interviews, Essays, and Filmography,* by Wheeler Winston Dixon. 1992
32. *Memoirs of a Professional Cad,* by George Sanders, with Tony Thomas. 1992
33. *The Holocaust in French Film,* by André Pierre Colombat. 1993
34. *Robert Goldstein and "The Spirit of '76,"* edited and compiled by Anthony Slide. 1993
35. *Those Were the Days, My Friend: My Life in Hollywood with David O. Selznick and Others,* by Paul Macnamara. 1993
36. *The Creative Producer,* by David Lewis, edited by James Curtis. 1993
37. *Reinventing Reality: The Art and Life of Rouben Mamoulian,* by Mark Spergel. 1993
38. *Malcolm St. Clair: His Films, 1915–1948,* by Ruth Anne Dwyer. 1997
39. *Beyond Hollywood's Grasp: American Filmmakers Abroad, 1914–1945,* by Harry Waldman. 1994
40. *A Steady Digression to a Fixed Point,* by Rose Hobart. 1994
41. *Radical Juxtaposition: The Films of Yvonne Rainer,* by Shelley Green. 1994
42. *Company of Heroes: My Life as an Actor in the John Ford Stock Company,* by Harry Carey Jr. 1994
43. *Strangers in Hollywood: A History of Scandinavian Actors in American Films from 1910 to World War II,* by Hans J. Wollstein. 1994
44. *Charlie Chaplin: Intimate Close-Ups,* by Georgia Hale, edited with an introduction and notes by Heather Kiernan. 1995
45. *The Word Made Flesh: Catholicism and Conflict in the Films of Martin Scorsese,* by Michael Bliss. 1995
46. *W. S. Van Dyke's Journal: White Shadows in the South Seas (1927–1928) and other Van Dyke on Van Dyke,* edited and annotated by Rudy Behlmer. 1996
47. *Music from the House of Hammer: Music in the Hammer Horror Films, 1950–1980,* by Randall D. Larson. 1996
48. *Directing: Learn from the Masters,* by Tay Garnett. 1996
49. *Featured Player: An Oral Autobiography of Mae Clarke,* edited with an introduction by James Curtis. 1996
50. *A Great Lady: A Life of the Screenwriter Sonya Levien,* by Larry Ceplair. 1996

51. *A History of Horrors: The Rise and Fall of the House of Hammer,* by Denis Meikle. 1996
52. *The Films of Michael Powell and the Archers,* by Scott Salwolke. 1997
53. *From Oz to E. T.: Wally Worsley's Half-Century in Hollywood—A Memoir in Collaboration with Sue Dwiggins Worsley,* edited by Charles Ziarko. 1997
54. *Thorold Dickinson and the British Cinema,* by Jeffrey Richards. 1997
55. *The Films of Oliver Stone,* edited by Don Kunz. 1997
56. *Before, In and After Hollywood: The Autobiography of Joseph E. Henabery,* edited by Anthony Slide. 1997
57. Ravished Armenia *and the Story of Aurora Mardiganian,* compiled by Anthony Slide. 1997
58. *Smile When the Raindrops Fall,* by Brian Anthony and Andy Edmonds. 1998
59. *Joseph H. Lewis: Overview, Interview, and Filmography,* by Francis M. Nevins. 1998
60. *September Song: An Intimate Biography of Walter Huston,* by John Weld. 1998
61. *Wife of the Life of the Party,* by Lita Grey Chaplin and Jeffrey Vance. 1998
62. *Down But Not Quite Out in Hollow-weird: A Documentary in Letters of Eric Knight,* by Geoff Gehman. 1998
63. *On Actors and Acting: Essays by Alexander Knox,* edited by Anthony Slide. 1998
64. *Back Lot: Growing Up with the Movies,* by Maurice Rapf. 1999
65. *Mr. Bernds Goes to Hollywood: My Early Life and Career in Sound Recording at Columbia with Frank Capra and Others,* by Edward Bernds. 1999
66. *Hugo Friedhofer: The Best Years of His Life: A Hollywood Master of Music for the Movies,* edited by Linda Danly. 1999
67. *Actors on Red Alert: Career Interviews with Five Actors and Actresses Affected by the Blacklist,* by Anthony Slide. 1999
68. *My Only Great Passion: The Life and Films of Carl Th. Dreyer,* by Jean Drum and Dale D. Drum. 1999
69. *Ready When You Are, Mr. Coppola, Mr. Spielberg, Mr. Crowe,* by Jerry Ziesmer. 1999
70. *Order in the Universe: The Films of John Carpenter,* 2nd ed., by Robert C. Cumbow. 2000
71. *Making Music with Charlie Chaplin,* by Eric James. 2000
72. *An Open Window: The Cinema of Víctor Erice,* edited by Linda C. Ehrlich. 2000

73. *Satyajit Ray: In Search of the Modern,* by Suranjan Ganguly. 2000
74. *Voices from the Set: The* Film Heritage *Interviews,* edited by Tony Macklin and Nick Pici. 2000
75. *Paul Landres: A Director's Stories,* by Francis M. Nevins. 2000
76. *No Film in My Camera,* by Bill Gibson. 2000
77. *Saved from Oblivion: An Autobiography,* by Bernard Vorhaus. 2000
78. *Wolf Man's Maker: Memoir of a Hollywood Writer,* by Curt Siodmak. 2001
79. *An Actor, and a Rare One: Peter Cushing as Sherlock Holmes,* by Tony Earnshaw. 2001
80. *Picture Perfect,* by Herbert L. Strock. 2000
81. *Peter Greenaway's Postmodern/Poststructuralist Cinema,* edited by Paula Willoquet-Maricondi and Mary Alemany Galway. 2001
82. *Member of the Crew,* by Winfrid Kay Thackrey. 2001
83. *Barefoot on Barbed Wire,* by Jimmy Starr. 2001
84. *Henry Hathaway: A Directors Guild of America Oral History,* edited and annotated by Rudy Behlmer. 2001
85. *The Divine Comic: The Cinema of Roberto Benigni,* by Carlo Celli. 2001
86. *With or Without a Song: A Memoir,* by Edward Eliscu. 2001
87. *Stuart Erwin: The Invisible Actor,* by Judy Cornes. 2001
88. *Some Cutting Remarks: Seventy Years a Film Editor,* by Ralph E. Winters. 2001
89. *Confessions of a Hollywood Director,* by Richard L. Bare. 2001
90. *Peckinpah's Women: A Reappraisal of the Portrayal of Women in the Period Westerns of Sam Peckinpah,* by Bill Mesce Jr. 2001
91. *Budd Schulberg: A Bio-Bibliography,* by Nicholas Beck. 2001
92. *Between the Bullets: The Spiritual Cinema of John Woo,* by Michael Bliss. 2002
93. *The Hollywood I Knew: 1916–1988,* by Herbert Coleman. 2002
94. *The Films of Steven Spielberg,* edited by Charles L. P. Silet. 2002
95. *Hitchcock and the Making of Marnie,* by Tony Lee Moral. 2002
96. *White Horse, Black Hat: A Quarter Century on Hollywood's Poverty Row,* by C. Jack Lewis. 2002
97. *Worms in the Winecup: A Memoir,* by John Bright. 2002
98. *Straight from the Horse's Mouth: An Autobiography,* by Ronald Neame. 2002
99. *Reach for the Top: The Turbulent Life of Laurence Harvey,* by Anne Sinai. 2003

The Hollywood I Knew

A Memoir: 1916–1988

Herbert Coleman
with Judy Lanini

Filmmakers Series, No. 93

The Scarecrow Press, Inc.
Lanham, Md., and Oxford
2003

SCARECROW PRESS, INC.

Published in the United States of America
by Scarecrow Press, Inc.
A Member of the Rowman & Littlefield Publishing Group
4720 Boston Way
Lanham, Maryland 20706
www.scarecrowpress.com

PO Box 317
Oxford
OX2 9RU, UK

British Cataloguing in Publication Information Available

Library of Congress Cataloging-in-Publication Data

Coleman, Herbert, 1907–
The Hollywood I knew: a memoir, 1916–1988 / Herbert Coleman.
p. cm. — (Filmmakers series)
Includes index.
ISBN 0-8108-4120-7 (hard : alk. paper)
1. Coleman, Herbert, 1907– 2. Motion picture producers and directors—United States—Biography. I. Title. II. Series.
PN1998.3.C666 A3 2003
791.43'0233'092—dc21 2002008823

Printed in the United States of America

∞™ The paper used in this publication meets the minimum requirements of American National Standard for Information Sciences—Permanence of Paper for Printed Library Materials, ANSI/NISO Z39.48-1992.

To my loving wife, Mary Belle
You were my life

Contents

Acknowledgments

This book has been thirteen years in the making, almost entirely from memory. When I began, I could see. Since then my eyesight has deteriorated, so I am now legally blind.

Without the help of many wonderful and caring people, this book would yet be unfinished. I am genuinely grateful to so many people whom I give my thanks, including my Indian friends for their warm hospitality and friendship.

My wife Mary Belle and my youngest daughter Melinda weighed my ideas and sustained me through the beginning years. My devoted thanks go to my daughter, Judy Coleman Lanini, who read and edited every word (many times) late at night after teaching all day. She was my eyes. Mr. Edward Ruttenberg of the law offices of Leopold, Patrich, and Smith has been my attorney and my confidant. Rosanna Little, English department chairman at Notre Dame High School in Salinas, California, helped me work and rework parts of the book. Tom Colley, executive editor of the *Bluefield Daily Telegraph* in Bluefield, West Virginia, answered many of my questions about Bluefield when I couldn't remember. Katrina "Katie" Brown read parts to me when Judy was busy. Jerry Brooks was extremely helpful in keeping my computer alive and working. What a friend.

My gratitude also goes to teachers, students, and Summit yearbook staff at Notre Dame High School who played an important role in the selection of the title of this book; to C. O. "Doc" Erickson, production manager, and Henry "Bummy" Bumstead, production designer, two very longtime friends who kept reminding me of items that I should not forget to include in this writing; and to Cristie Reich, an English teacher at Everett Alvarez High School in Salinas, who spent two years reading my manuscript and helping me to build confidence in my writing. Molly McRae is the special projects producer for the leading TV station, KPIX, in San Francisco. She never gave up making suggestions about the proper way to reveal my life's work. She is a wonderful friend.

Preface

There was a gentle rain blurring the view of the pure white faces of the two calla lilies and the still-to-blossom lilac bush in the garden outside the windows of my living room, where I sat lost in the memory of the sixty-seven wonderful years with Mary Belle. Three years, sweethearts. Sweethearts in the pure meaning of the word, way back in May 1928 when we first met. And sixty-four years, married sweethearts and lovers.

My memories of Mary Belle were shattered by the ringing of the telephone. It was my sister, Ruby Waterlyn, calling from her home in Salt Lake City, where she lived, and worked, as an independent research genealogist in Swedish ancestry. Ruby's husband, Lyn, had been before his death an artist noted for his desert and mountain paintings.

I had asked Ruby to tell me how and when the Coleman and Bond families (my mother's maiden family name) had come together in Bluefield, West Virginia. "Very soon after the end of the Civil War," she said, "Grandpa Coleman bought a farm near Crishenburg, Virginia." Shortly after the end of the Civil War, he and Grandma Charity moved in and, before he died in 1893, had four boys—Edward, Henry, Elmer, and my father, William Ezra—and ten daughters.

Late in 1893 Grandma Coleman sold the farm, divided the money among the children, and with the boys and some of the girls moved to Bluefield, West Virginia. Bluefield was a beautiful little city on the top of the Blue Ridge Mountains, a railroad center where coal cars from the mines down the mountains to the west were assembled and hauled in long trains to the shipping ports around Norfolk, Virginia, for shipment to Europe.

Papa and his three brothers found jobs with the Norfolk and Western Railroad. The Bonds, Mama's family name, were also farmers and had chosen the country around Pulaski, Virginia, just twenty miles from Bluefield, over East River Mountain, but almost a full day by train. Someway, Papa managed to travel to Pulaski where he met Alice Laura Bond. It was love at first sight. They were married in Pulaski in December 1893 and settled down in Bluefield where two daughters, Viola and Ruby Elizabeth, and four boys—Elbert, Ernest, Robert, and I, Herbert—were born. I followed Viola on December 12, 1907.

In 1914, when the demand overseas for Pocahontas coal from southern West Virginia fell dramatically, the Norfolk and Western Railroad was forced to reduce its losses by temporarily dismissing or transferring its younger employees. As one of the younger locomotive firemen, Papa had to accept a transfer, with his family, to Cliff Yards, West Virginia.

Chapter 1

Cliff Yards, West Virginia

My love affair with movies began a long time ago. More than seventy-two years ago.

It was 1916, just a few months before my ninth birthday. We were living in a little shack up in Cliff Holler, a short distance from a wide place in the railroad tracks where Papa worked as a fireman for the Norfolk and Western Railroad.

There were a few houses scattered along the Bluestone River in that southern corner of West Virginia.

For recreation, we swam "nekkid" in the prettiest river you'd ever see. Even where it was twenty feet deep, you could see the fish swimming over the blue rocks on the bottom. Those rocks were what kept the river clear and where it got its name, the Bluestone.

One day, word spread over the hills and up the hollers that a man was coming to Cliff Yard to show a movie that night. Most of us had never seen a movie. We'd seen the displays outside the movie house in Bluefield where we'd lived before shifting to Cliff Yard, but we'd never been inside it.

Long before dark, whole families from great grannies to tiny babies had come down from the hills and out of the hollers wearing their Sunday best—which meant, for the men, clean overalls and, for the women, fresh aprons and their best bonnets.

They spread their quilts on the railroad ties and settled down to wait for what they were calling "pitchers."

From the direction of the trestle that crossed the river, a man appeared. He was carrying a straw suitcase.

All conversation stopped as everyone turned to study the stranger. You could tell he wasn't from around these parts. Nobody wore a blue suit, red vest, tie, black patent leather shoes, and a bowler hat when they were out walkin' around the hills and hollers.

I didn't listen as he started explaining why he was there. He opened the suitcase and pulled out a projector, two rolls of film, and a dirty, white bedsheet. While the younger girls, pigtails flying, chased thousands of fireflies blinking their paths through the twilight, boys helped him stretch the sheet between two dogwood trees.

He then turned to face the crowd and said that he was charging a nickel a piece for us to see the picture, but if we couldn't afford it, we could see it for nothing.

He took off his bowler and moved among the people. A few who could dropped their money in the hat. He thanked us and went back to set up his projector.

At last, he started the machine, and magic appeared before my eyes.

A man, dressed like nobody I'd ever seen before—wide high hat, a handkerchief tied around his neck, leather vest, boots with spurs, and two pistols on his belt—was walking around a burned-out wagon train. He kept walking toward me, getting bigger and bigger until his face filled the whole bedsheet. He looked a lot like my grandma, except my grandma smiled a lot, and he didn't smile at all.

Suddenly, he looked over toward the railroad tracks, and I looked over there to see what he was looking at, but nothing was there.

Then the strangest thing happened. I looked back at the sheet and he was gone, and there were hundreds of Indians on horses racing down from the hills, screaming, and throwing spears, and shooting arrows. Some fell off their horses, horses fell, and then there were none; and there was the man again. He was shooting both pistols. He must have fired 100 times, and the strangest thing was, he never reloaded once. You'd never guess who he was: William S. Hart.

Although the noisy projector had wiped out the whisper of the breeze through the dogwood trees and the murmur of the river drifting past, I could plainly hear the war whoops, the screams of the Indians as they fell, and the thunder of the ponies' hooves as they bore down on the lone gunman. And above it all, there were the rapid blasts from the two pistols! And I was watching a silent movie.

I was too young to know what had just happened to me—I was hooked. It would be another ten years before I knew what I had to do.

It was spring 1916. I wouldn't be nine until December 12. My sister, Viola, whom everybody called Sis, my younger brother Bert, and I were walking home across the hills from school in Bramwell.

Tagging along was a twelve-year-old girl named Jillie Sue Winters. I thought she was kinda cute. Some of the schoolkids called her Silly Sue—but only behind her back, after she beat the heck out of the biggest boy who called her that. Sis was trying to hurry us along, but Jillie Sue wanted me to help her find some mayapples. We turned off the path into the woods, but Sis and Bert kept on going.

Pretty soon, Jillie Sue said she wanted to rest. We sat down on some damp grass under a great big chestnut tree. She began telling me about watching her pa breed his mare to the biggest jack (mule) you ever saw. She didn't leave anything to my imagination.

Then she got up, said she'd got her bloomers wet, raised up her dress and pulled them off, tossed them to me, and told me to hang them in the sun on a chinquapin bush.

When I came back, she was lying on the grass with her dress pulled up to her chin. She looked up at me with a big grin on her face. "Ain't nothing good as laying nekkid on wet grass. You oughta try it."

I wasn't sure I knew exactly what was about to happen, but I sat down beside her. She moved real close and asked if I'd ever seen folks breeding animals.

I told her I was no kid and knew how cows and pigs "got borned."

"Well, I'm gonna show you how babies get borned," she said. And wasted little time carrying out her threat.

The next time she tagged along and wanted me to help her look for mayapples, I made some lame excuse and kept on going with Sis and Bert.

I forced Jillie Sue from my mind and started talking about our move from Bluefield to Cliff Holler.

The train from Bluefield dropped me and my family off at the station in the little town of Simmons. Our few belongings were loaded on a wagon hitched to a scrawny mule, and Mama, holding our baby brother Bobby, got up on the seat next to the driver, and they were off on a twenty-mile trip, along the river, to our shack in Cliff Holler.

Papa led the rest of us, Sis, Bert, Ernie, Ruby, and me, along the railroad tracks, over the five, long, curving trestles crossing the Bluestone River, to Cliff Yards.

We found out later we would always have to use the railroad tracks to get to school in the winter. It was real scary when we'd be on the trestles and hear a train whistle. We'd run like heck to get to the end before the train appeared.

At Cliff Yard, we left the tracks and raced up the narrow holler, leaving Papa far behind. We splashed along a tiny stream, around an outcropping of shiny coal, and stopped and stared at the sight of the little shack. It sat on the top of a small shelf about twenty feet above the stream.

We waited for Papa and then climbed the path to the shack. It stood a couple of feet above the ground, with a post at each corner to keep it from falling down. A couple of steps led up to a narrow porch and the front door.

Beyond the shack and down the slope there was a heavy log pigpen with the stream running right through it. Off to one side of the pigpen was an outdoor two-holer: a wooden outhouse with a burlap sack for a door.

It wasn't all depressing. There were chestnut, maple, and dogwood trees everywhere. One of the dogwood trees, in full bloom, shaded a large basin, fed by a small waterfall of cool, sparkling water. It would be our only source of water for drinking, cooking, and washing.

I raced Sis to be the first inside, but she won, and I followed her through the door. Boy, was it small inside. Just a little living room where Papa's iron bed would take up most of the space.

Sis and Ruby would have a cot in the corner with Bobby's crib alongside. A small room off to the left with a curtain for a door would be where Grandma Bond, Mama's mother, and I would share a bed, with one bag filled with chicken feathers to be our mattress and another, our blanket.

Beyond the living room there was a long narrow room with a coal cookstove where Bert and Ernie would sleep and where all the cooking, eating, and washing would be done. The only light would be oil lamps. There wasn't a closet in the place. A line of nails on all the walls would have to serve as hangers for our clothes.

We went outside. Papa sat down on the steps to wait for Mama and the wagon to arrive. But the rest of us ran around exploring. We tried the water in the spring and fought to swing on the rope hanging from a limb of the chestnut tree until Papa got tired of the noise and sent us up to the holler to pick apples from the trees in a little orchard. The wagon got there just before dark.

Mama was exhausted from the long trip. She barely glanced at her new home, handed Bobby to Sis, and led us all inside.

I remember how she stopped for a moment in the main room. I heard her take a deep breath and watched her straighten her slender, tired body as she studied the place. She put her arms around Papa and said, "It'll do fine, Ezra."

Then, as usual, she got us busy getting our home set up. By the time the wagon was unloaded and the driver started back to Simmons in the twilight, Mama had a pot of beans cooking for supper.

Every Saturday Mama would build a fire out in the yard, fill the washtub with water from the spring, and, when it was hot enough, line us up. Sis first, because she was the oldest, then me, and on down the line. We'd strip off our clothes and climb in. None of us ever thought anything about being nude in front of the others.

Winter came early in 1918. It started snowing in September, and Mama caught a real bad cold. I didn't know it, but she was going to have a baby in December.

By the middle of October her cold had turned into influenza. I remember how thin she looked and how she was having a lot of trouble breathing.

The closest doctor was in Bluefield. Papa couldn't get him to come to the holler; and the wagon road to Simmons, where she could have been put on a train to Bluefield, was deeply drifted over with snow. He couldn't get anyone to try to make it with a horse and wagon.

I didn't know I was losing my mother. I didn't even know how much I loved her on the afternoon of November 24 when we were all crowded around her bed.

She was a beautiful young woman. Her dark brown eyes, smiling brightly, studied each of us and finally settled on Sis. "Take care of Bobby," she whispered softly.

Her eyes closed, but the smile remained.

I was too stunned to realize she was gone.

As the cries of the children began to fill the room, Grandma took charge and told Sis to take us all in her bedroom.

I didn't know it then, but Grandma had already planned to try to save the baby. She called for Sis, and she went back into the other room. We just waited. All we could hear was Sis crying softly.

It seemed like hours before Sis came and told me that Papa wanted me in the kitchen. As I entered the room and paused by the foot of the bed, Grandma turned to me, tears streaming down her face, and said in a soft voice, "We couldn't save the baby. Herbert, you better go help your papa."

Papa was just nailing the top on a small wooden box as I entered. He didn't look up at me as he said, "You'll have to help me bury your baby sister, Herbert."

We plowed our way through the heavy snow to the orchard, shoveled the snow aside, dug a deep hole in the frozen ground, and lowered the small coffin. We filled the grave and went back to the shack.

Mama was buried in a cemetery in Bluefield. Young maple trees covered her gravesite with a blanket of golden leaves in the fall.

Chapter 2

Bluefield, West Virginia

Papa moved us back to Bluefield. It was a real frontier town back in those days. The Norfolk and Western Railroad split the town in half. Our house was on the wrong side of the tracks. The business section was on the other side, and the wealthy people lived over the hill in South Bluefield.

I got a job selling the *Bluefield Daily Telegraph.* Before dawn each morning I was standing in front of the Matz Hotel where all the traveling salesmen stayed. From way back east, toward The Narrows in Virginia, I'd hear the first long drawn-out whistle of the giant steam engine racing west from Norfolk. Before the train pulled into the station, the salesmen and others would come from the hotel and head for the station. Very few of them ever failed to stop and buy my papers. I'd watch them rush away and then cross the streetcar tracks to the stone wall that separated the street from the railroad tracks below. I'd climb on top of the wall and stay there, watching that great passenger train speeding away into the Western Blue Ridges, the first rays of the rising sun mirrored in the windows of the last car.

I always got a funny feeling in my belly as I listened to the fading sounds of the engine's whistle. I'd wonder what it would sound like if I were riding inside one of those cars on my way to Hollywood. I'd also wonder what it would cost to ride on that train and where the money would come from.

I continued selling the newspaper. I also got a job delivering meat for Mr. Ford, the best butcher in town, every day after school and all day on Saturday for $1.50 per week.

Mr. Hudson, who owned the Hudson Grocery store next to Ford's, offered me $2.00 per week for the same hours, so I quit working for Mr. Ford and went to work for Mr. Hudson.

At fourteen, I was working for a civil engineer, Mr. Graham. He was a World War I Army captain on preliminary power surveys all over Virginia and West Virginia. He was also the Bluefield civil engineer and kept me with him for a number of years.

Summer 1925, with Hollywood and the movies firmly fixed in my mind, I figured I could learn something more about movies if I could get a job working at the Colonial Theater.

I don't remember the manager's name. He was real nice to me. He asked about the places I'd worked. He wanted to know about my school; and he listened to my tale of the movie I'd seen on the bedsheet at Cliff Yards and my ambition to go to Hollywood and make movies that he could show right there in his Colonial Theater.

I got the job.

The Colonial Theater was the showplace of southern West Virginia. Anyone arriving in Bluefield at twilight would be drawn to the grand foyer, where the theater's talented artist displayed his double life-size, cut-out color paintings of the picture's stars.

But it was the interior of the Colonial Theater that was most amazing to me. It had hundreds of comfortable seats and wide, carpeted aisles leading down to an orchestra pit. As the drapes slid aside revealing the screen, the organist would begin to play, his music timed and colored to the mood of the film.

The first time I watched those drapes slide aside, I saw on the screen a snow-covered mountain peak rising into the sky crowned with a circle of bright, gleaming stars and the words "A Paramount Picture." I knew then that someday Paramount would become my home.

I made sure I saw every new picture that came to the Colonial, including *Smilin' Thru.* I fell in love with the star of that movie, Norma Talmadge.

When the newspaper began running ads offering fabulous jobs at fabulous salaries everywhere in Florida, I knew I had to go there. With Papa's seniority, I got a pass on the railroad as far as Tampa. At the station I promised Sis I'd come back.

Twenty-six years later, on my way to Rome to assist Willie Wyler on *Roman Holiday,* I kept that promise.

Chapter 3

Florida

I left Bluefield on February 3, 1926, for Tampa. I was eighteen years old.

Within a week, I was hired by the Burns Engineering Company in Clearwater, Florida, and sent to help survey a town called New Port Richey, a few miles up the coast from Tarpon Springs. New Port Richey turned out to be swamps, citrus groves, rattlesnakes, and cottonmouth moccasins.

The pay was good, living was cheap, and I was putting away some money. I knew I'd made the right move when I left home.

The day we finished the survey I caught a ride to Bradenton. A new life, a new job, and a new girlfriend. She was the daughter of the owner of the store I worked in. She was beautiful and looked great at the beach, even in those old-time bathing suits.

Bradenton was a swinging town in 1926. Flappers were in, with "It Girl" Clara Bow haircuts, short skirts, and swinging hips. Wild parties and cars racing around with kids too young to handle the rotgut rum, gin, and beer.

I couldn't take the stuff. Or the wild parties. Half-drunk boys chasing girls too full of rum and Coca-Cola. Others dancing wildly to the jazz music coming from a Victrola. Half-nude girls jumping into the pool. One yelling, "Skinny dippin'!"

A moment later, boys' and girls' swimsuits would come flying out of the pool. Waiters carrying large trays of food would come from the house. They, and their trays, were sent flying when young men tackled them.

What I saw there, and at my job jerking sodas in the drugstore, kept me from most of the parties.

Sundays I was a Red Cross lifeguard at Bradenton Beach. Our main job was getting everybody out of the water when sharks were seen coming too close to the beach.

Every summer all the lifeguards were required to enter a three-mile, rough-water swimming race just off Bradenton Beach. During the race I didn't give the sharks one thought; I was busy trying to keep up with the leaders. I finished third and then began worrying about all the sharks I'd been swimming with.

On the Saturday following the rough-water race, the owner of the store where I was working and his daughter invited me to have dinner with them.

"Please don't say no, Herbie. You're my date."

The dinner was at Bobby Jones's winter golf club just south of Bradenton. I had my first taste of imported gin and Scotch.

It was easy to see that it wasn't the first for Bobby Jones. He was weaving more than a little bit when he made his speech. He was a friend and a hero to all the golfers present, and they wouldn't let him stop.

I was overwhelmed by the beautiful snow-white tablecloth, the china, the stemware, the embroidered napkins, and the number of silver spoons, forks, and knives around my plate. I began to compare that table with our table in our little shack back in Cliff Holler. Plain planks, red oilcloth tablecloth. One spoon, fork, and knife.

I told my girlfriend I'd never know which knife, fork, or spoon to use. "Don't worry, Honey, half the people don't know. And the other half don't care. Think of what we'll be doing after dinner. Dancing. Walking in the garden in the moonlight. We'll be together tonight. Just the two of us."

Later that summer, 1926, a killer hurricane roared across Florida. In Bradenton the police were busy warning the people to be off the streets and under cover by nine o'clock.

I was working that night. By nine we locked the doors, and as we stepped out on the sidewalk, a large metal signboard, carried by the howling wind, came at us. We jumped back just in time to avoid being beheaded. The walk home was a nightmare, fighting the hurricane-force wind, climbing over overturned cars and broken and uprooted trees, and skirting fallen power lines. I arrived home soaked to the skin by the driving rain.

A local newspaper reporter, named Mayberry, had been coming in for lunch. I'd told him about my plans to go to Hollywood, and one day he told me that he and his wife were leaving for Hollywood in three days and would take me along in their car for only $50.00; I couldn't believe it. I could ride all the way to Hollywood for only $50.00? I'd planned to work until I had $500.00 in the bank. I knew I had $320.00 in my account. My mind raced over the figures: $50.00 to Mayberry; fifteen nights for a room at $2.50 per night; food for the trip, about $40.00. Great! I could arrive in Hollywood with about $200.00. I told Mayberry we had a deal.

Chapter 4

Hollywood

The sun was still high in the bluest sky I'd ever seen when Mayberry pulled alongside the curb in front of a row of lower-middle-class houses and bungalow courts just a block north of Santa Monica Boulevard at Normandie.

He told me to wait, and then he and his wife hurried along a narrow walk between two rows of a small stucco court. I watched them enter a door at the end of the walk. I got out of the car and studied the area. Down the street, two bare-chested men were working on an old car parked on a lawn. Across the street two angry kids were fighting over a bicycle. This was not what I'd expected Hollywood to look like. Not small, old stucco houses with postage-stamp lawns and scrubby trees. I thought of our shack in Cliff Holler, the ground covered with natural grass and all those flowering dogwood trees.

I heard Mayberry calling. I took my suitcase and joined him. He gave me a blanket, towel, and soap; opened the door to one of the courts; and said, "This is yours as long as it's vacant." Well, it was already vacant. No furniture, not even a chair. He handed me the key and started away, but I stopped him with an angry outburst: "What about my money?"

He turned back and slumped against the door before answering, "I was sure my brother would lend me the money to pay you back, Herbie, but he doesn't have it. He's been out of a job for over eight months, and they're living on what his wife makes managing these courts. I've asked him to borrow the money, but the banks have already turned him down. I'll pay it all back as soon as I get a job. I promise you that."

I remember that conversation as vividly as if it had taken place just yesterday. The money I had loaned him, from the first $50.00 near Shamrock, Florida, to the last $25.00 in Yuma, Arizona, came to a total of $210.00 out of my $270.00. Of the remaining $60.00, I had just $11.30.

I can't remember what the new Mayberrys looked like. To me, they've become just two faceless people. Nor can I remember what they fixed for supper.

Those five frightened, desperate people seated around the Mayberry kitchen table that night more than sixty-two years ago, lost in their own troubled thoughts, were silent except for an occasional mumbled word or two.

When everyone had finished eating, the Mayberry ladies cleared the table and went into the parlor. While the host brought coffee to the table, the other Mayberry pulled a paper from his pocket and held it up. "There's over thirty newspapers in and around Los Angeles on that list," he said. "I'm sure to land a job on one of them and start paying you back. Every cent."

"Besides the money," I told them, "I need a map showing where all the studios are and how to get to them."

The elder Mayberry went into the parlor and returned with a sheet of paper. He sat down beside me and began to explain what he had drawn. "That X is here, the corner of Santa Monica and Normandie. I've drawn in all the main streets of Hollywood. They all run north and south or east and west, and I've put a number in for each studio. See number 1, there at Western and Sunset Boulevard. The Fox Studio."

The next morning, as I studied Mayberry's map, I felt adrenaline surging through my body. I wasn't surprised. It always happened when I was about to take an important step, and this had to be the most crucial time in my life.

I walked up Normandie to Sunset, had a twenty-cent breakfast at a one-arm coffee shop on Sunset, bought a copy of the Hollywood *Daily Citizen,* and searched the want ads for possible jobs in the studios. There wasn't a single offer.

At the corner of Sunset and Western, I stopped and stared across the street at a one-story office building and a wide gate in a wall farther down Western. Most of the people going in the building were well dressed, but the men entering through the gate seemed to be workmen. Everyone knew the old watchman who was dressed in rumpled pants and shirt, sat on a nail keg, and greeted them all by name.

I waited until the traffic through the gate slowed to a halt and then crossed the street and said, "Good morning." He pulled a half-eaten cigar from his mouth and studied me for a moment before growling, "Good mornin' yourself, kid." I told him I was looking for a job and asked who I should see. "I ain't heard 'bout no hirin'," he said. "And if there was, they wouldn't be hirin' no kids."

I told him that I looked younger than I was. That I was born in 1907 and would be nineteen in three months, but he wouldn't buy it. He looked off at the sound of a car's horn and the squeal of brakes and pulled me aside.

I turned and saw the biggest, fanciest car I'd ever seen sweeping toward the gate. The uniformed chauffeur was sitting outside in the open, and inside there was a real beauty waving at the watchman. As the car disappeared between the stages, the watchman asked me, "You know who that was in the limo, kid?" I could only shake my head. "That was Miss Janet Gaynor, kid. She's gonna make a picture with George O'Brien called *Sunrise.*"

I left the gate, walked down Western to the next street, turned along the studio wall, and stopped by an open stage door where workmen were busy building a wooden set. A carpenter, hammering away, paused to wipe the sweat from his face and came to the door for a breath of fresh air.

I thought maybe he could help me, so I asked him how I could get a job in the studio. "You don't look old enough to have a trade, young fellow. You have any training?" he asked. I told him some civil engineering was about all. "Unless you know someone," he said, "you'd have to be a journeyman carpenter, electrician, or painter to land anything."

He must have seen how disappointed I was because he told me he'd nose around at lunchtime to see if anyone knew of an opening and told me to check with him later that day.

I walked along Sunset to Gower, where the sidewalk was crowded with cowboys of all ages and descriptions. I stopped to eavesdrop. Most of the talk was about their chances of getting a job from any of the Poverty Row western producers that day.

I noticed one man, his western clothes a cut above that of the others, leaning against the wall. His hat was pulled low over his eyes, and one foot, in polished boot, was drawn up and resting against the wall. He was smoking a thin cigar and seemed to be a loner.

Now and then someone would come from some door and read off the names of a few cowboys, who would hurry to follow him inside.

After a while, the crowd began to thin, but the loner still remained. Ignoring the others, I crossed the walk, leaned on the walk beside him, and asked him if I had to be a cowboy to get a job there. He looked me over before answering, "Just about." I told him he didn't look like the others and asked if he worked in pictures. He nodded his head and told me he knew every director who worked on Poverty Row. That almost every day one of them would need an actor and tell his assistant to go get Tex. "I'm Tex. Pay's good, too. Some days I get two, three jobs."

I told him I'd come to Hollywood to get in the movie business. He pointed at the departing cowboys and told me that they came every day hoping for a day's work, knowing only a dozen or so would be hired. It was the same at every studio, not only for extras but for almost every job. He told me how the Hollywood Chamber of Commerce had been running ads in papers across the country since 1921, warning that out of every 100,000 people who found work, only five would reach the top in the studios. I told him I'd take the odds. He wished me luck, and I walked away, feeling sure he meant it.

I left Poverty Row. Walked along Sunset to Warner Brothers. I didn't like the look of that big white building with its line of giant columns. It reminded me of one of those southern mansions where all the rich people lived. It scared me a little, but I knew I had to give it a try. When I went inside, a man sitting at a desk barely listened to my story before dismissing me.

I decided that was not my day, so I went to a little park up above Hollywood Boulevard and sat under a tree to decide how to approach Paramount the next day.

By the middle of the afternoon I was back at Fox. When the carpenter saw me, he came over. But his news wasn't encouraging. Every department was full up, he told me. "Give me your name," he said. "If I hear of an opening, I'll leave a note with the watchman. You keep checking with him."

I tore a corner off the newspaper, wrote my name on it, handed it to him, and thanked him for everything he was doing for me.

It was dark when I got back to the court. The Mayberry apartment was dark, and Mayberry's Ford was missing.

The next morning I followed the map Mr. Mayberry gave me. At Vine and Melrose, an arrow indicated that I should follow Melrose to Bronson, where another arrow would show me the way to the studio. It pointed left. As I turned and looked up at the great arch, and the sign PARAMOUNT PICTURES, a surge of adrenaline flooded my whole body.

This was where my future lay. I knew it!

I joined the fifty or so people who stood in little groups around the gate. After a short wait, a real pretty girl came from inside and called for the people for the Sutherland picture to line up. About fifteen joined her. She checked their names as they passed through the gate. I took a chance and stopped beside her as the last one entered. I said, "Good morning."

She smiled and asked my name. When I told her, she checked her list and told me I wasn't on the call. When I asked what she meant, she told me that extras had to be registered at Central Casting and get their jobs through them. She was real nice and told me what extras did. She saw she had a real greenhorn on her hands and took me into her office. She told me Famous Players–Lasky had bought the Bronson Studio and moved in just months before, hiring more people than they needed and then laying off the ones they found they didn't need. "It's too bad you weren't around then," she said. "You might have been hired and been one of the lucky ones that were kept on."

I remember how I turned away so she couldn't see how the bad news had affected me. But she knew and attempted to ease the pain. She opened a booklet, copied off seven names, and handed the list to me, telling me they were the names of the department heads I should contact.

It wasn't easy thanking her, but I stumbled through it somehow. She invited me to stop in anytime and let her know how things were going.

I bought a writing tablet and some envelopes, went to the little Hollywood library, and wrote a letter to each of the men on the list. I gave them the Mayberry's address, but no phone number, and asked permission to telephone them. Within two hours of hearing their names, the letters were in the mail.

Then I had a great idea. Why not write to department heads in all the major studios? I started calling around, giving all kinds of stories to studio operators to get names. And it worked. I wrote more than thirty letters, mailed them, and checked Mayberry's mailbox daily for answers.

After more than a week of waiting with nothing arriving from any of the studios, I knew I had to find a temporary job outside the studios. I was almost broke, living on grapes and stale bread I bought from a little Japanese market.

Every day I answered, within walking distance, all the ads listed in the local papers. But it was a waste of time. There would be a sign saying the job had been filled.

More and more, I was thinking of home. Beginning to tell myself this dream of mine was all wrong. That I was out of my league, that my future was the railroad, where all the Colemans had spent their working lives.

But I still tried to hang on to my dream.

Then, one day, Mrs. Mayberry shattered that dream. She told me I had to move in two days because the court had been rented. She was obviously very upset. I told her how much help she had been since I arrived from Florida.

I left the court and went for a walk to sort things out. I was surprised that I'd accepted Mrs. Mayberry's news so calmly. It was easy to see I had to call all the people I'd written to, and if there were no positive responses, I'd find a way to get back to Bluefield.

Mayberry was climbing down from his Model T as I returned to the court. He stuck out his hand in a friendly greeting. He pulled some rumpled bills from his pocket, counted out $11.00, and handed them to me, saying he had earned $22.00 selling ads for a newspaper in Long Beach and wanted me to have half of it.

I told him I was going home and asked him to take me to the Southern Pacific Station in downtown Los Angeles. He asked for my Bluefield address and promised to send me the rest of my money when he got a regular job.

I went into the court, added the $11.00 to my $1.59. I never forgot that $1.59.

I pulled the Norfolk and Western Railroad pass from my wallet and studied it. I remember, it said Atlantic Coast Line, Tampa, Florida, to Petersburg, Virginia, N&W to Bluefield. I had used passes many times, and usually the conductors would just glance at them, punch them, and stuff them in their pockets. I was hoping they'd do the same on the train out of Los Angeles. If not, there was always the freight train.

When I saw Mayberry coming, I turned away so he couldn't see how upset I was at having to leave Hollywood and go back to West Virginia.

As I got in the car, he handed me a Hollywood *Daily Citizen* and pointed to an ad that he had circled with a pencil. "That's a new ad," he said. "Wasn't in yesterday's paper. You can check it out. It's on our way." I thanked him but told him I'd had it and was going home.

We started for the station. Less than ten minutes later, Mayberry pulled to a stop and pointed to a small building, "There's the drugstore that had the ad in the paper. You want to check it out?"

I told him to forget it. He started off toward downtown but kept insisting that I check it out. After a dozen or more blocks of listening to him, I agreed. He made a U turn and drove me back to the drugstore.

Mayberry stayed in the car while I went inside.

At first I thought the place was deserted, but then I noticed an old man at the prescription counter in the back. There was a soda fountain near the front door with ten stools. Then another man appeared from somewhere in the back. With his heavy, thick, black eyebrows and his jutting jaw, he looked downright mean. He was carrying a large white porcelain pot with steam rising around the cover. He dropped the pot in the steam cabinet and turned to ask if I was there about the job.

When I told him I was, he looked me over, and a smile replaced the scowl on his face. "The ad says, 'With experience,' young fellow." I told him about my past jobs, and he told me the job was mine. "Your hours will be 9:30 to 3:00 p.m., two hours off, then 5 p.m. to 10:30, Monday through Saturday. $27.50 a week."

I got my suitcase from the car and thanked Mayberry for everything. I watched him drive off. I never saw him again.

Without asking if I'd had breakfast, the man told me to eat something before the lunch crowd began pouring in.

I wondered where they would "pour in" from because there didn't seem to be any place for many people to be working around Melrose and Van Ness.

But "pour in" they did. From 11:30 until 2:00 the place was overrun with customers, mostly men in shirtsleeves; a few in suits, ties, and hats; and a few well-dressed women. I didn't have time to ask where they came from or even listen to their conversations.

By 2:30, we'd served the last of the lunch crowd, and I had a chance to ask my new boss, Joe Fornier, where they worked.

"Famous Players–Lasky Studio, where they make those Paramount Pictures."

"They walk all the way from the studio to have lunch here?" I asked.

"Do you know where the studio is?"

I told him I'd been there looking for a job. "It's at Bronson and Marathon."

He pointed out the window to the west along Melrose. "Paramount's right behind that Western Costume building. One of these days one of our customers that work there might invite you to come and watch them shoot a picture. If they do, take them up on it. You might like what you see."

I was glad he was too busy to see my reaction to what he had just told me.

A few minutes later, Joe left for the day. I closed the fountain at three. Slowly sipped a cup of coffee while I tried to put that exciting day in perspective. Despair at nine. Fear that I was too late when I walked through the door of the drugstore at ten. Stomach churning from hunger and fright as Joe studied me before telling me the job was mine. Then the discovery that Paramount was right there! That I might be invited inside! It was enough!

I did have a future in films! And this job would open the door for me!

In summer 1927, a man started coming in every day for lunch. For dessert, he always asked for hot—really hot—apple pie with a slab of ice cream. Everybody seemed to know that friendly man, and I soon learned that his name was Joe Robbins and that he was the head of Paramount's transportation department. Well, his pie got hotter and hotter, and the slabs of ice cream got bigger and bigger! So did his chins and his belt size.

The big day arrived. It was the first week of September 1927. Joe came in late for lunch. By the time he finished his dessert, all the others had left the fountain. As he paid his check, he surprised me by asking, "How'd you like to work for me?"

"More than anything in the world," I told him. "When?"

He wanted me to start the next day, but I told him I couldn't walk out on Mr. Fornier. I'd have to give him time to get someone to take my place. He said the job would wait and asked what my salary was.

"$27.50 a week," I told him. He promised me the same. For seventy hours, seven days a week, and fifty cents an hour overtime after seventy hours. He said I'd be driving a Model T, mostly around town, and wouldn't have to worry much about working on Sundays.

It was 8 a.m. the morning of September 10, 1927, when I walked through the Famous Players–Lasky Studio gate to start a career that would last exactly thirty-two years.

Joe was waiting when I walked into the transportation office. He introduced me to Mary Eicks, the dispatcher, whose greeting was very short. I decided, instantly, that she was a tough broad. I discovered that she was an angel to all who worked in that department. She became a lifelong friend.

Joe and I went into the large garage where a shiny, black, new Model T Ford touring car was parked. He told me to take him for a short drive. Fortunately for me, it had a self-starter, so I didn't have to crank it.

I got it out of the garage without stalling. Got through the studio streets without hitting anybody or anything. I ignored the stop sign at Van Ness and turned into the traffic without stopping.

I could feel Joe's feet press down on the floorboards and prayed he'd forgive me for that mistake. I followed his directions and somehow got us back safely and without a scratch on the car.

In less than an hour I was off on my first assignment. "Go to ladies wardrobe," Mary Eicks said. "They have someone to go downtown."

That someone turned out to be a skinny young girl who told me her name was Edith Head. She said her job was to find material for the costumes Travis Banton designed. She made no secret about her determination to see, on the screen, in giant letters, "Costumes by EDITH HEAD."

I wasted no time finding ways to meet as many department heads as I could, but I was careful not to mention a job. I wanted to look and listen. Find out where I could learn.

Drivers had to stick close to the garage, so I had little chance to watch a movie being made. But I did have fun watching directors and movie stars at play. Clara Bow's bungalow was right next to the transportation office, and when she wasn't in a film, her place was jumping.

But Clara had some problems. Booze, boyfriends, and one powerful ex-boyfriend, B. P. Schulberg, the new head man at Paramount. Rumor had it he got his job by bringing Clara Bow from FBO to Paramount. Later he dropped her for Sylvia Sidney.

Clara was a very pretty young girl, always smiling and happy. Her parties were never what we'd heard and read about Hollywood parties. Never any loud arguments or any obnoxious drunks around her bungalow. She should have been Paramount's biggest star. But Schulberg kept putting her in things like *The Plastic Age,* when he should have been casting her in top productions.

I didn't see any tears around the studio when he was sent packing. Emanuel (Manny) Cohen was brought out from New York to replace him.

Within six months, I was assigned to run film back and forth between the studio and the Paramount laboratory. When I delivered the film to the cutters, I'd hang around and watch them work. I soon discovered that most of them had been with Famous Players–Lasky from the day the company started making pictures. They worked in tiny crowded rooms under heavy pressure and seldom spent any time on a shooting set.

However, there was one cutter, Otho Lovering, an easygoing, cheerful person, who had time to explain and demonstrate what film cutting was all about. When he found out I was determined to become a director and producer, he told me to forget cutting and get into production.

I followed his advice and tried to convince Sam Jaffe, head production manager, to let me stand by on a shooting company and learn how to become an assistant director; but he let me know, in no uncertain terms, he didn't want me hanging around the stages.

I wasn't about to let Jaffe stop me. I slipped onto stage 4, just across the street from the garage, to watch director Eddie Sutherland work. When Jaffe heard about it, he barred me from the stages.

For days I was afraid I'd lose my job. But my boss told me to forget it, that his department was independent of the production office. "Don't give up," he advised me. "You'll make it if you keep trying."

One evening, I was told I'd be working all night as a seventy-year-old French taxi driver in a picture, *Seven Days Leave,* starring Gary Cooper.

I wondered, "Why me?" I'd already worked all night the past three nights. I didn't complain. Just got a uniform from wardrobe and went to makeup, where they plastered bushy gray eyebrows and a droopy gray moustache to my face. Drew black lines down my cheeks and said, "That oughta make you look seventy, kid." Nobody laughed when I got to the set. Not even Coop.

The first few months of 1928 were a bust. The studio was busy, but no one seemed interested in that kid from Cliff Holler, with that wild, wonderful West Virginia accent.

I kept telling myself, "Stop worrying. It was eleven years ago when I saw that seven minutes of film and knew I'd give up everything to become a success in the movie business. And don't forget," I told myself, "it was just seven months ago I walked through those Paramount gates. One of these days I'll get a break. Maybe sooner than I think."

It was the middle of May when the break came. Without a doubt the greatest break I would ever have in my entire lifetime.

Carvel Agner, a friend and fellow driver at Paramount, introduced me to his girlfriend, Mary Belle Powell, the prettiest sixteen-year-old senior in Hollywood High School. When Carvel started talking about dates, she told him, "No more dates until I graduate from Hollywood High in June. I promised Mom I'd graduate first in my class, and I'm going to keep that promise. From now on, after school and nights, I'll study at the Melrose Library, but I'll take a break from church on Sunday mornings at the Melrose Methodist Church."

I would tease her later in life that Carvel knew all that and she was really giving me that information.

One morning my old Model T was missing, and parked in its place was a light blue, four-door Model A Ford with a powerful four-cylinder engine. Joe Robbins came from his office, handed me the key, and said, "There's a lot of horses under that hood. Don't let them run away with you."

Chapter 5

Wolf Song

I found out how powerful those horses were about three o'clock one morning, late in September 1928, in a driving snowstorm.

I was looking for June Lake Lodge, somewhere high in the Mammoth Mountains, and had stopped quickly when a giant tree, almost hidden by the wind-driven snow, suddenly appeared in my headlights. I got out of the car, stumbled around in the knee-deep snow, and discovered that I had reached the end of the road. But another road came from the left and disappeared to the right. I stood there in front of the headlights wondering which way I should go.

Well, I couldn't stand there the rest of the night, so I got in the car and took off to the left. About an hour later, the road ended against a high wall. I got out and discovered that I had stopped behind a big, dark building. I stumbled around in the dark until I found a door that would open and went inside.

I found myself in a real big kitchen. A man, wearing an apron and a chef's cap, was sitting at a table with a plate piled high with hash brown potatoes, country sausage, and fried eggs. He saw me come in and froze with his loaded fork at his lips. "Where the hell did you come from, kid?"

I told him about getting lost and asked where I could find June Lake Lodge. "You're in the lodge," he said. "But you can't stay here; it's leased to a movie company." I told him who I was. He sent me into the main room to get rid of my wet clothes while he fixed me some food.

The main hall was enormous, with a blazing fire in a great stone fireplace. I took off my wet jacket and boots and went back into the kitchen. The chef gave me a plate piled high with hot food.

I slept on a couch in front of the fireplace and woke up when I sensed somebody nearby. It was Jack Moore, the head of Paramount's livestock department. Former champion cowboy and still champion poker player.

I told him why I was there, my car full of furs that the *Wolf Song* company needed that day. He told me his car was snowed in and said he would ride out to the location with me.

Those furs would never have gotten to the location if Jack Moore hadn't stayed in the lodge that night. I didn't have the slightest idea where the Hot Springs location was or how to get there. But, slipping and sliding off the road and back on it, we made it.

When we pulled in beside the jumble of trucks, cars, lights, and people, the first thing I heard was Henry Hathaway, the assistant director, screaming at Ernie Johnson, the property man, about leaving the furs at the studio and what would happen to him if they didn't arrive by the time they were ready to shoot. The look of relief on Ernie's face made my drive through the snowstorm worthwhile.

My orders had been to drop off the furs and make the 400-mile drive back to the studio that day, but Jack Moore changed those orders. He told the production manager to assign me to his department, and I stayed for the whole location. I spent every minute I could watching Victor Fleming, the director, at work.

One day I was standing half hidden by the mass of equipment, when Gary Cooper appeared beside me with two cups of coffee. "Howdy, podner," he said, as he handed me one of the cups. I was so surprised that Gary Cooper, Paramount's big western star, would bother to bring a cup of coffee to a kid who wasn't even on the bottom rung of the ladder that I almost dropped the cup while stammering, "Thank you, Mr. Cooper."

"Call me Coop. All my friends do. You drive that little blue Model A Ford for Jack Moore?"

For the first time in my life, I was so tongue-tied I could only nod, so he went on. He indicated the set with a wave of his hand: "You have any questions about all this, just ask."

I wanted to ask him why, with all that sunlight, they needed all those big, powerful lights. But I didn't because I was afraid he'd think I was stupid. I was saved when Hathaway yelled out that they were ready for him.

Coop gave Hathaway a wave, turned back to me with a smile, and then, without another word, ambled back to the set. I watched him, his long, lanky body clothed in tan fringed buckskin, rough boots, and leather hat, join Hathaway, the actor Louis Wolheim, Victor Fleming, and a girl who sat beside Mr. Fleming with an open book on her lap.

They discussed the scene they were about to film. That girl seemed to have an important job. I saw her correct Fleming when he had Coop look off at something to the left. Fleming didn't argue with her; he just told Coop to look to the right. Then she whispered something in Ernie Johnson's ear. Ernie looked over at the campfire, silently thanked her, walked over, and moved a rifle to another position. I sure wanted to see inside that book.

The evenings in that great hall, with burning logs piled high in the fireplace, were wonderful. The whole company lived in the lodge and gathered in groups after supper. One card table was always crowded where Jack Moore gave high-stakes poker lessons. Others played checkers, bridge, or whatever.

There was a long leather couch near the fireplace that everyone left vacant. It was there that Coop, Fleming, and Hathaway would stretch out and discuss the film or just gossip.

One night after supper, Russ Welch, with his big Packard sedan, and I, with my Model A, were sent to Lone Pine, a little town down on the flatlands about 140 miles away, to meet Lupe Velez, who was arriving there on the train the next morning. Neither of us had ever seen her, but we didn't worry. Not many people rode that train to the end of the track in Lone Pine.

It was after midnight when we arrived in the deserted town. The single streetlight, the one light hanging over the door of the small Dow Hotel, and the glow from the window of the Rainbow Cafe did little to penetrate the heavy mist that filled the air.

We pulled in beside the café and parked by a large foreign touring car, with its side curtains up and loaded with luggage. As we walked past it, Russ pointed to a six-foot spread of longhorns, with a large brass plate engraved with a T/M brand mounted across the hood. He said the car must belong to someone who didn't want anyone to know who he was. We were laughing as we entered the café. We quit laughing at the sight and sound that greeted us.

A skinny, dark-haired Mexican girl was sitting at the counter in the back of the café, shouting at the old fry cook, who was standing with his back to her, slowly stirring something in a frying pan. A stream of filth spewed from her mouth in English and Spanish.

The only English I could catch was the "son of a bitch" she kept yelling. There were a lot of *madres* and *putas*, so that Russ, who spoke Spanish, said, "The old man's mother was a whore." He also translated a lot more of her disgusting words, words I'd never heard men use, much less women.

After the cook placed food before the girl and disappeared in the back, Russ said he'd make a bet that Mexican dame was Lupe Velez.

He walked back and sat down next to her and asked if she wasn't Lupe Velez.

She whirled on him. "Who the fuck wants to know?" she yelled. Russ told her who we were and that Paramount had sent us to meet her when she arrived on the train.

That really set her off. "You can go back up there and tell Fleming, and all the rest of that stinking Paramount bunch who asked me to ride that fuckin' train, to stick *Wolf Song* up their ass." She switched into Spanish and began yelling louder at Russ. He leaned close to her and said something in Spanish that stopped her cold. Then he switched to English and told her he was arranging rooms for her across the street at the Dow and that she could stay there if she wanted to.

As we turned to leave the café, I noticed a man in a chauffeur's uniform sitting on the stool nearest the door. Embroidered on his cap and on the pocket of his jacket was the same T/M brand we'd seen on the car.

We slept at the Dow, had a late breakfast, and headed back to the mountain location where the company was shooting. Hathaway wanted to know what happened in Lone Pine. We told him only what we wanted him to know. You can bet, neither Russ nor I ever drove Lupe or wanted to.

That night, when Lupe came down to supper and, for the first time, got a gander at that long drink of water ambling across the dining room, she changed from Tom Mix's Mexican spitfire to Coop's little lamb.

Tom Mix was the owner of that T/M brand, that car with the prize longhorns, and Lupe Velez. He had sent his chauffeur along to keep an eye on his property. But after meeting Coop, Lupe told the chauffeur to get lost. That was the last time we saw him. But not the last we heard from Mix.

He called Lupe every night. The only phone in the lodge was in the main hall, and everybody had to be quiet so she could hear him. But not Victor Fleming. He'd yell loud enough for Mix to hear, "Kees Tony for me, Tom!" Lupe never complained.

It was snowing the morning we left June Lake Lodge and started the long drive back to the studio. I paused for a moment at the intersection of the roads where I had stood that dark night and looked up at the giant tree that stopped me and kept me from plunging over the cliffs into June Lake.

For the three cowboys in the car with me, this was old stuff. Just another location. But for me, the past six weeks had been part of what every boy dreamed about. Being on a movie set, watching a director bring to life what a writer had created on paper.

I didn't know what *Wolf Song* was all about until I saw it in the Paramount Theater on Sixth Street almost a year after Fleming finished shooting. I wasn't happy with what I saw. Every time Lupe appeared on the screen, even in the love scenes with Coop, I'd see her sitting in that café in Lone Pine, filth spewing from her mouth.

One last word about *Wolf Song*. On one of the last days of shooting in the studio, I ran into Coop, who was hiding in a passageway peering out into the little studio park. He cut off my greeting and pointed out. There was Lupe, her back pressed against a little tree. Standing in front of her was an angry Tom Mix. I couldn't hear what he was saying, but whatever it was, Lupe suddenly exploded. She screamed at him, and her sharp fingernails reached for his face. Mix stepped back and watched as she stormed across the street and disappeared inside her dressing room. He ran his hand through his thinning hair, slapped his big white cowboy hat on his head, and like the ham he was, carefully adjusted it to a right angle and stalked off toward the front gate.

I turned to Coop. He was still looking off toward Mix. As Mix disappeared through the main gate, Coop looked at me, shook his head, and said, "Not nice, podner."

I've heard stories about Coop being madly in love with Lupe, that he moved in with her and would have married her but for his parents' dislike of Lupe's lifestyle.

There were also stories about Coop's "love affair" with Clara Bow. Well, none of us ever saw him around there. Besides, Clara had too many others joining her binges. Her favorite at the time was a young director, Eddie Sutherland.

There've been too many lazy biographers writing about Coop's supposed love affairs. Of course, he fell in and out of love with many of the beautiful actresses who worked with him. But the girls couldn't compete with his love for hunting and fishing in the high country.

Often, when he returned from one of his trips, he would invite me to dinner and send me home with a dozen ducks. "Tell Mary Belle to cook them for five minutes in the hottest oven she has. Remember. Five minutes only." She followed Coop's instructions, and they were perfect.

Chapter 6

Fighting Caravans

Fighting Caravans was planned by Paramount to be a big-budget, big western, special film for release in 1931.

Before we left the studio for Sonora, California, in the foothills of the Sierra Nevadas where the company would have its headquarters, my blue Model A was taken away and I was given a new convertible four-door Studebaker. I figured Joe Robbins decided I'd grown up and could be one of the location drivers.

My job was driving Jack Moore and his cowboy wranglers. While most of the company would live in Sonora, the wranglers had a camp with their own cook in Cooperstown. No town, just a couple of old ranch houses surrounded by corrals.

The shooting sites chosen by the director, Otto Brower, were spread out all over the gold country in the foothills of the Sierra Nevadas. Many of the most important scenes would be shot in the high Sierra Nevadas in the summer and dead of winter around the Dardanelles and Sonora Pass at 10,000 feet.

Just three miles from Sonora, where the company would be living while shooting some of the summer scenes, was Jamestown, nicknamed Jimtown. Behind the buildings along the only street was a string of small white cottages where the "fallen ladies," with the approval of the entire community, performed their civic duties.

One night, some of the wranglers and their cook drove up to Jimtown to visit the "ladies." They were sitting in the parlor, sipping the local rotgut, when one of the women entered and called out, "Next!" The cook rose to his feet and then, with a shocked expression on his face, slumped back in his chair. The woman ran from the room. The wranglers helped the sobbing man from the cottage. That woman was his ex-wife, the mother of his two sons who were living with their father in the camp at Cooperstown. The next day the cook and his sons disappeared. No one was ever able to find out what happened to them.

One of the men I liked to drive was the cameraman, Lee Garmes. Lee was one of Hollywood's most respected cameramen, and he was always willing to tell others how he produced his unusual and beautiful photography. He was protective of his men. He had a young film loader, Russ Harlan, who would one day become the equal of Lee and win an Academy Award. Russ was a handsome, six-foot, two-inch hunk with the looks of a future film star. He had been tested by Paramount, and the studio was considering giving him a contract. But Russ had other plans. He was determined to study Lee Garmes's work and learn photography.

He was to have difficulty learning anything about photography on *Fighting Caravans.* He was too busy fighting off Lily Damita. From the day she arrived in Sonora and got a gander at that young lion until the picture completed filming, she never left him alone.

The day the company moved to Calaveras Big Trees to film the scenes of the wagon train encampment, I had riding with me Garmes; Otto Brower; Charlie Barton, his assistant; Sid Street, the production manager; and Bobby Odell, the art director.

On the way, Garmes asked Otto to set up the wagon train so he could film the master scene late in the afternoon when the sun was low in the western sky. I waited all day to find out why Lee made that request. I didn't know I was to get a lesson in photography that would influence my work many years later.

Around three o'clock that afternoon, the property men began to fill the area with smoke. As it drifted up through the branches of the giant redwoods, long shafts of sunlight from the setting sun angled down through the thin, blue smoke, creating a scene reminiscent of a Remington landscape.

Shortly before we finished our work around Sonora, Sid Street became very ill. The doctor said he had influenza and wanted him to go to the hospital in Hollywood; but Sid refused and, when the snows came, moved the company fifty miles up the Sonora Pass road to the Dardanelles. For the first forty miles, we drove up a narrow, two-way road and then down into the small high mountain meadow of the Dardanelles along a narrow, one-way road, mostly carved out of solid granite. It was really scary driving along the edge of that road looking straight down, through the drifting snow, to a tiny mountain stream at the bottom of a deep, 1,000-foot gorge.

The Dardanelles was little more than a summer fishing camp with a few permanent summer homes. Most of the crew lived in great tents, some of which would collapse under the weight of the snow, with everybody pitching in to put them back in shape.

Within one week of our arrival in the Dardanelles, Sid's influenza turned into pneumonia, and the doctor ordered him to go home. The man who was sent to replace Sid was a hard-nosed, selfish, narrow-minded, uncaring unit production manager, Richard "Dick" Johnson, who would become an ever increasing problem for me until summer 1951.

He hated the assignment and, after a week of heavy snow, demanded that one of us drive him to the nearest phone so he could call the studio executives and advise them to bring the company home. We drew straws to see who would have the pleasure of plowing his way out of the valley, up that steep grade, and then down the icy paved road to Strawberry Lake and the phone. I was the winner; and slipping and sliding, we made it to the start of the steep grade and got about one-third of the way up before Johnson made the mistake of looking out his side of the car to see that we were only inches from the edge of the deep gorge. His face turned as white as the snow, and he demanded that I turn around and go back. "You said you wanted to go to the phone," I told him, "and if I can keep my wheels in these ruts and not slide over the side of this mountain, you're going to the phone." He was too shaken to answer, and by the time we got to the top of the grade, I decided he could forget the phone. I managed to get the car turned around after an hour of shoveling snow. I was almost as scared going down the grade as Johnson had been coming up.

Gary Cooper was one of the first to welcome us back to camp when we drove in. I never saw Coop drink alcohol, but he was so happy to see us, if I'd had a bottle right then, I think he'd have lifted a glass with us.

When it wasn't snowing, we worked long hours, night and day, trying to make up the lost days. There were fourteen drivers, and we all lived in one great big tent. We built our own fires and carried water for the big round tub we shared for bathing, and no one ever complained. At first we had a little bootleg gin and green beer, but that ran out, and, with the road closed to Sonora, we just made the best of it.

Once after working until three in the morning, I slept in until about nine. When I climbed out of my cot, I noticed one of the other drivers asleep in his cot across the tent. I couldn't see who it was; he had his head buried in the blankets. I filled the tub with hot water from the big round stove in the center of the tent, stripped off my flannel pajamas, and settled in the steaming water. After half an hour, relaxed and content, I climbed out and began drying myself. I heard a movement and looked across the tent. The driver turned over, pushed the covers aside, and stared at my "nekkid" body. Only it wasn't another driver. It was a pretty woman. The wife of one of the drivers.

There were no tears when Otto yelled "Cut" and the cameras stopped rolling on the last scene to be filmed around the Dardanelles.

Charlie Barton, his voice rising above the commotion, called out, "Let's get the hell out of here!"

But it wasn't that easy. It took the State Highway Department two days to plow the roads. With half the trucks leading the way for the cars and buses, we made it.

It's been over fifty years since I last saw *Fighting Caravans,* but I still have fond memories of those months in the gold country. Many members of the company became friends and have remained friends throughout all my years in the business.

I remembered the beauty of the photography. Lee Garmes at his best. The battle with the Indians and the dangerous fire on the river, where Charlie Quirk and the other stunt cowboys put their lives on the line with horses through the raging, turbulent water. And the wagon train's struggle through the high mountain passes in heavy snow.

Still, it wasn't Gary Cooper's best picture. The scenes between Coop and Lily Damita lack the most important element needed to give life to a relationship, "charisma." Maybe Lily left her charisma in the gold country with Russ Harlan.

Chapter 7

Skippy

Late in January, I was sent to San Bernardino, where Norman Taurog was directing the film *Skippy,* starring two nine-year-old kids, Jackie Cooper and Bobby Coogan. It was a simple story of kids planning to stage a show, starring themselves and Mitzi Green, to raise money to buy a dog license for their pup.

We were working in the Mexican area known as Shanty Town. At the end of the second week the rains came, and the company moved back to the studio to shoot interiors.

The rain that came along with us as we drove from Shanty Town to the studio spoiled my plans to take my girlfriend, Mary Belle, to the beach in my Model A Ford roadster.

She said, "It's too cold and wet out there. Let's stay in and surprise Mom with dinner ready when she gets home. And surprise her more by spending the evening with her."

Her mother, Leona, a beautiful lady who worked as manager of a Van de Camp bakery, was not only surprised; she was shocked that we were actually spending the evening with her, not at the beach. Within a surprisingly short time, Leona retired. Mary Belle wanted to know all about Shanty Town and San Bernardino. Then she asked, "What about the hotel we're going to stay in?"

"Honey," I said, "we're not going to stay in any hotel. They wouldn't allow two unmarried kids to live together in their hotel. It's illegal."

Even in the dim light in the living room I could see the smile in her beautiful blue eyes as she said, "You can make it legal." I was stunned. I'd wanted to ask her to marry me for a long time but didn't have the nerve. Now I could stop worrying.

We talked about running away and getting married, but in the end I knew it would be unfair to her mother. I've never forgotten the moment we told her. Leona was preparing to wash the dinner dishes. Mary Belle and I were seated at the kitchen table. Mary Belle got to her feet and rushed to hug her mother. "Mom," she almost whispered, "Herbie has asked me to marry him. And I've told him I've been waiting for him to ask me." As her mother pulled Mary

Belle into her arms, I heard her say, "I've watched you and Herbie falling in love for over two years. I knew this day was coming."

We were married on St. Valentine's Day, February 14, 1931, at the St. Andrew's Presbyterian Church at the corner of Wilshire Boulevard and St. Andrews Place. I gave the rector his $2.00 fee, and with what we had left, we started on a two-day honeymoon in Tijuana. We only got as far as Long Beach.

I'd carefully swept all the rice from our Model A, but when I opened the door in the hotel garage, at least a pound of it fell around the shoes of the grinning garage attendant. I was a little nervous as I checked in, but I had our marriage certificate in my pocket in case the clerk asked any questions.

The next day we made it to Tijuana, stayed the two nights in the cheapest hotel we could find, and then drove back to Hollywood and our little room and bath I'd rented on a side street. No bedroom, just pull the bed down out of the wall.

The company went back to San Bernardino when the rains stopped, and the studio didn't object when I took Mary Belle along so we could continue our honeymoon.

Watching Taurog direct those two kids, especially Jackie Cooper, taught me a lesson in psychology I was able to use throughout my long career. He told the property man to develop a close friendship with Jackie. Within days, Jackie worshiped the property man, and any time during the making of the picture when Jackie became unruly, or Taurog wanted him to cry, he'd tell the man he was fired, to go back to the studio. The propman would get in a car and be driven out of sight. It never failed. Jackie would break into tears, and Taurog would get the performance he wanted from the nine-year-old child.

A couple of weeks after the picture finished shooting, Taurog invited everybody who had worked on the picture to a party at the famous Montmartre Cafe. It was one of Hollywood's most expensive restaurants with music and a bar and was always crowded with movie people who wanted to be seen by Louella Parsons.

The Montmartre wasn't serving Taurog's guests bootleg liquor. Everything was real. Scotch from Scotland, gin from England, and bourbon from the best Kentucky distilleries. Most of us had never tasted the real thing, and a lot of us were flying high when the Feds showed up. A white envelope was passed to each one of them, and they split. A pompous, self-important maître d' announced dinner and loudly ordered the bar closed.

Waiters began serving the first course. It was a round, pink disk. I recognized it instantly. I'd seen them in urinals in public restrooms. Most of us laughed and pushed them away, but some who had enjoyed the booze too much dug at them with their spoons, while the maître d' hopped around like a pouter pigeon, insulting us for refusing to eat what he called imported "Russian caviar." When he stopped by Bill Kubich, a man with the strength and body of a gorilla, he pushed the disk toward Bill and loudly ordered him to eat. We all knew that when Bill was drinking, one should walk softly and talk quietly around him. We held our breath, but Bill just turned away.

Later, after the "Russian caviar" had been taken away and a perfectly broiled steak had been served, the maître d' foolishly approached Bill just as he was raising his fork to his mouth with his right hand. The maître d' grabbed Bill's hand and shouted, "Didn't anybody ever tell you that you eat with your fork in your left hand?" He had barely finished the sentence when Bill grabbed him by his collar and the seat of his pants and was propelling the startled, screaming man madly across the floor toward the wide-open windows overlooking Hollywood Boulevard, twenty feet below. It took a dozen men to stop Bill. He really would have pitched him out.

Taurog joined the group and introduced the maître d'. "He's a famous 'court jester,' well known back east. I thought he'd keep the party lively. But not this lively. His name's Vince Barnett."

Chapter 8

A Climb up the Ladder

When I went to work on a warm July morning in 1931, I found out I was in the right place at the right time. An independent producer, Charles Rogers, and director, Harry Joe Brown, had arranged to produce a film, *Madison Square Garden,* using the old Paramount ranch out in the valley across from Warner Bros.

On the first day on the way to the location, a young man sitting beside me in the car held an open screenplay. It was filled with handwritten notes, numbers, and lines. I asked him what he did on the picture and was surprised when he said he was the script clerk.

That girl on *Wolf Song* was a script clerk. At last I had a look inside the scripts they used. The more I'd watched the girls work, the more I knew that job would let me learn how to make a picture.

The young man told me that there were other male script clerks and that studios were anxious to hire more. He said he'd had offers from most of the studios, including Paramount. They needed a man for the hard, dirty locations where girls didn't want to go. He said speed and accuracy in shorthand and typing were required, and a good memory sure helped. I could hardly wait to get home to give Mary Belle the good news. But what I found when I drove into the garage wiped those thoughts away.

Joe Robbins was leaning against the fender of one of the cars, a troubled look on his face as he spoke to the circle of men who worked for him. "What I have to tell you," he said, "makes me want to get out of this business. But if I don't tell you, the front office will find someone else to do it."

We waited for him to give us the bad news.

"You all know the studio is in serious trouble, financially. Every department has been told how many men they can keep and what they are to be paid."

Joe was a sentimental man, who considered every one of us a friend, and was having trouble hiding his emotions. "When I tell you what they've decided for us, you might say to hell with it and walk out. I won't blame you if you do." He looked us over and then read from the paper in his hand. "Cut your driver list to the bone. There won't be any more weekly employees. All drivers will be paid sixty cents an hour, with a one-hour guarantee. They must be available twenty-four hours a day. Those not responding to a call to work will be given demerits. Anyone accumulating twenty-five demerits will be fired." He crumpled the paper into a ball and threw it away. "This new policy goes into effect next Monday morning." He went back to his office.

Some of us were speechless, but a few blew up and called the ones who had set those rules every dirty name they could think of.

Mary Belle and I were barely keeping our heads above water on the $27.50 a week. She had an envelope for each of our monthly bills and would place the rent in one, the electric in another, and so on.

There wasn't a job to be found anywhere. I answered every call from the department. Some weeks I'd bring home less then $6.00 or $7.00. Then I might be lucky and make $15.00 or $20.00.

After trying to live under those conditions for just a few months, we'd had it, and with drivers from all the studios we formed the first drivers' union in the film business. We were accepted in the International Brotherhood of Teamsters, Chauffeurs, Stablemen, and Helpers, Studio Local 399.

With the powerful international union taking charge, the studios agreed to reasonable working conditions and wages.

For the first time in many anxious months, we felt we were again part of the Paramount family.

June 3, 1933, was a day Mary Belle and I had been praying for. She even more than I. I'd promised to be with her when the baby arrived. Fathers didn't usually stay with the mothers when the babies came back in 1933. But when she asked me to be there, I'd said yes.

And I kept my promise, yelling for the nurses and the doctor every time Mary Belle took a deep breath. The nurses tried to get me out of there, but I wouldn't go, and I watched our first baby join us. We named him Dale. He was to fill our lives for only thirty-nine years. I let my shorthand and typing cool while I tried to learn how to become a father.

On the job, I watched the miles build up on the odometer and told myself I wouldn't be behind that wheel when it turned the next thousand miles!

It was a cold evening in February 1934 when I got home from work. After dinner I got my notebook and sat down to start my shorthand lesson. Mary Belle just sat there rocking the baby and staring at me. I waited for her to start dictating. Finally, she said, "School's out. No more practice. Your shorthand's faster and better than mine."

We both knew it was time I made a move.

A few days later, George Arthur, head of the cutting department and script clerks, listened as I told him what I'd been doing to prepare myself for the job. He pulled a master chart from his desk, studied it, and then told me that all the films scheduled for production during the winter and spring were to be filmed on the stages and that his girls would handle those. But next summer things might be different. He told me to keep in touch.

It was May 9, 1934, late in the afternoon. I had just arrived at the garage, tired, sweaty, and dirty from a long drive in the high country. I went to the time clock to punch out and found a note asking me to come to Arthur's office. You can bet I wasted little time getting there.

Louise Woodcock, George Arthur's secretary, gave me a big smile and a friendly greeting and told me to go into his office. I went in and waited for George to finish a phone call. He swiveled his chair around and asked me if I was ready to join his girls' club.

I'd practiced over and over exactly what I would say when that moment arrived. And walking from the garage to his office I'd fought to remain calm, but when he asked me that question, I became a blithering idiot. In spite of that, George laughed, picked up a screenplay, and handed it to me. I looked at the title, *The Last Outpost.* It was written by Phillip MacDonald, Frank Partos, and Charles Brackett. At the bottom of the page, handwritten, was "Herbie Coleman."

As I stared at that page, my thoughts raced back to that day at Cliff Yard when I saw William S. Hart and the Indians on that bedsheet and I'd begun to dream. Now my dream had come true!

George brought me back to reality by telling me I'd have to pass a shorthand and typing test that Louise would give me before I could transfer to his department. He waved away my awkward expressions of gratitude and told Louise to give me the tests the next morning.

By the expression on my face, Mary Belle knew something important had happened that day. She demanded to know what was in the envelope I had in my hand. I gave it to her and watched as she pulled out the screenplay. When she saw my name written on it, her face lit up and her eyes filled with tears. "You did it! Three years with your face in a shorthand book, thinking and writing symbols, was worth it!" Three years and one night more.

At dawn the next morning, Mary Belle was still at it, reading the dialogue from the script for the umpteenth time while I sipped coffee and filled what I called my visual memory and my steno notebook with shorthand.

At nine o'clock, I was sitting in Louise's office. She was behind her desk, and I was seated at a little table near an open window with a cold breeze whipping the curtains past my head. I was nervous and tense. I could feel cold sweat on my face and hands. Louise had already tried to put me at ease. She opened her copy of *The Last Outpost* to the first page and was ready to start.

I stared down at the open book. I could see every line of dialogue on the first page in my visual memory, with the shorthand symbols swimming over the English words. I heard words come from Louise without realizing what she was saying.

Automatically, the shorthand symbols for the dialogue sped across the notebook. Then her voice began to register on my consciousness. Where did those strange words come from? Unfamiliar names like Mesopotamia, Euphrates. They threw me. They shouldn't have, but they did, and I stopped writing.

Louise looked up at me and said she thought a thimble of gin would steady our nerves. When she went into another room, I checked her script. She'd mixed up the location description and scene instructions with the dialogue.

While we sipped the four-ounce "thimbles" of gin, Louise told me to go to the stock room where a typewriter and other supplies were waiting. Come back, she said, and type what she'd dictated, and I'd be in.

I grabbed my notebook and got the hell out of there, fast.

At the property room, I had a friend dictate what Louise had read, and I calmly recorded it in my pad.

Years later, Louise and I were having a drink at Lucy's Bar across the street from the studio. I raised my glass and saluted her. "Louise, I cheated on that test you gave me. When you went for that thimble of gin, I stole a look at the script you were reading from."

"So," she said, "I saw you from the room. But all the girls wanted you to succeed. They would have killed me if I had said no."

Chapter 9

The Last Outpost

I could hear the laughter from the others in the car at script girl Nesta Charles's hilarious string of dirty stories. She was the first girl I ever heard tell dirty stories that didn't sound dirty. The next was Carole Lombard, and her dirty stories even sounded cleaner than Nesta's.

But the jokes just didn't register. From the moment I climbed in the car at the studio early that June morning in 1934, my mind raced from subject to subject.

Almost seven years driving others. Were they wasted years? Would I spend seven years as a script clerk before taking the next step up the ladder?

What a ribbing I took from the staff and crew when I walked on the set out on the sand dunes near Palm Springs. I'd driven most of them many times in the past, and they were friends. But they'd never seen a script man and couldn't resist the temptation to kid me.

The Last Outpost was a story of two British officers, Cary Grant and Claude Rains, and their men escorting an Armenian group across the desert of Mesopotamia. Rains saves Grant from certain death during a battle with a Kurdish tribe. While Grant is recovering in a Cairo hospital, he falls in love with a nurse, Gertrude Michael, who is Rains's wife. When Grant recovers, he and Rains are sent to destroy an enemy fort. Rains is killed in the battle. Grant and Michael get together again, and their affair resumes.

Charles Barton, a friendly young man who had worked his way up through the ranks at Paramount, was assigned to direct the film. Charlie had assisted "Wild Bill" Wellman on a number of films, and they had become close friends. To his credit, Charlie had not been influenced by Wellman's almost brutal treatment of so many of those who had worked with him.

Charlie's approach was exactly the opposite of Wellman's. He would suggest, rather than order. Actors would try almost anything to be chosen to work with him. So would staffs and crews.

As a friend, I knew I was lucky to be assigned to his picture. Conditions around Palm Springs were perfect for what Charlie had in mind. He was a realist, and with the cloudy days and the strong winds whipping sand across the dunes and into the faces of the stars, Claude Rains and a newcomer—the arrogant, egotistical, pompous, ever complaining Cary Grant—the picture began to take on the quality of a John Ford epic.

Charlie was forcing Grant to bend to his will, and it was evident that Grant didn't like that little man dominating him. He considered himself a star and had asked for a big name director on the picture, but was turned down.

He tried to get Rains to help get a new director, but Rains told Grant, "Don't try using me to solve your problems. I'm very happy with Charlie's direction."

As shooting continued and reports from the front office became more and more encouraging, Charlie realized that the executives were not aware of how Grant's subtle, insidious action was affecting the performance of Rains and others in the cast. It reached the point at which Charlie decided that, for the good of the picture, he or Grant had to go.

He couldn't ask the studio to replace Grant. He would have to retake every scene Grant was in. The New York executives would never approve the tremendous increase in the picture's budget.

In a series of late-night phone calls to the studio executives, Charlie convinced them they must send a new director to take over.

One morning, before the cast arrived on the set, Charlie told us about his talks with the studio. He said that he would be going home that night and the new director would take over the next day. He asked us to keep secret what he had just told us.

Grant must have wondered what had happened overnight. He was ignored by everyone. The wardrobe man was slow to bring his coat and just tossed it on his chair. Nesta was always preoccupied when he fumbled his lines and looked to her for help. It was the same with everyone: the propman, makeup man, and hairdresser.

But Charlie wouldn't give up. It was his last day, but he worked just as hard with Grant as he had the first day.

He sent Grant home early in the afternoon and then invited Claude Rains and the other cast members to join him in his hotel suite as soon as they arrived.

It was only then that they learned of his decision.

The next morning the sign on the parking lot for the company read "Parking for 'THE LAST OUTHOUSE.'" It was what we dubbed the picture that day, and we still call it *The Last Outhouse.*

The new director, Louis Gasnier, a man few of us had ever heard of, arrived. He was perfect for Cary Grant. He adored the tall, handsome English actor and fawned over him.

Filming continued, but it wasn't the same. The harsh reality of life in the desert and dangerous mountain passes lost its punch. Gasnier was clever. Over the objections of the cameraman, Theodor Sparkhul, he staged every scene to feature Grant, even when the scene demanded the focus on Rains, or one of the other actors.

Sparkhul was a German, with a long and distinguished record as a cameraman in Germany and in Hollywood. If he thought the light wasn't exactly right for filming, he would have the scene slated "Shot under protest." More often than not, those shot under protest turned out to be the best.

Finally, the picture limped to a finish.

I never saw the final cut of *The Last Outpost*.

One trade paper, the day after the preview, compared *The Last Outpost* with a roller-coaster ride: exciting highs and depressing lows. Uneven performances, especially from Paramount's newest hopeful, Cary Grant.

I don't have to tell you who directed the highs and who directed the lows.

Chapter 10

Desert Gold

Not every film I worked on as a script supervisor, our new title, from 1934 to 1942 was filled with high drama, stress, or both. There was one stretch during which each picture gave us a laugh or two.

In fall 1935 I was assigned to a new production with the title *Desert Gold,* loosely adapted from another of Zane Grey's many western stories.

Jimmy Hogan, a former Paramount assistant director, was being given a second chance to direct after letting alcohol ruin his first effort.

We arrived at the location for the first day's shooting at eight o'clock on the high plains, about ten miles southwest of Palm Springs. The weather was perfect. The sun shining bright. A deep blue sky without a single cloud to worry the cameraman, Georgie Clemens.

Jimmy, full of fire, paced restlessly as he waited for the cast to arrive. We were all pulling for Jimmy. We knew his future rested on the success of *Desert Gold.*

He saw actors Bob Cummings, Leif Erickson, and Marsha Hunt leave the car that brought them from the hotel and head for the coffee wagon. "Coffee has to wait, kids!" he called out. "We're ready for a rehearsal."

The opening scene was very complicated, and by the time Jimmy was ready to roll the cameras, a heavy cloud covered the sun, casting a shadow over the plains, the mountains, and the location.

We had a unit production manager who dreaded being assigned to a location picture where he might be forced to make a decision on his own. He kept looking up at that cloud, asking Georgie Clemens about the weather.

What could Georgie say?

So the unit production manager rushed the ten miles to the hotel, called the studio executives, and told them about the weather. They said, "Bring the company back to the studio."

He hurried back and gave us the news.

We loaded up and headed out. By the time we got to Palm Springs, the sun was shining. He called the studio again and was told to go back to the location. We repeated that routine all day without shooting a single scene.

But all wasn't lost. We had a long scene we could shoot that night. Food from the hotel was served about dusk, and then the crew began to build the track for the camera, but a sudden downpour forced everybody to run for cover.

Jimmy refused to join us. He stood there in the rain, watching his future drift away like the piñon leaves in the nearby stream.

Then lightning flashing across the sky and rolls of thunder in the distance strongly suggested we head for the hotel.

But Jimmy wouldn't give up. He got us together and laid it on the line. It was: Shoot the ten-page sequence in the rain, or have the production office report to the executives. "Hogan's first day was a total loss. Now you wouldn't want Josef von Sternberg to come and take over, would you?"

Leif Erickson spoke for all of us: "Rain, or crazy Joe? Who's afraid of a little water? Let's get on with it."

The scene involved Erickson, a rugged western rancher, and Bob Cummings, an eastern greenhorn, stranded in brush country while trying to rescue Marsha Hunt.

Erickson is cooking some grub in a large frying pan over an open campfire while Cummings stands guard.

Jimmy wanted to open the scene with a big close-up of the frying pan, but he couldn't because the rain kept filling the pan.

Then, as Erickson warns Cummings about a possible Indian attack, Cummings brags about his Virginia ancestors winning their Indian wars and boasts about how he'll destroy the Indian chief and his men if they show up.

The Indians, in full war paint and with war bonnets and feathered lances and tomahawks, appear from the brush behind him and sneak up on the unsuspecting greenhorn.

It was too much for all of us. Even Jimmy had to laugh. The yellow, purple, orange, and red war paint was a mess. It was running down their faces and mixing with the brown body makeup on their wet bodies. The feathers on the bonnets were hanging limply and dripping with water. When the laughter died down, Jimmy said, "Dry them off, paint them up again, and get under cover 'til the rain stops."

It did, and Jimmy was a happy and sober man when he went to bed.

The studio picked up his option, and we joined up on another film a few months later.

The good news about Jimmy's new contract was dampened by the word that reached us. The executives in the marble halls had promoted Richard "Dick" Johnson headman in the production department.

Johnson was the same man who demanded I drive him to the phone up at Sonora Pass on *Fighting Caravans* when he wanted to report that the man he claimed as a best friend, Sid Street, had wasted the studio's money by moving the company up into the snow.

When I got back to the studio, George Arthur gave me the bad news. Johnson had moved the script supervisors into his department.

Johnson didn't have the guts to call us in and tell us we were off salary until a director asked for us. He just posted a notice on the bulletin board.

I dreaded going home after reading that notice. But Mary Belle wouldn't let me see how hurt she was. She just counted the money she'd saved and said we'd make it somehow.

Chapter 11

Poverty Row

With the depression still on us, jobs were almost impossible to find around the studios. I didn't want to let a man like Dick Johnson end my eight-year career at Paramount.

I'd been without any income for about three weeks when I got a strange phone call. A man's voice asked if I was Herbie Coleman. When I said yes, he told me to be at the corner of Cole and Santa Monica the next morning at six o'clock. Same salary I got at Paramount. Without another word, he hung up. He didn't tell his name or what company he worked for.

I didn't really care. It was a job, and I was there before six. So was the rest of the small group standing on the sidewalk waiting for the bus to take us to the location where the company would be working that day.

I discovered I was working for Sigmund Neufeld Productions, a company rated at the bottom of the totem pole. But who cared? It made pictures. We all piled in the old rented bus—the director, Sam Neufeld, and his staff and crew. I couldn't believe it. A total of eleven people to make a picture.

I read the script that the assistant director gave me on the way to the location. It wasn't much. A story about a young cowboy who was accused of some crime. I don't remember what he'd done, but he has to hide out in the high mountains until his girlfriend rides in and tells him he's been cleared. The "high" mountain location was a movie ranch just off the old road to Simi Valley.

I don't remember the names of the actors who were playing the parts of the cowboy and his girlfriend. They were waiting in their own cars when the bus pulled to a stop. Everybody scrambled from the bus. Sam didn't seem to mind that the location was completely fogged in. He hurried through the brush to some large rocks and yelled for the propman to build a campfire there.

The first scene was the one in which the hero is on the lam and is hiding out from the law. While he is cooking some grub over the campfire, his girl rides in and tells him he can come home. Well, Sam doesn't waste any time. He points back into the fog and tells the girl to ride in from there. I'd heard sounds of horses but hadn't seen any. The girl disappeared into the fog.

Sam told the hero to squat down and start cooking. I didn't see anything in the pan for him to cook. I looked around for lights, but there weren't any. Sound and camera said they were ready. Sam yelled, "Action," and the girl appeared out of the fog almost on top of the hero. The girl wasn't a horsewoman. She jerked her skittish horse to a stop and just sat there looking at Sam. He yelled at her, "You're supposed to get off and go over to your lover!" Then he yelled to the cowboy, "Go help her off and bring her to the fire!"

The camera had continued to roll, and when the scene was finished, I waited for the soundman to say the sound was ruined, but no dice. And the cameraman didn't complain about the actors looking into the camera when Sam yelled at them. I was to learn a lot about making a film while working for Neufeld, which was sometimes funny but always bad. Sam had completed filming less than half the scenes around the campfire when the sun broke through the fog. I was sure Sam would retake the girl's ride in, but when I asked him about it, I found out I was there just to make notes for the cutter.

It was the same during the six days Sam had to make the picture. Nothing mattered. The actors had no interest in matching their action. Sam would tell them to enter or exit in the wrong direction. At least I made sure they were wearing the right wardrobe. That was easy. Nobody had a change of wardrobe. While we were shooting the third picture, Neufeld made a deal with the crew: "You speed up a little and finish these pictures in five days, and you can have the sixth off, with pay."

We found out later why he made us that offer. He was paying his star $1,000 per day, and if the pictures were made in five days instead of six, he'd save a cool $1,000 on each picture.

The funniest day's work was on the second picture. It had three sequences around a ranch house out on what the script called "the plains." We went to a location up in the rocky hills outside Chatsworth. There was an old farmhouse standing where some film company had built it years before. The yard was flat, hard dirt, and there wasn't a blade of grass or a bush anywhere.

Scene 1 was the hero riding in and finding his five brothers dead on the ground outside the house. As usual, everybody left the bus at a dead run. Sam picked a spot for the camera, showing the yard and ranch house. He yelled to the small group of cowboys, "Five of you guys stretch out on the ground in front of the house. You're dead, so don't move."

Then he told the hero, I think it was Tim McCoy, "Ride out there a ways until I tell you to stop. On action, gallop in, pull up, and look down at your five dead brothers. But don't get off your horse." Within five minutes the scene was in the can.

Scene 2 was a shot of the farmhouse being blown to pieces. It would be used in the middle of the picture. Sam didn't waste a second. He left the camera where it was, told Tim and the dead men to get lost. The propman got under the camera with a box of dirt, and as soon as the camera was up to speed, he threw the dirt up in front of the lens. That was the house blowing up.

Scene 3 was a new ranch house that was supposed to be where the blown up house had been. But Sam didn't change a thing. The same old farmhouse. Not even a coat of fresh paint. Same old hard dirt. And still no grass or bushes. And the camera was still where it had been all morning. He didn't even laugh when he told Tim and the girl, "This is after the ranch house was blown up and the new ranch house has been built."

He said to the girl, "Let me see tears in your eyes as you watch Tim mount his horse." It didn't matter to Sam. They would be tiny figures on the screen. He wanted tears.

"Tim," he said, "just tip your hat to her and ride away into the sunset." We were shooing the scene at high noon, and I couldn't keep from laughing at Sam's directions to the cast. He turned and glared at me. But who could expect Sam, whose total budget was $12,000, to care if he had the setting sun in the last scene.

I couldn't help but think what a laugh Mary Belle would get out of my description of the day's work. But when I got home, she was already laughing. Before I could say a word, she said, "Dick Johnson just called and said, 'Tell Herbie to report at nine o'clock tomorrow morning.'"

She dropped the telephone on the table as she said, "I didn't try to hide the joy I felt when I said to him, 'He's working.' Then I stood there waiting for Johnson to say something, but after a long silence he hung up."

After five more films, I was happy to leave Sigmund Neufeld Productions to take a job on a Howard Hughes epic, *The Outlaw.*

Chapter 12

The Outlaw

The story of Billy the Kid has been told many times by filmmakers but, I think, never so stupidly as Howard Hughes's potboiler.

While a parade of expensive writers gave Hughes their versions of Billy the Kid's escapades, Arthur Rosson, an old-time western director, a still photographer, and I toured Arizona, Colorado, and New Mexico, searching for the perfect Indian village Hughes had insisted he must have for his picture. Just outside the little Tuba City, Arizona, Indian trading post, we found the tiny Moencopi Indian village. It was perched on the rim of a ravine overlooking fields of maize. Its low, sun-baked adobe huts with walls of beautifully faded pink brought Art from the car, shouting to the still man to grab his camera while the light was just right on the village.

We had spent over six weeks covering the Southwest and arrived back at Hughes's headquarters with hundreds of color photographs. Hughes selected Moencopi and threw out the rest of them.

Howard Hawks had agreed to direct the film from a screenplay, written by one of Hollywood's top writers, Jules Furthman. Why he had agreed to waste his time trying to please Hughes was a puzzle to his friends, until they learned about the pot of gold Hughes held out to him.

Hughes spent many months, and another small fortune, searching for the girl he wanted for the part of the sexy native girl, Rio. The first time I got a look at her, I knew why he'd picked Jane Russell.

As soon as Russell was set, Hughes went to work casting what I guess he considered the minor roles. Walter Huston for Doc Holliday; Thomas Mitchell as Pat Garrett; and an unknown kid, Jack Beutel, as Billy the Kid. Hughes and Hawks agreed that a number of additional huts were needed for the Moencopi Indian village and sent cameraman Lucien Ballard along to supervise the painting on the new buildings.

When we arrived at our tent-city headquarters across the road from the Tuba City trading post, we found that Ballard had destroyed the beauty of the Indian village by having the painters cover the faded pink with a coat of whitewash. Only his close friendship with Hawks saved his job.

I was happy that Ballard would have nothing to do with our unit. We had our own camera crew, one that had worked with Arthur Rosson in the past. Dick McWorter was the first assistant director.

The second assistant director, the lowest spot on the totem pole, was a friendly, young man who had never been around a movie set. Watching him work, I could see he'd move up fast. When World War II started, he enlisted in the Navy and served his years in the Atlantic Fleet. When the war ended, he moved to London and formed his own movie company. He was the man who originated, owned, and produced the James Bond films: Albert "Cubby" Broccoli.

Anyone who knew Howard Hughes could have predicted what would happen to the picture by watching Hawks that first day. A stagecoach with a broken wheel stood waiting for repairs. Hawks, calm and relaxed, was listening to Tommy Mitchell and Walter Huston rehearsing their lines. He told them to forget the crappy dialogue in the script. His idea was to ad-lib it. The propman opened an elaborate gun case and asked Hawks which of the dueling pistols he should give to Huston.

"They wouldn't use those," Hawks said. "They're supposed to be real western gunmen. They'll use the guns they've got in their holsters."

When the propman told him Hughes bought the dueling pistols just for that scene, Hawks told him, in no uncertain terms, to forget it.

Art got tired listening to all that ad-libbing and took his second unit off some twenty miles to begin shooting the scenes we had on our schedule. Hawks continued his habit of rewriting and rehearsing and was falling days behind his schedule. He set the pace, and everyone else strolled along behind. We were becoming bored as the weeks dragged along. The weather changed, and we began to have a little snow.

One night, after a light snowfall had left a dusting of white on the sagebrush, Carl Coleman, the propman on our unit, and I went for a walk down toward Moencopi. A quarter moon, half hidden by a thin curtain of clouds, cast an unreal glow over the mesa. We stopped for a moment to enjoy the view and the quiet that surrounded us before heading back to our tent city.

Before we had moved 100 yards, we heard strange voices coming from somewhere in the distance. We listened for a minute or two and then decided to investigate. Crossing the mesa to the top of a small rise, we stopped and looked down on an Indian encampment. It belonged to the twenty Navajo Indian men and their families Art had hired in Window Rock to work in the picture. They had carved out a hole thirty feet in diameter and about four feet deep, with a smaller hole in the center. A blazing fire in the small hole cast moving shadows over the women and children who lay snuggled under handwoven blankets and sheepskins.

On the far side of the hole, three men sat beating time on handmade Indian drums. Around and around the encampment other Indian men danced a kind of shuffling dance while chanting and singing an ancient Navajo tribal story.

Watching that strange ritual gave me an uneasy feeling. In a whisper, I said to Carl, "Let's get the hell out of here."

It began to snow heavily as we made our way back to the camp. When we got up the next morning, a foot of new snow covered everything—the ground, the tents, and our cars and trucks; and all shooting was canceled. With a weather report promising more snow for the next three days, Hawks gave everybody a holiday. Cars and buses were available for trips to the Grand Canyon and Flagstaff.

One of the wranglers got a bright idea. He and some of his buddies loaded Jack Beutel's little strawberry roan into a truck, drove it into Flagstaff, stuffed it into an elevator just about big enough for three people, took it up to the top floor, and locked it in Hawks's bedroom. If anything had happened to that horse, we'd have been in big trouble. We'd never have found an exact double for it and would have had to reshoot every scene it was in. The horse had been leased from a big ranch in Oklahoma; and the cowboy who brought all the cast horses from that ranch was Ben Johnson. Hawks promised him a career in movies if he would stay in Hollywood. He stayed and became a star in the movie *The Last Picture Show.*

I'm sure you've all heard how stars claim that they do their own stunts. But Tommy Mitchell wasn't one of them. He was scared to death of horses and would absolutely refuse to get on one. But there was one scene for which Hawks insisted Mitchell sit on his horse for a short dialogue scene. They brought his tame stallion in before the cameras. Four wranglers got on the ground, and each held an ankle. One held the tail, and one held the bridle. Tommy gingerly climbed up a ladder and settled in the saddle. Hawks got the scene he wanted, but I'm sure some of Tommy's fear had to be seen and heard in the film.

Hawks continued to move along at his usual leisurely pace, without a thought about the schedule. There was talk among the staff and crew about Hughes's pride in his *Outlaw* script and about his demand that nothing be changed. We all wondered how long he would allow Hawks to continue.

Well, the "bell tolled" one Saturday night.

We, the Rosson Unit, arrived back at the camp just at sunset to find everyone gathered around the office tent. Hawks was on the phone with Hughes. From what we could hear of Hawks's conversation, Hughes wasn't a happy man. Neither was Hawks when he appeared in the door of the office. You could see he hated to tell us the bad news.

He told us that we had all been fired and that we were to have dinner, pack, and take the cars and buses to Flagstaff, where Hughes had arranged for a special train to be waiting to take us back to Hollywood. He added that Hughes had said that we were not to come to the Hughes offices. Our checks would be mailed to us. I thought that was the end of that. But I was to have second thoughts about *The Outlaw.*

I went back to Paramount and was assigned to a film to be called *I Met Him in Paris.*

Chapter 13

I Met Him in Paris

Paramount was recovering from years of poor business at its thousands of theaters and had decided that the world was ready for a bit of fluff.

Claude Binyon, one of Hollywood's finest comedy writers, had given director Wesley Ruggles a story about fun and games in the high Alps. The stars were Claudette Colbert, Melvyn Douglas, and a rising young star, Robert Young.

We were all loaded aboard a special train and sent off to Sun Valley, Idaho, where a typical Swiss hotel with an outdoor ice bar and skating rink had been built in a small, snow-covered valley. On the side of the mountain, rising high above the hotel, a string of chalets added reality to the film's atmosphere.

Averell Harriman was waiting at the Sun Valley Lodge to welcome us when we arrived. He had come to his newest playground to open the lodge for the first time.

Harriman, a man I learned to admire and respect, was the president and principal owner of the Union Pacific Railroad and was developing Sun Valley as a new resort. With air travel still a distant threat to the railroads, and skiing fast becoming winter's top sport, Harriman knew Sun Valley would be a financial success.

One of the assistant directors told us to wear our heavy clothes and go directly to the location to begin shooting in the morning when the train pulled to a stop at the end of the track at Ketchum, a little village just three miles from Sun Valley. But the snow was coming down so fast that we got in the cars and buses and headed for the lodge.

We sat around the lodge all day, waiting for the snow to stop. Late in the afternoon, Ruggles said to his assistant director, Artie Jacobson, "Forget it. We'll try again tomorrow."

We were to hear Ruggles repeat that order many times in the future.

The crews and some of the staff were sent to their quarters in Ketchum, and the supporting cast went to Hailey, a small town about twenty miles away.

The top brass, stars, and a few lucky ones, me included, lived in luxury in the lodge.

When it wasn't snowing, we'd slip and slide along the icy roads to the locations and wait for Colbert to come to work. It became an even money bet with few takers which would arrive each morning: Colbert or a note to Ruggles saying, "I won't be coming to the set today."

Sometimes, we'd find something to fill in the day—but always with a great loss to the schedule and the budget.

And that wasn't Ruggles's only problem with Colbert. He'd be rehearsing a scene with her, and she'd suddenly stop and want a change in the dialogue. She'd look around and ask, "Where's Claude?" When Ruggles would tell her Claude was working at the lodge, she would tell Ruggles she wanted Claude to make the changes.

There were no phones between the set and the lodge, so a car would have to go get Claude.

One day we were scheduled to film a scene in which Colbert, on skis, makes a sharp, fast downhill turn. A short section of a ski run was built on the side of a hill about 100 feet from the main road. The crew had to carry the heavy cameras, the giant arc lights, parallels, and other equipment across a field covered with three feet of snow to reach the set.

On that particular day, those of us who took odds that Colbert wouldn't show up had to pay up. Right on time, her car pulled up. She sat in the car watching the laborers shovel a path through the snow for her and then climbed out and joined Ruggles beside the cameras.

Colbert's double, an expert skier, was waiting at the top of the short run. Ruggles told her he was ready. Colbert watched the girl come slowly down the run, make the turn, and stop. Colbert turned to Ruggles and demanded to know why the girl was going so slow and what she was wearing on her skis.

Ruggles explained that he would speed up the scene with the cameras and that her skis would have skins on them so she'd be able to make the turn.

"Wesley," she said, "I'm supposed to be an expert skier. My character wouldn't wear skins on her skis." And without another word, she got in her car and went back to the lodge.

Then there was the scene at a ski hut on top of Dollar Mountain. The art director, moving the lumber, windows, and everything else up there on the ski lift, had built the set where Colbert has to walk to the door and go inside. Somebody made a mistake that would force her to show her "bad side." She absolutely refused to allow the right side of her face to be photographed.

Despite the long ride up the ski lift, Colbert was smiling and happy when she got off the lift and turned toward the ski hut. The smile disappeared instantly when she saw the entrance she would have to make. I didn't hear what she said to Ruggles, but I saw her get back on the lift and disappear down the mountain. We went back up after the entrance was changed and shot the scene.

Colbert was difficult for Ruggles, Leo Tover (the cameraman), and others; but for me, she was a dream. She was the only actor I'd seen in my short career who came on the set knowing every word of the dialogue. She had rehearsed every look, every movement of her hands and body, and how and when she used each prop. When she was in a scene with others, I could forget what she was doing and watch the others.

Bob Young was one of the others.

One day, we were doing a scene in which he, a novice skier, is trying to escape being run over by four Austrian ski instructors, who are speeding down the steepest of the runs; sweeping back and forth across the slope; making fast, dangerous turns; and dropping closer and closer to the ravine where Bob is hiding. As each would reach the rim of the ravine, he would jam his ski pole hard into the snow and would go flying over Bob's head. The last skier's pole broke, flew in the air, and landed with the sharp steel point sticking up. The skier, losing his balance, tumbled over and over and came down on the pole, the steel point tearing the flesh and driving deep into the bone of his leg. Somehow he muffled his scream of excruciating pain.

Forgetting that the camera was still turning, the company doctor and some of the crew ran to help the man. From somewhere, a long sled was pulled alongside the skier. He was gently lifted onto the sled and, with the ski pole still in his leg, slowly lowered to the bottom of the run where an ambulance was waiting.

It was almost a month before we saw him back on skis again.

Those Austrian ski instructors, whom Mr. Harriman had brought to Sun Valley from their homes in Eastern Europe, were all young, handsome, and blond. Groups of beautiful, wealthy, young socialites were always waiting for them to show up every morning. Even the ones who were already expert skiers insisted on private lessons on the slopes and on the dance floor at the lodge.

One night, Ernie Laszlo, Leo Tover's camera operator, and I went to the Alpine Casino to invest a dollar or two at the tables. After an hour or so of winning and losing a few bucks at blackjack, I joined

Ernie at the crap table. I was never very good at shooting craps, but when the dice came around to me, I dropped a dollar on the table and threw a seven.

After I'd made six straight passes, Wesley Ruggles joined the crowd that had gathered around the table to see when my luck would change. He dropped ten bucks beside my winnings and urged me to make another pass. He kept doubling his bets until the owner of the Alpine put a limit on his bets. He was making a killing, whereas I kept hedging my bets. When I made the thirteenth pass, I heard bets being made that I'd make the fourteenth. I didn't, but I became a celebrity.

Almost everybody in the valley knew my name, and many of them wanted to back me if I'd go back to the Alpine with them. Mr. Ruggles was one of them.

I have to tell you about one certain ride up to the top of Dollar Mountain.

We had a very early shooting call. I climbed on the chair lift at six in the morning. The lift rose higher and higher, passing over one gorge hundreds of feet below and approaching a peak that rose almost to the chair I was sitting on.

Before passing over the second deep gorge, I turned to my right and looked off toward Baldy Mountain, where only the most experienced skiers were allowed to go. The sun was just breaking into view through the mist rising from the valleys, casting a thin, pink glow over the vast snow-covered landscape.

Suddenly, I felt my script fall away from where I'd placed it on the lift. I looked down and saw it land on the mountain peak just three feet below. Already my chair was over the second gorge. I looked back and saw Bob McCrellis, the property man, slip out of his chair and land in the snow. He picked up my script and waited for the next empty chair to come to him.

During the short time it took for my chair to arrive at the end of the lift, thousands of thoughts raced around in my mind. What if the snow had slipped away when Bob landed on the peak, and he had been carried away in an avalanche to the bottom of the gorge? What if the script had fallen out over one of the gorges? There were no roads into the gorges, and my "Bible" would have been lost forever.

In that book, I had recorded every scene Ruggles had made during more than six weeks of filming: what the actors wore, where and when they moved, what they did with the props, what they were doing with their hands and bodies throughout the scene, on what line the camera moved, on what line it stopped, and the endless notes for the cutter—what scene number was given to what scene, where each take of each scene started and stopped, and much, much more.

The very cold weather gradually changed, and warm breezes from the south began to melt the snow. It became difficult to find locations that would match the countryside we had been photographing.

Ruggles finally gave up and moved the company to the studio, while the art director built sets resembling Sun Valley in an icehouse in downtown Los Angeles.

One night I received a call from Lee Murin, Howard Hughes's executive for motion pictures. He told me that he was anxious to have me rejoin the Hughes organization. He said I was the only person familiar with the film that Rosson's unit had made in and around Tuba City and that I would be doing them a great favor if I said yes. He offered to pay my full salary from the day I was fired in Tuba City. He apologized for saying "fired."

Chapter 14

The Outlaw—Again

I saw little of Hughes during the first few months. I wandered around the studio waiting for the picture to resume shooting. I discovered I'd been assigned to the second unit again, with Otho Lovering directing. I wasn't surprised that Art Rosson hadn't been rehired. After all, he was a close friend of Howard Hawks, which in Howard Hughes's mind made him an enemy.

Hughes showed Otho a photograph of the desert and hills near Red Rock Canyon, just north of Mojave. "Make a shot of Mitchell on his horse riding along the edge of that ravine. I want him exactly one mile away from the camera. Use a fifty-millimeter lens. That lens records exactly what you see with your eyes."

Otho gave me a sidelong glance. I knew what it meant. Who didn't know how to use camera lenses?

We made the scene with Lucien Ballard as cameraman. I wondered how he got his job back. I guessed it must have had something to do with his original contract. I realized that Otho didn't trust Ballard any more than I did when I saw him go to the camera and take a close look at the lens Ballard used.

We looked at the film a few days later. All we could see was the landscape. Not even a dot moving along the ravine. Hughes's only comment was, "Do it again but have Mitchell one-half mile from the camera."

Otho made up his mind that he'd get what Hughes wanted the next time we made that 200-mile trip to Red Rock Canyon. He ordered the special effects department to make a dust machine to attach to the horse's saddle. They did, and away we went. We made the shot from half a mile away and then attached the dust machine—a large drum full of fuller's earth with a hand crank and a long cloth funnel hanging down near the horse's hind foot. By double cranking the machine, the dust poured out and rose in the air. Otho grinned and said, "If Hughes buys that, we know what we can get away with from now on."

In the projection room, we waited for Hughes to shoot down the plan, but when he saw the shot with the dust machine, he turned to Otho and said, "That's exactly what I had in mind."

More boring days passed while we waited for Hughes to begin filming, with himself as director.

I'd always admired Hughes as an innovative designer and builder of new airplanes and as someone who always flew the planes he built before turning them over to his test pilots. But after a few days standing by on the set watching his performance as a director, I thought he'd better go back to his airplane business.

I felt he should have canceled the picture when he fired Howard Hawks. But he had Jane Russell, all the money in the world, and Greg Toland, one of Hollywood's finest cameramen, to help him stage the scene so the editor could make some sense out of what Hughes gave him. He also was saved by accepting the advice, reluctantly offered, by Walter Huston.

Hughes was never satisfied with a scene until he'd filmed it over and over. Huston never complained about the number of takes; but not Tommy Mitchell. He'd cover his irritation for a time, but as Hughes continued to say, "One more," Tommy's control would vanish. He'd stomp around the set until he'd finally explode, but he was too honest and too professional to do that.

There was a lot of unhappiness on *The Outlaw* set among the cast, staff, and crew. Everyone was ordered to be ready to shoot first thing in the morning. We'd sit around and wait for Hughes to show up. He'd usually march in at three in the afternoon, well rested and ready to go. But he was kind enough to let us go home around midnight.

He had the same concern for his girlfriend of the moment, one of Hollywood's top stars. She'd show up around six o'clock, all ready to join Hughes for dinner. He'd barely acknowledge her presence on the set. At quitting time he'd take her along to the projection room until three in the morning. Only then would his chauffeur drive them to one of his favorite restaurants.

If that particular star got tired of such treatment, she'd split. Soon another star, more beautiful and glamorous, would arrive to take her place.

It was easy to see why Hughes ignored those ladies. His attention was focused on Russell. When he was shooting the scenes between Russell and Beutel in the hay, he seemed to forget that Beutel was in the scene. He told Toland to feature her breasts. I guess he didn't trust Toland because he was always looking through the camera. I noticed that he had the camera pointing directly at her, what he was calling "the two most beautiful mountains this side of Everest."

Hughes knew what he wanted. He was after an angle to sell his "turkey" and had decided the right angle was Russell's body, especially the upper half of that gorgeous torso.

He hired Russell Birdwell to develop a national campaign featuring Russell's body. Birdwell came up with a certain attention getter: He issued press releases with a story about Hughes's latest invention, a cantilevered brassiere Russell was wearing in *The Outlaw.* He also announced that a patent had been granted to Hughes. Not satisfied with those bright ideas, he went further and bought space in newspapers across the country saying that the cantilevered bras were now available.

That scam sure got the picture the publicity Hughes wanted, and stores all over the country were flooded with girls asking for "Jane Russell cantilevered bras."

We had a lot of fun with that gag. Guys would steal their wives' or girlfriends' bras, rig them up with wire in all kinds of crazy ways, and hang signs on them: "Cantilevered bras." Word was soon passed around that Mr. Hughes didn't appreciate the joke, and that was the end of that.

Hughes and Birdwell decided to create interest in the film by using negative advertising. Birdwell leased giant billboards all across the country and plastered them with pictures of Russell in the most provocative poses. I remember seeing one of them. It was Russell lying, almost nude, in the hay.

It was 1946 when Hughes finally premiered the picture in Los Angeles, almost ten years after Hawks started shooting in the Moencopi Indian village in Arizona. And it was still a turkey.

Chapter 15

The Light That Failed

I was happy to hear that I was to work with William "Wild Bill" Wellman on one of Paramount's most important 1938 productions, *The Light That Failed.*

Robert Carson, a gifted Hollywood screenwriter, had given Wellman a script that faithfully followed Rudyard Kipling's novel, a tragic tale of a British soldier, Dick Heldar, wounded in the war between the British and the Muhammadan religious leader, Madhi, around Khartoum in the Sudan. Ronald Colman, who was cast as Heldar, returns to England, leaves the service, and becomes a painter. His portrait of a cheap London prostitute, Bessie Broke, played by Ida Lupino, is a masterpiece.

As a result of the wound he'd received, a saber slash across the face, he gradually loses his eyesight. Bessie, who has fallen madly in love with Heldar, realizes that she can never have him and, in a rage, destroys the painting.

The location Wellman chose for the Sudan was some thirty miles outside Santa Fe, New Mexico. Bobby Odell built a series of tents along the edge of the Pecos River.

I met Wellman for the first time when he arrived in Santa Fe to start production on the film. We weren't formally introduced. He just gave me a brief glance when his assistant director nodded toward me and told him I was his script clerk. I hadn't expected anything more. One of the other script supervisors who'd worked with Wellman said that he had little use for us. He considered us a necessary evil.

Wellman was impatient to get started, and as soon as we had checked in at the hotel, we headed for the location. On the way, he sat hunched forward, his eyes fixed on the road ahead. Not a word was spoken. I kept wondering why he was so tense.

His mood changed instantly when we pulled up on the small knoll that overlooked the Pecos and the encampment. We climbed from the car, and he surveyed the area, turned to the art director, Bobby Odell, and exclaimed, "Exactly what I had in mind, Bobby!"

Then he pointed to the figure of a girl, dressed in denims, a shirt, and boots, lying on the grass at the far end of the row of tents. "She's part of the set dressing, Bobby?"

He didn't wait for an answer and, with a grin, told us he was going down there and tell her she was going to sleep with him that night.

We watched him stalk down the path along the riverbank, lean over the girl, and say something to her. I could only guess what he'd said, but it startled her, and she jumped to her feet. She didn't run away, just stood there listening.

Finally, he walked away from her and waved for us to join him. When we got there, he said to his assistant, "She wants to be one of the horse wranglers. Put her on the payroll."

She went to work but not the way Wellman had expected. She exercised the cast horses. She had worked on other movies in the Southwest; and most of the wranglers and stuntmen were friends. Well, Wild Bill's plans for that pretty cowgirl went right out the window. Every time he went near her, some of the men would find some excuse to join them.

One thing I remember most about Wellman's method of directing was the difference between his driving force, which infected his entire company, and Ruggles's calm, almost casual, low-key leadership. Everyone on a Ruggles set respected that sophisticated gentleman and went about their duties, quietly and efficiently.

No one ever tested Wellman's authority. Most actors were scared of him. But all of them knew that a part in a Wellman picture was a shot at an Oscar nomination.

I began to realize that each director I'd worked with had special skills I should remember and serious faults I'd better forget when I became a director.

With only a week's work left for the first unit, Wellman announced that his assistant director, Joe Youngerman, would direct the second unit. I was surprised at his choice for such an important assignment. Joe had little or no experience as a director and, I felt, little imagination, something absolutely essential for such an important job.

I had another surprise coming. Youngerman went to Wellman and arranged for me to stay on the second unit with him.

I'd worked with Joe on some pictures in the past and had noticed his problems when he was staging action with the background people. He had trouble articulating his desires to them. I shouldn't have worried so much. Wellman had selected the finest and most daring stuntmen in the business, Cliff Lyons, Kenny Cooper, and a rising young daredevil horseman, Yakima Canutt, to do the dangerous stunts Bob Carson had outlined in his script.

Cliff had been working quietly with Kenny and Yak on plans for new, different, and more dangerous horse falls that would help Youngerman satisfy Wellman's appetite and, at the same time, line their pockets with folding money. Wellman got what he wanted, and so did the three stuntmen.

There was one scene in which they rode in as fast as their horses could go up a very steep hill. Near the top of the hill, the horses reared straight up and then fell over backward on top of the three men. One of the most dangerous stunts I ever saw.

We exchanged the Pecos for the studio, where Wellman was having his troubles with Colman. When I walked on the stage where Bobby Odell had built the drawing room set, I saw Wellman and Colman sitting together in the far end of the set. It was obvious that they were engaged in a serious argument. Colman was calm and composed; but Wellman, his jaw shoved close to Colman's face, was angrily telling Colman that he had made his decision and didn't want Colman to broach the subject again.

Ted Sparkuhl was sitting by his camera waiting for Wellman to finish his argument and get back to work. He told me that Colman had been pressing Wellman to dismiss Ida Lupino and replace her with Vivien Leigh; and Wellman had finally had it.

Ted shut up instantly as Wellman, ignoring my appearance on the set, dropped down in his director's chair, glared at Colman, and barked, "You've had your last rehearsal. Now I'm gonna take it."

He looked around the set and shouted, "Where's Lupino?"

She answered from a distance: "Right outside the door, Bill."

When she heard him call out for action, she entered and closed the door. One could see she had studied the girls who paraded along London's Curzon Street and Shepherd Market. Her makeup, hair, and wardrobe—in fact, everything about her—was the character Bessie.

As the long scene progressed, Wellman centered his attention almost entirely on Lupino. His eyes revealed his appreciation for the way Lupino was bringing life to the character.

"Print it!" he shouted, as he pushed himself to his feet and gave Lupino an affectionate hug. "Kid, you were perfect!"

Colman didn't like being ignored. He told Wellman he needed another take, but Wellman was already walking away with Lupino.

That was the first I'd seen of Wellman directing a woman; and it made a lasting impression on me. It was hard to believe that a roughneck like Wellman could hide the fact that he was deeply sentimental.

I walked on the set one day and found him sitting alone in the dim light, reading one of the bound volumes that Odell had used to fill the shelves of the library. When he saw me come in, he tossed the book on a table and walked into his stage dressing room. I picked up the book and was surprised to see that he had been reading Elizabeth Barrett Browning's poems, *Sonnets from the Portuguese.* If I'd told people back then that Wild Bill Wellman read love poems, they would have said I was crazy.

The next day started with Wellman joking with the staff and crew while waiting for Colman to show up. When he walked in, things changed. He argued with Wellman about everything: The dialogue needed a rewrite. Wellman would approve a scene, and Colman would say he needed another take. He'd stop in the middle of a scene, saying somebody had moved around the camera and distracted him. "I can't play a blind man with people running all over the place!" he would complain.

One day he said he couldn't go on unless something was done to prevent the distraction; so sheets of black cloth were hung around the set, from each side of the camera to the corners of the set. Only Wellman, Ted Sparkuhl and his crew, and I were in Colman's sight.

The only relief from that nightmare was the day I had to rush from the set to be with Mary Belle for the birth of our first daughter, Judy.

Wellman didn't try to hide his dislike for Colman, and the atmosphere on the set became almost unbearable at times. I wasn't unhappy when the picture was finally completed.

I read a review of *The Light That Failed* years after it was released that said something about Colman being a gifted artist. I wouldn't argue with that. He was a gifted artist, but he was also the most insecure actor I've ever worked with.

Ida Lupino walked into *The Light That Failed* almost unknown, at least I'd never heard of her, and walked out the last day a star.

The weeks with Wellman were weeks spent learning how to produce a movie. How a talented director, with a vivid imagination and unlimited vision, could bring the written word to life on the screen.

I didn't know that day when Wellman called "Cut!" for the last time on *The Light That Failed* that my next assignment would be a six-month vacation with pay.

Chapter 16

Reap the Wild Wind

Art Rosson and I had continued our social contacts following his dismissal from *The Outlaw,* and we were both pleased that we were to work together again. This would be our third film. I'd met him for the first time on the train en route to Wyoming and Montana for DeMille's *The Plainsman.*

Five members of our small second unit, including the cameraman, Dewey Wrigley, and I were playing poker. I was having one of my rare winning streaks when a slender, gray-haired man, wearing white silk pajamas, came out of his drawing room at the end of the car. I was the only member of the crew who didn't know Art. Dewey introduced us and asked him to join in if he wanted to. He wanted to and took little time teaching me a thing or two about the fine points of the game.

Even the second unit of a DeMille epic was a giant, expensive undertaking; and *Reap the Wild Wind* would set a record. Our schedule would take months to complete and would have us traveling all over the United States. Plane travel was rare back then, but I didn't care. I loved riding trains. The first location Art had selected was at the Azalea Gardens in Charleston, South Carolina. He'd been told to come early because the blossoms were fading fast. But *Reap* (nobody wanted to use the whole title for the next six months) wasn't getting off the ground very fast.

DeMille was determined to make it the most lavish of all his blockbusters. He was telling everyone, especially the newspapers, that *Reap the Wild Wind* would be his and Paramount's 1940 Academy Award winner.

Only one thing prevented us from leaving for the Azalea Gardens: the money to pay for DeMille's expensive spectacle.

Would the executives at Paramount's New York office approve of DeMille signing seven of Hollywood's highest-paid stars? Designing and building expensive sets, including a sunken sailing ship with a dozen of the most expensive Oriental rugs in its hold, which would be ruined by the salt water? And there was the giant twenty-foot mechanical squid that had to be designed and built to operate by remote control deep under the ocean surface. Also, the quartet of DeMille's favorite writers, Jeanie Macpherson, Alan LeMay, Charles Bennett, and Jesse Lasky Jr., who had dreamed up the idea of trapping John Wayne and Ray Milland in the hold of the sunken ship, plus a few other incidentals: such as the locations all around the country, the costs of staffs and crews, and the always bloated overhead.

DeMille had a real strange contract with the studio. He and the board of directors would agree on a budget. Whatever he spent over the budget figure, he had to pay for out of his own pocket.

DeMille had a man, Eddie Salven, who was an expert at hiding fat in the budget. But Paramount had its own experts who could sniff out every shred of pork. They would play their game of hide and seek until somebody gave in, and the budget would be approved.

We were waiting for the news in Art's office. He was grinning when he came through the door. "You all better go home and pack. We leave on the Southern Pacific, eight o'clock tomorrow morning."

It was almost two in the afternoon when we arrived in Charleston. We checked in at one of the finest hotels in that part of the country, grabbed a quick lunch, and headed for the Azalea Gardens.

The custodian in charge of the gardens was waiting when we arrived. He told Art that he was afraid we'd arrived too late because most of the blossoms were gone. Then he led us inside.

I stopped and let my eyes wander around what Art had described as "a floral wonderland." It was a floral wonderland. Long shallow moats of still water, reflecting a deep blue sky, dotted with pure white marble-like clouds, separated narrow fingers of land covered with what looked like a solid mass of soft pink azaleas. But the picture was flawed by dead and dying azalea blossoms. The pink had turned to a dirty brown. One large bush just across the nearest moat had lost all its blossoms. They littered the bank and floated on the blue water.

"You're right," Art told the custodian, "we are too late. But maybe we can still find azaleas somewhere else."

When we arrived back at the hotel, Art asked Andy Durkus (the production manager), Dewey Wrigley (the cameraman), and me to meet him in his room in an hour.

He was hanging up the phone as we joined him. He told us he had just been talking to the manager of the Paramount Theater in Atlanta. He told Andy he might have found a way to save the Azalea Gardens. The manager said that there was a company in Atlanta, famous for its artificial flowers, that might be able to provide us with all the blossoms we'd need. "I told the manager you'd be in his office at eight tomorrow morning, Andy. He'll take you out to the factory. Buy all he has and get back here as fast as you can." Andy told Art he didn't even know where Atlanta was or how to get there.

"You'll find a way, Andy. Besides, I hear the grits are great down in Georgia."

Andy left the room in a hurry. He was back two days later with four big boxes of beautiful pink crepe azaleas. With Art leading the way, everybody pitched in, and before dark every bush near the camera looked like the pictures the custodian showed us of the garden at its best.

While we were tying the fake blossoms on the bushes, and the painters sprayed the bushes in the background with pink watercolor, we made sure no pictures were made. If DeMille should find out what we'd done, he'd cancel the picture and wait for the next season. DeMille saw the film and said, "I've never seen the Azalea Gardens look more beautiful."

The weather and the Charleston city officials gave us complete cooperation during the days we were filming in and around the city.

Then, with just two days remaining on our Charleston schedule, Art led us to one of Charleston's most beautiful areas. The Ashley River bordered a long street on one side. On the other side, a high wall, running the full length of the street, partly concealed expensive colonial homes. Their upper verandas looked colorful, with hanging baskets of flowers in full bloom, overlooking hidden gardens.

But Dewey was unhappy. He told Art he couldn't handle that bright southern sunlight on the street and walls. He suggested painting shadows with black watercolor.

The city told Andy that it was okay but to wash it all away when we finished shooting. He sent the painters into the city for the paint while we moved to another location.

Art had an uncanny ability, which DeMille had long recognized, to capture on film the true atmosphere of any time in history. That was why, I think, he had planned to film some scenes around the Two Meeting Street Inn at South Battery Park. That famous old colonial home was built in 1890 and is still one of Charleston's most admired landmarks.

Early in the afternoon we went back to the first location and found that the painters had used heavy black oil paint instead of watercolor. Andy went crazy. He fired the painters and told them to get out. The paint wouldn't dry, so we were through for the day. We were back on the street at dawn and completed two days' work in one day. We packed our clothes and left that beautiful city on the first train to Savannah. We left Andy behind to tell the city officials how he was going to restore the area to its original condition.

Our next stop was Miami. We stepped off the Atlantic Coastline train in unbearable heat and humidity. We knew we didn't want to hang around that city under those conditions, so we headed straight for the Hialeah Race Track. One of the features of the track was its infield, where large flocks of flamingos lived.

The script called for some shots of flamingos in their native habitat. An art director from the studio had changed the infield to a reasonable likeness of a jungle area where wild flamingos might nest.

The birds ignored us while we ran around with the cameras and shot everything Art wanted. The moment he okayed the last take, we climbed into the cars and headed for Key West. Our driver turned out to be a native Key Wester, living and working in Miami. He was happy to be going home for a few days. When he discovered that we were making our first trip to his city, he began a running commentary: "Lucky 'yawl' don't come to the Keys a couple of years ago. This 120-mile bridge wasn't finished 'til last year."

We were standing outside the hotel at dawn the next morning waiting to photograph the sun rising out of the waves of the gray Atlantic. But the mist wouldn't go away, and by the time the sun broke through, the dawn effect we needed was long gone.

We had to try to get that shot for the next five dawns, before the mist came along and we got a sunrise that Art said, "Even C. B. might like."

The scene showing the sun setting in the emerald green waters of the Gulf of Mexico with the actors moving about in the foreground was easy. Key Westers, or whatever they call themselves, claimed that the sunsets seen from Key West were the most beautiful sunsets in the world. I had to agree until I saw the sun set in the Arabian Sea, with the Chinese fishing nets ballooning high above the shore at Cochin, one of the most colorful seaports in Kerala, India.

We finished our work in and around Key West and headed out on the Overseas Highway for the mainland. Cars were waiting for us at the station in New Orleans, so we drove directly to New Iberia. A light rain was falling as we drove down a tree-lined street of that beautiful little city to the Fredrick Hotel that would be my home on *Reap the Wild Wind.*

The *Reap* script called for scenes of the flamingos returning to their nesting places in the evening. We couldn't film that action at the Hialeah track. Someone had suggested Avery Island near New Iberia.

The word was that we'd find the biggest flock of flamingos this side of South Africa. We should have gone to South Africa for the flamingos and to Avery Island for the azaleas.

Early the next afternoon we went to the island, where an official of the Avery Island Company met us and led us to Bird City. On the way, we went through the Jungle Gardens, with its forests of dogwood in full bloom, stands of magnolia, live oak, and giant timber bamboo from China. The official pointed to the fields of papyrus from the Nile Valley, camellias from Japan, and holly from England. But for me, the highlight of the drive was the azaleas: "30,000 plants!" the man said. Dewey wanted to reshoot everything we'd filmed at the Azalea Gardens in Charleston.

Our still photographer had a field day. We almost had to drag him away when our guide suggested that we get along to Bird City. We climbed out of the cars at Bird City, where more than 100 giant, white birds were resting in the tall trees ringing the lake, where others stood in the water on spindly legs.

Art turned to the guide and asked, "Where are the flamingos?"

"There are no flamingos on Avery Island, Mr. Rosson. This is a sanctuary for snowy egrets. Shortly after sunset you'll see thousands of them coming home from their feeding grounds."

Art turned down the guide's offer to take us on a tour of the Tabasco factory and the salt mines. We watched him drive away. I then stood around wondering what we should do about the flamingos. Finally, Art made his decision: "C. B. bought the fake azalea blossoms, maybe we can fool him with the egrets. We'll give it a try. If we don't get away with it, we'll have a long rest on the boat to South Africa."

Long before sunset, Dewey had the cameras in place, and we settled down to wait for the birds to pour in. But they didn't pour in. Now and then small flights would circle in and land in the trees. Dewey began pacing around, watching the sun dropping lower and lower, checking the light with his meter. In disgust, he told Art, "That's it. I can't get an exposure. Wrap up the cameras, boys."

As I climbed out of the car at the hotel, I noticed a wide smile had replaced the glum expression Art had on his face when we left Avery Island. He invited us to join him for a drink in his room. We wasted no time getting there. I knew he'd found a way to get around the egret problem, and I couldn't wait to hear it. He refused to tell us anything until we'd all been served; then he held up his glass and said, "To a double whammy on C. B. We'll shoot the egrets leaving the sanctuary. With the sky filled with all those birds, none of his yes-men can point at the screen and yell, 'Look C. B. They're not landing. They're flying away.' And even C. B. won't know we shot it at dawn."

We were ready and waiting when the boss egret quacked, "I'm hungry! Breakfast time!" And away they went. We got everything we wanted and were out of New Iberia on the Southern Pacific the next morning.

When we got back to the studio, DeMille gave Art a painting done by his art director, Roland Anderson. It was a picture of a sailing ship, *The Southern Cross,* tied up at a dock with slaves loading cargo aboard. *The Southern Cross* was some 170 feet long from bowsprit to stern, with masts almost as tall. In the foreground was a small wooden office with slaves moving around between the office and the ship. "When you shoot the loading of *The Southern Cross,*" DeMille said, "copy Roland's painting."

We all knew what DeMille meant when he said to "copy Roland's painting." He meant every detail. The distance from the office to *The Southern Cross.* The ship from stem to stern. The top of the masts. The clothes the slaves wore. Everything.

There wasn't a harbor from San Diego to Santa Barbara where we could stage that scene. None of the piers was long enough or wide enough.

Art finally settled on a lumber company's dock at Wilmington, near San Pedro. The workers cleared away their lumber. Art placed stakes indicating the stern and the bowsprit of *The Southern Cross* and then started walking backward, looking through a camera finder. He backed into the fence between the dock and a main Wilmington street and still couldn't see both ends of the ship.

"To hell with Roland's painting," he said. "C. B.'ll scream when he doesn't see the whole ship and the top of the masts. Well, we'll do it here and be off somewhere else when he sees the film."

We made the mistake of being on his set when he came from the projection room after seeing that scene. He was almost running as he came through the stage door and yelled for Art. As he reached the camera, the chair boy made sure his high stool was under DeMille's butt as he sat down without looking. And the mike boy had the mike at DeMille's mouth before he could utter a word.

Most of the people who worked with DeMille would disappear when he was abusive. But not Art. He walked up to DeMille and asked, "You wanted to talk to me, C. B.?"

DeMille held up Roland's painting. "What happened to the rest of the ship and the masts that are on Roland's painting?"

"There isn't a dock in this area large enough to shoot the scene exactly as the painting," Art calmly answered.

"Well, go find one or build one. You understand me, don't you?"

Art didn't bother to answer him. He just sauntered away.

The front office asked Art to keep stalling. When the picture got over budget and DeMille discovered he'd have to pay for retaking the scene, he decided he liked Art's scene we'd shot at Wilmington.

Our unit was scheduled to stage all the scenes inside the holds of the sunken ship, using doubles for John Wayne and Ray Milland.

The sets were built in a tank at Malibu Beach, and we went into action. Art would spend a day rehearsing the doubles in their diving suits with Curly Linden, the camera operator, in his diving suit watching through his underwater camera. When all the bugs were worked out, we'd all go home while the special effects crew spent the night filling the tank with water from the Pacific Ocean. It was slow going. We discovered that the movement of the doubles was entirely different when they were working underwater from their movement with the tank empty. So was the camera.

We lost the entire first shooting day. Dewey Wrigley had ringed the catwalk around the top of the tank with giant arc lights to light the set below. But he didn't know that the beams from the arcs would bend at the surface of the water and miss their targets.

The studio lost the entire day, but we didn't. When the doubles were told that they were finished for the day, they went diving for lobsters. All of us went home that night with sacks of lobsters. It became a daily routine.

Overnight, large plate glass windows were put into frames and floated on the surface of the water. That solved Dewey's lighting problems.

Then he found that he had a bigger problem he couldn't lick. Unless the sun was shining to reflect the blue sky on the water, the water would be an ugly gray and we'd have to sit and wait. We waited a lot more days than we worked.

But that was a minor problem compared with what we encountered when we started shooting the scenes with that squid. We went through the same routine. Dry tank rehearsals with the squid and the doubles. The squid worked pretty good while it was dry, but fill the tank and start cussing.

Then came the day we were scheduled to shoot the scene in which the squid's arm was supposed to move in, wrap around the ladder (stairs), and break it away, leaving Wayne and Milland trapped in the hold of the ship.

Well, that damned stubborn animal refused to do the scene, wet or dry. For two days I watched the special effects men try again and again to make it work.

I began to wonder why Art or Dewey didn't try doing the scene in reverse. What we called "back-cranking." Wrap the arm around the ladder, start the cameras, and pull the arm away. What the audience would see was the arm going in and wrapping around the ladder. I thought maybe the cameras wouldn't work that way. I was afraid I'd show my stupidity if I suggested they try it, so I kept my mouth shut. I waited a while and then joined Art and Dewey and timidly asked if that wouldn't work.

They turned and stared at me for a moment and then looked at each other and started to laugh. I felt my face begin to burn with embarrassment. "Why in the hell didn't I think of that?" Dewey asked himself. "We've done these kind of things that way a thousand times!"

It worked the first time we tried it. DeMille was so pleased with the result that he gave Russ Brown, the head of special effects, one of his prized Jefferson half dollars, something he gave to those who did something great for him. And Russ Brown wasn't even on the location when the scene was filmed.

We'd had it with the foggy June days. Sitting around, day after day, waiting for the sun to break through. We even got tired of "cutthroat hearts." But, weeks behind schedule, we walked away from that tank and that squid happy that it was over.

I wasn't happy with what I learned when we got back to the studio that night. "DeMille wants the second unit to stand by for a few weeks."

I knew what that meant. I would have to sit around on the stage watching that self-appointed King of Hollywood abuse everybody on his set who was less wealthy and lower on the social scene than himself.

My friend and longtime assistant, Clem Jones, told me of a nasty scene in Florida when he was on the DeMille picture *The Greatest*

Show on Earth. They were shooting in a very large circus tent filled with tourists and local people, who the Paramount publicity department had enticed into showing up to see Jimmy Stewart, Betty Hutton, and the other stars.

DeMille had finished a rehearsal of a scene. Everyone was waiting quietly for him to start shooting. Suddenly, Clem was startled to hear him call out, "I want every assistant director I have to line up around the track."

Clem said, "Not me. Not in a hundred years! I'd heard him too many times. So I stayed right where I was and watched those poor bastards march out there to be shamed by that egotistical exhibitionist."

DeMille asked his audience to take a good look at those men who called themselves assistant directors. In a voice dripping with contempt, he told his embarrassed audience that it was no wonder he had to do everything himself. Then he ordered the men to get out of his sight. He was always at his abusive best when strangers were around.

I saw an example of how he operated when I was standing by on his set during the filming of *The Plainsman.* The scene was staged in a military barracks. Word had come to the cavalrymen to pack and get the hell out, fast.

Eddie Salven, DeMille's trusted assistant, had rehearsed the actors, giving each of them bits of business to create that scene of danger. A group of distinguished business executives, on a tour of the studio, arrived on the set just as DeMille came from his dressing room and told Salven that he was ready to see a rehearsal. The rehearsal had barely gotten under way when DeMille jumped up and rushed into the set, screaming at everyone, "Hasn't anybody read my script? You're supposed to be trying to get out!"

He shoved the mike boy, who had just gotten to his side and was trying to put the mike in place, into a corner, picked up a bedroll and threw it across the set, and picked up another and threw it in another direction. "There! That's what I want! Action! Now let me see some action!" I saw him take a look to see how the business executives were reacting to his direction. The chair boy was quick to slide his stool under DeMille's fanny as he sat down beside the camera, without bothering to check to be sure it was there.

I had only one encounter with C. B. DeMille. Because I was the script supervisor on the second unit of *Reap the Wild Wind,* I couldn't refuse to be on the set when DeMille shot the close-ups of Milland and Wayne in the hold of the sunken ship.

The first scene was a close-up of Milland, standing beside the stairs that the squid had torn away. Before DeMille arrived on the set I had the special effects men place a tangle of air hose in exactly the position they were in, to match the second unit work. That was one of my responsibilities.

DeMille arrived at the camera, and the chair boy and the mike boy went into action. He took one look at the set, reacted to the air hoses, and loudly, over the mike, demanded to know what they were doing there. I told him they matched the second unit shots. He gave me a dirty look and said he was directing actors, not air hoses, and ordered them taken away.

I walked off the set and never worked on a DeMille picture again.

Chapter 17

Safeguarding Military Information

In 1940 I was working on a forgettable low-budget film on one of the Paramount stages when one of the assistant directors, Joe Youngerman, walked in holding up a thin script. He told me he was going to direct his first picture and asked me to read the story he held in his hand.

After dinner I sat down and looked at the title page. It read *Safeguarding Military Information,* written by Preston Sturges. It took me less than ten minutes to read what was supposed to have been written by one of Hollywood's finest screenwriters. But I could tell it wasn't Sturges's work.

The story opened with Walter Huston, in the uniform of an Army major, standing by a desk in a large auditorium. Facing him were a couple hundred young men. And thirty-six pages later, it closed the same way.

In between were shots of the soldiers and shots of Huston droning on about the danger of revealing military secrets.

How could the government approve such a hopeless script? Hadn't Joe read the material before he accepted the assignment? If he did, I asked myself, how could he fail to see that those young boys—ordered to report to the projection room after a full day crawling through mud, water, and dirt, climbing walls, and running miles through brush and over mountains—would be asleep on their feet, with the message floating unheard, high over their heads?

When Joe came in the next morning, I handed him the script and told him he'd better get out of that assignment.

He felt I was wrong. After all, he said, "Washington had approved the script."

I finally asked him if he knew why they wanted it made into a movie. He was a little put out at the question. "Of course," he said, "they want the soldiers to see the danger."

"That's the point, Joe. They want the soldiers to see. If you make this, they won't see. And they won't hear either."

I waited for his reaction and then made him an offer. "See if you can get the office to replace me for the few days left on this turkey.

I'll write you a script you can direct. One I guarantee the government will be glad to approve."

I got the relief and went to work. Joe read the first two pages, came into my office, and asked me to let him share writer's credit. "No way," I told him. "That's all my work."

Four days later I handed him a new script with the opening and closing scenes very much like those in Sturges's script. I used a few shots of Huston and the draftees. Then I wrote scenes showing military men in various situations, carelessly revealing secrets that are overheard by possible spies. Huston's voice covers the scenes.

I stayed on the picture as the script supervisor.

I didn't believe Sturges had written the script that bore his name. I was to find out, fifty years later, that he had written a memo about writing it, claiming that he had participated in the shooting of it and that he had included some of his own experiences in the movie. He never appeared on the sets during the five or six days we were in production. And every scene, with the exception of those in the auditorium, was mine.

I was astonished that he had made those claims. He was at the height of his career at that time, in demand at every studio in town.

Although that was the first script I'd ever written, I never considered it a big deal and never included it in my résumé.

The last official government production I was involved with was one on conservation. I don't remember its title, but I do remember who starred in it: Robert Benchley. I was familiar with Benchley's style, and when I read the script, I was sure he'd written it himself. So I told myself to leave it alone. I enjoyed watching him ad-lib his way through the picture. I gave up trying to correct him when he changed his dialogue. His ad-libs never lost the importance of the message he was determined to deliver to the American people.

Chapter 18

Beau Geste

I had a big smile on my face as I walked into George Berthelon's office. He looked up at me, handed me a new screenplay, and said, "This'll wipe that smile away."

When I saw the title, *Beau Geste,* and Wellman's name as director, I wanted to throw the script in the wastebasket.

"Read that, then take a look at the *Beau Geste* the studio made in 1925. Bill Wellman's going to produce and direct a new version, and he's agreed to stick close to the original version. You'd better keep notes on what you see. You know Wellman. He'll expect you to know that picture like the back of your hand."

I ran the silent *Beau Geste* four times. It was an exciting film, and Ronald Colman stole the show. But I missed his great voice. Ralph Forbes made a very good John Geste. I was never a fan of Neil Hamilton, who was the third brother, Digby Geste.

Wellman's Gestes would be three of my favorite Paramount stars: Gary Cooper, Ray Milland, and Robert Preston.

"You're disappointed with the assignment?" George asked. "I thought Wild Bill was your favorite director. Anyway, you must be his favorite. He asked for you."

I knew I had to take the assignment. Jobs were scarce at all the studios, and I might be out of work if I refused to work with Wellman again.

So I just followed orders and left the studio with the rest of the gang in a convoy of cars, buses, and trucks for the location in Arizona.

How different that trip toward Yuma was from the drive along the same road in 1926, when I was on my way to Hollywood. I was riding in the backseat of a new Packard sedan, instead of the backseat of that 1922 Model T Ford. But I did miss the roller-coaster feel of the old plank road.

We turned off the highway onto a road leading up and over high sand dunes into a flat sand area called Buttercup Valley. The road ended at a large encampment established by the Anderson Boarding and Supply Company.

The tent city was laid out in the shape of half an old wagon wheel. The hub was the office, dining, projecting, and recreation tents. The spokes leading away from the hub were streets lined with tents for Wellman, the stars, other cast members, the staff, and the crews. Farther along were large tents for the extras and equipment.

Bill Anderson greeted us when we filed into the dining room. He knew many of us from previous locations, and he never forgot a name.

At a table near the center of the room sat Gary Cooper, Brian Donlevy, Ray Milland, Robert Preston, J. Carrol Naish, and Brad (Broderick) Crawford.

Wellman was surrounded by Joe Youngerman (his assistant), Ted Sparkuhl (his favorite cameraman), and Charlie Barton. Charlie had been Wellman's assistant before moving up to director. And Wellman had cast Charlie as the comic character, Paddy McDonigal. We were all happy Charlie was on the picture. With his wry sense of humor, he could, with one word, save anyone from a Wellman tongue-lashing.

Each department had its own table. The production staff invited me to join them. We gorged ourselves on Anderson's usual offerings of platters of thick, juicy steaks, New York or T-bone, roast prime ribs, vegetables, salads, and giant bowls of ice cream, pies, and cakes, all made in their kitchens.

It was a fun evening. Many of us had worked together on other pictures, and most of us had struggled to keep our heads above water during the depression. We were happy to be employed again.

Even Wild Bill had a slight smile on his face. We wouldn't see him smile many times after that first night.

Out of sight, behind some high sand dunes, Bobby Odell had built Fort Zinderneuf and a small oasis of foam-rubber palm trees. It was a hard fifteen-minute climb through soft sand to the fort.

We faced many problems during the days we were in production. With the taste of Bill Anderson's rare prime ribs and chocolate cake still with me when I woke up that first morning, I was ready to go to work. Even the dusting of yellow sand that had settled on everything in my tent didn't bother me. I soon learned to accept sand as a way of life. Sleep in it. Walk on it. Wear it. Everything except eat it. Somehow, Anderson's people managed to keep it out of our food.

I watched Wellman stalk up toward the fort with his head lowered against the blowing sand. He wasn't wearing a hat, and the sand was sticking in his shock of wiry, gray hair. The scowl on his face didn't seem to faze the old-timers who had worked with him on other pictures, and their calls to him were happy ones. All they got in return was a growl.

He came straight to me. Those who had arrived with him ducked away. They could sense that something unpleasant was about to happen and wanted no part of it.

"I know you looked at the old *Beau Geste*," he growled at me. "Don't ever mention that picture to me!"

He walked away through the swarm of workmen busy preparing for the first shot. That Colman *Beau Geste* disappeared from my memory instantly.

Well, craziness became bedlam that first morning. Assistant directors outside the fort were rehearsing the Tuareg tribesmen. Those inside were directing the legionnaires to their places up on the parapets.

Wellman, followed by Louis Van Der Ecker, a former legionnaire and the technical director, rushed around checking the soldiers, their uniforms, and their equipment.

Electricians were stringing cables and hauling heavy lights to the tops of high parallels. Cameramen, sound crews, grips, and others were busy preparing their equipment. Over all the noise, you could hear the first assistant yelling directions to the minor actors.

By the time Coop, Donlevy, Preston, Milland, and the other stars arrived on the set, Wellman had worked out their movements with stand-ins and was stomping around, anxious to get going.

I asked Clem Jones, the chief second assistant director who had worked with Wellman on many pictures, if he knew why Wellman was being so rough on everyone on the first day. He told me that Wellman's wife was expecting a baby very soon and that he had made it clear: "Come hell or high water, I'll be with her!"

Clem laughed and said, "We'll get our share of that hell before we finish this location."

By lunchtime, the master shot of the Tuareg attack was in the can, and we were on our way. As the days rolled along, we kept close to the schedule, but Wellman wasn't pleased. He demanded more and more speed. If he had to wait for anything, he'd blow his top.

One Sunday morning Coop dropped by my tent for a visit, and we got to talking about Wellman's attitude. After a while, he changed the subject. I can remember that conversation like it was just yesterday. Coop said, "You know, Rocky and I have a new baby, don't you, podner?" He didn't wait for an answer. "She'll be two in September."

I'd never seen him so serious and so proud.

I told him I knew about her and that they'd named her Maria. He smiled that wonderful, shy smile of his and said, "And Dale has a new baby sister, doesn't he, Herbie?"

I was surprised for two reasons. It was the first time he'd ever called me Herbie. And that he knew about Judy's birth.

"Saw the report about Mary Belle and the baby in the *Paramount Parade.* The Studio Club still sends me the paper."

He ambled around the small living room and stopped beside me where I sat with my script open. A dozen sheets of yellow onionskin paper rolled in my typewriter, half-filled with scenes copied from the script.

"Don't you ever take Sundays off?" he asked. "What's that you're working on?"

"One of these days Wellman's going to ask, 'Is there anything more I can shoot while I'm in this setup?' You can bet I don't want him to sit there fuming while I search through the script. So when he asks, I'll just hand him these pages."

Well, I didn't have to wait too long. One day we were shooting a scene with Ray Milland, crouched in the foreground, firing through an opening in the wall at the Tuaregs down below on the sand.

As soon as the scene was over, I pulled out the yellow sheets and ran a line through the scene we had just filmed.

Suddenly, the pages were ripped from my hands. I turned and looked up at Wellman, who sat beside the camera, just above me. He was thumbing through the pages. Then he glared down at me.

"Since when did a fuckin' script clerk think he could tell me how to shoot my picture?" he shouted.

"That's my list, Mr. Wellman, not yours."

"Where's my copy?" he demanded.

I took a copy from my briefcase and handed it to him. He studied it for a moment and then gave my copy back. "You got copies for everybody?" his voice a little less demanding.

I handed him the remaining copies. He gave them to Youngerman and told him they would shoot from my list. "Pass them around and get everyone ready."

Joe glared at me and stalked off.

"What made you think of this?" Wellman asked. His voice was almost friendly.

"All these openings are exactly alike, and all that sand down there looks the same. Just change the Tuaregs and put Coop, or Donlevy, Brad Crawford, or any of the other legionnaires there in place of Milland."

I didn't expect any thanks from Wellman and didn't get any.

Youngerman came to my tent that night complaining that I should have given the list to him and let him give it to Wellman.

Well, maybe so. But a lot of the guys around the studio felt that Youngerman found ways to take credit for things that others did. To my sorrow, I was to discover years later that they were right.

Wild Bill got wilder as shooting continued. One day he heard Van Der Ecker, the technical director, giving some instructions to a group of legionnaires. Like a wild bull, Wellman charged across to Louis, shoved his jaw into Louis's face, and shouted at him: "Who in the hell do you think you are, giving orders to my actors?"

Embarrassed, Louis turned and started walking away. Wellman blew his top. He hurled the heavy metal microphone at Louis, striking him in the back. Louis staggered a couple of steps, straightened up, and without looking at Wellman, disappeared inside the fort.

You can bet everybody walked softly and spoke quietly around Wellman the rest of that day.

That same night something happened that could have ended my movie career. I'm a little embarrassed by how I let the sand, wind, exhaustion, anger, self-pity, and, most of all, being separated from my family influence my actions.

I'd refused an invitation to a birthday party for Nick Vehr, one of Wellman's favorite actors, whose wife had sent down real Russian vodka and Nick's favorite Russian food for him and his friends. When I didn't show up, some of Nick's friends came and forced me to go to the party with them. That was the first time on the picture that I'd allowed anything to interfere with my work.

It didn't take long for me to join in the fun. The party was in high gear and I'd just shifted into second, when Charlie Barton rushed in and told me that Wellman, Coop, Milland, and everybody else were in the projection room waiting for me to show up.

I told Charlie to go back and tell the bastard he could see the film without me for once. Charlie said I was going into that projection room, even if he had to ask Nick to carry me.

I knew he meant it. I told him if he forced me to go, Wellman and everybody there would be sorry. It wasn't leaving the party that bothered me. I was just sick of *Beau Geste* and the whole mess.

There was complete silence, and I could feel the tension that showed on the faces of everybody as I entered the tent. Then the silence was shattered as Brian Donlevy scratched a match to light a cigarette. Wellman turned at the sound and saw me standing there. He exploded to his feet and shouted at me, "You, you. . . ."

Before he could utter another word, I cut him off by shouting even louder: "Wellman, you've treated everybody on this picture as your personal slaves! We've all worked our asses off to help you and never complained! I roll out of bed at five every morning to search the script for ways to help you finish! Miss dinner every night to type the day's reports! Rush in here to listen to you dictate comments to Tommy Scott about the rushes! Back to my tent where the studio driver is waiting for me to type them. Then, if I don't say to hell with eating, I go to the kitchen where, even at midnight, one of the cooks is waiting to feed me!"

I didn't wait for him to answer me. As I walked out the door, I heard him say, "We'll run this tomorrow night."

I didn't sleep much that night. I kept waiting for the production manager to show up with the news that Wellman had told him to get me the hell back to Hollywood.

The next morning was cold and windy. As I sat on a camera dolly outside the fort, almost everyone in the crew who passed me had some comment about what Wellman would do to me when he arrived.

I saw Wellman appear over the dunes from the direction of the camp. For the first time, he was walking alone. Was he in such a foul mood that everybody was ducking him? I'd almost convinced myself that he might forgive me, but that thought vanished from my mind when I saw him head directly toward me, his boots jamming down hard into the sand. His arthritic hands permanently clenched in menacing fists.

He paused beside me for a moment before saying, "I don't blame you for last night. I didn't realize you could hate this fuckin' place as much as I do."

He didn't give me a chance to apologize. Just went on to pin Sparkhul where he had the camera set up outside the walls of the fort.

With all the problems we had at Fort Zinderneuf, we finished days ahead of schedule and hurried back to the studio to watch Wellman frighten the life out of the inexperienced newcomer, Susan Hayward, whom the studio had cast in the romantic role of Isobel Rivers.

Those of us who had known and worked with Gary Cooper, some on more than twenty films, knew that *Beau Geste* was the last film he would be making for Paramount on his old contract and he would be leaving the studio. We were sorry to see a friend go away.

I was sure Wellman would remember that unhappy scene in the projection room and demand someone new on his next Paramount picture.

For the next five or six months I worked on a series of low-budget films, including a couple of Dorothy Lamour South Sea island jungle pictures, filmed mostly in Palm Canyon near Palm Springs.

One morning when I arrived at the studio, I found a message to report to the production office. When I walked in, Dick Johnson told me he was assigning me to Wellman's next picture, *Reaching for the Sun.*

I couldn't believe it! Not after that scene in the projection room. I wondered if Johnson had heard about it and was punishing me by shoving me off on Wellman.

But I kept my mouth shut, took the script, and left the office.

Chapter 19

For Whom the Bell Tolls

I had mixed feelings about *For Whom the Bell Tolls.* I was happy to finally get away from Wellman but not pleased at the thought of being away from Mary Belle on her thirtieth birthday. I knew I'd miss the baseball games with our eight-year-old son, Dale. And swimming with our beautiful three-year-old daughter, Judy.

Sam Wood was the producer-director. I knew he'd directed the Marx Brothers in *A Night at the Opera.* But I hadn't seen the picture.

I don't remember what writer's name was on the script that George Berthelon handed me. It wasn't the final screenplay and was more of a guide to be used for filming the winter sequences.

I read the script that night, then got a copy of Ernest Hemingway's novel, and shared the experiences of Robert Jordan as he helped the Spanish guerrillas defeat the fascists.

The final screenplay would be written by Dudley Nichols, but we wouldn't see his work until late the following spring.

It was warm that morning early in September 1941, when the *Bell Tolls* company drove away from Paramount in a convoy of cars, trucks, and buses for the location high in the Sierra Nevada Mountains above the little gold-mining town of Sonora.

Old Route 99, a narrow, two-lane, paved road with sharp twisting turns, skirted along the rim of the ridge between a wide place in the road called Castaic Junction and a little wider place in the road called Gorman. Then came Lebac, where 99 plunged almost straight down between high walls of a canyon to the floor of the San Joaquin Valley. That section of the road was notorious for the number of trucks that lost their brakes and, gathering speed, plunged off the road or crashed into traffic, killing their drivers or other motorists.

Leaving Bakersfield, Old 99 was still a two-way road, but now it was built up some eight feet above the surrounding cotton and hay fields. Harvesting equipment, some horse-drawn, slowed the convoy to a walk.

The road up the San Joaquin Valley had changed little during the twelve years that had elapsed since the day in 1929 I drove up the valley on my way to Sonora for the picture *Fighting Caravans.*

Twelve hours after leaving Hollywood, we pulled in at the Sonora Inn to have dinner. I'd been fighting a cold for a couple of weeks and wasn't feeling so good, so I skipped the food and slumped down in a chair in the lobby.

Eddie Salven, Sam Wood's assistant director, took one look at me and called the company doctor. He felt my head, took my temperature, and told me I should forget going up into the high country.

I didn't know at that very moment, when I told him I was going up there, that I was making a decision that would affect my whole career.

Late that same night, we arrived at the Dardanelles. It was the same little place in the valley, just below Sonora Pass, where we'd lived when filming the snow scenes for *Fighting Caravans.*

This time I wouldn't be living in a tent with thirteen drivers and one driver's wife. On one side of the valley there was a low, red building with eight doors that opened to reveal a narrow bedroom, a shower, and a toilet. It was quickly dubbed "the Cribs." Don Robb, the production manager, pointed toward it and told me to take my choice.

Early the next morning we piled into the cars. Wood had brought along on that preproduction unit William Cameron Menzies, the famous production designer/director; Ray Rennahan, Technicolor's top cameraman, and his crew; and the gaffer, key grip, property man, and construction foreman and his crew.

After the snow started falling, the rest of the unit—sound, makeup, wardrobe, and others—would arrive, along with Joseph Calleia, whom Wood had cast as El Sordo, and his band of rebels.

Fortunately, we arrived near the rock peak Wood had previously selected for the spot where El Sordo and his men would be trapped, without meeting anyone driving down the narrow one-way dirt road from the top of Sonora Pass. We held our breath while our driver fought to keep his wheels in the deep ruts as we crossed a long dirt slide.

We left the cars on the road and struggled up the 100-yard rocky path to the top of the peak.

Sam didn't waste a moment. Followed by Menzies and Rennahan, he hurried to the edge of the rock where the bare ground fell sharply away to a stand of tall pines far below. Sam told the construction foreman to move down the slope and he would tell him where to place the giant fake boulders that were on the trucks back at the Dardanelles.

In the car on the way to the location, Sam had told me to keep precise notes on everything he said during the survey, and I was ready when he described the changes he was making to the set.

Together, he, Menzies, and Rennahan agreed on the location of each of the boulders that were to serve as protection for the army during the battle.

Sam then moved a few steps away from the edge and surveyed the scene through the camera finder. He moved around a bit and then settled on the spot he would have the camera for the first setup. "Right here," he said, in a voice loud enough for everyone to hear. "I want the camera here for the first setup."

While he held the finder, the key grip measured the height and drove an iron rod deep into the rock.

I spent the days waiting for the snow, climbing the mountains around Sonora Pass with Sam and his staff looking for the locations he would use in summer 1942 to stage the scenes with Jordan, Anselmo, and the others in the summer sequences.

He would select one location for the shot of the bridge when Anselmo pointed to it, when he and Jordan paused on the trail.

The location for the scene between Anselmo and Jordan was picked on the side of a mountain miles away. For the close shot of Jordan in the same scene, another location on another mountain was his choice. For Anselmo's close shot, still another mountainside. To make it seem that all the scenes were shot in the same location, the same gnarled, twisted limb of a storm-weathered pine tree was placed in each scene.

Then, another picturesque location would catch the eye of Menzies, Ray, or Sam, and we'd be off again. Maybe one of the angles picked first would be suitable, or maybe it wouldn't.

My book was soon bulging with mountain names, roads, trails, and distances to each. Pretty soon I was beginning to wonder whether I would be able to make sense of what I'd written in it.

In November, we began to have some snow, and Sam sent for the rest of the shooting unit and the actors, including Joseph Calleia.

Don Robb had rented giant tents to house the horsemen, the wardrobe, the equipment for the horses, and the action props.

It was snowing heavily the day the buses and trucks arrived with all those horses and men.

We were scheduled to start shooting two days after the arrival of the soldiers, but when we rolled out of bed that morning, we knew we'd never get out of camp that day. It stopped snowing about noon, and the state highway patrol plows spent the rest of the day and most of the night clearing the road to the top of the pass.

I wish I could tell you the date we started filming on *Bell Tolls,* but I can't. But I sure remember everything that happened that day.

Sam Wood and I were the last to drive out of the camp and head for the location. The path from the road to the set had been trampled down, and that made it easy to climb up and join the others.

Ray had the camera set up over the iron rod that had been driven into the rock when Sam picked the setup weeks before.

One of the crew saw us coming, drew two cups of coffee from the container, and handed one to me and the other to the director. Sam smiled at the man as he accepted the hot drink. But as he turned to speak to Rennahan, the smile disappeared from his face and the coffee went flying into the snow. In a loud, angry tone, he demanded to know what the camera was doing in that position. Rennahan pointed to the iron stake and reminded Sam that it was the spot he'd selected. "Lens five feet, eight inches, above the rock."

Sam wasn't convinced. He turned to me and ordered me to read what he'd said when he picked the camera setup. I opened my book and, as quick as I could, found what I'd written. "Mr. Wood," I told him, "you said, 'I want a 35-millimeter lens, five feet, eight inches above the rock exactly over that iron stake.'"

He was angry when he told me I hadn't been listening to his instructions. At that moment, I realized that Wellman wasn't such a bad guy after all.

He continued to argue with Ray, insisting he'd said he wanted the camera on a six-foot platform set back far enough for the camera to include part of the rock.

As usual, the key grip was always prepared. Off to one side he had three knockdown wooden platforms. In less than five minutes, the camera was on top of the tallest one, and Wood, without a word of thanks, had climbed a ladder and was staring through the lens at the 100 mounted cavalrymen waiting in the woods for his instructions.

Over a microphone, with the volume turned as high as it would go, he repeated what he had told them in a meeting the day before. "Ride back in the trees until you're out of sight. When you hear a gunshot from up here, ride in as fast as you can. Spur your horses up the slope toward the camera as far as they'll go. Then when you hear a volley of shots from up here, turn your horses and race back into the woods. The more confusion you give me, the better I'll like it. Remember, we have to get it right the first time. Let me know when you're ready down there, Eddie!" he shouted to his assistant.

Sam got what he wanted in that one take and then began to explain the action he wanted in the next scene.

Between the shot we'd just completed and the scene Sam was about to shoot, showing the cavalrymen running from the woods and charging up the slope, there would be a shot showing El Sordo and his men scraping up mounds of snow, dirt, and pebbles for protection from the soldiers bullets.

I tried to point this out to Sam, but I couldn't get his attention. He was too caught up in yelling over the microphone at the soldiers. Finally, I told Bob McCrellis, the property man, to build the mounds.

When Sam saw those mounds, he exploded. I thought he was going to jump off that six-foot platform. Screaming over the mike at everyone standing around the platform, and without waiting for an answer to each question, he demanded to know what the mounds were doing there. Who put them there, and who ordered it be done?

I answered the last question. "I did Mr. Wood."

"You!" That little single-syllable, three-letter pronoun was devastating. He didn't need to scream the rest of the sentence. It was all there. "Stupid! Idiot! Slide back under the rock!" And more.

Then he ordered the mounds removed. All the time complaining about the millions he was losing because of what I'd done.

Why hadn't I taken the Sonora doctor's advice to go back to the studio and let somebody else take Wood's abuse? I decided I'd keep my mouth shut. Keep the cutter's notes and when we got back to the studio, walk out on Wood.

But I knew it was my job to advise the director when he was about to make a mistake that would cost Paramount a lot of money. So with the cameras turning and just before he shouted action, I told him that if he made that shot without the mounds, then he'd have to come back up there and retake the scene after another snowstorm.

He turned and stared down at me. He didn't say anything. I guess he was afraid of what he might say if he opened his mouth.

While the soldiers battled their way up the slope, I glanced up at Sam and saw that he had his eyes fixed on me. Not once did he look at the action the cameras were recording.

The moment the scene was finished, over the mike, and in the same loud voice, he apologized to me. He said that I was right and he would do it my way after it snowed again.

We moved off the rock and continued filming. Fighting bad weather until a really big storm covered the tracks on the slope, we moved back to the rock and started over with the battle between the soldiers and El Sordo.

We were losing the sun real early those first days in December. About three in the afternoon of Sunday, December 7, Rennahan told Sam he'd lost the light and he'd better call it a day.

We were on our way down the path toward the road when Carl Reynolds, one of the drivers, came running up the path shouting, "The Japs have bombed Pearl Harbor! I just heard it on the radio!"

I joined in the angry outburst against the Japanese and then hurried to the car to get more news of the attack. But with the static on the radio at that altitude, we couldn't make sense out of what the announcer was reporting.

We expected more news when we got back to the Dardanelles, but reception was just as bad down in that little valley, surrounded by all the high snow-covered mountains.

I was sure Sam would tell the state highway people to get busy plowing us out of there. But I was wrong. He passed the word that we would stay there until we'd finished shooting the battle sequence.

For the next four days, an angry and resentful company rushed to complete filming. When those three planes appeared over the peaks of Sonora Pass, dropped their dummy bombs, and the granite rock exploded spraying boulders high in the sky and down into the stand of pines where most of the company was hiding, we knew we'd be going home. We knew we'd return the next summer to resume location shooting.

I hadn't seen Sam Wood since late December, when he'd finished running all the film we'd shot in the snow. One day early in March, he called and asked me to come to his office.

I was surprised at his almost friendly greeting. He told me to move into the room next to his office. I knew *Bell Tolls* was scheduled to begin shooting again late in May around Dardanelles and Sonora Pass and wondered why he'd want me around so soon.

He wasted no time putting me to work. He gave me a copy of Hemingway's book and said, "Here's your Bible. If I ask you what

Hemingway had Jordan or anyone say or do, I don't want you wasting time searching through the book for an answer."

A few days later, I found a 250-page *For Whom the Bell Tolls* screenplay on my desk, with a note from Sam telling me to read it and write him a report. I found out that the studio paid the writer $50,000 for the script. I told Sam it was little more than a condensation of Hemingway's book.

I don't think my report had anything to do with Dudley Nichols writing the final script. He was probably already hard at work. I hoped Hemingway would come in to see Sam and I'd have a chance to discuss his book with him.

I don't think Sam wanted him around. They didn't walk the same political path, and Sam wouldn't want Louella Parsons telling her boss, and Sam's close friend, William Randolph Hearst, that he was cozying up to Hemingway.

Gary Cooper had long been set as Jordan. I was sure happy when I heard that good news. Casting was under way for the other major roles.

I overheard a conversation Sam was having with someone on the phone. He told that person that he didn't care what the Paramount executive said, he would never accept Vera Zorina. He and Coop had agreed on Ingrid Bergman for Maria, and David O. Selznick, who had her under contract, was just waiting for a starting date.

Vera Zorina was a young actress and talented dancer Paramount had under contract. The studio planned to showcase her in *Bell Tolls* and build her into a major star.

I watched the parade of stars as they passed through Sam's office. It was a slow process, but he finally okayed Akim Tarmiroff, Katina Paxinou, Arturo de Cordova, Vladimir Sokoloff, Fortunio Bonanova, and a host of distinguished and talented actors.

DeMille had reclaimed Eddie Salven as his assistant. George Berthelon appointed Joe Youngerman as Sam Wood's first assistant director.

I told Joe about a spot I'd picked out on the bank of the Tuolumne River at the Dardanelles. A ranger in charge had promised to bulldoze a road from the meadow and have the area cleared for a house trailer I'd bought to live in with Mary Belle and the kids. Joe went right out and bought one for his wife Molly, his children Arthur and Barbara, and himself.

It was near the end of May when we pulled away from our home in Sherman Oaks. Our trailer was overloaded with camping equipment, bicycles, pots and pans, food, and bags of oranges picked from the trees in our back garden.

By the time we started up the Ridge Route, the convoy of Paramount cars and buses had already left the Grapevine and was headed up the San Joaquin Valley.

Our 1938 Ford sedan handled that heavy, double-wall, steel trailer over Old Route 99 without missing one beat.

Late in the afternoon, somewhere north of Fresno, the trailer started weaving, making it difficult for me to keep us on that narrow, two-way road that was built up some six feet above the deep ditches on each side. I couldn't find a turnoff and had to stop where I was, completely blocking one lane. I got out and found I'd blown a tire on the trailer.

I was stunned. I hadn't thought of buying a spare tire. I looked around. All I could see in every direction was farmland. There wasn't a house anywhere.

I knew I had to get a ride to the nearest town, buy a tire, get it on that house trailer, and get out of there before somebody crashed into us.

There was very little traffic along that road back in the 1940s. I tried to flag down each car that passed, but no one would even slow down. I was about to give up when an old, battered pickup truck chugged to a stop behind the trailer. An elderly Japanese farmer climbed out and offered to drive me to a garage in Madera, a little town about ten miles away.

He stopped at a small garage on the edge of town. With rationing, I couldn't buy a new tire, but the owner sold me a retread, drove me back, and changed the tire, all for only $10.00.

We started off again. I was getting worried. I didn't want to get caught on that road after dark. Then, just as the twilight faded into blackness, I heard a loud bang, and the trailer started weaving again. I stopped, climbed out, and, just as I expected, saw that the tire I'd bought at Madera had blown out.

Just as the last time, there was only farmland everywhere. But off in the distance I could see a single light and a building.

I got Mary Belle and the kids settled on a bank well away from the car and trailer. Anyone could have crashed into them in the darkness.

I hated leaving them there in the darkness but started off toward that light. I couldn't believe my eyes when I arrived at that building. Old tires were piled everywhere. A man came from the building, dug around until he found one the right size, and told me that he wasn't sure it would last long enough to get me to Sonora but I could have it for $2.00. I'd have been grateful if he'd said $20.00.

He threw a couple of smudge pots and the tire in the back of a pickup, told me to climb in, and drove me back to the car. On the way, I kept praying I'd find Mary Belle and the kids safe. They were. Everybody had managed to pass without hitting the car or trailer.

The flame from the smudge pots gave him protection from the few passing cars and light while he changed the tire. He refused the money I tried to give him and drove away.

We headed out again for Modesto. I kept waiting for that old tire to fail, but it didn't.

We got to Modesto after everything was closed for the night. Mary Belle had been telling me that Judy was running a fever.

We turned off 99 onto the road to Sonora. By that time, Mary Belle was so concerned about Judy that she insisted we pull off and spend the night in the trailer. On a dark deserted side street, I pulled under some trees and shoved bicycles and boxes aside to open the beds.

About nine the next morning, we finally pulled to a stop in front of the Sonora Inn to find a worried Sid Street pacing the sidewalk.

He had sent the others off on the drive to Dardanelles while he waited for us to arrive. He told us he'd called out the California highway patrol at midnight, and they'd been searching Highway 99 all night.

I asked Sid if he could find a doctor to check Judy's temperature. When he examined her, he told us she was suffering from bronchitis. Mary Belle said she'd take the kids back home, but the doctor said that the high altitude would be fine for her. He was right; Judy never had another bronchitis attack.

We made it up to the Dardanelles without any more trouble, not even one more blowout. That $2.00 tire was still on the trailer when we sold it a year later.

The forest ranger had been true to his promise to prepare the trailer site along the riverbank. He'd even had a stone barbecue built and a private chemical toilet installed. But nature had provided the perfect touch. A giant, hardwood tree lay just beyond the fireplace. Its trunk, the bark long past having turned to dust, was without a blemish. Wind and driving rain had polished the trunk and its branches a gleaming silver-gray. We backed our trailer into position facing the river, leaving space for Joe to park nearby.

The first Saturday night we invited Coop and some of our other friends to a barbecue. It was an event that would continue until we completed shooting in the mountains and moved back to the studio.

Only Coop had a standing invitation, and he never failed to come. He had fallen in love with Judy, and she with him. In a way, she was replacing his daughter Maria, who was with her mother at their home in Southern California. One minute after he lifted her on his knees, she had him laughing. She was also able to have that wonderful, silent man tell her children's stories.

Those Saturday nights were also filled with music. Charlie Quirk, a longtime friend, was up there with five of his cowboy stuntmen friends to double the cast when the script called for dangerous stunts. They were also country and western singers and guitar players. Charlie was a trained musician and often played with symphony orchestras.

As soon as supper was over they'd find favorite places on the trunk and branches of that tree and begin. Even the children stopped running around and settled down with the adults to enjoy their beautiful soft harmony.

Even though Sam Wood was a hard-nosed, unapproachable man, we were a happy company. Everyone but Sam. And he had a reason to be unhappy. Paramount had taken a stand on the part of Maria. And so had Sam. He told them he'd refuse to shoot any scene that included the character Maria.

Despite his stand, the studio had Vera Zorina's hair cut short, created Maria costumes for her, and shipped her up to the location.

Sam refused to acknowledge her presence. Most of us liked her. She was a lonely figure. She'd come to the location every day but never near the set. We'd see her wandering around in the distance.

One Friday, Sam told me I'd better cancel our barbecue for the following Saturday night to see a test of Ingrid Bergman the studio had made.

After dinner at the Sonora Inn, we sat around until midnight, when the theater was available. We waited until all the local people had left the building, locked the doors, and waited for Bergman to appear on the screen.

What we saw was Ingrid, dressed as Maria, and an actor playing the part of Jordan, sitting beside a campfire in a stand of pine trees.

It was the first time I'd ever seen her, and as the scene progressed, I began to see why Sam and Coop had chosen her for Maria.

Suddenly, from somewhere off the scene, a voice rang out, "Hold it, please." The actor and Ingrid paused and looked toward the camera. Then the voice spoke again. "Leave the camera running." Then into the picture, the head and shoulders of the director appeared. It was Ralph Murphy. Ralph was a little man, barely five feet, six inches tall. He asked Ingrid to come forward. He wanted to talk to her. When she got to her feet and approached Murphy, everybody in the projection room started laughing. She loomed over him from the top of the two-foot platform where the set was built. Added to that was her six-foot height. The top of Murphy's head barely reached Ingrid's waist.

After some brief comments, he walked out of the picture. Ingrid went back to her position by the fire, and Murphy's voice told her to resume the scene.

It was apparent the test had been made to show Sam that Ingrid was too tall for the part.

Sam was outraged. He viewed it as an insult to his intelligence, as it certainly was. He phoned the head of the studio and told him that if Bergman wasn't at the location Tuesday morning, then he was walking off the picture.

Sunday morning, Zorina was on her way back to Hollywood. A lot of us were sorry to see her go. I thought the studio had treated her unfairly. The attempt to force Sam to accept her, I think, ruined a promising career. I can still see her running through the forests with the wind ruffling her short hair.

Ingrid Bergman was not an easy person to know, but she was easy to fall in love with. Mysterious, sensuous, and shy. I thought she wanted to be accepted but was afraid of revealing her true feelings to anyone. She was a joy to watch as she performed. She was Maria.

Each day when dismissed, she would go back to the home Sid had leased for her, never to be seen until she answered her call the next morning.

Sam Wood gave our son Dale an exciting present for his ninth birthday. He had Pat Williams, the wardrobe master, tailor a fascist soldier uniform to fit him for the scene of the guard on the bridge, as seen by Coop and Sokoloff.

Bob McCrellis, the propman, gave Dale a miniature wooden rifle, and Sam had Dale walk a narrow plank out to where the bridge ended over a deep gorge.

Why did Sam use Dale instead of a full-grown man? He was doing a matte shot, a long shot. Only the part of Dale walking the plank would be retained. Everything else would be replaced with a painting of the bridge, the high mountain range, and the sky.

We kept on schedule all summer. Sam was almost a friend by the time we completed our work. Early in September, we packed up and headed out for Yosemite National Park for two days of shooting before going on to the studio.

I remember Sam gathering the entire cast together in a corner of the stage to listen while I read from Hemingway's book the scenes he would be filming that day. To say I was nervous reading to that distinguished group would be the understatement of the year, but I got through it without stumbling too often. Sam even said I was okay.

Summer and fall 1942 passed too quickly. It was almost fifteen years from the day I started working at Paramount when Sam said "Cut" at the end of the last scene he would direct on *Bell Tolls.*

The following day, after viewing the last day's rushes, Sam asked me to come along to his office. He didn't waste any time when we got there. He picked a camera slate (a numbering board that is photographed before each take) and handed it to me. It read "*FOR WHOM THE BELL TOLLS*, Director, Herbert Coleman."

I thought it was a bad joke and waited for Sam to explain. He told me that what I was reading on the board was true.

Warner Bros. had threatened him with a lawsuit if he didn't show up the next day to start his next picture for them.

"I told the front office that you were going to direct all the remaining scenes," he said. I stared at him. I couldn't believe it. A bitter argument on top of that granite peak in the snow a year ago. Now a promotion from script clerk to director!

When I recovered and started to thank him, he brushed it off.

We spent part of the afternoon going over the script. I told him how I thought the scenes should be handled. He made a few suggestions. Some I agreed with, but on others I took a strong stand for my approach.

Before he left the studio, he said that if anyone interfered with my work, to give him a call and he'd take care of it. Never did a director get better cooperation than I did. Everyone in the studio was behind me. They were determined to see that I was a success.

Sam came by a few evenings to see how I was getting along. He'd watch a rehearsal and then leave. He never interfered.

George Berthelon called me into his office the day after I finished shooting everything on my schedule. He told me how pleased he and the front office were with the work I had done on my schedule.

George added, "Are you ready for your next assignment?"

I answered, "Not with Bill Wellman?"

George grinned and said, "This morning, you're an assistant director. You've earned it."

That same day, I joined the Screen Directors Guild, now the Directors Guild of America. It wasn't long before I began to think I should have joined the Gofers Guild. It was "go for this" or "go for that"; but after a while, the running stopped, and I settled in as a regular second assistant director, with the choice assignment of the year.

"You'll join Buddy Coleman on Billy Wilder's new film, *Five Graves to Cairo,*" Berthelon told me.

Chapter 20

Five Graves to Cairo

I don't remember the year Billy Wilder joined Paramount. I do remember wondering who he was. From the moment he first walked onto the lot, he drew attention to himself. He was perpetual motion. With his first step, he was in high gear. And his mind was always in overdrive.

Five Graves was not the first screenplay Billy and Charles Brackett had written together. Their romantic, suspenseful story *Hold Back the Dawn* was given to the untalented director, Mitchell Leisen, who failed to capture the mood and suspense Billy and Brackett had instilled in the screenplay. When Billy saw what Leisen had done to their story, he told the studio he'd direct his own future screenplays.

Five Graves to Cairo was adapted from a 1917 Lajos Biro play. The star was Franchot Tone, a British Army enlisted man, posing as a hotel flunky whom he had found dead in the basement of a small hotel in a village somewhere near the Mediterranean Sea in North Africa. The owner of the hotel was Akim Tamiroff, in a role completely opposite the brutal Pablo of *For Whom the Bell Tolls.*

Anne Baxter, a more American girl you'd never find, was memorable as a French maid in the hotel who hates the British for leaving the French soldiers behind at Dunkirk. A wonderful cast included Erich von Stroheim, Peter Van Eyck, Miles Mander, and Fortunio Bonanova.

The picture opens with the African Corps of Field Marshal Rommel capturing the village and taking over the hotel. Peter Van Eyck mistakes Tone for the dead servant, a Nazi spy who had infiltrated the British lines and had been keeping von Stroheim informed about their movements.

The Germans capture a large group of British soldiers and bring them to the hotel. Miles Mander discovers that Tone is a British soldier trusted by the Germans and orders him to find out how von Stroheim manages to move his African Corps across the desert without visible supplies of fuel, food, or ammunition. Tone discovers that the "five graves to Cairo" is really von Stroheim's five secret hidden fuel supply depots, just as Van Eyck finds the body of the dead servant in the basement.

The hotel is rocked by an air raid as Tone and Von Eyck fight to the death. Tone kills Van Eyck and hides his body.

Von Stroheim sends Tone to Cairo to arrange for a big victory celebration when he arrives in the city with his African Corps. He then discovers that Van Eyck has been murdered.

To protect Tone, Baxter claims she killed Van Eyck. Tone manages to reach the British forces near Cairo and tells them of Rommel's hidden supply depots. He joins a tank group, enters the battle of El Alamein, and fights his way back to the little hotel, where Tamiroff tells him that Baxter has been executed by Rommel for killing Van Eyck.

With that flawless, perfectly paced, suspenseful, yet witty film, Brackett and Wilder became Hollywood's top producing, writing, directing team.

For the desert scenes, we went back to Buttercup Valley in exactly the same location where I'd spent those miserable months with "Wild Bill" Wellman on *Beau Geste.* Same sand dunes. Same blowing sand. Just one thing different: we swapped the bitter cold wind for a blazing sun and never a whisper of breeze.

The U.S. Army was still training tank crews in desert warfare and had a contingent working in Buttercup Valley. They knew we were coming and didn't seem happy to add picture work to their dawn-to-midnight duty.

But after just one day waiting in the shade while Billy rehearsed and our crews prepared each scene, we were all friends. They didn't even say no to Billy when he asked them to power their way up a steep soft dune. They just smiled at each other and climbed inside their hothouses.

The first tank left the hard-packed floor of the valley and started up the dune. It didn't get very far before it stalled. The tracks kept turning and digging the sand away until the tank was resting on its belly. It sat there until a giant crane was brought in to lift it back to the valley floor.

But none of the problems we continued to have seemed to bother Billy. And his sparkling, nimble wit kept all of us happy and anxious to help him.

I don't remember how many days we were shooting on the Paramount stages, but I do remember the days, happy days, watching Billy directing his magnificent cast. He was never quiet or stationary. Always pacing or discussing the scenes with his actors.

I learned a lot working with Billy Wilder on *Five Graves.* I would have become a much better and wiser filmmaker if I could have been at his elbow on just one picture as his script supervisor. But that could never happen. When he made his start as an American director, in 1942, with the screenplay he and Charles Brackett wrote, called *The Major and the Minor,* starring Ray Milland and Ginger Rogers, I was already working closely with Sam Wood on *For Whom the Bell Tolls.*

I had begun to think *Five Graves* would become the first picture ever made without one day of unhappiness. I should have known better. Not with Erich von Stroheim around. He was playing the part of Rommel or should have been playing that part. It looked to me like he was playing Field Marshal von Stroheim: arrogant, superior, and supremely egotistic.

One day he was lying in bed, waiting impatiently for Billy to come from his stage office and start the scene, when one of the studio escorts brought three uniformed Air Force officers and their wives onto the set. I recognized the Pacific Area ribbons all of the young men wore under their gold wings. I saw von Stroheim glare at them and then yell for Billy's assistant, Buddy Coleman, who joined him and listened as von Stroheim, waving his arms toward the officers, told him to get those people off "his" set.

Fortunately, the visitors were listening to something the escort was telling them and didn't see or hear von Stroheim. Buddy came over and told me to do what von Stroheim wanted. I told Buddy that if von Stroheim wanted them out, he'd have to do it himself. I also told Buddy that those men were risking their lives so von Stroheim could lie around in that bed and be overpaid all that money.

When Billy came from his stage office and saw the group of people, he hurried to greet them. He spent some time describing everything about the scene he was about to film. He pointed at the glowering but silent von Stroheim and then had them sit beside him while he made the scene.

Chapter 21

China

The day after we finished *Five Graves,* I joined the few assistant directors to whom the draft boards had not yet said, "Here's your invitation to join the Army and see the world, kid." I'd watched friends such as Chico Day, Holly Morse, Ralph Axness, Mel Epstein, "Cubby" Broccoli, and others disappear from the studios.

Paramount had applied for a deferment for me, and it had been granted. I found out later that the script I'd written, *Safeguarding Military Information,* was responsible for the studio getting that deferment.

I know it lifted Mary Belle's spirits. She'd never expressed the deep concern she felt for our two children, Dale, who had just turned ten, and Judy, now five, if I were called to active duty. She was sure she could find a job somewhere. But would it pay enough to meet the mortgage payments on our first home we'd built in 1936 and to support her and the children?

China quickly followed *Five Graves.* It was an original script, written by Frank Butler, who was known around Paramount as the Story Doctor. He was one of the studio's most valuable executives. Although Butler was third in pecking order in the story department, after D. A. Doran and Frank Cleaver, his gifted talents touched almost every screenplay that found its way to his desk. And almost every script did, on direct orders from Barney Balaban, president of Paramount Pictures Corporation. Butler began working as an extra for Famous Players–Lasky even before I walked into the studio in 1927.

Butler's script was a story about the Chinese people struggling to live and escape from the invading Japanese army.

Producer Jules Blumenthal signed John Farrow to direct the film and Hal Walker as director of the second, or action, unit.

Three days before the Walker unit was scheduled to leave for Phoenix and the Adams Hotel where we would live, I was sent there to interview and select the Chinese youngsters we would use in the picture. It was the most important assignment I'd been given since becoming an assistant. But I wasn't worried. I'd always been fond of the Chinese and got along great with all of them.

What a shock I had coming. I had the name of the Chinese gentleman who represented the Chinese community in all motion picture activities. I think his name was Chui, but I'm not sure. I dialed the number I'd been given. Almost on the first ring, I heard a man's voice. I introduced myself and was surprised when Chui said, "I've been expecting your call, Mr. Coleman." When I tried to explain why I was calling, he said, "Of course you can drive out, Mr. Coleman. But it will be a waste of your time and mine."

How did he know I was in town and wanted to see him? With that thought and his statement about my coming being a waste of time tumbling around in my mind, I decided to hell with lunch. I took a walk while I tried to sort things out. But the minute I stepped outside the door into that hot, dry breeze sweeping down the street, I said to hell with that also.

At three on the dot, I reached for the doorbell, but before I could press it, the door opened and Chui stood there. He offered his hand and invited me inside. As we sat down, he said, "You've been wondering how I knew you were coming to Phoenix, Mr. Coleman?" I told him he was right.

"The Phoenix papers have been full of stories about your studio's plans to make a picture called *China* in this area. And it follows, you will need our people to make your film look like it was filmed in China?" It was so obvious, I wondered why he'd asked the question.

"You're right, sir," I answered.

I was stunned when he told me that the Chinese community had decided to refuse to cooperate with the Hollywood movie people in the future. When I asked him for an explanation, he hesitated for a moment. I could see he would rather not talk about it, but then he told me the whole sad story.

"The last movie company from Hollywood that came to Phoenix and asked to use our people was produced and directed by one William Wellman. At first we were happy to have our people working with him, but it wasn't long before they began to tell us about his abusive tactics. His vulgarity. And more. That was too much. It was the day the picture ended, we made our decision. I'm sorry I cannot help you, Mr. Coleman."

I told him Hal Walker was a man who grew up with Paramount Pictures. His reputation was spotless, and he was a gentleman. I could see I wasn't getting through to him. I told myself I wasn't going to fail on my first important mission for the studio. Various schemes flashed around in my mind. Then the solution, or what I hoped would be the solution, came to me.

"Mr. Chui," I said, "we have two days' work where we need just one young Chinese girl, in her late teens, as a double for one of Hollywood's finest Chinese actresses whose scenes will be filmed at the studio. Let me choose the double and film the two days. Then, based on her report, decide if you'll allow the other people to work with us."

I waited, anxiously, for his decision, but he sat silent. Then I said, "Mr. Chui, I'm taking a big financial risk, bringing a large shooting unit, about 100 people, plus equipment, buses, trucks, and cars all the way to Phoenix because I know the people we'll bring with us."

I began to have some hope when he said, "Plan on an interview at ten tomorrow morning. I'll make some calls and phone you at the Adams at seven tonight." I gave him two large photographs of the Chinese actress I'd mentioned and told him I'd like the double to look as much like her as possible. Then I got out of his house as fast and as gracefully as I could.

Chui called promptly at seven. He had discussed my proposal with his committee. The committee members were impressed with the risk I was taking and agreed to go along, under certain conditions. He added, "You will accept personal responsibility for the safety of the children, and you will be with them when they are picked up at their homes in the morning and stay with them until they are returned to their homes in the evening." I thanked him for what he'd done for me and Paramount and gave him the number and ages of the children we needed. He told me where the interview would be held.

Still, I didn't sleep too good that night. I'd begun to wonder what would happen to me if that double gave Chui a bad report. Who was I to make such an important decision? Maybe I should have called the studio and asked what I should do. No way, I reminded myself. You're a big boy now. If you want to spend the rest of your life being a gofer, then call your boss every time you have a problem.

I called the studio the next morning and asked all the department heads to choose, very carefully, the people they were sending to Phoenix.

Chui met me at the door of the building where he'd assembled around eighty girls and boys. I took one look at the bright, beautiful young Chinese girls and handsome boys who were waiting, hopefully, to be the ones I would choose for the movie.

When they discovered I'd arrived, the laughter and chatter were replaced by a silence, broken only by the sounds of the girls running to line up on one side of the room and the boys on the opposite side.

I told them about the movie and described the scenes they'd be working in, the long hours on dusty, dirt roads, and the mud and rain and added, "If any of you would rather not work under those conditions, please step aside." Every one of them stood in place.

Then I grinned and said, "You've disappointed me. I was hoping all but twenty girls and twenty boys would take advantage of my offer and make my job easy."

That broke the tension that had been building. I spent some time chatting with them about their schools, their past experiences in movies made around Phoenix, and their hopes and plans for the future. We were having a great time, but I was dreading the moment I'd have to send over half of them back to their homes. But I got through it without making any enemies.

Choosing the photographic double was easy. There was only one candidate. At first glance, I thought she was the real Chinese actress. Her report to Chui at the end of the first day's work eliminated any lingering doubts he may have had. He called me with the good news.

Working with those kids became a joyful experience, and by the time we finished our work there, we'd become close friends. So close in fact, that the day we "wrapped" they honored me by taking me on a traveling dinner to all the best Chinese restaurants in Phoenix. Plus, they came to the station to see me off when we left for home.

Wellman's conduct threatened to eliminate Phoenix as a favorite China look-alike. And *China* left its mark on the whole state of Arizona. The screenplay called for a large group of soldiers on motorcycles leading the Japanese forces, racing for the mountain pass, to round a sharp curve at high speed and crash into a cable the Chinese had stretched across the road. The first motorcyclists, all top Hollywood stuntmen, were caught by the cable and thrown violently to the road. The leader was seriously injured. He was rushed to a hospital in Phoenix. His recovery was slow and painful.

The studio's recovery from the cost was also slow and painful. Arizona law required payment to him for the entire length of his recovery at the salary he was paid for that day's work. I'm not sure, but I think it was $750.00. The total bill amounted to $234,000, all for one minute before the camera.

You can bet your life, Hollywood found other states in which to film its movies until Arizona changed that law.

Chapter 22

Here Come the Waves and *Blue Skies*

Here Come the Waves was a choice 1943 assignment. Mark Sandrich was one of Hollywood's top producer/directors. All the assistant directors looked forward to working with him.

Sandrich had to be good to handle Betty Hutton in two roles. She was always a "handful" in one. As twin number one, Rosemary, and twin number two, Susie, Betty Hutton meets Bing Crosby, America's favorite singing star, and his friend, Sonny Tufts. Rosemary falls for Bing, but Susie lets him know she has no use for him. It's a great comedy situation for Bing because he can't tell the twins apart.

Paramount had gathered the perfect team to make *Waves* a winner.

The captain of the team, Mark Sandrich, in his midforties, had been a successful director for over fifteen years. Still, he was little known outside the movie industry. For those of us who were fortunate to work closely with Mark, it was easy to see why. When reporters for newspapers or magazines would appear on the sets and attempt to make him the center of their stories, he would move the conversation to the story and the stars.

Mark believed the name Sandrich would sell few tickets at the box office. And he knew that as long as his pictures made a lot of money, he could choose the stories he wanted to make and the actors to star in them.

The only thing I knew about Betty Hutton was that she'd been a singer with Vincent Lopez and that she was blond, loud, and obviously knew somebody important in the front office. She often marched across the grass of "Cohen's Park," past a little fountain, and into the "Marble Halls," what all the old-timers called the administration building. Those guys in the Marble Halls were passing the word that she'd become a major star.

The first time I read the *Waves* screenplay, written by Alan Scott, Ken Englund, and Zion Meyers, I wondered, How in the world could Mark Sandrich remember, from day to day, from scene to scene, the pace, the mood, the character of Rosemary? Of Susie? Mark had been around a while. He'd handle it, I told myself. But there was Hutton. She'd have the same problem and lacked his experience.

I decided I'd stick as close to Mark as possible. I did. And what I learned was invaluable throughout my career.

Bing had on his staff a boyhood friend, Leo Lynn, a happy-go-lucky man who was always there for us if Bing became a problem. Bing respected him and would listen to him.

After *Waves* closed, I drifted along with the current for a year or so helping other assistants, mainly on pictures directed by John Farrow. I think they were *Hitler's Gang* and *Wake Island.*

Then one day, Mark Sandrich called and asked me to come to his office. I got a big smile from his secretary as I entered the outer office. She came around her desk. "He's waiting for you," she said as she opened the door to Mark's inner office.

Mark was sitting behind his desk, leaning over an open screenplay. He looked up and grinned as he called out, "Come in, Herbie." He pointed to a chair, asked me to sit down, and then settled back onto his black leather chair. He was not a man to beat around the bush. He usually got right to the point, but for a moment he left me to wonder what was on his mind. He swung his chair around and stared out the window overlooking Cohen's Park, then turned to face me, and began reminiscing about events that occurred while he was shooting *Waves.*

"I couldn't help but notice the interest you took in every scene I staged. I could tell by the expression on your face that at times you didn't agree with my direction. I kept waiting for you to say something. But you never did. Why didn't you?"

I stared at him for a moment. "Mark," I said, "I was remembering all those Fred Astaire, Ginger Rogers musicals you directed years before, and I was wondering how you could switch, so easily, from what I've always considered much easier films to direct to a complex subject like *Waves* with Betty Hutton playing twin sisters. And besides, any second assistant director caught criticizing a producer/director would be fired, and I'm a second assistant director."

"Not anymore, Herbie," he said. "Starting today, you're my first assistant. We're going to do another Crosby musical, *Blue Skies.*"

He handed me a copy of the script. "Read it. Think about it. Read it again. Take a week; then we'll talk."

I was in a daze as I walked out of his office holding that screenplay in my sweaty hands. I fought to bring some order over the thoughts racing around in my mind. The new salary. More than double what I'd been making. What a blessing for Mary Belle in her struggle to make ends meet. Another giant step up the ladder for me. How many years had it taken for me to reach this plateau? Almost eighteen years.

Blue Skies, starring Bing Crosby, Fred Astaire, Joan Caulfield Wolfe, Olga San Juan, and Karolyn Grimes, was to be Paramount's banner film for the year.

I went with Mark to the music room to hear Irving Berlin play and sing the tunes he'd composed for the story. Composer? You bet! He was the best. Piano player? He was no Ray Turner. Singer? His voice covered a range from minus zero to plus zero. But he could sell a song, and I sat there hearing not Berlin's voice but, rather, Bing's, singing "White Christmas," "Blue Skies," "Puttin' on the Ritz," and a dozen others.

The first day was a very big production number, one of thirty, with Bing involved in every camera setup. I told Bing I'd call him at noon the next day and tell him what time we'd need him. He said, "I won't be home." He wrote something on a piece of paper and handed it to me. "Call that number." From the look he gave me, I knew it wasn't his wife Dixie's phone number. I showed it to Leo Lynn and asked who it belonged to. "You don't want to know, Herbie," he said after a brief glance at the piece of paper. "And burn it after you call him. He'll have a new number for you the next time you have to call him."

The next morning, Mark and I were having coffee in his stage dressing room. I could see that he was anxious to get going on his new picture.

"I'd like to talk to Bing about a change I have in mind for this scene, Herbie. Ask him to come to the stage as soon as he's ready."

"He's not in the studio yet, Mark. I told him I'd call him at noon and tell him what time to be here."

By the look Mark gave me, I knew I'd goofed. But he didn't blow his top like Wellman, or Hathaway, or so many of the top directors. He merely said, "I'll talk to him after lunch."

At exactly twelve o'clock, I called the number he'd given me. I heard the lovely voice of a bright and cheerful young woman answer. I gave her my name and asked for Bing. "He's taking a walk on the beach," she said. "I'll have him call you the moment he comes back." She wasn't sure what time that would be.

I was pacing back and forth around the stage, checking my watch every five minutes, waiting for Bing to return my call.

Finally, just a little after 1:30, somebody called out, "Bing's on the phone, Herbie." I got there as fast as I could and told Bing we'd need him to come right in, that Mark wanted to talk to him and rehearse the first scene on the stage.

I was shocked when he said, "Tell Mark to rehearse it with the double, Herbie." He didn't give me time to plead with him, just a cheerful, "See you at nine tomorrow." And he was gone.

Mark took the news calmly but warned me that Bing couldn't be trusted. "Always give him a definite call, even if you're not sure of the time," he said.

We were not prepared for the terrible shock when we were told about Mark's sudden death from a massive heart attack. The news wiped from my consciousness everything about the picture except for the little bit I've told you.

Within days, Sol Seigel was set as producer. He brought in a little known director, Stuart Heisler, to replace Mark.

George Berthelon called me in and told me that Heisler refused to accept me as his assistant. He added, "I'm afraid you'll have to wait a while for another first's job. But you won't have to stay on *Blue Skies* as a second."

Mary Belle took the bad news better than I did. But I wasn't surprised. She could always adjust better than I could.

Chapter 23

Frenchman's Creek

Frenchman's Creek was a turkey that should never have been allowed out of its gilded cage.

The stars were Joan Fontaine, Arturo de Cordova, Basil Rathbone, Nigel Bruce, Ralph Forbes, Harold Ramond, Cecil Kellaway, Billy Daniels, and a supporting cast of forty-three actors and Mitchell Leisen's "boys." Joan Fontaine was "loaned" to the production by David O. Selznick, to whom she was under contract.

The screenplay was written by Talbot Jennings and was based on Daphne du Maurier's novel. It was directed, or misdirected, by Mitchell Leisen, a man who paraded his homosexuality with a touch of elegance. I once saw him coming along the sidewalk by the director's building. He was wearing perfectly tailored walking shorts, surely from the men's shop he owned up in Hollywood, where he spent too much time personally fitting his male customers' trousers, knee-highs, white stockings with colored tassels, and shoes with tingling bells.

The Pacific Coast highlands above San Francisco, near the little village of Albion, were chosen to represent England's Cornish coast. The exterior of Fontaine's mansion was built near the Navarro River where it emptied into the Pacific Ocean.

An ancient, little red pirate ship that had been moored in Balboa Bay at Newport Beach for many years was leased from its owners, moved up the coast, and moored in the Navarro River.

Dick McWhorter was the unlucky first assistant who drew the job of assisting Leisen. George Berthelon said, "You're Dick's assistant, but you're also responsible for overseeing the wardrobe department. Edith Head's slow to get the sketches to Leisen, and he's been slow in approving them. Ride herd on both of them."

That job became a nightmare. I never saw such a mass of sketches. Thirteen period gowns for Fontaine. At least three costumes for each of the main cast. Then Leisen's "boys," most of them little more than atmosphere players. It was easy to get Mitch (that was Leisen's nickname to everyone except me; I called him Mr. Leisen as a way of keeping my distance from the bastard) to come to the wardrobe fittings of his "boys." He'd raise holy hell if he found even the slightest wrinkle in the expensive glove leather used to make the costumes for his bloodthirsty pirates, especially the costumes for his lover, Billy Daniels.

Billy was small in stature; but he stood tall among those in his profession, choreography. He was a magnificent dancer. I don't think he had an enemy in the world. He also had a great sense of humor.

One day, Alan Ladd and I were standing in the door of Alan's dressing room when Billy came along the sidewalk. As usual, the smile that covered his face revealed the happiness he felt with everything around him. Alan, reacting to the clicking sound of Billy's hard, built-up heels, called out, "Mornin' Billy. You're walkin' tall this morning."

"Hi there, Laddie," Billy answered. "You oughta try wearing your lifts on the outside. Make you walk a little taller, too." It was a good-natured exchange between friends.

As the day for the start of the picture drew closer, I asked Joan Fontaine to meet with Leisen to discuss her costumes. When Leisen walked into Edith Head's office, Joan handed him a thick, sealed envelope. He glanced at it and asked, "What the hell is this?"

"It's David's instructions to you," she answered.

"Instructions?" he screamed. "Instructions about what?"

"How you are to direct me," she answered with a smile.

Leisen threw the envelope in her face, spewed some epithets I can't repeat here, and stormed out of the room. Joan shrugged her shoulders, turned to her lady friend, and sighed, "Eleven weeks with that?" Then she said to me, "I'm still sticking to my plans, Herbie. We're driving to the location. See you when we get there." She was too professional to allow Leisen's rudeness to disturb her composure.

Watching the love scenes with de Cordova and Fontaine, I had to marvel at de Cordova's concentration. His mind had to be on his real love waiting down the coast in San Francisco. He had been involved with Lupe Velez for years. The same Lupe from 1928 on *Wolf Song,* whom the studio had barred from ever showing up around the *Frenchman's Creek* location. De Cordova complained but had to settle with running off to San Francisco every time he had a day off. Lupe and de Cordova were quite an item around that time.

They were living in a small cottage in the Longridge Estates, about a dozen blocks from our home in Sherman Oaks. Lupe was one of those who didn't give a damn what the wives thought, and I'd bet my life she'd stand naked in those big view windows and take her time closing the drapes.

My feelings about Lupe, formed that night in the Rainbow Cafe in Lone Pine, had never changed. If I'd heard she was mowing her front lawn, stark naked, I wouldn't have used her street to drive home.

Paramount spent a lot of money on the picture, especially on the lavish sets. Sam Comer won an Academy Award for his outstanding work as set decorator.

I think Leisen himself destroyed any possibility of the picture winning an Oscar by making the "bloodthirsty" pirates a joke. The opening shot of the pirates is a close shot of Billy Daniels seated comfortably on the deck of the ship. Mitch spent a lot of time getting his position just right. His legs crossed just so. A lock of hair carefully moved to curve just above the eyebrow. The hand-knit stocking cap, designed by Leisen himself, with its long trailing end adjusted time and time again, hung down over Billy's left shoulder.

The musical director handed Billy an ancient string instrument that looked to me like some kind of mandolin and watched him strum through the number he was to play. Now, Leisen was ready to present his "pirates" to his public.

The time did come when I learned to respect Mitchell Leisen. I walked on a stage at Universal years later, after I'd become a producer. A very small unit was rehearsing a scene for a half-hour television show called *Markham.* Each segment was filmed in just two days. I was shocked to see Leisen standing behind the camera, just as he always stood when directing his most important pictures.

A mutual friend told me the whole tragic story. Leisen had earned a fortune as a producer/director. He owned an apartment house, his very successful tailor shop, a 139-foot schooner moored in Balboa Bay, and other assets. He followed his tax adviser's advice and, for years, deducted his sailing ship as a business expense. However, the IRS decided that he wasn't entitled to the deduction. He lost everything when he had to pay back taxes and interest from the day he bought the ship.

No one ever told me who gave him the job at Universal, but I'm sure it was Lew Wasserman. He's supposed to be a hard man, but I know different. He'd never let a friend down.

Chapter 24

The Emperor's Waltz

One day in 1946, I was asked to come to Billy Wilder's office. When I arrived, he got right to the point. "I've got a problem," he said, "and I need your help. Buddy's tied up on another picture and won't be finished in time to prepare *The Emperor's Waltz.*"

He was talking about Buddy Coleman (no relation), who had been his first assistant on all his pictures. "You've worked with me. After you've read the script, you'll be able to prepare an honest budget and give me a schedule I can live with. When Buddy completes work on his picture, you can turn everything over to him. Will you do this for us?"

"Buddy knows about this?" I asked Billy.

"He does," he answered. "We'd both like to have you stay with us for the whole picture."

I was happy to have the responsibility of telling Billy what his picture would cost, what scenes he'd film each day, and in what order they'd shoot. And a million minor details. But I would certainly leave the picture before Billy started shooting. I had no intention of staying on as Buddy's second assistant.

The Emperor's Waltz was a story of an American phonograph salesman, Bing Crosby, who, along with his pet mutt, arrives in Austria to set up shop and make a million bucks selling Thomas Edison's newest invention, the phonograph, to that music-loving nation.

I was sitting in Bing's dressing room with a tall, cool drink when he asked, "You wanta discuss the hair you're taking to Jasper, Herbie?"

I'd never heard girls referred to as "hair" before, but I knew what he meant. "We hadn't planned on taking any girls to Jasper, Bing."

He grinned at me and said, "I don't think I feel this picture, Herbie."

"Bing," I said, "I think we'd better go talk to Billy."

He was in no hurry to leave his cool office, but I finally persuaded him to come along. I told Billy what Bing had said. Billy turned to him and said, "But, Bing, there isn't a scene in what we're shooting in Jasper where we can use girls."

"Now I know I don't feel this picture," Bing smiled at Billy and left the office.

He felt better about the location when Billy wrote in a shot of Bing looking off scene and seeing some girls milking cows as he strolled along a mountain path singing "Friendly Mountains."

Bing gave me a list of ten girls. They were young and beautiful, and all of them could have been cover girls. They did make the location more acceptable.

Somebody had been showing the girls how to milk cows, and they were faking it pretty good when Billy shot the scene. But I'd bet that the closest any of them had ever been to a cow was a milk carton.

Before Billy asked me to help on the picture, he had already selected Jasper National Park in the Canadian Rockies to substitute for the Austrian Alps.

The airlines were on strike when the company was scheduled to travel to Jasper, so Hugh Brown, the production manager, arranged for a special train to move the equipment and the cast, with the exception of Crosby, Wilder, and his staff.

I agreed to supervise the trip with one condition. Mary Belle was expecting our third child, and I would be free to come home to be with her.

The morning we were scheduled to board our train, I was standing with the conductor at a door leading out to the tracks, checking our people aboard, when I heard a distant outburst, "Darling!"

I looked down the long corridor toward the street entrance and saw Joan Fontaine, arms up-stretched, rushing toward me. When she got to me, she threw her arms around my neck and gave me a big hug. I couldn't believe it! Not after *Frenchman's Creek.*

That evening, I was sitting by the window of my compartment watching the lights coming on in the streets of the little towns our "special" was passing through and listening to the click of the car's wheels on the steel tracks. It was a sound I'd always enjoyed as a kid, riding on a giant steam engine with Papa, watching him kick open the door of the firebox and sling a heavy scoop of coal twenty feet onto the roaring fire.

The porter from Fontaine's Pullman car came to tell me that Miss Fontaine wanted to see me. I looked up Jimmy Rosenberger, Buddy Coleman's assistant, and took him along.

When we got to her drawing room, we found her sitting alone. She'd changed her clothes. She was wearing clinging white silk pajamas and looked surprised at seeing Jimmy. "I thought we might have dinner together while we talk," she offered.

I lied. "I'm sorry, Joan."

All she wanted to say was that she was tired and didn't want to talk to the press at stops along the way. It only took a few minutes for me to think of a way to keep them away from her. I tried it out at the first stop. When they crowded aboard and asked for her, I told them she was in her room, in her pajamas, probably in bed by now. "If you had asked for an interview, she would have been happy to see you."

They apologized for not contacting me and left the train without realizing they'd been hoodwinked. I used the same tactic all the way, adding that "Miss Fontaine was unhappy that the press was ignoring her."

Billy gave a champagne party for everyone the night we arrived. He was his usual genial host, and everyone was ready to go early the next morning. Only the weather kept the company from staying on schedule.

I had little to do but found myself beginning to be drawn too close to the daily operation. Buddy was turning to me rather than to Jimmy. If I allowed that to continue and anything happened to Buddy, they would turn to me. No way, I told myself. Jimmy is a competent assistant. He's been waiting a long time for his chance to step up. That night, I called Mary Belle and asked her to send me a telegram saying that the doctor wanted me to come home immediately. When we arrived at the lodge from filming on a distant location, Hugh Brown handed me the telegram.

Alice Melinda Coleman, 9 pounds, 12 ounces, joined the rest of the Coleman family at St. Joseph's Hospital in Burbank at 9:45 p.m., June 28, 1946, one *month* after I had received Mary Belle's telegram to hurry home!!

Chapter 25

Calcutta

There was a lot of talk about Alan Ladd's new picture, *Calcutta.* When John Farrow was chosen to direct the film, I assumed that Joe Youngerman would be his assistant. He'd assisted Farrow on his last few pictures. But Joe wouldn't be available for the picture.

Henry Ginsberg, the executive in charge of all of Paramount's West Coast activities, had given Joe a big promotion. He was brought into the Marble Halls as assistant to Ginsberg to supervise budgets on forthcoming pictures.

Farrow was given to me. At least that's what I thought when George Berthelon told me I was "it" and to hop up to the art department where Farrow was in a meeting with Franz Bachelin, the art director.

Farrow barely acknowledged my greeting when I walked into Bachelin's office. During a discussion about the sets, Farrow accepted a phone call. I heard him say, "I'm trying to get you away from DeMille, Eddie. Do what you can. I still want you to be my assistant." He handed the phone to Bachelin and resumed discussing the sets. He knew I'd heard his talk with Eddie Salven, DeMille's assistant, but offered no explanation. DeMille told Eddie to forget John Farrow and *Calcutta.*

During World War II, writers had spread the news of the American flyers who kept supplies flowing into Chungking, China, from Calcutta. Too many of our slow DC3-cargo planes were shot down by the Japanese, but our flyers never gave up.

Most of the studios were turning out romanticized tales of what was called, back then, "flying the hump," and Paramount joined in. Seton I. Miller wrote an original screenplay that had little to do with "flying the hump" but was right for a character Alan Ladd had been perfecting for himself that, as his agent, Sue Carrol (who later became his wife), convinced him, would make him a star as a tough, uncompromising, but fair fighter for law and order. Miller's script was exactly that.

I couldn't believe my ears when I heard that Gail Russell had been cast as the female lead.

The first time I ever saw Gail Russell was October 1942. We were filming the "sleeping bag" sequence for *For Whom the Bell Tolls* on one of Paramount's stages. Only the whispered voices of Coop and Ingrid Bergman disturbed the silence that surrounded us.

I heard someone move nearby. I looked around and saw Russell standing almost hidden in the shadows under a light platform. She was staring, transfixed with wonder at the beauty of the performances of two of Hollywood's finest artists.

She must have sensed that I was looking at her, for she turned toward me and then faded back into the darkness. When Sam called "Cut" at the end of the scene, she had disappeared. A few days later, one of the young contract actresses introduced us. The first thing I noticed about Russell were her beautiful blue eyes. But she was so young and so shy. She seemed almost ready to run. Maybe she should have.

There was a contract director, a handsome but immoral man, from whom those girls who knew him shied away. He moved in, and soon she was lost.

I didn't see much of her between 1942 and 1946. She was busy studying under Bill Russell in the talent department and singing and dancing with LeRoy Prinz, head of the dance department.

I understood why she was cast when we met in Farrow's office a few days after I was assigned to the picture. Something had happened to her. The blue in her eyes seemed to have faded. She was no longer the eager, trusting young schoolgirl I'd met in 1942. I could also see that she was completely dominated by Farrow. She was too anxious to please him.

Calcutta opened the way to a friendship between Alan Ladd and myself that would grow closer as the years sped along, until his tragic death almost twenty years later.

I left the meeting in the art department with little enthusiasm and went to my office and read the 135-page script without stopping. I then leaned back in my chair, closed my eyes, and started reflecting on the problems I faced on my first picture as a first assistant director.

All I knew about Calcutta I'd learned from reading *National Geographic*. My first job was to find a technical director who knew Calcutta like the back of his hand. But the research department had already solved that problem or thought it had. It had hired an East Indian, Paul Singh, the same Paul Singh who would play the part of Mul Raj Malik.

There's an old Indian truism, "All Sikhs are named Singh. But all Singhs are not Sikhs."

Research showed he couldn't be a Sikh because Sikhs are forbidden to ever cut any hair from their bodies throughout their lifetime.

Paul Singh was clean shaven and wore a molded hat shaped to look like a turban. I soon became convinced that the closest he'd ever been to India was Southern California.

Farrow agreed on a starting date and then threw a monkey wrench into the works. He said, "I won't start on that day unless you have real Indians from India working on the sets."

Central Casting had less than a dozen Indians listed in its files. It, the studio's casting department, and Paramount contacts around the country went into action. But after days of a frantic search, they told us to forget it.

Then one day a friend of mine dropped by my office to tell me about a camp down in Wilmington filled with hundreds of Indian sailors.

Margie, the head of Paramount's extra (or atmosphere) players, and I made a beeline for Wilmington. My friend was right. The camp was crowded with Indian sailors. They were Indians who were brought by the shipload from India to British Colombia and then moved to Wilmington a few hundred at a time when the shipyards were ready to deliver the next Liberty ship.

Paramount's legal department went into action. First, it had to get our government's permission to allow them to work in this country. Then, the Indian government had to approve, which it did. The Indian authorities said, "Work it out with the Indian Seamen's Union."

The Screen Extras Guild wages had to be paid both to the Indian Seamen's Union and to the Screen Extras Guild. In other words, we had to pay twice for the same part. The studio provided free lunch!

"It was a deal," the studio told them.

To meet the lunch agreement, we had stage 4 at the studio assigned to us. The east end of the stage was given to the Hindus, and the West end, to the Muslims. In the center of the stage, two giant electric ranges were placed back to back, with the chefs of each sect facing each other but preparing entirely different food for their groups. Jimmy Rosenberg and I were invited to have lunch with the Indians. The Muslims one day, the Hindus the next.

All the Indians sat on the floor in groups. They'd reach into a single large pot, always with their right hands, for the mutton or fish, blazing hot with curry powder. Rice, often with saffron, was always available.

My lunch and Jimmy's were served in beautiful brass bowls, inlaid with porcelain flowers, elephants, and Nataraj dancers.

The Indians did lend a touch of reality to the picture, but using a little village street on the back lot of a little studio out in Culver City as Calcutta was a joke. And using a small dirt strip, somewhere up in Antelope Valley, as Dum Dum Airport, the international airport for eastern India, was an insult, as K. S. Vaidyanathan, the general manager of Paramount Films of India, told me when I visited his office for the first time in January 1967.

I didn't learn much about directing by watching John Farrow on *Calcutta.* To begin with, I didn't much like his style. He was cold, arrogant, and superior. He never seemed to know how he'd stage the action in a new set. He'd stroll in, swinging his cane (his affectation), hang it over his arm, and walk around the empty set gazing through the camera finder, trying to figure out what to do. He'd finally stop and tell the cameraman, the distinguished veteran Johnny Seitz, to put the camera there. Then he'd disappear into his stage dressing room to be joined later by some of the young and beautiful would-be actresses.

Filming went along smoothly until one Monday morning when actor Gavin Muir failed to show up. He was in every scene planned for that day. Jimmy Rosenberger, my assistant, called every number he could think of trying to locate Muir. We gave up around eleven and moved to another set, losing half a day.

In the afternoon, the search was turned over to the police and the sheriff's department. Thursday morning, Muir was found in a motel near Malibu with a woman. Joe Youngerman wanted me to fire Jimmy.

"Blame it on Jimmy, and I'll walk off the picture," I said.

"If you don't, John will ride Muir until the picture is finished," Joe responded.

"Good. He deserves it. And if making second assistants suffer when people like Muir fail to show up is part of a first's job, then find somebody else to finish this picture. I'll leave with Jimmy."

Jimmy and I were there at the finish.

Chapter 26

A Shoddy Tale

I can't remember the date, but I know Joe Youngerman hadn't been in his new job very long when he asked me to come to his office in the Marble Halls.

I was surprised when he asked, "What would you say if I told you we're bringing Dick Johnson back?"

A lot of things flashed through my mind. Everyone knew why the studio fired Johnson in 1940. There was no way we could keep out of the war in Europe, and Paramount would need someone in that job whom everyone would want to work for.

Now, six years later, with the war just a bad memory and experienced filmmakers standing around the gates of all the studios looking for jobs, Joe could bring his old friend back. If Johnson reverted to his old hard-nosed, uncaring ways, who cared? And what about Paramount, struggling to survive in 1940 with Johnson in charge, the studio's income a bare $7 to $8 million, and the estimated income, in 1946, over $44 million?

Did they need a cutthroat production manager to increase their profits? What was happening to the studio I was so proud of?

All that passed through my mind in seconds. I knew the answers to all the questions.

"What about George Berthelon?" I asked. "He'll be stepping up. We'll have a new job for him. And stepping right out the front door in a couple of months," I said.

I walked out, thinking back to 1939, when we came back to the studio from the Key West location on *Reap the Wild Wind* to find that the script supervisors were now reporting to Dick Johnson, not to the cutting department.

My first run-in with Johnson occurred at a budget meeting on *Blaze of Noon*. Budget meetings were held before the start of filming on every picture, always with the studio production manager presiding.

My direct responsibility was the "Bits and Extras" budget. How many extras we would need in each set and how much they'd be paid.

Blaze of Noon was the first budget meeting where I ever faced Johnson. I knew he was just waiting to cut me down to size. There was no love lost between us. I'd lost all respect for him on that drive up that snow-packed road out of the valley of the Dardanelles back in 1929.

He was having a bad time of it. Most of the department heads were resisting lowering their budgets. He looked at me and demanded, "Let's see how much you're going to take out of your budget. You're overloaded on the first set—150 extras on the carnival set?"

He almost came up out of his seat when I told him to double that figure.

"They've built the set on two levels with a Ferris wheel, merry-go-round, and more sideshows than we really need." He glared at me. He was losing face before everyone.

"We'll discuss it after the meeting," he said. We never did. I got the 300 people. The ice grew thicker and colder between us, until he was eased out again in the mid-1950s.

This was to be my second picture in a row with John Farrow. There would be many more: *The Night Has a Thousand Eyes; Alias Nick Beale; The Big Clock; Copper Canyon; Beyond Glory; California*; *Red, Hot and Blue; Submarine Command*; and *Botany Bay.*

I guess Henry Ginsberg thought he had a permanent team. But he found out differently one day when he, Farrow, and I were walking down dressing room row. He said, "John, it was a great day when we decided to team you and Herbie Coleman. Your pictures all make a good profit. They always finish on time and within the budget. Must be a mutual admiration society."

"It's not exactly that, Henry," Farrow replied. "Herbie's just waiting for his back pay check so he can slap me in the face with it." He wasn't kidding. Henry turned, looked first at John and then at me, wondering just what was behind John's statement.

I still had to threaten to leave the studio before the executives would put another assistant with Farrow. But that wouldn't happen for years.

Chapter 27

California

I always liked making westerns, and *California* was a choice assignment. But if I could have had my druthers on who to direct, I'd have picked someone like George Marshall, with whom I had worked on *Forest Ranger.* Or John Huston, a director for whom I had great respect.

Ray Milland, Barry Fitzgerald, and Barbara Stanwyck were the stars. I'd worked with Barbara on Wellman's *The Great Man's Lady* as script supervisor and was happy I was going to be with her again. And this time in a more important position.

The picture got a big, big budget for a Farrow production. Twenty giant, canvas-covered Conestoga wagons, each drawn by four horses, were transported to Arizona for the scenes of the wagon train moving toward California. Men were sent to Tuba City to round up 120 Indian covered wagons and teams, along with their owners, wives, children, grandmas, grandpas, dogs, horses, and cattle.

Farrow refused to go to Arizona to choose the locations we would need. He told the front office to send Joe Youngerman, and he'd shoot on the locations Joe selected. Just one day before we were scheduled to start shooting, Farrow and I were met in Flagstaff by one of the studio's cars.

We headed out on the road that led to Tuba City, the same road we'd traveled so often when we were living there on *The Outlaw.* Farrow seemed little interested in conversation on the sixty-mile drive to our headquarters at Cameron. I was asking myself, Why Cameron? It was not even a wide place in the road. Just a tiny, old Indian trading post that barely rated a glance before you would fix your attention on the narrow, old, iron bridge that crossed a twenty-foot-deep wash.

The most important scene to be filmed in Arizona shows the entire wagon train arriving at a point in the high, rugged mountains where they can see the "Promised Land." High rugged mountains? Around Cameron? For as far as you could see at Cameron there was nothing but vast, flat prairies, with low, bare, rolling hills on the horizon.

Cameron was crowded with trucks, loaded with lights, props, and other equipment. Across the highway from the trading post, the Indians had established their camp. The 120 wagons and horses were scattered around. Smoke was rising from the countless fires where the Indian women were preparing food for their husbands and fathers, who stood around in groups waiting for instructions. The Anderson Boarding and Supply Company had established its kitchens and other tents on the grounds of the trading post.

As the driver pulled to a stop in all that confusion, Farrow turned to me and asked, "Where are all the mountains?" I told him there were no mountains anywhere in that area.

"Then what are we doing here?" he demanded.

"Maybe we'd better find a phone so you can call Joe and ask him. You said you'd shoot the locations he picked."

From the car, we could see propmen and construction workers working on the rim of the wash. They were building rigs to lower wagons from the rim to the floor of the wash about twenty feet below. "We can't shoot here, Herbie," he said. "What're we going to do?"

I told the driver to take us to Sedona. Back through Flagstaff and down the narrow, steep, twisting road to one of the true garden spots in all of Arizona. At least it was in 1947. The only signs of civilization at Sedona were a little store and a single gas pump. It should have been preserved as a national treasure. Rising above the sparkling stream, beyond the store, there was a bright red table with a tall spire rising toward the white fluffy clouds in a bright blue sky. I told the driver to cross the stream and take the road to the left. It skirted the backside of a rugged red mountain. Halfway up that road, I asked the driver to stop.

Farrow was all smiles as he climbed out. He looked straight across a steep slope to a series of cliffs between the road where we stood and the red mountain.

Turning to his left, he looked out past the end of the red mountain to the Promised Land, a vast level plain with no sign of civilization.

"How did you know about this place?" he asked.

"We drove up here when we were looking for locations for Howard Hughes's picture, *The Outlaw,*" I told him.

On the way back to Cameron, I told Farrow we could find enough work around Cameron to keep us busy for a couple of days, using some of our Conestoga wagons, while we moved all the Indians and Anderson's commissary to Sedona. That worked out just fine.

I wasn't surprised that Joe had picked Cameron. Joe had little imagination and was unable to visualize what a scene would look like. Cost always colored Joe's actions. What a sensation that move from Cameron to Sedona became, those 120 Indian covered wagons stretched out alongside that highway, moving at a snail's pace, surrounded by the families of the drivers, extra horses, cattle, dogs, and countless children. Tourists must have thought they were seeing the exodus of the Navajo Indians.

We drove out one night to see how the Indians were getting along. As far as the eye could see, there were fires around each of the 120 wagons. What a sight! Five days after leaving Cameron they arrived in Sedona.

Two days later, we were ready to film the scene, but Farrow stalled. He wanted clouds in the sky. I couldn't blame him. I'd have done the same thing. But word came from the studio: "Shoot it. We'll put the clouds in later."

Of course, they didn't. Back in those days, it wasn't technically possible.

We rehearsed the scene all morning and part of the afternoon, and just before the sun was ready to go down over the distant plains, Farrow called, "Action."

Farmwomen, men too old or too ill to work, and children of all ages began streaming in from the right, striving to keep their footing as they descended the steep slope near the camera.

The camera panned with them to include men on the tops of the high cliffs some distance away, lowering wagons down the face of the sheer rocks. Other men at the foot of the cliffs were hitching the teams to the Conestoga wagons. Drivers climbed to the seats and, with the camera panning, headed across the steep slope toward the red mountain.

The camera began to include the 120 Indian wagons, strung out in a line far ahead of the Conestogas. Beyond the Indian wagons, men, carrying sheets nailed to poles, doubling for covered wagons, were already moving along a narrow trail halfway up the side of the red mountain.

The camera continued to pan to the left to include the wide opening between the red mountains and the distant plains of the "Promised Land," California!

California! The real California wasn't good enough.

Arizona made a better California.

Chapter 28

Copper Canyon

Copper Canyon brought us back to that garden spot, Sedona, where we'd filmed *California*. It was John Farrow again. This time he would direct a screenplay written by one of my favorite writers, Jonathan Latimer, adapted from a story by Richard English. There's not much to talk about on that story of Ray Milland, who, dressed in the uniform of a Confederate soldier, is hiding from the Union Army.

Hedy Lamarr is Hedy Lamarr. Sexy, of course. Otherwise, why was she in the picture? The love scenes between her and Ray created some excitement.

Lamarr was riding high at the time and had some clout around the industry. The studio agreed to her agent's terms, which included a provision that all her scenes would be filmed in the studio. As a result of that agreement, two long, expensive streets had to be built, one on location and another on a studio stage.

Another demand, less expensive but a distinct annoyance, was that a chaise lounge would always be placed beside the camera. No eyebrows were lifted when word was passed that Miss Lamarr needed to be on her back at every opportunity. But you could hear some pointed comments.

With just two days left to finish our location shooting, Farrow told me he was going back to the studio to work with Latimer on the script: "You know what's left to be shot around here. You'll have to do the chase with Milland."

That situation led to my first serious run in with Dick Johnson since he was brought back by Youngerman. "Why did John Farrow come back to the studio when there is still work to be done there with Ray Milland?" he demanded to know.

"Why don't you go to Farrow's office and ask him?" I suggested. "You want me to cancel the rest of the filming and come home?"

He didn't answer, he just broke off. That set the tone for our relationship for the duration of his stay in his job.

There was one amusing incident that occurred before we completed filming on *Copper Canyon*. Right at midnight one Saturday night, I got a call from the operations desk at the studio. Lew Foster, a longtime friend, was on duty at the time. "You've got a problem," he said. "A Mister Hakim just called and asked me to tell you Miss Lamarr would be sick on Monday and wouldn't report for work."

Lew wanted to know if I was going to change the call for Monday's work if Lamarr didn't show up. "No," I told him. "Just give me Hakim's phone number."

Because I was now wide awake, I decided I'd read a while. I divided my time between my book and the clock on the wall. At three o'clock on the dot, I dialed Hakim's number. He didn't answer immediately, so I just let it ring. Finally, a sleepy man's voice came on the line. "My name's Herbie Coleman," I said. "Let me speak to Miss Lamarr."

"Miss Lamarr isn't here," the voice answered.

I asked if he was Mr. Hakim and if he was the one who called the studio with word she'd be sick on Monday. He admitted he'd made the call.

I asked how he knew Miss Lamarr would be too sick to come to work on Monday. He couldn't come up with much of an explanation, so I told him to tell Miss Lamarr I would have a car with the studio's doctor at her home at 5:30 Monday morning. He would examine her, and if, in his opinion, she was able to work and she didn't report to makeup at 6:30, I would cancel all work for the day at a cost of some $80,000. Maybe it's worth $80,000 of her money to enjoy a day in bed, I added. I guess she decided it wasn't, because she was in makeup at 6:30 and on the set at nine. And she looked as sexy as ever.

Chapter 29

The Big Clock

I was once asked what I thought of Charles Laughton.

As an actor, in most everything he did, he was superb. As a person, he was a "pompous old poop." A pompous old poop? Why? Well, I could give you many reasons. I'll just tell you one tale.

Around ten o'clock one morning when I was about to leave for location to direct a second unit on *The Big Clock,* I decided to stop by the stage to see how John Farrow was getting along without me.

To my surprise, when I stepped on the stage, there was absolute silence. Except for one light focused on Farrow, Laughton and the camera crew were sitting around the camera. The stage was black.

The shot they were lined up on was a big close-up of Laughton that should have been in the can by 9:15. I asked Farrow about the delay.

"We can't shoot," he said. "They've lost Charles's shoes."

"This is a big close-up of his face. What do his shoes have to do with that?"

Laughton spoke in a voice filled with indignation. "How do you expect me to have the proper posture without my proper shoes?" I quickly decided not to give him the answer that was on the tip of my tongue. Instead, I asked Pat Williams, the wardrobe man, how much Laughton's heels were built up. "An inch and a quarter," he told me.

Laughton watched the head grip place a board, exactly an inch and a quarter thick, on the floor where he was to stand. "Your heels on the edge of that board should give you the proper posture, Mr. Laughton," I said.

He didn't bother to answer. He just got to his feet, stared at me so angry he couldn't speak, and then marched off the stage. "There, John," I told Farrow. "He'll cool off and march back in after he runs around the Marble Halls telling anybody who'll listen how I've abused him."

Laughton came back. They did the scene. His shoes were found in the bedroom of his home. They still got the day's work finished in time.

The first day Laughton came to Farrow's office before the start of the picture, he heard my "Wild, Wonderful Cliff Holler, West Virginia," accent. I saw him puff up his head, tilt it back, and stare down at me over his noble nose. I could sense the words he decided not to throw at me: "Why cawn't you learn to speak the King's English?"

We didn't have to order the air conditioning turned on that hot summer when Laughton was working. The chill between the two of us was enough to keep the stage almost frigid.

Big Clock had a lot going for it when Oscar time arrived in 1948: Milland's performance, Farrow's direction, Maibaum's screenplay, Roland Anderson's imposing sets, the always superior photography by Johnny Seitz.

Farrow had good reason to believe that he had a chance to win for best direction, but Joseph Mankiewicz won with *A Letter to Five Wives*. He also beat out Dick Maibaum for best screenplay for the same picture.

When I was assigned to *The Big Clock*, it was the seventh picture in a row that I'd been ordered to work with John Farrow on, and I thought that was enough.

I hadn't been learning much on the others, but on *Big Clock* I had my first lesson in how suspense, if properly developed, could grip and hold an audience.

Hitch would give me a doctorate in suspense many years later.

Chapter 30

The Great Gatsby

Just a few days after we finished *Big Clock,* Alan Ladd asked me to drop by his dressing room. "How'd you like to get a new director on your next picture?" he asked with a laugh. "Sue [Alan's wife] is in Henry Ginsberg's office right now, telling him we want you on my new picture, *The Great Gatsby.*"

"Who's the director?"

"Elliott Nugent. You know him?" Alan asked.

"No. I do remember seeing one of his pictures about three years ago. *Up in Arms.*"

"I think you and Elliott will get along just fine."

F. Scott Fitzgerald wrote a novel that, far more than any other, paints a true picture of life among the amoral society of the late 1920s in the New York suburb known as the West End. It focuses on the jaded youth of the established rich, with their imported open Dusenberg roadsters racing around the city, with kids too young to handle even the imported Scotch, gin, and beer their parents were all too willing to buy for them. It's also about the gangsters and bootleggers who paraded their wealth, their ribald rowdy women, and their guns, with contempt for both the law and the public.

Ladd was one of the richest and boldest of the latter group. We find him driving into the West End in his imported open car. With him are two of his henchmen, Elisha Cook Jr. and Ed Begley. Ladd is looking for a mansion he can buy. One that will allow him a place among the old, established rich. He finds one, an enormous estate, and moves in. His new mansion sits across the bay from Betty Field's mansion. Ladd points it out to Begley and tells him about Betty, whom he knew in Louisville, Kentucky, as Betty Faye. Who now calls herself Betty Buchanan.

Ladd begins throwing expensive parties. Wild men and wilder women. Booze and bathing suits. (Well, not everyone was always in bathing suits. At least, that was the way I'd planned the action with the atmosphere people. But Nugent wouldn't go for it.)

In the script, the first party Ladd gave was around the swimming pool. The camera was shooting past a half dozen tables in the foreground where young men and girls were really whooping it up. One of the girls had on one of the briefest bathing suits the Censor Board would allow us to use. During the scene, one of the guys in a tux would pick her up and attempt to throw her in the pool. They struggle, and both go in. Others were drinking and dancing the Charleston to the loud, swinging music of a large orchestra. One girl was pouring champagne over her boyfriend's head. One young man near the camera was passing a champagne bucket across the pool to another young man near the door to the large drawing room from which Ladd, Ruth Hussey, and Macdonald Carey would come to join the party.

When everything was ready, I asked Elliott to take a look at the rehearsal.

Everything was going according to the plan. As Ladd and the others crossed behind the man with the bucket, he threw the bucket back to the first man. But, as instructed, he threw it short. The first passer ran and leaped for it, landing with a big splash in the pool.

Elliott turned to me with a puzzled look and asked, "Herbie, what is all that?"

"That, Elliott, is a sample of what parties were like back in the 1920s. I know. I went to a few parties in Bradenton, Florida, the summer of 1926 and saw scenes much wilder than the one you just saw. Fitzgerald wouldn't allow Gatsby's parties to go that far, but he should have."

"It's much too much," replied Nugent. "Let's not have the champagne bucket bit. And the two going into the pool distracts too much from the entrance. Does the orchestra have to play so loud? Maybe the dancers can slow down a bit. Let's have everyone in their dress clothes. Sipping their champagne is fine. They can be having a fine time talking and laughing."

I said, "Elliott, why don't you tell the people all that?"

He did and added a bit of his own action. He called to one of the people standing at a table near the door to the drawing room, "When Mr. Ladd crosses behind you, please raise your handkerchief and wave it toward the camera." Then he chose a girl at a table near the camera to see him waving. "You recognize him as your date. Get to your feet and run around the pool to join him. I think that will do it," he told the girl.

I tried to convince him that the party was dull. That it didn't establish a true picture of events in the 1920s. I didn't win.

I was surprised when Dick Maibaum didn't order a retake after he saw the rushes the next day. But I wasn't surprised when, months later, the executives saw a rough cut and ordered some stock footage of action I'd wanted from the start added to the picture. Scenes of cars overloaded with overloaded girls and boys waving and yelling, driving madly down crowded streets, were bought and cut into the print.

The second amusing incident occurred when we were in the drawing room with the camera fairly close to the open door leading from the main corridor into the drawing room. Ladd, Macdonald Carey, and Ruth Hussey entered through the door. As they came forward speaking the lines from the script, the camera, holding the three in full figure from head to foot, retreated across the wide, bare parquet floor.

I could see that Alan was very uncomfortable. Carey was a full head taller than Alan, and Hussey was at least two inches taller, as well. Usually, I'd handle a situation like that by having Alan walk on planks to correct the height problem. But this was different. Because the camera would show the bare floor behind them as they followed it, any planks on the floor would be seen.

Johnny Seitz was still lighting the scene when a possible solution came to me. Maybe, if I had boom tracks laid on the floor and had the carpenters cover them with matching parquet, Johnny could flat light them so they would blend with the rest of the floor. When I asked Johnny about it, a big smile appeared on his face. "You bet I can, Herbie. But I'll need a little time." Johnny was always as concerned with Alan's height as I was.

I sent everyone away for an early lunch.

The carpenters did their job, and Johnny wasted no time relighting. Then the fun began. Because there were no shadows on the floor, it looked flat. People would start across the floor, trip over the hidden planks, and fall flat on their faces. The first to fall was Alan, but all he did was turn and thank me.

While the film was in production, Alan lived the part of Gatsby. His moods offstage were in perfect harmony with his Gatsby character.

Of course, I had my usual run in with Dick Johnson. It happened in the budget meeting before all the studio department heads. They were resisting his demands for cuts in their budgets. He was waiting for me. "I want every ounce of fat out of your budget." He had his pencil poised over the "Bits and Extras" paper.

"I've got some good news for you, Dick. Let's go back to the sets. You can take out that $10,000 Hans Dreier has for the boat set. I've found a stock shot of a boat and matching set in storage. Farciot showed me the matching transparency plates. Nugent's okayed it all."

Johnson was ready to explode. He closed the meeting and told me to come to his office. I followed him along the corridor. As soon as the door to his office closed, he turned to me and said, "I wish you'd learn to let other department heads defend their own budgets."

"I thought you'd be happy about that $10,000."

"That $10,000 stays. It's in there to pay for Henry Ginsberg's vacation in Hawaii. And forget what I've just told you."

Chapter 31

Red, Hot and Blue

Red, Hot and Blue! And back with John Farrow! But after Elliott Nugent, Farrow wasn't such a bad assignment.

The star of *Red, Hot and Blue* was Betty Hutton, who was riding high in 1949. She could pick and choose her stories and directors. There would come the day on *Blue* when she'd regret accepting Farrow.

Frank Loesser, whom I'd never known as an actor, was interesting in the part of a gangster. But his real contribution to the success of the film was his songs, including "Where Are You Now That I Need You?" "Hamlet," and "I Wake Up in the Morning Feeling Fine." They were perfect for Hutton.

And Billy Daniels. He created the dance numbers for Hutton. It was his final number that caused the earthquake the last day on our schedule. Betty had worked long and hard to perfect the difficult solo number we'd scheduled a full day to film. I'd asked her to report at 8:30 in the morning to show Farrow and the rest of us the dance she'd purposely concealed from us.

Farrow arrived on the stage a little after eight. He seemed preoccupied as he walked directly into his stage dressing room and closed the door.

Less than five minutes later he came out and asked for Hutton. I told him her call was 8:30. He wasn't satisfied and said he wanted to see the dance at once.

I walked away to keep from blowing my top. He called Billy Daniels and asked him to do the number. For at least ten minutes Billy stalled: "Betty has never allowed me to dance her numbers for anyone. She wants you to see it Hutton's way."

Farrow insisted so strongly that Billy went up on the stage and began the number. He was a gifted little man. Not even Astaire could excel his graceful, fluid moves.

Even I had forgotten Betty. No one heard the stage door open. Only an explosive, angry outburst stopped Billy cold. "What the hell's going on here?"

Betty Hutton didn't wait for an answer. "Who made Billy show my number?"

Farrow didn't have the guts to answer her. Before I could get to her, she stormed off the stage. Except for the slam of the stage door, there was absolute silence. I followed Farrow into his stage dressing room. "What do you think?" he asked.

I told him I thought he made a fool of himself when he forced Billy to dance. When he wanted me to go after Betty, I told him we'd better give her a chance to cool off.

I waited a full hour and then walked slowly down the street to her main dressing room. We'd become friends during the summer while we were in production. She was a hard, demanding woman who'd been around. Her climb up the ladder was slow and painful.

When I knocked on her door and asked to see her, there was silence. I waited a while, and when I knocked the second time, she opened the door and let me in. "If you came here to ask me to come back, you're wasting your time, Herbie. Not until that bastard Farrow's gone and a new director's sitting in his chair."

"You've told Henry Ginsberg?"

She shook her head. Betty had one of the finest agents in the business. I think his name was Abe Lasfogel, but I'm not sure. I am sure he was one of the most respected agents in town. It was time to get him involved. I suggested she call him and have him see Ginsberg immediately. I told her I'd go back to the set and stall until I heard from her.

When I walked on the stage, Farrow was sitting in his dressing room, entertaining his "beauties" of the day. He came out, looked past me toward the stage door, and asked, "Where's Hutton?" I told him she'd be along later. That we'd let Danny Fapp, our cameraman, complete his lighting, send everyone to lunch, and be ready to shoot around two o'clock. I knew by then all hell would be a-poppin'. Two o'clock arrived, but Hutton didn't. She and her agent were meeting with the brass, so we all just sat around and waited.

As expected, Dick Johnson blew in and wanted to know why I'd told Billy to do the dance. I pointed to Farrow's dressing room where John was still surrounded by his "beauties." "There's your problem, Dick. He made a big mistake, and you don't have to tell me it's costing the company big money."

I knew he didn't have the guts to face Farrow. He left the stage, and I grabbed another cup of coffee.

I wasn't invited to the meetings in the Marble Halls. Betty called me around four and said she'd be on the stage ready to shoot at nine the next morning.

I was happy that long boring day was over.

But that long boring day wasn't over, as I discovered just after midnight when the telephone woke me from a sound sleep. The voice I heard when I picked up the receiver sounded like Betty Hutton's. But I wasn't sure. It was a soft voice, with tears in it. Hutton crying? I couldn't believe it. She didn't let me wonder too long. "Herbie, I know I agreed to work tomorrow, but I've changed my mind. The thought of having that bastard staring at me all day makes me sick. You'd better tell the studio to have a new director there in the morning."

I could tell she meant it. I knew I'd have to find words, damn quick, to change her mind. I didn't keep her waiting very long. "Betty, everybody in the studio knows what happened yesterday. The call sheet went out, so they know you agreed to come to work. If you don't show up, Farrow will spread the word all around this town that you're afraid of him."

I heard her explode. She didn't reach Lupe Velez's peak, but she wasn't far behind. "I'll be there! And you tell that son of a bitch, if he says one word to me all day, I'm gone!" Then, in a kinder and softer tone, she said she hoped I'd have a good night's sleep.

I was on the set early the next morning. I took Danny Fapp and Billy Daniels aside and told them what we all faced that day. "I'll have Betty show you the entire dance as soon as she gets here. Billy, for the rest of the day when Farrow asks to see a rehearsal, you step in."

When Farrow strolled in swinging his cane, I told him the facts of life. He had the good sense to go along, but there was a feeling of impending doom hanging over us all day.

When Farrow said he was satisfied with the last scene, I invited everyone to the usual "wrap" party on an adjoining stage where our unit manager had arranged an elaborate buffet supper, with a bar and a small orchestra.

Betty had left the stage the minute the last scene was completed. I was sure she'd come back for the party. She sure did. And she brought along presents for the entire staff and crew. Way back then, stars always passed out expensive gifts, and Betty had the reputation of giving the most lavish presents of anyone.

She joined in the fun, and when the eating, drinking, and dancing began to slow down, she began passing out the loot. She'd reach into one of her boxes, pull out a beautifully wrapped gift, call out the name on the tag, and walk out among us to present it, along with a kiss.

As she continued to pass out the gifts, I began to wonder about Farrow. He sat there, watching all that with a half smile on his face. Would she have something for him?

She came to where I was standing and handed me a small, beautifully wrapped present and gave me a kiss. When I opened it later, I found a solid gold pen and pencil set. The pen was engraved with the words, "To Herbie Coleman, with my love, Betty Hutton." My present was the next to last. After the kiss she went back to the raised platform, turned to face us, and announced, "There's just one present left in this box. It's yours, Mr. Farrow. If you want it, you can come and get it."

What a slap in the face. Would he go up and get it? We all watched.

He did.

Betty told me later that his present was a rare first edition he'd been trying to find for years.

Chapter 32

Submarine Command

I was tired of Farrow but didn't complain when I was handed the script of *Submarine Command.* With that title, I was sure it would be a change from the studio stages to the open sea.

It was an original written by Jonathan Latimer. Joseph Sistrom was the producer and a good friend. Henry (Bummy) Bumstead would be the art director. Charles Lang was the cameraman. Charlie was always in demand, especially by the female stars.

The Navy gave us complete cooperation. We could film our interiors aboard the *Broadbill,* a submarine docked in Wilmington used for training. And two active submarines docked in San Diego. We also could use facilities at the San Diego Naval Training Station. All had certain restrictions. We could only film the active subs at their restricted training area, some thirty-five miles out to sea.

I was happy to be working with Bill Holden again and to watch his remarkable natural interpretation of Commander White's role. To me, he was always Bill Holden. The audience always forgot he was Bill Holden.

Many years after the film was released, I read a review of *Submarine Command* that contained some deliberate lies about Bill's conduct while we were making the picture. It mentioned that Holden was drunk most of the time. I never saw Bill take a drink during the entire picture. As a matter of fact, he was on a health kick at the time. I used to kid him when we were dining together. He always gulped down a handful of vitamin pills.

It was December 31, 1949, when *Submarine Command* went before the cameras. No one could understand why we opened the picture on New Year's Eve. Something to do with taxes was the only explanation offered.

We shot a scene between Bill Holden and Peggy Webber, the widow of Bill's superior officer, at her home in San Diego. He tells her of the death of her husband: "We were on the surface close to the Japanese coast the day World War II ended. Commander Rice was on the deck of the *Tiger Shark.* A flight of Japanese planes came out of nowhere and opened fire. Commander Rice was seriously wounded. To save the *Tiger Shark* and its crew, I ordered the sub to crash dive. After the attack, we searched the sea for the commander and the deck crew. None of them were ever found."

After that one day of filming, the picture was closed down for planning, casting, and preparation.

The first time I climbed down inside the *Broadbill* and saw the tiny space in the main control area where most of the scenes were to be staged, I asked myself, "How could Dick Johnson give this picture to Charlie Lang?" Charlie used more lights than any cameraman in Hollywood. Put Bill Holden, William Bendix, and all the rest of the actors needed in that confined space, and he'd have to light it with flashlights. Here we go again, I thought, another fight with Johnson. Fortunately, before we went into production, I found a way to correct that impossible situation.

There was a cameraman, Lionel (Curly) Lindon, under contract to the studio. We'd grown up together and were close friends. He'd started as a film loader and worked his way to the top. Dorothy Lamour refused to be photographed by any other cameraman.

But Curly had a big problem. He drank too much. Not on the job, but every night he could be found across the street from the main gate in Oblaths bar. What Curly did after he left the studio was nobody's business. But somebody made it his business, and Johnson fired Curly. I heard about it and went looking for him. Of course, I found him at Oblaths. I made a deal with him. "Put down that drink and give up drinking day and night from this moment until the end of shooting on *Submarine Command,* and I'll get you the picture." He promised and kept his promise. I told Johnson I'd go to the front office if he didn't go along. Curly got the picture and, two years later, more than repaid me for my good deed.

Among the scenes on my second unit schedule was a shot of the commander's body lying on the deck as the sub dives to escape.

I had a waterproof camera secured in the rigging. Placed the double for the commander in position. He agreed to lie there until the rush of water carried him out of the camera range.

Everyone went below, and the captain ordered his crew to dive.

We were sitting in the projection room two days later waiting to see the rush of ocean water carry the commander's body overboard! What we saw was the double running out of the scene. But we were lucky. As he ran out, his cap fell off and remained in the scene, whirling around in the turbulent water. What the audience saw was just the cap. I was commended for my creative talent!

Chapter 33

Branded

Following *Submarine Command,* I was assigned to work with Byron Haskins on *The Naked Jungle,* starring Charlton Heston and Eleanor Parker. And for the last time, assigned to work with John Farrow on *Botany Bay,* starring Alan Ladd and James Mason.

On to *Branded,* and four wonderful months with the gifted, sensitive, former cinematographer Rudy Maté.

The photography had to be magnificent, and it certainly was. Charles Lang Jr. was the cameraman, with Rudy Maté beside him.

And the cast! Alan Ladd was never better. The lovely Mona Freeman at her best.

Charlie Bickford? Never a question to anyone but director C. B. DeMille. Charlie never accepted the Hollywood notion that DeMille was second only to God (some thought the numbers were the other way around). While performing in a DeMille epic, he made the mistake of standing on principle in an argument with the Master.

Principle wasn't a word in DeMille's vocabulary. He didn't know the meaning of the word. Bickford would bend to his will or be out. Charlie wouldn't bend. DeMille used his influence to have Bickford barred from films for many years.

Principle became an issue during the filming of *Branded.*

One night, I was in my room in the hotel in Douglas, Arizona, where we were staying while filming the scenes around the Lavery ranch some seventy miles east of the city, when Charlie Bickford came to see me. He was waving some new script pages in the air. In his deep, booming voice he wanted to know why the script had been changed: "The scene where I rode and broke that crazy outlaw bronc made me agree to do this picture! Now the scene's been rewritten, and Ladd's going to ride that horse! Why?"

"You know why, Charlie. He's the star of *Branded,* and riding a mean, crazy horse is spectacular. You know Sue Ladd. She read the script and got to the producers. Alan hasn't even seen those pages. There's his copy on the bed."

"You'd better get the studio on the phone right now, Herbie. I'm through 'til this is straightened out."

"Charlie, you had all of us with you in your fight with DeMille; but no one could help you, and you lost. And you'll lose here. Is it worth all that?"

"It's the principle of the thing."

Principle! There was that word again. He was right, but he lost again. He reported back to the set, and we went on with our work.

Why had Charlie come to me with his problem that night? Mel Epstein, the producer, was his man. But Mel wasn't on the location, and I guess Charlie felt that a kindred soul was right down the hall. Although we lost some time while they settled things, nobody held anything against Charlie.

Branded was a happy company, despite Dick Johnson getting in the act again.

Word arrived on the set while we were shooting down in Salt Canyon. We'd moved our headquarters from Douglas to Globe, Arizona, for a complete change of scenery for the Mexico sequences. "Starting next Monday," the message stated, "no production personnel would be paid unless they were assigned to a picture."

Production managers would replace first assistant directors at assistant directors' salaries. First assistant directors would replace second assistants at seconds' salaries, and second assistants would be dismissed.

No one would be recalled unless needed on a shooting company.

Some of the assistants we had with us on our two shooting units had their pay cut two days after we received Johnson's message.

What was Johnson trying to prove with this squeeze on his staff? Did Paramount need those few bucks so desperately? What had they done with that $73.5 million of working capital they had just a couple of years ago?

Chapter 34

Carrie

I'd heard conflicting stories about William Wyler. On his sets he was a demanding, driving, inflexible man, refusing to accept less than absolute perfection from his cast. Not even the most distinguished film stars would dare ask why when he would say, after twenty, fifty, or eighty takes, "Let's do it again."

And then there was the other Wyler. The one sitting across the desk from me. And I liked what I saw. A small man with slightly graying hair, a face lined by the horrors of the war in which he'd served with distinction as an Air Force combat commander. And eyes, with the most sincere smile I'd ever seen in any of the many directors I'd worked with. He seemed relaxed, but there was more than a hint of energy bound up inside that stocky body.

When he asked for the names of his pictures I'd seen, I told him *Wuthering Heights, Mrs. Miniver,* and *The Best Years of Our Lives.* He led me into a discussion of each of them.

I didn't realize what was going on until halfway through the first picture. He wanted to know, without asking directly, my views on the story, performances, sets, music, and, most importantly, photography.

I hadn't prepared myself for such an intensive examination, but he seemed pleased with my reports.

His secretary kept our cups filled with strong black coffee, while he told me about his new venture.

"Are you familiar with Theodore Dreiser's work?" he asked.

"I've read just one of his books. *Sister Carrie.* I didn't like it very much."

"Why not?"

"It was a simple but powerful story, drowned in an ocean of extraneous storytelling. I understood Carrie's determination to escape the dreary future she faced in Columbia City and everything that happened to her in her struggles in Chicago and New York. But I had a hard time accepting her selfish, callous treatment of Hurstwood as he sank deeper and deeper toward his suicide."

"And Hurstwood?"

"Frankly, Mr. Wyler. . . ."

"Willie."

"Yes, sir. I found myself disliking Hurstwood more and more as I turned the pages of Dreiser's book. I kept asking myself, Will he ever realize where his entanglement with Carrie was leading? I found Drouet the only person in the story I could root for."

The smile that had disappeared from Willie's face reappeared at the mention of Drouet, as I told him what I thought of *Sister Carrie.*

"You maybe found a kindred spirit in Drouet?" He didn't wait for, or expect, an answer. He picked up a screenplay from his desk and handed it to me.

I stared at the title page. The word *CARRIE* stared back at me.

"You're going to help me make Carrie and Hurstwood as believable as Drouet. That's not the final shooting script, but you can use it for budget and schedule. I wouldn't want anyone to see those until we've studied them and agreed I've got the time and money I need."

The final screenplay that Ruth and Augustus Goetz delivered to Wyler roughly followed Dreiser's book.

I have a vivid memory of the opening scene. It is a shot of Jennifer Jones as Carrie trudging along a narrow, dirt road lined with tall trees along one side. On the opposite side there is open farmland showing the effects of drought and misuse. She is carrying a small bag that contains the few cheap clothes she owns and is taking to Chicago, the city of her dreams.

Preparing the budget was easy. Willie had already approved the set sketches and drawings that Art Director Roland Anderson had given him. And the budget department was busy figuring the cost.

Just a year before *Carrie* became a reality, Willie produced and directed a big-budget period film, *The Heiress,* at the studio; so all departments were familiar with his requirements and soon provided us with their individual budgets. Only the schedule remained to be worked out and approved by Willie.

I didn't have the slightest notion of Willie's past working habits, so I spent a lonely afternoon in a projection room viewing *The Heiress.*

I checked *The Heiress* production reports until I had a pretty good idea of how many pages a day Willie was able to cover.

When I placed the schedule and budget on Willie's desk, he spent less than ten minutes studying the top sheet of the budget, where the total cost of *Carrie* was revealed. He turned to me and asked, "You're happy with this figure?"

"I am, if you okay that schedule."

I could see Willie was right at home with a schedule board. He looked at the name of the set, noted the number of pages in each, and counted the number of black strips that indicated how much time I'd allotted to each set. He stopped checking at the end of the first week. "Two pages a day in Drouet's apartment?" he asked.

"You need more time, Willie?"

"No. I think we can do more."

"With cameraman Victor Milner?"

"I'm not sure we'll take Milner on *Carrie.* We'll think about the cameraman a while before we make a decision."

He handed me the schedule board. "We'll go with your schedule."

As I started out of his office, he stopped me with, "Larry Olivier says he wouldn't want anyone to call him Sir Laurence. Pass the word that we're all to address him as Larry."

Usually, the days just before the start of a new picture were filled with problems that had to be solved instantly. I expected most of them to be hectic days. But not on *Carrie.* Willie's calm, relaxed attitude fooled everyone. I watched Willie move around Drouet's apartment with Roland checking every detail of the set and its dressing.

When we got back to his office, he told me he was going to New York for about ten days. "While I'm gone, I want you to bring in Jennifer and Eddie Albert and do the wardrobe tests. Don't just stand them up in front of a backing and have them turn around to show off the clothes. I want to see them in character. Write a scene with movement and dialogue. Something around five minutes. Be sure and let me see them standing together. Jennifer's worried she's too tall for Eddie."

I wrote a seven-page scene in Drouet's apartment, opening with Jennifer in the living room. Through the open bedroom door, Eddie can be seen packing to move out.

He brings his suitcase into the living room and joins Jennifer in a close shot. At the end of the scene he kisses her and leaves.

I sent the scene to both of them with a note telling them when I'd make the tests. Jennifer called me late that same day. She liked the scene but wanted to know how the tests could be filmed with Willie in New York.

When I told her I'd be directing, she insisted that she couldn't possibly play such an important scene without Willie being there to guide her. We had a long talk about the picture and her character as I understood it, and she agreed to the tests. She confessed that her concern was that Willie would think she was too tall for Eddie. I promised I'd have her sitting on the couch when Eddie came to her side.

On the morning of the tests, I rehearsed the scene as I'd promised. I secretly told Eddie about Willie's request to see them standing together; and he agreed to pull her to her feet before kissing her good-bye. Jennifer, an experienced and proud professional, didn't resist when Eddie gently pulled her to her feet.

She continued in character, watching Eddie take his suitcase and leave the apartment. She didn't move until she heard me say, "Cut." Then she turned toward me and smiled. "You broke your promise, Herbie. But I forgive you."

Before we started shooting, we went out to the MGM back lot, Bowery Street. Willie chose a high camera setup from where he'd film the street with all its activity for the four seasons.

The day we filmed the scenes on the street, Willie made only one change in the action we'd laid out. In the fall sequence, I had, in the center of the screen, a landlord kicking a destitute family out of his building. Some of his workmen were carrying their bits of furniture down the steps of the brownstone and loading them on a horse-drawn wagon.

After the scene was over, Willie, almost whispering, said, "Let's do this one again. Have the landlord standing with a family, happy they've found shelter. And the workmen carrying the furniture into the building. If I do it your way, certain people will say, 'There he goes again, trying to make us look cold hearted.'"

Late in the afternoon, before we were scheduled to film the first scenes with Olivier and Mrs. Hurstwood in the Hurstwood home, Willie told me he'd decided to recast the part of Mrs. Hurstwood. We left the stage and went directly to his office.

"I'm going to try for Miriam Hopkins," he said. While he started dialing her number, I got on the phone to Frank Richardson, head of the wardrobe department. I couldn't reach him. He'd already left the studio.

Willie's luck with Hopkins was just as bad. We sat around trying the phones, eating Willie's supply of Russian caviar.

I finally reached my friend, the unflappable Frank Richardson. He told me not to worry. They had a new dress form for Hopkins. He'd get Edith Head, and all the help needed, to have the dress ready for shooting the next morning. Just let him know if Hopkins is set.

Willie surprised me by asking if I knew why he'd insisted on having me on the picture. I told him no but that I was very happy he did.

He tried Hopkins's number again and then began, "When I was in Washington getting my staff together, I saw a training film, *Safeguarding Military Information,* supposedly written by Preston Sturges. But an officer in G2 told me a script clerk at Paramount by the name of Herbie Coleman rewrote Sturges's thirty-five pages of Huston telling a room full of tired kids how they should protect military information. I tried to get you but found you had a wife and two kids and Paramount had you deferred. I made up my mind we'd work together someday."

"And having me write that scene for the test?"

"I knew you could write a documentary. I wanted to see how you'd handle drama."

He went back to the phone. Just after nine o'clock, he was telling Hopkins about the starring part the Goetzes had written just for her.

Then he turned her over to me. I told her a car would be at her home in Laguna Beach at four the next morning. The driver would have a script she could read on the way to the studio. Edith Head would need her by five for fittings. I'd have breakfast served in Edith's office. Wally Westmore would be waiting in makeup.

She had a hundred arguments why it wouldn't work but finally gave up and agreed to everything. To my surprise, everything did work perfectly.

At nine the next morning, she walked on the set looking like she'd just come off a long vacation.

Larry Olivier, Jennifer, and Eddie Albert were three of the finest and most professional actors I'd ever worked with.

Besides his insistence that we call him Larry, Olivier had two other requests. The first was a moment of absolute silence before each take. He told me he needed that moment to review the scene in his mind before Willie called, "Action." I had no problem with that request. I also liked the stage quiet before we went for a take.

The second request wasn't really a request. He had it in his contract that his hours on the set were nine to six. At exactly six, he was gone. Larry and I had a lot of fun with that. Each day, a little before six, he'd show me his watch, which would read exactly six. I'd accuse him of setting it ahead and show him mine, which I'd turned back a few minutes. He never walked off if we were already in the middle of a scene.

But one day I thought he was going to leave the stage when, after around thirty takes of a very dramatic scene, Willie said to him, "Let's try it again, Larry."

Larry exploded, "For God's sake, Willie, what do you want?"

Quietly, and with his usual friendly smile, Willie answered, "I want it better, Larry."

When he was completely satisfied with the performances of his cast, Willie would turn to his script supervisor and tell her to print takes two, seventeen, and forty-three. What a memory he had. To recall what he wanted to use from each take was remarkable. No other director I'd worked with had that ability.

I watched Willie lead his cast through scene after scene, skillfully adding to the depth of feeling the Goetzes had instilled in their magnificent screenplay.

He was careful with the composition of every camera setup and the positions of his actors throughout the entire scene.

A scene in which Jennifer tells Olivier she is leaving him will explain what I mean. It was a simple scene to stage. Jennifer watches Olivier arrive in their squalid apartment. She watches him slowly cross to a tall chest where he stops with his back to her. I could see she was struggling to find exactly the right words to end their tragic affair. Then, as Olivier reached with both hands toward the back of his neck to loosen his collar, Willie gave Jennifer the cue to tell him, "I'm leaving you, George."

His hands froze. Willie let the camera run. Olivier's hands began to tremble. Still Willie refused to cut the scene.

I doubt there was another director anywhere who would play such an important scene on an actor's hands and never show his face.

Jennifer leaves, and it isn't long before Olivier ends his life with gas from the kitchen oven.

I remember many times when Willie's unmatched imagination lifted scenes beyond their projected heights.

I wasn't happy at the thought of losing the friendship that had grown between Willie and myself as we approached the final day of shooting on *Carrie.*

But Willie had plans for me. He asked me to stay with him on his next picture, *Roman Holiday.*

Chapter 35

Roman Holiday

The first time I heard the name Audrey Hepburn was the day Willie told me he'd cast her as the princess of a mythical European country in his new film, *Roman Holiday,* opposite Gregory Peck. He showed me a large photograph of her in the costume she was wearing in the New York stage production of *Gigi.* I don't remember anything about that costume, but I'll never forget her eyes. They were set wide apart and seemed to be saying, "The world's a wonderful place. I am your friend. Please be my friend."

I didn't want to read the *Roman Holiday* script in my office with the phones ringing and friends dropping in, so I drove the sixty miles to our home on the waterfront at Balboa, walked out across the sand, and sat on a dune with the waves breaking just below.

The title page showed the screenwriter was Ian McLellan Hunter, based on his own original story. Before I'd finished reading the first thirty pages, I was asking myself, Could Willie Wyler so quickly wipe from his consciousness the stark reality of *Carrie* and Hurstwood's suicide and revel in presenting to his movie fans what I was reading? If any of you ever saw the picture, you know he could and did.

It was here on Via Margutta in Rome that Willie and I almost reached the end of our association.

We had decided I would prepare and rehearse the scenes in which Audrey comes from the tunnel onto busy Via Margutta, a short, narrow street crowded with tourists, searching for the objets d'art sold in Rome's famous artists' colony. With Via Margutta running almost exactly north and south, the sun would cross from the tall buildings on the east and disappear behind the buildings on the west side in less than an hour.

Long before the sun began to creep down the buildings on the west side of Via Margutta, I was satisfied with the action I'd staged. The moment it began to touch the heads of the people on the crowded sidewalk, I went inside the courtyard and told Willie we were ready to go. He was filming the scene in which Audrey borrows half of Greg's 2,000 lire. When she asks him if he can spare all that money, he tells her it's only about $1.50.

Willie stalled. "One more take, Herbie, then I'll be right out."

Ten minutes later, with the sun almost flooding both sides of the street, I went back in. Willie was still shooting the same two shots of Audrey and Greg. I still remember the take number on the camera slate. It was thirty-seven. The minute the take was over, I asked Willie to drop what he was doing and come out. Again he stalled. A few minutes later I was after him again, the third time.

When the sun began to leave the east sidewalk and crawl up the buildings on the east side, I went after Willie and told him it was almost too late to shoot the two master shots. "I'll be right there, Herbie."

I was standing by the camera when he rushed out into the street. His one glance at the street was enough. He looked over at Franz Planer, "Too late, Franz?" he asked. When Franz nodded, Willie turned and loudly berated me for not insisting he come out earlier.

For the first and last time as an adult, I lost my temper. Willie and I stood face to face, in front of the staff, crew, and all those people on the street, loudly blaming each other for failing to get those expensive scenes.

Suddenly, I saw Franz laughing at us. I pushed past Willie and marched over to Franz and said to him, "Your turn will come someday soon." I was wrong to argue with Willie. He was the producer and director. If he wanted to pay 450 people to come back another day, who was I to criticize him? But the incident didn't damage our growing friendship. We shot the scenes the following day.

Kenny Deland, a production manager, and Walter Tyler, one of the top studio art directors, were sent to Rome to prepare the location portions of the film. Kenny didn't like what he found there and asked to be replaced. Charlie Woolstenhulme was the lucky choice—or, as he grumbled later in Rome, victim.

Just a couple of weeks before I was scheduled to leave for Rome, Willie told me that the studio had asked him to produce the picture entirely in Rome and asked me to stay with him.

I talked it over with Mary Belle. I hated leaving my family for the estimated three months I'd be away, but we decided that the extra income was too important to turn down.

If I'd known that early May morning, when Mary Belle, Dale, Judy, and Melinda stood on the Union Station platform to see me off on the Santa Fe Chief, that it would be the middle of November before we'd be together again, I don't think I'd have said good-bye and climbed aboard.

Charlie Woolstenhulme, Kenny Deland, and Walter Tyler were at the airport when I arrived in Rome about nine that night. "We'll drop your bags at the hotel and go out to dinner to celebrate," Kenny told me.

When I asked what we were going to celebrate, he said, "Your arrival in Rome and me going home."

We climbed out of the car in front of the old Grand Hotel. I took one look at all the streets that came together at the hotel. They were packed with cars, scooters, and motorcycles, racing their engines and blowing their horns. I wondered aloud how in the world anybody got any sleep. "It's the same all over Rome," Walter said. "You'll get used to it."

After I'd signed in, the clerk handed me a note. I opened it and read it out loud. "Come to my room the minute you arrive. I must see you tonight." It was signed Henry Henigson.

"Who's Henry Henigson?" I asked the others.

"He's someone Paramount hired to oversee the production. He'll let you know who he is. You're going to love him," Kenny answered with a laugh. "Forget calling him now or forget dinner. He'll burn your ears for hours."

I didn't give Henigson a second thought and went with them to a fabulous dinner club. It was way past midnight when we got back to the Grand. Along with my room key, the clerk gave me another note from Henigson. "Come straight to my room when you return from dinner, regardless of the hour." I handed it to Kenny and told him to give it to our boss when he got back to the studio.

What I found when I walked into my room didn't improve my opinion of Henigson. It was big enough, but the view of Rome was an old brick wall that allowed me only a narrow sliver of Via Vittorio Emanuele Orlando, the street that passed in front of the hotel.

With the memory of Henigson's demanding note and the noise of the motorcycles and cars roaring past, with horns blasting, I got very little sleep and was in no mood to listen to Henigson when I was introduced to him in the lobby the next morning.

"Oh," he said, "so you're the new man who refused my request for a meeting?"

I told him I'd be available from nine to five while preparing for the start of the picture. Just give me a call. He wasn't too happy with what he'd just heard but didn't answer me. He just disappeared into the dining room.

Henigson had selected for our offices a wing of Cinecitta's administration building, facing the main boulevard leading out of Rome. I followed Walter along the corridor where carpenters and painters were busy completing our quarters.

Henigson had chosen the quiet side of the building overlooking the studio's gardens for the accounting department, art department, casting department, and cashiers.

Across the corridor, with windows opening on one of the busiest streets around the city, with streetcars, buses, trucks, and other traffic roaring past, he'd prepared the offices for Willie and the rest of us.

I went straight to his office and suggested he'd made a mistake with Willie's quarters. I reminded him of Willie's problem with noise. He refused to discuss the matter with me.

I went to my office, which was next to Willie's, and began breaking down the new script, a rewrite of Hunter's screenplay by one of England's brightest writers, John Dighton.

A few days later, Henigson came in and told me to make the schedule forty-eight days. I told him I wouldn't schedule *Roman Holiday* in forty-eight days, even if we were making it in Paramount's Hollywood studio. He really got upset and informed me that he was in charge and I would follow his orders.

In no uncertain terms, I let him know my only boss on the picture was William Wyler and that Willie and I would decide how many days we needed on *Roman Holiday.* That was the last I heard from Henigson on that subject.

Willie, his wife Talli, and their two daughters arrived and were settled in the Residence Palace until a permanent home was found for them. Willie wasted no time getting to Cinecitta. He took one look at his office and asked why I'd allowed Henry to pick that spot.

I told him about my argument with Henigson. He said, "Let's go tell Henry the facts of life." We did, and within an hour the carpenters were busy tearing out the accounting offices and moving Willie and me to the quiet side of the hall.

The first real problem Willie had to solve was an unexpected reluctance by the Italian government to approve the screenplay.

He heard a whisper from someone with good connections in the government to hire a certain Italian writer to make changes in the script. He got the job but was not given screen credit. I don't remember any of his suggestions showing up in Hunter and Dighton's final screenplay.

We were able to hire one of Italy's finest assistant directors, Piero Mussetta. He brought along some great assistants, George Zambon and Carlo Lastricati. Years later, Carlo became a successful producer in Rome.

Although Wally Westmore received screen credit as Audrey's makeup artist, Wally wasn't even in Rome. Her Italian makeup artist was Alberto De Rossi. Alberto was an artist and acted like an artist. He had an assistant who carried his makeup kit. He would kneel beside Alberto, open the kit, and hand him each item, lipstick, eye shadow, whatever; and when Alberto finished Audrey's makeup, he would close the kit and move away. He was always ready to jump back if Alberto decided to make some slight adjustment to her makeup.

Willie completed the casting, bringing from Hollywood Eddie Albert, Hartley Power, Harcourt Williams, and Margaret Rawlings. Among the many top Italian stars he cast were Tullio Carminati, Paolo Carlini, and Claudio Ermelli.

I was happy when Willie picked Franz Planer as the cameraman. I'd never worked with him, but I knew he was a great photographer. Franz became a favorite with everyone on the picture. Robert "Bob" Swink arrived shortly before we began shooting. He'd been delayed at the studio finishing up final editing on *Carrie.*

The end of the first week after Willie's arrival I told him that Walter, Charlie, and I were planning to go to Pompeii the next day to see the ruins.

"Please, don't," he said. "I need the help of all three of you. I hope you'll spend every spare moment looking for sites that the American public will appreciate seeing in our picture. If you'll do that, I'll pay your wives' expenses for a tour of Europe for two weeks when we finish shooting."

Only Walter Tyler had his wife come over. Charlie wanted no part of Rome when the picture closed production. I left with only a few days left to shoot.

Willie found a home for his family and moved from the Residence Palace. Walter, Charlie, and I moved into his vacated apartment. There were three bedrooms, three living rooms, three bathrooms, and a tiny kitchen not much larger than a closet. We drew straws for the rooms. I drew the one with the kitchen and was elected cook. "Breakfast only," I declared. There was a family grocery store just down the street.

I had to do the shopping because I could speak Italian. Or thought I could. The owner of that grocery store and his wife would begin grinning the moment I stepped through the door. They knew they were going to hear the strangest sounding Italian, flavored with what was left of my Wild Wonderful Cliff Holler, West Virginia, accent. But like locals everywhere, they were pleased when they heard Americans trying to speak their language.

Audrey Hepburn and her mother, two lovely ladies with whom I would enjoy an occasional dinner, arrived.

Luigi Zaccardi, one of the finest gentlemen it was my pleasure to ever know in the picture business, advised Willie and me to be at the railway station early on the morning Gregory Peck and his family were scheduled to arrive. "Mr. Peck is almost a god to the Italians," he said. "Half of Rome will be waiting for his train to come in. And everyone of them will be shouting 'Saint Gregorio' over and over."

Luigi was right. It took a dozen policemen to open a lane for our three cars to reach the entrance to the station. It took almost that many to get Greg through the shouting crowd to his waiting car.

I asked about his wife. He told me that Paris had made arrangements for her group to leave the train at a station about thirty miles from Rome.

That afternoon, I took Greg out to Cinecitta to meet Henigson and to collect the expense money listed in his contract. And it was no trifling sum.

Henigson was his usual ungracious self. He didn't bother to rise from his chair behind his desk and acknowledge my introduction. He grunted, opened a drawer, took out a thick bundle of those foot-long 1,000-lira notes, and threw them at Greg. They struck him just below his chin. He made no attempt to catch them and just let them drop to the floor. They were still lying there when we turned and, without a word, walked out. Greg told me later that further business between Henigson and himself would have to be done through me.

The weather was really getting uncomfortable, hot and very humid, when we were scheduled to begin filming. Willie had made a decision to use the French schedule when shooting interiors.

The day before we started shooting, we had a meeting on the stage at Cinecitta, where Walter had built Peck's tiny apartment in Via Margutta. Willie gave Franz Planer the camera setup and left the studio. When we left, Franz had the lights in place and was ready to go.

Willie had told me he'd pick me up the next day at twelve sharp. Long before then, I was standing in front of the Residence Palace. I saw his Cadillac turn onto Via Archimedia and come racing toward me.

His first words to me as I climbed in beside him were, "Vacation's over, Herbie. Time to go to work."

He had a grin on his face and a twinkle in his eyes, but I knew he meant every word of it. He was keyed up and anxious to get to Cinecitta. During the few minutes it took us to get there he said, "I don't want anybody on this picture bringing their problems to me. Tell them to come to you."

We drove through the studio gates without stopping, up the main street, and around some stages and pulled to a stop at our door. Willie looked around at the deserted streets and asked, "What's going on here? The studio looks deserted. Where's our people?"

I found all the stage doors padlocked and followed Willie as he stormed into Henigson's office, demanding to know why his company wasn't on the stage.

Henigson answered, "You told me you wanted to follow the French schedule."

"Right!" Willie said. "Shoot from one to seven!"

"No, Willie," Henry said, "French schedule in Rome means everyone arrives at the stage at one. I thought you knew."

All I knew about the French schedule was that one American director, who'd returned from making a picture in Paris, told me how much he liked it: "Make the first take at one o'clock. Shoot straight through until seven. No stopping for lunch. No interruptions. Great!"

Walter, Charlie, and I kept our promise to Willie to spend all our spare time searching for interesting locations to stage scenes in natural locations.

Once, when we'd worked until after two in the morning, we started roaming around the city. When we paused to look around the Pantheon, who should pop into view but Willie. He was also searching the city. On the spot, the Pantheon was selected as the location for Rocco's Cafe.

I was stepping aside more and more, letting Piero Mussetta take over as first assistant when we were staging scenes with large crowds. My Italian wasn't good enough to give instructions to them, and Piero would have to translate.

Willie and I decided that the company would operate more successfully if I would oversee the whole production. Things did seem to move more smoothly.

I'd ride to the studio with Willie each morning. If either of us had a problem, we'd solve it on the drive. I would check the day's work with Piero and go to my office. The thing I missed most was being in touch with the cast, especially Audrey. And, I was to discover within a week, it went both ways. It was a Saturday night, and I'd just arrived at my apartment when Audrey called. When I asked if she had a problem, she said, "Our problem is you, Herbie. Where have you been all week?" She didn't wait for an answer: "Mother and I want to have dinner with you tonight. Tell me you're available, and we'll pick you up in about an hour." The only person who could have kept me from being available that night was Mary Belle, and she was 9,000 miles away in Newport Beach.

We dined at a wonderful restaurant, The White Elephant. We talked about hundreds of things. *Roman Holiday.* Our hopes for the future. Our families. And our childhoods.

I was to enjoy dinner with Audrey four more times. Once with her mother and three times with Audrey alone.

Her stories about the horrible war they'd endured were fascinating.

I walked on the set the morning Audrey was scheduled to work for the first time in her white shirt and brown skirt. During the rehearsals, I kept looking at her. Something was wrong with her appearance. I couldn't figure out what it was at first. She looked thinner. Then it came to me. She wasn't wearing the "falsies" she'd had on when I made her tests in New York.

I asked Willie if he'd decided to forget them. He took one look. "You'd better have Anna Lisa take care of it."

Anna Lisa Nasolli Rocca was our wardrobe attendant. A beautiful teenaged Italian girl from somewhere up north near the Italian–Swiss border. Unlike the dark-skinned, brown-haired, brown-eyed southern Italian women, Anna Lisa had bright blue eyes, red hair, and a fair complexion dotted with the cutest freckles.

When I told her what Willie wanted, her face turned the color of her hair. It took her almost a minute to compose herself enough to blurt out, "Mr. Coleman, she's wearing them." With or without them, I thought she had the cutest figure of anyone I knew. And I still do.

It wasn't long after we moved into Willie's vacated apartment at the Residence Palace that Walter, Charlie, and I realized we would have to have an increase in our living allowances. I couldn't ask Willie to discuss our problem with Henigson. After all, he'd made me the problem solver.

I expected an argument from Henigson and got one. He said, "You're getting all the budget will allow. You'll have to live with it."

"Give it to us in lire, Mr. Henigson, or I'll raise our allowance to a just figure and use the dollars I have with me. The studio will reimburse what I spend and charge it all to your dollar account."

I was using my trump card on him. I knew the studio wanted *Roman Holiday* produced entirely in Rome, using as much as possible its enormous frozen blocked funds. If I spent my dollars, they'd ask him embarrassing questions about what was really a very minor matter.

Henigson was a clever cookie, but he had one fatal fault: he never thought anyone was as clever as he was.

We got the increase. More than I'd requested.

Just eight days after that unpleasant scene in Via Margutta where I'd told Franz Planer he would soon have his "day" with Willie, he asked me to have dinner with him. We went to Tre Scalini on the Piazza Navona and had dinner on the terrace. Franz seemed nervous, reluctant to explain why he'd asked me to come with him. Franz was proud of his reputation as one of the world's finest cameramen. He was a friendly man, easy to know, and easy to like. I just waited.

Then he opened up: "I'm going to throw you a curve, Herbie. I have to leave the picture. I hate to walk out with the scenes on the river coming up. But I have to. Shooting all day and prelighting half the night is too much."

He sure did throw me a curve. Before choosing Franz as his cameraman on *Roman Holiday,* Willie looked at the work of all the available top men in Hollywood. He didn't want to repeat his *Carrie* mistakes, whereby he started with Victor Milner, replaced him after a week, and then fired Milner's replacement within days. He had started out again with the third cameraman, who lasted less time than any of the others. So Willie brought back Milner, who finished the picture.

I tried to keep calm. I even ordered some of Tre Scalini's famous *gelato chocolatti* (chocolate ice cream), but after only a taste or two, I told Franz I'd better get busy.

Within minutes after I got back to the Residence Palace, I had Eduard deSegonzac on the phone. I asked him to send me films of all the top French cameramen who weren't working. "I want them here on tomorrow night's plane."

Kay Selby, a top Paramount executive in London, was next. "Not to worry, Herbie," she said. "Just have somebody meet the plane."

On our way to Cinecitta the next morning, I told Willie about Franz and about the pictures I expected from Paris and London. He took the news calmly, at least on the surface, but for the rest of the drive to the studio kept silent.

The first thing he did when he walked on the stage was take Franz aside for a long talk. When they came back to the camera, Franz had a smile on his face. From that moment until he left Rome to go back to his home near Hollywood, he was again the calm, relaxed, confident artist we all knew.

The planes from London and Paris brought a total of five pictures, three London productions and two French. At eight the next morning, I was in the projection room. I ran, for almost six hours, the ones Kay Selby sent first and then ran the two French pictures. There was no question in my mind that Henri Alekan's work was the best.

When Willie finished his work on the location, he came straight to the studio. After watching parts of the two London films, he switched to Alekan's picture. I kept waiting for him to say no, but he ran the whole picture and told me to tell Henry to have Alekan in Rome the next day.

After working alongside Franz for a couple of days, Alekan took over, and Franz left for home. Everyone had become friends with Franz, and we were sad to see him go. I went with him to the airport and watched him disappear inside his plane.

It was at that moment that I realized it was time for me, too, to leave.

The company was moving smoothly. Willie was happy with Piero, and there didn't seem to be any real problems looming ahead.

I was getting homesick. I missed the kids, and Mary Belle's forty-first birthday was only two weeks away. I had a talk with Willie. He said he needed me and asked me to stay until the end of the month.

As the day I was to leave approached, Willie asked me to postpone my departure. I agreed to stay on. I had mixed feelings about leaving the picture before it was finished.

But one day, Willie started talking about postproduction problems. How much he would miss having Paramount studio people with him. Postproduction on a picture like *Roman Holiday* in Rome could take six months or more. I knew I had to get out before I got involved.

We finally agreed on a firm date in late October.

I told Henigson to make arrangements on the Rome Express to Paris and a first-class cabin on the *Mauritania* from Le Havre to New York. He pulled my air tickets from a desk drawer and tossed them on his desk. "You flew over here. You can go back the same way."

"Forget it, Mr. Henigson," I told him. "You keep the tickets. I'll make my own arrangements and pay in dollars. The studio will take it out of your dollar budget."

The next day, Henigson asked me to come to his office. When I walked in, he handed me a cablegram. It was from Jack Karp, the executive legal counsel at the studio. I don't remember the exact wording, but it confirmed, in unmistakable language, what I'd told him. Outwardly, Henigson was the same old Henigson, but with the first words I heard coming from his mouth, I realized that the cable had really affected him.

"I've talked to the travel people about your reservations on the train. I called the Paris office about a first-class cabin on the *Mauritania.* DeSegonzac said he'd take care of it." He also asked if rooms at the George Cinq would be okay. I told him that would be fine and thanked him for everything he'd done for us.

He started to turn away but stopped and slowly turned back. "Why does everyone avoid me? Why won't they let me be part of the team, Herbie?"

I was shocked at what I'd just heard. It was the first time he'd ever called me Herbie. I usually heard a cold "Coleman" or, around others, "Mr. Coleman." And suddenly, there was a caring person hidden behind that cold forbidding exterior.

"For me, Henry, you made it impossible."

My opinion of Henry Henigson was formed before we ever met because of those cold, domineering notes I received at the hotel the night I arrived. "For Gregory Peck, it was the reception he received that first morning in your office when you threw that heavy bundle of lire in his face."

I said, "There's still time, Henry. Just let the others know who you really are."

I thanked him for everything and went back to the stage. It wasn't easy saying good-bye to all those wonderful filmmakers I'd worked with the 140 days I'd been in Rome.

Willie was the hardest. We went outside and sat in the shade of a flowering tree. Willie said to me, "I need you with me right to the end. I've known for a long time how unhappy you were away from your family, and I understand why you must go. I'll be making another picture here before we move back to the States. I'd like you with me. Let's try and work it out."

Luigi Zaccardi, an assistant to Pilade Levi, Paramount's chief executive in Italy, saw me off the day I left Rome. Luigi and I had become close friends. He was always there to help us solve difficult problems.

Chapter 36

Forest Lakes, Colorado

It was cool that early summer morning where I sat on the deck of our home in the high Colorado Rocky Mountains, opening a letter I'd just received. A letter that years later would cause me to ask myself, "Why didn't I burn it unopened?"

It was from a man who signed it Donald Spoto. He wrote about his plan to write a biography of Hitchcock and wanted me to grant him an interview.

He sent along a book entitled *The Art of Hitchcock.* It was a review of each of Hitch's films. I thought it was honest and well written. He also included his résumé, listing the biographies he'd written, his education, and his work with young students. Granting Spoto an interview was a decision not easily made. Would he report my views honestly? I thought.

I finally decided, mistakenly it turned out, that I could trust him. Mary Belle agreed with me and surprised me by suggesting that we invite him to share our home while he was in Colorado.

I gave Spoto the news and met him when he arrived at the airport in Durango a few days later. It was easy to pick him out from the few men leaving the plane. He was carelessly clothed. Slacks, sport shirt, and hatless. I guessed him to be about thirty-five. His handshake was firm and brief.

As we drove the twenty miles to our home, I told him I would be happy to answer any questions about my years with Hitch, starting with *Rear Window* and continuing on through *North by Northwest, The Alfred Hitchcock Hour,* and, some years later, *Topaz.* Nothing more.

Mary Belle met us when we arrived. Spoto thanked her for opening our home to him. He was impressed at the beauty of our valley and the deer grazing nearby. Mary Belle led him to his quarters. He quickly stowed his gear and joined me on the deck. He seemed to be having a little difficulty breathing at the altitude at which our home sat, at 7,500 feet, but he wasted little time getting down to business.

If I'd known he intended *The Dark Side of Genius* to be the title of his unauthorized biography, I would have been forewarned and would not have granted him the interview.

Donald Spoto's numerous misquotes, mistakes, and outright inventions damaged and destroyed many close friendships. The loss of my friendship with Vera Miles, a lady for whom I had and still have deep respect and affection, was, I believe, caused by Spoto's unfounded statement indicating a possible hidden affair between Hitch and Vera.

Over the years I've often thought that Spoto came to our home looking for something he could use as the beginning of a book in which he could destroy the reputation of my friend, Alfred Hitchcock. I had to ask myself, Did Spoto have a grudge against Hitch? Was he jealous of Hitch's success? Or was it the lure of money from the sale of his book? Did he have trouble seeing me through the flood of swirling dollar bills and the book jacket with that devastating title, *The Dark Side of Genius,* he carried in his mind?

Spoto kept his promise to send me an early autographed copy of his book. I skipped around in it until I came to the chapter on *Rear Window.* It is a rambling tale, hard to follow. I wasn't too unhappy at what I was reading until I came to an item in which Spoto mentions John Michael Hayes leaving Hitch's office, after a few preliminary meetings, to write the screenplay of *Rear Window.*

Preliminary meetings, indeed! Hayes typing for days as Hitch dictated the entire screenplay is "preliminary meetings"? In this item, Spoto had broken his solemn promise to report my story accurately and honestly. Was Spoto, and/or Hayes, attempting to discredit Hitch's creative work on the screenplay? I forced those disturbing questions from my mind, only to have others aroused when I happened to see, on television, men discussing our film *Vertigo.* One of the men mentioned Spoto's book about Hitch and praised it for its historic accuracy and how important it would be for students in film schools.

Hearing this, I knew I had to place before the public the true facts about Alfred Hitchcock, for Spoto certainly did not.

Chapter 37

Rear Window

Mac Johnson and I stood on a stage at Warner Bros. watching Grace Kelly and Ray Milland rehearse a scene for the film *Dial M for Murder.* Mac, a friend and the art director with whom I'd worked on other pictures, had been assigned to design the sets for *Rear Window.*

Sitting under the camera in a director's chair, with the name Alfred Hitchcock spread across the back, was a short, heavy-set man in a black suit and matching black tie. His thinning gray hair lay flat against his head, and his numerous chins overflowed the collar of his shirt.

He was unlike most of the directors I'd worked with. His hooded eyes and composed features showed absolutely no emotion, no reaction to the tense scene he was watching.

Kelly finished her last speech and walked off the set.

Hitchcock quietly said, "You have it," pushed his heavy body from the chair, and crossed to where we stood waiting. He paused beside us and acknowledged Mac's introduction with a short, "Mr. Coleman." He didn't offer to shake my hand. "Be with you shortly, Mac."

He turned away and walked into his stage office, a converted dressing room.

When he called us in, he pointed to the only chair in the room and said, "You may sit there, Mr. Coleman."

I was surprised he'd remembered my name.

He opened a cigar box and extended it to me. "Care for a cigar, Mr. Coleman?" He didn't seem pleased when I told him I didn't smoke. He ignored Mac, who already had a lighted cigarette between his tobacco-stained fingers.

He selected a cigar for himself, carefully examined it, closed the box, put it aside, took a wooden match from the table, and proceeded to light the cigar. I noticed he barely allowed the end of the cigar to touch his lips. It was a ritual I would see repeated for the next twenty-five years. With the cigar business settled, he sat back and waited for Mac to show him plans for the *Rear Window* sets.

I sat silent, as did Mr. Hitchcock, while Mac unrolled the plans and laid them on the table. I marveled at the way Mac had solved the problem of building an entire Greenwich Village block of brick buildings, a street, an alley, and Jimmy Stewart's second-floor, two-room apartment on one stage.

I became aware, however, of the fact that Mr. Hitchcock didn't seem to be listening. I could see his reflection in the mirrors that covered all the dressing room walls. His eyes were fixed on me.

He didn't know I was also trying to figure out what lay behind that inscrutable mask.

"We're clearing stage 17 and the basement under the stage floor," Mac droned on. "Cut away the entire floor, leaving only enough room on the west end for Jimmy's apartment. The courtyard will be on the basement floor. There'll be an alley between the main building and the side building on the left, opening on a street where street action can be staged. The east end of the stage will be covered with a painted backing that Bob Burks can light for day, sunset, and night."

Mac had been talking with his attention centered on the plans. He finished his spiel and waited for some comment from Mr. Hitchcock.

To my surprise, Mr. Hitchcock asked me, "What do you think, Mr. Coleman?"

"I think Mac will win an Oscar for set design, Mr. Hitchcock."

"Do you have any questions, Mr. Coleman?"

"I had one, Mr. Hitchcock, but it's been answered."

"What was your question, Mr. Coleman?"

I was getting a little tired of that Mr. Coleman bit, but I hurried to answer him. "There's a rumor around Paramount that you intend to film *Rear Window* using the same technique you used for *Rope.* One full 1,000-foot reel a day. A 9,000-foot picture in nine days. But with Mac's set, you can't film it that way."

"You'll decide the number of days we need to produce *Rear Window* after you've read our screenplay, Mr. Coleman."

There it was. I'd suspected all along I'd been sent with Mac to allow Hitchcock a look at the man someone had recommended he accept as his assistant director on his first production for Paramount. I didn't much like the idea of having Hitchcock, or any other director, looking me over the way one would a pet dog before agreeing to buy it. Well, if he doesn't like the way I part my hair, or my Cliff Holler accent, he can take one of the other first-class first assistant directors on Paramount's payroll.

I was about to reveal my thoughts when a voice from the doorway of the office called out, "Why, Herbie Coleman, does Paramount know you're hanging around the Warner Bros. lot?"

I didn't have to turn to see who it was. I'd worked with Ray Milland on many pictures at Paramount and had directed him at times when the films' directors were unavailable. His vaguely disguised English accent was all too familiar. And we were friends. Now I knew who had recommended me to Hitchcock.

Mac and Hitchcock discussed the sets until someone called out that they were ready for another rehearsal.

By the time we got back to the studio, my boss, Frank Caffey, had been told that Hitchcock wanted me to be his assistant. "Mr. Hitchcock would like you to join him on the Warner stage at ten tomorrow morning," Frank said.

Would I have refused the Hitchcock assignment if I'd known what an impact, good and bad, my decision would have on my family, myself, and my professional career? I've never been able to answer that question. To myself or to anyone.

Hitchcock didn't greet me with a handshake when I entered his office the next morning. In fact, I never saw him shake hands with anyone. I saw some very famous, important people offer their hands and look puzzled when he didn't seem to notice.

He did allow a brief "Good morning, Mr. Coleman" to escape his lips before going through the cigar routine. Then he settled back on his flowered sofa and began, "Mr. Coleman, there are a few details about my working habits you will want to know. The only staff I'll be bringing with me are Bob Burks, my cameraman; his camera operator, Bill Shurr; and his camera assistant, Lenny South. I'm leaving the selection of the rest of my staff in your hands."

"I have a personal secretary, but she works at home. When I move to Paramount, I don't want to find a secretary sitting outside my door. They interrupt my work with their constant questions. Herman Citron, my agent, has already arranged a four-office suite in what I understand you all call the Marble Halls. One of those offices will be yours. Work closely with Mac on the big set. Come out any time you have a question or a suggestion about our project."

I asked him when we could expect to have a script. He told me he wouldn't select a writer until he'd completed *Dial M.*

I moved into the Hitchcock suite and started thinking about choosing the Hitchcock staff. For unit production manager, there was only one candidate: Clarence "Doc" Erickson. He'd been with the studio for a number of years, working in the budget department, and had just been promoted.

I worried most about the film editor. It wasn't a matter of who I wanted. George Tomasini would be the perfect choice. A tall, handsome young man, he had an infectious smile. Just his appearance on the set would relieve any tension building up. He hadn't been a first cutter very long, but he was already much in demand.

There were a number of top film editors with whom I'd worked: Archie Marshek, Stu Gilmore, Artie Schmidt, and, of course, Otho Lovering. They'd become my friends, and I respected their work. I really fussed over that problem for days but in the end went with George.

Before we'd reached the halfway mark on *Rear Window,* Hitchcock was giving George complete freedom on the first cut. Their relationship quickly turned into a friendship that lasted until George's untimely death on a fishing trip to the High Sierras, after he'd completed editing *Marnie,* his tenth consecutive picture with Hitch.

On one of my trips to see Hitchcock at Warner Bros., he held up a large painting of the Greenwich Village set. Sitting in his wheelchair with a pair of binoculars held to his eyes was the figure of Jimmy Stewart. Through Jimmy's apartment window, which faced the courtyard, Mac had painted the courtyard windows of the apartment building across the yard. He had included the alley and the street in the distance.

"In most of those windows over there," Hitchcock said, "we'll have stars and other important members of the cast with whom I'll need to have intimate conversations. Discussions I'd rather others not overhear. You wouldn't expect me to talk with them using a loudspeaker would you, Mr. Coleman?" From the amused expression on his face, I knew he thought he'd thrown me a curve.

"Certainly not, Mr. Hitchcock. You'll be able to be as intimate as you like."

I asked George Dutton, the sound department's top man, "You know those little receivers we hide in actors' ears when we're filming dance scenes? Like they have to hear the tempo of the music while they talk?"

Because he had solved that problem with the introduction of sound, he knew exactly what I was talking about.

"You are asking me if we could put a wire around the whole stage so you can talk privately with anyone wherever they are on the stage?"

Gary Cooper and my son, Dale Coleman, standing on the miniature bridge that Gary was to destroy in For Whom the Bell Tolls.

On the set of California, *celebrating my 42nd birthday with, left to right, film editor Eda Warren, Ray Milland, Barbara Stanwyck, and director John Farrow.*

Celebrating my 46th birthday with (far right) James Stewart and Grace Kelly, on the set of Rear Window.

With Alan Ladd and my assistant, Harry Caplan, on a break from filming Branded.

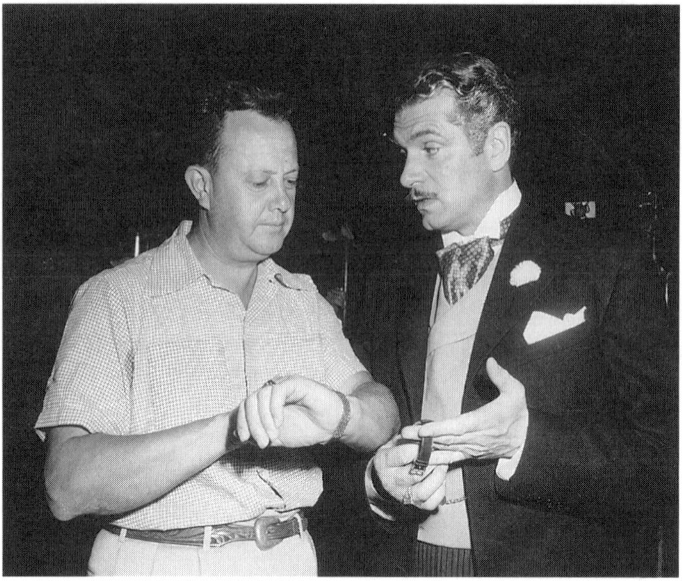

Sir Laurence Olivier and I compare our watches on the set of Carrie. *Since Larry's contract required that he work only from 9 a.m. to 6 p.m., he thought the workday had ended. His watch showed 6:30 p.m., although my watch displayed 5:30 p.m.*

With Jennifer Jones, a great lady, on the set of Carrie.

On location in Rome to film Roman Holiday. *Gregory Peck, Audrey Hepburn, William Wyler, and I sit outside of the Roman Forum as we wait for traffic noise to subside. After midnight, we filmed the scene where Greg finds Audrey asleep on a bench.*

Alfred Hitchcock with Judith Evelyn, "Miss Lonely Hearts," on the set of Rear Window.

Henry Fonda hands me a piece of cake during his birthday celebration on the set of The Wrong Man.

Alfred Hitchcock, James Stewart, and I share an amusing moment while filming Vertigo.

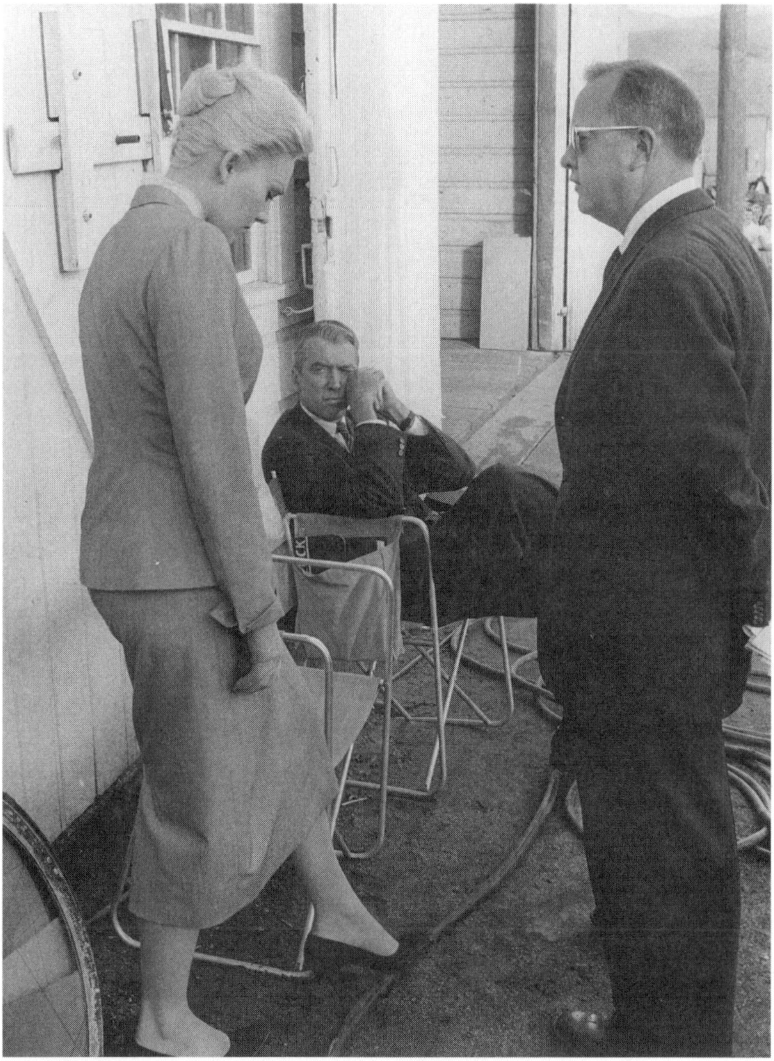

At Mission San Juan Bautista to film Vertigo. *As James Stewart looks on, I refuse Kim Novak's request to return to Los Angeles for the weekend.*

While in Bombay for the series Maya, executive producer Frank King and I are deep in conversation.

I told George it would be for Hitchcock to talk with his actors.

"We've never been asked to try that before. But we'll give it a try and find out." He did, and it worked perfectly.

Just a day before we went in production, Hitchcock and I were standing in Jimmy's room looking at the apartments across the courtyard. The noise from the busy workmen was almost deafening. Hitchcock asked me, "What have you done about all that noise, Mr. Coleman? You wouldn't expect me to shout my directions to my actors?"

"Of course not, Mr. Hitchcock." I pointed to a microphone hanging on a corner of the set. Below the mike were buttons and the actors' names. "All you'll have to do, Mr. Hitchcock, is pick up that mike. Push the button for the actor you wish to speak to, and a muted bell will be the signal for the actor to pick up his receiver and listen to your instructions. And the greatest thing about that system is they won't be able to talk back."

Hitchcock didn't seem to be as happy with the idea as I thought he would be. But he was all smiles when he tried it out after we started shooting.

I was told only what I needed to know about Hitchcock's contract with Paramount. He would produce nine pictures for the studio. Four would be Paramount productions; the other five would be Alfred Hitchcock productions. Paramount would finance and distribute all of them. A car and driver would be assigned to him, and the cost would be added to each production.

A few days after he finished shooting *Dial M for Murder,* he called and asked if I'd be kind enough to drive out to his home in Bel Air. His home was a lovely cottage surrounded by lawns and flower gardens. Moments after I rang the doorbell, the door opened, revealing a tiny, smiling blond lady in form-fitting white shorts and a slightly soiled short-sleeved shirt. In one hand, she held a broom and, in the other, a small wastebasket.

Immediately, in a voice ringing with friendship, she said, "You must be Herbie Coleman. I'm Alma. Hitch is waiting in the living room." She indicated the direction I should go and added, "Go right in." I fell in love with Alma before I turned away and remained in love with her until the day she passed away.

Hitchcock didn't try to rise from his place on the down-filled cushions of the long sofa that filled most of the space under the windows that overlooked the Bel Air Country Club. He was dressed exactly the way he was each time I'd visited him on the *Dial M* set.

Even in the comfort of his own home, his tie was in place, and his coat was properly buttoned.

I soon realized he hadn't called me out there to discuss business. He wanted me to know Alma, to show me his home, and for me to understand his lifestyle.

He was proud of his collection of fine paintings. We strolled through the house and around the gardens.

Alma joined us from time to time. She was interested in my family. I had to describe Mary Belle.

We returned to the living room. Mr. Hitchcock poured a mild vodka and tonic for me and a glass of white wine, his favorite, Sancerre, for himself. I noticed he kept looking around for Alma, as he downed it quickly. I found out later that she was concerned about his drinking and he didn't want to worry her. I left after promising to have his car at his home at ten the following morning.

We had little time to talk about the picture when he came to the office. Executives kept dropping in to welcome him. Herman Citron was anxious for him to make a decision on the writer for the screenplay.

Mac came in with more detailed plans for the Greenwich Village set. Hitchcock suggested a few minor changes he would like Mac to make in Jimmy's apartment.

I didn't see much of Hitchcock during the days that followed his visit to the studio. He divided his time between postproduction on *Dial M* and short vacations at his ranch, among the redwood trees in the Santa Cruz mountains, overlooking the Pacific Ocean.

When he did come in, he would stroll into my office, go to my coffeemaker, pour himself a cup, bring it to the soft leather sofa, place it on a table, and leave it there until it was stone cold before drinking it. It was a routine he would follow throughout our long relationship.

Almost nothing was said about *Rear Window.*

Then, before I was aware of where other questions were leading, I was telling him my life story.

Late in May, he agreed with MCA's suggestion to hire a novice screenwriter, John Michael Hayes, to write the screenplay.

Hayes arrived at the studio sometime early in June.

It was the same routine every day in my office. Coffee, gossip, and an occasional comment about the story they were going to write. I thought they'd never get down to work on the script. But late one day, after the usual goodnight cocktail, Hitchcock said, "Mr. Hayes, tomorrow morning we commence work on the screenplay."

Hitchcock and I were having our morning coffee in my office when Hayes joined us. Hitchcock allowed Hayes to sit for a moment and then told him it was time to get to work. Turning to me, he said, "Come along, Mr. Coleman."

I could see by the expression on Hayes's face that he wasn't happy that Hitchcock wanted his assistant director around while they were writing.

We went into Hitchcock's office. He indicated the typewriter and chair I'd had the office service provide for Hayes. After another dirty look at me, Hayes sat down, ran a sheet of paper into the typewriter, and typed the opening scene as Hitchcock dictated.

I sat there and listened in amazement as Hitch, pacing slowly around his office, described in detail the opening scenes. The camera movement through the window of Jimmy's apartment to the apartments across the courtyard. A half-dressed ballet dancer, seen through her open window. And action in other apartments. Then to Jimmy's leg in a cast. He stopped for a moment and turned toward Hayes. A smile replaced his usual somber expression: "I've decided to have Jimmy asleep when Grace makes her first appearance in our film."

As he described her approach to Jimmy and the close shots of Grace waking Jimmy with tender kisses, I began to realize that Alfred Hitchcock could put more than sex and suspense in his films.

Obviously pleased with his vision of the opening scenes for *Rear Window,* he resumed his pacing and his description of the scenes for the picture. A composer in an adjoining apartment. A honeymooning couple who move in next door. A married couple who live directly across the courtyard. He continued to describe the other important neighbors. Who they were and how their lives affected the thinking and actions of Jimmy.

The routine of Hitch dictating and Hayes typing continued for many days. Schooldays for me and maybe for John Michael Hayes, also. We were receiving a graduate school course in screenplay development.

The day he dictated the final scene, Hitch told Hayes to take a copy of the script and add the dialogue.

We watched Hayes take the pages from the typewriter, add them to the stack on the table, and leave the office.

Hitch took one of his Havana cigars from the box on his desk and said to me, "Come along, Mr. Coleman, we'll salute *Rear Window.*" We went into my office, where a well-stocked refrigerator was waiting. While we were enjoying the first salute, Hitchcock asked for my opinion of the story.

"You've told me you have Jimmy Stewart and Grace Kelly. Do you think anybody will believe Jimmy when he resists Grace Kelly's advances?"

"I'm surprised, Mr. Coleman. Have you forgotten Jimmy is in a wheelchair with his leg in a cast?"

We talked through the second salute. I told him I thought that it would be disturbing to go away from the Greenwich Village set to Gunnison's office. He didn't agree.

On September 12, 1953, a little after five in the afternoon, Hayes gave me what he called his screenplay. But it was more like the treatment I'd heard Hitch dictate, with dialogue added. Some good. Some very good.

While we waited for the starting date of November 27, 1953, to arrive, Bob Burks was busy with the largest crew of electricians, grips, and other workers, prelighting the largest set ever constructed on a Paramount stage.

I was beginning to worry that Hitchcock was about to become only a shadow of the man I'd met on the *Dial M for Murder* set, when he was kept busy rushing back and forth to the stage to approve Mac's changes in the set, set dressing, and many other details.

Hitchcock often had Hayes in his office working on the final screenplay, the dialogue he'd instructed Hayes to provide.

With Jimmy Stewart, Grace Kelly, Thelma Ritter, and Raymond Burr firmly committed to the project, he quickly added Judith Evelyn and Jesslyn Fax to the cast. He took great care in the selection of the composer. He wanted a talented musician/actor in the part, someone who could actually compose a hit song during the hour and fifty minutes the completed film would run. Ross Bagdasarian got the part and did his best. Unfortunately, time didn't allow Hitch to cut to Ross often enough to make the plan a success.

With the main cast set, Hitchcock said to me, "It is your responsibility, Mr. Coleman, to select the actors for the remaining parts. When you're satisfied you have the right girl for Miss Torso, keep her away from the dance department. Give her a record of our music and let her create her own dance."

I looked at a lot of film and interviewed a lot of girls before finally giving the part to Georgine Darcy. She had everything the part required—beauty, youth, a gorgeous figure, and limited acting ability—and was an excellent ballet dancer. I let her read the script and then took her to her apartment on the stage and pointed out the various moves Hitchcock would want her to make. She took the record and left the stage after promising not to make her ballet moves too professional.

The parts of the bride and groom, the sleepers on the fire escape, and other minor roles went to people with whom I'd worked on other films.

The happiest days before we started shooting were the ones when Grace Kelly would come to the studio. I deliberately scheduled her meetings with Edith Head on wardrobe for a full day, knowing she'd be finished with Edith in a couple of hours, and then arrange a meeting with Hitch on another day. Any excuse to have her around. I soon decided she was absolutely the most beautiful girl I'd ever seen. Even more beautiful than Elizabeth Taylor was when I first met her in 1937.

My respect for that lovely lady soon was replaced with affection. And then, like every man who had the great, good fortune to work closely with her, I fell in love with her.

We received John Michael Hayes's final corrected screenplay late in the afternoon of September 12, 1953. I remember the date and the time because it was Mary Belle's birthday. My assistant, Clem Jones, had a mimeograph machine waiting to make copies. That same evening, copies of his screenplay were sent to everyone working on the picture, including Jimmy Stewart, Grace Kelly, and the rest of the cast.

Spoto inaccurately, and more dramatically, reports that Hayes gave the screenplay to Jimmy, who was so impressed with the script that he agreed to star in the film and take a share of the profits instead of a salary. The truth is that Jimmy and Hitch had agreed to produce *Rear Window* through Patron, a company they owned.

November 27, 1953, finally arrived, and filming began. We were a very happy company. With Hitchcock, it was still Mr. Coleman and Mr. Erickson. We'd been shooting for at least two weeks when Hitchcock answered my "Good morning, Mr. Hitchcock," with, "Will you and Mr. Erickson call me Hitch?"

"We will, if you'll call us Doc and Herbie," I told him.

One day I scheduled a half day with Jimmy in his apartment and then a move to another stage to film the scenes in Gunnison's office.

As Hitch and I were walking to the new stage, he stopped, looked at me for a moment, and then asked, "Do you still think it's a mistake to cut away from the Greenwich Village set to Gunnison's?"

I was shocked at the question. It had been over two months since I'd made that statement. "Yes, Hitch," I answered.

"Then cancel the move to Gunnison's office," he said.

"If I do, we'll have nothing to do this afternoon. The set is ready, and Gunnison and the other six actors are waiting. All it will cost us is a little film. And you'll have it if you change your mind again." We went on and filmed the sequence, but it was never used.

We were back home on stage 17 the next day, filming the scene in which Grace climbs the ladder and goes through the window into Burr's apartment. I wasn't too happy that Hitch wouldn't use the stunt double I'd hired for the stunt.

When I called lunch, the lights went out, and everyone scattered. Everyone but a small group of electricians, who settled down for their usual noontime poker game in Miss Lonely Heart's apartment. I grabbed a quick sandwich, came back to Jimmy's apartment, and settled down in his wheelchair for a catnap. I was half asleep when someone landed in my lap, threw her arms around my neck, and gave me a great big kiss. I opened my eyes and saw Grace smiling at me. "Don't be mad at Hitch, Herbie," she said. "I talked him into letting me climb the ladder."

Before I could answer her, a flashbulb exploded. When my vision cleared, I saw our still photographer, Jack Kaufman, standing there reloading his camera.

The next morning Grace called me into her dressing room and gave me a copy of the picture. That was thirty-eight years ago, and I still have it.

The day the filming ended, Hitch presented me with a picture of himself: a big close-up of his face, framed by a camera finder, and the face of his cameraman. In his handwriting are the words "To Herbie. From your assistant, Hitch."

Hitch, Grace, Jimmy, and I walked out of stage 17 together. Grace stopped, turned, and looked back through the open door at the Greenwich Village set. "You know, Hitch. It's like leaving a home you've grown up in."

Then, ignoring the cold winter drizzle, we stood there watching the stage lights go out until the set was lost in total darkness.

For the first time in my long career in the picture business, I was given an editing course in fine tuning a film. I sat for days in the "stop-and-go" projection room watching Hitch tell George, "Add six frames there. Cut two there." Running the picture back and forth. Time and time again.

Then, one afternoon, we ran the picture from start to finish without a single interruption. When the light came on, Hitch sat there staring at the blank screen. George waited, anxiously, for some word of approval for his work on the picture.

Finally, Hitch said, "I think we have a movie."

I was to learn that "Thank you" was not a part of Hitch's vocabulary.

The critics and the public agreed with Hitch's statement, "I think we have a movie."

Chapter 38

To Catch a Thief

While Hitch and John Michael Hayes were busy turning David Dodge's novel into what seemed to be merely a light comedy caper on the French Riviera, Bob Burks, Mac Johnson, Doc Erickson, and I flew to Cannes to prepare to film the picture all along the Côte d'Azur from St. Tropez to Monte Carlo.

The last thing Hitch said to me just before we left the studio was, "Stay away from picture postcard locations. Let the world see the French Riviera is more than a playground for the idle rich."

The first thing I did after settling down in the Carlton Hotel was to head for the nearest photographic gallery to find photos of the most beautiful landscapes, seascapes, and a mountain villa for Cary Grant's retirement home, a setting important in *To Catch a Thief.* Grant, known as the "Cat" during his days as an infamous jewel thief, lives quietly in retirement after serving a short term in prison for a jewel theft.

Most of our days were spent riding around in an old car, with the constant rain seeping through the canvas top soaking our clothes. When we complained, Doc would say, "Do you want to spend all our money on a limousine or save a little for the Carlton bar?"

We covered the three auto routes from Nice to Monte Carlo. Along the Grand Corniche at the crest of the mountain, the view was breathtaking. Cap Ferrat, Cap d'Ail, and other less known fingers of landscape jutting into the Mediterranean featured summer villas and mansions of the world's aristocrats.

The Bass Corniche followed the coastline closest to the sea. We drove past the colorful port of Villefranche, the home of the U.S. Sixth Fleet, and then through the tiny village of Beaulieu, with its world-famous restaurant, Le Reserve.

The Bass Corniche would be Hitch's selection for a chase, but it was too heavily traveled for our purpose.

The Moyen Corniche followed a middle course, halfway between the other two. One of my favorite ancient villages, Eze, looks down on the Moyen Corniche. I knew I would use this route for part of the chase.

We photographed Monte Carlo from end to end, including the Palace Monaco, the future home of the star Grace Kelly. I selected a section of the quay on the harbor where Mac would build the Charles Vanel (Bertani) restaurant.

We toured the backcountry above Cannes, Antibes, and Nice searching for Robie's villa, the most important set needed for the picture. We photographed six of the best, including one high in the Alps near Digne and another closer to the colorful village of St. Jeanine, standing on top of a ridge in the background.

That left only the road for scenes in which the police chase Robie's car from his villa toward the coast, until it's stopped by a flock of sheep in the roadway.

This chase was especially important as it gave us an opportunity to show the high mountains and villages above the Côte d'Azur. I only had to drive along this road one time to know I'd found what I'd been hoping for. It led from Digne, through Barreme, to a series of turning, twisting curves, including one just above Castellane, where our helicopter pilot, John Crewdson, barely escaped crashing against the canyon walls.

Despite the steady rain drenching the airport at Nice when we boarded the plane for home, I was excited about returning to the Côte d'Azur.

The door to Hitch's office was closed the morning I got back from Cannes. When Hitch joined me a few minutes later, he ignored my friendly greeting with "I trust you have a new writer waiting in the wings."

Astonished, I blurted out, "For *Thief*? What happened to Hayes?"

"Not for *To Catch a Thief*," he said. "For our next story, whatever it might be. Hayes sent Ned Brown [a literary agent at MCA] to tell me he wants to direct the next script he writes for us."

"And you agreed with Ned?" Hitch knew I was joking.

"I asked for a list of writers MCA represented. I think Mr. Hayes will understand the message."

That ended all discussions about future writers until the end of *To Catch a Thief*.

Spoto discarded the true story I'd told him and wrote one of his own. How Hitch had given the book, *The Trouble with Harry*, to Hayes before Hitch left for France to begin filming *To Catch a Thief*. That could not have happened without my knowledge because I would have had to approve the commitment of Paramount's money for the deal. The book *The Trouble with Harry* was given to me just before we completed filming *Thief* on the Paramount stages.

I handed Hitch a stack of the pictures I'd brought back from Cannes. I'd deliberately placed the most beautiful picture on top. The one of the harbor at Monte Carlo, with the yachts of the rich and powerful moored on the bright blue water and the sky filled with fluffy white clouds.

His first comment was, "I thought we'd agreed no picture postcard locations."

I told Hitch if he didn't want beauty in *To Catch a Thief,* we'd better find another country in which to film the picture.

"Well," he said, "when you're directing the second unit, don't dwell on it."

He was happy with the pictures of the first chase but asked me to be sure to include a scene of Robie's car passing the picturesque St. Paul du Vence restaurant nestled in a saddle of the hills above Antibes. This little restaurant, with its small outdoor terrace, was known locally as one of the Côte d'Azur's most romantic spots for dining under the stars.

I still wonder how Hitch knew about St. Paul du Vence. Had he read about it, or was he a secret romantic?

The first Thursday after I arrived back at the studio, Alma came for lunch with Hitch and me. I had laid out on my desk the location pictures of the second chase, the police chasing Grant and Grace Kelly from Cannes to Monte Carlo.

Alma studied the pictures and moved the ones of the Bass Corniche aside. She kept a few of the Grande Corniche and concentrated on the Moyen Corniche. "I think the Moyen Corniche is the route Grace should take," she said. "It's so beautiful."

I couldn't keep from grinning at Hitch. He wasn't about to argue with Alma. I'd already discovered that he had the greatest respect for her judgment on all aspects of his films.

I sat and listened as she ad-libbed the entire chase, which was not yet on paper. When Hayes wrote the screenplay, he followed Alma's chase almost to the letter.

I was told that the front office had agreed with Hitch that, in addition to my work as second unit director, I would also assume the duties of supervisor. Frank Caffey added, "Without credit or increase in your second unit director's salary."

I guess that was one of the ways Hitch was going to keep the budget down to the $1 million figure he'd been saying would cover the cost of the picture.

I watched Doc and Danny McCauley, the gentle, quiet, unassuming, but highly efficient gentleman I'd arranged to replace me as Hitch's assistant, wearing out their pencils adding numbers to the budget sheets. I wasn't surprised when I saw that the figure had more than doubled Hitch's $1 million figure.

Hitch was startled when I gave him the news. "Tell Doc I want the budget at $1 million. I'm not planning big sets or great crowds, and I don't want the casting department overpaying the actors we select in Paris. I want to shoot in natural interiors in Cannes. Keep the budget tight."

I told Hitch I believed him when he said that $500,000 would be enough for *Rear Window* because he and Jimmy would be off budget. But the picture still cost a little over $1 million. "There's no way *Thief* can be made for less than $2 million."

He groused about it a little but gracefully gave in and quickly forgot that the studio would expect us to meet the $2 million.

It was a little harder for me to talk him into making *Thief* as one of his four Paramount productions. He also gave in on that proposal, but I don't think he ever forgave me. It was a great financial success and the only picture we made as a Paramount production.

I could see we'd never have a complete screenplay by the time we were scheduled to leave for Cannes, so I asked Hitch if he was planning to take Hayes along. "I don't want him around while we're shooting over there," he said. "Tell him to work here in the studio." I seem to remember I allowed him to come to Paris, but I'm not sure. I know he never came to Cannes.

Paramount's doctor decided that all the people going to the South of France needed a series of shots to prevent them from catching all those terrible diseases in that far-off underdeveloped nation.

Shots had never been a problem for me, so I let Lillian Rock, the studio nurse, slip a needle in my arm. Within minutes, my temperature soared. Lillian was frightened when it passed the 104 degrees mark. She called Dr. Strathern at his office in Hollywood. He came immediately and gave me an antidote.

By six that evening, my temperature was down to 100, and he allowed me to be driven to our home in Balboa. Soon my temperature began to climb again.

Mary Belle called our doctor in Newport Beach. He was out of town, so his new associate came. He gave me a brief examination and said I had a kidney infection. I told him I was supposed to leave for the South of France the next day.

"I'll give you a double dose of penicillin," he said. "If your temperature's normal tomorrow morning, you can go." Joe Casala, a close friend, was with us when the doctor arrived. He stayed with me while Mary Belle went downstairs to show the doctor out. Immediately, my body caught fire. I climbed out of bed and headed for the shower. "I've got to get in the shower, Joe. My body is burning up." Halfway to the bathroom door, my sight began to fail. I called to Joe, "I'm going blind. I can't see!"

That was the last thing I remember. Joe ran out on the balcony, calling for the doctor, but he'd driven away. Mary Belle called the hospital and told them what had happened. They told her to get me there as quickly as possible. "Don't wait for an ambulance," they said. "There's no time for that."

Joe and a neighbor carried me on a chair to a car and rushed me to the hospital. A nurse was waiting outside with a needle when we arrived. The first twenty-four hours were anxious ones for the doctors and my family. Four days later, quiet and troubled, I left for Cannes.

Danny and Doc, who shared a large suite with me in the Carlton, often found me deeply absorbed in the Bible, a practice I'd abandoned as a youth.

Hitch flew in a few days later. We gave him no rest. We piled in cars and headed for the villa we'd chosen on top of the mountain. When we arrived, the fog was so thick that Hitch wouldn't get out of the car to take a look.

"Let's see the one you liked at St. Jeanine," he said.

He didn't reveal his opinion about the St. Jeanine villa until we walked onto the veranda, with its view of St. Jeanine in the background. He turned to Doc. "The people who own this place will let us work here, Doc?"

"For the right number of francs, we own the place," he assured.

With Robie's villa settled, we drove to Monte Carlo to show Hitch the Bertani restaurant that Mac had under construction. Hitch didn't bother to walk down the long flight of steps to the quay. He stood by the wall that ringed the car park, looked out at the harbor of Monte Carlo, with all the multimillionaires' enormous yachts moored on the placid blue water, up to his right at the Palace Monaco, the home of His Serene Highness, Prince Ranier Grimaldi, turned to Mac, and almost allowed a smile of approval to show. "It will do, Mac," he said.

I waited until we got back into our car before noting, not too seriously, "If it's too beautiful here, we can move the restaurant over to the loading docks."

He knew I was kidding. "It's done now. Somehow, I'll make it work."

The next day, I took Hitch over the high mountain route Grant's housekeeper would take to lead the detectives away from Grant's villa. From there, we went to the Moyen Corniche. We drove slowly along and stopped occasionally so I could show him the locations for the various stunts.

There is a scene in the picture in which the two detectives who are chasing Grace and Grant crash their car when a chicken runs across the road. I told Hitch I would do a scene in which Grace just misses a chicken that "didn't cross the road."

It would start across, see the car coming, and turn back just in time to miss being hit. "You could spend weeks trying to get a chicken to do that," Hitch said.

"If I don't film it in two takes, Hitch, I'll give it up."

"It might get us a laugh," he said. "And it's your second unit."

I waited until the last day of my schedule before giving it a try. We couldn't undercrank the camera to give the appearance of the car going full speed. So it came flying up the road at sixty miles an hour. The chicken strolled out on the road and disappeared in a cloud of feathers. That was the first part. Again, we came flying up the road, and the chicken strolled across the road from the right. Disappeared in front of the car, reappeared on the left side of the car, and strutted off the road to the left. There we had the second part.

It took the special effects department over a week to get the chicken to turn around. The scene sure got the laugh we wanted.

Hitch flew alone to Paris to select the French cast.

The most important was the role of the restaurant owner, Bertani. Hitch chose a noted French actor, Charles Vanel, for the part, even though he could speak almost no English.

The second most important role was a girl for the part of Danielle. Brigitte Auber was the easy winner.

Hitch, Doc, Danny, Paul Feyder (Danny's French assistant), and I went to the dock at Cannes to meet Cary Grant when he came ashore from the French liner he'd vacationed on from New York to Cannes. It was the first time I had seen Cary in person since *The Last Outpost,* back in May 1934. When Hitch introduced us, I saw a momentary puzzled look appear on his face, but it disappeared as quickly as it appeared.

Doc pointed to a shiny new black Lincoln limousine he'd leased in London. A uniformed English chauffeur was standing beside the open rear door. "There's your car, Mr. Grant. We brought it over from London. Your chauffeur's name is Barclay." Although he'd just met Doc for the first time, he hugged him as he exclaimed, "How thoughtful of you, Doc. But you shouldn't have gone to all that trouble."

"The studio said it was in your contract, Mr. Grant."

"Please don't be formal, Doc. I want everybody to call me Cary."

For a moment, I thought Cary had changed from the haughty, arrogant Englishman of the early 1930s; but within three weeks, I decided I was wrong.

One morning, he cornered Doc with, "Doc, why do I have to ride around in that limousine with everybody staring at me. Get rid of it. I'd like a little open car with someone my age, dressed in ordinary clothes, for my driver."

Doc delivered the car and driver Cary wanted and shipped the Lincoln back to London.

Another couple of weeks passed before Cary groused, "I'm not happy with the car and driver you've given me. Why can't I have the car my contract demands?"

Doc had to bring the Lincoln back by air.

Then Cary surprised us all. From that moment until the finish of the picture, he cooperated fully with everyone.

Grace arrived a few days later on the Blue Train from Paris, followed by Charles Vanel and the rest of the French cast. John Williams and Jessie Royce Landis came from London. With their arrival, we were ready to go.

The evening following Vanel's first appearance in the picture, he called and asked if he could come and talk to me. While I waited for him to arrive, I wondered how that would be possible, for my French was about on the same level as his English. I could see he was very upset and worried about something. He paced around my room and then paused to gaze out the window at the moonlight on the Mediterranean Sea. When he turned toward me, I indicated a chair and asked him to sit down.

For over an hour we fumbled around, each trying to understand the other. For a while, I thought it was hopeless; but with the aid of my well-thumbed dictionary, I understood that he was trying to say, "It's too much. I lose Bertani trying to remember the English words. Monsieur Hitchcock must be disappointed with my performance." I convinced him that he must trust Hitch's judgment. "Don't be surprised if Mr. Hitchcock doesn't thank you after a scene. He never says 'thank you' to anyone." He was smiling when he left the room.

One day at the flower market in Nice, Doc gave me a cable that had just arrived from Hollywood. I opened it and saw that it was from one of Hollywood's top agents. It read, "Have firm offer from studio for you to direct pilot new series *Nurses.* Stop. Only your acceptance needed to seal deal. Stop. Cable your answer immediately."

Doc was reading over my shoulder. He called for Danny to come see the cable. Hitch wanted to know what we were excited about, so I handed him the cable. He read it and then handed it back without a word.

Later in the afternoon, he took me aside and asked me what I was going to do about the *Nurses* offer. I told him I had never walked off any job until it was finished but that if the *Nurses* job was still available after I completed the second unit, I would accept it.

"Hold your answer until after dinner tonight," he said. "I have something I want to discuss with you."

Dinner was at Le Reserve, the famous restaurant in Beaulieu, just a few miles west of Monaco. We sat at a table overlooking the Mediterranean Sea, with the rising moon reflected on the calm water. Hitch wasted little time getting to the cable. After asking Alma if the wine was satisfactory, he said, "If you will reject the *Nurses* offer, I'll have a position for you that will be much more important for your future career. I can't tell you what it is until the boys [Lew Wasserman, the head of MCA, and his agents] arrange it with Paramount." I told him I'd give him my answer the following morning.

As soon as I got back to my room at the Carlton, I called Mary Belle, told her the story, and asked for her advice. She gave me the same answer she always did when I asked what I should do. "Make your own decision. I'm with you whatever you decide to do."

Doc and Danny were waiting when I got off the phone. We all agreed that there was only one position in the Hitchcock organization he could be thinking about: an exciting job of producer!

I was earning $650.00 per week as second unit director. He couldn't offer less than $1,000, important money back in 1954. I trusted him and told him at breakfast the following morning that I accepted his offer.

Hitch finished his work on the Côte d'Azur and flew back to the studio to film the interior scenes.

The helicopter and the pilot, John Crewdson, whom Doc had brought from England, were waiting on the little Cannes airstrip when Wally Kelly (director of photography on my second unit), Doc, and I arrived. We got aboard and headed for Digne.

We followed the route I'd decided to use for the first chase. It looked better from the air than from the road. I asked Crewdson to leave that area and let me check out another road on a higher mountain. To get there, we had to cross a deep gorge. I was sitting beside the pilot and began getting a little worried as we got closer and closer to the mountain on the opposite side of the gorge. We made it but not by much. I guessed about four feet. That settled it. We flew back to Digne and followed the road through the little villages.

As we approached the ancient town of Castellane, the road turned sharply into a very narrow canyon. Crewdson pulled the helicopter almost straight up to avoid the unexpected rush of air that came pouring down on us.

I told Crewdson to stay out of there when we filmed the scene. We flew over St. Paul de Vence but found it impossible to make a shot of the chase passing the restaurant. Hitch was so excited when he saw the chase that he forgot to ask why I hadn't included St. Paul du Vence.

We rehearsed each scene from the helicopter until the timing was just right. When the scenes were filmed, I was sitting at the airport hoping Wally and Crewdson were shooting the scenes exactly as we'd rehearsed them. I couldn't be in the helicopter. There wasn't room for me after that VistaVision camera was loaded aboard.

I had to wait until we were back in the studio to find out. I shouldn't have worried. What I saw on the screen was absolutely perfect.

Parting with the French staff and crew was painful. We'd become friends. I had the greatest respect for them as dedicated filmmakers and looked forward to working with them sometime in the future.

I had lunch with Hitch the day after I arrived home from Cannes. You could never tell by looking at him what was in his mind; but that day he seemed pleased about something. There was a hint of a smile in his hooded eyes.

"Lew and the boys have been meeting with Jack Karp about your new job," he said. "You will be my associate producer, with all the authority and responsibilities you would have if your title was producer. We'll work together on selection of stories, writers, and casts. The budget will be all yours. You'll have total control over all spending." Before he could continue, Danny McCauley called him to the camera. That ended our discussion about the new job.

I spent the next two days in the projection room with George Tomasini, Doc, and Wally Kelly looking at all the film we'd shot in France. We were all happy with what we saw. But I couldn't just walk away and leave George and Hitch with the job of putting all that film in some sort of continuity.

For a week or so, I cut the Grace/Grant chase, starting with the scene of them driving away from the Carlton Hotel and the shots of the cars along the Moyen Corniche. I timed the transparency plates to the dialogue between Grace and Grant, added the stunts, and came up with a 900-foot reel.

When I asked Hitch to run it with me, he said, "Let's wait until tomorrow. Alma will be in for lunch, and we can all see it together."

Alma, George, and I were waiting when Hitch arrived in the projection room. He'd come directly from the stage and was anxious to see the film and get to his office where lunch was waiting. He sank down beside Alma on the soft, black leather seat and said, "If we're ready, George, let's have a look at Mr. Coleman's chase."

There wasn't a single reaction or comment from Hitch during the running. However, I was happy to hear Alma when she saw the shot of the two cars crossing the high bridge over the gorge, with the little village of Eze perched on the peak overlooking the Moyen Corniche. Alma said to Hitch, "When I suggested Herbie include Eze in the chase, I wondered how he could find a way to get the shot." She made other comments, always in undertones for Hitch's ears only.

When the running ended, Hitch turned to me and said, "Alma seems pleased with what you've done with her chase, so I suppose I'll have to go along." Faint praise—but more than I expected.

Later that afternoon, Alma said that the chases would be reviewed as an outstanding highlight of *Thief.*

I took a short vacation. It didn't last very long. Hitch called and urged me to come back. I couldn't figure out why. Doc and Danny were still with him and could handle any problems that came up.

Chapter 39

The Trouble with Harry

The next morning I was on the stage before Hitch arrived. Doc and Danny were surprised I'd been asked to come back so soon. "We're ahead of schedule," Doc assured me. "No complaints from anyone. Not even from the Marble Halls."

I watched Hitch cross the stage. He was walking with a brisk and jaunty air; I guessed that the fact he'd been dieting, and had lost so much weight, gave him all that energy. He wasn't even breathing heavily when he joined me in his dressing room. Steam was no longer rising from the coffee that waited on the table beside his chair. He would leave it untouched until it was stone cold. I knew he had something on his mind when he didn't bother to ask about my vacation. Still, he went through the cigar selection, inspection, and lighting up routine before picking up a small book that lay on his desk.

"Here's your first assignment on your new job," he said, as he handed it to me. I glanced at the title, *The Trouble with Harry*. The author was J. Trevor Story.

"Is this the one you're going to let Hayes direct?" I asked with a laugh.

His answer was a slight smile. "I haven't yet told Ned Brown that Hayes will be allowed to write the screenplay." He indicated the book; "Read it and let me know what you think."

By the time we met for our usual lunch in his office, I'd read the book twice. I wondered why Hitch had chosen *The Trouble with Harry*, a strange little story with absolutely no suspense and little mystery, to follow *Thief*.

When I posed that question to Hitch, he said, "I've always wanted to do a black comedy. This story is perfect for that."

"We'll make Harry our second Alfred Hitchcock production and make it for a price. A low-budget film. Without high-price stars. We'll cast it with New York stage actors. You'll have to use the book to prepare a budget. Leave the director's space blank."

Five days later, in my office, when I handed him his usual single, goodnight cocktail, I gave him the rough, hurry-up budget figure. He almost dropped his drink when I said, "$1,013,000."

"$1,013,000! That's impossible! I told the boys I could make the picture for $450,000!" He didn't shout as loud as I thought he would.

I said, "Hitch, I can make *Harry* for $450,000, but you can't."

He didn't take my statement with too much grace. "What do you mean? You can? But I can't?"

"You can't because your name is Alfred Hitchcock. I can because my name is Herbie Coleman. You'll pay more for the story. Everybody who works for you expects to be, and is, paid more. You'll take a full staff and crew from the studio. You'll have to hire two New York crews, one to standby on the set with your Hollywood men and one to work with me on the second unit. I'll hire local film crews and rent equipment. You'll travel to New York in two drawing rooms on the Super Chief. I'll fly alone. You'll stay in your usual suite at the St. Regis and entertain your friends and the press at Twenty One, the Colony Club, and the Stork Club. I'll have a room at the Lexington and eat at the Automat. If any reporters come to see me, I'll have a bottle in my room."

Hitch ended my argument by asking me to get the figure down a bit. I shuffled a few accounts and gave him a new figure just over $900,000. The total production actually cost $1,030,000, just $17,000 over my original guess budget.

We wanted to make the picture in an area with the most beautiful foliage. I decided to take a look around New England. I felt sure I'd find acres of giant maple trees with gold and crimson leaves shimmering in the breeze.

Hitch suggested I take Mary Belle and the kids with me. "They'll be back in school when we're shooting back there, and you won't be able to bring them along when you join us."

He got no argument from anyone in the Coleman family. Dale decided to stay home. He wasn't about to give up sailing his *Toroa* in all the important offshore races.

The last thing he said to me before he left the office was, "Call Hayes in and give him the book, and tell him to get started on the screenplay. Let him understand he's not to change one word that's in the book."

Hitch arranged it all. A drawing room for Mary Belle and me. And an adjoining compartment for Judy and Melinda. Wine for each meal delivered to the private dining room he'd reserved for us on the City of Los Angeles train.

A limousine was to meet us at the Grand Central Station when we arrived in New York. A suite in the Plaza Hotel. And the proper publicity in the New York papers announcing my new position with the Alfred Hitchcock Company.

The studio sent a car to take us to Union Station in downtown Los Angeles. On the way, we stopped at the studio. I wanted to leave some instruction with Bob Burks regarding the transparencies he would be photographing while I was away.

Danny told me that Frank Caffey would like me to stop by his office for a short meeting. When I got there, Frank told me he was no longer my boss. "Starting today," he said, "you'll report only to Jack Karp and Mr. Hitchcock." He paused, reluctant to continue, and then asked, "Have you settled your salary with Mr. Hitchcock?"

I told him I'd left that up to Hitch.

"I think you made a mistake, Herbie," he said. "Herman Citron told Jack that Mr. Hitchcock would agree on a salary of $375.00 a week."

I sat there stunned at that insulting figure.

Then I stood up and told Frank about the *Nurses* offer I'd turned down when Hitch made the statement, "If you'll turn down the *Nurses* offer, I'll have a job that will be much more important for your future career." I paced around his office until I was able to control my anger and then told him I'd worked at Paramount for twenty-seven years and neither the studio nor I had ever violated a trust. "I agreed to do *Harry*, and I will. But the day the picture ends, I'm through with Paramount and Hitchcock."

Before he could reply, I walked out, got in the car with my family, and asked the driver to take us to the station. Mary Belle and the kids were too excited about the trip to notice the anger I was fighting to mask.

The kids didn't care much for the private dining room. They preferred to be out among the other passengers. Mary Belle wasn't happy with it either. She didn't like travelers staring in on us as they passed along the corridor. We gave it back to the Union Pacific the second day.

Judy read a review of the play *Pajama Game* and asked if we could see it while we were in New York. I promised her I'd have the Paramount office get tickets for us.

The Paramount office had bad news for Judy. It said *Pajama Game* was sold out for at least a year. Maybe President Eisenhower could get a ticket or two for himself and Mamie. But Richard Nixon and Pat could forget it.

We flew to Boston to meet with the New England Council, an organization devoted to the development of tourism in the area. Walter

Raleigh, the executive vice president, already had a tour of the best maple groves from Boston to the Canadian border planned for us.

After a tourist's tour of the city, I rented a car and we started on our search for the perfect maple grove. I had in mind an area of rolling hills with stands of color trees as far as one could see. Small villages with historic high-steepled, white churches. Covered bridges. Lakes and streams. We followed all the side roads from Boston to Nashua. Then on to Peterborough, where we stayed a few days.

Daniel F. Eneguess, the director of the Monadnock Region Association, showed us everything for miles around. I was impressed and placed Peterborough high on my list. Next, we surveyed the countryside around Keene before moving on to Concord. From Concord we drove to Glendale, on Lake Winnupescukee. A quick look around the lake, then on to a lodge in the hills above White River Junction.

Raleigh had made reservations for us. He wanted us to stay at President Eisenhower's favorite mountain retreat. We followed the manager down a winding road, through a heavy stand of pines, to a cabin beside a small lake shrouded in a ghostly mist. He told us to come back to the lodge soon for dinner.

I was called away from the table to take a phone call from Raleigh. He told me he was in trouble and needed my help. He said he'd had a call from Clifford Miskelley, the director of the Vermont Development Commission, complaining bitterly because I hadn't been to Vermont. I told Raleigh I would call Miskelly and arrange a meeting. I wasn't too happy with Miskelley for being so rough on Raleigh, so I waited until we left the dining room to make the call. When he came on the phone, I told him Mr. Raleigh had suggested I save Vermont until the end of my survey. "You'll find what you're looking for up there," was the way he'd put it.

We met at White River Junction the next morning.

Miskelley was just the opposite of the picture I'd had in my mind since Raleigh's call. Despite the fact he'd left Montpelier at four that morning to be in White River Junction at seven, he was smiling as he shook my hand. I found him to be friendly and anxious to help. I told him the story of *Harry*. He asked for a couple of days to plan a tour of the areas he thought would be best for our picture.

The drive up to Montpelier along the White River, to the rolling, tree-covered hills of Vermont, dismissed from my mind Peterborough, Keene, and all the other places we'd covered.

Miskelley was waiting at the lodge in Montpelier when we arrived. He'd brought along a photographer. We had coffee while Miskelley unfolded a map of the area and pointed out the spots he suggested we check.

I told Cliff the most important location was the giant maple tree where the body of the dead stranger would be discovered. I wanted the tree to be on a hilltop with the landscape falling away in every direction. Second in importance was the place where we would build the country store and roadside stand where the artist's paintings would be sold. There is a scene in the picture in which the artist arrives at the little stand and sees that none of his pictures have been sold. He looks across the dirt road at the village compound, an acre of lush grass enclosed by a white fence, with a few cows quietly grazing. He turns back and asks the owner of the stand, "Do you think we'd do better on Fifth Avenue?"

I wanted to find a place where we could have the stand and the compound all together. Cliff took me directly to East Craftsbury. It was exactly right.

Beyond the stand there were two giant elm trees more than 300 years old. The compound was in the right place, with a few old homes in the distance. We covered the area with pictures, received permission from the owners to use it in the picture, and moved on.

Near East Craftsbury we found all the less important locations we needed. The home of the widow of the dead body. And the home of the spinster, where she entertains the old sea captain.

At Morrisville I arranged to rent an old gymnasium in which to build the interior of the widow's home for a cover set where we could shoot during bad weather. That left only the problem of quarters for Hitch, Alma, Mary Belle, myself, the stars, and the staff.

A few miles higher up in the mountains from Stowe, the owners of an inn called the Lodge at Smugglers Notch agreed to move out and give Hitch and Alma their suite. They also had enough rooms for the rest of us.

Everybody else would be housed in Stowe, a popular ski resort.

We said good-bye to Cliff at the Montpelier airport and took off for New York, stayed overnight at the Plaza, and flew home the next day.

Hitch had completed filming on *To Catch a Thief* before I got back and was at Revue filming his first *Alfred Hitchcock Presents,* a new half-hour television series. The set was a large trailer park. As I drove in, I saw Hitch sitting beside a beautiful young lady who was wearing a real sexy costume. If you could call nothing but a long man's shirt a costume. When I joined Hitch and the girl, he introduced us with, "Vera, this is my feature films' producer, Herbie Coleman. Herbie, Miss Vera Miles, the star of my movie, *Revenge*." Before Hitch could continue, his assistant called him to the camera. After Hitch walked away, I asked Vera if *Revenge* had anything to do with the provocative costume she was wearing.

"Everything," she said. "We live in that trailer over there. My husband and I. After he goes off to work, I come out in this costume, stretch out on that cot to get some sun. What I don't know is a man has been watching me. One day I go inside for a drink of water. He follows me inside and rapes me. When my husband comes home, he finds me crying hysterically. When I'm able to tell him about the rape, he gets his gun. Leads me to the car, and we go in search of the man. We didn't have far to go. I see a man entering a building. 'There's the man!' I cry out. My husband grabs his gun, follows the man inside the building. There's the sound of a shot. My husband comes back, gets in the car and tells me the man will never rape another girl. We start off again and I see another man walking along the sidewalk. I point at him and tell my husband, 'There's the man who raped me!'"

I told Vera that Hitch picked the perfect title and the perfect story for his first television film. I wanted to add, "and the perfect girl."

We were silent for a moment and then Vera asked, "Did Mr. Hitchcock ever tell you he might be interested in offering me a contract?"

I told her I'd been away and asked why she wanted to know.

"My agent has a meeting at Fox this afternoon at three. But if Mr. Hitchcock is interested, I'd rather sign with him."

"If he is Vera, I'll see it includes feature films."

As soon as Hitch was free, I asked him if he was planning to offer Vera a contract.

"What do you think?" he asked.

"Well, she's young. Beautiful and sexy. If she can act, we've got a new Grace Kelly."

"I'll talk to the boys about it."

"You'll have to talk to them in a hurry. Her agent has a meeting at Fox at three this afternoon to sign with them."

"Call Herman and tell him why he has to drop everything and get out here in a hurry."

By lunchtime, the deal was signed. And it did include feature films.

During the lunch break, he studied the photographs I'd brought back from the survey and agreed on the spot. East Craftsbury was right for the little store where John Forsythe's painting would be displayed. "When am I going to meet the art director, Henry Bumstead, you've promised would join us?" Hitch asked.

I had to tell him Bummy was tied up on a difficult picture and couldn't get away: "John Goodman will be with us on *Harry*. I've worked with him many times. He's good. And you'll like him."

Hitch had three more days shooting on *Revenge*. The day after he finished, we met in our offices at Paramount. John showed us his plans for all the sets he would build in Vermont. Hitch approved John's plans and, after he left, asked Doc, "Can you get everything arranged so we can start shooting back there the minute we complete 'fine tuning' on *To Catch a Thief*?"

"No problem, Hitch," Doc said. "We'll be out of here sometime tomorrow."

After Doc left, Hitch wanted to know when I was going to New York to complete the casting on *Harry*. "Has anybody back there suggested anyone for Harry Roger's widow, Jennifer?"

"Not even a hint." After a moment I asked, "Vera Miles?"

"All wrong. You said it the other day. Young. Too young. Beautiful. Too beautiful. Sexy. Too sexy. I thought we'd settled on a ordinary small-town girl."

"Sorry, Hitch. I guess I'm still thinking about that $450,000 figure." He accepted it as the joke I meant it to be. "I'll leave with Doc and the others tomorrow. I'll call you from the St. Regis when I get in."

Doc put the sets in work in East Craftsbury and came back to New York to line up the New York crews.

I was busy working with Balaban, the head of casting for Paramount in New York, culling the lists of candidates he'd assembled for the various roles.

The part of Mrs. Wiggs, the owner of the country store and stand, was eventually won by Mildred Dunnock. The role of Miss Graveley, a spinster who falls in love with a sea captain, went to Mildred Natwick.

From the very beginning, Hitch had planned to cast Edmund Gwenn as Captain Albert Wiles, the retired old sea captain; John Forsythe as Sam Marlowe, the eccentric artist; Royal Dano, the county policeman; and Jerry Withers as the son of the widow, Jennifer Rogers.

With the start date of *The Trouble with Harry* just around the corner, and the problem of finding a Jennifer weighing heavily on my mind, I fortunately remembered Judy's constant plea. "Try to see *Pajama Game* this time, Daddy."

When I discovered that Frank Loesser had written the music for *Pajama Game*, I called his office. He gave me his house seats for the matinee the next day.

I can't tell you the story of *Pajama Game*; but I can tell you I sat fascinated by the performance of the star, Carol Haney. The moment the curtain came down, I told Doc I'd found our girl. "Carol Haney's exactly the one I've been searching for."

"Carol Haney?" Doc said, opening his program to show me a notice announcing in the absence of Miss Haney, her understudy, Shirley MacLaine would assume her role.

I hurried to the manager's office, and asked him to introduce me to MacLaine. He called backstage but she had already left the theater.

I went directly to Balaban at the Paramount office, and asked what he knew about Shirley MacLaine. "Not much," he answered. "I know she's in the chorus of *Pajama Game* and an understudy for Carol Haney."

When I asked if she'd ever been in a movie, he said, "Hal Wallis had an interview test made of MacLaine, but nothing ever came of it." He told me Wallis had the test in his office.

I called Hitch and told him I'd found our girl. He wanted to know all about her. I said I'd only seen her once, from the fifteenth row of the theater. He asked if I was going to test her in New York or send her out to the studio so he could test her. I told him I didn't want a test made. He drawled out very slowly, "This is your first picture as a producer, and you're going to use an untested actress in the starring role?"

I told him about the interview test Hal Wallis had made of Shirley and asked him to have Danny borrow it from Wallis and show it to him.

Hitch called me early the next morning and in a completely unemotional voice said, "I signed your girl."

Hitch and Alma joined me in New York. He was anxious to meet Shirley. So was I. I called Balaban and asked him to bring her to the St. Regis the next day.

I was standing at the window of their suite the next morning, staring out onto Fifth Avenue, watching the rain pouring down on the people hurrying along the sidewalks. Hitch sat engrossed in the London *Times*.

Hitch looked up from his newspaper and drawled, "Stop pacing, Herbie. You're making me nervous. Your girl will arrive presently."

As I started for the window, the phone rang. I picked it up and heard the desk clerk say, "There's a girl here who says she has an appointment with Mr. Hitchcock." I heard him ask her name. "Her name is Shirley MacLaine."

I asked him to send her up and then told Hitch he was about to meet his star. He looked over the top of his newspaper and asked, "Wouldn't it be correct if you said, 'Your star,' Herbie?"

I hurried to open the door when the doorbell rang. Standing there was the most pitiful figure I'd ever seen. She couldn't be the same bright, bubbly, bouncy actress I'd enjoyed for two hours in *Pajama Game*. Rain was dripping from her drenched, short red hair to her rain-soaked trenchcoat. I glanced down at her feet. The worn loafers she was wearing were run down at the heels and looked like she'd been tramping around in the rain for hours. When I looked up, she was holding out her hand and a wonderful, bright smile covered her pixie face.

"I'm Shirley MacLaine," she said.

I took her hand, told her my name, and invited her inside.

As I helped her off with her trenchcoat, I noticed that the collar was stained with makeup. Underneath, she was wearing a worn, light brown sweater and skirt.

It didn't take long for Shirley to impress Hitch. He recognized immediately that he was talking to an educated, sophisticated articulate young lady, and it was obvious to me, he was enjoying the conversation and in no hurry to end it.

I hated to break in, but we had to meet John Forsythe at Twenty One. John had asked me to let him get away by two o'clock to attend another important meeting.

But after such a pleasant morning talking to Shirley, Hitch was relaxed and in no hurry to get down to business when we met John at Twenty One. He couldn't make up his mind about the proper wine he should order. Then he dawdled over the luncheon menu. That settled, he began to talk about the clothes he wanted on the dead body.

First, it was the jacket. "One of those blue jackets with the silver buttons and the two slits at the back," he said. "A striped shirt with French cuffs and extra-large silver cuff links. One of those wide, handpainted silk ties from Sulka. Blue and white plaid, wool socks and those shoes with the tassels."

I saw that John was becoming increasingly nervous. I thought it was because he was going to be late for his next appointment, but he made no attempt to leave. He was still sitting at the table when Hitch and I left for a meeting at Paramount. I asked him later why he'd remained behind. He grinned and said, "I was afraid to get up from the table. I was wearing everything Mr. Hitchcock said he wanted on the dead body."

The next day we flew to Montpelier, where the New York chauffeur was waiting with his limousine to drive us to the Lodge at Smuggler's Notch.

Hitch checked out the owner's suite and came out smiling. It started to rain as Doc drove up with John Goodman, Bob Burks, Howard Joslin (Hitch's new assistant), and the rest of our staff.

Hitch wouldn't agree with the suggestion to postpone a look at the locations until the rain stopped. We paused at the country store and little stand and climbed over an old split-rail fence into a pasture to choose a camera setup for the opening shot. While we listened to Hitch describe how he would stage the scene, a small herd of curious brown and white milk cows came from the trees and paused in a circle behind us. They were attentive and seemed to understand everything Hitch said. When he pointed off in the direction he wanted Royal Dano's old car to drive in, they turned as one to follow his outstretched arm. They reacted the same as I'd seen humans who were watching us do when we were filming in public places.

We continued the survey, with Hitch asking for very few changes in the sets. When we entered the gymnasium, the rain was pelting down on the tin roof; it sounded like we were inside a snare drum. Hitch looked at me with raised eyebrows. I told him we were covering the roof with canvas to kill some of the noise, but we'd have to replace all the dialogue. He accepted my explanation without comment.

When Hitch heard about Shirley's marriage to Steve Parker, a popular New York choreographer and dancer with whom I would form a warm friendship over the years, he grumbled, "Why couldn't she have waited until we finish this picture? I don't want him up here on this location. I want her thinking about Jennifer day and night." He paused and then added, "Especially at night."

I told Hitch that the lodge was a public place and her husband had every right to join her there. I promised to keep him from coming to the sets. That seemed to placate him.

One large table in a corner of the dining room was reserved for Hitch, Alma, Teddy Gwenn, Doc, Mary Belle, and me. A couple of extra chairs were left vacant. Almost every night Hitch would invite someone to join us for the evening. Everyone tried to be in place before Teddy arrived. Otherwise, he would insist on pushing himself, painfully, but cheerfully, to his feet as they approached the table. He would remain standing until all the ladies were seated, then slowly lower himself back down onto his chair. Halfway down, his arms would give out, and he would drop, with a thud, onto the hard oak chair.

The rain that welcomed us to Vermont the day we met the audience of friendly milk cows in the pasture near Mrs. Wiggs's country store continued to plague us. We would plan a day among the maple trees only to find a steady drizzle outside our rooms at Smuggler's Notch that would send us to our tin-roofed gymnasium in Morrisville.

Hitch never complained.

As soon as I saw that there were no problems, I would join my second unit to sit around and wait for the sun to break through the clouds and watch the rain strip the golden leaves from the trees. Then we'd go in search of another grove the rain had left untouched.

On our schedule there was a scene of Captain Wiles and Miss Graveley crossing a lake in a small boat. The perfect light was early in the morning. Our unit was ready to shoot at eight o'clock.

With doubles for Teddy Gwenn and Mildred Natwick sitting in the boat out in the middle of the lake, a sudden squall pelted them with sleet. They dried themselves in a nearby cabin, and then we tried again. Finally, the sun broke through late in the afternoon, and we got the shot.

I was a happy man when I walked into the gym. I knew Hitch would also be happy. I'd managed to mark off one scene we must have. He saw me come in, caught my eye, and looked away. I followed his look and was shocked to see Shirley and her bridegroom, Steve Parker, sitting in the semidarkness. It was obvious they were not discussing her role in *Harry*.

I sat down beside Hitch and listened while he reminded me of my promise to keep Steve away from the shooting company.

Burks finished lighting the set, the interior of Jennifer's living room, and asked for a rehearsal. Howard Joslin assembled the cast and came for Hitch.

I joined Steve and had a serious talk with him. I told him that if I were directing *Harry*, I'd be happy to have him around. "But Hitch is a different kind of animal. He believes that with a husband, even worse, a bridegroom, hanging around, the actress would have difficulty concentrating on her role in the film."

Steve apologized for breaking his promise, and that was the end of that.

When we got a break in the weather, we'd get a couple of days outside, the rain would come again, and back to the gym we'd go.

I soon saw we'd run out of cover sets in the gym before we completed the exteriors and had a meeting with John Goodman and Doc.

John said he could reproduce the set around the big maple tree on a stage at the studio. "No big problem," he said. "I'll do the trunk of the tree and lower branches with foam rubber. Paper leaves are available in Hollywood. A painted backing and some color bushes."

I didn't let Hitch in on what I was doing.

We continued to fight the weather.

One night Hitch and I were driving back to the lodge from Morrisville when snow began hitting the windshield. Pretty soon the wipers had trouble brushing it aside. By the time we reached the lodge, the ground was covered with an inch of snow.

Hitch climbed from the car, took a long look around the area, and then turned to me, "Tell me, Herbie, who picked this location?"

I knew he wasn't criticizing my judgment about selecting East Craftsbury. I guessed he was about to ask me how he was going to complete his picture, which he did as soon as we reached his suite.

I told him what John was doing at the studio. He was silent for a time. I broke into his thoughts to tell him he had four days left in Jennifer's home, and that Doc would go back to the studio with him.

"I'll take my camera crew and a couple of helpers, all of us and our equipment, in one bus and wander around the back roads of New England filming scenic shots to keep alive the feel of autumn you've already established in the picture," I told him.

Mary Belle and I stood with Cliff Miskelley watching our chartered planes take off from the Montpelier airport, and disappear quickly in the low, dark clouds that threatened to give us more snow or rain.

Bill Kelly, our second unit cameraman, and his small crew were waiting in the bus. We joined them and were off.

I was certain only of one scene I wanted to film. Weeks before, I'd seen a small covered bridge over a small stream about seventy miles southwest of Montpelier, so we headed for that spot.

We were lucky the snow hadn't reached that area. The rain had. We sat in the bus, waiting. As the hours passed, Bill became restless. He asked where we were going to stay that night. I told him not to worry, that we'd find a town somewhere along that old country road.

Late in the afternoon, the sun broke through the clouds, and we got the shot I wanted.

The rain came again before we had the equipment loaded back on the bus. No one complained about the weather. We were a dream team: six men and one very happy woman.

It was long after dark when we pulled into a small village. Our New York assistant director, Eddie Fay, found lodging for all of us.

We continued to wander along the back roads, filming farmers at work in their fields. And later, a gleaming, white church, with a very high steeple reaching for the sky.

Another scene was a stream tumbling down through a stand of white birch trees. The hill beyond covered with maple trees.

One day, just at sunset, we were driving through an area of rolling hills. I saw a corn field where the corn had been harvested, leaving rows of stubble a foot, or so, high. I called to the driver of the bus to turn up the next road. He was forced to stop when he reached a barbed wire fence. "I can't go any further," he said.

I told our grip to cut the fence. "I can't," he said. "That's private property."

I took his clippers, cut the wire, and pulled it aside.

We started up again. Along a rough farm road to another fence. Just beyond were the rows of stubble.

I called for Bill to give me a very low setup, crawled through the fence, and quickly picked a spot for the camera. The camera crew was as anxious to get the shot as I was. The sun was sinking lower and lower and the shadows of the stubble were growing longer and longer. The sun disappeared below the horizon while the camera was still turning. But we got the shot.

For another six days we continued our travels.

At the end of the sixth day, I called it off. We had everything we needed, and more. Most of it was used in the picture.

Mary Belle and I flew home. We were tired, but it was a wonderful experience.

Hitch still had a few days work left around the maple tree.

I sat through a running of the rough cut with editor Alma Macrorie. Shirley was simply wonderful. She wasn't the girl I'd seen in *Pajama Game*. She was a "down East" small-town girl with the ability to turn simple sentences into confusing questions that sent her listeners scrambling for answers. And, as I'd told Hitch, the timing of a Jack Benny or Lucille Ball.

The morning after Hitch, for the last time on *Harry*, said, "You have it." I was in my office packing my files into a stack of boxes piled upon Hitch's favorite couch. He walked in, looking for his usual cup of coffee, and stopped just inside the door.

I didn't even know he'd arrived until I heard him ask, "What's going on here, Herbie?"

"The picture's finished," I said. "I'm moving on. But before I go I want to thank you for the opportunity you gave me."

"What do you mean?" He seemed a little startled. "Our agreement wasn't just for one picture."

"It became that," I told him.

"I don't understand."

"Did you know my salary was to be $375.00 a week?" I asked.

"The boys said Jack Karp approved that amount."

"Jack Karp approved that amount? Or did Herman Citron tell him that's what the Hitchcock Company wanted it to be? I'm not angry, just disappointed."

I went back to my packing. Hitch waited a moment and then went into his office and closed the door.

I was still packing when Herman Citron came rushing into my office. He said he wanted to have a talk with me and asked if we could go outside.

We walked out and sat on one of the wrought iron benches overlooking the little fountain in the lawn, known as Cohen's Park, named after Emanuel (Manny) Cohen, a former head of Paramount Pictures.

Citron started with, "You've made Hitch very unhappy."

"Why did you ask to talk to me?"

"Hitch told me to find out what you wanted."

"Herman, I've been with Paramount for twenty-seven years. This place has been my home. All I've ever wanted was to remain in this home. But you've ruined that." I got up and started for my office.

Citron asked me to give him ten minutes with Jack Karp. He was back in less than five with an offer I couldn't refuse. The new deal would be retroactive to the day Hitch handed me the book.

I returned to my office. Hitch came in just after I'd thrown the last empty box out a window.

We had our usual nightcap. Neither of us ever mentioned what happened that day.

We were in the projection room the next morning, waiting to see the rushes of the scenes he'd made the previous day. Out of the blue, he asked, "Do you think our new picture should be a remake of *The Man Who Knew Too Much*?"

"*The Man Who Knew Too Much*? I don't remember ever hearing anything about a picture by that name."

"Didn't you ever see any of my pictures before we started working together?" he asked.

"I did see one," I told him. "*Shadow of a Doubt*. Damn good picture, Hitch. Teresa Wright was wonderful. We've got to find a story for her."

He didn't want to talk about anything but *The Man Who Knew Too Much*. I told him I'd find a print somewhere and take a look at it. I did and couldn't believe Alfred Hitchcock, one of the world's top filmmakers, could have made such an old-fashioned spy story. He was waiting to hear my reaction to the film.

"Well?"

"All I can say, Hitch, is you and films have progressed together."

I could see he was hurt by my spontaneous unrehearsed comment. I've regretted all my life for having made that unkind statement. But it was the truth.

"What do you mean?" he asked.

"Today, you'd never have your hero walk into the dental office of the master spy and, when caught, tell him you need to have a perfectly good tooth pulled."

As we continued to discuss the possibility of bringing the picture up to date, we agreed we'd go ahead with the project.

Hitch didn't want to make the new film in the snows of Switzerland. He'd already picked Marrakech, French Morocco, as the perfect alternate to St. Moritz.

We dropped *The Man Who Knew Too Much* to get back to *Harry*. There remained the selection of a composer, the "fine tune" editing, and the preview before we could turn our attention solely to the new project.

I'd never met Bernard Herrmann, the man Hitch brought in to compose the music, but I knew him by reputation as a distinguished composer and conductor of serious music. When we were introduced, I could believe he deserved that reputation. He looked the part; short, stocky, a thick shock of unruly black hair covering most of his brow, his face seemingly frozen in a threatening scowl. He dominated his audience, especially those musicians dominated by his appearance, his musical knowledge, and his baton. I didn't know that Bernie, a highly educated, articulate, sophisticated gentleman, would accept as his equal an uneducated, inarticulate man with a wild, wonderful, Cliff Holler, West Virginia, accent. He did, and over the years we became close personal friends.

Hitch didn't ask Bernie to let him hear the score before we all assembled on the scoring stage to record the music. There were smiles on the faces of the musicians as they played through the main title. One could anticipate the beauty of the Vermont landscapes by the lilt of the music, punctuated with an occasional hint of danger, especially over my credit. A show of friendship for me by my friend.

I even heard a muffled chuckle from Hitch when he heard the phrase Bernie had composed for the scene of the sea captain sneaking past the deputy sheriff, with his rifle concealed under his coat.

With the encouragement of Joseph B. Johnson, governor of Vermont, we held the world premiere of *The Trouble with Harry* in Barre, Vermont. A vast crowd of invited guests was treated to a wonderful New England dinner in a large auditorium.

Sitting with Hitch and Alma on the dais were governor and Mrs. Johnson, Shirley MacLaine, Jules Stein (the CEO of the Music Corporation of America), Mrs. Stein, Herman Citron (the MCA agent who took care of Hitch's affairs at Paramount), and Mrs. Citron.

The night before the premiere, Shirley discovered that her husband, Steve, had been assigned a table with Mary Belle and me, down below on the main floor. She came to see me, blaming Hitch for barring Steve from the dais. I was able to place the blame where it belonged, on the man from Paramount's New York office who was in charge of the premiere.

Cliff Miskelley was master of ceremonies for the affair. Standing on the stage, he introduced the guests seated there. Then began talking about how *Harry* happened to have been filmed in Vermont.

Without mentioning my name, he went through his first meeting with a Paramount executive in White River Junction, our travels together throughout the state to find the perfect sites for Hitchcock to use.

He described the problems that had to be solved before the start of production, told the whole story behind the scenes, and concluded by comparing the making of a successful motion picture with the success of a winning football team. Only with a great blocking back, running interference for the star running back, can a football team be successful. The blocking back on *The Trouble with Harry* was Herbert Coleman. He pointed down at me. I knew I had to get up and bow to the crowd. I was embarrassed. He had given me more credit than I deserved. Then he added, "And his beautiful wife, Mary Belle Coleman." We had to urge her to stand up and accept the applause of the assembled guests.

From the applause at the end of the running of *Harry*, we felt we had a hit.

Mary Belle and I joined Hitch and Alma at breakfast the next morning. I told Hitch we wouldn't be going back home with them. "Mary Belle and I have accepted an invitation from Governor Johnson to join him in his office tomorrow. He wants us to know what the filming of *Harry* in Vermont means to his state."

With the premiere out of the way, my authority and influence over *The Trouble with Harry* ended.

Hitch said he was going to stop over in New York and discuss the publicity tour on *Harry* with Barney Balaban and would see me in the studio.

When Hitch came back to the office, he told me that New York had decided to open *Harry* without the usual Hitchcock publicity tour.

The picture opened in a little theater down a side street off Fifth Avenue, across from Saint Patrick's Cathedral. The theater lacked a marquee, and one would have to walk along the side street, and stop in front of the theater to know it even existed.

The New York executives went even further in their efforts to dismiss *The Trouble with Harry* as being unworthy of a large and expensive campaign, despite the fact that every Alfred Hitchcock film in the past had been "sold" to the public by a mammouth media campaign.

"Word of mouth will make *The Trouble with Harry* a winner," they told Hitch. He bought it. The public didn't. "It must be a flop," they told themselves. "There's nothing about it in the papers or on TV."

Chapter 40

The Man Who Knew Too Much

I spent the first week after returning from the preview of *The Trouble with Harry* arranging Hitch's trip to Paris for the French dubbing on *To Catch a Thief.* Then he went to St. Moritz for his yearly Christmas anniversary holiday. We'd already agreed to let John Michael Hayes start on the screenplay of *The Man Who Knew Too Much* while Hitch was away.

The French dubbing on *To Catch a Thief* was completed on schedule. Hitch was back in the office in early January, eager to go to work on the screenplay of our new project.

I was away from the studio when Hayes came in with the pages he'd managed to write on *The Man Who Knew Too Much.*

When I came back, Hitch was sitting at his desk, the London *Times,* untouched, beside Hayes's work.

He pushed the pages Hayes had given him and, without a word, indicated that I should take a look. I took the script into my office where I could read without Hitch staring at me, waiting for my reaction.

When I finished reading the material, I walked back into Hitch's office and told him I thought we would have to develop *The Man Who Knew Too Much,* the same way *Rear Window* was written.

We agreed that Hayes's ability to write sophisticated dialogue was an asset. But his *Man Much,* as we were calling it, was sadly lacking in form.

We needed an experienced scriptwriter to construct a framework wherein the story could be told. It didn't take Hitch long to make up his mind who that writer should be.

"Call London. Ask them to find out if Angus MacPhail is available," he said. "If he is, have them send him over right away."

Angus was available, and less than a week later I went to the airport to meet a man about whom I'd heard so much during the years I'd been working with Hitch.

Angus was a distinguished member of the London Film Society in 1925 and worked through the years as a top film editor, story editor, and screenwriter. He was an important member of producer Michael Balcon's company when Hitch made the original *The Man*

Who Knew Too Much; and he worked on the screenplay with Charles Bennett, Edwin Greenwood, D. B. Wyndham-Lewis, A. R. Rawlinson, and Alma Reville.

I wasn't prepared for the man who walked from the plane. He was tall and very thin. His lined face and protruding nose sat atop one of the longest thin necks I'd ever seen. But it was his low, cultivated voice that drew me to him.

I guess he liked what he saw in me because we became instant friends. He trusted me from the beginning and relied on me to protect him in our strange country.

We drove directly to our offices. Hitch greeted his old friend as if he'd just said "good night" the previous day. I could see there would be a good bit of gossip before they'd get down to work, so I left them alone.

"Angus is frail," Hitch said. "He looks forward to his 'before'-dinner glass of wine. We'll keep his working hours from nine to three. He remembers everything about the old *The Man Who Knew Too Much* and is excited about working on our new screenplay."

Under Hitch's strong hand, Hayes and Angus were working well together; so I took Doc Erickson and flew to Paris.

While Doc was busy with visas, travel arrangements, and gathering up the French francs for our trip to Marrakech, I met with the officials in the French Foreign Office to tell them about our plans for filming in French Morocco. They wanted to read our screenplay before sanctioning our work; but I was able to tell them the story well enough to gain their permission to go to Marrakech for the survey.

All I knew about Marrakech I'd learned on the terrace of the Carlton Hotel in Cannes from some of the jet-setters, "the beautiful people," whose pursuit of pleasure took them from Paris, to Cannes, to Deauville, to Marrakech.

The flight from Paris to Casablanca was boring. The few passengers on the plane were mostly businessmen and early vacationers. Not a single jet-setter among them.

In Casablanca, we were switched to a tiny Air Atlas plane for the flight to Marrakech. It was filled to capacity and more. The aisles were a conglomeration of packages and djellaba-clad figures who were seat hopping and talking with their friends. Bundles filled the overhead racks, some hanging down to the heads of the seated passengers.

When we landed in Marrakech, we battled our way through customs and immigration and out to the limousine the hotel had sent to meet us.

Our first meeting was with Mr. Matzloff, the head of the Tourist Office. He had some experience with movie companies and was anxious to have a Hitchcock film produced in Marrakech. We spent the afternoon with him discussing our requirements for the picture. He arranged a meeting for us with a Mr. Fines, the head of the French Commission, in the Marrakech Town Hall. When we arrived at Fines's office the next morning, he introduced us to a Mr. Baylor, the head of municipalities, and his associate, Mr. Lerin.

They seemed a little bored as I told them the story of *Man Much,* but when I started telling about the chase through the crowded streets, ending with the stabbing of one of our stars, they came to full attention.

"The scenes you've described up to the murder of one of your men would give us no problem, Mr. Coleman. The people of Marrakech respect us and will obey our requests to cooperate with you. But your murder scene presents a very great problem. By the way, Mr. Coleman, when do you plan to start here in the city?"

"Mr. Hitchcock has just starting work on the screenplay. There's considerable work to be done before we can actually come to Marrakech and start shooting, Mr. Baylor."

"You must complete your work in Marrakech and be out of the country before the start of Ramadan. It will be a condition in our approval of your request to make your picture in our country."

I agreed to abide by all the limitations the Marrakech authorities wished to include in our agreement.

Lerin found us a top-notch commercial photographer and accompanied us when we toured the city, photographing areas we thought Hitch would want to use.

I told Lerin I'd like to photograph a few homes for a scene I believed we would need for the picture. He made a telephone call and then drove us to a lovely home on a palm-lined street. On the way, he told us about the Villa Taylor. "The home of the Count and Countess de Breteuil, Villa Taylor, should interest you. During World War II when your President Roosevelt came to Marrakech to meet with Prime Minister Churchill, the count moved out and gave his home to the president. Mr. Roosevelt loved the view of the city and the Atlas Mountains from the villa. Each day just before sunset, he was carried in his wheelchair to the roof where he could have a moment to rest and relax in the gentle, cool breeze that drifted down from the snow-capped mountains."

The count, an aristocratic French gentleman, showed us around his gardens and his home and led us to the rooftop while repeating some of the story his friend Lerin had just told us. He said that we were free to use the Villa Taylor in our picture, if Hitchcock wished.

I decided to see a little more of French Morocco before going back to the studio, so I rented a car and driver and toured Fez, Meknez, and Rabat on the way to Tangiers, where we would board a plane for home.

On the flight home, I began to realize that Baylor's warning about Ramadan had thrown us a wide curve. Before we could go into production in Marrakech, we must have the final screenplay covering those exteriors.

Also, the scenes of the attempted assassination in the Royal Albert Hall during the concert had to be written to allow Bernard Herrmann time to compose the music to be recorded and filmed in the Albert Hall.

I met with Hitch, Hayes, Angus, and Doc in my office the morning after I arrived home. I gave them the news—good and bad.

Overnight, the still department processed the photographs from Marrakech. Hitch was quick to select the ones he would use. I told them about the script we would need for Marrakech and London.

Before Doc and I left for Marrakech, I signed Bernard Herrmann to compose the music and conduct the orchestra in London. He knew we'd planned to ask him to join us again and was waiting for my call.

Jimmy Stewart had agreed to star in the role of the husband. Doris Day wasn't my first choice for his wife; I wasn't sure she could handle the scene in which Jimmy tells her about the kidnapping of their son. But Hitch had unshakable faith in her. He was right. She was excellent. Christopher Olsen won the role of the son.

While Hitch, Hayes, and Angus shuffled their pages around and worked hard to solve our script problems, I went down the hall to report to Jack Karp.

I laid it all on the table. I told him of the possible danger of having to return to Marrakech after London. Jack had become my strongest supporter at the studio and wasted no time agreeing with me to go ahead with the project.

Hitch and I met for our cocktail after the others had gone home for the night. I asked him if he felt comfortable leaving the screenplay in Hayes and Angus's hands.

"I settled that this afternoon," he said. "Hayes will write the dialogue. Angus will keep him on the right track. I made it clear to Hayes that Angus speaks for me on storyline. And he's not to stray from the path we've laid out. Hayes wanted to come with us to Marrakech or work in London. I told him to work here in the studio. I don't want him on the set." With the pressure on, Hitch, Hayes, and Angus delivered the pages needed for Marrakech.

Hitch had asked me to borrow Lois, the script supervisor who'd been working for him on his television series, *Alfred Hitchcock Presents*, but Universal refused to release her. I told Hitch that I'd find someone in London for the London and Marrakech work and Lois would join him when we came back to the studio. That someone turned out to be Connie Willis, a bright, bubbly spirited, happy young lady who would become an important member of our company.

Hitch, Alma, and I left for London to cast the important roles of Mr. and Mrs. Drayton, Buchanan, the prime minister, and the ambassador.

Doc followed us a few days later with Bob Burks, Howard Joslin, Hitch's assistant director, Henry (Bummy) Bumstead, the art director I'd been fighting to have assigned to our Hitchcock company, and other key members of our unit. We took them on a quick tour to the important sets we'd film when we came back from Marrakech. Then Doc took his group to Marrakech.

Doc had everything under control when we arrived in Marrakech. The staff, crew, and equipment from Hollywood had checked in and were ready to go, as well as the English film workers who would stand by in Marrakech and take over some of the more important duties when we moved to London.

Hitch had been concerned about the food he would find in that Muslim country and wanted me to have Dover sole flown from London. I stalled, waiting for his reaction to the food he would be served at a marvelous restaurant—a favorite of mine—Dar Es Salaam. He wasn't too keen on going there his first night in Marrakech, but Alma insisted; and the three of us rode across the Souk and went inside.

I watched Hitch's face as we stopped by the desk of the maître d'. His usual somber expression deepened as he watched a group of Moroccan men sitting on low cushions beside a low table, as they reached into a large copper tray with their right hands, rolled up balls of couscous and popped them into their mouths, gulped down glasses of steaming hot tea, and pulled strips of meat from the roast lamb that sat in the center of the couscous.

Only the appearance of the maître d' prevented him from escaping what I was sure he considered a dreadful scene. His expression changed instantly when the maître d' greeted him. "Good evening, Mr. Hitchcock. Welcome to Dar Es Salaam. We are honored by your presence."

He indicated that we should follow him and led the way to a table prepared for foreign guests. Hitch didn't know I'd phoned the maître d' and arranged it all.

Hitch forgot about the Dover sole when he tried the sole caught fresh that day from the cold Atlantic waters off the Moroccan coast.

Chapter 41

More Tales of *The Man Who Knew Too Much*

The day Alma qualified for American citizenship she joined a large group of people from many countries in the federal courthouse in Los Angeles, stood with them, and took the oath of citizenship. She'd often told me how much she wanted Hitch to also become an American citizen.

One evening, after our second and last cocktail of the day, when I again brought up the subject, Hitch surprised me by agreeing to make Alma happy if I would arrange for the judge to come to his office. I told him I thought it could be arranged; but I felt he should stand with all the others in the federal court and listen to the judge explain the responsibilities and duties of American citizenship. He agreed to go downtown if I'd go with him.

On the drive to the federal court building, Hitch was silent, lost in thought, staring straight ahead. Then he opened up a bit. "Herbie," he said, "have you ever wondered why I never gave in to Alma's wish that I give up my British citizenship?" I had to admit, it had never entered my mind.

"The Hitchcock name goes back almost to the beginning of the British Empire. It isn't easy giving up a lifetime surrounded with British tradition and history."

I asked Hitch if he was having second thoughts about going ahead with the citizenship.

"Alma would never forgive me. Or you either, Herbie. Not after you've brought me this far. She's coming, isn't she?"

"Doc's trying to find her and bring her to the courthouse," I told him.

There must have been 300 people already standing in the room when Hitch and I walked in. They were from all walks of life: Asians, Europeans, men, women, and children. Some were obviously poor; others were middle class; and, I guessed, a few were upper crust. The judge was an imposing figure sitting on the bench above the crowd. Hitch listened impassively to the solemn lecture.

It was a proud moment for me. And Hitch admitted years later, it was a proud moment for him.

We drove to Perinos restaurant on Wilshire Boulevard where our entire staff and executives from the Marble Halls were waiting to congratulate our newest American citizen. As champagne glasses were raised, Alma came rushing in. Hitch couldn't hide the smile that covered his face when she hugged and kissed him and exclaimed, "Hitch! You did it! You finally did it!"

Then she turned to me. "Thank you, Herbie. I'm happy you didn't wait until Dolores found me. Hitch might have changed his mind." Then, in front of all those guests, she gave me a big hug. Doc got his hug when Alma discovered he had arranged the party.

We met with the head of Paramount's music department to discuss the song we would need for Doris Day. Jay Livingston and Ray Evans were given the assignment.

Shortly before we left for London, I was asked to come to the music room to listen to a strange song they called "Que Sera, Sera." Ray played the piano while Jay sang. It was a catchy tune, but would it fit in? Doris Day, sitting at a piano, singing to a group of distinguished diplomats in an embassy in London?

When they finished the song, they all turned to me. Someone, I can't remember who, asked, "Well Herbie?" I thought it over for a moment and then told them I just didn't know. I asked them to wait while I went to bring Hitch.

He listened while they performed again. The impassive expression on his face revealed nothing. It didn't take him long to make up his mind. As usual, he didn't thank them for what they'd given him. He just agreed with everyone that it was the right song. It sure was. It won an Oscar for the composers.

On the plane to London I began to worry about Angus MacPhail having to deal with Hayes while Hitch and I were 8,000 miles away.

Once under way in Marrakech, I pushed the Hayes–MacPhail script problem aside to concentrate on keeping our company reasonably happy in the heat, humidity, and dust and the approaching Ramadan.

I asked George Tomasini to come to Marrakech to discuss the film we'd been sending him. I wanted to be sure we were amply covered before moving to London. George brought the completed screenplay to me. I looked at the title page and was shocked to see that it read: *The Man Who Knew Too Much,* screenplay by John Michael Hayes.

Angus MacPhail's name was missing. He should have been given equal credit with Hayes. I kept the screenplay hidden until we got to Hitch's suite that evening. We settled down under the cool, swirling breeze from the ceiling fan to enjoy our before-dinner cocktails. I opened the envelope and took out the screenplay.

It got Hitch's attention immediately. "Let's have a look." I handed it to him without comment.

He started to open it but glanced at the title page and stared at it for a moment. Then, for the first time, I saw an angry look cross his face. "How could he have left Angus's name off the title page?" he almost shouted.

"Are you surprised Hayes would do such a selfish thing?" I asked.

He didn't bother to answer my question. "You've read the script?"

I told him I had.

"Does it have any serious flaws? Anything the three of us can't fix?"

"Nothing we can't handle," I answered.

"Then call the boys. Tell them we're finished with Hayes. And I mean, today! I don't want to see him or talk to him again! Ever!"

We demanded that the Writers Guild of America give Angus McPhail equal credit on the screenplay, but the Writers Guild, with absolute authority to assign credit, refused to give Angus the credit he so deserved.

We started *Man Much* with the scene showing Ben, Jo, and the boy driving up the boulevard in a carriage, turning in on the curving drive to the front of the Mammounia Hotel.

A couple of amusing, and not so amusing, incidents occurred during the filming of that scene. On the first rehearsal I noticed two Arab girls reacting visibly to our stars in the carriage. I'd hired two Moroccan assistants to assist as interpreters: one who spoke only Arabic and French and one who spoke French and English. I took the two of them with me and joined the girls. I cautioned them against noticing Jimmy Stewart and Doris. My words were translated by the first assistant into French. The second changed it from French to Arabic. One of the girls started laughing and said in perfect American English, "Mr. Coleman, I was educated at UCLA. I understood everything you said." I hired her on the spot as an additional interpreter.

The other incident wasn't so funny. As the carriage pulled to stop, Ben and the others got out and started up the steps toward the glass doors of the Mammounia. Halfway up, flashbulbs started flashing inside the glass doors.

Hitch stopped the scene and turned to me with raised eyebrows. I went inside and saw Doris Day's husband, Martin Melcher, standing there with his camera pointed toward our camera. Hitch was a little cool toward him for quite a while but eventually forgot about it.

One day Hitch had a lot of trouble getting just what he wanted from Hank. When the scene was completed, he came to me and asked why I'd cast Chris in the part. I told him it was because Chris was a fine young actor.

"Your problem, Hitch, is you don't know how to direct children. You use the same language with Chris you use when you're talking to Jimmy, Doris, or any adult."

He didn't argue the point. I thought that was the end of that; but months later, after the picture was in release, he walked into my office and laid a copy of the *Hollywood Reporter* on my desk. I glanced down at an article he'd circled with a heavy, black pencil. It read: "Christopher Olsen nominated for an Academy Award as Best Supporting Actor in the Alfred Hitchcock film *The Man Who Knew Too Much.*"

I looked up at him. A self-satisfied smile covered his face. "So, I don't know how to direct children?" He'd been waiting patiently all those months to prove me wrong.

While Hitch was busy with the first unit, I took my crew and filmed the scenes on my schedule: the bus from Casablanca en route to Marrakech. Its arrival at the bus station. Doubles for the stars driving in the carriage from the bus station to the Mammounia. And the transparency plates to cover. We had full cooperation from everyone.

As the days passed and the weather became extremely hot, and the start of Ramadan stared us in the face, we doubled and redoubled our efforts to complete our work.

Hitch finished everything on his schedule and retired to his suite to work with Alma on the script, while I started filming the last two days of my schedule in the Souk.

Armed soldiers were around in the crowds, who were becoming increasingly sullen and angry about working for me in the sweltering heat and humidity without food or water from sunrise to sunset.

I got through the first day without any serious trouble, but Ramadan started the next morning. When we arrived in the Souk, armed soldiers were posted on rooftops overlooking the area. By noon the crowds were becoming hostile.

Salmi came to me and asked me to suspend filming immediately and get our cameras out of sight. That ended our work in Marrakech.

We packed up and flew to London.

Kay Selby, an executive in Paramount's London office, had everything laid out so we could get right to work.

Benny Herrmann was waiting to conduct the London Symphony Orchestra in his exciting reorchestration of Arthur Benjamin and Wyndam Lewis's "Storm Cloud Cantana."

We completed our work in London and returned to the studio.

Angus rejoined us. He'd been working on the screenplay and had many suggestions for minor, but subtle, changes in many of the scenes remaining to be filmed.

Our usual routine was quickly established. A quiet, steady, happy company. Happy to be home again. But there was little rest. Hitch and I joined George every day in the projection room. Lunch was served on trays as we reviewed the rough cut that George had put together while we were away. Twice, when we returned to the stage after the runnings, Hitch, peevishly, asked why George had made some, I thought, minor cut in the film: "Why did he do that?"

The third time he asked that question, he added, "But what else should I expect from an ex-projectionist?"

I was surprised at Hitch. That didn't sound like the Hitchcock I'd come to respect. So I asked him: "Is that what you say to your friends when I've made a decision you didn't like? But what else should I expect from an ex–truck driver?" I never heard him make another remark like that about anyone.

The picture was completed without any serious complications. Hitch and Alma went back to the ranch for a rest. George finished the rough cut. We ran it together, and then I called Hitch and told him we were ready for him to come back and "fine tune" the picture. There wasn't too much he needed to do before I called in Benny Herrmann for a music running. While Benny was busy adjusting the timing of his already completed musical composition to the final cut of the film, Hitch and I were working out travel plans for an "around-the-world" publicity tour for our last two films, *To Catch a Thief* and *The Trouble with Harry.* He and Alma would leave immediately after Benny finished scoring the picture.

We joined Benny on the scoring stage and for two days watched him criticize, dominate, and sometimes rave at the Paramount orchestra, until the last chord was recorded. The moment the last musical note faded away, Benny's attitude changed completely. Smiling broadly, he thanked the players for their attention to his complicated composition.

A few days later I held a private running of the picture for Jimmy and his wife Gloria and Alma, Hitch, and George. As we left the theater, Jimmy, who seldom expressed an opinion about the editing of one of his pictures, told us he thought we needed to change how Doris looks at the prime minister and the assassin in the lobby of Albert Hall.

"Well, Herbie. What are you going to do about it?" Hitch asked.

I replied, "I'll have Bummy build a small section of the Royal Albert Hall lobby. Send photographs of the three women directly behind Doris to Kay Selby in London and have her buy, or rent, their clothes. Get it all together and make the shot."

I saw Hitch and Alma off on the Super Chief the next morning.

The publicity department had everything laid out for their trip. Stopover a day in Chicago, on to New York for a week, the *Queen Elizabeth* to London, a week there at Claridges. Next, Paris, Madrid, Rome, Cairo, Bombay, New Delhi, Calcutta, Bangkok, Singapore, Tokyo, Honolulu, and then finally home.

There were many meetings with Paramount distributors, and the press was at every stop. It took over forty days, a tiring but necessary journey. That was the way Hitch helped sell his pictures.

Before he left London for Paris, I'd filmed the scene with Doris. At the secret preview in Glendale, California, I had the sound department record the entire soundtrack of the picture, including the sound of the audience's reactions, and airmailed the tapes to Rome. Unfortunately, Hitch had completed his work in Rome and left the city for Cairo and Bombay. Rome shipped the tapes to Bombay. The tapes played tag with Hitch from Bombay to Tokyo. They finally tagged him at the Paramount office in Tokyo.

When Hitch left Rome for Bombay, and the other cities of the subcontinent, I decided to take Mary Belle on a vacation in the backwoods of Northern California. I'd only been back a day when a reporter from the Associated Press, Bob Thomas, and others from the national press started calling my home asking what I knew about the Hitchcocks' disappearance on a flight from Bangkok to Singapore. One of them suggested that the news was a publicity stunt to build interest in his latest pictures. I told him, "Trying to hide Alfred Hitchcock in a Thai jungle was like trying to hide an elephant on the skating rink at Rockefeller Center."

When I arrived at my office later that day, I met Dolores Stockton, the new secretary the stenographic department had suggested I might find acceptable. Acceptable? She was a tall, beautiful, blue-eyed blonde with the figure and carriage of a Sophia Loren. She was a welcome addition to the Hitchcock company, and we became her new protective family. She told me that word had spread around the studio about Mr. and Mrs. Hitchcock's disappearance and that everybody was waiting to hear from me.

I was still spreading the lie that they were safe when Benny Herrmann walked in. He was wearing his usual scowl and sported that shock of unruly, black curly hair with the one curl down his brow that he continually rolled around with one finger when he was deep in thought. It was only 10:30 in the morning and already, as "Bummy" Bumstead, once said, "his clothes look like he's just been shot out of a cannon." They were obviously expensive. Tailored tweed jacket with unmatched trousers. Dark, cashmere, sleeveless sweater; gray shirt unbuttoned at the neck; and carelessly tied dark tie.

I watched and listened as he paced around the office, reliving his days with the London Symphony. Right in the middle of his discourse, he suddenly stopped pacing, turned to me, and said, "We want you and Mary Belle to come to dinner tomorrow night. Lucy is calling Mary Belle." He had it all planned. "She can ride in with you tomorrow. They'll have the whole day together." There was to be no argument. He went back to his pacing.

To many, Bernard Herrmann was an arrogant, uncompromising, dictatorial conductor. But to the musicians who responded to the baton he sometimes used as a lash, he was a master who demanded, and received, perfection. He never lacked their complete respect.

Hitch called me from Tokyo to tell me that their plane was forced to bypass Singapore and head straight for Tokyo because of heavy storms. They'd landed for fuel at some tiny out-of-the-way town before reaching Tokyo. He also told me the sound tapes were a success in Tokyo. "Why didn't you send them to me in London?" he asked. I just let it pass.

The Man Who Knew Too Much was a huge success. Jack Karp asked me to drop by his office. "*The Man Who Knew Too Much* is the fourth picture on Hitch's contract, Herbie, and only one has been a Paramount Pictures production. We hope your next film will be a Paramount production."

I shared that dream with Jack. But it turned out to be a pipe dream. I was destined to leave my home for a sometimes unhappy period at Warner Bros. to produce a film, *The Wrong Man.*

Chapter 42

The Wrong Man

Hitch and Alma ended their "round-the-world" publicity tour for Paramount with a tiring nonstop flight from Tokyo to Los Angeles. That 28,000-mile journey left them tired but happy to be home. Hitch was anxious to get back to work. But, as it turned out, not on either of the Paramount projects we'd been considering. Hitch said, "The boys," meaning MCA, "have told me Warners is demanding I fulfill the contract I have with them to direct the one picture remaining under that contract."

Herman Citron brought in a *Life* magazine that had a story written by Maxwell Anderson called *The True Story of Christopher Emmanuel Balestrero.*

I thought it was too dull and colorless. I expected Hitch to have the same reaction to the story. When he came into my office for our evening cocktail, he listened silently while I listed my reasons why we should pass on the Balestrero story. "This is a simple story about a man who the audience is told at the very beginning is not guilty of the robberies he's accused of committing.

"He leaves his wife's insurance policy with the girl at the insurance office. No robber would be that stupid.

"He is an educated man who must have some knowledge of his civil rights yet doesn't protest when the detectives take him around to the various stores he's supposed to have robbed and make him restage the way the robbery was committed.

"He knows the effect his absence will have on his wife, but he fails to demand his right to make the one phone call all prisoners are allowed to make.

"Will the public accept, as the hero of the story, a man so spineless, he allows himself to be shuffled around like a puppet on a string?"

I reminded Hitch of the three basic elements he'd always made the main pillars upon which he'd constructed his screenplays: suspense, romance, and spectacular landscapes on which to present his stars. "You'll have to abandon your successful time-tested practice of building suspense by revealing to the audience, but not to the hero, who is staging those robberies."

Hitch agreed that everything I'd said was true but explained, "Jack Warner has already paid me to do the picture. I agreed when he suggested we have Maxwell Anderson write a treatment. Anderson's calling it *The Wrong Man*. We'll meet with him when we move into our offices at Warner Brothers."

"Not we, Hitch." I said. "I have no intention of breaking my tenure with Paramount. Not after thirty years. We'll let it drop for the time being."

A few days later, Jack Karp told me he was happy *The Wrong Man* wasn't being offered to Paramount and that, if I wanted to help Hitch with the picture at Warners, he would arrange to loan me to the studio for the one picture.

I agreed to do the film with the understanding that I was the producer, although my screen credit would still be associate producer. But I wanted it clearly understood by everyone that I answered only to Hitch on any decisions I made.

Hitch decided to keep his office at Paramount. I moved to Warners and began putting together our staff. Naturally, for our production manager I wanted Doc Erickson. But he was on an important Paramount picture, and they wouldn't let him go. Henry "Bummy" Bumstead wanted no part of Warners. But I was lucky when I called Danny McCauley. He joined me the next day. Bob Burks, our cameraman, and his staff were standing by waiting for a call to come in.

During early meetings with Maxwell Anderson, we discovered that he had researched the Balestreros' family lifestyle thoroughly. Their marriage and struggle to overcome the problems that come to every family. Even the fact that Rose bought their clothes in a Queen's basement store.

Hitch was quick to use what he'd learned about the basement store: "We won't need to ask Edith [Head] to design the wardrobe for Rose Balestrero. We'll buy her clothes in that same shop."

Weeks went by before Hitch revealed that he'd been thinking about Vera's clothes when he said, "You keep referring to Vera as our new Grace Kelly. The public won't accept her as our new Grace Kelly if they see her, for the first time, in those basement store clothes."

I surprised him when I said I'd talked to Edith about designing some clothes for Vera to wear when he took her to New York and introduced her to the press. She had some designs ready and was waiting to show them to Hitch.

"There's only one thing wrong with your plan. Alma and I have absolutely no wish to go to New York at this time. She's busy with her gardens and our granddaughters. I'm enjoying sleeping in my own bed for a change. You, Herbie, will take Vera to New York. I don't need the publicity. But Vera and the picture do. And a little publicity won't hurt you too much." With that settled, as far as he was concerned, he asked me to call Edith and have her come right over.

Two weeks later, after I'd approved a payment of $5,000 of Jack Warner's money to Edith for her work in making Vera's clothes, Vera and I spent ten days in New York meeting the press, radio, and television. Dining at the best restaurants and being seen around town.

During those days I found Vera to be a young lady, eager to succeed as an actress. A lady with high moral standards, which she would protect whatever the cost. We parted, firm friends, at the end of the New York journey.

Hitch was happy with the reports coming in about our trip but was getting a little unhappy sitting around waiting for Anderson's treatment on the screenplay.

Mary Belle invited Benny Herrmann and his wife Lucy to dinner at our big home on the bluff at Newport Beach. As usual, Benny kicked off his shoes the moment he walked into the living room. After dinner we sat on the balcony and watched the sun sink into the Pacific over the west end of Catalina Island. I told Benny the *Wrong Man* story and asked if he'd compose the music for the film. "For Warners?" Benny exploded. "They'll never let me on the lot!"

"They'll not only let you on the lot," I told him, "they'll give you a raise from your $15,000 to $17,500."

Benny couldn't keep from laughing. "I'd like to see Jack Warner's face when you tell him you've signed such a contract."

Henry Fonda made everybody happy by accepting the starring role of Christopher Emmanuel Balestrero. Vera Miles would be his wife, Rose. Anthony Quayle was miscast as Frank O'Connor. Most of the remaining cast members were from New York.

I moved to New York, used my suite at the St. Regis Hotel as an office, and went to work.

Among the many problems that had to be solved before we could go into production was Bob Burks's New York cameramen's union problem. Bob had told me that Richard "Dick" Walsh, the head of International Alliance of Theatrical Stage Employees (or IATSE), the organization that represented most film workers, including the cameramen, had assured him he could be our cameraman, even if we filmed 100 percent of the picture in New York. I trusted Bob but wanted to hear Dick Walsh say the same thing.

I met with Dick and also with the head of the cameramen's union, I don't remember his name. Dick agreed that he'd told Bob he could be our cameraman in New York. The head of the cameramen didn't agree and told me he'd already assigned their top man to the job. When I pointed out to him that, if he refused to cooperate, I'd have to move 50 percent of the picture back to Hollywood and every union member in New York would lose months of work, he still refused to cooperate.

Sherman Billingsley, the amiable, sophisticated gentleman who owned the Stork Club, was happy to allow us to use his name and club in the picture. He knew the publicity his club would get, not only in the States but all around the world.

Before the word got around that I was in New York preparing to film the Balestrero story, I managed to meet, secretly, the two detectives who first arrested Balestrero and drove him around to many of the stores in Queens they thought he'd robbed.

But I ran into a stone wall when Johnny Graham, our New York production manager, and I asked the New York City police for their cooperation. They wanted no part of the Balestrero story. They were trying to keep secret the fact that their forces had severely violated Balestrero's civil rights. I had a meeting with one of their highest officials. His name was Arm. He was completely uncooperative. He told me that the police department was no longer allowing film companies to photograph their facilities or use their equipment. His attitude changed when I told him about a New York film company that was using some of their rolling stock that very day. He still refused to allow us to interview any of their officers.

Angus MacPhail flew in from California. I got him settled in a hotel near the St. Regis. Alma and Hitch arrived by train a few days later.

I got them all together, including Maxwell Anderson, in Hitch's suite at the St. Regis, and we got to work on the screenplay.

It was some two weeks before Hitch, with Angus's help, decided on the changes he wanted Anderson to make in the first draft of the screenplay. Maxwell went home to make the changes.

One afternoon, the telephone in Hitch's living room rang. I picked up the phone and listened as someone on the other end identified himself as Warner Brothers' Hollywood comptroller. He started to ask a question about my unlimited expense account. I blew up and yelled, "How dare you ask me such questions?" and then slammed the phone down.

Hitch asked about the call. I told him to forget it. He demanded to know what I'd heard on the phone. When I told him, he marched past me, picked up the phone, and asked the operator to get him Lew Wasserman at MCA in Beverly Hills.

When Lew answered, Hitch told him to go out to Warners and tell Jack Warner, if I received one more call from the studio, I'd walk off the picture. And so would he. Within a half hour, Steve Trilling called and apologized for the call the comptroller made and promised I'd never get another call from anyone at the studio.

Hitch then called the desk and asked that the manager please come to his suite. When he arrived, Hitch asked about other available suites. The manager said there was one just like Hitch's and the Presidential Suite on the top floor. Hitch said we'd take a look at the Presidential Suite. It was an enormous suite with an entry, a living room with floor-to-ceiling tinted glass windows open on three sides of the hotel, a dining room and kitchen, two bedrooms with adjoining studies, and three bathrooms. "I think Mr. Coleman will be happy here," he said to the manager.

I told Hitch I was happy with my suite.

"Well, I'm not happy with your suite," Hitch said. He asked the manager to have my things moved to the Presidential Suite immediately.

My present suite was costing Warners $300.00 per day. That phone call from the comptroller cost Warners an additional $700.00 per day. The Presidential Suite was $1,000 per day. And I was in that suite for at least two months.

Word had spread around New York that Hitch was determined to talk to every detective and police officer who had any role in Balestrero's arrest and imprisonment. One day, I received a call from a woman who refused to give me her name but told me she was a Warner Brothers' attorney. She said she had an avenue to the top man and wanted to know exactly what we wanted.

I gave her a brief verbal outline of the story we were working on. She said she'd call me back the next afternoon. She was as good as her word, up to a point. She said, "The wheels are turning," and then broke off after telling me she would call again the next afternoon.

This time she had a surprise for me. She said, "It's all arranged. Place $5,000 in small, old bills, in an envelope addressed to Warner Bros. Leave it with the St. Regis Hotel bell captain. I'll have it picked up. Mr. Hitchcock will be notified when the meeting will take place."

I told her to forget it and called Steve Trilling. I told him about the calls and that Hitch and I wanted nothing to do with her. Steve promised to start a quiet investigation. The whole affair ended there as far as we were concerned.

Our problems with the New York police were eased somewhat when I hired a retired detective, George Groves, as a technical adviser on police matters. He was highly respected by his former superiors at the Central Headquarters in Lower Manhattan.

Frank O'Connor, who by this time had realized his ambition to become district attorney of Queens, offered to serve as overall technical adviser. I was reluctant to accept his offer. I had to ask myself, "Would he be completely objective when advising Hitch about his involvement in Emanuel's affairs?" Hitch had confidence in O'Connor, so I had to agree to hire him.

Hitch's confidence in O'Connor was somewhat shaken when we met with Judge Groat, who told us about O'Connor's failure to protect Emmanuel, or Manny, when one member of the jury complained about listening to more testimony against Manny.

Meanwhile, Hitch was busy with the casting. I was happy with every choice he made, with one exception. I thought Anthony Quayle was entirely wrong for O'Connor. Quayle was a distinguished actor, handsome, highly educated, and articulate. He would have been perfect if O'Connor had been a partner in one of Wall Street's most prestigious law firms. I think Hitch was influenced by O'Connor's appearance when he met him after he became the district attorney.

I was sure O'Connor had changed considerably from the man who sat in that little office in the Victor Moore Arcade.

With the casting problems ended, I asked Steve Trilling to send Bob Burks and his staff, including Frank Ferguson, Bob's gaffer, and the rest of the Hollywood staff and crew to New York. Warner Bros. trucks, with lighting, grip, and props, arrived in New York seven days later. I called Vera Miles and asked her to join us. I told her I'd meet her at Kennedy Airport. Henry Fonda was already in New York ready to go to work.

Hitch and Alma went with Vera to the basement clothing store in Queens to select Vera's clothes.

Hitch, Alma, and I were having dinner in the Stork Club's Cub Room one evening when Sherman Billingsley joined us. "Mr. Coleman," he said, "my club is yours from midnight Saturday until 11:30 Monday morning. Just allow time for our guests to leave the club at midnight before you start moving in. And be sure your equipment and people are out before noon Monday."

I took him at his word and decided to film the scenes inside the Stork Club first on the schedule. On Friday, we were all ready to go. The atmosphere people had been selected and given the time to report to the club on Saturday. Staff and crews were on salary. Equipment was rented and loaded on the trucks.

Late Friday afternoon I got a call from an angry Sherman Billingsley. He said, "I've just been told you plan to bring what you call 'extra people' into my club tomorrow. I didn't agree to allow you to replace my regular guests."

I pointed out that we needed people who would be paid to follow our orders for the thirty-six hours we'd be shooting, but he refused to compromise. I finally ended the conversation, "Mr. Billingsley, you're not a man of your word." Before he could reply, I hung up the phone. I knew he could refuse to allow us to use his club in the future, but I could build the set in the studio with what it would cost us to shoot the scenes in New York.

I called Danny McCauley and gave him the news. "We'll go to Cornwall tomorrow and shoot the scenes where Fonda and Miles go to the Idleweiss Farm to find their alibi witnesses. If the couple you cast as the owners are not available, bring some people over to the St. Regis and let Hitch recast."

So, instead of the warmth of the Stork Club on that Saturday, we found ourselves in a snowstorm in Cornwall. The snow let up enough to allow us to cover everything we needed in the one day.

Billingsley called me on Monday and said that he'd misunderstood our requirements for the use of his club and we could do it our way.

Despite our problems with the New York City police department, we completed our work and moved back to the Warner Bros. lot in Burbank.

I don't remember having any serious problems with anyone at the studio. Steve Trilling was especially helpful.

Benny Herrmann wanted to stay away from the studio as long as possible, so I had George Tomasini run each cut reel for Benny at Paramount.

Trilling asked when I wanted Ray Heindorf to run the picture. I asked why I would want Heindorf to see the picture: "Don't you remember the copy of the Herrmann contract I sent you?"

He agreed he'd seen the contract, but Jack Warner still wanted Heindorf. I still refused to accept Heindorf; Benny was the composer. He also received the $2,500 raise I'd promised him.

Trilling also told me that Warner wanted to make a present to Vera of the $5,000 personal wardrobe I had Edith Head design for her to wear on the publicity tour in New York. It must have been embarrassing for Steve to tell Warner that we'd already given the beautiful clothes to Vera. The happiest day for me on *The Wrong Man* was when, for the last time, I heard Hitch say, "You have it."

We moved back to our offices at Paramount and drove to Warners to complete postproduction work on the picture.

I was notified about the preview of the picture. Mary Belle went with me. It was held at a theater in Huntington Park. We had to sit through the running of the scheduled picture, called *The Mole Men,* something weird about men who slithered along just under the surface of the ground. The audience was an unruly collection of young people who loudly talked back to the actors, whistled, and, from what I heard later, were probably making love in the back rows.

The Wrong Man received the same treatment.

I was disgusted and mad as hell as Mary Belle and I crossed the lobby and headed for the street. A young man stopped me and told me that Warner would like me to join him in the manager's office.

I could feel the hostility that filled the room when I walked in. Warner was seated behind the manager's desk, surrounded by a half dozen or so of his hired yes-men. I was sure Warner was remembering the Heindorf–Herrmann deal and how we had upstaged him on the wardrobe present to Vera.

His first words to me were, "Well, Mr. Coleman. What do you think?"

"I think, Mr. Warner, it was idiotic to preview a Hitchcock picture in this theater on a Friday night with that crowd and that picture, *The Mole Men.*"

I sat there as Warner and his henchmen did their best to embarrass and humiliate me. His men were careful to agree with everything Warner said.

Finally, he turned to me and asked, "Well, Mr. Coleman, what do you want us to do with your picture?"

"I want you to leave this picture alone. I don't want a thing changed until you have another preview with a picture that will attract a Hitchcock audience." I got up and walked out.

I got what I wanted. The second preview was held in a theater in Encino. The other picture was *High Society.*

I think *The Wrong Man* was the wrong picture made at the wrong time by the wrong people. But it gave me the opportunity to work with a dedicated actor and gentleman, Hank Fonda.

Chapter 43

Flamingo Feather

I can't remember just how Laurens Van der Post's story, *Flamingo Feather,* happened to end up on our schedule, but Hitch and I agreed that if we could get the South African government to allow us to film the story, it could be a blockbuster.

Jack Karp and the entire Paramount organization were happy we were back on the lot with a project containing all the Hitchcock elements that almost guaranteed a winner at the box office.

Very briefly, it was a story about a foreign government's attempt to secretly gather a vast crowd of the underprivileged, mistreated, black South Africans and train them to overthrow the all-white government. The foreign government would, of course, become their new master. The "flamingo feather" was to be the signal for the uprising to begin.

I asked Doc Erickson to arrange two connecting drawing rooms for Hitch and Alma and compartments for himself and me on the Super Chief to New York; and a first-class stateroom for the Hitchcocks and separate first-class staterooms for the two of us on the *Queen Elizabeth.*

A week at Claridges in London. Rome by air, a week at the Excelsior Hotel in Rome. Then on to Johannesburg by air.

I knew Mary Belle would be unhappy when I'd tell her about another long absence from home. But she had to be told. Sunday morning when we returned home from church, I laid it all out. I was speaking slowly, trying to find the right words to make her understand that I didn't really look forward to leaving her and the kids. Before I finished telling her the whole story, the smile that was in her eyes when I started speaking had gradually disappeared.

She rose from her chair and went into the bathroom, closing the door as she entered. I heard the water running in the basin. It seemed like hours before she came back. I could see she had been crying. She sat down, reached across the table, and took my hand. "Honey," she said, "the same day your boat leaves New York, Dale will graduate from Orange Coast College, Judy will graduate from Newport Harbor High, and Melinda will graduate from Balboa Elementary. They are looking forward to that day having their father with them when they're handed their diplomas. They can show their friends the father who has been missing so often when they needed him." She pulled her hand away and in almost a whisper said, "If you're not there, I'm leaving you!"

For a moment, I sat there stunned. Then I got to my feet, took her in my arms, and promised, "We'll both be with the kids."

Hitch didn't take the news too graciously. He grumbled we'd be losing valuable time. "We could be discussing the story, choosing a writer and the cast."

Even if what he said was true, and I knew it wasn't, all we'd be doing on the train and boat was enjoying the scenery, the food, the wine, and stimulating conversation. I wasn't about to endanger the most important things in my life, my marriage and my family.

I told Doc he could go along with Hitch, but he said, "I think I'll wait and go with you." I asked him to see that Hitch and Alma got off all right on the train. He told me later that Hitch was still grumbling that we were letting him down.

I had a wonderful time with Mary Belle and the kids. She was right, the kids did have fun showing off their father to their friends at the graduations and the parties.

Years later, I realized Hitch had never forgotten my refusal to go with him. Hitch, Sir Michael Balcon, and I were dining together. Hitch surprised me when he said, "Michael, Herbie Coleman knows more about producing a movie than anyone I've ever known."

Sir Michael turned to me, grinned, and said, "That was quite an endorsement, Mr. Coleman. You must remind Hitch about what he just said when your contract comes up for renewal."

Then Hitch spoiled it all when he said, "But he has one fault. He thinks more of his family than he does his job."

Doc and I flew to London just in time to grab a car and drive to South Hampton to meet Alma and Hitch as they came ashore from the *Queen Elizabeth.* During the ride back to London, Hitch let us know the pleasures we'd missed by flying over instead of taking the *Queen Elizabeth.*

Despite the fact that Hitch had spent a week with the press in London while on his world tour, he was not unhappy that they were waiting when we arrived at the Claridges Hotel. I told Hitch about a meeting I'd arranged with Laurens Van der Post later that afternoon.

He felt I should sound out Van der Post first and arrange a formal meeting for us on our way back home.

Doc was with me when we arrived at the Van der Post home in the country. Mrs. Van der Post was a quiet, charming lady. Her husband, who was waiting for us on their wide, shaded veranda, was a slight, slender gentleman. He made no attempt to conceal the fact that he was very happy we'd chosen his *Flamingo Feather* for a major motion picture.

The long English twilight had faded into darkness when we thanked the Van der Posts for their hospitality and the valuable information he had given us.

"Africa," he'd said, "possibly the best scenery in the nation. Baentoland. M'beya, the beautiful capital city of Swaziland. And Ruanda, for the mountains of the moon. And there were others." He'd already written or cabled friends all over Africa asking them to help us with any problems that might arise.

Riding back to the hotel, troubling thoughts began disturbing the enthusiasm I'd felt about the project. I pulled Van der Post's list from my pocket and studied it. I realized instantly that logistics would be a tremendous problem for Doc.

Johannesburg, and the surrounding area, was a must.

Thousands of atmosphere people, many of them seven-foot Watusi warriors in their white flowing robes and ever present eight-foot spears. Next, how would he ever manage to transport all those thousands to the beautiful mountains Van der Post suggested we would need?

By the time the driver stopped the car at the door of Claridges, I was ready to cancel the trip and go back to the studio. Maybe we'd jumped into *Flamingo Feather* too soon. Hitch had insisted we visit all of the country, mix with, and understand, the people, before selecting the screenwriter and going to work on the script. He got no argument from me. I knew Hitch had to see for himself what we were getting into.

Official London offered no objection to our plans to film *Flamingo Feather* in South Africa. The authorities even arranged for lunch with the governor general in Cape Town.

Hitch wanted us to go to Rome via Madrid to discuss the starring role with Cary Grant. I wasn't high on Grant for the part. I told Hitch we'd meet him in Rome and warned him not to let Grant consider their meeting as a commitment for his services in the picture. He went on to Madrid after agreeing that a suave, sophisticated English gentleman might not be just right. The character might turn out to be more of a rugged, tough, middle-class ex-military man.

Doc and I flew to Cannes to renew friendships with the French film workers who'd helped us make *To Catch a Thief.* The film workers were all away on an American film somewhere in the French Alps, but the same "beautiful" people were crowding the beach across the street from the Carlton during the day and grabbing every seat on the Carlton Terrace bar during the cocktail hour.

We enjoyed dinner at La Reserve the first night. Our plan to have dinner in Monte Carlo the second night was spoiled by a phone call from Paramount's Rome office. Luigi Zaccardi, a friend from *Roman Holiday* days, said that Hitch had called from Madrid asking him to find me and ask me to meet him at the airport in Rome the next afternoon. Luigi told me that Hitch's plane would arrive at three o'clock.

Doc and I caught a flight from Nice to Rome the next morning.

At the Paramount office, I asked the chief of publicity if he'd arranged for the press and photographers to meet Hitch. He laughed and said, "When Hitch was here on his world tour, they got everything from him they would need for the next dozen years. They would laugh at me if I even dared ask them to be there."

I told him publicity was the only reason we were stopping in Rome on our way to Johannesburg.

"I'm sorry, Herbie. There's really nothing I can do."

We had a big surprise waiting at the airport. The place was crawling with photographers and newspaper reporters. I thought the publicity man had been pulling my leg and asked him how he'd gotten all those people together on such short notice. He didn't answer me. He joined the group for a moment and then came back to tell me they were not there for Hitch. They were waiting for the arrival of the French boxer, "Dummy" Cohen, who was arriving for a bout with the Italian champion. "We've got a problem, Herbie. Cohen's plane arrives after Hitch's. But I've made a deal with some of them to fake it when Mr. and Mrs. Hitchcock come down the steps from the plane. They'll flash some bulbs, but they won't be taking any pictures. Hitch will never know the difference."

Hitch did ask a few times why the newspapers were not printing any of the pictures they made at the airport. He always said his arrival at the Rome airport was the greatest publicity reception any Paramount publicity department had ever arranged. Rome was little more than a stopover to spend a few days enjoying the wonderful pasta available in hundreds of the finest restaurants in the world. I had to leave the fun and food to Hitch, Alma, and Doc. I'd caught a lousy cold and spent the three days in bed before we caught our flight to Johannesburg.

Johannesburg turned out to be just another modern city. Nothing to really write home about. I called on all the people Van der Post had suggested I meet.

The owner of the biggest theater chain in the country assigned George Noble, one of his top associates, to travel with us. We flew from Johannesburg to Cape Town to have lunch with the governor general, a round trip of more than 2,000 miles all in one day.

We were discouraged with everything we found around Johannesburg, so we flew to Durban, a seaport city on the Indian Ocean. Durban was much more colorful than Johannesburg.

Doc rented two cars with drivers, and we drove to M'baban, the capital city of Swaziland. Mr. Fowler, one of Van der Post's friends, had made reservations for us at a lovely little hotel, the Swazi Inn, and was waiting to show us the country of which he was justly proud. The rolling hills were dotted with groves of beautiful trees, many of them with flowers in full bloom.

Hitch agreed we'd have to find a place in the story for Swaziland.

Word of our presence in South Africa had already reached Pretoria. The officials there promised their full cooperation if we came back.

Even before we arrived back in Johannesburg, we knew *Flamingo Feather* was a lost cause. The Watusi we wanted were not there. The treeless Drankensbergs were more hills than mountains. And they were the least of our problems.

We decided to make the rest of the trip a vacation and flew to Livingstone, Southern Rhodesia, to see the Victoria Falls.

One of the tours the visitor to Livingstone is offered is a boat trip on the great Zanzibar River. We took the bait and climbed aboard a small powerboat. I didn't like it when the driver headed downriver. I could see the current increase as we neared the top of Victoria Falls and thoughts of that boat's engine failing crowded everything else from my mind. I was about to demand that he turn and head upstream when the driver, grinning at us, turned around. I guess it was his way of giving us a treat. After lunch, we stood and watched the mile-wide river rush over the edge and fall almost 400 feet into a narrow gorge. The spray came back and enveloped us. The roar of the falls was deafening. I was surprised when Hitch suggested that we climb down the narrow, steep path to the bottom of the falls.

The following morning, about two-thirty, we left Livingstone to drive to the Wankie Game Preserve. We were told we'd have to arrive at Wankie around four to see the wild animals on the prowl.

We were crowded into a tiny station wagon. The Rhodesian driving the car had small, round wooden casks in the lobes of his ears. I had to plead, then demand, that he slow his pace. Around three, driving through a forest along a narrow road, our headlights revealed a black man in a torn, discarded army overcoat standing alone. I asked the driver about him. He said, "He's waiting for a ride to his job in Livingstone." Less than 100 yards farther along the road, we were forced to pause while a pride of about thirty lions ambled across the road. I asked the driver about the danger to the man we'd just passed. "Oh, they're not man eaters." He tossed it away.

We arrived at Wankie just before dawn and were lucky to see more lions, cheetahs, and other wild animals. We didn't actually see a hunt, but we did see a lioness dragging the carcass of a small animal in the distance. We parked on the top of a small rise with an unobstructed view for miles around. There wasn't a tree, bush, or rock within a half mile of us. All the wild animals had disappeared.

The driver wanted to return to Livingstone. "You'll see no more animals today," he said.

We decided to have lunch and then leave. Despite the warning the Wankie officers had given us not to get out of our car, even for a moment, Doc and I got out, stood back to back beside the open doors of the car, and started to eat our sandwiches. Doc watching off in one direction, and I, the other.

Suddenly, with absolutely no warning, two beautiful white cheetahs went streaking past not 100 feet from where we stood. Well, two frightened men scrambled back into that car and slammed the doors.

The next day we flew to Nairobi, Kenya. We didn't have to get out in the middle of the night to drive to the game preserve in Nairobi. It was almost part of the town. We found out that lions had occasionally wandered right into town.

We took a quick tour of the surrounding territory just in case we'd find a story that would need such a location and then flew back to London.

Hitch invited his sister, Nellie Ingram, to come to the States with us aboard the *Queen Elizabeth.* We drove to South Hampton and boarded the ship early on the morning of July 25. The fog that slowed our drive to South Hampton got thicker and thicker as the ship slowly moved down the river to the English Channel and headed for Le Havre to pick up passengers waiting at that French seaport city. We were cruising at about twenty knots with the visibility less than half a mile when whispers of a collision, between the Italian liner *Andrea Doria* and another ship off the American shore, began spreading around the *Queen Elizabeth.*

As passengers began complaining loudly about the speed of our ship in the heavy fog, the captain announced that the rumor was false and continued to speed toward the French coast. Later that day we learned the truth. The *Andrea Doria* had gone down, and many passengers were lost. Even that shocking news did little to lower the spirits of the fun-loving passengers. The dining, drinking, dancing, and possibly even sex continued as the ship sped across the Atlantic.

Doc and I parted company with Hitch, Alma, and Nellie and flew home while they enjoyed another week of slower travel on the Super Chief.

That ended our, and Paramount's, interest in *Flamingo Feather.*

Chapter 44

Vertigo

With *Flamingo Feather* fast fading from our memories, we turned our attention to our next production: an adaptation of the novel *D'entre les Morts,* by two French authors, Thomas Narcejac and Pierre Boileau.

Vertigo, the title we finally gave the picture, almost ended my association with Hitch.

The first faint danger signal appeared when Hitch suggested that we have Maxwell Anderson write the screenplay. I knew little about Anderson before he was engaged to write *The Wrong Man.* I never felt comfortable with his approach to *The Wrong Man* during the days we were working on the screenplay with Hitch and Angus MacPhail in Hitch's suite at the St. Regis Hotel in New York.

I was afraid we might lose the stark reality faced by that Stork Club bass fiddle player while he was in the clutches of a force determined to put him away.

Hitch finally tired of my opposition to Anderson and insisted that I call Irving Lazar, Anderson's agent, and make a deal. "I'm not willing to risk that much of Paramount's money on Anderson," I told him.

That didn't stop Hitch. He had someone in the story department, Herman Citron or some other MCA agent, make the deal with Lazar.

Anderson and Hitch held story conferences. I attended but only as an observer. Anderson returned to his home in Connecticut to write the screenplay.

Hitch and Alma returned to the ranch.

I took Mary Belle with me on a location survey in and around San Francisco. Hitch was anxious to use Muir Woods, some distance north of San Francisco, for one of the most important sequences in the picture. I'd never visited Muir Woods and drove directly to check it out.

My first look at the dense grove of trees convinced me I'd have to find an alternate. We followed the ranger who was waiting to take us inside. He led us along a path just wide enough for us to walk single file. He warned us not to step off the path, for the roots of the 1,000-year-old giant redwoods were barely covered by a thin coating of soil.

Not a glimmer of sunlight was able to penetrate down through the closely growing forest. I described to the ranger the scenes we would want to stage in the forest: how we would want to bring in heavy lights, cameras, and other equipment; how electricians and other workmen would have to move off the path.

He told me to forget Muir Woods. I knew Hitch wouldn't easily give up on Muir Woods, but there were many groves of great sequoias we could use.

Muir Woods was a disappointment; but our second location, a museum where Jimmy would see Madelaine with the portrait of Carlotta, was to become a welcome surprise.

Crossing the Golden Gate Bridge on our way back to the city, we turned to take a look at the Palace of the Legion of Honor Museum. It stood on a hilltop overlooking the Pacific Ocean and the entrance to San Francisco Bay. The director of the museum took us on a tour of the building and allowed me to photograph the art gallery. I didn't bother to visit the other museums on my list.

In a booklet praising San Francisco's finest restaurants, someone had underlined Ernies. Mary Belle and I stopped there for a cocktail early in the evening. We didn't tell anyone who we were or what we were doing there.

The turn-of-the-century bar we saw when we entered Ernies was the best example of an early California tavern I'd ever seen, and I'd seen most of them. But it wouldn't work for us. However, the bar and dining area in the Ambrosia Room upstairs were perfect.

I went to the San Francisco Police Department seeking a retired police officer I could hire as a contact man, guide, and technical adviser.

"There's only one man I would recommend to you," the police captain said. "Morrie Reardon, a retired detective lieutenant. He's respected by everybody in the city."

He was right. I hired him, and he became our friend and adviser.

Morrie was proud that he'd never carried a gun during his entire career as a police officer. He always rode in the front seat of the car, and each time we approached a church, he would slip his hat from his head and replace it after we'd passed it. Everybody respected his devotion to his faith, and we never let him know we were watching him.

I gave him a list of the places we would need for the picture: a small mission with a graveyard; an imposing turn-of-the-century, two-story, wooden home that a powerful, wealthy man might build for his mistress; a home that a retired detective might own; and a few minor sets we would need.

A home at the corner of Gaff and Eddy was by far the best for the Valdez home. Morrie liked a number of sites on Telegraph Hill for Jimmy's home; but I decided on a small house on a steep hill across the street from a grammar school where the playground was filled with Chinese children.

With San Francisco well covered, we said good-bye to Morrie and drove to Carmel to check out Hitch's choice for the old Spanish mission. The Carmel Mission was beautiful. It was one of the most imposing missions I'd visited anywhere along the California coast. But it was too closed in by busy streets with noisy traffic.

Our daughter, Judy, a student at San Jose State, had suggested that we take a look at the Old Mission San Juan Bautista. So we left Carmel and drove there.

I could almost hear Hitch dictating the mission sequences as I stood looking across a vast square of bright green grass to an open space with a view of the early Mexican cemetery in the distance. On the left side of the plaza there was a long, low, single-story stucco building with doors opening into rooms every ten feet. A wide walkway, paved with flat stones worn thin by generations of faithful worshipers, under a tiled roof, gave relief from the hot noon sun. The roof was supported by an arcade, the entire length of the building.

At the far end of the arcade, the high San Juan Bautista Mission dominated the area. Only the very high mission tower was missing. No great problem for us. For the master shot, we could do a glass shot and paint in the tower.

On the right side of the square, there was a connecting line of two-story wooden buildings. On the ground floor, rooms still displayed original period furniture; upstairs there were rooms where local government officials ruled over the people.

The right corner of the square from where I stood taking photographs was occupied by a two-story open stable with buggies and wagons. Near the opening, a full-sized replica of a beautiful gray stallion stood ready to go.

Now the big question arose. Could we get permission to stage our action in and around the mission church and the other buildings?

A few minutes later, I was sitting in the presence of Father Michael Sullivan, the monsignor of the Diocese of Monterey, a quiet, reflective man who listened without comment to the story of *Vertigo*. I didn't gloss over how a movie company's massive invasion of the mission could disrupt the peace and quiet one felt upon entering the park.

Father Sullivan thanked me for my honesty and suggested that we take a walk around the mission grounds. As we strolled along in the shade of the arcade, he told me the history of San Juan Bautista and of his own determination to establish a boys' school on the mission grounds.

I offered to donate a substantial sum toward his goal if he would agree to allow us to film the mission scenes at San Juan Bautista. He didn't answer immediately.

Before we left San Juan Bautista, Father Sullivan sat me down in his study and gave me his decision. "I appreciate your honesty about the problems your filming here might present to our community, Mr. Coleman. I trust you and look forward to your returning with Mr. Hitchcock."

In due time, Maxwell Anderson's screenplay arrived. I knew the moment I read the title he'd given to our story that he'd been floating in the clouds while he was writing it: *Listen Darkling*. What in the world did it mean? Today, I can't remember a single line of his dialogue or anything else about the script.

With the help of a lot of hot coffee, I managed to struggle through the script, start to finish. Still somewhat bewildered, I tried again. It was no use. The second reading didn't help, so I placed a call to Hitch at his ranch above Santa Cruz. I told him that Anderson's script had arrived and that I would send it to him that evening.

"Ollie will meet the plane and deliver it to you by cocktail time."

"Is it all that important? You've read it?"

I told him I had.

"Well?"

There was a lot he left unsaid in that one-word sentence. I waited for him to complete the sentence.

"What do you think?"

"If I answer that, you'll say I didn't want Anderson to have anything to do with our story and I'm not being fair with him."

Hitch wasn't to be denied my reaction to what I'd read and wanted me to tell the whole story.

"I'll do this much," I told Hitch. "I'll read you one scene from his script; then you can judge for yourself." I didn't search through the pages for a particularly badly written scene. I just opened the manuscript and started to read. After only three or four pages, he stopped me with a painful cry, "What did he do that for?"

"I don't have the slightest idea," I told him. "What do you want me to do with the script?"

"Burn it!" he replied.

"What about a new writer?"

"I'd rather hear about your survey."

I told him I'd join him at the ranch with the pictures two days later. He asked me to bring Mary Belle along. "She and Alma can have a few days together while you show me the places you like best."

We arrived at the ranch in the early afternoon. It was a wonderful day. A cool breeze ruffling the leaves on the trees was a welcome relief from the heat we'd felt driving down the valley from the airport.

We sipped champagne and nibbled at the cold quiche lorraine Alma had prepared for a mid-afternoon snack. Alma took Mary Belle away to show her their new walled garden with the newly installed Braque ceramic tile, with his famous *Birds in Flight* design.

As I was laying out the photographs I'd selected to show Hitch, he surprised me by saying, "The 'boys' have found you a new writer, Herbie." I waited for him to explain. "Alec Coppel. He wrote a splendid screenplay for Alec Guinness, *The Captain's Paradise.* He'll be waiting for us when we get back to the studio."

I let it go at that. The next morning, Al Latta, who would be our driver captain on *Vertigo,* arrived at nine, and we were off to Muir Woods.

A new ranger was waiting to escort us. He was a fan of Hitchcock films and was anxious to please us. As we walked along the narrow path, Hitch told the ranger how perfect Muir Woods would be for his picture.

"I want Madelaine to feel the world is closing in on her. The density of the trees is a wall around her. There's no escape. Only suicide is left." He stopped in an area where the ancient trees almost overlapped and started walking away from the path. Alarmed, the ranger called out rather sharply, "Mr. Hitchcock, come back! No one is allowed to step from the path!"

"But I must have freedom to move about to stage my scenes. Our workmen will be moving equipment all around."

The ranger told Hitch that no movie company had ever been given permission to film in Muir Woods, and he was sure they would not make an exception for us.

Driving back to San Francisco, Hitch asked if I was willing to give up on Muir Woods.

"No," I said. "But there are two groves of giant redwoods I've worked in. One, the Calaveras Big Trees northeast of Sonora, and one on the top of the ridge above Santa Cruz. For Calaveras Big Trees, we'll run Gary Cooper's picture *Fighting Caravans.* And George Marshall's *Forest Rangers* for the grove above Santa Cruz. You can decide if either is suitable for what you have in mind."

Our next stop was the Palace of the Legion of Honor Museum. A quick look was all Hitch needed. "Fine," he said.

He didn't even get out of the car at Jimmy's house. He liked the idea of tying the home to the Chinese school.

Victor and Roland Gotti were waiting when we arrived at Ernies.

Although the restaurant was open only for dinner, they'd called in some of their staff. Hitch declined their offer to prepare lunch for us, using his usual excuse that he was on a strict diet. The real reason was that he was thinking of his big thick cut of prime strip beef that Alma would have waiting when we got back to the ranch.

I watched Hitch's face when they led us into the Ambrosia Room and bar upstairs. I saw a faint smile replace his usual somber expression and knew Ernies was in, if they would allow us to use the restaurant. We left Ernies, assured by Victor and Roland that everyone in their organization would cooperate fully with us. They sure did. For the Ambrosia Room and the bar, Henry Bumstead built one at the studio. Victor ordered, from their fabric manufacturers, the ruby red silk wall covering. They removed all the pictures and other decorations from the walls and gave Bummy silver, china, crystal, napkins, menus, tablecloths, and other items they used in the Ambrosia Room and bar.

And more than that, they came to the studio and appeared in the picture. Victor was the host. Roland became the bartender, and other staff members were waiters and captains.

Neither Hitch nor I was anxious to leave the Gotti brothers, but I wanted to arrive at the Mission San Juan Bautista a little before sunset, so Hitch could see the area in its best light, with the sun casting long shadows of the arcade across the grassy plaza.

I'd asked Father Sullivan to be available to show Hitch around the mission and tell him the history of San Juan Bautista, but he'd been called to Monterey. One of his parishioners had been seriously injured in an accident.

Even the thought of his dinner waiting at the ranch couldn't pull Hitch away from San Juan Bautista. I could almost hear his thoughts as he stood on the sidewalk, slowly letting his eyes move along the arcade to the church, then across the plaza to the two-story buildings, finally fixing on the stable.

"Let's have a look inside the church," he said.

A little light from the fading sun came through the narrow windows high up on the side walls. A single-wide aisle, paved with the original square stones, led to the altar. It was cool and quiet inside the mission. "Do you think Bob can light this place?" Hitch asked.

"I'm glad he's the cameraman. I'd hate to have his problem, but he'll get the job done. He's never let you down yet, has he?" I asked Hitch.

An hour later we drove away from San Juan Bautista. We were having cocktails on the patio, with the moon rising above the tops of the redwoods, encircling the house and gardens.

The next day we flew back to Los Angeles. Hitch went right to work with Coppel.

I sent Doc Erickson and Bummy to San Francisco to make arrangements for filming at Ernies, the old mansion on Eddy, Jimmy's house, and the Palace of the Legion of Honor Museum.

"I have an agreement with Father Sullivan on filming his mission, so you won't have to talk money with him," I told Doc. They didn't rush through that assignment. I thought they'd never get back. Doc said it was tough tearing themselves away from their new friends, Victor and Roland Gotti.

It wasn't long before I realized Hitch was becoming dissatisfied with Coppel. He was reluctant to dismiss the second writer on *Vertigo* and, with faintly disguised misgivings, sent Coppel off to complete the screenplay.

We had agreed *Vertigo* would be the picture to make Vera Miles a major star. One of the scenes, designed to convince Jimmy that Madelaine was unbalanced, had him seeing her seated before a portrait of a woman in a nineteenth-century costume and the identical hair dress Vera would be wearing.

I decided to have the portrait painted in Rome. A color photograph of Vera in costume and with the strange hair dress was sent to the Paramount office with a request that a full-length portrait be painted with only two changes: the color of the hair and the face of Vera to be replaced with the face of an aristocratic Spanish lady.

The painting we received from Rome was a disaster. Something a beginner in a junior high school might produce. Hitch wanted me to try again with an English artist. The result was a little better but still unsatisfactory.

Gordon Cole, head of the property department, showed me some portraits by a local artist. I thought we had the right man until he asked to meet Vera. That little gray-haired old man fell in love with Vera and delivered a picture of an angel.

I was beginning to wonder if we'd ever have the painting by the time we started shooting in San Francisco; then I remembered John Ferren, the artist who did the paintings we used in *The Trouble with Harry.* Fortunately, John was in town and agreed to paint the portrait. You've seen the results in the picture.

Hitch tired of waiting for Coppel's script and went back to the ranch with Alma.

That afternoon, I answered my phone and heard the voice of a man who was obviously a little angry. After telling me his name was Irving Lazar, agent for Maxwell Anderson, he informed me that I had violated the terms of our contract.

I don't remember exactly what I told him, but I let him know that I had not signed a contract with him or Anderson. The conversation was beginning to steam when he told me I'd failed to authorize a payment of $15,000, three weeks from the date of the delivery of the first draft. When I told him I wasn't going to approve that or any other payment to Anderson, he broke the connection.

A second call came from Lazar a couple of weeks later. This time he was more than a little angry. I felt he was determined to scare me into giving in. When I'd had enough, I told him I hoped he would sue me and give me the opportunity to read from the witness stand, for all the world to hear, what kind of shit producers had to accept from some writers.

His voice was deadly when he replied, "My writers don't write shit." Again he broke the connection.

I knew he called Jack Karp and complained about my refusal to settle the Anderson matter when Jack called me and asked why I was being difficult.

I reminded him of the handshake agreement we had when I accepted the offer to work with Hitch. I was to be consulted before writers were hired to work on every Hitchcock picture. I added, "I still don't know who signed the contract with Lazar, and who authorized the payment of $35,000, and how much more Anderson was to be paid." Jack said that the second payment of $15,000 should have been paid when I received the first draft and the final payment of $15,000, upon delivery of the final screenplay.

The third call I had from Mr. Lazar was almost friendly. He said, "Mr. Coleman, if you'll send me a check for the $15,000 due now, I'll write off the final $15,000." I told him the check would be in the mail within an hour.

A month or more passed before I received the fourth and really surprising call. Lazar said, "Mr. Coleman, one of these days you're going to leave Mr. Hitchcock. When you do, I want to represent you." I thanked him for the offer and told him I'd call him when I reached that crossroad. After we'd talked about the problems in the studios and the limited opportunities available for producers, we broke off, promising to keep in touch.

It took a few minutes for me to sort out what that call might mean for me. I knew talented actors, directors, and writers whose careers were at a standstill because they were unable to find an agent—not a Lazar but *any* agent—to represent them. And here was Lazar asking to take me on. Was I ready to step away from the security I had at Paramount? I wasn't sure and decided to wait a while longer before taking such an important step.

Lazar wasn't willing to wait. Call number five came a short time later. He asked for a meeting at his office the next day. I'd seen photographs of him in the newspapers, had watched him on television, and knew what he looked like; I looked forward to meeting him in person. I found him to be pleasant, open, and direct. I didn't offer, and he didn't ask, where I'd come from or how I had reached the position I held with Paramount and the Hitchcock organization. I let him know I wanted to wait a bit longer before entering the independent field and wanted to direct, rather than produce, movies.

He asked if I had a project ready to go. I told him I had a screenplay, *The Day before Tomorrow,* written for me by James Edmiston from my own original story.

I left the meeting convinced that he was much more interested in helping me move further up the ladder than in any possible agency fees he might receive.

Call number six came very soon. Lazar told me he'd arranged a meeting for me with Buddy Adler, the head of Twentieth Century–Fox, to discuss *The Day before Tomorrow* project.

I found Adler to be the friendly, interested executive everybody who knew him said he was. He listened attentively to the story. He asked about the budget and who I wanted for a producer. I told him about Doc Erickson. He agreed to Doc.

Then, a question about the cast. I told him I planned to use Vera Miles as the female star.

"A fine actress. Not a big draw at the box office yet. But I'll take her. And John Landon? You need an important star in that role."

"Robert Wagner has read the script. He'll do it for us," I said.

"Not Bob," Mr. Adler said. "He's under contract to Fox. You'll have to bring a star to us who will agree to a three-picture contract. Do that, and we have a deal."

I didn't go back to Lazar for help. He'd given me the meeting with Buddy Adler and would consider me capable of carrying on from there.

Doc and I were talking to a number of possible candidates when Adler suddenly died. We were not surprised that his replacement wasn't interested in our project. He, like others in his position, preferred to start fresh with his own program.

Problems with *Vertigo* were forcing us to turn our attention back to the picture, so we pushed *The Day before Tomorrow* from our minds.

Coppel's script arrived. It was a far better treatment of the *Vertigo* concept than Anderson's, but it was still not good enough. Hitch knew he would have to devote a lot of time and work with Alec Coppel.

Vertigo was a joint venture, similar to *Rear Window,* between Hitch and Jimmy Stewart, with Jimmy starring in the film.

Vera Miles, on the verge of becoming a major star in the role of Madelaine and surely the happiest actress in town, was waiting restlessly for the start of production. Tom Helmore was set in the part of Gavin Elster, Madelaine's husband, a wealthy owner of a giant shipyard, and also a former college classmate of Jimmy and Midge.

Barbara bel Geddes, I was happy to discover, accepted the role of Midge. What a joy it was to watch her perform. Ellen Corby would be the manager of the old hotel. Konstantin Shayne was set as Pop Leibel, the owner of a bookstore.

Jack Karp, with Barney Balaban, the president of Paramount, studied my budget at Jack's office in New York, and Balaban went along with Jack's approval of the project.

The coffee and gossip hour in my office each morning had ended completely. Everyone connected with *Vertigo* was anxious to get the picture into production.

I set October 15 as the start date, with filming in San Francisco and San Juan Bautista first on the schedule. On October 12, Doc and I joined Hitch and Alma at the ranch. Danny McCauley, Bummy, Peggy Robertson, our new script clerk, Bob Burks, and his staff drove to the Munrus Hotel in Monterey, where they would be staying while we were filming at the mission and the other locations we'd selected in the area.

Doc and I were sharing the large bedroom just above the downstairs living room. The morning after our arrival, Doc was sleeping late while I was working on a screenplay I called *Mission? To Marrakech!!* an original story that grew out of our experiences in Morocco on *The Man Who Knew Too Much.*

I heard the telephone ringing loudly in the room below. Some time passed before I heard Hitch's voice respond to the caller, "Why, hello Lew." There was a long wait before I heard him say, "Does Gloria really believe Jimmy needs two and a half months' rest before we start?" I knew the caller had to be Lew Wasserman. There was another pause, and then Hitch said, "I'll talk it over with Herbie and call you back."

I shook Doc awake and shocked him by asking what it would cost us to postpone the picture until January 2, 1957. He was in and out of the shower in ten minutes. By the time we heard the call to brunch, we'd arrived at a figure of a little over $100,000, without overhead. I told Doc we were not supposed to know anything about the call.

Brunch on the patio was champagne, green salad with lobster that Hitch ignored, of course, and perfectly broiled New York strippers. As usual, Hitch's steak rapidly disappeared. He was not one to toy with his food. He waited, impatiently, for me to finish eating. When Alma went into the kitchen for coffee, he leaned close and whispered in my ear, "We've got to talk."

I followed him inside along a corridor to an old, heavy, wooden door. He opened it and indicated that I was to follow him. He fumbled around in the darkness until he found the chain hanging from a center light in the ceiling. I'd been a guest at the ranch many times but didn't even know that room existed. It was an old wine cellar with hundreds of bottles of wine in the racks along the walls.

Hitch closed the cellar door and whispered the news I already knew. "What do you think it will cost to postpone for two and a half months, Herbie?"

I ran through the figures Doc and I had used to arrive at the $100,000 and added that the figure was without overhead and that, if we postponed, I would carry everyone who was on salary.

"Do you think we should postpone?" he asked.

I gave him the reasons I felt we should. I said, "Jimmy is a full partner on *Vertigo.* He knows what the delay will cost him. He wouldn't ask us to postpone unless there was a serious reason he should. We don't want an unhappy star on our hands for sixty days, do we?"

Hitch was happy with my decision and called Lew. Within an hour, Jimmy called and thanked us.

I gave Doc the news. He called Danny at the Munrus and told him to take everybody back to the studio. Hitch and Alma decided to remain at the ranch for a few days.

I saw a big change in Hitch's disposition when he came back to the office about two weeks later. He wouldn't talk about his problem. We were having lunch the day after he arrived. He was about to take a bite from the large ground sirloin steak on his plate, when he suddenly dropped his fork and hugged his stomach.

He brushed aside my suggestion that I call Dr. Tandowsky.

"It's nothing, Herbie. I'll be all right in a minute or so."

The pain seemed to go away, and he finished his lunch. But for the next few weeks the same thing kept happening, until he was forced to see his doctor.

Hitch had been suffering for years with a serious navel hernia that Tandowsky had been keeping an eye on, and he told Hitch it was time to take care of it.

The operation in late November was more serious than his doctors expected it to be. Hitch's recovery was slow and painful. Dr. Tandowsky told me, "Mr. Hitchcock will need a lot of rest before starting his new picture. I'd say he could be ready to go by March 1st."

Shortly before Christmas he began coming to the office for a few hours a day. One morning after he'd poured himself a cup of coffee and settled down on the couch, he surprised me when he said, "Herbie, I've decided you need a new writer. Mr. Coppel's script is still not good enough."

He called to Dolores Stockton, his secretary: "Dolores, call Kay Brown in New York. You'll find her number in my address book."

Kay Brown was a highly respected literary agent in New York and a longtime friend of the Hitchcocks. When she came on the line, he told her our problem and the story of *Vertigo.*

And he asked for her help in finding the right person to do the screenplay. Without a moment's hesitation, she told Hitch that the right man for the job was the brilliant playwright Samuel Taylor.

We were both familiar with Taylor's very successful Broadway play, *Sabrina Fair.* And his work with Billy Wilder on the screenplay they adapted from his play. It was the first time since Hitch first started talking about Maxwell Anderson that I felt we were after the right man.

Sam liked the idea of working with Hitch and accepted the assignment. On January 17 I arranged to meet Sam in San Francisco. We toured the locations in San Francisco, including Ernies. Then drove to San Juan Bautista to look over the mission. Then on to Hollywood, where his lovely wife Suzanne was waiting in the apartment Doc Erickson had arranged for them.

The following morning when Sam joined us in my office for coffee, it was like old friends. I thought for a moment Hitch was going to shake Sam's hand, but he reverted to style and gave Sam a big smile and a welcoming, "Welcome to the club, Mr. Taylor."

"Sam, please, Mr. Hitchcock."

"Hitch, please, Sam."

Gossip and coffee lasted barely half an hour. Then Sam and Hitch decided it was time for work. They disappeared into Hitch's office. We had lunch together in Hitch's office, and then it was back to work.

Sam would meet with Hitch every morning at Hitch's home. Then Sam would disappear into his office in the writer's building and go to work.

Pages rolled from his typewriter with amazing speed. I was beginning to believe we would make our March starting date, until my phone woke me at 4:00 a.m. at our home in Newport Beach. It was a frantic Alma I heard when I answered. "Herbie, Hitch is terribly ill. He's asking for you. Can you come right away?" I could and did. I was at their Bel Air home in record time. Hitch looked at me the moment I walked into his bedroom: "Find Tandowsky, Herbie! He must come!" The words came between gasps for breath.

I took Alma into the living room and told her Tandowsky wasn't available. I knew he was out on the Pacific somewhere studying the heartbeat of whales.

I telephoned Lew Wasserman and gave him the bad news. He was there in minutes. I told Lew about Tandowsky. He called his physician, one of the most important doctors on the staff of the University of California, Los Angeles, Medical Center. He responded almost as quickly as Lew.

When he walked into Hitch's bedroom, he took a quick look at Hitch and told him he must have an operation without delay. "I've just had an operation," Hitch told him.

"For what?" the doctor asked.

"A navel hernia," Hitch replied.

"It's not a hernia now, Mr. Hitchcock. You have gallstones. We must get you to the hospital immediately."

Hitch was rushed to Cedars of Lebanon Hospital, with red lights flashing atop the ambulance. Little time was lost before he was wheeled into the operating room, where a team of top surgeons was waiting. The gallstone operation was a complete success. The doctors told me that Hitch needed months of complete rest. In his suite in the hospital only Alma, Pat, and I were given permission to visit him. I was warned not to discuss any business. They said, "He should be able to resume work by June 1st. We'll see." So June 1 became our new starting date at the Old San Juan Bautista Mission.

Vera Miles heard the first television broadcast about Hitch's second operation and called me. "I've got to talk to Hitch, Herbie!" She was not the calm, thoughtful Miles I knew so well. Her voice revealed a deeply troubled young lady.

"Impossible," I told her. "The doctors have limited visitors to Alma, Pat, and me. The telephone has been removed from his room. The doctors have warned me against discussing any business with Hitch."

"But I must, Herbie," she insisted. "What I have to say can't wait."

I was startled at the words I heard coming from my mouth. "Are you pregnant, Vera?"

"Yes," she answered. "How did you know?"

"I didn't, but what else could be so important?"

She ignored my question. "I knew I was pregnant when you told me I was set for the picture, but with the October start date there was no problem. Even with the new date of January 2nd, the picture would have been finished before anyone would know. But with this delay, it's impossible. You've got to find another girl."

That about ended that conversation. It also ended Hitch's dream of creating a new major star with Vera. For the rest of his life, he refused to blame Jimmy Stewart's request to move the original starting date back almost three months so he could have a vacation as the root cause of our problems.

I called Lew Wasserman and gave him the bad news. He knew he would have to find a star to replace Miles, without having a chance to talk to Hitch. Lew was, without question, the most powerful dealmaker in the film world. There wasn't one major studio's top executive whose door wasn't always open to Lew.

He walked into Harry Cohn's office at Columbia and walked out with an agreement to give Jimmy Stewart to Cohn for his next picture in exchange for Kim Novak for *Vertigo.*

I continued my usual visits to Hitch's suite at Cedars of Lebanon every morning without giving him the Novak news. One morning I arrived to find Hitch fully dressed for the first time. His first words to me were, "How long have you known that Vera Miles is pregnant?"

"About five weeks. How long have you known?"

"About five minutes."

"How did you find out?"

He pointed to the telephone on his bedside table. "Hedda Hopper just told me."

"How did that thing get in here?" I asked.

"I let them know I was paying for that phone." He walked to a nearby chair, sat down, and sipped at a waiting cup of cold coffee before asking, "Well, who is my new Madelaine?"

I told him about Lew's deal for Novak.

"What's our new starting date?"

"The doctors tell me you should be well enough to go back to work about June 1st. We'll see."

They let him go home to recuperate but warned us to make him take it easy.

Sam resumed his daily conferences with Hitch at his home. There wasn't too much left to be done on the screenplay. Early in May Sam gave us his *Vertigo* screenplay and left for his home in East Blue Hill, Maine.

The screenplay was beautifully written and contained elements we'd never dreamed of. Sam had introduced a new character he called Midge. She was an artist with an apartment with a large picture window revealing the city of San Francisco seen in the distance. She had met, and fallen in love with, Jimmy when they were classmates in college. She wanted to marry, mother, and protect him forever. But Jimmy wasn't ready for marriage and might never be ready.

Sam knew he had to create a person close to Jimmy from whom the audience could learn about his background. Why he suffers from acrophobia. Someone with whom Jimmy could discuss his problems. Midge became an invaluable member of the cast.

June arrived, along with the latest bad news: Kim Novak wouldn't report until she took the six-week vacation her contract with Columbia stipulated. She was going off to Europe, and nothing was going to stop her.

I called and asked Kim if she was willing to meet with Edith Head to discuss the costumes she would be wearing in the picture. She was not only willing; she was anxious to cooperate.

With still another delay staring us in the face, Hitch decided to fly to New York for one last talk with Sam Taylor on some minor details in the screenplay. I arranged for Sam to fly down from his home in Maine. They met for a few days at the St. Regis Hotel. Hitch flew home, and Sam mailed us the changes long before they were needed.

Soon after meeting Edith, Novak flew off to London, Paris, or wherever. She wasn't about to have anybody spoil her vacation with phone calls.

I'd become convinced we would start shooting within a week of her return, but I was in for another round of bad news.

Novak arrived back on time and then refused to report to us because Harry Cohn had promised her a share in the loan-out fee Cohn was charging Paramount for her services and had then reneged on his promise. Most, if not all, stars were paid a weekly salary. The difference between that sum and what a studio received on a loan out belonged to the studio.

"My share or forget it," she apparently told Cohn.

We sat and waited while they haggled throughout most of the summer. Cohn blinked first, and we finally started shooting the Old San Juan Bautista Mission exactly a year after Hitch and I stood in his wine cellar and told Lew Wasserman we agreed to the postponement.

Hitch and Alma left for the ranch the morning after we walked off the stage for the last time on *Vertigo.* I'd promised Mary Belle a holiday in Hawaii but had to ask her to wait a little longer. It wasn't the first time we'd had to postpone our vacation.

Bernard Herrmann was hard at work on the score for the picture. He and Lucy invited us to dinner at their home out in the valley on

Bluebell Avenue. It was never difficult to find their house on that quiet tree-shaded street. It was the one almost hidden by flowering vines that covered the entire front wall and porch. The chilled wine and can of Beluga caviar, almost buried in a large silver ice-filled bowl, were waiting on a table beside the quiet water of the large swimming pool.

We'd just settled down when Benny's beloved cat parade commenced. I never knew how many he had. One in particular always headed straight for Mary Belle. I guess that kitten thought we loved cats. But it was the other way around. Cats were crazy about her. I watched Benny watching Mary Belle and knew he was studying her to decide if she was worthy of mothering one of his children.

I figured he'd made a decision when he took me to his music room to play what he called "Madelaine's theme." Two pianos, keyboards facing each other, with only enough room for a swivel chair between them, dominated the small room.

Benny offered no explanation for such an unusual arrangement. He sat down before one of them. His whole body seemed to change. His shoulders rounded, and his head bent forward toward the keyboard. His stubby fingers gently caressed the keys, and the soft sound of a haunting melody filled the room.

A few days later I ran the picture for Benny and then later ran it for the sound and effects editors. I asked Hitch to come from the ranch for the "fine tuning." We spent a week in the "stop-and-go" projection room with George Tomasini. It was "Add a frame here. Cut a frame there." Never anything like "Let's cut this sequence" or "Shift this around." Editors didn't have that luxury with a Hitchcock film. The way the screenplay was constructed and the picture was directed left George with no options.

Hitch and Alma returned to the ranch to wait for the call to come back for the scoring session. But that call never came.

Benny completed the music composition and the arrangements and was ready to conduct the Paramount orchestra when the American Society of Composers, Authors, and Publishers (ASCAP), of which Benny was a reluctant member, called a strike against all the studios. Faced with the possibility of a very long delay while the producers and ASCAP argued, I decided to score the picture overseas. The London musicians union agreed to allow their members to work for us.

ASCAP ruled that Benny couldn't conduct the orchestra anywhere in the world. I was happy I wasn't around when Benny got the news. It was enough when he walked into my office and vented his feeling against ASCAP, England, America, the rest of the world, and most of all, the LIBERALS, meaning me. But we parted friends when I promised I'd take with me a music editor, Birnbaum—a man in whom he had great confidence—and my promise to hire Muir Mathieson to conduct the orchestra.

To further soothe my feelings, Benny dropped by our home the Sunday before I left for London. Snuggled in his arms was that same little, long-haired gray kitten. He handed it to Mary Belle. "His name's Babo." He pulled some pages from a pocket. "Here's how you care for him, what you feed him, and when, the name and address of his vet. It's all there." It meant nothing to Benny that his vet was seventy miles away in North Hollywood.

Birnbaum turned out to be very much like Benny. Together, they arranged the music cues on the print of *Vertigo* that I would take with me.

It was snowing when we landed at Heathrow Airport in London, and it continued to snow or rain throughout our stay in the city. I would learn that Birnbaum had little love for either.

Kay Selby, the Paramount executive who made life in London less difficult on *The Man Who Knew Too Much,* was waiting when we walked into her office. We'd talked on the phone, and I expected to find everything ready for us. But Kay had some disturbing news. "The first day I could get Muir Mathieson, the symphony orchestra you wanted, and a recording studio all together at the same time was. . . ." She named a date nine days later.

I called Hitch and gave him the news.

He arrived the night before our first day's recording.

Mathieson and the orchestra were waiting when we walked into the scoring room. Everyone was on a high at the end of the first day.

Everything was in order when we arrived the next morning. Just as Muir was about to give the cue to record the first section of the music, a stranger walked in and called Muir aside. What he said really upset our distinguished conductor. He then introduced himself to us as the head of the Musicians Union in England. He told us his organization had held an emergency meeting the previous night and had agreed to support the ASCAP strike. The musicians didn't agree when they heard the news but had to pack their instruments and leave the stage.

By the time we got back to Claridges Hotel, Hitch had made up his mind to go home. "What now, Herbie? Where do you go from here?"

"Maybe Rome. Or Paris. Any country that will work with us."

"Not us, Herbie. I'm going home. Let's hope the strike is over before you have to move out of England."

I drove with him to Heathrow that evening to see him off.

Birnbaum followed Hitch the next day. "You told me I'd be free in ten days. I have to report to MGM next Monday."

I think it was more like the rain, the snow, and the smell of the kippers that made him abandon me.

For the next week, everyone in the London office jumped in to help me find what I needed to record Benny Herrmann's music.

My first choice was Rome. No dice. The same news from Paris, Stockholm, and Brussels. Then Vienna came through. The managing director of Paramount's office in Vienna called and said, "We have the facilities, the symphony orchestra. Just bring Mathieson and come on down."

I left London on a BEA plane. The sky was filled with dark storm clouds, and a light snow was streaking past the windows of the plane as we neared Vienna. I looked up at the beautiful English stewardess who leaned over my shoulder and with a bright smile said, "Mr. Coleman, when you see the Danube, will you tell me if it looks blue or gray?"

"Why do you want to know?"

"If it's blue, it means you're in love," she said.

"What color does it look to you?" I asked.

Her smile increased, and her eyes glowed: "Always blue."

She was first off the plane. I watched her run through the snow and jump into the arms of a tall, hatless, blond young man. Of course, with the sky covered with the storm clouds, the Danube was a muddy, brown river.

Paramount had put me up in a lovely hotel, the Sacher, in the center of town.

Twelve days after arriving in Vienna, I joined Mathieson and a wonderful orchestra in a recording studio. After one rehearsal, Muir came to me and told me he was confident that Herrmann, Hitch, and I would be happy with what he would be able to accomplish here in Vienna.

I arrived home thirty days after leaving for London for four day's work. The ASCAP strike was still on. Benny was still as bitter as he was the day he walked into my office to give me the bad news. He grumbled about the quality of the recordings but had to accept what he heard.

While I was away, Hitch and George had been working with the sound and effects editors and were ready to go for final mixing as soon as I got back with the music. The mixing went smoothly except for an occasional outburst from Benny that Hitch would squelch by lowering the dry end of his Havana cigar from his lips and softly remarking, "Now, Benny."

Barney Balaban, the president and CEO of Paramount, came out from New York, ran the picture, went back to his office on Times Square, and spread the word that *Vertigo* was Hitchcock's finest picture.

We decided to hold the world premier at the Fox Theatre in San Francisco before an audience of invited guests, distinguished citizens, the mayor of San Francisco, critics from the most important newspapers, and the general public.

Vertigo was a huge success. Many in the audience actually cheered when the lights in the theater came on at the end of the picture. Critics were unanimous in their praise of Hitch's direction and the performances of Jimmy Stewart and Kim Novak.

The Gottis had closed Ernies to the public and had invited all Paramount guests to a cocktail party and dinner after the preview. It was a gala affair.

With the successful premiere of *Vertigo* behind us, we decided that there wasn't a single change necessary and turned the picture over to the Paramount executives.

Balaban was anxious to get the picture into the theaters and ordered the prints be distributed without delay.

Hitch came into my office late one afternoon. I could tell that something was preying on his mind and that he was having trouble putting his thoughts into words. But a single vodka and tonic loosened his tongue. "I'm not convinced we should have used the scene in Judy's hotel room where we see her thoughts of Madelaine going up through the trap door and disclosing Elster throwing the body of his dead wife from the tower as she writes the good-bye letter to Scottie."

My first astonished reaction to such a suggestion from Hitch was, Who had he been talking to about that part of the picture? I had my instant suspicion: Joan Harrison. But she wasn't at the preview. She hadn't seen the picture.

"But, Hitch," I said, "there are many reasons you shouldn't think about removing that scene. Don't you remember our conversation when you came into my office and told me how Sam Taylor had solved our problem of turning *Vertigo* from a mystery story into what we always wanted, a Hitchcock suspense film?"

"But Herbie, people have said we couldn't hold the audience if we have that scene in the picture."

With Harrison in mind, I asked him, "What people?"

He dodged answering my question. Instead, he suggested we freshen our drinks. I was too disturbed to join him. "Why don't we have George cut that scene and take another look? Call Jimmy and Gloria. See if Sam and Suzanne Taylor can fly out from Maine. Bummy, Doc, Bob Burks, Danny, and others from our staff, and get their reactions."

George had to tell his boss, Chuck West, the head of the cutting department. Of course, Chuck hotfooted it to Jack Karp. Jack wanted to know what we were doing with Balaban's favorite picture. I told him he had nothing to worry about. "When Hitch sees the film without that scene, he'll say, 'Leave the picture alone.'" I had to promise Jack I'd call him after the running and tell him Hitch's decision.

"I don't care when you call, Herbie. As late as necessary," Jack said.

It took a while to get them all together. Hitch had arranged a table at Chasens after the running. I didn't even look around to see who came to see the picture. Even though I hadn't invited Joan Harrison, I wasn't surprised to see her sitting right beside Hitch.

There wasn't an audible reaction to anything during the two-hour running. But the instant the screen went blank and the lights came on in the projection room, she jumped to her feet and yelled out, "Hitchy! How could anyone want your picture to be seen any different from this?"

There was absolute silence from everyone else in the theater. I got up and walked away from the others. After a brief moment Hitch joined me. "Well, Herbie. That's it." I told him the silence in the room should tell him he was making a big mistake. He didn't like that, and we began to argue.

We were standing face to face. Our voices were rising. Finally, he'd had enough and gave me the first direct order he would ever give me in all the years we worked together. "Release it just like that."

I pushed past him, crossed through the silent group, and hurried out of the theater. Before I'd reached the corner of the camera building, Jimmy Stewart ran after me. "Herbie," he said, "you shouldn't get so upset with Hitch. The picture's not that important."

"Is Hitch right, Jimmy?" I asked.

"No," he said.

"Then why didn't you speak up, Jimmy? He has the greatest respect for your judgment. You're a partner in *Vertigo,* and that change is going to cost you a lot of money."

"It isn't worth it, Herbie. Forget it and come along to Chasens with us."

"No thanks, Jimmy." I turned away and walked to my office. Called Jack and gave him the bad news. Looked around for some boxes to start packing. I'd made up my mind to get away from Hitch and his whole organization. I couldn't find any boxes, so I locked up and went home.

I hadn't planned to go to the studio the next day, but around noon George called and wanted to know what he should do with the picture. "You'll have to come in. Chuck [West] won't let me do anything until you come in and give us written orders."

I went in and found out that making that cut in the picture wasn't as simple as I'd thought. Prints had been delivered to exchanges all over the country. Every exchange had to return that one reel.

I had to find Benny Herrmann and have him come in and adjust the music. He wasn't a happy man when he heard the news.

We ran that section of the picture. He blew his top when he saw where the cut came: Judy, standing in her room, her face showing the strain she's under. He'd written soft, almost romantic, music to play over her, blending into the heavy, dramatic chords for the chase up the tower stairs into the bell tower. And just the reverse from the bell tower to the close-up of Judy.

Between George and me recutting that section and Benny and Paramount's experts on the mixing panel, we finally got a somewhat less-than-perfect result.

Five hundred reprints of that reel were shipped to the exchanges, and they were ready to distribute them to the theaters when all hell broke loose.

Jack Karp called me to his office. I'd never seen him upset before. He was a kind man with his emotions always under control. But not that morning. "Where's Hitch?" he asked.

"Up at his ranch. Why?" I asked.

"I just had a call from Barney Balaban. I've never known him to be so angry. He wanted to know what you've done to *Vertigo.* He said that after all the great statements he's made about the picture, he arranged a private showing for the top critics in the East. And calls have been coming in from all of them that *Vertigo* is a disaster. He wants Hitch in my office tomorrow morning. He'll telephone us at nine sharp."

I went back to my office and started calling. The transportation department would make reservations from San Francisco to L.A. Tickets would be waiting at the airport. Ollie, our San Francisco limousine driver, would leave immediately for the ranch and have Hitch at the airport in time to catch the six o'clock flight.

With those arrangements out of the way, I called Hitch. Our relationship, strained from the confrontation at the Joan Harrison running, had not reached the level we'd enjoyed before that event. I told him about the travel arrangements. He was startled by the news of Balaban's call to Jack.

"Have you told Lew [Wasserman] about this?" he wanted to know.

I told him I'd thought it best not to involve Lew until after he talked to Balaban. I added, "If you want my advice, I don't think you should talk to Lew either."

Balaban must have made his point very quickly the next morning. It was just 9:18 when I heard his secretary, Dolores, say, "Good morning, Mr. Hitchcock." There was no response from Hitch.

I looked up. He was standing in her office looking through my secretary's office into mine. "Put the picture back the way you had it." He turned away, went into his office, and closed the door. The mental picture of Hitch disappearing into his office was deeply disturbing.

Never during the weeks that had passed since that distressing evening in the projection room had either one of us attempted to explain it away. His trusted friend, Joan Harrison, had placed him in an embarrassing position. He had been hurt, and I felt his pain.

Chapter 45

No Bail for the Judge

From the Paramount executive offices on Times Square in New York to Jack Karp's office on the Paramount Studio lot at 5451 Marathon Street in Hollywood, there was joy and happiness at the critical and financial success of *Vertigo.*

Hitch had long since forgiven Barney Balaban for forcing him to restore the bell tower–Helmore scene to the picture. It took him a long time to admit that he was wrong and I was right in fighting to keep it in.

We were searching carefully for a story to follow *Vertigo,* finally selecting a novel, *No Bail for the Judge,* written by Henry Cecil Leon and published under his pseudonym, Henry Cecil. The judge was to be played by John Williams. Lawrence Harvey would be a society jewel thief.

Audrey Hepburn was cast as the judge's daughter, a barrister in his court.

No Bail for the Judge was a story about an Old Bailey Court judge walking home late at night. When he sees a taxi bearing down on a small dog, he runs to save the poor animal. He falls, striking his head against the curb, knocking himself unconscious.

When he wakes up, it's morning. He's in a small attic room lying across the nude body of a young woman, his hand clutching the handle of a knife buried deep in her back. Convinced he's responsible for her murder, he turns himself in and is held without bail while Scotland Yard investigates the crime.

Returning to her home where she lives with her father, Hepburn surprises a society jewel thief, Laurence Harvey, attempting to steal her father's fabulous jewel collection from a wall safe. Anxious to continue to conceal his criminal activity from his friends in London society, he agrees to help Hepburn solve the mystery of the prostitute's murder.

Harvey rents a small apartment and hires a number of retired British army officers to pick up prostitutes and bring them to the apartment where he can question them. The police become suspicious and arrest the girls who are going in and out of the apartment house.

Meanwhile, Hepburn, frustrated at the slow pace at which Harvey's plan is progressing, decides to pose as one of the girls. She's among the prostitutes who are arrested and taken to Bow Street Police Station and questioned. With no proof that the girls have been accepting money for any illegal activity, the police are compelled to release them.

London's head pimp (who but Hitch would make him the son of a duchess?) is waiting outside Bow Street Station. One look at Hepburn is enough for him. He must have her immediately. She gets in his car. He drives her out to Hyde Park and takes her out behind the bushes where she submits to him.

The case reaches its climax when the judge is brought to trial in England's highest court, Old Bailey, the same court where Judge John Williams had presided.

One quick reading of the novel convinced both Hitch and me that there was only one man to write the screenplay, Samuel Taylor. He accepted the assignment after reading the book and left his home in East Blue Hill, Maine, with his wife Suzanne to join us.

We agreed before Sam started work on the screenplay that we would take a look at prostitutes in action—meet and talk to some of them, if possible.

"Bummy" Bumstead and I were first to arrive at the airport in Los Angeles to catch the American Airlines flight to New York en route to Heathrow Airport in London. Bummy showed me his new and different passport he'd just received. Suddenly I remembered that my passport was in my file at home in Newport Beach. Carl Reynolds, our driver and an old, old friend, left immediately to pick it up and bring it to the airport. Just then Hitch and Sam Taylor arrived. When I told them about my passport, Hitch asked, "Why don't you come over tomorrow?"

I told him, "Hitch, with or without a passport, I'll bet you I'll be standing inside England when the rest of you arrive at the customs officer."

And I was right. The American Airlines agent in New York told me to go to the first uniformed airport officer I saw the next morning and tell him I had made a big mistake. I left my passport lying on our counter.

When I told that to the uniformed officer at Heathrow he said, "Sir, you have made a big mistake. Come with me." He led me into an office where a distinguished gentleman, with much gold braid, sat at a desk. When I repeated my story, he said, "Welcome to England, sir. With thousands of foreign ladies coming into England every year, you can imagine what a small thing a missing passport can be. Welcome to England, sir."

When Hitch, Sam, and Bummy arrived at the customs officer's counter, passports in hand, I was standing inside England, laughing at them.

Jet lag confined us to our hotel the first day in London. But on day two we were ready to meet the "girls."

Jim and Linda Swarbrick, two of London's finest photographers, had promised to photograph the "girls" who frequented Shepard Market. They would make still pictures and sixteen-millimeter movies we could use for casting, wardrobe, makeup, and hairdressing back at the studio in Hollywood.

But when we got out of the car across Curzon Street from the market, Jim said, "Mr. Coleman, most of those girls know us from movies we've worked on around here. They'll never allow us to take their pictures."

I borrowed his movie camera and walked into the market. There were a few well-dressed girls hanging around in doorways. The moment I brought the camera up to take a shot, they disappeared into doorways and up stairs like rats running from a cat. I faked taking shots of displays in windows and other things around the market.

Soon one of the girls came back down the stairs and stopped near me. I turned and in my "Wild Wonderful Cliff Holler, West Virginia," accent asked her, "Is this the place they call Shepard's Market?" The accent and the *s* on *Shepard* assured her that I was just another American tourist. She became real friendly. I was hers. Soon other girls came out into the open, and I got all the pictures we needed.

At dinner that evening, Hitch turned to Bummy and asked, "Mr. Bumstead, how do you propose to duplicate the rooms where the prostitutes perform with their clients? We must be correct in every detail. It would be helpful if you make your photographs with movement. You understand what I mean."

Of course, Bummy knew he was kidding about the action. He told Hitch he'd find some research somewhere.

That wasn't enough for Hitch. He told Bummy he wanted to see actual photographs of the rooms.

"Hitch," I asked, "who're you afraid of offending if the rooms are just figments of Bummy's imagination? The prostitutes? Their pimps? Or the 'marks' the girls pick up? You think they'll demonstrate outside the theaters?"

"Just see that Bummy comes home with those pictures, Mr. Coleman."

We'd heard there was a place somewhere in London where the pimps gathered late at night to wait for their prostitutes to turn over their earnings of the evening. Sam thought it might add color to the story if he could find a way to work it into the script.

A prominent Fleet Street journalist, who was trusted by the London underworld, had visited the place and gave us the address. "Tell your driver to drop you off, then drive away and be back to pick you up exactly fifteen minutes later. Act just like American tourists who have wandered in by mistake. Let them hear your American accents, and at the very first sign anyone of them suspects you, get the hell out."

Following his advice, we arrived outside a building in a completely deserted section of London. A single dim streetlight in the distance did little to relieve the darkness and the sense of danger I felt as our car drove away.

Before us, a long, narrow, steep flight of stairs led down to a single door. As we started down, Sam asked, "Where's your camera?" He grinned. "Hitch will want to see photographs."

"He'll accept what we tell him or come over and see for himself," I answered.

We stepped inside a large basement room. Off to one side was a small bar with a coffeemaker, a few bottles, and a bartender lounging against the back bar.

There was one unoccupied table near the door that we headed for. No one among the crowd of pimps and their girls sitting around the twenty or so tables noticed us. But I sure took a good look at them. Especially the pimps. Maybe it was my very vivid imagination working at breakneck speed that made every one of them a killer with a razor-sharp knife or a gun hidden in his clothes.

A few "girls," late arrivals, came in and hurried to join their pimps. We'd been there only about five minutes when two "girls" arrived. To my dismay, one of them was the woman I'd talked to at Shepard Market. She glanced at me and a puzzled look replaced the smile on her face.

I watched her join a pimp, sitting alone near the back wall. She said something to him as she sat down. They both looked in our direction. In a whisper, I told Sam it was time we followed the journalist's advice and got the hell out of there. We got up and, fighting the urge to run, walked slowly toward the door. With every step, I could almost feel the point of a pimp's knife plunging between my quivering shoulder blades. Lucky for us our car arrived just as we reached the sidewalk.

We spent a couple of uneventful days at the Ascot racetrack. With my usual luck at the races, I dropped a few pounds. Hitch was the only winner.

We had no problem attending a trial at the Bow Street Police Station. Bummy was able to get all the research photographs he needed to reproduce it at the studio.

Old Bailey was a different story. Hitch, Sam, and I were allowed to sit in the VIP section and watch the trial of a man and woman who were accused of running a degrading, vicious child pornography ring.

The courtroom was an imposing narrow rectangular room. At one end, the judge sat at his bench high above the floor. His clerk sat at his desk a little below the judge. To the right of the judge, on the same level, there were a dozen or so comfortable seats for VIP visitors.

On the end of the courtroom, opposite to and at the same level as the judge's bench, there was a box where the accused stood, guarded by uniformed police officers. Barristers and the prosecuting team operated from the narrow floor below the judge. The judge was a dignified gentleman, wearing red robes and a handsome white wig. His clerk was also wearing red robes and a white wig.

My request to take photographs in Old Bailey had been denied, so I'd brought a small sketch pad with me and was quietly drawing a plan of the courtroom and recording details of the proceedings. I looked up from my sketch pad in time to see the judge, without looking in our direction, lean over and speak quietly to his clerk. The clerk got up and disappeared through a door.

I was sitting above and a couple of rows behind Hitch and Sam. Suddenly, I became aware of someone's head almost touching mine. I turned and was startled to see the clerk close to me. "I beg your pardon, sir," he whispered. "Taking notes of court proceedings and sketching is forbidden in this court."

I told him I was unaware of the restriction and apologized. When I offered to give my sketch pad, he told me I could keep the notes I'd made but to please stop what I'd been doing. He retreated back up the steep stairs of the VIP section and soon reappeared at his desk.

We watched the trial reach its conclusion. The judge, looking sternly across the room toward the accused man and his wife, said they were both guilty and sentenced them to long prison sentences. The man, a short, overweight, disgusting-looking individual, moaned and would have slumped to the floor but for the presence of the two officers.

I still had to get photographs of everything I'd seen in Old Bailey. The judge's and clerk's costumes. Pictures of the courtroom so Bummy could accurately reproduce it in the studio.

Out of respect for Hitch, the judge's chief aide allowed us to bring Jim and Linda Swarbrick into Old Bailey late one night and make the photographs. He put on the judge's robe and wig and then the clerk's robe and wig. I made a solemn promise that I would destroy the photographs and negatives the moment we were finished with them.

We continued our leisurely survey. I had to keep pressing Hitch to get what we needed and get back to the studio and start working on the screenplay, but it was slow going.

Except for my meeting with the "girls," we still hadn't covered Shepard Market. At dinner one night, he agreed we'd go there the next morning. When I suggested leaving the hotel at nine, he countered with 10:30. We got away about eleven.

As usual, Hitch warned Bummy against overbuilding the sets. As we stood looking over the market, he said to Bummy, "Measure from the corner of that display case across to the right, and I'll stop you when I know how much of it I want you to build."

Bummy hooked his tape measure on the corner and started moving as Hitch had directed. He'd barely moved three feet before Hitch called out for him to stop. "That's it, Bummy. In the studio, just build that much. Not an inch more."

Of course, I would approve Bummy's plan to build the entire front of Shepard Market. As Bummy was writing down his measurements and the Swarbricks were taking photographs, Sam Taylor said, "Hitch, I haven't had breakfast. I must have something to eat."

"We're in the right place, Sam. Cunningham's is just next door." He turned to me: "Let's take a short break, Herbie, and pop into Cunningham's for coffee."

We did pop in. Not only for coffee but for champagne, brunch, and lively conversation until almost four that afternoon. That ended our London survey completely.

Hitch had not given in on the photographs of the girls' workrooms. I talked to the journalist who'd advised Sam and me on the pimps' meeting hall. He strongly advised me to give it up. "It would be even more dangerous than going down into the pimps' meeting room."

"There isn't a girl in this town who'd take that chance. She'd be signing her death warrant if her man saw your picture and recognized the room. Forget it or fake it," he advised.

We flew back home. Sam and Hitch were ready to abandon the long morning coffee klatches. They would arrive early and get to work.

I wasn't with them very often. I had to prove to Jack Karp that we could make the picture within a reasonable time period and for a limited budget. "It won't be another *Vertigo* river of money," I promised him.

I was in London when they completed the screenplay. I can't remember if Sam had gone back to his home in Maine when I arrived back at the studio. I read the script. I thought they'd equaled the suspense, the color, and the brilliant dialogue of *Vertigo* and certainly had added some amusement, sadly lacking in *Vertigo.* But I was surprised and disturbed by the scene in which the "girls" are dismissed from the Bow Street Police Station.

Hepburn comes out of the police station with the others, goes with the head pimp out into Hyde Park, and submits to him behind a clump of bushes.

I waited until cocktail time to discuss with Hitch what I'd read. When I got to the Hyde Park rape scene, I told him I thought he and Sam had made a serious mistake in the way they'd developed the scene. Or, as I put it, "failed to develop the scene."

"What do you mean? We failed to develop the scene?" Hitch was a little upset.

"You missed the chance to continue the sequence. Hepburn wouldn't submit to him so readily. She'd play him like a fine chess player. Build his desire while she draws from him any information about her father's involvement in the murder of the prostitute. Another thing. The selection of Hyde Park in which to stage the scene. Millions of visitors from all over the world have strolled through Hyde Park.

"Lovers walking hand in hand. Families gathered on holiday. It's just not believable," I said. "And, Hitch, don't forget Hepburn has recently starred as a nun in *The Nun's Story.* Like every dedicated actress, she'll live that part for years to come. When she reads that scene in the script, she'll refuse to do the picture."

"We won't let her see that sequence until we're ready to film it," he said.

"No, Hitch," I said. "I've known and respected Audrey ever since I directed her tests for *Roman Holiday* in May 1952. Her ethical and moral standards are unequaled by anyone in our industry. She'll walk right out of the picture when I hand her the pages. And she won't come back. I can't risk allowing Paramount to lose all that money."

"What are you going to do about it, Herbie?" he asked.

"She's in Durango, Mexico, starring in *The Unforgiven*. I'm sending the script to her." Hitch wasn't at all happy with my decision. I mailed the script directly to Audrey, bypassing her agent, Kurt Frings.

A few days later, Jack Karp asked me to come to his office. When I walked in, I wasn't surprised to see Frings sitting there. "Kurt, tell Herbie what Audrey said about his script."

"Audrey said, 'I wouldn't be caught dead in that picture.'"

I asked Frings if she said why. "That scene in Hyde Park," he said.

"What are you going to tell Hitch?" Jack asked.

"Exactly what Audrey said."

"Do you think it's wise to tell him that?" Jack asked.

"Jack," I said, "it's tell the truth or lie. I'm not good at lying."

It took me less than one minute to walk from Jack's office to mine, but in that short time, my memory carried me back to the day at our shack in Cliff Holler when Papa, with his homespun philosophy, let me know the value of truth and trust.

I was late getting home after school. Mama was out in the yard, bent over a washtub scrubbing Papa's overalls, what we called "overhalls" way back then. When I stopped to give her a hug, she told me Papa was in the kitchen packing his supper box.

What she said worried me. Papa was always down at the Yards firing up his engine by this time. I wondered if he'd found out that I'd gone swimming after recess and had missed my geography lesson.

When I walked in, he was standing at the coal stove, pouring himself a cup of hot coffee. He didn't say anything to me. Just carried his coffee back to the rough-plank kitchen table. Sat down, poured his coffee from his cup into his saucer, raised the saucer to his lips, and began sipping it. Finally, he fixed his eyes on me and asked, "How did your teacher like the map of the United States you made last night, Herbert?"

There it was. Papa knew I'd played hooky. But how in the world had he found out? I was flustered and stammered out a confused story.

Papa listened quietly, all the time sipping at his coffee. When I stumbled to a halt, he put his saucer down and said, "Herbert, fibbin'"—it was what he called lying—"is all wrong, and you know it. Tell one fib, then you got to tell another one to cover the first one. First thing you know, you're all tied up in fibs, and people won't trust you. The two most important things in life are truth and trust. Always remember that, Herbert."

He got up from the table, pulled out his gold Hamilton pocket watch, and studied the time. "Walk me down to the Yards, Herbert. Bring the coal scuttle. You can bring back some coal for the stove."

I followed him out of the kitchen, repeating to myself what I'd just heard him say: truth and trust.

I called Audrey in Durango and discussed the script with her. "Is it the scene in Hyde Park that caused you to tell Kurt you wouldn't be caught dead in our picture?" I asked her.

"Yes," she answered.

I asked if she'd reconsider if that scene were removed from the script.

"Herbie, I've always wanted to work with Mr. Hitchcock. Take that scene out and tell me when you want me to report."

Hitch and Alma were up at the ranch. I called and told him what she'd told Frings and about my conversation with her. I could sense the anger he felt when he said, "Tell Paramount they must make her report when you call her or I will cancel my contract."

We found a way to end the stalemate. I asked Audrey to come in to approve Edith Head's wardrobe designs before going to her home in Switzerland for the vacation her contract provided. While she was on her vacation, the studio announced that she was pregnant and would have to withdraw from the picture.

The project was abandoned when Hitch refused to replace her.

With *No Bail for the Judge* out of the way, Mary Belle and I took a brief vacation. The morning after I returned to the studio, Hitch walked into my office for his coffee. He placed a book on my desk. "Take a look at our next production. We're moving to MGM for that one," he said.

He then filled his cup and walked to the couch, noticed I'd ignored the book, and, with raised eyebrows, waited for an explanation. I asked if he'd read it. "Not yet," he said. "Herman Citron just gave it to me this morning."

"Hitch," I said, "Dale brought that book home months ago; he was all excited about making a great movie with it. I'm going to tell you what I told him. I don't think we want to spend three months out on the ocean aboard a rusting, battered old freighter, the *Mary Deare,* in stormy weather or aboard oceangoing sailboats, powerboats, even rubber rafts in the cold Atlantic. Maybe even worse, building sections of the *Mary Deare* on rollers in the tank on stage 15, rocking it violently while giant wind machines blow heavy rain over the set and over everybody on the stage.

"There are no beautiful people, or beautiful scenery, and the love interest is missing for two-thirds of the story. When the love interest does enter the scene, the loving is strictly lukewarm. And it's the mystery story to end all mystery stories. I think Sam [Taylor] would run like hell the other way if we asked him to write the screenplay."

Hitch had finished his coffee and was staring at me as he selected one of his favorite Havana cigars. "That's it? You have no other objections to our getting involved in the project?"

I knew he was kidding because there was a hint of a smile in his eyes. "I could find others, Hitch," I told him. We left it at that. Hitch went into his office to look over his mail. The picture was made some time later with Gary Cooper as the star. If I had known Coop was part of the deal, I might have had second thoughts about the project.

Chapter 46

North by Northwest

I knew Hitch had cleared his head of any thoughts about *The Wreck of the* Mary Deare when he began talking about a story that had been building in his mind he was calling *The Man on Lincoln's Nose.* Often in the past, when the conversation would lag, he'd spell out bits and pieces of the story.

It had all started at a luncheon with a newspaper reporter who suggested that Hitch make a film about an important New York executive who is mistaken by some Eastern European country as a spy, determined to destroy them.

He was unable to dismiss the idea he'd been working out in his mind—a chase story starting with the stabbing death of a diplomat from behind the Iron Curtain in the Delegates' Lounge at the United Nations.

Hitch went out to Metro and told the story to Sol Siegel, the head of MGM. When he came back, he didn't need to tell me we'd be moving to Metro. The smile on his face was enough.

Siegel wanted us to take Ernest Lehman as the writer of the screenplay. I would have preferred Sam Taylor, but Lehman was under contract to them. I'd never met him, but I knew he was a highly respected writer with a long list of successful scripts to his credit.

Siegel asked me to come to the studio to discuss the project. I'd known him at Paramount when he produced *Blue Skies.* He got down to business immediately. "Mr. Coleman, we've allotted $2.5 million to your project." I asked him if he'd discussed that figure with Hitch.

"I brought it up with him. He told me money was part of your responsibility. But he indicated he was interested in keeping costs down. He would personally see that the art director didn't overbuild the sets." He would have gone on, but I interrupted his dream.

I told him I'd heard that same story on every one of our pictures. "Did you see our film *Vertigo*?" I asked.

"Of course. I see every one of his pictures."

"When we were preparing that picture, he told Henry Bumstead, our production designer, to keep the size of the sets to the absolute minimum. You may remember the scene in the shipbuilder's office between Jimmy Stewart and Tom Helmore. The scene could have been staged on a set with only two walls.

"The plans Hitch approved had two levels with seven walls, with windows revealing shipbuilding activity. The set was built in sections on rollers to allow each section to be placed before the transparency screen. I don't expect him to be less demanding on this film."

Next I asked, "Did you discuss cast with Mr. Hitchcock?"

"Only that Cary Grant seemed right for the part."

"Well, Mr. Siegel, the story will be developed for Grant and Grace Kelly, if Hitch can lure her back to Hollywood. He feels it's quite possible despite her strong statements to the contrary. With Grant and Kelly, or someone in the same category, we're headed for an extremely costly picture. If $2.5 million is your limit, I'd suggest you forget this project. I'm sure Jack Karp and Barney Balaban will be happy to have it at any figure after the success of *Vertigo.*

"If you want to go ahead knowing all I've told you, I'll do the best I can to bring the picture in without wasting one dollar of Metro's money. But I'll never agree to start with a cutoff at $2.5 million."

I thought we'd reached an understanding, but a storm would be blowing in before we finished shooting.

When I told Hitch about the meeting, he said, "They'll come around."

We moved our offices to a suite in the Thalberg Building at Metro and went to work.

Hitch and I flew to New York to survey the area before he and Lehman started work on the screenplay. I warned Hitch to avoid discussing the assassination sequence with anyone when we went to see the Delegates' Lounge at the United Nations. The official who showed us around did his best to "worm out" of Hitch just how we planned to use the United Nations in our picture. Before we left, he told us that they would have to read our screenplay before approving our filming there.

From New York we headed for Rapid City, South Dakota. When we reached Minneapolis, we were forced to change planes to reach Rapid City. At lunch with a local newspaperman, Hitch described the chase around and over the presidents' sculptures, down the nose of Lincoln to his lips.

As he talked, Hitch sketched it on a paper napkin, highlighting the progress of the stars with little dots. "We're calling the film *The Man on Lincoln's Nose*," he said.

After lunch, Hitch and I flew on to Rapid City. After a day working out details of how we would film the chase, we returned to the studio.

Disturbing news was waiting for us. The newspaperman had written full details of his interview with Hitch. It was published on the front page of the local newspaper. The sketch Hitch had drawn was shown along with the interview. Letters of protest flooded the paper, including one from someone who wrote, "Let that English filmmaker go back to England and have the actors climb around the Queen's nose!"

I received word from the Department of the Interior that our permit for filming at Mount Rushmore had been revoked. After extensive negotiations, the department sent an important executive to discuss the problem with Hitch and me. When we invited him to join us for lunch, he told us that he had been told to accept absolutely nothing from us. Not even a cup of coffee.

He was a fan of Hitchcock films and helped us work out a plan that would allow us to go ahead with the picture. We could build a life-size portion of Lincoln. Just his lips, chin, the tip of his nose, and his shoulders.

Our stars could make their way across the shoulders of Lincoln but were forbidden to touch him.

Bummy Bumstead was working on an important Paramount picture, and the studio refused to let him join us. Robert "Bob" Boyle, whom I'd known at Paramount, was available. I knew he'd worked with Hitch on *Shadow of a Doubt*, and he accepted the assignment. I didn't know how lucky I was. Working closely with Hitch, Bob designed a series of set pieces of the monument and combined them with photographs that could be used as point-of-view shots of the monuments or transparency backgrounds before which the stars could perform their dangerous stunts. Portions of the rubble carved from the faces of the presidents were reproduced in foam rubber.

To photograph the shots of the faces, Bob and a photographer were slowly lowered by ropes from the tops of the heads, time after time, day after day, by park rangers for any camera angle Hitch might want.

Meanwhile, Ernie Lehman, under Hitch's guidance, was busy turning out the screenplay that Hitch was now calling *North by*

Northwest. When he first proposed using that title, I pointed out the contradiction in terms. "You can't read a compass right to left," I told him. "You read it clockwise. Every sailor will be insulted and writing about our carelessness."

"Good!" Hitch responded, "great publicity for the picture!"

He remembered that statement when he told the Universal publicity department to advertise *The Birds* as "*The Birds* Is Coming." He got what he wanted. Educators all over the country complained that it was difficult enough to teach youngsters proper grammar without having a leading filmmaker like Hitchcock hamper their efforts.

Cary Grant agreed to star as Roger Thornhill, a wealthy Madison Avenue advertising executive. Lew Wasserman assigned the task of signing Grant to Herman Citron, who, without consulting me, gave Grant a starting date two months before we would be ready to start production.

Hitch, still hoping that Grace Kelly would leave the Monaco throne to star as Eve Kendall, an undercover American secret agent, was resisting Metro's attempt to push one of its contract stars, Cyd Charisse, as Grant's costar. Siegel was supported by Edd Henry, who, like Herman Citron at Paramount, Arthur Park at Warner Bros., and George Chasen at Disney, looked out for MCA clients in those studios.

But I had my own choice for the part, Eva Marie Saint. With help from her agent, Lawrence Turman, who worked for the Kurt Frings Agency, I won.

James Mason was cast as Phillip Vandamm, head of the Far East spy ring. Jessie Royce Landis as Clara Thornhill, Grant's mother. Leo G. Carroll as the Professor, secretly the top American counterintelligence agent and Saint's boss. Selecting the man to play Mason's assistant, Leonard, was an interesting event. Hitch and I were casting some minor parts, including a cop who would work one day in Chicago and two days near the end of the shooting period—a total of four days, including travel to and from Chicago. Metro's casting director brought in a tall, dark young man with piercing eyes and an intense attitude. We took a quick look. Hitch and I looked at each other. I asked the young man to wait outside for a moment. As soon as the door closed, Hitch asked, "Who are you thinking about?" "Leonard," I answered. Hitch told the casting director to get him. His name was Martin Landau. It was the start of a brilliant career for a deserving and talented actor.

We wanted Edith Head to come with us as costume designer; but she refused to leave Paramount, even for us. The sketches of the costumes for Saint, presented to us by the designer assigned to us by Metro, proved unsuitable.

We decided to dress Saint with clothes from the Bergdorf-Goodman collection in their "Duty Room." I took Eva Marie there. Together, we selected the costumes we felt best suited for each sequence. We asked the lady in charge to show Hitch a couple of dresses for each change, before showing him our selection. It worked perfectly. When I brought Hitch to the store, he bought every costume we'd chosen.

Hitch had long wanted to, somehow, get back at David O. Selznick for the continuous flow of memos he and other directors received from him. *North by Northwest* gave him the perfect opportunity. He told Lehman to write the opening scene, in which Grant leaves his office to go to the Plaza Hotel, with Grant continuously dictating to his secretary along the corridor, down in the elevator, in the lobby of the building, along the sidewalk, in the taxi to the hotel, and to the doorway of the Plaza. Although it was an inside-the-industry joke, it worked and got a big laugh.

I saw that scene repeated one morning at the St. Regis Hotel. Hitch and I were waiting for the elevator on the fifth floor. When it arrived, the door opened, revealing Selznick and his secretary. Although he'd known Hitch for years, there was no acknowledgment. Selznick went right on dictating. When we crossed the lobby and headed for the outside door, he was still at it. As they disappeared into the dining room, the secretary was still trying to keep up with his rapid discourse.

There were many frustrating and irritating moments during the filming of *North by Northwest*. But there were also many amusing incidents that occurred, such as the day we were shooting the scene of Grant, Landis, and the two assassins getting out of the elevator in the lobby of the Plaza Hotel. The camera was in place, holding on the bank of elevator doors. The lights were blazing. The lobby was filled with visitors, photographers, and reporters. All was quiet. The elevator, crowded with Grant, Landis, the assassins, and just plain passengers, was waiting at the second floor for the cue to come down.

Suddenly, the elevator doors next to our elevator opened, and two bewildered people started to step out. When they saw all of us staring at them, they didn't know whether to step back into the elevator and close the doors or to run for the outside—or what the hell to do. So they just stood silently staring at the mob of people. Those two beautiful people were Elizabeth Taylor and Eddie Fisher. It was the first time their affair was revealed to the public. Eddie was still married to Debbie Reynolds.

When authorities at the United Nations read the final screenplay of *North by Northwest,* they turned thumbs down. They would not allow us to film anything on or inside U.N. property.

On the exterior of the U.N. Plaza where the public crosses the vast open area to enter the main public U.N. building, we had to see Grant arrive by taxi, pay the driver, pass the uniformed guards at the gates, cross the plaza, and enter the building. Another important scene was the arrival, by taxi, of the two assassins, one of whom follows the route taken by Grant.

I'd managed to become friendly with an important person in the U.N. security forces. He agreed to allow us to film the two shots under certain conditions. There was a gate into the U.N. property off First Avenue, a little south of the public entrance. "Have your cameras at the gate at exactly 9:00 a.m. I'll leave the gate unlocked for five minutes. Don't be one minute late. You won't have a second chance!" The New York camera crew blew it. They got caught in a traffic jam and arrived too late. Now, I had to find another way to film the scenes.

Anyone who's been around moviemaking very long knows about hiding cameras in vans with curtained sides: Park the van, and when ready, lift little doors just big enough for the camera lens and film the scene. I decided to give it a try. At the U.N. public entrance, there is a little half circle at street level, large enough for two or three cars to stop for a short time. The plan was to pull the van into position. Grant, in one taxi, was parked a short distance up First Avenue. The two "assassins" were in a second taxi just behind Grant's. The cue for Grant's taxi to drive in was when I walked past the van.

The moment the van parked, I started walking past the guards' position. One guard stopped me with, "Mr. Coleman, you've parked your camera van on United Nations property. Please move it immediately." I was surprised more by hearing him call my name than by his knowledge of the hidden camera trick. I dismissed Grant and the others and began looking around for some other way to shoot the scenes we had to have. I found it on Second Avenue.

On the east side of the street workers were dismantling a tall building. The foreman gave me permission to wander around. I knew that a hidden camera, with a long focal-length lens, could film everything we needed.

We shot the scene with Grant. Everything worked fine until he got almost to the entrance, when the gate guard realized who he was and began looking everywhere for our hidden cameras. He'd never seen the "assassins" and paid no attention to the one who entered the building.

With those two scenes in the can, I had just one more shot to make: a shot from the curved driveway along the sidewalk to the line of tall flagpoles and flags of all the nations in the distance. We would use this scene as a transparency background for a scene of Grant getting out of the taxi before entering the U.N. building and also for a shot of the assassin getting out of the taxi and following Grant. We couldn't put an open camera on the curved driveway, so I used a station wagon filled with luggage and clothes hanging from hooks all along the windows. Hidden under the luggage were the cameraman and his assistant. The driver of the station wagon and his passenger were dressed like California tourists. The passenger got out and began shooting pictures in every direction.

Meanwhile, the cameramen slipped a suitcase aside and began filming the scene. Suddenly, a uniformed guard at the delegates' entrance in the distance became suspicious of the station wagon and began walking down to investigate. Two members of our crew who were watching from across First Avenue hurried across and began asking him the meaning of the flags. By the time the guard had gone through all the nations, we had all the footage we needed and drove away.

Sol Siegel's budget arrived for my approval and signature. I didn't bother going through the detail figures. The top sheet was enough: $2.5 million. I returned it to Siegel, unsigned. Before we'd completed filming in New York, I received another budget with the same figures, which I returned unsigned, and reminded Siegel about my statement that I would never sign a budget that didn't reflect the true cost of the picture. I knew he had to be in trouble with Metro's home office, to which he must have given the $2.5 million figure. If he could get my signature on the budget, I would be the one responsible for allowing the picture to go $2 million over his budget. I wouldn't be at all surprised if I found out that someone at the studio had forged my signature and sent the budget on to New York.

We finished our work in New York without any serious problems and moved on to Chicago. During dinner on the train, Hitch asked where I planned to shoot the scenes with the crop-dusting plane attempting to kill Cary Grant. I told him I would look over the area between Chicago and Indianapolis before making a decision. "Remember," Hitch said, "the area has to be absolutely flat with nothing he can run to for cover in any direction."

While he was busy filming the Chicago sequences, I rented a plane and searched all over Indiana and Iowa without finding what we needed. I decided I had to find it somewhere closer to Hollywood.

We completed the Chicago filming and moved to Rapid City and the Mount Rushmore Monument, where we filmed all the scenes, including the monument and the exterior of the center building. Including Grant viewing the heads of the presidents and his talk with Leo G. Carroll and the arrival of Mason, Eva Marie Saint, and Leonard. Also, Saint running to her car and driving away and Carroll loading Grant's "body" in a station wagon and disappearing in the distance.

With the work around Mount Rushmore completed, I moved the company back to the studio.

Almost every day, Hitch was pressing me to find the location for the crop-dusting scenes. Metro had given a two-passenger plane to Robert Taylor during World War II to quiet his demands for an increase in his salary, which was frozen by the government during the war. I was a little nervous flying around in that old plane but agreed to use it. I asked the pilot to head up San Joaquin Valley. Near Blackwells Corner, a little crossroads center on the highway between Bakersfield and Paso Robles, I found what I was searching for: a paved highway with a dirt road coming from nowhere. And as far as I could see there wasn't a tree, a bush, or anything that Grant could run to for safety when chased by the crop duster.

The location was perfect, except for the absence of a cornfield. A few miles away, a farmer had planted a few acres of corn. He agreed to sell me three acres. Bob Boyle had his men drive spikes through boards, bury the boards in the ground, and a few days before we arrived to film the sequence, cut the corn, move it to our location, and stick each cornstalk on a spike. I wasn't sure the little cornfield would satisfy Hitch, but he didn't complain when we arrived to shoot the sequence. I held my breath each time the plane dived at Grant. I expected the rush of air to blow our cornfield into the next county. But the cornfield was still standing there, a little droopy, when we drove away on the last day of filming.

For the scene of Mason's plane landing near his home at Mount Rushmore, we picked a dirt strip skirting highway 101 near Moorpark, shot it late in the day, and printed it for night. The result wasn't all I'd hoped it would be. I decided to take one last look at the scene before telling our editor, George Tomasini, to use it. I joined George in the projection room. We were about to turn the lights out and start the film when Sol Siegel's "hatchet man" (I can't remember his name) walked in. It took only a couple of minutes to run the film. When the lights came on, I told George to cut it into the picture. Siegel's man stood up and said, "Mr. Coleman. We've decided you're responsible for the budget of this picture going $2 million over the budget." I waited for him to go on. "If you'd told Mr. Hitchcock the picture would cost over $4 million, he would have cut the screenplay to fit our $2.5 million." His statement was so ridiculous I didn't bother to answer. I just walked out and went back to the stage where Hitch was working.

He was sitting in his stage dressing room lighting one of his Havana cigars. I sat down beside him. He lowered the cigar from his lips and solemnly said, "I've just learned why you've allowed this picture to go $2 million over budget." I waited for him to continue. "If you had told me we could not meet Metro's budget, I would have cut the screenplay." His attempt to be serious was too much. Hitch seldom allowed himself to laugh out loud, but he gave in.

"I just heard the same statement from Siegel's man," I told him. "Where did you hear it?"

"From Mr. Siegel. You just missed him."

The next complaint came from Cary Grant. He walked up to me on the stage and demanded to know when I was going to finish the picture. I could sense by the tone of his voice that he was spoiling for an argument. "After today, five days with you. Why do you want to know?"

"Because I'm working for nothing!"

"$5,000 a day is nothing?" I asked.

"Every dollar of that $5,000 goes to the Internal Revenue Service," he said.

"You were the one who insisted on going on salary two months before our start date. Your guarantee of $450,000 was all paid to you before we started shooting."

"When Herman Citron told me Hitch wanted me for the picture, I told him I had an offer from Fox and I would take the one that started first. When I told him the start date of the Fox picture, he told me Hitch would start two weeks before Fox."

I knew I had to find a way to calm Grant, or Hitch would have an unhappy and probably uncooperative star on his hands. The solution for our problem came later that same day. I got Cary in his dressing room and started to say, "Cary, work for us the last five days for nothing." Before I could finish my proposal, he exploded. "That's what I'm doing now!"

"Hear the rest of it, Cary," I insisted. "You're taking a vacation in London as soon as we finish. Work for nothing the next five days, and I'll give you a drawing account for 5,000 English pounds for just one press interview on *North by Northwest*."

He calmed down considerably while I talked. I gave him a moment to think about my proposal and then added more bait. "Tax free," I said.

As I left his dressing room, I saw him reach for his telephone. I expected Stanley Fox, Grant's attorney, to drop in sometime that day, and I wasn't disappointed when he joined me on the set within an hour.

"What's this crazy proposal you made to Cary? That he work the last five days for nothing? We have a contract, you know."

"According to Cary, that $25,000 goes directly to the IRS. I'm offering 5,000 pounds tax free for one hour with the press in London."

He joined Grant in his dressing room, and when he came out, he told me we had a deal.

We finished the picture and moved back to our offices at Paramount.

North by Northwest was a huge success at the box office, not only in the States but all over the world.

Robert Burks was nominated for an Oscar for his photography but failed to win. It was the same for George Tomasini's editing.

We were outraged that Robert Boyle didn't win an Oscar for his universally acclaimed set design. Being nominated was little solace.

After failing to win an Oscar for *Vertigo,* Hitch had become convinced that his peers would never acknowledge his talents. At times, he would become discouraged. But with the arrival of another challenging story, he would quietly resume his role of Master of Suspense.

Chapter 47

A Career Decision

Suggestions about our next project were coming in from all directions, but nothing arousing any enthusiasm arrived. Hitch was content to rest for a while. He and Alma went north to the ranch. Left alone, I began to reflect on the years that had passed since I joined the Hitchcock organization and the major events that had changed the course of my life.

The first, of course, was meeting Hitch at Warner Bros. on the set of *Dial M for Murder.* The second event was the arrival in Nice, France, on *To Catch a Thief,* of the cable offering me the job of director on the pilot of the new television series *Nurses.* And Hitch's counteroffer of a great, and profitable, executive position with his company, which I accepted.

The third was my first serious disagreement with Hitch, which happened on *Vertigo* when I opposed his selection of Maxwell Anderson to write the screenplay. Hitch won the argument, but in the end, he lost.

I won more than just getting the right man to write the screenplay. I won the respect of Hollywood's finest agent, Irving Lazar. He told me he wanted to be my agent when I left Hitchcock. Only in our industry would one know how important that offer would be to my career in films.

Next came *No Bail for the Judge* and my decision to let Audrey Hepburn read the screenplay with the objectionable scene in Hyde Park, which resulted in the cancellation of the picture and a brief chilled atmosphere in the office. The more I thought about the years we'd been together, the more I realized time was slipping away and I had to make a move if I was to reach the goal I'd set for myself the day I walked into the Paramount Pictures Studio thirty-two years before.

When Hitch returned to the office, he brought along a book with the title of *Psycho,* written by Robert Bloch. "Read it, and we'll talk," he said.

An hour later I went into his office, laid the book on his desk, and asked why he wanted me to read material his TV unit would be producing.

"It's not for them. I'm going to try something new. Finance it with my own money. $500,000. Lew [Wasserman] invited us to come to Universal. We'll use their contract people. Cameramen, soundmen, everyone. And no overhead charge."

"What about the people who've been loyal to you, Hitch? Bob Burks? Bummy? Edith Head? George Tomasini? And all the others?"

"We can't afford them, Herbie."

"Neither can you afford Sam Taylor. Or Ernie Lehman. Who do you have in mind for the script?"

"Joan's recommended a bright young television writer who has written some good things for her. He's coming in to see us."

There it was again. Joan Harrison! Her meddling in the editing of *Vertigo* cost Paramount thousands of dollars and almost caused me to end my association with Hitch and Paramount. And now she's pushing herself into the feature arm of the organization. This was a violation of the agreement between Hitch and me that provided that she would have nothing to do with the features and I would stay out of *Alfred Hitchcock Presents.*

I didn't like what I saw when the writer came to see us, and I got out of the meeting as gracefully as I could. They met two or three times, and then Hitch let him go back East with his "friend" to write the script.

Hitch was up at the ranch when the script arrived.

After skimming a few pages, I called him and told him I was mailing the script to the ranch. He asked me to read the whole script and call him before mailing it.

I read it twice. I thought about it a long time, trying, unsuccessfully, to find a single scene written with an understanding of what Robert Bloch had tried to convey to his readers.

Hitch answered my call with a single word, "Well?"

"If I tell you what I think of his work, you'll say 'You didn't like him, so how can you be objective?'"

"That's your word. Tell me, is it good enough?"

"I'll read you one scene, Hitch, and you decide for yourself." I read the last scene in the script, in which the girl, Vera Miles, goes down into the basement and discovers the body of Tony Perkins's mother. It went something like this: "Vera turns the chair around, the body falls to the floor revealing the glass eyes and the painted face of a rag doll."

I heard Hitch almost gasp for breath before asking, "What did he write that for?"

"I don't know, Hitch. What do you want me to do with the script?"

"Burn it. We'll have to find a new writer."

I didn't burn it. I sent it to the story department with orders to file it and forget it.

Hitch was in no hurry to get back to the studio. And I began to have too much time to think about the future. My urge to get away became an obsession. It began to disturb Mary Belle and the kids. "You've got to end this. We are your family. Not Hitch and his films. Tell him and get it over with."

I turned for comfort to my closest friends at the studio. When I asked Jack Karp if he would break the news to Hitch, he said, "Herbie, this is something only you can do. Not me, Herman Citron, or even Lew Wasserman."

Hitch came back from the ranch and started a search for the new writer. He sensed that there was something growing between us but waited patiently for an explanation. Then came the day I knew I had to break the news.

He and Alma were going back to the ranch after he finished shooting one of his half-hour shows.

When I got up that morning, after a restless night, I skipped my usual swim and drove directly to our church to seek the advice of our minister, James Stewart. Jim, a World War II Navy fighter pilot, had become our friend the day he came to our home on the oceanfront to ask us to become members of his new Presbyterian church in Costa Mesa.

To my dismay, the doors of the church were all locked. I turned away and drove on to the studio. I'd told Hitch I was going to drop by the stage where he was shooting.

He was behind schedule and pushing his staff to finish so he could make the last plane to San Francisco. While I waited, I rehearsed over and over the words I would use to break the news.

The streets around the stage were dark and deserted when we came from the stage.

He headed directly for the waiting limousine.

I just blurted out, "Hitch, I've decided it's time for me to move on."

He stopped dead in his tracks and stared at me. His usual somber, expressionless features revealed nothing. Then he asked, haltingly, "Would a full producer credit and more money change your mind, Herbie?"

I told Hitch it was now or never. Not another word was spoken. He got in his limousine and drove away. During the two weeks he and Alma remained at the ranch, I wrote him a long letter, revealing in detail my reasons for resigning—concluding with my burning ambition to become an independent producer, writer, and director.

I gave it to Dolores with instructions to clear Hitch's desk of everything but the letter before he returned. Continuing postproduction on *North by Northwest* prevented me from clearing my office before they came back. I was at my desk. The doors to Dolores's office were open when Hitch walked in.

Without even glancing toward where I sat, he disappeared into his office without acknowledging Dolores's greeting. His door was still closed when I left for the day.

This routine continued for a number of days. Then one morning, I looked up to find Hitch standing in my doorway. "Do you need me for anything, Herbie?"

I asked if he'd care for coffee. He nodded and helped himself. He settled in his usual spot on the couch. "Do you still feel the same about leaving, Herbie?"

"I'm afraid so, Hitch. But if there's anything I can do to help get *Psycho* off to a good start, just tell me what it is."

He asked me to stay and help with the casting. And make the deal with Wasserman to film the picture at Universal.

He was not enthusiastic about my choice of Anthony Perkins for Norman Bates. He admitted he'd never seen Perkins in *Fear Strikes Out.* He agreed to look at the first reel of the picture. I told the projectionist to stop the running after the first reel, but Hitch liked what he saw and sat through the whole picture. When the lights came on, he said I was right and signed Tony for the part.

I wanted Maureen O'Sullivan for Marion Crane, but Hitch signed Janet Leigh. There was never any disagreement for Lila Crane. Vera Miles was a sure bet for the part. No one could have been better.

I arranged a meeting with Albert Dorskin in his office at Universal to discuss the terms under which Hitch would move to their studio and produce *Psycho.*

I was surprised to find Lew Wasserman sitting in Dorskin's office when I arrived. We exchanged the usual studio gossip, and then Lew got up to leave. Just before he disappeared through the door to the outside, he turned to Dorskin and said, "Make Herbie the same deal we have with Universal."

I managed to call to him before he closed the door, "Lew, Hitch told me there would be no overhead charges!"

He didn't react. Just kept going and closed the door. Dorskin answered for Lew, "That's right. We'll charge you no overhead."

"What do we get free for agreeing to move this project to Universal?"

"Offices. Projection rooms. Stage space. Cameras. Lighting equipment, grip equipment. Sound. Everything you're getting, and paying for, at Paramount."

"Guaranteed?" I asked.

"Office space and projection rooms. Everything else when available. If we get busy and have to rent equipment, you'll have to pay for it," he answered.

"No deal, Mr. Dorskin. That's the oldest scam in our business. Assign your equipment to your own productions, and rent equipment for outsiders."

I had Paramount's budget department make comparative budgets, using our 25 percent overhead added to the cost of the picture. And the same budget using Universal's approach to picture cost, with free office space and projection rooms and renting all equipment.

I showed Hitch the savings he could realize if he made *Psycho* at Paramount, but he still decided to make the picture at Universal.

Friends wanted to have a farewell party for me on my last day at the studio, but I asked them to forget it. They did bring a cartoon signed by many with whom I'd worked during my thirty-two years.

Hitch joined me for our final cocktail. I had trouble concealing my thoughts. I could see he had the same problem. For me it was like telling an older brother good-bye. We got through it somehow.

Hitch's final words were, "Alma's not happy you're leaving." He didn't say how he felt.

The twilight was fading fast as I watched him drive away. I walked toward the front gate. Tom, the uniformed officer, sitting in his little cubbyhole, called out, "Good night, Herbie."

He didn't know I wouldn't be coming back, or he would have said, "Good-bye."

I walked through the gate, moved a short way down Bronson Avenue, and turned to take one last look at the high arched entrance with the words "Paramount Pictures" inviting the world to enjoy its films.

Chapter 48

Whispering Smith

Word spread from studio to studio that I'd left Paramount, and on the third day of my "retirement," I got a call from Alan Miller, the president of Revue Productions, the television arm of MCA, the giant talent agency that had purchased Universal.

I'd met Alan, or, as his close friends called him, Pinky, when he was an MCA partner spending much of his time representing Hitch.

His nickname had been with him since childhood. Given to him because of his rosy complexion. He was a tall, slender, friendly gentleman, with tremendous executive ability. He invited me to join him for lunch the following day.

I sat with him in the Universal dining room and listened while he made me an offer I knew I couldn't refuse.

"You know Audie Murphy, don't you?" he asked.

"I've considered Audie a friend of mine from the first day he reported for work on a film called *Beyond Glory*. John Farrow was the director. I was his assistant."

"Would you like to be working with him again?" Pinky asked.

"Maybe, when my vacation is over," I told him.

"The job I'm going to offer you can't wait a month, or a week, not even a day. We have a series *Whispering Smith* starring Audie and Guy Mitchell that's stalled because Audie is not happy with the first eight shows. I want you to take over. Look at the eight. Try to save them. Do whatever you want with them.

"Rewrite, direct the retakes. Have them ready by the date they go on the air. Our contract with the network is for twenty-three shows. I'll give you a contract for saving the eight. And a separate contract as producer/director/writer for the remaining fifteen."

At four that afternoon, when I left Universal, I had an unbelievable contract, an office, and a private parking place with my name painted on it. What I liked most about the contract was my position. For the first time in my career, I was in complete charge. At least I thought so. I had a big surprise coming.

A few days after I reported to the studio, Mary Lou Stewart, the most competent secretary I ever had, came into my office and told me that Dick Lewis had tried to walk past her and come into my office unannounced. "I stopped him. He's pacing up and down my office right now. Mad as a hornet."

"Who is Dick Lewis?" I asked.

"Your executive producer. Didn't you know you have an executive producer?"

I smiled at her. I had already become fond of her. Especially the way she ran the office—and me.

"I do now. Send him in."

He didn't waste time trying to impress me that he was the most important person on *Whispering Smith.*

"Alan Miller tells me you're discarding two of my *Whispering Smith* films. Why didn't you come to me? Didn't you know I am the executive producer of this series?"

"I didn't even know you existed until my secretary told me you were waiting to see me."

"You're to put those other two segments back on your schedule."

"They're dead and buried as far as I'm concerned. Take your complaint to Alan Miller."

He stared at me, "On your way out ask Miss Stewart to come in," I said.

His face flushed at the insult. He was, obviously, so angry he couldn't speak. If he ever talked to Pinky about it, it stopped there.

I asked Audie to work with me on the writing. He brought along a man in whom he had complete confidence, Willard Willingham. I'd known Willard ever since he was a kid living on the Paramount Ranch out in Malibu Canyon. He was one of the most daring stuntmen and had worked for me many times as a stunt double for Alan Ladd and others. He was very close to Audie and had been working with all the writers on Audie's pictures. I agreed to have him work with me.

The schedule on the series was for two segments to be filmed in five days.

Two days on the stage and a half day on the Denver Street and sheriff's office on the back lot. Each segment with a different director.

I was rehearsing a scene on the remake of the first of the six shows on the stage, the silence broken only by the words spoken by the actors.

Suddenly, the silence was shattered by the sound of the stage door opening and a man's voice shouting, "Coffee wagon!"

All the lights on the set were extinguished, and everyone rushed out the door to the coffee wagon parked just outside. I couldn't believe what was happening. I asked my assistant if this was a regular event.

"Every morning and afternoon," he said.

I checked my watch and checked it again when all had returned to their places, and I was ready to resume the rehearsal. A little over half an hour lost. The scene was repeated in the afternoon. The total loss of shooting time was about an hour.

I asked my assistant to call Paul Donneley, the studio's production manager, and have him come to the set. When he arrived, I told him I wanted coffee, rolls, and doughnuts on the set the following day and everyday *Whispering Smith* was shooting. "And the company will pay for it," I told him.

He told me he didn't have the authority to grant my wish.

"You'll have to see Mr. Dorskin," he said.

When Al Dorskin refused to agree to charge the coffee and doughnuts to the company, I told him if it wasn't on the set when I arrived the next morning, I would go to Lew Wasserman.

Donneley came back to the set and told me they would have the coffee and things on the set the next morning. "You pay for it with your personal check, and I'll pay you back in cash. But don't let the other producers know." Naturally, I spread the news, and soon every set had free coffee and rolls.

I was casting on one *Whispering Smith* that I would direct, I can't remember its title. It was a story of an old western woman who was raising her teenaged daughter to seduce Whispering Smith, so her teenaged son could challenge Whispering to a shootout and kill him. Her husband had been an outlaw whom Whispering had killed in a fair fight. The old woman was bent on revenge.

The Revue casting director suggested I interview someone that Revue thought had more than his share of talent. Into my office walked a sandy haired, pleasant young man. I watched his reactions to the story and told him the part was his. He turned out to be one of the finest producers, directors, and actors around today, and he got his start on *Whispering Smith*. His name was Robert Redford. I don't think he considers me the best director he ever worked with. How could he? Two and a half days to film forty pages, sixteen pages per day.

The next morning we moved to the exterior sets on the Denver Street. Before the cast arrived, I showed Lionel (Curly) Lindon, the cameraman, my plan for the half day we had to cover all the scenes in the script.

"Twenty-six setups for the gunfight alone!" he said. "Impossible!"

"You tell me the order you'd like me to stage the scenes, Curly, and you can report to the next director at one o'clock."

Curly shook his head doubtfully and looked around the street. "Well, the sun will hit the west side of the street first, so we'll start there. Then cover the north side. By that time the sun will be high enough to shoot to the south. We'll leave the east side for last. You're going to drive your script supervisor nuts trying to keep the looks and movements straight."

Curly took charge. He kept his crew on the run. At 12:30, I turned the company over to the next director.

Just five days after I finished on the street, the cutter (that's what we called them back in the days before they started calling themselves editors) said he was ready to show me the final cut of Redford's picture.

The projection room was filled with some twenty people when I arrived. Dick Lewis was sitting at a desk with a light shining on a script. The cutter was sitting next to him. The constant loud conversation from everyone almost completely covered the dialogue from the cast. By the end of the first reel, I'd had it and walked out.

Mary Lou told me the running was SOP—standard operating procedure at Revue. "Every department sees the picture at the same time. I'll bet no one told you each reel of your picture had a different cutter, and each cut his reel the way he wanted to."

I met with Pinky Miller and told him that I was going to see my pictures alone and that others could see it after I approved it.

Alan said, "You're the producer. It's your series. Do it your way."

Lewis had to accept Alan's decision. I knew he would search for some way to get even.

Lew Wasserman and Pinky were satisfied with the shows I was turning out. But unexpected trouble was soon to be upon us. The Writers Guild of America called a strike. Of the twenty-three shows we were to deliver to the network, sixteen were completed.

I had three scripts ready to go before the cameras, and guild writers were at work on the final four but were forbidden to continue to work for us. The studio offered to provide nonunion writers to complete the work on the four.

Audie agreed that we should produce the three and postpone the final four until the strike was over. I told Pinky of our decision.

"You'll have to select someone to produce those three," Pinky said. "We have something else for you. The Writers Guild has approved an independent company, J&M Productions, to produce a series, *Checkmate*, here at Universal, using the members of their guild. If you have an agent, tell him to see me." I told him Larry Turman at the Kurt Frings Agency was representing me.

I turned the final three *Whispering Smith* shows over to Willard Willingham. He would produce them, and I would supervise his work.

Chapter 49

Checkmate

Larry, all smiles, came to me after his meeting with Pinky.

He told me that MCA was offering me a seven-year contract, $1,000 per week to start. Every perk I'd told him to fight for. "They're high on you, Herbie. I'd advise you to sign."

Checkmate would be a CBS-TV prime-time special, directly under the supervision of Guy della Cioppa, the head of CBS. I'd met Guy and had great respect for him.

I was pleased when Pinky told me that Maxwell Shane would produce alternate episodes of *Checkmate.* "You'll each have your own unit and be completely independent of each other." Max Shane had a long and distinguished record as a screenwriter. If Pinky had asked my opinion of a second producer, I would also have selected Max.

CBS gave a big party to introduce Max and me to the organization and the press. Guy was very friendly, and I left the party happy to be with them.

The studio wanted us to use the back lot as the exterior of the Checkmate Detective Agency offices. I refused to go along and went to San Francisco. I've forgotten the exact location of the building we used. As long as I remained with the series, it was filmed in the city of San Francisco. But as soon as I quit, they went back to Universal's back lot and used the Colonial Street as San Francisco. It gave the series the feeling of being in the Deep South. They were more interested in the money they would save than in authenticity.

Sebastian Cabot was the unanimous choice to be the senior partner of the firm. I was cool on the studio's choice of Tony George as second in command and reluctant to accept Doug McClure, but they convinced me that we needed a young, handsome leading man to attract the youthful audience.

I asked Stirling Silliphant to write my first script. You may remember him. He won an Oscar for his screenplay *In the Heat of the Night.*

I also brought in one of my favorite screenwriters, Jonathan Latimer, who wrote the screenplay for *The Big Clock.* I asked Jonathan to write a script for Laughton with some of the feel of *The Big Clock.*

Laughton, a very wealthy San Francisco businessman who has been receiving threats on his life, comes to Checkmate. The detectives' most serious problem is finding someplace to hide Laughton while they solve the mystery of why he is being threatened and by whom.

Jonathan and I came up with what we thought was an original plan: Let Laughton grow a grubby beard. Dress him like a poor fisherman and have him among the men who come daily to sit on the Monterey pier holding a fishing rod.

Pinky Miller read the script and was enthusiastic about having Laughton, whom he had once represented, take the part.

Laughton was living in an old, stucco mansion at the very end of Curzon Street in Hollywood. We arrived about noon. At my first knock, the door was opened by Laughton's butler.

"Mr. Laughton's waiting for you by the pool." He pointed to a path leading around a corner of the house. We fought our way along the broken cement walk, pulling the untended bushes aside until Laughton came into view. He was sitting beside the pool.

It was obvious that the sandstone pool hadn't been cleaned for weeks. Laughton didn't rise to greet us. He couldn't. His pants were open, and his testicles were exposed to the hot sun. His explanation was brief: "You know my problem, Alan." He didn't bother to cover himself.

He listened, without comment, while I told him the story from the first scene up to the point where I described him sitting among the fishermen. Then he exploded, "Mr. Coleman, why would you ever think I, Charles Laughton, would sit around with filthy, smelly fishermen on a dirty pier? And of all things, pulling slimy fish from the water!"

"But it wouldn't be Charles Laughton sitting there, Mr. Laughton. It would be Mr. Baxter."

"People would always remember Charles Laughton with that beard. There are other artists for you, Mr. Coleman."

We left soon after our conversation, and on the way back to the studio Pinky told me about Laughton's cancer.

It was about that time I found out that Dick Lewis was back in my life. He came to my office with a copy of Silliphant's screenplay and wanted changes and additions made. I told him to put them in writing and I would study them.

After he left, I went to see Pinky, who explained that it was necessary to have someone check on the material Max and I were considering. "You and Max might be having writers working on similar stories. Dick Lewis will only keep you both advised about what the other is doing."

I discovered that Lewis was letting his friends outside the business read our scripts and was bringing their suggestions to us. I decided *Checkmate* was not for me. I had two additional scripts in work and would leave the studio when they were completed.

I went to Pinky and told him of my plans. He pleaded with me to sign the contract. When I told him I couldn't work with someone for whom I had no respect, he said, "It won't be long before you will be an executive producer." We left it at that for the time being.

I had a writer working on a script in which a shy, wealthy young girl in fear of her life slips away from her New York home on East 61st Street. At the San Francisco airport she sees the man she has been fleeing from. Desperate at finding herself in a strange city, she finds the name of the Checkmate Detective Agency in the phonebook and goes to its headquarters.

I had chosen a newcomer for the lead part. She was everything we wanted. Beautiful. Shy. Like a fawn about to flee from the hounds baying in the distance.

Lewis came to me demanding I cast one of MCA' s clients, Anna Marie Albergetti, in the part. I'd met Anna Marie one night down by the Tiber River under the Ponte St. Angelo when we were filming some of the scenes on *Roman Holiday.* She was a charming girl. An actress I'd welcome in the right part. But she was far from the shy creature we'd described in the screenplay.

I would have accepted her as a partner in the Checkmate agency. Even Laughton would have accepted her as the person to save him.

I told Larry to discontinue dealing with the studio and walked away from what could have been a wonderful association with Pinky Miller and Lew Wasserman.

Offers from various independent producers in the television field were considered and rejected. I'd made up my mind to return to features as a director.

Chapter 50

Posse from Hell

Although Larry Turman was convinced that I'd made a mistake turning down the offer MCA had made, he knew Universal was planning to approve Gordon Kay's production of a new Audie Murphy western to be called *Posse from Hell,* and he wasted no time selling me to Gordon.

The screenplay, written by Clair Huffaker from his own novel, at first glance seemed to be just another tale of escaped convicts riding late at night into a small frontier town called Paradise, killing the marshal, and kidnapping the town's prettiest girl.

But a closer look at Huffaker's work revealed he had given his screenplay an important new element. He wrote how the lives of a posse of seven men, all but one, a greenhorn from the East, natives of Paradise, are changed as they track the killers of the marshal and the kidnappers of the girl.

I was shown a test of an actor for the part of the leader of the outlaws. But it was not the actor who caught my attention.

It was the actress in the scene. A young New York actress, Zohra Lampert.

I was drawn to her by the same feeling I'd felt the afternoon in New York when I saw Shirley MacLaine in *Pajama Game.* I met with her the following day and, after a brief conversation, told her the part was hers.

A few days before we were scheduled to start filming *Posse from Hell* on one of Universal's stages, I took Cliff Stone, our semiretired, top-notch cameraman, to Lone Pine. At each site I explained how I would stage the scenes and listened to Cliff's suggestions. When we arrived back at our headquarters at the Dow Hotel, he took me aside and said, "In over thirty years as a cameraman, this is the first time any director has ever taken the time to choose the locations for the best light. And the time of day to be there ready to go. If you'll stick to your schedule, I promise to give you a beautiful picture." I did, and he did.

It was cold the morning we were scheduled to start shooting the picture on one of the Universal stages. At six, I dived naked into our unheated pool. Pulled my daily fifty laps. And thirty minutes later, I was on my way to Universal Studio, sixty-five miles away.

Posse from Hell wasn't the greatest project that was going before the cameras in 1962. The budget was modest, and Audie wasn't the greatest star to appear in a movie that year. But he was my star, my friend, my hero, and a hell of a good actor in the right part, and Clair Huffaker had given him that part. It was up to me to see that it all came out on the screen.

When I walked on the stage, I could feel the friendly atmosphere my friends and coworkers had prepared for me. The camera was ready; the crew was putting the final touches to the lighting. My director's chair was in its place under the camera. But it wasn't a regular director's chair. It was different. The frame was solid oak. The seat and backrest were hand-tooled cowhide with my name in black letters. Attached to one of the arms was a similar hand-tooled leather attaché case.

As I stood looking at it, Willard Willingham joined me. "Can you guess who had that made for you?" he asked.

"Audie, for sure," I answered.

I took off my topcoat and dropped it over the chair. When Audie arrived, he saw my coat covering the chair and asked, "What's the matter? Are you ashamed of it?"

"No." I answered. "I haven't earned it yet. When I walk off this stage tonight, sure all of us gave our best today, I'll be sitting in that chair when you arrive tomorrow morning."

At six that evening, when Ray Gosnell, my assistant, called out, "Wrap it up!" I didn't walk off that stage. I was so keyed up, my feet were six feet in the air. When Audie arrived the next morning, I had my butt firmly planted in the chair.

During the day, a telegram arrived from Hitch. It said, "Remember, it's only a movie." It was a phrase he often used when someone came to him with a problem.

We finished the interiors and moved to Lone Pine. We were a happy company, and our filming continued without any serious problems until a sudden storm swept down from high mountains and left a blanket of snow over the Alabama Hills.

Clair Huffaker's story gave a feeling of summer heat, and I'd kept that impression dominant from the opening scene of the picture in which Murphy answers the call from his friends in Paradise to hunt down Marrow and his vicious gang.

Then, one morning at breakfast, I sat looking out the window of the restaurant, watching the snowflakes drifting down, wondering how I could fit snow into the film without destroying the mood I'd established.

Suddenly, the answer came to me. I remembered John Ford's great western, *Stagecoach.* His film was a story of movement across the West. He used the weather he found each day. Sun, rain, or snow, the stagecoach raced on. I remembered what I felt about the cold, early dawn with the sun not yet above the eastern horizon. The heat of a shadowless noon. The sunset with the long shadows of the pinnacles stretching across the Monument Valley landscape.

Our film was also a story of movement. The outlaws, followed by our posse, kept on the move. If Ford could disregard continuity on his major, expensive production, so could I on our modest film.

I called Ray Gosnell and said, "This snow isn't a disaster, Ray, it's an asset we could never have afforded. Let's get everyone out to the Alabama Hills as fast as possible." I wasn't worried about complaints from our cast, staff, or crew. I'd known from the first day they were with me.

During the day I began to pray the snow would continue until we completed filming the sequence. My prayers were answered. And Universal's executives were happy with the results.

The weather changed again, but we continued to shoot while Universal's location department found a suitable substitute.

They sent up photographs of the Fox Ranch near Malibu Canyon. One look, and I told our production manager to get us there as quickly as possible.

We didn't have Mt. Whitney as a backdrop, but the rugged range seen in the distance served us well for the scenes in which, following a second sadistic attack by Morrow and his gang, Murphy finds Lampert abandoned and left to die in the badlands. She is placed on a travois, and her uncle is told to get her back to Paradise. Also, the location was perfect for the final scene of the picture, in which Murphy and Lampert visit the Paradise cemetery where fresh graves and wooden crosses mark the final resting places for the marshal, Rudolph Acosta, and the six other victims of the outlaw gang.

Only the marshal's grave is decorated with flowers. Murphy kneels, takes a single flower, and places it on the grave of the Indian who gave his life to save others in the posse.

Lampert lets her eyes wander across the graves, turns to Murphy as he rises with her back to the camera, and tells him that there were good people in Paradise.

Murphy tells her there are still good people in Paradise. She wants to know who they are. He names three men. She raises her hand to her head as a sudden gust of wind disturbs her hair. But the hand stops in midair as Murphy softly adds, "You." All of her hope for Murphy's respect and love is revealed in the trembling hand. Only then did I allow the audience to see her face.

When I was working with Willie Wyler on *Carrie* with Lawrence Olivier and Jennifer Jones, I watched Willie use the same director's touch for the most dramatic moment in the picture. Olivier had given up everything in life for his love of Jones, a dirt-poor farmer's daughter, who had used him to climb the social ladder in Chicago. After months of poverty in an attic room, Olivier comes home from another day of trudging, hopelessly, around the city searching for a job, any job. His clothes are wet, dirty, and ragged.

Jones watches him cross the room. As he reaches a dresser, with his back to Jones and the camera, his hands go to the collar button at the back of his neck. But Willie never allows them to get there. He nods to Jones.

"I'm leaving you," she says.

His hands pause in midair and begin to tremble.

I'd waited ten years to find an opportunity to steal that touch from Willie.

I'd been blessed with a wonderful staff and crew on *Posse from Hell.* Frederic Knutson, one of the finest editors in the business, called and said he was ready to show me the rough cut. All I could say after the running was, "Fred, I just saw a picture better than the one I directed."

Everyone at Universal was happy with *Posse from Hell,* and the critics were kind to me.

I didn't have to wait long for another offer. Another Audie Murphy picture, at Twentieth Century–Fox.

Chapter 51

Battle at Bloody Beach

Richard "Dick" Maibaum, an old and respected friend from my days at Paramount, with whom I'd worked when he was the producer of *The Big Clock,* signed me to direct *Battle at Bloody Beach.* It would be a Twentieth Century–Fox release, and we would be headquartered at the old Fox Studio at the corner of Sunset and Western, the studio where I'd first tried to get a job on that September morning in 1926.

The memories of that day passed from my mind. I drove across the street to the entrance and gave my name to the guard. He pointed down the studio street and said, "You'll find your name on a parking place down the street on the left. There's an entrance to the executive building along that path to the right."

The corridor of that old building didn't have the marble floor of Paramount's Marble Hall, but it did have my name in large gold letters on the door of one of the suites. I didn't have my wonderful secretary, Mary Lou Stewart. In fact, I had no secretary at all.

Dick came in from his office down the hall. I told him he'd given me a screenplay that gave me the opportunity of presenting Audie in a role reminiscent of his *To Hell and Back* film. I told him I could give him a picture he would be proud of, if he gave me the actors and the schedule that would give me time to develop their relationships.

Lionel "Curly" Lindon, the fastest cameraman in our business, would give me more time to work with the cast. "You know Chico Day, Dick? You give me Chico and Curly, and you can take a day out of whatever schedule you give me."

He promised to have the unit production manager, "Colonel" Harold Knox, go after them. Knox reported back a few days later. "'Curly' Lindon is in Europe on a picture and won't be available. Chico Day is on a picture at Paramount and won't finish in time to prepare our picture. Besides, his salary is way above what we have in the budget. Kenny Peach will finish the picture he's working on. I've talked to him. He knows you and would like to work with you."

"Kenny will be fine. He's a very good cameraman. Let's sign him before someone else grabs him."

Knox gave me a list of first assistants. I'd heard of some of them, but everyone was from the independent field. I passed on everyone on the list. I was determined to have Chico with me. I called him. He told me Knox had offered scale. "And besides, Herbie," he said, "I won't have time to prepare your picture."

I asked him if he'd take the picture if I would do the preparation and see that he was paid $750.00 a week.

"$750.00 a week! They'll never go for it," Chico said.

"I'll have Knox call you again. Give him the $750.00 figure. He'll come running to me. I'll show him how he can afford it."

Knox was in a tizzy when he reported his conversation with Chico. "You'll never believe what Chico asked for! $750.00 a week!"

"Get your pencil and paper, Harold," I said. "How many extras do you have in the budget to double as guerrillas and Japanese soldiers?"

"Fifty," he answered.

"How much will you save if I tell you forty-five will do? Salary, overtime, food, and housing? Costumes? Rifles and ammunition? Stunt adjustments?" Harold had been around the picture business. He stopped adding and said, "Chico belongs to you." It wasn't long before Knox had joined the "Chico Boosters Club."

"Where's the location for the battle around the subchaser?" I asked Dick.

"Catalina Island," Dick answered, enthusiastically. "You want to take a look at it? How about tomorrow?"

A studio car dropped us at the dock in San Pedro. An H-10 water taxi was waiting. A stiff wind was sending a spray of cold channel Pacific in our faces. I began to get a little worried as Catalina Island became visible in the distance.

I'd sailed our racing sloop *Toroa* many times on a course almost exactly like the one we were following. I knew we would land somewhere close to Long Point.

I asked Dick, "You haven't picked a cove on the north side of Catalina, have you?"

"The cove is exactly the same as I've described it in the script, Herbie. Wait 'til you see it."

The water taxi stopped 100 feet or so from the beach. "I can't go in any closer," the boatman said. "You'll have to row in from here." Dick and I climbed into the rubber raft and headed for the beach through the swells. I saw Dick was beginning to have doubts about getting ashore. We made it by wading the last few feet when the raft grounded.

I took a quick look around at the cove. The sun had reached only about one-third of the west end of the beach and it was almost eleven o'clock.

The rest of the beach to the east was in deep shadow. I told Dick we were in serious trouble. "Kenny Peach won't like this. He'll be forced to use lights most of the time. I won't be able to shoot in continuity, but I've had that problem before and can manage."

We spent some time trudging around in the soft sand discussing the scenes scheduled for filming in the cove. We climbed aboard the old subchaser they' d brought over to the island and tied up, the stem deck barely above the water, midship and bow well up on the beach.

I looked at the area below deck where I'd stage the scenes with all the cast during the battle. It reminded me of the crowded interior of the submarine we used on the Bill Holden film, *Submarine Command.* Only that interior was like a ballroom compared to this old hulk.

On the way back to San Pedro, I told Dick about a cove very much like the one we'd just left. "John Farrow owns a cove just west of Malibu Beach. I'm sure he'd lease it to us. It faces south, and we'd have sun all day. There's a narrow road leading down to the beach from the top of the hill. It has every advantage missing on Catalina, including the fact that it is only an hour or so from the studio. You'll save on living expenses for the staff, cast, crew, and all those extras. This time of year we're bound to have days we can't shoot around the beach, and we can have cover sets in the studio."

I left my best objection to Catalina for the last. "Dick," I said, "remember the trouble we just had getting ashore from this boat? Think how we're going to transport everyone from Avalon to location by water taxis. Have landing craft waiting offshore. Have everyone, especially the older actors, struggle to transfer from the water taxis to the landing craft to get ashore."

Dick countered with arguments. "Herbie, that old subchaser is not watertight. It would sink to the bottom of the channel the moment it was pulled off the beach. It was the only one we could find anywhere on the West Coast."

That ended my attempt to move the location to Farrow's cove.

The Sunday following our trip to Catalina, I got a call from Knox early in the morning. He told me we were in serious trouble and asked me to come to the studio immediately. When I asked why, he said our subchaser had sunk during the night.

"That's not my problem, Harold," I told him. "It's yours."

"I talked to Mr. Maibaum," he said. "He suggested I call you."

By the time I got to the studio, Knox had half the studio in my office. I listened to his tale of woe. How heavy swells had broken the ropes the construction men had used to tie the boat on the beach, and it had slid back and gone under. "Only the top of the mast is visible above water."

The solution to the problem was so obvious I was surprised somebody hadn't brought it up. There must be a half dozen marine salvage companies in San Pedro. "Harold, why don't you call around and make a deal for one of them to raise the boat and put it back on the beach?"

By the time the boat was back where it belonged, Chico Day had come to work. When World War II started, Chico enlisted in the Navy. In a very short time he was sent to the Pacific as a chief petty officer in charge of underwater demolition teams.

I asked him to go to Catalina and supervise tying off that old tub so it wouldn't sink with all of us down in the hold.

Chico had them dig holes in the sand down to bedrock, drill into the granite rock, and attach steel cables from the bow of the subchaser. That ended that problem.

Casting went smoothly until I insisted on Gary Crosby for the part of Sackler. I was strongly advised against taking a chance with him. Rumors had it he was becoming an alcoholic and would let me down. I'd first met Gary when he was about ten years old. I was the script supervisor on a Bing Crosby feature. I think it was *Rhythm on the Range.* Gary and his three younger brothers came on the stage dressed in their military school uniforms. I'd watched him grow into a young man and had followed his struggle to succeed in the film and music business. I finally got tired of arguing and told everyone, "Set Gary in the part."

He was everything I'd hoped he'd be. One night at Avalon he called and asked to come to my room. He was a little disturbed about a scene we were filming the next day. Almost every night someone would call with a problem. There was always alcohol on a table for them if they wanted an after-dinner drink. I got up to hide the bottles but stopped. What would Gary do? The bottles were still on the table when he came in.

During our conversation, I saw him glance toward the liquor a couple of times. I asked if he'd like a drink. When he nodded yes, I told him to help himself. He mixed a weak vodka and tonic and sipped it while we talked.

That was the only drink he had while we were making the picture. He was excellent in his role, and I never had a more cooperative actor.

I'd read the screenplay written by Maibaum and Willard Willingham from Dick's original story. *Battle at Bloody Beach* was a story about the Japanese occupation of the Philippines.

I thought the audience would need a break from the tension and violence. Even a good laugh might fit in here. I told the property man to choose the tamest fighting cock, keep it in a cage far removed from the others, and have Blanco alone feed it. I wanted the cock to feed from Blanco's hand.

The morning we shot Blanco catching the cock, I told Chico to be ready at dawn. No lights. And only Kenny Peach and his assistant, the propman with the cock, and Blanco. I told Kenny to grind off thirty feet. Then I gave Blanco the cue to back into the scene on his hands and knees holding out his hand full of chicken feed. I then gave the propman the cue to let the cock follow Blanco. It worked perfectly the first time we tried it. The camera was running backward and what was seen on the screen was the cock backing into the picture with Blanco following holding out his hand trying to entice the cock to stop and take the food.

The cock backs out of the picture followed by Blanco. There's a long pause, over which I had the sound department dub in a loud squawking. It got the laugh I'd hoped it would.

The day after we finished shooting on the picture, I sat with Dick Maibaum in the projection room to see the rushes of our last three days of work.

The cutter, I'd already discovered he didn't deserve the more dignified title "editor," whom the executive producer, Robert "Bob" Lippert, hired for the job, told us he would be ready to show us the rough cut in three or four days.

I joined Dick in the projection room unaware that I was going to spend the most miserable two hours watching how that cutter had mangled my film.

When the lights came on at the end of the running, I walked out without a word to anyone, got in my car, and drove home.

Dick was as concerned as I was about correcting the many mistakes I thought were made in the rough cut. I told him I would spend as many days in the cutting room as necessary to have the picture we'd all worked so hard to make. It meant putting many sequences back in daily form and starting from the beginning. It was a tiring job, and I was never entirely satisfied with the result.

One day while I was busy with the recutting, my agent brought me a screenplay. "Jack Karp wants you to direct this." He said with a smile, "For $25,000." For *Posse from Hell* and *Battle at Bloody Beach* I was paid $10,000 each. And this would bring me back to Paramount.

"Jack would like you to read it tonight and meet with the producer, Bryan Foy, tomorrow morning."

"I'd do anything for Jack and Paramount, but why must I drive all the way from Newport Beach on Sunday?"

"Foy has to be in Boston on Sunday. You won't have to come in to Hollywood to meet him. He lives on the bay just a few blocks from your home. He's expecting a call from you tomorrow morning."

I waited until I got home to read the screenplay. I've forgotten the title, but it was something like *Ladies of the Big House,* a story about a women's prison.

Stella Stevens was to be the star of the piece. I can't remember why she'd been sentenced to serve a long term in a prison with a warden who uses his power to shorten her stay in jail if she will become his housekeeper and satisfy his enormous sexual appetite.

There was even a scene in which, in the middle of the night, the prison alarm system broadcasts a prison break. The camera is centered on a door that opens into Stella's bedroom. Almost instantly after the alarm sounds, the door opens and the warden rushes out pulling up his pants. I'd read enough to know I wouldn't take the job. How could I face my children if my name was on such a film and they had watched it with their friends?

I made up my mind. I wouldn't meet with Foy the next day. Late Saturday afternoon he called and asked about the meeting. I didn't want to embarrass either of us and told a little white lie, hoping he'd be satisfied and agree to cancel the meeting. He suggested an early meeting the next day. Knowing he was leaving for Boston, I told him my church came first. When he told me he wasn't leaving for the airport until late in the afternoon, I decided the only thing I could do was meet with him and tell him exactly why I wasn't interested in directing his film.

His home on the bay was an expensive bungalow with an enormous swimming pool, just a few feet from the clear blue water of Balboa Bay. I found Foy to be a pleasant, friendly man who spent some time escorting me around the house and gardens. We settled down by the pool. He started the meeting by asking what I thought of the screenplay. I told him I didn't think I was the right director for his picture.

When he insisted on knowing why, I said that the Stella Stevens character wasn't one who could generate sympathy from an audience. Certainly, I had no sympathy with a woman who'd bring her young child into such an environment.

"Don't you feel sympathy for her when her child falls to her death from the balcony?" he asked.

"No. I disliked her even more. After all, if she hadn't committed the crime for which she was in prison, her child would still be alive." We continued the discussion, covering every objection I raised from page 1 to the end.

Foy asked if I'd consider accepting the assignment if he would let me rewrite the screenplay. I told him I would think it over and give him my decision when he got back from Boston.

By the next morning I knew I didn't want to go back to Paramount with a rehash of a story I disliked so much. I called Jack Karp and fully reported the result of our meeting and my decision to refuse the assignment.

Jack thanked me for my honesty and pulled the project from his schedule. Foy took it to Warner's, where he found a more sympathetic executive and director.

I returned to the cutting room and worked hard to build the secondary relationships without losing any of the action and the triangular love affair among Benson, Ruth, and Julio.

Kenny Peach's photography conveyed a sense of the Philippines that helped keep the picture moving.

Robert Lippert, the executive producer, made it all worthwhile in his gracious acceptance of the final result of our combined efforts.

Chapter 52

An Unhappy Interlude

My son Dale, happy with his job as an assistant director on the Paramount film *The Carpetbaggers,* starring Alan Ladd, came home and told me that Alan would like me to have lunch with him if I was free.

I sat with Alan in his stage dressing room the next day and nibbled on a sandwich, listening to a story, when I immediately realized that someone was trying to involve Alan in an impossible plan. He told me about a director, someone he didn't know. I knew the director as one whose career was built on a large number of low-budget films for minor companies.

Alan said that the director had told him he had obtained the rights to produce a television series based on the film *High Noon.* And he wanted to form a company with Alan as the executive producer and star. And himself as producer and director. I sipped my coffee while I let my mind sort out all the problems the director would have to solve before he could present his plan to Alan.

High Noon was a tremendous winner at the box office. There was a large number of wealthy people in town who still had a piece of the action. The company that financed the project. Gary Cooper, the star. Freddy Zinnemann, the director. The composer, whose music was as popular as the picture. And others. Unknown to the director, I went over all of this with Alan and told that him it was unlikely the director had a written agreement with everyone involved.

Alan asked me to meet with the director and sound him out.

I met him a few days later at a restaurant near the studio. He was a little man, about Alan's size, with short gray hair and a pleasant demeanor. I listened to his story. Exactly the same story Alan had told me. Well rehearsed, I thought. When I asked to see the signed release agreements, he told me that he didn't know I'd want to see them and he'd left them at home. "Another clue pointing to a shady deal," was my reaction to that bit of news.

I agreed to another meeting a few days later when he promised to let me examine the papers. We met all right. But again there were no papers. He confessed that he had hoped Alan would let him use his name to put the deal together.

When I told Alan about the second meeting, he thanked me for spending all that time protecting him. He then said, "Dale told me you're busy writing a new screenplay. What's it about?"

"You remember that old film Paramount made back in the 1930s, *If I Had a Million*?"

Alan laughed as he nodded his head. "You can never make that again. Too many millionaires around now."

"Mine's going to be about the other side of that coin. *If I Didn't Have a Billion*."

"How's it coming along?" Alan wanted to know.

"I'm beginning to think I should go out and live like a bum to get more ideas."

"Herbie," He said, "doesn't Mary Belle ever get tired of having you around the house all the time? Why don't you come and work in my Ladd building out on Wilshire? You can use the office right next to mine. It's quiet there, and all you'll have to pay for is your own phone and parking in the underground garage. Sue [Alan's wife] runs the place and checks on those things."

He kept pressing me, even calling me at night, until I finally gave in.

I always tried to get to the office around nine in the morning. Alan usually arrived around ten. He'd go into his office for a while and then join me. He was always happy to be talking about all the films we'd made together, starting with *Calcutta* and ending with the last film we made together, *Branded,* and its great director, Rudy Maté.

Then things began to change. He'd be asked to go into his office to take a telephone call. He'd usually be gone for a half hour or so. When he returned, he wouldn't be the same Alan Ladd who had left to take the call. His face would be contorted. He would be angry. And I could tell he'd been drinking.

One day he came back so out of control that he slammed his fist against the wall so hard I was sure he'd broken it. Then he turned to me and uttered one word, "Sue." I knew when he came in the next time, almost out of control, and said, "You want to bet me a quarter I won't dive through that window?" that I had to find a way to help him. We'd been close friends for too many years to let that go on.

"Laddie," I said, "you've got to get away for a while. Call Paul Baxley [a close mutual friend], get on a ship, and take a long cruise. Go around the world."

"I can't, Herbie. Sue controls all the money."

I was shocked, but I shouldn't have been. We, who were close to Alan, knew that Sue was involved in every moment of his life. His contract with Paramount. Choice of screenplays. Casting. Wardrobe. Anything he wore in his films belonged to him after the picture was completed. Sue was completely in control of his career and, as I had found out, his very life.

I knew I had to get away. For Alan's good, as well as my own.

I waited a few days and then called Alan "Pinky" Miller and asked him to come to Beverly Hills and have lunch with me. He countered with an offer for me to join him at Universal. He listened, patiently, to my story and agreed that a move away would be best for both Alan and myself.

He was confident that a place could be found for me at Universal. "I've always admired Alan and wished many times we could have him with us at Universal."

One morning I was late getting to my office. Shortly after I arrived I got a call from a friend asking where I'd been all morning. He told me that somebody at Universal had been calling all over town trying to find me: "All I can tell you is she has a very strong British accent. It sounded important."

I sat there staring at the telephone trying to remember any woman at Universal with a strong British accent. Then it came to me. Bea, Norman Lloyd's secretary, had a very strong accent. And her voice hadn't changed since I'd last talked to her. The moment she heard my voice, she broke in, "Herbie, Norman's been trying to reach you all morning. Can you come out here right away? I mean, right now."

"I'll be there before you put the phone down, Bea," I promised.

Norman was all smiles when I walked into his office. We shook hands, and he pointed to a chair. "Don't relax in that," he said as I sat down. "I'd like you to join us on our new series, *The Alfred Hitchcock Hour,* as a producer/director. If you and Manning O'Connor [the executive in charge of TV deals] can come to terms on a deal."

I'd known Manning for years. He was a gentleman. And a gentle man, I thought, until we began to discuss money. He offered half of what I was getting when I was producing, writing, and directing *Checkmate.* "Why do you think I would accept such an offer, Manning?"

"Easy," he said. "Then we needed you. Now you need us." But he said it with a smile. We continued haggling for a while until we reached a sum that we thought was fair to both of us.

Chapter 53

The Alfred Hitchcock Hour

I went back to Norman's office. He told me he was happy that Manning and I were still friends. "And you are now a member of *The Alfred Hitchcock Hour.*"

He gave me a script, *Three Wives Too Many.*

"I want you to study this script and tell me next Monday what changes you think are necessary. Teresa Wright has agreed to star in it. I'd like you to be ready to start shooting in ten days."

I was about to leave his office when he added, "There are a few strict rules Hitch has imposed on us. Each segment must be completed within the $129,000 he receives for the completed film. And no producer on the series is to approach Hitch. If you have a problem, come to me and I'll take it up with him."

I told Norman it was okay with me. "Makes a lot of sense. With me and three other producers running to him with our problems, he'd get tired of the series in a hurry."

I took the *Three Wives* script and left the office. I knew I had to break the news to Alan, and I wasn't looking forward to facing him. But when I arrived at my office, he was sitting at my desk laughing at the new pages I'd written on *If I Didn't Have a Billion.*

He looked up as I entered and asked, "Jack Benny seen this yet?" But he stopped at the sight of my serious demeanor and the *Three Wives* script in my hands. "You haven't quit working on this for that, whatever it is, have you, Herbie?"

"I'm afraid I have to, Alan. Money's going out pretty fast for our big new home in Newport Beach. Norman Lloyd offered me a job I couldn't turn down."

I told him how much I'd enjoyed the days we'd had together. He suggested we go somewhere for lunch and talk about it.

We left the restaurant, unaware that it was the last time we would ever see each other again.

The news came of his tragic death in Palm Springs, on January 29, 1964; rumor had it, it was suicide. But despite the anger I saw in him so often in his offices in the Ladd building, I never believed it was suicide. His death left a void in the lives of the Colemans and others who'd enjoyed the friendship of Laddie.

Sad to say, it also led to the complete and unhappy break between Sue and the Colemans. When Sue announced in the press that she was leaving the coffin open so Alan's many fans could say goodbye, I knew I had to stay away. I wanted to remember him as the happy friend he'd been through all the years we worked together.

On the Paramount lot, a few weeks later, Sue and I came face to face at the corner of a building. As we halted, our faces inches apart, she spat out, "I hate you!"

The screenplay *Three Wives Too Many* was a story of a gentle, young homemaker, Teresa Wright, whose husband, a traveling salesman, spends too much time away from home visiting the wives he has in three different cities. When Wright learns the truth about her wayward husband, she goes visiting each of the women.

We finished the film well within the budget. Norman ran the picture with Hitch and came back to tell me that Hitch wanted me to make a cut in a scene in which Wright confronts the first wife.

"He had the cutter mark the exact frame to make the cut and choose the close-up of Wright to use next," Norman said.

I told Norman I wouldn't approve the change because the attitude of the two was exactly opposite in the two cuts.

"But Hitch has made his decision," Norman insisted.

I called Hitch's office and arranged to see him. He seemed a little cool at first. I explained why the scene couldn't be edited the way he wanted. I could almost see that scene running back and forth in his mind as he reviewed the film with and without the cut. He allowed a slight smile to appear in his eyes before announcing, "It's only a movie. Your movie. Do it your way." I've often thought Hitch deliberately ordered that cut as a test to see if I would fight for what I thought was right, even on a TV show. He then surprised me by inviting me to join him for a good-night cocktail.

Finding stories suitable for the series was a real problem for everyone.

Some writers would come in to pitch their ideas. Their first acts were always well developed. The second, less so. The third, nonexistent. Other writers, or their agents, presented synopses and sometimes fully developed scripts written specifically for our program. My memory of those two and a half years is a jumbled whirlpool of pages spinning in the air. But we, and the series, somehow managed to survive.

Then came that tragic morning of November 22, 1963, when my hero, and the hero of millions of Americans, failed to survive an assassin's bullet fired from the window of the Dallas Schoolbook Depository Building.

I was in a happy frame of mind. The network executives had just called to thank me for the film they'd just reviewed when a greatly disturbed Bessa, Norman's secretary, rushed in to tell me to hurry into Norman's office. "The president's been shot!" I joined Norman and others who were standing stunned at what they were watching on his television set. I don't remember anyone saying anything, or even moving, for what seemed like hours. The ringing of the telephone broke the tension, and everyone started to talk. Norman answered his phone. I remember him saying, "Right, Lew. I'll spread the word." Then he turned to us. "Lew said, 'There's to be no pause. Work is to go on. It's what the president would expect of us.'"

Work did continue. But the shock of what we had just seen was too great. No one seemed able to concentrate. We were spared the knowledge of the disasters that would result from Oswald's finger squeezing the trigger, sending that bullet speeding into the head of our President John F. Kennedy.

The tragic event, for a time, wiped from my memory the films I'd made for the series. I do remember a little something about two of them. I was checking my weekly *Reader's Digest* for ideas when I noticed a quip at the end of one article. Something about a psychology professor at an eastern university who, as a test, inserted an advertisement in the town's newspaper stating "Murder for Hire."

The more I thought about that quip, the more I felt we could do something with it. I called in one of my favorite writers. Together we developed a story of a similar professor and a similar situation. The twist we gave the story was that a young man answered the ad and hired the professor to find and murder the husband of the woman with whom he was having a mad love affair. Neither of them knew that the man the professor was to murder was the professor himself. It was his wife the young man was romancing. I can't remember the name we gave the episode or the cast, except for the actor who played the young lover. His name was Richard "Dickie" Dawson. Most will remember him as the original host of *Family Feud*.

The other story I remember was called *Night Nurse*. It was about a man chained to a bed in the detention section of a hospital. He is cared for by a nurse, who apparently has fallen in love with him. The prisoner also is apparently in love with the nurse. He convinces her that they can have a life together if she will help him escape.

During a rainstorm she opens the locks that bind him to the bed and takes him to the apartment where they will live. She is stunned when the door to the apartment is opened revealing a mob of thieves, murderers, and their "broads." One of the broads rushes to shower the prisoner with kisses and orders the nurse to get out. The nurse, her hopes of a life with the man she's helped to escape from a long prison sentence, leaves the apartment with taunts from the gang ringing in her ears. She slowly makes her way down the long flight of stairs where a group of police and detectives are waiting. "They're in room 210," she tells them.

It' s only then that we reveal she was part of a plan to capture the entire mob. She stands watching the officers silently move up the stairs.

The reason I remember that episode so vividly is that it gave me the opportunity to direct one of the finest actresses it had been my good fortune to know during my long career: Coleen Dewhurst. It was her brilliant performance that prompted the network, and Hitch, to present *Night Nurse* to the television viewers for their reaction to *The Alfred Hitchcock Hour* series to restore interest.

Hitch and the network agreed to close *The Alfred Hitchcock Hour* because finding suitable stories had become an expensive and endless unproductive task.

I went home to happily enjoy the task of proving to Mary Belle and our three children, Dale, Judy, and Melinda, that there really was a loving husband and father in their lives.

Chapter 54

Nevada Smith

In June 1965 Frank Caffey, executive production manager at Paramount, a friend for many years, and my former boss when I was an assistant director, invited me to lunch. When I arrived, Rowland, his secretary, nodded toward Frank's closed door, gave me a mysterious smile, and said, "He's waiting. Lunch is laid out in there." No wonder his smile was mysterious. Frank never invited anyone to have lunch with him in his office. "What's up?" I asked myself.

Frank got up from his desk as I entered and headed toward the lunch spread out on his conference table. "Why lunch in here, Frank? Am I barred from the executive dining room?"

"Let's eat and then talk, Herbie."

We gossiped while we ate. Mostly about Hitch and his last picture, *The Birds*. "Have you seen it yet?" Frank wanted to know.

"Yes," I answered. "Hitch arranged a private showing for me. Just George Tomasini and I."

"Talk around town it's one of his best, if not his best. What do you think?"

"I'll tell you just what I told Hitch, Frank. Technically, a close second to *Vertigo*. The cast, lacking the skills to challenge the stars you've always demanded in the past. And you stumbled badly in one scene, Hitch."

"That must have shocked him."

"No, Frank. As always, he expected me to be honest in my review of his work." His hooded eyes continued to grip mine while he waited for my explanation. "You had me, Hitch, and I'm sure you'll have your audiences as frightened as Tippi Hedren was from the moment of the first seagull attack. The tension grew exactly as you must have planned."

Sitting there in the studio projection room, without the advantage of playing off the emotions of a crowded theater, I found myself gripping the armrests of my seat. "And then you allowed Hedren, a woman who would scream at the slightest sound, to hear in the dead of night a faint, mysterious, incomprehensible sound; leave Rod Taylor sleeping; climb a long flight of stairs; open a closed door;

go inside; and close the door behind herself. Look up at a flock of seagulls ready to attack her through a large opening in the roof. It was the closing of the door that was most disturbing."

"How did he answer that?"

"He said, 'I had to have her trapped. With no means of escape.' Fortunately, Dolores arrived with a chilled bottle of champagne Hitch had planned to use to toast *The Birds.* And toast it, or them, we certainly did."

"Do you miss working with him?"

"Sure. Just as I miss working with Willie Wyler, Wesley Ruggles, Mark Sandrich, Sam Wood, Norman Taurog, and way back when 'Gentle' George Marshall, who really meant it when he said, 'You're not to worry. It's only another movie.'"

"You didn't mention Henry Hathaway."

"I was always able to avoid working with Henry Hathaway."

"Until now."

I asked him what he was getting at.

"How would you like to become a unit production manager?"

"Why would I want to step back twenty years to a job I performed just once?"

"For the producer's fee you received on your last picture."

He didn't wait for my answer. "I've got a real problem on Hathaway's upcoming picture, *Nevada Smith.* Every top production manager in town has refused to come aboard when they discover they'd have both Hathaway and Steve McQueen to deal with. Andy Durkus [the oldest, in point of service at the studio] threatened to resign if I assigned him to Hathaway."

"What about Doc Erickson?"

"He turned me down cold. Wouldn't even discuss it after I mentioned McQueen's name."

"Does Henry know you're asking me to come aboard?"

"He's in his office right now waiting for your answer."

"I'll listen to what he has to say, Frank."

He had plenty to say. How happy he was we would finally have a chance to work together after all the years we'd been friends. I thought "friends" was stretching it a bit. What a great script we were given by John Michael Hayes. Art Director Tambi Lansen had the sets in work up in Owens Valley, Mammouth Mountain, and around Baton Rouge, Louisiana. Sections of Abilene were also built in other locations some distance from Bishop.

The main street of Abilene was built on a great pasture in the Inyo National Forest near the summer resort at Mammouth Mountain, where we would be living in the Mammouth Mountain Inn and surrounding motels.

The last major set was the Indian tribe's tepee village alongside a meandering stream below Indian Hot Springs near Convict Lake. I watched Tambi pressing his staff and crew to complete work on the various sets. I asked what I could do to help. "The way these sets are spread out over all these mountains and Owens Valley, I could use someone to oversee some of the set. We need more transportation. Cars, buses, and trucks. Bob [Robert] Benton's trying to dress all the sets with one car and one truck. He could use an assistant and more set dressers."

I called Frank. He sent Al Roelof, an art director I'd worked with in the past, to help Tambi. Al Latta arrived to solve the transportation problem. My first priority was to open and staff an office in Bishop. Fortunately, a longtime friend, Carl Andre, who for years had been film star Joel McCrea's double, and Carl's wife owned the Frontier Hardware store in Bishop. He was highly regarded by Hollywood's film community as an honest and responsible citizen. Carl agreed to become my representative and quickly had the office open and working efficiently.

The studio had hired an accountant who'd formerly worked at Columbia. He was sent to Bishop to report to me. He didn't last long. While I was back at the studio spending some time with Danny McCauley on the budget and schedule, the auditor gave a big expensive party for Owen Valley big shots and charged it all to the picture. He also bought expensive clothing for himself. When I became aware of his misconduct, I had him replaced with Frank Parmenter, a longtime assistant director at the studio.

The reason Andy Durkus and Doc Erickson refused to work with McQueen became apparent to me when Coffey told me about McQueen's contract. "The studio must provide him with a motor home and a 1965 air-conditioned convertible Lincoln or Cadillac limousine. Both have been delivered to his house. We know his wife is using the limousine. He drove the motor home to Palm Springs, and on the way back he wrecked it. He wanted it rebuilt to his specifications: the interior on two levels. Expensive carpets. And a built-in piano. Joseph Levine, the executive producer, approved $25,000 to cover the costs. You'll have to provide a driver when he takes it to the locations. He has a special twelve-cylinder sports car he's going to drive to Lone Pine. He wants to park it somewhere where no one can touch it."

Al Latta had a section of the local garage boarded off to protect the car. When McQueen arrived, he raised hell until Al let it be known that he was looking for a private garage for the car. Almost every housewife in town offered her garage free for Steve. The winner parked her car on her lawn, and his car sat inside, unused, for the duration of our shooting period.

McQueen's stand-in arrived with McQueen's pickup. In the back of the pickup was McQueen's off-road dirt bike. I kept wondering when that Lincoln limousine would arrive, but his actress wife kept it at home for her own use.

Hathaway and the entire company settled in their quarters in Bishop. Just two days remained before filming the opening scene in which the three outlaws, Karl Malden, Arthur Kennedy, and Martin Landau, ride in where McQueen is filling barrels with water from a small stream. I received word that our permit to use the stream in the picture had been withdrawn. I chartered a small plane and flew to Bakersfield to attempt to have the permit restored. I told the authorities I would be personally responsible for protecting the stream from any damage during our filming. They believed me, and I flew back to Lone Pine with the treasured paper in my pocket.

The opening day of production, I'd spent the morning in conference with Bill Murphy, chief park ranger of the Mammouth District, at his office at Mammouth Mountain. When I arrived back at our Bishop office, Parmenter told me that Howard W. Koch, the West Coast chief of Paramount Pictures, had called asking me to tell Hathaway that Suzanne Pleshette had turned down the part of Pilar. I drove up to the stream location and waited until Hathaway finished filming the scene in which the three outlaws ride in to question McQueen. I didn't want the others to hear me deliver the message, so I took him aside. I'd barely gotten the words out before he began to bow to every point of the compass, almost shouting, "I've been told from the west! I've been told from the south! I've been told from the east! I've been told from the north! Pleshette has turned down the part!"

I stared at him and then, without a word, turned away and drove back to the office. I walked in and asked Parmenter how Hathaway already knew about Koch's message. "I thought it was important, so I wrote him a note," Parmenter said.

I've never been so close to hitting anyone as I was when he deliberately placed me in such an embarrassing position. "From now on, stick to your accounting and leave the thinking to others," I told him, "or you'll be on your way back to the studio."

After dinner I went to Hathaway's room and talked to him. "Over the years I've heard stories about your treatment of those who, for various reasons, were forced to work with you. But I'm not one of those. I took this job as a favor to Frank Caffey, Howard W. Koch, and Paramount. I'll stay on here and work my ass off to help you make a good picture, but if you ever embarrass me again, I'll do exactly what I did today except for one thing, I won't stop at the office, I'll keep going until I get home, and you can find someone more hungry than I am to take your verbal abuse."

He made a feeble attempt to smooth things over: "We've known each other ever since you arrived on the set of *Wolf Song* in the winter of 1928 at Indian Hot Springs, where we'll be working again in a few weeks. You know what I said didn't mean anything."

"Maybe not to you, Henry, but a hell of a lot to me. One thing I've always received from everyone with whom I've worked in this business was respect, and I'll expect the same from you in the future." That was the end of that.

The next morning, at breakfast, he threw his arms around me and apologized before the whole company. Although we never became friends, our working relationship couldn't have been better.

With the opening day of shooting in the Bishop area rapidly approaching, Frank Caffey called and read me a letter he'd received from Columbia, telling about the trouble the staff members were having with the Teamsters' Union in Baton Rouge. He said they'd advised us to move our sets to another state. "What do you think we should do?" I told him I'd fly down to Baton Rouge and find out firsthand what was going on.

Elmer Rogers, the construction foreman in charge of building the sets around Baton Rouge, an old friend from Paramount days, met me at the plane.

With him was a man who would become a lifelong friend, Robert (Bob) Carter, a tall, easygoing gentleman whose face was always covered by an engaging smile. Bob, with his father, owned the Charles Carter Construction Company, which had been contracted to build our sets.

Neither of them had heard about any trouble with the Teamsters' Union. "They've certainly given us no trouble." For three days I telephoned the office of Edward Partin, the head of the Baton Rouge Teamsters' Union, asking for an appointment with him. Each time, a secretary would tell me that Mr. Partin was unavailable or out of the state or would offer some other lame excuse. Bob Carter invited me to a business party and introduced me to a "Mr. Williams," the Baton Rouge coroner. "Bob tells me you've been trying to see Ed Partin," he said. "Are you free at ten tomorrow morning?" he asked. When I assured him I was, he told me to knock on Partin's door exactly at ten.

I didn't exactly knock on Partin's door, but I did walk into his outer office to be greeted with a smile by his secretary. "Go right in, Mr. Coleman. Mr. Partin is expecting you." Ed Partin was an imposing figure. Six foot two or three and a ready smile. He was dressed in tan slacks and a checkered brown, short-sleeved sport shirt.

He rose from his chair behind a large cluttered desk and shook my hand.

"I've been expecting someone from Paramount Studio to show up here and ask why we're giving Columbia so little cooperation. Some months ago, a man walks into this office without an appointment and says he's from Columbia and they're coming down here to make a major motion picture. He says they are going to have to rent a lot of equipment, cars, buses, and trucks and hire a lot of our drivers. Then he makes a not-too-subtle hint there was money in it for both of us. My first impulse was to pick him up bodily and throw him through that window. But I kept my hands on my desk and told him flatly, if Columbia showed up in Baton Rouge, they would be in deep trouble.

"I didn't know anything about him. First, he'd insulted me. Second, he could have been a plant of Jimmy Hoffa's. I'd been worried Jimmy would try something like that ever since I went to Tennessee and testified for the prosecution about his attempt to bribe one of the jury in his trial.

"Bring your company down here, Mr. Coleman. We'll do everything we can to help you make your filming in Louisiana a success."

We shook hands, and I left his office with my mission completed in about fifteen minutes. I don't think I spoke more than thirty words.

Something clicked in my head, and I was recalling the first of my many serious problems with Steve McQueen. We were shooting in the forests around Mammouth Mountain when Bill Murphy, the chief park ranger, sent word for me to come to his office forthwith. He was the man from whom I'd received permission to work in the Inyo National Forest and who I'd promised to protect the district and its many tourists from all harm. We'd developed a very friendly working relationship and were on a first name basis. "Herbie, a very serious problem with Steve McQueen has placed your shooting permit in jeopardy. I've had reports, almost daily, of his riding his off-road motorcycle at very high speed on the public roads under our supervision. Now he's riding it on paths reserved for hikers. This morning, a family with small children strolling along a narrow path were forced to jump for safety when McQueen came roaring around a sharp turn at a high rate of speed. I'm sorry to have to tell you this, Herbie, but he's not to ride that bike inside the boundary of the Inyo National Forest again. If he does, your permit is null and void and you'll have to move out."

I drove straight to where Henry was shooting the scene in which Max first meets Jonas Cord, the gun dealer. When I arrived, everyone was having lunch. McQueen was sitting off to one side with his stunt double. I joined them and told McQueen that there was something I wanted to discuss with him in private. "Anything you have to say to me, you can say in front of him," he said.

"Fine with me. Tell him to put that bike of yours in that pickup and leave it there while we're shooting anywhere up here in the national forest."

He didn't answer me. He just threw his plate on the ground and stalked off to where Hathaway was sitting in the shade of a giant pine reading his script. I was too far away to hear what he was telling Henry, but from his gestures, I guessed he wasn't very happy with me. When I approached them, McQueen moved away. "Steve just told me if you stay on this picture, he'll walk," Henry said. "What's it all about?"

"Nothing serious, Henry. Just one more report to Bill Murphy about McQueen riding his dirt bike anywhere in the Inyo National Forest, and you can sit still while I find a new location to move and rebuild all your sets."

"What can you do to stop Steve?" Henry asked.

"I've told him to keep his bike on his pickup. If he doesn't, I'll have the sheriff's men put it in cold storage until we finish up here."

I guess Henry relayed my threat to McQueen. Anyhow, the bike remained tied down in the pickup for the rest of our work in that area.

We finished all the California locations and moved the company to the studio for the nine days we had scheduled for the interiors.

I stayed with Henry the first day to be sure there were no real problems.

Then, with Mary Belle, we flew to New Orleans where Al Latta, our driver captain, and his wife Margaret, old friends from my driving days, met us. I asked Al to take us to Baton Rouge through New Iberia, that beautiful little city I'd talked about so often. I wanted to find some friends from the past but could find not even one. From New Iberia we drove past many of the old plantations and settled down in a lovely suite in the old section of the Bellmont Motel.

Bob Carter arrived, and, along with Tambi Larsen and Elmer Rogers, we drove out to Port Vincent, where the big prison set stood on the bank of the beautiful blue waters of Coyell Bay. On a tributary of the Amite River, giant cypress trees, festooned with gleaming, silver-gray moss, rose from the water as far as I could see. It was a setting Willie Wyler would have chosen, but Hathaway? I was surprised he had selected this beautiful, peaceful paradise in which to build a prison, where cruelty and brutality would rule.

Bob Carter, a real southern gentleman in his middle thirties and a very wealthy man, was enjoying his first encounter with moviemakers. He was determined to become a part of our company. He kept asking if there wasn't something he could do to help us. I told him I was looking for a man to be our contact with the local authorities to help me solve problems that were bound to show up during the weeks we would be shooting around Baton Rouge. "You couldn't afford to take that job. It only pays $50.00 a day."

"I'm just the man you're looking for," he said. "And I'll do it for nothing."

"Sometimes it's a twenty-four hour a day job, Bob. It's yours, if you want it. But the day, or night, will come when you'll be sorry you took it." I was wrong. For the next five weeks I handed him some almost impossible problems to solve. He never complained. The smile never left his face.

The second week in September, Hurricane Betsy roared out of the gulf and headed up the Mississippi toward Baton Rouge. It presented Bob with his first, and biggest, problem. On the evening of September 10, Bob, Mary Belle, and I were having dinner at the Village Inn on the edge of the city. Rumors spread fast that the eye of the storm would pass directly over Baton Rouge. By eight-thirty, most of the diners had hurried over their food and left the inn. At nine sharp, the manager of the restaurant came to our table and told us he'd just been ordered to close and send everyone home. We forgot dessert and coffee and got out in a hurry. Fortunately, Bob had parked close to the entrance.

The wind was so strong that branches were breaking from the trees and flying around us. We made it to the Bellmont and inside our three-room suite.

Mary Belle spent the night running from window to window, watching roofs tearing away from the Bellmont's buildings and windows of parked cars blowing out from internal compression. Having lived through the 1926 hurricane that devastated Fort Lauderdale and sank every boat in Tampa Bay, I foolishly dismissed Betsy and went to bed.

My memory of the sights and sounds I saw and heard the morning after the storm is devastating. Uprooted trees and broken branches covered the roads.

Downed power lines and transformers threatened to electrocute any of the careless pedestrians who ventured out in the rain. Power was out in most places, including the Bellmont.

My first concern was the safety of our employees. But everyone came through it without any serious injuries. My second concern was our prison set. After a cold breakfast, Henry Rogers, Tambi Larsen, Bob Carter, and I joined Al Latta and started the twenty-five-mile drive to Coyell Bay. It was stop and go the whole distance. City and parish crews, working in water sometimes reaching above their knees, were hard at work clearing the roads. With more than a mile still to go, we were forced to abandon the car, slog through ankle-deep water, and climb over fallen trees to reach the prison compound. If I'd known cottonmouth moccasins could strike while swimming under water, I would never have stepped from the car.

We stopped dead in our tracks the moment the prison set came into view. The buildings seemed untouched, and none of the trees close to our set had been uprooted. But every strand of the beautiful silver-gray moss now littered the still waters of the bayou. Hundreds of bloated dead fish floated belly up on water that had turned from blue to an ugly black.

I told Bob Carter now was the time he started earning his $50.00 a day. "You'll have to help Elmer get workmen out here to replace the moss. Clear the bay of all those fallen trees, and scoop up those stinking fish." The ever present smile never left his face. I don't know where he found the manpower, but when I went back to the set the next morning, workmen were swarming all over the place. Within a week, the place looked much as it did the first time I saw it.

The one thing they couldn't correct was the black water. We left that for another time.

Bob's next job was finding us a power launch to use as the prison boat. He wasn't having much luck until he tried the deep backwaters. At Bert's Boat Works at Madisonville, he stumbled upon Bert Chatellier, who had an old oyster lugger. I made a deal with Bert, and Elmer managed to make it look like a prison boat. It was powered by a gas engine, and Henry wanted to see puffs of smoke coming from the smokestack. We had a pretty sharp special effects man from the studio. He asked Bob to find a dry cleaner's pressing machine. "I can convert it to provide steam coming out of the smokestack if you'll also get me a DC generator. It can't be an AC/DC generator. That wouldn't work."

The pressing machine was no problem, but a DC generator? Bob discovered that every DC generator in the South was tied up providing electricity to hospitals and other priority establishments. The smile was missing when he made his report to me. "Not a chance in the world of finding a DC generator, Herbie," he said.

The smile came back when I told him I'd have one brought down on the plane bringing Henry and the rest of the company to Baton Rouge. I asked the special effects man to call the studio and tell them exactly what kind of generator he wanted.

Henry arrived right on schedule with McQueen, Arthur Kennedy, Suzanne Pleshette, Howard Da Silva, and the rest of the company.

Within an hour, Henry, Danny McCauley, Lucien Ballard, and all the key department heads were on the road heading for Coyell Bay. Bob Carter and I trailed along while Henry checked out all the buildings, the set dressing—every little detail. He didn't congratulate Tambi or Robert Benton, the set dresser. Neither did he complain about their work. That was enough for them. It was in the warden's office that he threw a hardball in Bob's direction when he told Benton he wanted a fresh alligator skin on the wall behind Da Silva's desk.

"There's no way we can get him a fresh alligator skin," Bob whispered to me. "Alligators are a protected animal. It's against the law to kill one."

"Henry won't be shooting in the warden's office the first two days. That gives you almost seventy hours, Bob. Plenty of time for an overpaid contact man to fulfill Henry's minor request." I grinned at him. The smile hadn't disappeared from his face, but it wasn't as bright as I'd seen it at times. Bob begged off going back to the prison set with Henry and the rest of us the following day. "Got to find that alligator skin," he told me. When we arrived at the prison set, the first thing Henry brought up was the ugly, black water of Coyell Bay. Ballard thought he could put some color back into the water if I could get some green vegetable dye. I sent Al Latta to the nearest phone to tell Bob Carter to drop the hunt for the alligator skin, buy some green dye, and get out to the set as fast as possible.

He showed up an hour or so later with two small bottles of dye normally used to color bakery goods. It was poured into the water and stirred up with an outboard motor. Ballard thought it would do. I told Bob to buy all the dye he could find and have it on the set by dawn the next morning. That time the smile disappeared completely. "But, Herbie, those two bottles were all my people could find in the whole city." "At dawn tomorrow morning, Bob."

I didn't have too much hope he could deliver on that one, but I'd underestimated him. He went back to his office and put his whole staff to work. Night had fallen when they discovered that the dye was manufactured at St. Martinville, a small town just north of New Iberia, in the center of Cajun Country. I told him to buy all they would sell him. He sent one of his men who was fluent in Cajun dialect.

In the back of his pickup, when he arrived on the set the next morning, were two fifty-gallon drums full of enough dye to color all the water from Baton Rouge to New Orleans. Bob had delivered again.

It was after midnight that night when I answered the phone and heard the excited voice of Bob Carter. "Mr. Hathaway will have his fresh alligator skin on the wall of the warden's office tomorrow morning by nine o'clock!" he said.

He didn't wait for my reaction to what he'd said. "I was on my way home tonight when I heard on my radio somebody had shot an alligator in his yard. I headed for the nearest police station. Found out where the animal was. Bought it on the spot. A taxidermist is busy skinning it right now. You can go back to sleep now." I could hear the joy in his voice and knew his smile was wider than ever.

But it wouldn't last very long. The next afternoon when our special effects man unpacked the generator that had arrived from the studio, he discovered that someone had disregarded his instructions to send a straight DC generator. What he found was an unusable DC/AC machine. He hurried to the phone and called the studio. They had the generator he must have, but there were no flights to Baton Rouge until the next day.

I turned to Bob again. "A DC generator? Forget it, Herbie. If there was one available anywhere in the South, hospitals would be fighting over it."

I grinned at him. "Don't need it until seven tomorrow morning, Bob. Good luck."

Again his entire staff went to work. At midnight they gave up and went home.

Bob took his girlfriend, Sarah Jane Watson, an executive at the Sears & Roebuck store in Baton Rouge, to a very late dinner. When he told her why he was so late, she told him she had the answer to his problem. "We have a DC generator sitting in our store waiting for the customer to pick it up. Let's get some of your men out there right away and sneak it out. I'll take care of the owner if he shows up tomorrow."

The insistent ringing of the telephone woke me from a sound sleep. I wasn't a bit surprised to hear it was Bob. I was surprised at the joyful tone of voice: "Did I wake you?" Before I could answer, he continued, "I just wanted you to sleep peacefully knowing your generator will be on your prison boat before Henry arrives on the set this morning." With that, he hung up.

McQueen's pickup, with the bike and the motor home, arrived at our headquarters at the Bellmont Motel to join the 1965 convertible air-conditioned Oldsmobile Touring Car Al Latta had managed to rent for McQueen's private use. He took turns driving the car or the pickup and riding the bike to the prison set some twenty-five miles from Baton Rouge. I knew McQueen's use of his motorcycle and cars someday was going to cause us big trouble.

Mary Belle and I spent days riding around in pirogues through the swamps and bayous, searching for colorful areas to replace the hurricane-damaged locations Henry and Larsen had selected close to Baton Rouge. Most of them were some ninety miles west of the Mississippi River. We would arrive very early in the morning at a little Cajun village. Someone knowledgeable about that section of the bayou would help us into the tiny native boats and then paddle us through forests of giant cypress trees growing from beds of beautiful water lilies.

It was after nine when we got home from one trip through a nasty bayou to find Peppe Lenzi, one of Danny's assistants, waiting outside our quarters. He told me that Henry wanted me to come to his room the moment we got in.

I'd never seen Hathaway so serious and disturbed as he was when I walked into his room. Before the door had closed behind me, he began, "Herbie, something happened today out at the prison set that could end our filming in Louisiana. We were shooting a close shot of Steve standing in front of the prison barracks. The location was crowded with photographers, writers, and visitors.

"I'd just said 'Cut' when a big redheaded man pushed his way past the camera, picked Steve up by his shirt collar, shoved him against the wall, and said, 'Listen to me, you ex-jailbird, you've used your own car or motorcycle on company business for the last time! From now on, you'll ride in a car driven by one of my union drivers.' Then he dropped Steve like a sack of potatoes and walked away.

"Steve says he isn't coming back to work until you make that man apologize to him in front of the whole company."

"Henry," I said, "President Johnson himself couldn't make Ed Partin apologize to Steve McQueen."

"Will you talk to him? Somehow we've got to get through the next few weeks and give Paramount the picture we promised them."

I walked over to the building that the owners of the Bellmont had built to please the film stars, whom they hoped to attract during the increasing film production around Baton Rouge. I stood for a moment, looking at something Roland Anderson, Cecil B. DeMille's art director, might have designed as an Egyptian mausoleum. A flight of eight steps, narrowing in length from some nineteen feet, led up to eight-foot high, heavy hand-carved double doors.

I climbed the steps and rapped on the door. I heard a bolt thrown, and then it silently opened barely three inches. I found myself looking into the business end of a thirty-eight-caliber police special revolver pointed directly between my eyes. Behind that gun were the eyes of a madman. I saw the cylinder, loaded with dreaded hollow-nose bullets, slowly revolve as the hammer was pulled back and locked into firing position, with a snap that sounded like a crash of thunder just above my head.

"What the hell is this, McQueen? Get that damn thing out of my face!"

His eyes shifted to search the area behind me.

"What's this I hear that you had to see me tonight? You want to talk? Open that door or forget it!"

He lowered the gun and opened the door just wide enough for me to enter. I'd never been inside that apartment before. It took me a few seconds to look it over. I was standing on a large, tiled entry. Through an open door at the right I could see an enormous circular bedroom with floor-to-ceiling, half-rounded tinted windows. I followed McQueen down a flight of eight stairs to an immense, circular living room, the floor on a level with the grounds outside. Through expensive glass curtains covering the eighteen-foot glass wall I could see a private circular swimming pool.

McQueen sat down and laid the revolver on a table just inches from his hand. In a bolstering tone, he told me a story much like the one I'd heard from Henry, except he left out the part about being called a jailbird and being picked up like an empty sack.

"You're going to make him come out to the set tomorrow and apologize to me in front of the whole company, or I'm walking out!"

I said to him, "McQueen, you've been around the picture business long enough to know the studios have contracts with unions all over the world, and when you sign a contract to appear in a Paramount picture, you're bound by the same agreements. Or maybe you or your agents are not smart enough to read the small print."

He pointed toward his telephone. "Either you call him right now and get him to agree to show up on the set the first thing in the morning or find something to shoot without me."

I'd had enough of his pettiness, and besides, I was tired and hungry. I leaned my face close to his and told him the facts of life. "Your call is leaving for the location at eight o'clock tomorrow morning. I'll have a union driver in your car. You can ride with him or ride with Hathaway. If you're not in one of those cars, I'm going to call Howard W. Koch and have you taken off salary. In addition, we'll deduct from your contract every dollar it costs us to sit here waiting for you to come back to work." Without another word, I walked out.

McQueen rode with Henry the next morning. Al put a union driver in the Olds, and after a couple of days, McQueen seemed to be content to ride back and forth in the backseat. He and the driver never became friends. It wasn't something the driver wanted anyhow.

I was becoming concerned about being away from the shooting company so often and asked Frank to send someone down to Baton Rouge until my survey was completed. Bill Gray, an assistant production manager, arrived. With him was an electrician our gaffer had asked for. It was very late at night when they arrived at the Bellmont. The loud ringing of the phone by my bed woke me about midnight. It was Gray asking me to come to the desk right away. When I walked into the lobby I saw and heard an obviously drunken electrician loudly raising hell about the room he'd been told was his. And a desk clerk that had all he was going to take from the electrician. He was telling Gray, "Get that drunken man out of here before I call the police. We don't allow such people to live here in the Bellmont."

When my attempts to calm the man proved useless, I told the clerk to call the police. Gray spoke up, "I wouldn't do that. You'll have the union down on us."

"I know you wouldn't do that, you don't have the guts."

When the police arrived and listened to the details of the uproar, they told me they wouldn't book him; they'd just put him in a cell by himself and let him cool off. "You can pick him up after eight in the morning."

I told Gray to get him a ticket on the first plane back to Los Angeles. I went with Al Latta to the police station the next morning. When I gave the sergeant on duty the name of the electrician, he asked, "Black or white?" When he saw I was puzzled by his question, he explained, "If he's white, he's in one section. The blacks are in another."

The electrician didn't know I'd spent a sleepless night trying to decide whether to give him another chance. I'd decided I probably would if his night in jail had made him realize how wrong he'd been. And he would apologize for his previous conduct. But when an officer brought him to us, he was even more belligerent than he was at the Bellmont. We drove him to the airport and saw him aboard the plane.

I knew I'd miss all the new friends I'd enjoyed working with, but I was happy my problems with McQueen were finished. Finished? I should have known he'd find a new way to make life miserable for Henry and me.

I'd left the filming on the paddle-wheel cattle boat for last. The crew arrived at five o'clock in the morning, down in a little river town in Plaquemine Parish, to load the cattle, generator, lights, and other equipment aboard. I watched the water level rise closer and closer to the deck level as each 1,000 pounds came aboard and wondered if we'd be swamped once we were out on the Mississippi. We were ready to cast off when Henry arrived. He came directly to where I stood on the bridge. "You can forget the trouble you've had with Steve in the past, Herbie," he said. "When you hear what I'm about to tell you, you'll realize you've got a real problem on your hands."

I waited for him to continue. "Steve came to my room just as I was about to leave this morning and told me an incredible story. He said he was in a bar down in the French Quarter when a beautiful young dame joined him. He didn't remember how long they stayed at the bar or how he got back to his room. The next thing he knew it was morning, when he woke up to see that same girl standing, nude, next to his bed. She was talking on the phone, and the first words he heard were, 'Mom, you'll never believe who I slept with last night. Steve McQueen.' The next words were, 'Sure, I told him I was only sixteen.'" Henry continued, "He says you'll have to protect him from the police."

"Henry," I said, "this one he'll have to handle himself." I wasn't about to put myself in the position of being an accessory after the fact to a federal crime.

Henry said, "Help me through the last two days on the picture. Listen to what he has to say. Try to think of some way to cheer him up."

"No dice, Henry." I walked away.

Danny McCauley had arranged for McQueen to come down the river in a speedboat and meet the stern wheeler on its way to the shooting site.

When he climbed aboard, he came directly to where I stood near the noisy paddle wheel. He told me the same story I'd heard from Henry.

When he finished, I told him he had a lot of nerve coming to me for help after shoving a loaded gun in my face at the Bellmont.

He stared at me for a moment and then walked to where Henry was discussing the setup for the first scene with Danny and Lucien Ballard. He said something to Henry, and then the two of them walked over to the railing and started a long conversation. When it was over, Henry came to me and told me that McQueen had threatened to get out of town before the police could arrest him.

I told Henry to send McQueen to me. He came right over and waited to hear what I had to say. "Because of my loyalty to Paramount, I'm going to do something I never dreamed I'd have to do to save a picture," I told him. "I won't offer to tell the police what you've done. But I'll answer truthfully any questions they ask about your conduct last night. Here's what you're to do when we finish our work today: I'll have Danny send Peppe Lenzi with you in that speedboat. You'll land at Saint Gabriel where a car will be waiting to take you to the Hilton Inn. It will drop you at the back entrance. I'll have my wife move our things to another room. Go to our room. Order your dinner from room service and don't leave the room. Tomorrow morning the car will take you back to Saint Gabriel where the speedboat will be waiting. Tomorrow night when we're finished with you, you'll be taken directly to the airport. You'll board the first flight to Los Angeles." He had the nerve to ask me to arrange for his exercise equipment to be sent to his home. I told him to get one of his gang to take care of it.

Henry got what he wanted from McQueen and asked me to direct the scenes of the stern wheeler's trip down the Mississippi. Two days after he took his company back to the studio I finished filming those scenes.

Chapter 55

Maya

November 1966, Martin (Marty) Shapiro, one of General Artists Corporation's agents, called to say that Frank King, the president of King Brothers Productions, had made an important offer for my services as director of a series, *Maya,* which would be produced entirely in India.

Over the years I'd heard stories about the King brothers. They were not known as producers who hired the top filmmakers in the industry. Their priority was getting the best filmmakers they could hire, only if they would accept the minimum salary demanded by the Directors Guild of America.

"I'm not interested in working for the King brothers," I told Marty.

"Frank King has made an offer I think you should consider. He wants to meet with you right away. Today, if possible. I think you should go out to Metro and listen to what he has to say."

I let Marty talk me into the meeting.

When I walked into Frank King's office at MGM, he introduced me to his older brother, Maurice (Morrie), his attorney, and his associate producer, Harry Franklin. There was no small talk. Frank started to tell me his plans for the series. I interrupted him immediately with, "Mr. King, if I'm interested in this series when this meeting is over, and you're still interested in me, I want you to know I wouldn't think of going to India for a year unless my wife goes with me. And we live and travel first class." I heard his attorney mutter under his breath, "That damned Directors Guild."

Frank seemed pleased with the idea of Mary Belle going along.

"Fine with me, Mr. Coleman. With your wife around, I know you'll have your mind on your job. Not on some dark-skinned Indian beauty."

He spent some time telling me what the series was all about.

A young American boy, actor Jay North, arrives in Bombay to search for his missing father, a noted white hunter. The authorities, who are convinced his father is dead, rule that he is to be sent back to the States. North runs away with the Indian police in hot pursuit. He meets an Indian boy, Sajid Khan, who has an elephant, Maya. The police believe Sajid has stolen the elephant and are determined to run him down and arrest him. Jay and Sajid join forces and travel throughout India, becoming involved in various situations.

King said he would be using the same German technicians he used on his successful feature film, *Maya,* also produced in India. He added, "The equipment is already on its way to Bombay by boat."

I scanned the paper he handed me. I was surprised a crab dolly (a platform for the camera with four small wheels that allows the direction of the camera to be changed during a scene at any time and in any direction) was not on the list. When I asked about it, Franklin answered for Frank, "You won't need a crab dolly."

I ignored him and said, "Mr. King, the concept of the *Maya* series I just heard was one of movement. Do you expect me to have the actors ride in on the elephant, stop and read the lines, then resume their mad dash to escape from the authorities?"

I began to view Frank King in a new and more favorable light when he turned to Franklin and gave him an order, in a tone that left no room for further discussion. "Have a crab dolly in Bombay before Christmas, even if you have to fly it over."

I listened to Frank praise the talents of the German film crews that had worked for him in the past, especially the cameraman, Gunter Sempfleben.

I left the meeting after telling Frank privately that I could see problems with his associate producer. He told me the title was meaningless. "He's really my unit production manager on the series. You'll answer to no one but me."

Marty Shapiro had no trouble with Frank King over the conditions I wanted in my contract. On my fifty-ninth birthday, December 12, 1966, I signed the contract that would tie me to India for the next year.

I was to arrive in Bombay the morning of January 2, 1967, to direct thirteen of the twenty-six episodes of the *Maya* series.

All the Hollywood movie producing companies had immense amounts of blocked rupees in the Reserve Bank of India that could only be used for production of movies in India, executive travel, and living expenses. Frank was as good as his word, and I was given first-class tickets on United Airlines to New York and the same accommodations on Air India from New York to Bombay.

To avoid the press of holiday travelers, I left Los Angeles on December 28 and stopped over in Rome to visit with my old friends, "Doc" Erickson, his wife Connie, and their beautiful four-year-old daughter, Dawn.

At the airport on the morning of January 1, I noticed a group of Americans standing together. As I entered the first-class section of the Air India 747 jumbo jet, I saw them head back into the overcrowded tourist section. At three o'clock on the morning of January 2, when we landed at Santa Cruz Airport in Bombay, Morrie King met the plane and introduced me to the group of American strangers: Writer Bill Stuart; Art Director Frank Sylos; "Bluey" Hill, an assistant director from London who would become my friend and right arm; and the lone woman in the group, Countess Trudy Von Trotha, the script supervisor from Munich, Germany. I'm not sure, but I think Harry Franklin was also in the group. All of the people in that group had violated the terms of their unions by flying tourist class.

With Morrie there was a small, intense Indian Muslim gentleman, Rashid Abbasi, one of the finest production managers in all of India. He was a man for whom I would learn to have tremendous respect, for his honesty and ability. It was the start of a close friendship that would last sixteen years.

Rashid loaded us into a chartered bus, and we started on a journey that is as vivid in my memory now as it was on that cold, early drive into the city. Men, some wrapped in thin blankets, others wearing only their pajamas or dhotis, huddled together to fight off the chill; and whole families making their homes in giant concrete pipes, strung along an open ditch.

By the time we reached the Nataraj Hotel, our home until we moved to Srinagar, Kashmir, in May to escape the monsoon rains, the stench had been left behind, but the memory of that first drive in from the airport still haunts me. In the early 1970s, they moved the slaughterhouse away from the city and filled in the swamps.

Before we arrived at the Nataraj, Frank King had chosen rooms for all of us. Mine turned out to be an oversized broom closet. I called Marvin Chomsky, the director who had signed to direct the other thirteen episodes of *Maya,* and asked if he was happy with his room. He was a little disappointed Frank hadn't given him a suite, as our Directors Guild contracts required. I told him I was on my way to Frank's office to demand a suite and asked if he cared to come along.

Frank King would have made an excellent actor. He told me he'd done his best to get both of us suites but that the hotel didn't have any available. I told Frank I'd just talked to the manager and two suites were available. He didn't argue when I told him that Marvin and I were moving. One of the suites faced the sea, and the other was on the side. We matched for the seafront suite, and Marvin won.

Frank sent Marvin to Agra to photograph scenes of doubles of Jay North and Sajid Khan riding Maya past the Taj Mahal and other beautiful scenery to be used for title backgrounds. I stayed to help Frank get the company organized with a business office, stages at Mehboob Studios, and locations that could be used for the series. Bluey Hill, who had been Frank's first assistant on the feature film *Maya,* took me around the countryside.

Each day I'd meet a new member of Frank's staff. Rashid Abbasi was already taking charge of the staff and crew, most of whom had worked with Frank in the past. There was an ex-movie star, Karan Dewan, who had signed on as the casting director.

Others I met included Krish Krishnaswamy, a welcome addition to the two American auditors, John Sided, and Norman Webster, from MGM; and Ansari, an Indian gaffer, the title given worldwide to the top electrician on a picture. Gaus-uddin, a retired navy ship's carpenter, was our Indian grip. He became a trusted friend.

Then there was a man who would become, along with Rashid, close to Mary Belle and me. He was a camera assistant whom I would one day have the personal satisfaction of promoting to head cameraman on my film *Return to India.* His name was Rohinton Behramsha. He and his family were Parsis.

There also were Ram Yadaker, a fine art director, Ram Ramanlal, a top camera operator, and Baba Sheikh, a production manager from Afghanistan.

Each film had its own choice tale to tell, beginning with *Satira,* the first of the series to go before the cameras in Bombay, which I directed, and continuing through to the last, which I produced and directed in Srinager, Kashmir. Some were dangerous. Some skirted on tragedy.

Shakut Khan, the owner with his two brothers of Mehboob Studios, the largest motion picture studio in India, offered to play the role of an Indian maharajah in *Satira.*

Paul Sylos and Ram Yadaker had built the exterior and interior of the village post office outside Bombay on the grounds of the Aarey Milk Colony.

The opening scene of the picture is a very young, beautiful princess asking the postmaster for mail from her betrothed prince who is away in college. The postmaster, played by one of India's favorite actors, David Abraham, takes mail from a slot and comes to the princess.

We see, as he shuffles the mail, a letter addressed to the princess. I wanted to convey, without dialogue and without a cut in the scene, the fact that there was a letter for her. I wanted the audience to become suspicious of the postmaster.

Two Indian films were in production at the Milk Colony the day we arrived to film the scene. As I was rehearsing the scene using the crab dolly, the directors, cameramen, and some of the crews of the Indian films came to watch. They'd never seen movement with the camera the way I was using it. Most Indian films were shot using cameras in fixed positions. After I'd completed filming the scene, I invited each of the directors and cameramen to ride the dolly and watch the scene through the camera.

In one episode, *The Treasure Temple,* another segment I directed while we were still living in Bombay, we had two narrow escapes. We were filming at night in the National Park at Kanhari, where Buddhists had carved great rooms from a mountain of solid granite. Outside the caves, as the rooms were called, a wide, flat expanse of granite, polished by the feet of millions of tourists, allowed access to the porches where fifteen-foot statues guarded the entrance to the rooms.

The scene called for Jay North, Sajid Khan, and an American archaeologist, bound hand and foot, sleeping on a pile of rubble in the foreground, while in the background a giant tiger enters and explores the caves. During the first rehearsal, the tiger followed the path he'd been trained to follow, but instead of entering the caves, he charged our actors. Instantly, the trainers and the crew, all with long, sharp-pointed bamboo poles, rushed in to protect our people. The trainers rehearsed the tiger a few times, and when we shot the scene, the animal performed correctly.

The second incident was even more frightening. I barely prevented the death of Sajid or Jay, I can't remember which of the boys it was. The scene was staged around the entrance to an opening in the hillside where the archaeologist was digging a tunnel to search for the "treasure" under the "Treasure Temple."

Jay North had carelessly left his rifle at the entrance of the tunnel while he was busy with Maya.

Jairaj, one of my favorite Indian actors, playing the part of the archaeologist's henchman, was to come from the tunnel, pick up the rifle, and place it against the side of the boy's head. As always, I'd warned Mohan, the property man, against handing an actor a gun until he'd given it to me so I could inspect it.

During the first rehearsal, when Jairaj picked up the rifle and shoved it against the boy's head, I screamed at him to aim it toward the sky. I took it away and opened it. I broke into a cold sweat at what I found there. A live round. Mohan told me that the German grip had given it to him. The grip brought me an open box that had live rounds, blanks, and dummy ammunition, all mixed together. He told me Harry Franklin had given it to him.

I was outraged by Franklin's stupidity. When he walked on the set later that afternoon, I humiliated him before the whole company. Later on, when I agreed to also produce the series, I sent Franklin back to the studio.

Frank King sent me a script for *The Demon of Kalimira,* a story about the mysterious disappearance of villagers while they are at work or play.

At high noon Jay and Sajid ride in on Maya. They stop and stare off at what seems to be a deserted village. Deserted by villagers and animals. But why is a potter's wheel turning? But where is the potter?

A child's swing moving back and forth. But where is the child? A rocking chair rocking. But where is the person who was rocking? And there is other evidence of people having been in the village.

Slowly, frightened villagers come from their huts and tell the boys about an animal, an animal they've never seen, carrying off their friends.

The boys decide to stay in the village and help the people rid it of what they believe are the acts of an angry god.

They know it has to be a tiger, and they set a trap to destroy it. They ask the headman of the village to tie a water buffalo to a stake in the center of the village. Jay, with his rifle, will wait in a tree, and when the tiger attacks the buffalo, he will kill it. But I wanted the public to believe that this particular tiger was a tiger with superhuman intelligence.

I asked our animal trainer if he could train the buffalo to remain absolutely still if I had the tiger disregard the buffalo and go after Jay. He said it could be done if I would give him a few days to train the buffalo.

Here is how I filmed the killing of the tiger. I made a shot of the deserted village square. Jay passes the buffalo and gets into position on a limb of a giant tree. We show the village from his point of view.

Next we see the tiger appear at the corner of a building and survey the square. We see his eyes center on the buffalo. He suspects a trap, and his eyes go to Jay in the tree. He disappears behind the building. Then he appears again, and we move the camera along with him. He passes the buffalo without even glancing at it. His prey is Jay up in the tree.

Jay hasn't seen the tiger since it disappeared behind the building and is unaware that the tiger is after him. The tiger climbs the tree and comes into view on the same tree limb behind Jay. As the tiger is very close to Jay, a shout from Sajid alerts Jay, and he turns just in time to save himself by firing one shot that causes the tiger to fall to the ground dead.

I thought *The Demon of Kalimira* was one of the most exciting episodes of the *Maya* series. But I was outraged when I saw it back at the studio. The cutter hadn't used any of the shots of the tiger disregarding the buffalo. The scene was filmed to convince the audience that the tiger was superhuman.

Yash Johar, a close associate of Dev Anand, one of India's top producers, directors, and stars, who owned his own production company, called on us, bringing an invitation to a dinner party Mr. Anand was giving at his home, in honor of Shirley MacLaine.

We didn't know Shirley was in India and found out later that she didn't know we were in Bombay. It would be a great surprise for all of us.

Dev Anand's home was overcrowded with journalists, photographers, movie stars, and a sprinkling of just plain folks like us.

Mary Belle and I were standing near the fireplace talking to an Indian couple we'd known for some time when the entry door opened and Shirley entered, wearing a green sari, surrounded by a group of leading Indian artists.

She was greeted by a sudden burst of applause. The photographers, followed by the reporters and others, crowded around her.

Suddenly, she spotted us and, with a scream of delight, ran pell-mell through the crowd, threw her arms around my neck, and kissed me. "What are you and Mary Belle doing in India?"

She didn't wait for an answer but, rather, turned to the crowd and called out, "This man, Herbie Coleman, gave me my first part in a movie. *The Trouble with Harry.*"

At dinner in the open patio, with the gentle, cool breeze flowing in from the Arabian Sea, we were seated beside Shirley. She turned the conversation from the beauty of the country and her love for the people to my experiences with Indian filmmakers while producing

Maya. She interrupted my long discourse about the cooperation I'd received from those well-trained and dedicated men and women in the Bombay film world to ask, "Do you think it possible to produce an expensive major screenplay entirely in India?"

I told her that I was positive it could be done but that there were many major problems to be solved before a commitment was made to move a company to India.

"If your series isn't renewed, or if you decide you want to move on, call me when you get home. I've something in mind you might like to take on," she said.

For a short time, Frank got me involved in the production of a film, *The Year of the Cricket.* I agreed to guide his girlfriend, Mary Murray, in the preparation of the film that would be filmed around Bombay.

But Murray, an untested producer, and I were unable to establish a satisfactory working relationship, so I bowed out. I was getting restless waiting for word on the series and, around November 1, resigned, and we left for home.

Chapter 56

Every Time a Heart Beats

Shirley MacLaine answered my call with a "Come on up."

When I arrived at her home, there was little gossip and small talk as we sat in her spacious but comfortable living room. I listened with interest as she told about her plans to make a major motion picture in India she called *Every Time a Heart Beats.* Meaning that every time a heart beats, somewhere in the world, another child is born.

It was a story about an American woman gynecologist, Shirley, who goes to India to help in India's struggle to encourage birth control. Waiting at Dum Dum Airport in Calcutta when she arrives is a young, handsome, Indian doctor of gynecology who has been assigned to work with her.

Dev Anand would play this doctor. In the scene at Dum Dum, the audience would discover that the film has its lighter moments when the customs inspector, ignoring Shirley's pleas to pass a tightly packed suitcase, releases the locks. Out of the suitcase pops every known contraceptive device ever invented.

There is another funny sequence. In a small village somewhere away from the big cities, Shirley demonstrates the proper use of a condom by rolling it out on a thick bamboo stick. She leaves a supply of condoms for the villagers.

When she returns to the village, she sees that the men understood exactly how they were to use the condoms. In front of each little hut, a bamboo stake had been driven in the ground and a gleaming white condom had been rolled down on it.

That scene would draw a mild rebuke from Harrish Khanna that would disturb Shirley when she read his report on the synopsis.

She told me she would write the screenplay and direct the film. She then added, "Herbie, I hope you'll join me as coproducer." I asked her to hand me the contract so I could sign it. She told me she would have her attorney, Ben Neuman, call me in a few days. She gave me a copy of the synopsis, and a hug, and asked me to call after I'd read and thought about her rundown.

Ben Neuman called and asked for a meeting at his office in Beverly Hills.

I found Neuman to be a small man, a little overweight, with thinning gray hair and a friendly open disposition. I also found him to be a little too sharp.

"Mr. Coleman," he said, "Shirley tells me you've worked as a producer in India for the King brothers." I waited for him to continue. "She also told me you had agreed to join her as her coproducer." I waited for him to get to the reason for that meting.

He shuffled through some papers, found the ones he wanted, and placed them before me. "You'll see in that contract we're offering you two contracts. The first is for the survey in India: $750.00 a week for six weeks. The second is . . ."

I shut him off with an outburst, "You can forget the second! And the first! If you wanted to insult me, you could have made that offer on the telephone. You said, 'We are offering.' Did you and Shirley discuss that contract?"

"Discussions between attorney and client are privileged. You must know that."

"Well, if your client wants a production manager to go to India, she can call the Directors Guild, and they'll send her a list of the available members."

I turned and walked out of his office.

On my drive home I asked myself, "Was this Shirley's attempt to repay me for the opportunity I gave her to rise to the absolute top of her profession, when I cast her in my first film as a producer and her first as an actress? Didn't Neuman learn from Frank King that my salary for my last week on *Maya* was $3,250.00?" And they were offering $750.00.

For the rest of that day and the next, I refused to accept Neuman's phone calls. But when he called the morning of the third day, I agreed to a meeting that afternoon. I'd been giving a lot of thought to Shirley's story and the possibility of making a very good picture that would help India in many ways. The most important, of course, was helping that great country in its fight to slow the enormous flow of babies born in a nation unable to provide for them.

And there was Mary Belle. She loved the people and the country. A year moving around India would give her the opportunity to continue her study of its culture, Hinduism, and Buddhism.

I met with Neuman that afternoon. It didn't take long for us to reach a figure fair to both of us, and on December 27, 1967, I signed a contract with the Parker Company, the name of Shirley and her husband Steve Parker's company, to coproduce *Heart Beats.*

I discovered that her film would have moments of gentle humor but would be a serious attempt to promote birth control in a nation where the women, including Prime Minister Indira Gandhi, desperately wanted to end the exploding birth of babies.

Naturally, as Shirley and Dev Anand travel throughout that vast subcontinent, they become romantically involved.

Shirley would write, direct, and coproduce the screenplay. Richard Attenborough would have an important role in the picture and would direct when she was acting in scenes.

Shirley told me that Charles Bludhorn, the CEO of Gulf & Western, the parent company of Paramount Pictures, had agreed to finance and distribute the picture but that he wanted me to take a unit production manager from London. I told Shirley I wouldn't agree with that suggestion. I'd already decided to take Curtis Mick from Paramount. I wanted him with me when I met with top Indian government officials.

"There are a number of obstacles for foreign filmmakers that have to be removed before we will want to produce *Heart Beats* in India," I told Shirley. "The first and most important is the Indian income tax, assessed on one's worldwide income if one remains in India more than ninety days during the financial year that begins on April 1 and ends on March 31.

"The only time period for filming in South India is November through February, all in one fiscal year. We'll have to decide if we can prepare, shoot the picture, and get out in less than ninety days.

"The second is the requirement that four copies of a complete shooting script be submitted and approved by the Ministry of Information and Broadcasting in New Delhi before the Ministry of Finance will release the necessary blocked funds from the Paramount account.

"I've established a friendly business relationship with Harrish Khanna, the deputy secretary of the Ministry of I&B, who is the final authority on script approval, and I believe he will give his approval based on the synopsis.

"The third is the rule that a complete budget be submitted to I&B when the screenplay is given to them."

Shirley talked about her tour of the country, especially about the villages she'd visited and wanted me to take a look at. I remember there was one village in Orissa State she was fond of. She gave me copies of the pictures she'd made during her tour.

When I left Hollywood for Bombay, I felt Shirley fully understood that we had better than a 50–50 chance of making a success of the project.

Curtis flew out from Paris, where he was preparing another Paramount picture, and joined me at the Taj Mahal Hotel where we would stay while in Bombay.

K. S. Vaidyanathan, known to everyone as K. S., the chief officer for Paramount Films of India, Pvt. Ltd., a man I still treasure as a close friend, handed me bundles of rupees and a few very important tips on dealing with the people in New Delhi.

We flew on to New Delhi and registered at the Oberoi Intercontinental Hotel, where I met many of Oberoi's men from the Oberoi Palace Hotel in Srinagar.

I called Harrish Khanna at the Ministry of I&B and was invited to join him the same afternoon. While I described our mission, I saw him studying Curtis. He was satisfied with what he saw and was ready to accept Curtis as another of the "good" Americans. When my tale of *Heart Beats* ended, he asked for the shooting screenplay. I handed him the synopsis. He shuffled through the pages, looked up at me, and asked, "This is it?" I wanted to get out before we got into a discussion about the synopsis, so I told him we'd take a quick look around the country and drop in on him in a couple of weeks.

We flew to Calcutta to check out Dum Dum Airport and then on to Shirley's Orissa village. It was a step up from the poor villages surrounding Bombay I'd used in *Maya.* The people were well fed, and their costumes were colorful. I was concerned about the number of villagers who had been maimed by that dread disease, elephantiasis.

We checked out the remaining villages Shirley had selected during her tour. She'd made wise choices.

I gathered the official documents promised by the various Ministry of Finance departments and flew home.

Shirley was starring in a Universal film, *Sweet Charity.* The news she had for me was anything but sweet. She told me there had been trouble on *Charity,* forcing a change in producers. They were weeks behind schedule. She also said she wouldn't finish *Charity* early enough to go to India, write the screenplay, and be ready to start shooting on November 1. "You'll have to postpone the start of the picture until November 1, 1969."

In Bernie Donnenfeld's office at Paramount, we called Charles Bludhorn in New York. He had no interest in a year's delay on *Heart*

Beats. "It's a topical subject. A year from now, people who go to see our movies will have something new on their minds. Do it now or forget it."

Shirley didn't take the news of Bludhorn ducking out with grace. We were sitting in her living room talking about *Heart Beats.* Then, for a moment we were silent, lost in thought. Shirley broke the silence by asking, "That afternoon when you saw me in *Pajama Game,* what caused you to decide, at that very moment, I was right for Jennifer Rogers in *The Trouble with Harry?*"

I should have answered, "Intuition." I've lived my whole life intuitively. But I didn't. What I heard coming from my mouth shocked me even more than Shirley. She was too much the lady and actress to show her dismay at the sexist remark she'd just heard.

We resumed our discussion about *Heart Beats,* but it wasn't the same. At the door, we said good-bye. A good-bye that was different from all the previous good-byes. To my sorrow, it was the final good-bye.

I went back to my Paramount office, told my secretary to pack everything she could find—pictures, contracts, Indian government documents, anything to do with *Every Time a Heart Beats*—and send it all to Ben Neuman's office in Beverly Hills. That done, I said good-bye to *Every Time a Heart Beats* and, for a time, to Paramount.

Chapter 57

Topaz

A few days after I walked away from Paramount, Hitch called and invited me to lunch and a private running of his last picture, *Torn Curtain.*

Lunch was waiting in his large, private dining room, a room that was added when Lew Wasserman moved the music department to a new location and gave the whole building to Hitch. It included two private offices, one for his meetings with his television associates and a much larger one for his feature film operation. Three secretaries' offices. A private projection room. A large drafting room, and offices for the art director, the screenwriter, assistant directors, and the production manager.

Hitch was on his usual diet—a piece of meat and a glass of wine. The piece of meat was a large sirloin steak, and the glass of wine was from a bottle of his favorite French Bordeaux. As we sat down, he glared at the glass of milk beside my very rare hamburger. "Herbie," he drawled, "don't you know that stuff is for baby cows?"

I grinned at him. "We eat baby cows. Guess their mommy's milk can't hurt us."

He turned his attention to his lunch and then looked up and asked about my Indian project. "The grapevine has it, your Shirley MacLaine project at Paramount won't get off the ground this year."

"Not this year or ever, Hitch. Bluehorn told me to make it this year or forget it. His lame excuse was *Every Time a Heart Beats* is a topical subject! I asked him how the struggle to stem the flood of babies born every year, all over the world, could be topical. He wasn't interested in discussing the subject. And that was the end of *Heart Beats.* And her *Sweet Charity* won't finish in time to get started this year."

The food and wine were long gone before Hitch stopped asking about making pictures in India. Then he started talking about his latest picture, *Torn Curtain,* a film he'd made while I was tied up on *Nevada Smith.* "You've seen every picture I've made since *North by Northwest* but *Torn Curtain.* It's ready to go in the theater. Will you take a look?"

I sat alone in Universal's largest theater. *Torn Curtain* wasn't up to Hitch's standards.

Hitch was in his office waiting with the ice tinkling in the cocktails he'd mixed for us when I arrived to give my report on the picture.

"I had the feeling you didn't expect another *Vertigo* with *Torn Curtain,* Hitch. There are qualities missing in this picture that made the others so successful. The camera work, for instance. Jack Warren isn't Bob Burks. I thought Bob was all set. Why did you drop Bob and Bummy? And we all miss George Tomasini and his sensitive touch. And Benny Herrmann. After eight straight pictures you let him get away.

"But what bothered me most was the scene between Paul Newman and Ludwig Donath. How could Newman, a brilliant scientist, hope to compose a meaningless formula on a blackboard and have an equally brilliant scientist wipe it away and reveal the secret formula known only to himself?"

Hitch didn't answer immediately. He called to his secretary, "Sue, Mr. Coleman needs another cocktail. And add a block of ice to mine." He held up his empty glass. After Sue left the room, Hitch thought a moment and then said, "Your criticism of that scene reminds me of your feelings about the scene in *The Birds* where I let Tippi Hedren enter that upstairs room where all the seagulls were waiting. I think I told you then I had to have her trapped with no means of escape from the seagulls. I let Brian Moore, who wrote the screenplay, convince me the scene would work. You're the first to disagree." Hitch wasn't upset by my frankness. He expected it. He knew I would lay it all out.

He was enthusiastic about his next project. He told me that Lew had bought for him Leon Uris's book *Topaz* and that Uris was hard at work on the screenplay. "It will be a film with landscapes equal to *The Man Who Knew Too Much,*" he said. "And more suspense than *Vertigo.*"

I thanked him for the lunch and wished him luck with *Topaz.*

I forgot about *Topaz* and went back to work developing, with Dick Nelson, a young writer in whom I had great confidence, an original screenplay of mine, *An Italian Affair.* Gossip columnist Hedda Hopper helped create studio interest with an item in her column.

Work on the screenplay was interrupted by a phone call from Paul Donneley, the head of production for Universal, inviting me to lunch at the studio. There would be many times in the months ahead I would regret accepting that free lunch. "Herbie," he said, "Hitch wants you to help him on his new film *Topaz.*" His next statement was something of a shock. "As production manager."

I sat silent as Paul tried to sell me on the idea of stepping back to help my old friend. The more he talked about Hitch's need to have my help, the more I began to suspect that he and the studio wanted me to accept the job. They evidently thought they would have more control over my spending if I was under their direct control.

After two very expensive films, *The Birds* and *Marnie,* was the studio trying to move Hitch back toward less costly pictures like *Psycho*?

I'd long heard hints that I always pushed Hitch to demand perfection. And perfection was costly. Ask Sol Siegal. I always suspected he spread the word that I was responsible for spending double what he'd budgeted for *North by Northwest.*

Well, I told myself, if that's what they have in mind, they have a surprise coming. I told Paul to call Billy Hunt, an attorney with whom I'd signed to handle my affairs.

The day I reported to work, Donneley gave me a budget they'd prepared and told me to move into one of the offices in Hitch's bungalow.

I remember little of Uris's screenplay. Hitch wanted to talk about cast. In my new position, I was a little hesitant about offering my opinions until Hitch repeatedly pressed me to speak up.

My first choice for Andre Devereaux, who posed as the French commercial attaché in Washington, D.C., but was actually the top French intelligence officer, was Yves Montand. Hitch had MCA check on Montand. They reported that Montand could be had but would insist that Catherine Deneauve be cast as Nicole Devereaux. Hitch wasn't about to have an actor, any actor, dare invade his domain, and Montand was gone.

Hitch decided to concentrate on casting the American actors before leaving for Paris. Only one American would work on locations in Europe, and Hitch had already given the role of Michael Nordstrom to John Forsythe.

Hitch was anxious to get to Europe; complete the casting of the actors needed in Copenhagen, Wiesbaden, and Paris; and put *Topaz* before the cameras.

He wasn't happy with what he'd received from Uris and grumbled constantly about the need for a new writer. By the time Hitch, Alma, and I arrived in London and were settled in Claridges Hotel, he'd decided to act. He called Samuel Taylor at his home in East Blue Hill, Maine, and said, "Sam, can you catch a plane for London today?"

"Not today, Hitch," Sam told him, "but I could tomorrow." When he told Hitch he hadn't read *Topaz,* Hitch said, "Buy a copy and read it on the plane coming over." He added, "I'm not happy with the Uris screenplay and want you to give me a new script."

Sam was as good as his word. Universal's New York staff had him on a plane to London the following night.

He'd had little sleep, having spent most of the night reading Uris's book. But within an hour after arriving in his suite at Claridges, Sam joined Hitch and they went to work. Hitch told Sam, "I'd like you to write the scenes covering Copenhagen, then you can go back to Universal and work there. There's a large comfortable office for you in my building."

Sam was not only one of the finest writers it was my good fortune to know, he was one of the fastest. And he knew Copenhagen as well as he knew his hometown, San Francisco. Still, I was surprised when he handed us the script.

Before Hitch would let Sam leave for Hollywood, he decided to take him along to Stockholm, where he planned to meet with Ingmar Bergman and seek his advice on casting the Russian KGB official, Kusinov, his wife, and his daughter.

"I want actors unknown in the States," he told us. One of the first things Hitch said to me when I joined him on the project was, "I want the opening of *Topaz* to have a documentary feel."

The Universal staff made all the arrangements for our journey to Stockholm. One of their men met us with a limousine when we arrived at the airport. Soon after we arrived at the hotel, Hitch and Sam were on their way to the studio to meet Bergman. His suggestions of Per-Axel Arosenius for Kusinov and Sonia Kolthoff for Mrs. Kusinov proved to be just what Hitch was looking for. I don't remember where the daughter came from; I think she was cast in London.

I was making the arrangements to return to London when Hitch surprised us all. "While we're this far north, I think we should take a quick look around Finland for the movie I plan on making after *Topaz.*

"I have a book, *The Short Night.* We'll need a big home somewhere in the lake country. There's a big exciting chase between a Russian train and a car from Helsinki to the Russian border."

Sam was reluctant to make the trip but was persuaded by Hitch to come along.

Universal had no contacts in Helsinki, but the people at our hotel in Stockholm arranged rooms at a hotel in Helsinki and a car to meet our plane.

The car failed to show up at the airport in Helsinki. I put Alma, Hitch, and Sam in a taxi and told them to go on to the hotel.

I arrived at our hotel almost an hour later than Hitch and the others to find a message from Hitch to come to his suite as soon as I checked in. I expected to hear a complaint about his suite. Instead, he wanted to know why I'd stayed behind at the airport. "And leave all our luggage sitting on the sidewalk for anyone to steal?" I asked him.

"But we've always stayed together in the past."

"Hitch," I said, "you know as well as I, the responsibilities of a production manager are a little different than those of a producer."

The mask that always seemed to conceal his thoughts fell away, and a surprised look appeared on his face. "I don't understand," he said. "Production manager?"

"It's the job Donneley said you wanted me to take to help you on *Topaz,* Hitch."

Without another word, he picked up the phone and asked the operator to connect him with Lew Wasserman at Universal. I didn't want to hear what Hitch was going to say to Lew, and despite Hitch's insistence, I went to my room.

Less than ten minutes had passed when I heard a knock on my door. It was Hitch. He took a look around my single room before giving me the news. "You're back in your old job," he said. "Lew will see to it. Credit and salary."

He took another look around my room. "Move into proper quarters, then join us in my suite for a drink. Sam knows of a great restaurant here in town. He's already made reservations."

It was a great restaurant. Hitch took one look at the first course, an immense red bowl filled to the brim with what looked like little bright red legs. He said he was back on his diet.

He tried to turn away as Sam and I dug in, breaking open the legs and sucking out the delicious meat. I don't remember the Finnish name for them, but back in the streams around Cliff Holler we used to call them crawdads.

The waitress managed to convince Hitch that he would enjoy the sole from the cold waters around Finland. He and Alma did, and Hitch insisted on dining at the same restaurant each evening we remained in Helsinki.

I found a travel guide who listened to my story and suggested that we center our search for the proper lake and little island around the city of Hemilina.

We moved there and found just what Hitch had in mind. For three days we traveled, mostly by boat, for miles and miles. The deep blue lakes, the sky always filled with thunderheads, the stands of tall straight birch trees, and the white bark accented with black broken patches were an added photographic inducement to lure us back for the film.

We returned to our hotel in Helsinki. I was anxious to get back to London and get things going on *Topaz*. But Hitch wanted to take a drive out to the Finnish–Russian border where the climax of *The Short Night* would be filmed.

We left Helsinki early on a Sunday morning. The weather was perfect, and the driver of our limousine was a fountain of Finnish/Russian history.

For lunch, he stopped at a famous roadside restaurant. As we entered the building, four men near the entrance were just turning away from their table, heading for the cashier. One of them recognized Hitch and started applauding. Instantly, others in the crowded restaurant began joining in the applause. Hitch was beaming as the owner escorted us to a table. The four men who were about to leave when we entered returned to their table and sat there for a full hour while we were dining.

Hitch was a little surprised that after the greeting he had received when we entered the restaurant, not one person came to our table for his autograph.

We drove on to the border, where our driver stopped some distance from an outpost where two armed uniformed Russian soldiers stood guard. There wasn't a building in sight, nothing but the railroad tracks leading off into the Soviet Union. We got out to stretch our legs. As I made a series of photographs, the soldiers stood, silent and watchful, but did nothing until I pointed my camera in their direction. That brought them to full attention. By their actions, they let me know that I was not to make any pictures of them or the border.

While all this was going on, a small group of children appeared from the forest. Some of them recognized Hitch and ran for his autograph. Our driver explained that Hitch's movies were very popular in Finland and that there was a school hidden in the forest.

Back in Helsinki, we discovered that there was a Russian passenger train at the station. I was able to get permission to take a look at it. "You can walk around the coaches," I was told, "but you will not be allowed to go aboard or make any photographs." There were a number of similar intercontinental trains in the States that could double for the Russian ones.

Hitch and I sat together on the flight back to London. He was enthusiastic about filming *Short Night* in the places we'd scouted. I dampened his enthusiasm when I pointed out the impossibility of disrupting an entire railway system for his film. The Russians would never allow us to use their equipment.

"Then where would you suggest we film *Short Night*?" he asked. "Where would you find lakes like those around Hemilina? And forests of birch trees similar to those in Finland?" I told him I didn't know but that I'd seen pictures of Wisconsin that looked interesting. That ended any conversation about *Short Night* until one night in the Villa d'Esta Hotel at Lake Como months later.

While we were vacationing in the North Countries, Universal sent to London for Wallace (Wally) Worsley, their top unit production manager. By the time we arrived back he had everything organized. The production office was open with a top English staff hard at work.

Hitch and I had already decided on Jack Hildyard as the director of photography. Fortunately, he was available and willing to team with Hitch.

Sam Taylor flew off to Hollywood to resume work on the screenplay.

Alma, Hitch, and I moved to the Hotel Plaza Athenée in Paris and went to work in earnest selecting the cast. Universal began pushing Hitch to sign Montand. Hitch refused. Long before we left for Paris Hitch had decided that the only non-European member of the cast would be John Forsythe, who would be an American intelligence officer. In Paris, our search for the French intelligence officer, André Devereaux, became a problem that had to be overcome in a hurry. Guillo Ascarrelli, Universal's top executive in France, suggested that an Austrian actor, Frederic Stafford, living and working in Rome might fit the bill.

I flew to Rome and invited Stafford to dine with me at the Eden. I liked what I saw when he walked in. Tall and trim. His stride and bearing reminded me of General Maxwell Taylor, of *The Beyond Glory* days. His accent was similar to the accent of the people with whom I'd worked in Vienna, Austria, when I was there recording Bernard Herrmann's score for our picture *Vertigo.*

I called Hitch and told him I wasn't sure Stafford was our man and asked him to come to Rome and test him.

I met him when he arrived in Rome the next morning. We met with Stafford later that day. He and Hitch spent some time together that afternoon. At dinner that night at the Excelsior, Hitch said he had the same slight question about Stafford being the man we were searching for but wanted to go ahead with the test. The test was filmed at Cinecitta. We looked at the test when it arrived and decided to go ahead with Stafford.

Jay Kantor, the chief of Universal's foreign operations, was pressing Hitch to accept Dany Robin for the part of Nicole Devereaux, the wife of André Devereaux. She turned out to be an over-the-hill former French star. I thought she was unattractive, cold, self-centered, selfish, and, as I was to discover too late, prone to cheat a bit financially.

Claude Jade was a perfect choice for the part of Michelle Picard, and Michel Subor, for François Picard. Two of France's finest character actors were also selected: Philippe Noriet for Henri Jarre and Michel Piccoli for Jacques Granville.

Edith Head arrived with the sketches for Dany Robin, and Head supervised Balmain's company in what he called "executed" Head's designs.

Mary Belle arrived from home and joined us at the Plaza Athenée. Bummy Bumstead, our production designer, joined Worsley and the other American staff at the ancient, but comfortable, Raphael Hotel.

Filming in Copenhagen went smoothly. We were a happy company. No personality clashes. Hitch even accepted the English crew's insistence on tea breaks in the afternoon.

With only three days left to complete the Copenhagen schedule before the company would move to Frankfurt to film for one day the scenes at Wiesbaden, I decided to fly down to Paris and straighten out problems that had come up on Piccoli's contract.

I called Fred Surin, our French production manager, and asked him to arrange a car to meet us at Orly and a room at the Plaza Athenée for the one night I planned to be there. Fred had been ill, so I told him it was not necessary to meet us at Orly when we would arrive after midnight. But when Mary Belle and I arrived, Fred, looking very tired, was standing at the gate. I was a bit angry that he had disobeyed my order not to meet us. "Fred, didn't you understand me when I said there was nothing important enough to have you meet us?"

"But there is, Herbie," he said. "You've had your French shooting permit revoked."

I stopped dead in my tracks. I was stunned. If what he said was true, it meant that we couldn't shoot anywhere in France. Our whole project was in danger of going down the drain. What had happened to cause the French government to take such drastic steps? Possible solutions, none practical, began swimming around in my mind. I forced those thoughts away and asked Fred, "What's the story?"

"The French ambassador in Washington advised Paris to cancel the permit because *Topaz* would do great harm to France."

By the time we reached the hotel, I had a plan of action I had to put into work immediately.

I called Universal and asked for Lew Wasserman. "Mr. Wasserman is on his way to Washington," his secretary told me. "There's no way I can reach him right now. Will Edd Henry do?"

I asked her to get him on the line. There was no love lost between Edd Henry and myself. We had nothing in common. When he came on the line, I told him it was imperative that Lew arrange for me to meet with Sergeant Shriver sometime that same day. Shriver was the U.S. ambassador in Paris and a friend of Lew's.

When I climbed out of bed after a sleepless night, there was a message that the meeting had been arranged. I was to be at the American embassy at two o'clock that afternoon.

I took Guillo Ascarrelli along. We were ushered into Shriver's large, beautifully decorated reception room. After a short wait, he came in. He was a busy man and soon turned from a brief discussion of conditions at Universal to ask, "Mr. Coleman, do you think your mission is on the ambassadorial level?"

"Yes, I do, Mr. Ambassador because the French ambassador in Washington placed it on that level." He waited for me to explain. "To film our story in France, we were, as always, required to submit a copy of our screenplay to the French embassy in Washington. It was approved, and the permit was soon in our hands. Evidently the ambassador had second thoughts about allowing *Topaz,* a story about a ring of top-level French intelligence agents who were spies for the Russians. The ambassador called Paris and had the permit revoked. Universal has a small fortune tied up in *Topaz,* and unless the French reissue the permit, I'm afraid I'll have to recommend to Mr. Wasserman we cancel further work on the picture. Mr. Hitchcock has two more days of work in Copenhagen and one day in Wiesbaden before arriving in Paris for some three weeks of filming."

Ambassador Shriver was on his feet before I'd even finished speaking.

"We'll be in touch with you before the day is over, Mr. Coleman. Perhaps we'll find a way to help you." With that, he walked us to the exit and then turned away.

At five that afternoon, Fred Surin called to tell me he had the permit.

Hitch finished his work in Copenhagen. I met him at the airport in Frankfurt and gave him a brief report on the permit problem. The scene at the airport in Wiesbaden in which Forsythe escorts Kusinov and his family aboard an Air Force plane for the flight to Washington was completed, and the whole company moved to Paris.

Until we arrived at the soccer stadium to film the duel between André Devereaux and Jacques Granville, there's not much to tell about the days and nights spent filming in and around Pairs.

The script covering the Paris sequences, which we received from Sam Taylor, hard at work in his office at the studio, made Hitch a happy man. He often said how lucky we were that he had discarded Uris's screenplay.

Then came the dawn when we were preparing to film the second of our scheduled days in the football stadium—the gun duel between Devereaux and Granville.

I'd left Hitch at the hotel and gone on ahead when he was waiting for an important telephone call from his home in Bel Air. He didn't get out of his car when it pulled to a stop in the stadium. His chauffeur hurried to where I was standing and told me, "Mr. Hitchcock would like you to join him."

I could see that he was trying to conceal the pain and stress he was feeling. "Herbie," he said, "you're going to have to take over. Alma is seriously ill. You know how to pick up from where we left off yesterday. Can you spare Wally to come with me and help me get out on the first plane?"

Minutes later, I watched his car speed away from the stadium. I directed the remaining scenes of the gun duel between Devereaux and Granville and moved the company to Washington, D.C., where Hitch joined me at the Hotel Hay Adams.

Although Alma was recovering from her illness, her doctors convinced her that she should remain at home while we were filming the Washington exterior scenes.

I knew we were going to have problems with one very important scene. It was the arrival of Air Force One with the Kusinovs and

John Forsythe at Andrews Air Force Base. Hitch wanted two limousines, bearing a group of American intelligence officials, to pull to a stop at the foot of the landing stairs as Forsythe and the Kusinovs came from the plane.

Lew Wasserman's personal generosity and his unequaled ability to raise funds for the Democratic Party came to our rescue here, as it did when I needed to see Sergeant Shriver in Paris. At my request, the major who had been assigned to us while we were filming at Andrews had received permission from the president to allow us to use Air Force One for one hour only on the coming Thursday.

On that Thursday morning, I stood there with my eyes glued on my watch as the last seconds ticked away. The "mule," the tow truck, was just out of camera range waiting to hook onto Air Force One and tow her back to her hanger, when I heard Hitch's familiar, "You have it."

The rest of our work in Washington went smoothly, and we moved on to the studio where Bummy was busy completing the interior sets.

We'd received word that the authorities in New York had refused to allow us to film the scenes around the Teresa Hotel in Harlem: "too dangerous to stage these scenes in Harlem at this time." When I agreed to join Hitch on *Topaz,* I'd been told that permission to shoot in Harlem had been approved and that the budget had been prepared with Harlem as a location. Now we would have to build the exterior of the Teresa Hotel and a large section of the street. Bummy flew to New York to make photographs of the hotel and the adjoining buildings.

I sent word to Paris to send Michel Piccoli and Phillipe Noiret to Hollywood. I sat beside Hitch while he shot the scene in Pierre's café with Stafford, the two French actors, and a supporting cast of superb players. As the cameras rolled, I glanced at Hitch and saw a smile of approval appear on his face. It was a look I'd seldom seen during the years we'd worked together. It reminded me of the look I saw when he shot Grace Kelly's introduction in *Rear Window.* The smile was still there when we paused for lunch in his stage dressing room. "You're a happy man today, Hitch," I said.

"And why shouldn't I be?" he asked. "With the cast you gave me. And one of the finest scenes Sam has ever given me. The rest was easy."

"I have some news that will keep you happy, Hitch. I've finally found someone who can get into Cuba and get the photographs we need of the airport in Havana and the Cubans unloading the missiles from the Russian freighters. He works for a British company. He flies in from Mexico City. Has good friends in the Cuban military," I said.

"You gave him the list of everything we want?"

"Yes," I said. "He read it once, then tore it up and threw it in the trash. When I asked him if he could remember everything on the list, he said, 'Can you guess what would happen to me if any of Castro's men found that list on me?'"

The photographer returned from Cuba with everything we'd asked for. For some unknown reason, the Cubans refused to allow him to photograph the caves, which wasn't a big problem for us. We'd already dropped the scenes around the caves. However, we were surprised at the scene of the unloading of a Russian freighter. The photographer was using a thirty-five-millimeter handheld movie camera. What we were looking at was four armed guards standing by the gate of a high chain-link fence. Behind them, a Russian ship was being unloaded. Suddenly, the guards became aware of the fact that the camera was recording their actions and the unloading of the ship. Two of the guards aimed their rifles at us and started coming forward. The cameraman kept the camera running until the rifles were filling the screen. That scene raised a puzzling question. Our picture was being produced in 1965, six years after President Kennedy told Khrushchev to get his missiles the hell out of Cuba. What was Russia sending Castro that he wanted to keep the newly elected president of the United States, Richard Nixon, from knowing about?

Now that we knew what the Cuban port and the Russian ships were delivering to Castro looked like, I had to find a port where we could film the scene of Cubans unloading missiles. I checked every port on the West Coast from San Diego to San Francisco in an attempt to find one similar to the port in Cuba.

Nothing worked. I had to settle on a pier at Wilmington, California. I took Al Whitlock with me. We climbed a high tower and looked down on a real mess. On the pier below us, great piles of lead balls waiting to be loaded aboard a freighter bound for Japan blocked the harbor water. Some distance away, another pier jutted out into the harbor. Beyond the pier was open water. In the distance, the San Pedro hills completely blocked our view of the Pacific Ocean. Below the hills was the city of San Pedro. I was ready to climb down from that tower when Al surprised me. "I can take out that pier and all those piles of lead balls and replace it with water," he said. "I'll take out the hills and put in the Pacific Ocean. I'll paint in the Russian freighter. You can stage your action on the pier. Have a high boom swinging your missile from the ship to the pier. Just keep your boom and the missile in the sky above my painted ship."

I staged the scene just as Al Whitlock had suggested. It worked fine.

I wasn't unhappy when we finished the "fine tuning" of *Topaz.* The duel in the soccer stadium between Stafford and Piccoli gave us our biggest problem. Duels, by their nature, are a slow-moving process. Solemnly, the instructions are given by the referee. You walk at a mandated pace. So many steps. When we tried to speed it up, the whole concept was destroyed.

I stayed with Hitch through the first preview. The public didn't complain, but the "Black Tower," those around Lew Wasserman, put the pressure on Hitch to shorten the ending of the picture, and the duel was dropped. In its place, a shot of the door to Granville's home with a pistol shot ringing out was substituted.

Would the public accept a B-picture ending to a Hitchcock film? It was not creative thinking. Had imagination deserted those around Hitchcock? I'd been away from the project a long time before that controversy arose.

I first heard about the offscreen pistol shot ending when I received a call from Charles Greenlaw, one of Lew's top assistants. He asked me to come to his office in the Black Tower.

When I arrived, he handed me a few pages and told me Hitch had asked him to call me. "There's a new ending to *Topaz.* Hitch is anxious to have you help him with it. He's at the Villa d'Esta in Chenoble, Italy. Call him after you've read it. You can use your old office in the Hitchcock building." I left his office and headed for my office but changed my mind when I noticed the time. Four-thirty in California. After midnight at Lake Como.

At home, I read the few pages. Before I'd finished, I thought this had to be a joke. A bad joke. But if they were serious, it had to be stupidity. It went something like the following.

On the tarmac at Orly airport outside Paris, two giant airliners stand side by side. One an American Airlines four-engine jet Stratocruiser, the other, a giant Russian Aeroflot. A sign at the bottom of the stairs leading up to the door of the Aeroflot announces that it is a flight to Moscow. The sign at the stairs to the American Airlines plane announces that it is a flight to Washington. André and Nicole enter and climb the stairs of the American Airlines plane. Halfway up the stairs they see Granville enter and start up the stairs of the Aeroflot. He sees André and Nicole, stops, waves goodbye to them, and then enters his plane. André and Nicole return his salute and then enter the plane bound for Washington.

I couldn't believe the French would allow Granville to walk out of France a free man after they discovered he was a traitor.

I called Charlie and warned him against submitting the new ending to the French ambassador in Washington. I told him that our original shooting permit was still valid.

I called Hitch the next morning. He was happy I would help him again. He dismissed my question about Granville getting away right under the noses of the French authorities at Orly by reciting the escape of the two British spies, Philby and McLean.

"But Hitch," I protested, "they didn't grab a taxi to Heathrow, get on an Aeroflot plane, and fly off to Moscow. They first flew to, I think it was Athens, and caught a Russian plane there."

My protest got nowhere, and I agreed to fly over to Paris, pull everything together, and then have him come to join me and direct the scenes.

Fred Surin was waiting for me when I arrived at the Plaza Athenée. He got right to work. At Orly, he found the authorities cooperative. Out in the center of the airfield there was a large space reserved for the use of any airline on a temporary basis. Fortunately, Frederic Stafford, Michele Piccoli, and Dany Robin were in town. I set the date for filming three days later.

I called Hitch and gave him the news. "Hitch," I said, "there's a Alitalia plane leaving Milano at nine o'clock Thursday morning. There will be tickets for you and Alma at the airport. You'll arrive at Orly at twelve. You won't have to go through customs.

"I'll be waiting with a car when you get off the plane. We'll drive directly to where the planes and the cast are waiting. When you finish shooting, I'll drive you back to the terminal. Seats are reserved for you on an Air France plane leaving at six. You'll be back in Milano in time for dinner."

At 10:00 Thursday morning, everything was in place but the American Airlines plane. One of the officials was waiting for me. "I'm sorry, Mr. Coleman, but our plane was delayed in London. It's now scheduled to land at 11:13. The moment the last passenger leaves the plane the captain will taxi directly over here. It should be on those marks [he pointed at the place I'd selected] twenty minutes later." With that, he climbed in his car and headed back toward the terminal.

I watched nervously as each plane would appear in the distance, turn into the landing path, land, and taxi away. Air France. Lufthansa. El Al. BEA. Everything but American Airlines. Then it appeared. I glanced at my watch. Nine after eleven. I watched the passengers slowly leave the plane. As the last one headed into the terminal, the plane turned away from the gates and slowly moved down a short distance, waited for another plane to clear the runway, and then headed directly for us. When it was finally in position, a flight of steps was pushed against the forward door. When it opened, a short muscular man in a captain's uniform came bounding down to the ground and almost ran to where we were standing. "Who's in charge here?" he demanded.

"My name's Coleman," I said. "I guess I'm your man."

"Do you know you've placed my airplane in danger of being destroyed?" He didn't wait for an answer. He pointed toward the plane. "I'm responsible for the safety of that plane until I kill the engines at the terminal."

I told the captain that I was sorry for the inconvenience but he should really discuss the matter with his superiors at American. Mad as hell, he turned and, like a fighting gamecock, marched off to a waiting car that roared away as he dropped onto his seat.

Hitch arrived right on time. The filming went smoothly, and I drove him back to the terminal. In the lounge, we enjoyed a cocktail while he waited for his plane to Milan. I told him I was taking a late plane to London. "I've made arrangements to have the film processed at Technicolor," I said. "If you can drive down to Milan on Saturday, we can look at it there. I'll leave for home on Sunday and give the film to your editor at the studio."

"You seem to be in a hurry to get home," he said.

"I've been offered a job on a television series at Universal. Norman Lloyd is having trouble with the star of his show and thinks I can be of some help."

I watched Hitch board his flight to Milan.

Saturday morning, Technicolor gave me the negatives and the prints. At 3:30 that afternoon, Hitch, Alma, and I sat in a projection room in Milan and watched the running of what I was convinced would never be seen by the public.

When the running was over, Hitch had his driver take us to a wonderful restaurant. It was in the high-rent district. We sat at a sidewalk table and marveled at the architecture. Overhead, for a whole block in all four directions, an arched glass structure covered the streets and sidewalks.

During our late luncheon Hitch invited me to be his guest at the Villa d'Esta for a few days.

We arrived there just at sunset. I've enjoyed wonderful hotels around the world, but the Villa d'Esta would forever be my favorite. Nestled safely in a forest high above Lake Como, the hotel presented a view of unspoiled beauty.

As we parted in the lobby, Hitch said, "We must celebrate tonight. Cocktails in our room in half an hour."

We didn't linger long over the drinks. Hitch centered the conversation on the dinner he'd already notified the maître d' to prepare. When we arrived in the dining room, we were escorted to the table the management always reserved for him. It was close to a high, wide window. As we settled in our chairs, the window began to disappear, silently, into the wall above. A gentle, cool breeze brought the fragrance of lilac blossoms into the room. Hitch began comparing the view we were enjoying to the view from his room at the hotel in St. Moritz.

But his description was lost on me. The fragrance of the lilacs had brought memories of the lilacs around our shack back in Cliff Holler. I was seeing my two brothers and sisters, Mama and Papa, and Grandma Bond sitting around our rough-board table having supper. A red oilcloth covered the table. Supper was boiled beans and sowbelly. Mama had made my favorite cornbread laced with crackling—"hickory-cured sowbelly." Through the tiny window, just past Grandma's shoulder, a gentle spring rain was beginning to distort the view of the lilac bushes near our spring. I watched Papa push the beans onto his knife with his fork and then slide the knife into his mouth. I'd always wondered how he could keep from cutting his mouth. I heard Bobby, our two-year-old baby brother, start to cry, and Mama say to my oldest sister, "Sis [it was what everybody called Viola], rock the baby for me, please." Mama never ordered any of us around, and she always said "please" when she asked us to do anything.

I was brought back to reality when I felt Alma's hand on my arm and heard her voice, "Herbie, come back to us. Where have you been?"

"Sixty-two years and 8,000 miles from here, Alma. Back when I was a little boy living with my folks in a shack in a place called Cliff Holler. But this is not the time or the place to discuss past history."

Hitch was much too absorbed with his dinner to notice our conversation. Alma let it drop for the moment but insisted that I tell her of my youth, time and time again, until many months later when Mary Belle and I were guests at the hacienda on the mountaintop above Santa Cruz. Hitch had retired soon after dinner. We were sitting out on the patio under the circle of giant redwood trees when Alma said, "Herbie, I've waited too long to hear the rest of your boyhood. Tell me now. Everything."

I began when we saw, for the first time, our little shack sitting on the ledge under the chestnut and dogwood trees and stopped when I walked through the gates of Paramount.

The following day we boarded a power cruiser Hitch had rented for a trip around Lake Como and had lunch at a famous restaurant situated on a small island out in the middle of the lake. Hitch had talked a lot about dining there a number of times in the past.

It began to rain as the boat operator kept up a running commentary in a strange language. I knew it was Italian because I recognized some words and phrases. It was not the Italian I'd learned in Rome. A wide smile covered his bearded face as he heard my garbled Italian. But we got along.

As we neared the island, Hitch pointed toward an old and obviously abandoned landing. "Stop there," he called to the boatman. In a volley of his northern Italian dialect, he told Hitch that the proper landing was around on the other side of the island. Of course, all this sailed over Hitch's head, carried away by the wind that was beginning to drive the rain into our faces.

I translated what I could of the boatman's words, but Hitch wasn't about to agree. He kept insisting that the boatman turn into the landing. The boatman turned to me. I just shrugged my shoulders and nodded toward the landing.

As we got out and started up an old vine-entangled path, I heard the boatman call out in almost recognizable Italian, "That goes to the back entrance. You can't get in that way!"

Hitch ignored his warning. We continued to push our way to some steps leading to a back porch stacked with boxes and barrels blocking a doorway, if one existed. Fortunately, the porch was covered. I told Hitch to wait in the lea of the porch while I found my way around to the entrance. I tried going around both sides of the building before returning to the boat and asking the boatman to take me to the proper landing. He looked back up the path and asked, "Senor Heetch?" I told him to forget about "Senor Heetch."

We were at the proper landing in minutes. I invited the boatman to come have lunch with us, but he turned into the comfort of the cabin, opened a large basket, pulled out a bottle of wine, and asked me to join him.

The path to the main entrance was clear of vines. I ran to the door where a giant of a man stood in the shelter of an overhang. He held out his hand in welcome. "You're alone?" he asked. I told him about Hitch and Alma waiting at the back. I followed him as he ran across the dining room, through his busy kitchen, calling for help. After a ten-minute struggle, the door was opened and a path was cleared through the boxes to where Hitch and Alma stood shivering.

Alma gratefully accepted the warm fluffy towel that Padrone Benvenuto Puricelli, the owner, placed around her shoulders, but Hitch brushed his aside. Puricelli led us to a table where a waiter soon arrived with a great loaf of warm bread fresh from the oven. Hitch and Alma accepted Puricelli's suggestion to try the local trout, caught that very morning. A wide smile covered Puricelli's face when I told him I'd been away from Italy too long and had been dreaming about osso buco.

"Osso buco! Domineca specialita, the Sunday special," he said. And we were there on Sunday. Needless to say, we left the restaurant pleased we'd endured the rain and the struggle to reach Puricelli's.

While Alma and Hitch rested, I took a long walk along a winding path in the forest. When I returned to the hotel, I found a message waiting: "The ice cubes are getting cold. The cocktail hour is upon us." It wasn't signed. It didn't need a signature.

Alma was still resting when I arrived. Hitch seemed in a serious mood. He toyed with his glass of wine. Finally, he opened up. "Alma and I have been talking," he said. "We would like to have you come back to us. This time, with the credit you deserve. Producer. And the money that goes with it. Ship the *Topaz* film to the studio and go directly to Finland to prepare *The Short Night.*"

"It won't work, Hitch. Edd Henry will see to it. He and I have never been in agreement on anything. He's never forgiven me for pushing Eve Marie Saint in *North by Northwest.* He and Siegal had agreed on Cyd Charisse and thought they'd sold her to you. And the word around town is that Lew Wasserman was tightening the purse strings. Adding my salary to your budgets when you average one picture a year will be too much."

"Will you come back?" he asked.

I told him I would, if he could arrange it.

"Then leave it to me, Herbie."

I flew home still convinced Hitch wouldn't be able to make the deal. I know he tried when he got back to the studio, but those in the Black Tower refused to go along.

Topaz ended our professional association but not our social life. We lunched together from time to time, and he invited me to screen his subsequent films, *Frenzy* and *Family Plot.*

Index